Society, Culture, and Drinking Patterns

Edited by

DAVID J. PITTMAN
Washington University

and

CHARLES R. SNYDER
Southern Illinois University

Society, Culture, and Drinking Patterns

JOHN WILEY & SONS, INC.

New York · London

Contributors

Selden D. Bacon
Robert F. Bales
William M. Bates
Kettil Bruun
Robert Buechley
Marshall B. Clinard
Ralph G. Connor
Theodore L. Dorpat
Peter B. Field
C. Wayne Gordon
Joseph R. Gusfield
Dwight B. Heath
Joan K. Jackson
E. M. Jellinek
Mark Keller
William R. Larson
Joseph J. Lawrence
Edwin M. Lemert
Wendell R. Lipscomb
George L. Maddox

Milton A. Maxwell
Joan McCord
William McCord
Patricia O'Neal
Ernest G. Palola
Peter Park
Arthur Pearl
David J. Pittman
Lee N. Robins
Earl Rubington
Walter H. Sangree
John R. Seeley
Ozzie G. Simmons
Charles R. Snyder
Gregory P. Stone
Robert Straus
Archer Tongue
Harrison M. Trice
Albert D. Ullman
J. Richard Wahl

to Barbara, Bertha, and Willie
and Patricia

Preface

This book aims to bring under a single cover a wide selection of the best current social-science research on drinking patterns, normal and pathological. Our purpose has been not only to consolidate knowledge by collating a variety of studies in a rapidly growing area of research interest but also, through preliminary systematization and editorial comment, to point out the interrelations of various studies and to suggest, directly or by implication, some of the avenues along which future research might fruitfully proceed. Although major emphasis in this undertaking has been given to the work of sociologists, the book as a whole must be said to be interdisciplinary in nature, at least to the extent of including studies conducted in the traditions of cultural anthropology and social psychology, as well as sociology.

A few words on the background of the book will help further to clarify our rationale in preparing it. The idea for this book originated with the Committee on Alcoholism of the Society for the Study of Social Problems. Over the years the Society has established committees to foster research and social action in such areas as mental health, crime and delinquency, community development, occupational problems, and alcoholism, to mention only a few. One of the main concerns of these committees has been to collate and publish the results of research with the object of synthesizing knowledge, if only in a provisional way, in areas where specialized studies have multiplied at such a rapid pace that it is virtually impossible for scholars and interested laymen to grasp their interrelations and broader meanings.*

---

* Three books, emanating from the work of these committees and treating of community organization, mental health, and sexual behavior, have already appeared under the auspices of the Society for the Study of Social Problems.

It was this general concern, coupled with an acute awareness of the chaotic impression created by the proliferation of studies in its own area of interest, that prompted the Committee on Alcoholism in 1957 to set up a subcommittee to study the desirability and feasibility of preparing a collection of social-science studies centering primarily on patterns of drinking alcoholic beverages and, more narrowly, on alcoholism. The following year the subcommittee unanimously recommended that work should begin on such a book, a recommendation which was heartily endorsed by the Executive Committee of the Society. In due course, the membership of the Committee on Alcoholism selected David J. Pittman and Charles R. Snyder to serve as editors. This book is thus the outgrowth of considerable study and planning on the part of the Committee on Alcoholism, as well as the end product of the efforts of the editors and contributors.

The organization of the book reflects a compromise among three basic interests of the editors. It was first necessary to develop an outline sufficiently broad to embrace the varieties of studies of drinking patterns extant in sociology and in such closely allied fields as psychology and anthropology. Second, it was our wish that the various parts should unfold in a meaningful sequence and, given the limits of our present knowledge, comprise a reasonably coherent whole. It is this second concern which principally governs the movement of the book from a consideration of drinking patterns in comparative perspective to the context of our own complex society, through to a more sharply focused discussion of alcoholism, and thence to responsive movements and systems of control. Finally, it was our desire to order these diverse materials in a sociologically relevant way. From our standpoint, there is nothing precious about the framework resulting from our efforts to reconcile these ofttimes conflicting interests; it will have served a useful purpose if it begins to highlight important gaps in systematic knowledge in addition to making clear what is known. We particularly hope, however, that the framework of organization will heighten awareness of the relation of studies of drinking patterns to the larger totality of sociological facts, concepts, and theories.

In selecting materials for inclusion in this book, we have not relied exclusively upon works already published. From the outset, a concerted effort was made to learn of research in progress both in this country and abroad and to encourage the presentation of reports of such research in this book. Of the thirty-five chapters composing the book, twelve represent abridgments, excerpts, or reprintings of previously published material with varying degrees of modification by the editors. The remaining twenty-three chapters are original contributions, written and edited especially for this book. In this latter group will be found both critiques and syntheses of studies in particular subareas and reports of new research.

By emphasizing the sociological approach and centering attention upon drinking patterns, we in no way intend to depreciate the value of other approaches and interests in the study of man's relation to beverage alcohol.

Investigations of the physiological and psychological effects of alcohol on the human organism, descriptions of the techniques of manufacturing alcoholic beverages or of the economics of their distribution, treatises on the moral and theological implications of drinking and drunkenness, evaluations of differing clinical programs for alcoholics—these and a host of other subjects may be of great significance for other purposes but are quite beyond the scope of this book. With regard to alcohol and human behavior, we would certainly agree that such fields as experimental psychology, physiology, biochemistry, and psychiatry have much to tell us of importance in terms of their own universes of discourse. However, we are convinced that, in trying to understand phenomena such as ranges of variation in drinking patterns and differential rates of alcoholism, the sociological approach affords the proper terms of analysis. Although the present book hardly begins to exhaust the potentialities of the approach, we trust that it will at least provide ample testimony that man's use and misuse of beverage alcohol cannot be seriously comprehended without reference to the socio-cultural plane of his existence.

Our book is directed toward two major groups of readers. First, it should be of value to those social scientists—teachers and researchers—who are generally concerned with or who are specializing in the relationship between alcohol and human behavior. In the university setting, the book may prove useful as supplementary reading for courses in social problems, criminology, social psychiatry, deviant behavior, and social disorganization, and it should be useful to researchers in these fields. Second, the book should be of interest to professionals and laymen in so-called applied fields directly concerned with the problems of drinking and especially with alcoholism. This would include psychiatrists, social workers, physicians, judges of municipal courts, health educators, ministers, and temperance and beverage-industry leaders. Persons connected with the large number of international, national, state, and local programs on alcoholism may also find this book of interest in their diverse educational and policy-making activities. Yet we would underscore again the fact that our major purpose has been to consolidate social-science research and to stimulate scientific inquiry in an area where systematic investigation is still in its infancy and not to popularize the results of scientific endeavor in a well-established field.

Inevitably, in a work of this kind, there is much indebtedness to many persons, on the part of both editors and contributors, which must go unacknowledged. We editors would like, however, to express our particular thanks to Mark Keller, editor of the *Quarterly Journal of Studies on Alcohol*, for his wise counsel. Special thanks are also due Ellen Bennett, Ruth Bruce, Josephine Dickson, and Elizabeth Seuss for their help in preparing the manuscript for publication and in handling the extensive correspondence connected with this task. We are grateful also to Ruth Bruce and Marilyn Harrington for editorial assistance, to our colleague Herman R. Lantz for many valuable suggestions, and to Judith Lantz for preparing the index. In addition, we are indebted to Southern Illinois University for support and encouragement, and particularly to Willis G. Swartz, John O. Anderson, and the members of the Graduate Research Committee, as well as to Talbert W. Abbott, Paul J. Campisi, and John W. Voigt. Likewise we are indebted to Washington University faculty members, Nicholas J. Demerath, Edwin F. Gildea, Alvin W. Gouldner, and Eli Robins. Also, we are grateful for the cooperation of the Rutgers Center of Alcohol Studies. Finally, we wish to express our appreciation and thanks to the contributors who made this book a reality.

DAVID J. PITTMAN
CHARLES R. SNYDER

Saint Louis, Missouri
Carbondale, Illinois
April, 1962

Acknowledgments

We express our appreciation to the following publishers and authors for permission to reprint excerpts and/or articles from materials which have been copyrighted.

1. American Anthropologist, Ozzie G. Simmons, "Ambivalence and the Learning of Drinking Behavior in a Peruvian Community," Tucson, December 1960.
2. The American Sociological Association, *American Sociological Review*, Gregory Stone and William Form, "Instabilities in Status: The Problem of Hierarchy in the Community Study of Status Arrangements," New York, 1953.
3. Family Service Association of America, Elise de la Fontaine, "Cultural and Psychological Implications in Case Work Treatment with Irish Clients," New York, 1940.
4. The Free Press, Marshall Sklare, "The Jews: Social Patterns of an American Group," Glencoe, 1958.
5. Victor Gollancz, Ltd., Victor Gollancz, *The Pub and the People*, London, 1949.
6. Herbert Jenkins, Ltd., Sir Henry A. Robinson, *Further Memories of Irish Life*, London, 1924.
7. Journal of Studies on Alcohol, Inc., New Haven, Conn.:
8. Longmans, Green and Company, Ltd., Edward MacLysaght, *Irish Life in the Seventeenth Century: After Cromwell*, London, 1939.
9. The Macmillan Company, Conrad M. Arensberg, *The Irish Countryman*, New York, 1937.
10. Mills and Boon, Ltd., Robert Lynd, *Home Life in Ireland*, London, 1909.

a. Selden D. Bacon, "Alcohol and Complex Society," in *Alcohol, Science and Society*, 1945.

b. Robert F. Bales, "The Therapeutic Role of Alcoholics Anonymous as Seen by a Sociologist," *Quart. J. Stud. Alc.*, 1944.

c. Kettil Bruun, "The Significance of Roles and Norms in the Small Group for Individual Behavioral Changes While Drinking," *Quart. J. Stud. Alc.*, 1959.

d. John Dollard, "Drinking Mores of the Social Classes," in *Alcohol, Science and Society*, 1945.

e. Dwight B. Heath, "Drinking Patterns of the Bolivian Camba," *Quart. J. Stud. Alc.*, 1958.

f. Joan K. Jackson and Ralph G. Connor, "The Skid Road Alcoholic," *Quart. J. Stud. Alc.*, 1953.

g. E. M. Jellinek, "Phases of Alcohol Addiction," *Quart. J. Stud. Alc.*, 1952.

h. Mark Keller, "The Definition of Alcoholism," *Quart. J. Stud. Alc.*, 1960.

i. Boyd E. Macrory, "The Tavern and the Community," *Quart. J. Stud. Alc.*, 1952.

j. David J. Pittman and C. Wayne Gordon, "Criminal Careers of the Chronic Drunkenness Offenders," *Quart. J. Stud. Alc.*, 1958.

k. Charles R. Snyder, *Alcohol and the Jews*, 1958.

l. H. M. Trice and J. Richard Wahl, "A Rank Order Analysis of the Symptoms of Alcoholism," *Quart. J. Stud. Alc.*, 1958.

m. Albert D. Ullman, "The Psychological Mechanism of Alcohol Addiction," *Quart. J. Stud. Alc.*, 1952.

n. Albert D. Ullman, "The First Drinking Experience of Addictive and of 'Normal' Drinkers," *Quart. J. Stud. Alc.*, 1953.

11. St. Martin's Press, Inc., Albert D. Ullman, *To Know the Difference*, New York, 1960.

12. Stanford University Press, William McCord and Joan McCord, with Jon Gudeman, *Origins of Alcoholism*, Stanford, 1960.

13. The University of Chicago Press, *The American Journal of Sociology*, E. C. Moore, "The Social Value of the Saloon," Chicago, July 1897.

14. The University of Chicago Press, *The American Journal of Sociology*, David Gottlieb, "The Neighborhood Tavern and Cocktail Lounge, A Study of Class Differences," Chicago, 1957.

15. Yale University Press, Robert Straus and Selden D. Bacon, *Drinking in College*, New Haven, Conn., 1953.

D. J. P.
C. R. S.

Contents

DRINKING IN
ANTHROPOLOGICAL
PERSPECTIVE

Introductory Note. Emphasis in this book has been placed intentionally on studies of drinking patterns in the context of complex modern society, and particularly American society. Yet there are good reasons for beginning with a brief excursion into studies of drinking in non-literate societies which are the province of anthropologists. The advantages to be gained from such a procedure are several. Familiarity with anthropological investigations of peoples and cultures seemingly remote from our own helps cultivate a kind of detachment from parochial judgments which is needed in approaching a subject as fraught with emotion as the use of beverage alcohol.

At the same time, the momentary intellectual identification with the ways of other people which these investigations afford may bring into sharp relief crucial features of our own patterns of behavior and attitude, features that might otherwise have remained unnoticed. More important, perhaps, is the fact that anthropologists who focus their attention on relatively small homogeneous groups often are able to portray with boldness and clarity the larger social and cultural structures in which drinking patterns are anchored. The understanding that is gained highlights a goal toward which the necessarily fragmentary studies of drinking in our own complex society may strive, even though a firm grasp of the relevance of larger structures continues to elude us. Finally, anthropological inquiry opens up that wider range of fact which must be accounted for in any effort to generalize about drinking behavior, thereby paving the way for comparative sociology.

Important as they may be, these broad considerations yield only the most general criteria for the inclusion of anthropological work and hardly suffice to provide a rationale for the specific selections to follow. After all, barring

1

those concerned with the cultures of the minority of peoples who traditionally lacked beverage alcohol, virtually all ethnographers have had something or other to report on the subject of drinking customs, however incidentally, and in principle, we were at liberty to choose from the nearly
endless list of their works. Moreover, recent years have witnessed the development of a rapidly growing body of anthropological literature which
has deliberately sought to bring into clearer focus the drinking behavior of
preliterate and other peoples marginal to Western culture.*

Because of this situation and in the absence of any monistic principle of
selection, it is probably as important to indicate what we have not tried
to do in introducing the four studies that follow as it is to provide brief
justification for each selection. It has not been our purpose to sample the
anthropological literature representatively, either in terms of the varieties of
drinking patterns extant or in terms of cultural areas. Nor do we propose
to take the reader on a global Cook's tour by exposing him to smatterings of
drinking customs from each continent. On the contrary, each selection has
been made on the grounds of freshness and relevance to current theoretical
and methodological concerns in the study of drinking behavior.

Chapter 1, written by Walter Sangree, concerns drinking among the
Bantu Tiriki and should do much to dispel preconceived and stereotyped
notions of "drunken savages." This chapter describes a pattern of drinking
in which drunkenness is relatively infrequent and which could be designated as pathological only by reference to the most abstemious standards.
The particular merit of Sangree's study, however, lies in his ability to indicate the role of drinking in expressing and reinforcing Bantu Tiriki social
organization, notably the clan and age-grade systems, as well as certain key
aspects of the cultural tradition which this organization supports. The reciprocal effect which these structures exert in regulating drinking behavior
illustrates a theme which will be more fully developed later on. Here we note
that such an analysis makes it difficult to sustain popular individualistic
generalizations regarding why people drink—generalizations which derive
drinking from the psychic needs of individuals as such, without reference
to the social context. Also, the fact that Sangree's analysis brings into focus
the bases for persistence and change in Bantu Tiriki drinking (which is
under constant frontal assault from missionaries of abstinence persuasion)
may be taken as preliminary evidence of the validity of the functional approach in the study of drinking behavior.

In his discussion of the Bolivian Camba (Chapter 2), Dwight Heath offers
one of the most thoughtful descriptions of drinking and related behavior
which has appeared in the anthropological literature. Anyone who tries to
address to this literature rather elementary questions deriving from the
study of drinking patterns in Western society immediately runs afoul of the
lack of sufficient information to make clear-cut inferences and conclusions

---

* A useful bibliography of this literature is contained in the notes and references of
Chapter 2.

possible. Often enough, this is not so much a problem of poverty in descriptive material, although ethnographies vary greatly in this respect, as it is a lack of concern for negative evidence. In considering primitive societies where drunkenness is prevalent we may, for example, wish to know if something comparable to alcoholism exists, if manifestations of aggression or sexuality in the course of drinking are to be found, or if sequels to drinking such as the hangover or hallucinations are experienced. Of course the simple fact that such phenomena are often not reported may genuinely reflect their absence in certain primitive groups, but it may also reflect the failure of ethnographers to note their absence. It is characteristic of Heath, however, to assert positively that a variety of phenomena are *not* to be found in the Camba group even though drunkenness is widespread—an order of facts which may prove quite useful. Beyond this, his tentative interpretation of Camba drinking ritual as an institutionalized mechanism for stimulating interaction and dramatizing collective identification and solidarity in an otherwise vacuous context points to more general functions of drinking. In their drunkenness, tendencies toward isolation, and loose communal organization, the Camba provide a rather marked contrast to the Bantu Tiriki. Together these two societies concretely illustrate generalizations about the relation of drunkenness to different types of social structures.

Many observers of the American scene have called attention to the possible consequences for the perpetuation of drinking pathologies of cultural attitudes toward drinking which veer to the extremes of asceticism and hedonism. Attitudes of this sort bespeak that condition which Abraham Myerson (2) aptly summed up in the phrase "social ambivalence"—a condition which limits the development of stable attitudes toward drinking, restricts the meaning of the act to a hedonistic alernative, and insulates it from effective social controls. The upshot when drinking takes place is purported to be the kind of extreme and uncontrolled behavior the effect of which is to intensify the conflict and polarization of attitudes, activating a vicious circle of cause and effect. However sound such a view, a supposedly complementary hypothesis has emerged in popular and professional discussion which bears close examination, especially since it is liable to gross oversimplification. This is the notion that if only drinking were more thoroughly integrated in social custom and routine, ambivalence would be neutralized along with more extreme pathologies like alcoholism.

Acknowledging that there may be germs of truth in this idea, Ozzie Simmons proceeds to show, in Chapter 3, that the anatomy of ambivalence toward drinking is more complex than has been widely assumed. He describes a Peruvian mestizo community where drinking is highly valued, where the use of alcohol and drunkenness permeate adult interpersonal relations, yet where ambivalence is at once made manifest and communicated to successive generations by marked limitations on the drinking activities of youth. By focusing upon such seemingly disparate phenomena as the stresses in interpersonal relations among adults and the framework of respect relations which govern relations with youth, Simmons begins to localize sources of ambivalence toward drinking in the social and cultural structure.

In his emphasis on socialization and youth, Simmons provides useful material for comparison and contrast with our own patterns which are described and analyzed in a preliminary way in Section IV. To the perennial question as to whether or not youth in our culture should be allowed to drink, or to drink as do adults, Simmons' study speaks by way of implication. It suggests the prior question as to why this is apparently so problematic even in sectors of the society where drinking is common among adults, as well as the kinds of axes along which study of this question might proceed. His study also provides the outlines of a testable and orderly scheme for predicting the conditions which account for cross-cultural variation in attitudes toward youthful drinking—from encouragement and permission to proscription.

Field's study, in Chapter 4, aims at generalizing, on the basis of extensive and systematic cross-cultural study, about the factors responsible for the enormous range of variation in drunkenness in primitive societies. The method of cross-cultural comparison, at least when it has entailed extensive statistical analysis, has been the butt of serious criticism on a number of grounds. It has been asserted, for instance, that the abstraction and disassociation of custom from its setting which inheres in the method results in grave distortions of meaning. It is sometimes alleged that the quest for samples which will meet statistical criteria of adequacy fosters an unwholesome tendency to give equal credulity to sources of markedly unequal scholarly value. Other times it may be asserted that the supposed indices of crucial variables hardly tap or exhaust the dimensions in question.

In the face of these and other criticisms of the cross-cultural method we would be loath to plunge the reader into a morass of cross-cultural correlations without first providing him opportunity to ponder materials on drinking patterns described in relative depth and in particular cultural settings. Having given the reader such materials, however, we are pleased to include Peter Field's cross-cultural study of drunkenness in primitive societies which builds upon and modifies the now nearly classic study by Donald Horton (1).

The reader who is mindful of possible loopholes in the cross-cultural method and who has digested material on drinking patterns in particular cultures will discover places where the chain of inference in Field's reasoning appears tenuous or where his interpretations seem opposed to those of other authors. Whatever may prove eventually to be the most satisfactory total explanation, Field's findings seem clearly to indicate that the nature of the social organization is a crucial determinant of the extent of drunkenness in primitive societies. It seems equally clear that the degree of elaboration of durable and well-defined corporate kin groups is of far greater significance in this respect than is the presence, absence, or development of certain other types of social structure.

These findings will surely warm the hearts of those social scientists who have long since contended for a thorough consideration of variables of social organization in exploring ranges of variation in drinking patterns. They also lend support to lines of speculation and research which, broadly speaking, envisage the incidence of alcohol problems in complex society and various sectors thereof as dependent upon the vitality, dissolution, or resurgence of those social structures beyond the individual or nuclear family—be they based upon nominally familistic, ethnic, religious, or other criteria—which may reasonably be supposed to have a potential for organizing and controlling social life equivalent to that of the structures which Field sees as capable of inducing sobriety in primitive societies.* In consequence, Field's study will serve for many readers as a natural bridge for a return from the so-called primitive to a consideration of drinking patterns in modern society.

References

1. Horton, Donald, "The Functions of Alcohol in Primitive Societies: A Cross-Cultural Study," *Quart. J. Stud. Alc.*, 4:199–320, 1943.
2. Myerson, Abraham, "Alcohol: A Study of Social Ambivalence," *Quart. J. Stud. Alc.*, 1:13–20, 1940.

* See, for instance, the discussion of the Jews in Section III, Chapter 11.

chapter 1

The social functions of beer drinking in Bantu Tiriki[*]

Walter H. Sangree

The Tiriki people (*badiliji*) live in the southeastern portion of North Nyanza District, Kenya Colony. They are one of the twenty-two culturally similar but politically discrete Bantu tribes living in North Nyanza and Elgon Districts of Nyanza Province that are today collectively known as the Abaluhiya or Abaluyia.† British rule was established in Nyanza Province in the last decade of the nineteenth century. Since approximately the First World War, European influences have changed many of the life patterns of the Abaluhiya with increasing rapidity. Beer-drinking patterns, probably because of their intimate connection with basic aspects of Tiriki social organization, have changed less rapidly than many other Tiriki social patterns.

Pax Britannica and control of famine and disease have caused the dense initial population to increase probably several times over in the last 50 years; and as a result, serious overpopulation now exists in the southern portion of North Nyanza. Tiriki Location, the contemporary homeland of the Tiriki as legally instituted by the Kenya government, has a total area of just over 70 square miles, of which about 18 square miles are uninhabited

---

* This chapter was written especially for this book. The material used is drawn in large measure from two unpublished manuscripts (3, 4). The field work upon which it is based was carried out by the writer and his wife during a 16-month residence in Tiriki between December 1954 and June 1956. The field trip was made possible through a grant given the writer by the Fulbright program.

† Although based primarily upon his field work undertaken among the Abaluhiya Maragoli and Vugusu, Wagner's studies (5–8) give some insight into the general cultural traits of the group as well as an indication of the degree of variation found within Abaluhiya tribes.

6

forest reserve or mission lands. In the remaining 52 square miles, about forty thousand Tiriki make their homes and practice their traditional hoe agriculture. This brings the average population density in the inhabited part of the location close to 750 people per square mile.

Overpopulation is the most pressing reason for the Abaluhiya people's ever-growing practice of seeking employment in regions outside of Nyanza Province. As the population increases so does the absolute dependency on wages from jobs in East African urban centers and on European "Highland" farms lying to the east of Nyanza Province. Today probably over half of the Tiriki adult males are off-tribe (*mulugulu*) at any given time, for the most part performing wage labor. Mostly it is the men between the ages of about 18 and 40 who seek wage labor off-tribe; consequently, the tribal population appears to the visitor to consist overwhelmingly of women, children, and old men.

This study focuses on the functions of beer drinking in contemporary Tiriki. In order, however, to appreciate present day Tiriki attitudes towards beer, we must consider some background material on the nature of indigenous uses of beer, as well as data on European contact, especially missionary activity. In these first few pages, a brief picture of contemporary Tiriki is presented, and the nature of widespread mission-spawned activity is sketched. This is followed by a summary description of the bi-cultural nature of the indigenous Tiriki social organization. Then the principal organizational attributes of the clans and age groups are given, and the principal beer-utilizing ceremonies of each are indicated. Next the incidence and control of misbehavior while drinking, and drunkenness are discussed. In conclusion, the relationship between beer-drinking practices and the spread of Christianity is outlined.

The Tiriki Scene

The Tiriki scene, when viewed by the present writer for the first time, struck him as being ideal material for a Peter Brueghel landscape. Here was a bucolic beehive; the women were the workers, and the men were the drones. Women do the agriculture in Tiriki. Of a morning, women are to be seen everywhere. They balance water-filled kerosene tins on their heads as they climb homewards from valley streams; little groups of them hoe the fields; they spread maize kernels or beans to dry on huge flat-topped granite boulders that protrude at frequent intervals from the cultivated land; they carry loads of firewood back from the forest on their heads. Children are also much in evidence. Small boys brandishing sticks, some naked and some wearing dirty torn shirts, chase cattle out of maize fields back to the path and road edges where they are permitted to graze. Younger children, both male and female, race around in little groups in the occasional grassy spots, often playing soccer with a green mango or some other improvised ball— even while carrying their infant charges on their left hips.

Generally, the men do not become a conspicuous part of the scene until around noon. At that time the tribal elders leave the community meeting grounds, where they have passed the morning chatting and hearing cases brought before them for settlement. For the next hour or so they can frequently be seen sauntering along the pathways on their way to the nearest beer drink. Typical clothing for the Tiriki elder is an ancient army greatcoat, worn over equally ancient shorts, and two hats—one pushed down on top of the other. One can always spot an elder on the lookout for beer, for in his right hand he will be clutching an immense sheath, 7 or 8 feet long, which encases a beer-drinking tube, and under his left arm he will be carrying a battered four-legged stool. The beer pots are the center of the elders' social life. It is while seated around a communal pot in a banana patch and sipping beer through long tubes that the elders exchange gossip, recollect the exploits of deceased comrades, and discuss and, in effect, often settle disputes of one sort or another even before they are presented to them for arbitration in the community courts. Around midafternoon, when the elders' beer drinks are already well under way, the younger men who are not away working collect around beer pots of their own or settle in the back rooms of local African stores to drink European beer or illegally distilled liquor (*iwalagi*). Most of this younger set is comprised of men home "on leave" from jobs off-location and men who hold salaried positions in the administrative bureaucracy.

During the weeks following the semi-annual harvest when there is plenty of grain with which to make beer, drinks are virtually an everyday occurrence; from evening until after dark it is common to hear if not see old men chatting as they saunter home after a lively beer drink. In the words of the Tiriki elders, "It's a tough world" (*shibala shidinyu*) on those days when a beer drink cannot be found within walking distance.

Throughout most of the day one or another *askari* (tribal policeman or messenger) or headman can be seen pedaling his bicycle along the graded dirt automobile road that runs the length of the tribe, on his way to and from the location center at Hamisi. Occasionally an overcrowded bus traveling between Kisumu and Eldoret grinds by covering all it passes with dust. Mission-directed or mission-derived church and educational activities probably provide the passing traveler with more evidence of European inroads upon Tiriki life than either the British-sponsored tribal administrative system or the European transportational technology.

From any high point in Tiriki, several primary schools are usually visible; they are often located on hilltops, and they are easily recognizable from a distance because the long rectangular shapes of the thatched school buildings contrast with the thatched conical roofs of the ordinary round huts generally found in the homesteads. Children in rows doing calisthenics frequently grace the school grounds. On Sundays many of the schools, all of which are mission run, are used as churches. Women make up three quarters or more of most church congregations. After the Sunday morning services, processions form at the school-church grounds and then stream over the country paths under the midday sun on their way to banana grove "memorial services," singing and drumming syncopated songs of salvation.

The first Christian mission station was established in Tiriki in 1902 by a group of evangelically oriented American Quakers. Their mission at Kaimosi, Tiriki, known as the Friends African Mission, has remained the principal center of missionary activity in the tribe. In recent decades, the Salvation Army and the Pentecostal Assembly of East Africa (Canadian in origin) have also gained a considerable number of Tiriki converts. In addition, primarily since 1950 or so, Roman Catholic Mill Hill Mission activities, and the proselytizing efforts of several independent African Christian sects have met with growing success in Tiriki. Today a comprehensive network of community churches and primary schools, operated, for the most part, by African pastors and teachers, extends to within easy walking distance of everyone in the tribe. It will be seen that these mission-spawned church groups provide a very important core of religious beliefs and social loyalties for otherwise increasingly disorganized segments of the Tiriki population.

The Protestant missionaries in Tiriki operate intermediate schools for boys and for girls, a primary teacher's training center, a Bible school, and a well-equipped hospital, all of which draw students or patients not only from Tiriki but also from other tribes. The missions have been almost entirely responsible for the establishment and administration of the school system in the tribe, the value of which is becoming more and more appreciated by the Tiriki as they seek better jobs in Nairobi and other East African urban centers.

The weekly scene varies little from one part of the tribe to the next. The terrain and climate are similar enough to make the seasonal shifts in agricultural activities and abundance about the same throughout the tribe, but, as one proceeds northeast, the country grows less crowded, the huts are progressively further apart, and the rusticity is more pronounced. The hills and valleys are less precipitous, and there are fewer granite outcroppings; European-imported Australian eucalyptus trees more often break the eye's sweep, and large tracts of dense hardwood rain forests protected by the Friends African Mission and the African District Council preserve a picture of what most of northeastern Tiriki looked like as late as 1902 when the last elephant was seen roaming the area.

Social Organization and Drinking Patterns

The Tiriki indigenous social structure is a blend of two distinct social traditions. Tiriki social structure can be likened to a rope of three strands: clans (*zimbamba*), age groups (*maxulu*), and territorial units (*zisomo; zimbihiya*). The clan organization is clearly of Abaluhiya origin. Although clan groupings in Tiriki have been deprived of much of the political significance they generally retain in other Abaluhiya tribes, they are nevertheless the organizational arena in which a large number of the Tiriki's significant social relationships are carried out and the bulk of the tribe's cultural tradition preserved. The age-group and territorial organizations are, in contrast, of Nilo-Hamitic origin. Even though they supply the principal indigenous political framework for the Tiriki, the tribe remains Bantu in language and predominantly Abaluhiya in culture.

Clan organization supplies the underlying framework for the ancestor cult which is the tribe's principal indigenous religious system. Today the clan-based ancestor cult has largely been supplanted by Christian practices. The traditional ancestral supplications, so replete with beer-drinking ceremonials, are only carried out by a rapidly dwindling minority of tribal elders, but they are well remembered by all adult Tiriki, and they continue to color contemporary attitudes toward beer drinking. It seems relevant, therefore, to outline the nature of these ancestral supplications.

The homestead ancestral shrine (*lusambwa*) is the place where the rites of the ancestor cult are most often performed. Often (and preferably) the keeper of a homestead shrine is also the homestead head, and the eldest son of the deceased previous homestead head. The shrine is usually under the eaves of the granary in which the crops of the homestead's senior wife are stored. Eleusine from this granary is employed in making the beer (*malwa*) used in supplications at the ancestral shrine. The granary is usually about 15 or 20 feet in front of the entrance of the senior wife's hut.

The ancestral shrine, situated on the side of the granary facing the hut, consists of two parts. One part is a slender branch of the *lusiyola* tree which is renowned for its great size, toughness, and resistance to rotting. Known as the branch of the ancestral shrine (*musaala gu lusambwa*), it is placed so that it extends from the ground up to the eaves of the granary. The second part of the shrine is several—usually three—small stones, called "the stones of the ancestral spirits" (*majina ji misambwa*), that are planted around the base of the *lusiyola* branch. One stone is placed there for the deceased father of the homestead, the second stone for the present homestead head, and a third stone is added by the homestead elder, usually for his eldest son, after that son has a wife and children of his own.

Occasions characterized by trouble or stress and times of transition and celebration (which also inevitably carry elements of stress) traditionally give rise to supplications of the ancestral spirits at the *lusambwa*. Illness, for example, may induce a homestead head to hold a supplication. Perhaps, with a diviner's aid, the head will conclude that the illness has come because the ancestral spirits are feeling forgotten and consequently are no longer giving their strength to the people of the homestead. Thus, it may be decided to hold a special supplication and gathering of remembrance (*liluxiza*) at the ancestral shrine. Before the widespread acceptance of Christianity by the Tiriki, supplications and offerings were inevitably made at the ancestral shrine of the homestead principally involved on the occasion of wedding or funeral celebrations, at the conclusion of a youth's initiation, etc.

When a major supplication is to be held at the ancestral shrine, the homestead head has some beer brewed, usually by his first wife, and a specially selected chicken (*ingoxo ingasizwe*) slaughtered. Then, in the company of the community ritual elders (*bassalisi*) and as many other elders (*basaxulu*) of the community (both clansmen and neighbors) as wish to attend, the homestead's ritual elder puts a few drops of blood from the slaughtered bird on each of the ancestral stones. Next he places a bit of eleusine porridge or mush on the stones, and finally he tops the offerings with drops of beer. As the homestead ritual elder sprinkles on the beer he supplicates the ancestral spirits and asks their blessing. The supplication is generally simple and direct, and repeated at each stone. The following is an example:

> *Guga belu mungwi malwa bulahi!*
> *Xumenyi ni milembe!*
> *Bandu bosi bizanga; misambwa yanzi mungwi malwa bulahi.*
> *Xandi xujendi bulahi; xumenyi bulahi.*
>
> Our forefathers, drink up the beer!
> May we dwell in peace!
> Everyone is gathering; be pleased, oh ancestral spirits.
> And may we be well; may we remain well.

The traditional way of showing friendship or hospitality—indeed, of doing anyone a special favor in Tiriki—is to serve food followed by beer. Thus, it is quite in keeping that similar activity should be extended to the ancestral spirits when trying to restore their favor and aid. The ritual elders of the community, who come to help beseech the ancestors, eat the sacrificial chicken (on very special occasions, a goat or some other large animal may be used instead) and drink beer through beer tubes (*zinsexa*) from a pot placed between the ancestral stones. After the beer drinking is ended, a small pot of beer is left for the ancestral spirits dwelling too far away to partake of the main drink.

There are many different occasions, all more or less stressful, on which the ancestral spirits are beseeched and remembered at the homestead ancestral shrines. Not only are supplications at the *lusambwa* held as part of the regular *rites de passage* and at times of illness, but they also are performed as part of special lustral ceremonies (*miiluxa*) held to purify warriors after they have killed in battle (before tribal warfare was abolished), to restore peace between kinsmen or neighbors who have been fighting, and to neutralize the particular contamination (*buxwana*) believed to accompany the birth of twins. Also, the occurrence of any of a whole category of acts and events which the Tiriki and other Abaluhiya believe are unnatural and dangerous (*luswa*) demand that lustrations be held by the ritual elders to prevent disaster from befalling the individual, persons, or groups involved. Although many of these lustral ceremonies are not held at the ancestral shrines, it is common in conjunction with such ceremonies to leave offerings of food and beer and to supplicate the ancestral spirits at the ancestral shrines of the homestead or homesteads involved.

The Tiriki assume that the ancestral spirits are delighted to join any special gathering of living descendants, and a basic concern is that the ancestral spirits should feel that they are remembered and welcome participants at all such important occasions. All Tiriki agree that the ancestral spirits have a special predilection for beer; indeed the presence of beer is believed to be a beacon that will make the ancestral spirits aware of a special occasion among the living as nothing else will. Once attracted by the beer, the ancestral spirits are supposed to be flattered if they discover that they have not been forgotten at the festive gathering; pleased by the offerings of food and drink and the remembrance showed them, the ancestral spirits may be moved to grant the party makers their continued and even special support.

To this day, when a man of property dies, a beer-drinking postfuneral meeting (*lubego*) of the lineage and neighborhood is held to honor his memory and settle his estate. The inheritance patterns articulated on such occasions are in strict accordance with lineage and clan affiliations. Some of the more devout Christian relatives of the deceased join the women (who today are nearly 100 per cent Christian) in drinking tea on such occasions, but the majority of Tiriki elders persist in feeling that only a beer drink will really make the deceased feel kindly disposed towards his living relatives; certainly most pagan elders expect to have such a memorial beer drink held for them after they die.

The Tiriki age-group organization is not an indigenous Abaluhiya institution, the Tiriki assert, and all evidence indicates that the age-group organization is something they have received from the Terik.* During the last 150 or 200 years Abaluhiya lineage segments and family groups have been migrating from the north and west into the region, now known as Tiriki, which was already thinly inhabited by the Nilo-Hamitic Terik who are a herdspeople and an offshoot of the Nandi tribe. The Terik allowed the Abaluhiya to settle in the region provided they agreed to become incorporated into the Terik military organization.

The Terik age groups supply the principal organizational frame for their military regiments; thus, perforce, every Abaluhiya immigrant was obliged to undergo initiation into an age group, if of military age, and, in any event, to accept post-puberty circumcision and age-group initiation for his sons. Initiation converted the Abaluhiya immigrants into full-fledged members of the Terik tribe; thus these Abaluhiya immigrants became known as Tiriki (*badiliji*), the Bantu linguistic rendering of "Terik."

Differences of opinion and belief concerning female initiation (the Terik clitoridectomize the women as a prerequisite to marriage, while the Tiriki find the custom repugnant, and have constantly refused to do so) have

---

* The Tiriki are unique among the Abaluhiya in having joined with the Terik in their Nandi-type circumcision and age-group organization. No data on the Terik-Tiriki initiation and age-group organization has been published. However, the works of Huntingford (1) and Peristiany (2) do give accounts of the very similar Nandi and Kipsigis age-group organizations.

proved an effective deterrent to intermarriage between Terik and the Tiriki, and thus probably have in large measure been responsible for the Terik and Tiriki maintaining discrete linguistic and cultural identities in spite of their intense and extended military, political, and ritual interaction. Today the Terik are outnumbered by the Tiriki perhaps ten to one; but continuing respect is shown them by the Tiriki because they were the people who first permitted straggling remnants of Abaluhiya lineages to settle in the region, and first initiated these newcomers into the Terik age groups.

The Tiriki age-group organization has ramifications that extend far beyond the military realm. To this day it is of enormous political significance, and it affects directly or indirectly most of the major areas of social activity. The social groupings, rankings, statuses, and roles it institutes are manifest in everything from the largest tribal and subtribal groupings to everyday intrafamilial relationships. Indeed the age groups traditionally supply the principal political and ritual basis for Tiriki corporate action. The nature of the Tiriki age-group organization is, briefly, as follows.

There are seven designated age groups, each embracing an age span of approximately 15 years. The system is cyclical, a span of about 105 years being covered from the time a named group starts through the cycle to when it appears again at the cycle bottom. Boys are circumcised and initiated into an age group after puberty. The initiation involves an extensive cycle of rituals performed during a 6-month, initiate-seclusion period, and is held approximately every 4 years. Thus each age group generally receives recruits from three successive initiations.

Before the abolition of tribal warfare by the British around 1900, the age group immediately senior to the group still receiving initiates was responsible for carrying on offensive and retaliatory raids. At approximately 15-year intervals, handing-over ceremonies were held which caused each age group to move up a grade to the social functions of the group immediately senior to it, and which also opened a new age group to initiation. One result of these ceremonies, then, was the retirement of the warriors to positions of senior warriors, who mostly confined their warrior activities to advisory roles and defensive efforts, while the erstwhile initiates succeeded to warrior status. The former senior warriors for their part became judicial elders, and the former judicial elders became ritual elders.

The formal change-over ceremonies, held every 15 years, have not been held since before 1900—probably having been forbidden by the British in an effort to prevent the installation of a new group of warriors. The cycle of age groups, however, still continues; a new age group is now opened to initiation about every 15 years, simply in conjunction with the beginning of every third or fourth initiation period. Furthermore the graded statuses of the four adult age groups (in traditional terms: the warriors, the senior warriors, the judicial elders, and the ritual elders) are still observed, even though the social roles expected of group members in each status have changed considerably.

Initiation marks the change from the vastly inferior status of women and children to the full tribal status of manhood. In the strictest sense only a man initiated into a Tiriki age group is a real Tiriki; women and children are merely tribal appendages—Tiriki only by virtue of their husbands' or fathers' age-group memberships. A whole set of customs, attitudes, social responsibilities, etc., running the gamut from separation while eating and in most recreational activities to markedly different social responsibilities, divide the initiated from the uninitiated. Then, within the initiated portion of the tribe, the four graded social statuses mentioned above affect the type of social activities and the homestead, community, and tribal responsibilities undertaken by members of each age group. During the course of initiation, it is graphically and forcefully impressed on all initiates that one must show deference and respect towards members of age groups senior to one's own, and that members of the two "elder" age groups must be shown particular respect and honor. Also, a man regards others of his own age group as special comrades. When a choice must be made between age-group loyalties and other affiliations, both indigenous and of European origin, the age-group loyalties almost always win out.

Beer is as important to the ritual of initiation as it is in supplication ceremonies of the clan-derived ancestor cult, perhaps even more so. Indeed an under-average grain harvest usually militates for the postponement of initiation for a year because granaries must be full to supply the grain necessary for the four tribe-wide beer drinks and the many smaller beer drinks that tradition demands be held during the 6-month initiation period. The seclusion period following circumcision is divided into four major stages, each with its own ceremonial and instructional program, and the opening of every stage is marked by a beer drink held in the circumcision groves (*bibanda*) scattered throughout the tribe. Such a drink is attended not only by the initiates but also may be attended by all members of the tribe already initiated. In addition the arrangement meetings held by the elders before circumcision must all be lightened with beer, and several ceremonies which terminate initiation, held in the hilltop sacred groves of each subtribe, in the subtribal communal meeting grounds, and in the homesteads of the initiates, all call for the consumption of quantities of beer. Finally, the initiation elders in charge of the circumcision and initiation procedures, and their assistants, expect the families of the initiates to keep them well supplied with beer for refreshment during the entire initiation period.

Initiation occurs during only 6 months out of every 4 years (just in the last decade the initiation ceremonies have been abbreviated and the total initiation period length reduced to 3 months), but informal community beer parties, where men tend to gather around different beer pots according to age groups, are held with considerable frequency whenever sufficient grain is available for beer making. During the harvest season (the fertile soil and plentiful rainfall of Tiriki generally manages to produce two grain crops a year), it is not uncommon for two or more beer drinks to be held a week in a community, and it is rare indeed for a beer-thirsting elder not to be able to find a beer drink to join in another community within easy walking distance. After the harvest the frequency of drinks gradually tapers off. For a month or so before the new harvest, there is often no beer at all. This is the period when there is generally nothing home grown left to eat but beans (which are considered a very inferior repast indeed), and sometimes people must even buy grain from the north to sustain themselves. Although starvation is extremely rare during these periods, and actual famine conditions have occurred only three times during the last 50 years (each famine was quickly alleviated by government shipments of grain), people feel deprived; chatter constantly turns to "hunger" and thirst.

The informal community beer drinks reflect the Terik-derived multiclan community organization of the Tiriki, and do much to foster a sense of community solidarity. Community elders, after hearing and settling local disputes over such matters as divorce settlements, delinquent bridewealth payments, assault, adultery, property damage, and the like, retire to a beer drink whenever possible to rehash the highlights of the morning's proceedings and often to discuss—and sometimes, for all intents and purposes, settle—a case that they know will be pending in the near future. Also, at such gatherings, news is exchanged and perhaps opinions developed about current British administrational efforts at soil conservation, taxation, and livestock control; or perhaps the latest mission scheme is hashed over, such as a plan to build a church in a community where a rival Christian sect is already established. The most influential chiefs of every community regularly travel to the Tribal Center to attend the Chief's weekly tribal meeting, and it would be a mistake not to recognize how much the nature and the effectiveness of the chief's tribal policies are determined by the discussions the community elders hold around the beer pots.

Younger men of the junior age groups seldom join an elders' banana grove beer drink; but they often have concurrent drinks, sometimes in a neighboring grove but more often today in a nearby hut. Of course warfare, except for the occasional soliloquy on an adventure while in the King's African Rifles during the second World War, is no longer a topic of conversation and debate for the younger men, but the merits of various off-location jobs and of different European employers are often discussed; more strictly local matters such as amatory exploits and the latest neighborhood dance are also reviewed. Ridicule, generally in the form of jesting and mimicry, leveled during a beer drink against the individual or clique commonly felt to be indulging in undesirable behavior, serves as an important mechanism of social control within the community and tribe.

The frequent and widespread drinking of beer described in the preceding pages may have conjured up for the reader a mental image of chronic tribal overindulgence, in which life for most of the year is a never-ending round of drunken parties and hangovers. Actually this is far from the truth, for several reasons. In the first place, both traditionally and today neither the women nor uncircumcised youth take part in these drinking parties; indeed except for the occasional ceremonial sip, and filched gourdful, only the women past menopause have ever been permitted to drink beer. This, as we shall see later, significantly affected the spread of Christianity in Tiriki.

Second, Tiriki beer is low enough in alcoholic content so that it cannot normally be expected to produce intoxication unless drunk rapidly in rather large quantities. Made traditionally of eleusine flour (today mill-ground maize is substituted for hand-ground eleusine) which is roasted, watered, and then allowed to ferment in huge earthenware pots, the resultant thick fermented liquid is placed in somewhat smaller pots and diluted with hot water at the time it is drunk. Although a strainer at the end of each beer tube prevents the drinkers from getting the more solid portion of the brew, they are nevertheless sipping a thin gruel. The prevalent Tiriki feeling is that the stomach is full and the appetite for both food and drink assuaged before any but the mildest intoxication can occur. To the present writer's knowledge no laboratory analysis of the alcoholic content of Tiriki beer has been made, but he found that a couple of tumblers (about 15 ounces) of undiluted Tiriki beer, quickly quaffed, produced the same sort of mild euphoria and slight feeling of unsteadiness that he usually experiences after rapidly drinking two 12-ounce cans of American beer on an empty stomach.

The Tiriki elders, who probably frequently consume more than a quart of beer during the course of an afternoon's drinking, typically saunter home with bloodshot eyes, heavy breath, and unsteady gait, expressing their feeling of well-being through song, soliloquy, and effusive greetings to all passers-by. Nevertheless, the writer never saw an elder lose control of his actions as a consequence of his attending a community beer drink. If there are those who might actually become intoxicated from the beer, the web of social attitudes and expectancies around beer drinking evidently are such as to preclude their drinking enough to lose control or express their euphoria in a disruptive or abusive manner.

A mystical attitude of almost religious reverence is still widely held by the elders towards locally brewed beer, undoubtedly because of its traditional use in ritual and ceremonial occasions. The majority of the elders have given up maintenance of the ancestral cult ritual and have ceded religious leadership, at crisis rites and on other special occasions, to the Christian clergy. Of course, in doing so, they have disavowed major responsibility for troubles that befall the land and the people. They still feel, however, that the ancestral spirits are bound to be attracted by beer, and thus be near at hand at every drink. Even though the ancestral spirits may be no longer religiously supreme, the pagan elders still feel that no good and probably evil results from displeasing the ancestral spirits by misbehavior around the beer pots.

Traditionally beer drinks are considered an effective way of ridding oneself of the company of witches. The Tiriki say that the witches (*baloji*) are those individuals who because of an innate evil predisposition use both magical and natural means to bring harm and death to other members of the community and tribe. It is believed that witches fear to join the beer drinks because the ancestral spirits wouldn't tolerate the presence of witches, might cause them to sicken and die, and then relegate their ghosts to the bottom of Lake Victoria. Continued misbehavior at beer drinks (indeed, continued unusual behavior in any quarter of life) is grounds for suspecting an individual of being a witch; thus a man is prone to take seriously an admonition by the elders to behave with more decorum while drinking. Nowadays these traditional attitudes provide a subtle incentive for any person who has difficulty in holding his liquor to give up drinking altogether and become a pillar of one of the Protestant Christian churches in Tiriki, all of which preach total abstinence.

Some pagans interpret a man's conversion to Christianity as evidence of his being a witch, while the Christians, for their part, assert that the ancestral spirits are in fact nothing other than Satan's agents; some Christians even go so far as to say that the ancestral spirits are probably ghosts of deceased witches.

A growing number of Tiriki beer drinkers are essentially little concerned about the power of the ancestral spirits and have lost much of the traditional feeling of reverence towards beer. For them, the fear that misconduct while drinking may displease the elders, bring them the elders' curse, or, even worse, move the elders to direct their vast resources of magical power against them, serves as an effective deterrent against rowdiness while drinking, and indeed against chronic misconduct in any sphere of life. The elders have a virtual working monopoly over the use of destructive magic, because it is believed that using such magic deprives the practitioner of his fertility; thus only elders no longer concerned about having more children feel free to employ whatever power of this sort they may hold. Within the elder group itself misconduct at a beer party is extremely rare because the ostracism to which the delinquent elder will be subjected not only deprives him of the opportunity of attending future beer drinks but also bars him from the other regular judicial and social prerogatives of elderdom.

Drunkenness occasionally occurs in Tiriki today, and its incidence is probably on the increase. The writer knows of no case of drunkenness occurring from local beer alone. Sometimes a bit of local illegally distilled liquor (*iwalagi*) is added to the local beer, but seldom is the amount of alcohol drunk increased enough by this to result in anything more than a slight increase in the volume and speed of chatter around the beer pot. Instances of drunkenness are almost always the result of two or three friends acquiring a pint or more of illegally distilled liquor and then retiring to an empty hut or shady spot to quaff it off in a matter of minutes. This results in a few moments of extreme garrulousness and hyper-activity quickly followed by stupor and sleep.*

* The popularity of European-type bottled beer is on the rise among younger members of the tribe in spite of its high cost relative to the price of local beer. Legal European-distilled liquor, however, is out of the price range of all but a handful of

Seldom are Tiriki violent or destructive when drunk, and, unless a person tries to interfere with a beer party when in this state, it is not common for any corporate or community action to be taken against a drunken man. If an intoxicated person harms someone or destroys property, it is up to the injured party (or parties) to bring the matter either before the local court or directly to the British-instituted subdistrict court. The result of either action is usually that the defendant is obliged to pay the injured party appropriate indemnity, plus a small fee to the local elders, or a more substantial fine to the subdistrict court. The community, in the person of the community elders, occasionally takes action against an individual (or group) who has become troublesome in his use of local distilled liquor. To date it remains impossible for an individual or group in Tiriki to attain sufficient privacy either to make or to distribute locally distilled liquor for any length of time without the community elders becoming aware of the fact. Since to do either is a Crown offense, indiscreet, impolitic, or undesirable behavior on the part of any or all so involved may lead to tipoffs by the elders, arrests by the Kenya Police, and consequent jail terms for the offenders.

Persistence and Change

The preceding pages should suffice to show the close relationship between Tiriki drinking patterns and Tiriki social organization. Not only does beer have strong mystical connotations because of its constant traditional utilization in religious and ritual ceremony, but in addition it will be recalled that those not in the age groups—the uninitiated, the outcasts, and the strangers—were not permitted to partake in any of the beer drinks, except occasionally on a highly tentative basis.

The coming of the missionaries and the subsequent multitude of religious and social changes they have fostered have in no way destroyed the intimate relationship between drinking practices and social organization; indeed the missionaries have probably strengthened it. Certainly the course of missionizing in Tiriki has been strongly affected by both the missionary viewpoint on alcohol and the traditional Tiriki orientation.

The missionaries introduced a new notion to Tiriki, namely that beer is evil (*damanu*) and beer drinking a sin (*bwoni*). All the missions in Tiriki, with the exception of a small, rather recently established Catholic mission and one small, politically suspect separatist church, preach and profess that the drinking of alcoholic beverages is incompatible with leading a Christian life. During the early portion of the writer's stay in Tiriki,

---

Tiriki; thus those who seek hard liquor must almost invariably themselves distill or purchase the local version of "moonshine" (*iwalagi*). Made from sour maize mash, almost colorless and clear, it is very strong and often quite raw. Occasionally the wrong fraction of distillation occurs; several hours of agony preceded the death of one man who drank without restraint from an untried batch during the writer's stay in Tiriki.

missionaries reported to him that the Tiriki have been less receptive to Christianity than the surrounding Abaluhiya tribes, and that all but the most intelligent Tiriki men still reject Christianity because of the appeal of beer. The Tiriki elders, both pagan and Christian, very quickly made it clear to the writer that they themselves classified all beer drinkers as good Tiriki (age-group members in good standing), and all abstainers as Christians (and highly suspect, if older men). Thus abstinence has come to be a general symbol to both missionary and African of Christian church membership.

A review of who has been converted to Christianity, who have remained steadfast members, and who have become "backsliders," during the last 54 years (1902–1956) in Tiriki, reveals that, quite consistently, those who have become and remained Christians are either people who are uninitiated and therefore unqualified to participate in age-group beer drinks or people who have been discouraged or completely forbidden by the elders to participate in age-group activities of which beer drinking is an integral part. Indeed, during the first 25 years of missionizing, very few people except those excluded from the Tiriki age groups were attracted by the alternative affiliation and status offered by mission church membership. In other words, virtually all the converts to Tiriki missions during this period were tribal aliens, outcasts, women who wished to escape from uncongenial husbands, and children wooed by food and clothing or sent by their parents to work on the mission coffee plantation for money, and sometimes also to attend school.

Then in 1927 the government-appointed Tiriki chief, Chief Amiani, was converted to Christianity. Although a member in good standing of his age group when appointed as headman in 1911, he tried to continue in a senior-warrior, executive-type role as chief even after he had reached the age when his age group had retired to a judicial role. Thus, by 1927, his waning popularity both within his own age group and with the other age groups may have inclined him to turn to the missionaries for a new source of support and prestige.

Around 1932 the mission persuaded the converted Tiriki chief to legislate against Christian women being forced to brew beer for their pagan husbands. Women had customarily brewed the beer for their menfolk's beer parties, which are an integral part of initiated male sociability and also of the initiation feasts. The women, however, were never included in the parties. After this legislative decision, women started joining the churches in increasing numbers, and today hardly a woman can be found who is not a church member. Thus they have escaped the drudgery of brewing beer.

The chief's edict did not succeed in making Tiriki a beerless tribe; it did, however, shift the burden of beer preparation from the women to the men. Further, the traditional millet (eleusine) beer was completely forsaken for beer made from maize in which the fermentation process is seeded by the addition of a few millet sprouts. The shift to maize beer undoubtedly would have taken place even if the women had continued to make beer, because of its relative cheapness and its quickness and ease of preparation. Tradition, however, which assigned all grinding to women, obliged the men immediately to turn to maize flour as the base for their beer because maize could be ground into flour at the mission-introduced power mills, while eleusine had to be ground by hand.

Church membership has come to mean a great deal more to the women than simply an escape from beer-making. Traditionally, women's legal, economic, and principal religious statuses were all mediated through their agnatic or affinal male kinsmen. The churches have not really enfranchised women in these areas because the principal church authority positions are held by men. Today, however, husbands are often absent from home for extended periods of work in European areas, and the local church groups fulfill many of the social functions once performed by the adult men for the women of their homesteads. Not only do the church groups minister to the more strictly religious needs of the women, but also the village church pastor may act as a woman's jural representative in the absence of her husband, father, or brother. Finally, the women now organize agricultural work bees, with accompanying semi-formal tea parties, on the basis of local church affiliation. Indeed, church tea parties have become the women's equivalent of the traditional beer parties of the men.

During the last two decades the economic advantages of European-type schooling, which can be acquired in Tiriki only through mission-run schools, have become more and more widely recognized by both Christian and pagan. Consequently many pagan fathers have been sending their sons to school even though this often means that the sons have nominally become Christians. After adolescence most of these students submit to the traditional Tiriki initiation with its beer-filled ceremonies. In consequence they are regarded as "backsliders" by both the missionaries and steadfast African Converts. Many never reinstate themselves in the Christian churches and never return to school to complete their intermediate and secondary education. A minority, however, curb their appetite for tribal beer and sociability, make their peace with the missionaries, and return to school to complete their intermediate and secondary education.

Some of these go on to become primary school teachers and sometimes church pastors. Thence, with the aid of their superior education and mission and church backing, a man may achieve a position in the British-instituted tribal government. Shortly after getting the governmental job, he almost inevitably starts attending the community beer drinks of his age group. Consequently he gains the companionship and judicial support of the local and tribal elders, and is but little disturbed when he is suspended from his church leadership positions. Formerly a man usually lost his school-teaching job if he started drinking beer; but today, with a growing shortage of teachers, the missions seem to be more tolerant of beer-drinking school-teachers.

Today, just as 25 years ago, men excluded from the Tiriki age-group organization (uninitiated aliens, witch suspects, and outcasts), form most of the senior African mission church leadership in Tiriki. Young men, eager to further their education and help launch their political careers through mission affiliation, form most of the junior male Tiriki church membership and leadership. It is the uninitiated Tiriki, however, those who cannot and never could partake in the age-group beer drinks—the women and children—who comprise the overwhelming majority of Tiriki church membership. The Tiriki age-group elders are quite content with the younger men's present relationship with the missions; the younger men profit by mission education and church connections without incurring a lasting loyalty among aliens, witch suspects, and women, thanks to the missions' stand on beer.

References

1. Huntingford, G. W . B., *The Nandi of Kenya,* London: Routledge and Kegan Paul, 1953.
2. Peristiany, J. G., *The Social Institutions of the Kipsigis,* London: Routledge and Kegan Paul, 1939.
3. Sangree, Walter H., *Structural Continuity and Change in a Bantu Tribe: the Nature and Development of Contemporary Tiriki Social Organization,* unpublished doctoral dissertation, University of Chicago, 1959.
4. ———, *Anthrop. Tomorrow* (mimeographed student journal, University of Chicago), 7:5–11, 1957.
5. Wagner, Gunter, "The Political Organization of the Bantu of Kavirondo," in M. Fortes (Ed.), *African Political Systems,* London: Oxford University Press, 1940.
6. ———, *The Bantu of North Kavirondo,* Vol. I, London: Oxford University Press, 1949.
7. ———, "The Abaluyia of Kavirondo," in Daryll Forde (Ed.), *African Worlds,* London: Oxford University Press, 1954.
8. ———, *The Bantu of North Kavirondo,* Vol. II, London: Oxford University Press, 1956.

chapter 2

Drinking patterns of the Bolivian Camba[*]

Dwight B. Heath

An approach to evaluating the role of socio-cultural aspects of drinking behavior can perhaps best be made through the comparison of drinking patterns and associated traits in the different cultures of several societies. It is the anthropologist who has the conceptual tools, broad ethnographic knowledge, and opportunities for research of this kind. The most ambitious cross-cultural study in this field was undertaken by Horton (7) and was based on general ethnographic descriptions of seventy-seven primitive societies. His major conclusion was that "the primary function of alcoholic beverages in all societies is the reduction of anxiety."

One of the difficulties encountered in Horton's study was the frequent ambiguity or inadequacy of data pertaining to drinking as an aspect of culture. It is simply impossible for the ethnographer in the field to report in equal detail on every phase of the culture he is studying, however "simple," "primitive," or "homogeneous" that culture may appear. It is hardly surprising, therefore, that Horton found few systematic descriptions of prosaic and familiar drinking patterns in the anthropological literature. The orgiastic tribal drinking sprees so vividly depicted in many reports are not typical in worldwide perspective. Yet these uses of alcohol commanded more attention than social drinking in small groups or other less spectacular forms of drinking behavior.

* This chapter is a revised and somewhat shortened version of an article which originally appeared in the *Quarterly Journal of Studies on Alcohol,* 19:491–508. The field research upon which this study is based was aided by a grant from the Henry L. and Grace Doherty Charitable Foundation, Inc.

A few investigators have recently made studies specifically concerned with the relationship of drinking to other aspects of culture in primitive societies.* The discussion which follows adds to this growing literature a brief characterization of the culture of a relatively homogeneous society, the Camba of eastern Bolivia, together with a description of Camba drinking patterns and some tentative interpretations of the relationships between drinking and other cultural institutions. The peculiar relevance of such an analysis of this particular group to the study of drinking behavior in general should become apparent in the course of this discussion.

The Cultural Context

The Camba are a mestizo people. They are descendants of colonial Spaniards and local Indians, and their physical and cultural characteristics evidence both sides of their ancestry. In reality, the Camba constitute what might be called an "emergent society." They have rejected traditional tribal ways of life, yet have been admitted as a laboring caste only to the periphery of another society dominated by a small group of whites. Even today, Indians are "becoming" Cambas by assuming clothing, learning Spanish, and moving to haciendas as farmhands. Numbering about eighty thousand, the Camba occupy an area of alternating jungle and prairie which stretches north from the city of Santa Cruz in eastern Bolivia. Enormous distances and natural barriers have effectively isolated them from any regular or sustained contact with other centers of population. Hence the Camba comprise an enclave with a slightly modified colonial Spanish way of life, virtually surrounded by nomadic Indian tribes.

A primitive form of agriculture is the primary economic activity in this tropical lowland area. Trees are felled in a small plot of jungle land, the undergrowth is cut and burned, and rice, corn, or manioc is planted for a

---

* Bunzel's pioneering work (2), in which she compared the role of alcoholism in a Guatemalan and a Mexican Indian community, is a model of integration and interpretation. Alcoholism has been treated as a major focus of anxiety also in two Indian communities in Mexico by Viqueira and Palerm (17), and in two Indian and three white cultures which occur within a small area in the southwestern United States by Geertz (4). Honigmann and Honigmann (6) compared in some detail the drinking patterns and cultures of Athapaskan Indians and their white neighbors in a small Canadian trading post community. The function of alcohol in Mohave society was interpreted by Devereux (3) in the light of psychoanalytic concepts, while the drinking behavior of the Navajo was described by Heath (5), and that of some Salish tribes by Lemert (8, 9). Berreman (1) related inebriety to social strain among the Aleuts, as did Sayres (15) in three communities in rural Colombia. Marroquín (11) briefly described the use of alcoholic beverages by the Quechua in Peru, and Mangin (10) stressed the predominantly integrative functions of drinking among them. Rodríguez (13) summarized reasons which another group of the same tribe (in Ecuador) gave for drinking, and Sariola (14), in characterizing the drinking customs of the Indians of Bolivia, generalized Quechua patterns to other tribes. Platt's (12) description of traditional alcoholic beverages among the south African Bantu emphasized their socially integrative uses.

few years before the soil is exhausted and abandoned. Such an inefficient system is possible only because so small a population occupies a vast area of rich land—some of the larger haciendas are measured in terms of "so many days' ride by horseback" in different directions from the house of the landlord. Even on such estates no more than twenty tenant farmers are regularly employed because only a tiny portion of the land is cultivated at any time.

Although it is at most a few generations since their Indian forebears were lured or bought from the Chiriguano, Guarayú, Siriono, or Tapieté tribes by gifts of steel tools and alcohol, these farmers, who speak an archaic dialect of Spanish and wear clothing of Western cut, regard the neighboring nomadic tribesmen of today as "savages" or "barbarians." Virtually none of the aboriginal religion, folklore, or social organization persists among the Camba; some elements of handicraft and a few native words are all that has been retained of the indigenous cultures.

The Camba may be described as peasants. A few of them are independent farmers, living on isolated homesteads and cultivating small plots in order to grow enough produce to feed their families. The great majority, however, live as tenants on haciendas where they are given food, housing, tools, clothing, and a tiny token wage in exchange for their labor. These haciendas are rarely large-scale commercial enterprises. Enough produce is raised to feed the owner, his family and workers, and to provide a small surplus for trade in local village markets. Unlike most peasants, the Camba have no love of the land and are extremely mobile. The few who own small tracts of land live in isolation on their scattered homesteads. But the majority who work as tenants move about frequently, "just to try a new place," unless they are bound to a landlord by debt. Others live in isolation as squatters on the uncultivated land on the edges of the large estates, which they use as their own until dispossessed. Work patterns are such that cooperative effort is rarely encountered. Even during harvests on haciendas each man works a small area assigned to him, much as the small landholder works alone.

There is little opportunity for accumulation of capital in an economy which is neither marginal nor overproductive. The individual Camba is not beset either by the stress of competition or by subsistence anxieties. Especially insulated from strain are the tenant farmers whose few needs are met by their landlords and who accept a secure dependent status unquestioningly.

Geographic mobility is such that membership in neighboring groups is fluid and enduring friendships are rare. Wage work is conceived of as an impersonal business relationship, and there is no special loyalty to the employer or to the hacienda. The only associations which might be considered sodalities are the Farmers' Union, a pseudo labor organization which really serves only as an agency for political patronage, and the Veterans of the Chaco War, which dates from the early 1930's when virtually every able-bodied man in the country was fighting against Paraguay.

Although nominally Roman Catholic, the Camba have little knowledge of Church doctrine. They observe a few rites in a way which bespeaks magical faith rather than profound religious conviction. Fundamentalist Protestant missionaries have made some devoted converts, but their numbers are few. Perhaps the most striking feature of Camba religious life is that not one of the indigenous elements survives.

Just as in the religious and economic spheres social integration is minimal, kinship ties are tenuous, and solidarity is lacking. Common-law marriage is the rule and such consensual unions are extremely brittle. Often a man will leave a woman after 3 or 4 years and move to another area where he takes another wife. The deserted woman does not return to her family but works for a time until another man comes on the scene. Because the individual couple usually set up housekeeping independently, apart from either spouse's parents, the extended family of three or more generations, so common among primitive and peasant peoples, does not occur. The independence of the nuclear family is stressed, and geographic dispersion results in few cooperative enterprises.

Camba socialization gives little indication of severity, trauma, or discontinuity. Children are valued and well treated. There are no ceremonies marking the birth, but christening takes place as soon as the family comes to town where the church is located, usually within 4 months. Babies are swung in hammocks or cradled in the mother's arms most of the time until they begin to crawl and then they have almost complete freedom. Because the mother is always near, she can offer sympathy, petting, or the breast whenever an infant cries. Weaning is abrupt only when a newborn baby displaces an older child; otherwise he may nurse occasionally for comfort until he is 4 or 5 years old. Gradual toilet training is started shortly after the first birthday.

Children over 3 are left very much to their own devices, except that girls are sometimes obliged to care for younger siblings when their mother is occupied with a new baby. This they do ungrudgingly but with childish irresponsibility. Discipline is rarely severe and usually takes the form of a brief scolding; physical punishment is considered brutish. Aggression is rarely shown by adults or children. The family usually are together for meals, for siesta, and in the evening. The small one-room thatch hut is used only for sleeping and as shelter against inclement weather; otherwise most domestic activities center around the yard. Because of familial isolation there is little opportunity for group play. Children have responsibilities such as gathering firewood, carrying water, running errands, and so forth, but spend much of their time playing alone or with siblings until adolescence when, with no ritual observance, they assume the duties of adults and are ready for marriage.

The Role of Alcohol

The Camba drink a highly concentrated alcoholic beverage on their numerous festive occasions. Both drinking and drunkenness are the norm on these occasions and an integral part of their social ritual. Drunkenness is consciously sought as an end in itself, and consensus supports its value. Aggression and sexual license are conspicuously absent on these sole occasions when beverage alcohol is used. Moreover, there is no evidence whatsoever of individual instances of dependence upon alcohol comparable to alcoholism or addiction as it is known in the United States. These facts highlight the strategic significance of the Camba for the understanding of alcohol problems.

The Beverage. Despite an abundance of tropical fruits, palms, corn, manioc, and other foods from which neighboring tribes make beers and wines, the Camba do not make or drink home brews. After meals they take strong black coffee, and as a refreshment, an unfermented corn chicha. But their festive beverage is not so innocuous. It is probably the most potent alcoholic drink in customary usage.

Almost the only commercial industry in the area is the distillation of cane alcohol. The soil and climate are well suited to the cultivation of sugarcane. However, neither sugar nor molasses could have been sold for enough profit to cover the cost of the 2-month mule trek over the mountains—until recently, the only route to the nearest market city in the western portion of the country. The margin of profit from alcohol, however, was sufficiently great to justify the expense of transportation. Hence, nine distilleries are now operating. These range from a small homemade contraption which produces about 200 liters a day during the 4-month season, to a huge mill with modern French machinery and a daily capacity of 12,000 liters.

The product of these distilleries, called *alcohol,* is shipped throughout the country in 16-liter cans. Chemical analysis indicates that it contains 89 per cent ethyl alcohol. Watered to 30 or 40 per cent, *alcohol* becomes the *aguardiente* so often encountered in the Andean region. Among the Camba, however, it is not diluted. It is a colorless drink with little flavor but has an extremely irritating effect upon the drinker's mouth and throat. The Camba report that this burning does not diminish with habituation, and admit readily that they enjoy neither the taste nor the feel of *alcohol*. What they profess to enjoy is the drunkenness which it brings. On a particularly hot day, the acrid fumes which may bring tears to a seasoned drinker's eyes occasion good-natured jokes about the strength of the beverage and derision of the unseemly "tame" drinks of other peoples. A special advantage of drinking the pure *alcohol* which was frequently cited by informants was that "it kills the [intestinal] parasites" which infest virtually all of the Camba. Although the validity of this "medical" opinion is questionable, the Camba attribute "stomach trouble" and "liver sickness" among other peoples to their use of additives—water or fruit juice—which "spoil" *alcohol*.

In each village some shopkeepers sell *alcohol*, and on the haciendas it can usually be purchased at the commissary. Sometimes a shrewd speculator keeps a few bottles hidden in his hut so that he can resell them at night, when the normal sources of supply are closed, and realize a profit of 20 or 30 per cent. The standard unit of measure is the *botella*, a used beer or soda bottle with a capacity of 0.7 liters. The cost of a bottle of *alcohol* is equivalent to three days' wages of a farm laborer.

The fact that buying *alcohol* keeps men poor must not be construed as an indication of constant drinking or neglect of family obligations. The basic needs of a tenant and his family are met by his landlord, and cash wages represent only a small portion of a man's real earnings. This informal "social security," including care of the ill and aged, stems from an old strictly feudal system which has only recently undergone slight modification.

Occasions for Drinking. The Camba drink *alcohol* only during fiestas, but these are not infrequent. Every national or religious holiday throughout the entire year, including local patron saints' days, is such an occasion. There are no religious prescriptions or proscriptions about drinking, but the Camba sometimes confide that they are "putting one over" on the village priest when they have a party. *Alcohol* plays no part in the rites of the Church, and drinking during a religious service or procession is frowned upon. However, the rest of each holiday is devoted to carousal, and Carnival, the week preceding Lent, is treated as a week-long occasion for revelry. Peasants who come into town from outlying haciendas sit in small groups in the street and drink, while those at home often have "open house" for friends and neighbors. Each weekend, too, is an occasion for rest from the week's labors and for drunkenness in an atmosphere of companionship with whoever joins the party in a house or yard.

Rites of passage are also occasions for festive drinking. When the family return home from a christening, the godparent "sponsors" a drinking party.* After his wedding, the groom is expected to give a party for all comers. Some men have even given avoidance of this expense as their chief reason for not solemnizing a stable common-law marriage. Regardless of the age and sex of the deceased, a wake is another occasion for drinking, usually at the expense of surviving relatives. It is perhaps noteworthy, in marked contrast to American patterns, that the annual reunion of the Veterans of the Chaco War is a sober occasion when warm camaraderie reigns but drinking is completely absent.

Fiestas may last several days. Most people spend their entire weekends drinking; wakes last a night and a day; national and religious holidays are not only used to the full but almost always are stretched a day longer. The Camba recognize only two possible reasons for bringing a fiesta to a close —lack of *alcohol* and obligation to return to work. The former applies mostly to independent farmers (small landholders and squatters) to whom

---

* No special prestige accrues from "sponsoring" a party, and no one expresses thanks when it is over. In fact, the concept of "sponsorship" is used here simply as a convention for the more cumbersome phrase "providing the first bottle." The Camba do not think in such terms and no one "gives" a party; it is simply held "at so-and-so's place." When the "sponsor's" supply of *alcohol* is exhausted, other participants readily and without comment pool their funds to buy more.

no source of credit is available; tenants are permitted and even encouraged to take small loans from landlords who consider their extension of credit as cheap assurance of a stable labor force. The obligation to return to work, by contrast, rarely pertains to the independent farmer, who sets his own schedule, unlike the tenant who is assigned working hours. Most landlords have made a compromise which is effective in getting cooperation from their workers: the day following every holiday is also a day of fiesta, but after that everyone must go back to work. Thus the workers feel that they are getting an extra holiday on each occasion and return ungrudgingly when the time comes. In like manner, after a weekend people are resigned to the obligation of working through the new week.

Participants. It is probably a valid generalization that all Camba adults, except the few Protestants, drink *alcohol;* and most of them become intoxicated at least twice each month. Despite frequent and gross inebriety, alcoholism, in the sense of addiction, does not occur.

Drinking takes place only within a social context; solitary drinking is inconceivable to the Camba. Observed groups varied in size from three to sixteen, and were as often mixed as they were of men only. Women do not drink except with men. Kinship does not figure in any consistent manner or significant degree in the composition of such groups even during festivities connected with life crises, reflecting the dispersal of kinsmen and the tenuousness of relationship bonds. Usually unmarried men and women drink only in the company of married couples. Boys and girls (*muchachos* and *muchachas*) stand around but are not invited to join until they are considered "young people" (*jóvenes*), a status of maturity with criteria no less vague than those of adolescence in our own society. The youngest drinker encountered was 12; the oldest claimed to be 92.

Fiestas never comprise invited guests only—they grow by aggregation of neighbors, passers-by who are hailed from the road, and watchful "free loaders" who come uninvited. For this reason, they show no marked stratification by age, apart from the exclusion of children. In the course of a fiesta a group may expand considerably but would in no event subdivide into smaller units. Social class lines are so sharply drawn between the peasant majority and the landed gentry that these groups never drink together and, in fact, rarely mix in any social situation.

Drinking Ritual. The behavioral patterns associated with drinking are so formalized as to constitute a secular ritual. Members of the group are seated in chairs in an approximate circle in a yard or, occasionally, in a hut. A bottle of *alcohol* and a single water glass rest on a tiny table which forms part of the circle. The "sponsor" of the party pours a glassful (about 300 cc) at the table, turns and walks to stand in front of whomever he wishes, nods, and raises the glass slightly. The person addressed smiles and nods while still seated; the "sponsor" toasts with "*Salud*" (health), or "*A su salud*" (to your health), drinks half of the glassful in a single quick draught, and hands it to the person he has toasted, who then repeats the toast and finishes the glass in one gulp. While the "sponsor" returns to his seat, the recipient of the toast goes to the table to refill the glass and to repeat the ritual.

There are no apparent rules concerning whom one may toast, and in this sense toasts proceed in no discernible sequence. A newcomer is likely to receive a barrage of toasts when he first joins a drinking group, and sometimes an attractive girl may be frequently addressed, but there tends to be a fairly equal distribution of toasts over a period of several hours. To decline a toast is unthinkable to the Camba, although as the party wears on and the inflammation of mouth and throat makes drinking increasingly painful, participants resort to a variety of ruses in order to avoid having to swallow an entire glassful of *alcohol* each time. These ruses are quite transparent (such as turning one's head aside and spitting out a fair portion) and are met with cajoling remonstrances to "Drink it all!" Such behavior is not an affront to the toaster, however, and the other members of the group are teasing more than admonishing the deviant.

After the first 3 or 4 hours virtually everyone "cheats" this way and almost as much *alcohol* is wasted as is consumed. Also, as the fiesta wears on, the rate of toasting decreases markedly: during the first hour a single toast is completed in less than two minutes; during the third hour it slows to five minutes or more. A regular cycle of activity can be discerned, with a party being revived about every six hours. When a bottle is emptied, one of the children standing quietly nearby takes it away and brings a replacement from the hut. When the supply is exhausted, members of the group pool their funds to buy more; they send a child to bring it from the nearest seller.

The ritual sequence described above is the only way in which the Camba drink, except at wakes, where a different but equally formalized pattern of behavior is followed. At a wake there is still a single bottle and a single glass, but they are carried by an adolescent girl who is not necessarily related to the deceased. She stops in front of each male mourner and, if he nods, pours a glassful of *alcohol* and hands it to him. He looks around the room, nodding slightly and silently to all present, and they return the silent nod. He drinks in a single quick draught and returns the glass to the girl who continues making the rounds. A mourner may decline by simply shaking his head. Female mourners are not offered alcohol "because women always have so much sadness, they don't need it."

Behavior and Attitudes Associated with Drinking

A fiesta is a time for easy social intercourse. Despite the elaborately patterned behavioral sequence, drinking is not a solemn rite. There is usually a low undercurrent of nondescript small talk—conversations about the weather or crops, a few anecdotes, or simply recounting the events of the past week. Occasionally there is music—a young man may play the guitar and sing love songs, or men may form a band of flute, snare drum, and bass drum. In either case, men ask women to dance and couples shuffle awk-wardly around inside the circle while the drinking ritual continues.

The Camba usually begin drinking shortly after breakfast. A stomachful of *masaco* (a pasty mash of manioc and lard) retards the absorption of alcohol into the system. Nevertheless, as a party wears on, the effects of intoxication become apparent. After 2 or 3 hours of fairly voluble and warm social intercourse, people tend to become thick-lipped, and intervals of silence lengthen. By the fourth hour there is little conversation; many people stare dumbly at the ground except when toasted, and a few who may have fallen asleep or "passed out" are left undisturbed. Once a band or guitarist starts playing, the music is interminable and others take over as individual players pass out. The sixth hour sees a renewed exhilaration as sleepers waken and give the party a "second wind." This cycle is repeated every 5, 6, or 7 hours, day and night, until the *alcohol* gives out or the call to work is sounded.

During a lull, a woman may slip away to prepare *masaco* or bread, which is then put in a conspicuous place outside the circle where people may help themselves as they go to urinate in the shadows a few feet away from the group. No matter how long a fiesta may be, no other food or drink is taken, yet nausea was observed only once.

The general pattern of individual behavioral changes in inebriation is fairly standard. There is an appreciable increase in sociability during the early stages. The Camba peasant who is ordinarily taciturn becomes more voluble; his normal attitude of almost complete indifference to the world around him is replaced by a self-confidence which is shown in positive but not dogmatic expression of opinions. As he imbibes more *alcohol,* the in-dividual becomes befuddled—he thinks more slowly and has trouble voicing his ideas. There follows a sort of retreat inward; he stops talking, slumps in his chair, and may fall asleep. When he "comes to," the earlier euphoria is restored and he enthusiastically rejoins the party as though he had never withdrawn. Women usually "cheat" by swallowing a smaller portion of each draught, and they rarely pass out. Although they are no more subject to censure for drunkenness than are men, they claim to be more sensitive to irritation of the mouth and throat.

It is perhaps worth while to underscore a few ways in which this pattern of drunkenness differs from that of certain other peoples. For instance, among the Camba drinking does not lead to expressions of aggression in verbal or physical form, as is so often the case when alcohol overrides normal inhibitions to asocial behavior. Neither is there a heightening of sexual activity: obscene joking and sexual overtures are rarely associated with drinking. Even when drunk, the Camba are not given to maudlin sentimentality, clowning, boasting or "baring of souls." Drunkenness is con-sidered an inevitable consequence of drinking and, far from being despised, is highly valued and even eagerly sought by the men. Repeated questioning in various forms and contexts about their reasons for drinking inevitably evoked the same answer: "Just to get drunk" (*Para emborracharse, no mas*). The Camba have no conception of an ideal stage of drunkenness, such as "just feeling good," nor do they differentiate between stages of intoxication such as "high," "tight," and "drunk."

Because a Camba almost never leaves the permissive context of the drinking group while intoxicated, no one has occasion to condemn his behavior. Occasional untoward actions are explained and excused on the basis that "sometimes when a man is drunk he doesn't always know what he's doing." Among examples, which were not made much of, were a man's unwittingly stepping on a sleeping pig, failing to button his trousers after urinating, or burning himself by accidentally brushing against the globe of a lantern. Such minor misbehaviors are not held against the drinker nor does he feel obliged to apologize then or later. There is apparently no guilt associated with drinking, drunkenness, or drunken behavior.

Although it has never been explicitly formulated by the Camba, an implicit general system of reciprocity seems to hold with respect to fiestas. Whenever a peasant feels he can afford it, he buys a few bottles of *alcohol* and all comers are welcome. Often, in fact, a man will "sponsor" a fiesta when he obviously cannot afford it. A few unmarried men are notorious "free loaders" but are tolerated because they provide creditable performances on the guitar which add to the "atmosphere" of a fiesta.

Magical properties are not attributed to *alcohol* by the Camba, apart perhaps from its supposed medicinal value as an internal parasiticide. Drinking does not appear to have connotations of proof of masculinity, and individual differences in tolerance to alcohol go unnoticed. However, the fact that the investigator, a *gringo* (foreigner), drank with the Camba was to his credit and was made much of as a sign of true friendship even on his first day in the area. Indeed, he soon came to be called in consequence "very much a Camba" (*muy Camba*).

Hangovers and hallucinations are unknown among these people, as is addiction to alcohol. A farmhand will "snap out of" intoxication abruptly when the call to breakfast is sounded after a fiesta. He eats a bowlful of *masaco*, drinks a cup of black coffee, and then performs a normal morning of work. Sometimes on an especially hot day their systems are so full of alcohol that fumes from their perspiration make their eyes water, but neither their work nor they themselves show any ill effects. And so they labor quietly, diligently, apart, until the next fiesta.

Tentative Interpretations

An attempt has been made above to describe drinking patterns and their cultural context in sufficient detail so that other investigators may analyze and interpret them in terms of their own diverse interests and theoretical orientations. A few tentative interpretations will be offered here, however, to suggest approaches which may be fruitful in understanding the role of alcohol in Camba society. It is hoped that these may also suggest, by analogy, certain functions of alcohol in other areas and throughout history, although this analysis makes no pretense at comprehensiveness or finality.

The Camba data supplement those from other primitive societies which indicate that alcoholism is not a function of the alcohol concentration of beverages used, or of the quantities imbibed. While these people drink large amounts of almost pure alcohol, no instance of addiction was encountered, and drinking is completely restricted to specific social situations. Furthermore, the Camba convincingly demonstrate that extensive inebriety does not necessarily result in manifest troubles. An important contrast with most primitive societies which have marginal economies must be noted, however, in that the periodicity of Camba drinking cannot be attributed to irregularity of supply of beverage. Neither does their high rate of drinking appear to be correlated with obvious threats in the environment. In terms of the sources of anxiety on which Horton (7) based his ratings for cross-cultural comparison—subsistence, sexuality, and aggression—the Camba are virtually free from fears and it would be a dubious matter to attribute their drinking to any of those areas of insecurity.

If it be assumed that all human behavior is motivated and that the patterns of behavior which persist are those which are in some way rewarding to the individuals who comprise the group or society, then any attempt to understand the relationship of one aspect of culture to the broader ongoing socio-cultural system must deal with functions. The following is an attempt to suggest, by inference, some of the functions which alcohol may serve for the individual Camba, as a start in explaining the role of alcohol in that society.

The outstanding characteristic of Camba drinking is the elaborately patterned sequence of behavior which is the only context in which drinking takes place. The strict conformity and the implicit equality of communion expressed in the use of a single glass seem to make of drinking a socially significant rite. The importance of this factor cannot be fully appreciated without the realization that the rest of Camba culture is virtually lacking in forms of communal expression. The child is early trained to self-sufficiency which prepares him well for the relative isolation of adult life. Geographically dispersed nuclear families are virtually independent of each other, and kinship ties are tenuous and unstable.

There is also, as we have noted, little sense of identification with neighborhood, church, or voluntary associations. People live alone and work alone, with few opportunities for sociability throughout the week. Fiestas provide occasions for intense interaction, and drinking groups constitute primary reference groups which are lacking in other phases of Camba life. If it be postulated, in keeping with a universal implicit assumption, that there is some element of value inherent in human association per se, this function of alcohol can be seen to have enormous potential importance for individual adjustment as well as for social cohesion. To be sure, there are activities other than drinking which could fulfill the same function of facilitating social interaction. Comparative ethnographic data suggest that the act of drinking, like eating, may in itself have a peculiar significance as a means of expressing corporate solidarity. Furthermore, there are certain characteristics inherent in beverage alcohol which make it particularly suitable as a stimulus to sociability. Despite the over-all depressing effects of alcohol on physical and mental functions, an apparent stimulating effect has long been observed in group situations.

This illusion of stimulation is given by increased volubility and camaraderie which, presumably, result from the lowering of inhibitions and restraints which normally operate to limit the individual's rapport with others. This function would be of especial importance among persons whose experience is particularly individualistic and whose frequent or prolonged isolation results in introversion and a loss of the basic social skills of relating themselves to others in a meaningful way. The effects of alcohol in overcoming such personal reserve are quite rapid; but since alcohol is readily oxidized in the body, the effects are short-lived and its occasional use does not disable men from their normal round of activities. A similar function of alcohol may be cited in the frequent association of drinking with rare and sporadic occasions for social interaction in other highly atomistic societies or subgroups, such as sailors ashore after a voyage, cowboys or lumberjacks "on the town," the farmers of Chichicastenango at market(2), or the homeless men of "Skid Row" (16).

It is interesting in this connection to compare Camba drinking with that of the surrounding tribes to which they are closely related. Although detailed descriptions are not available, it is plain that each of the major groups which contributed to the Camba population had some form of indigenous alcoholic beverage even before the Spaniards arrived, and that their drinking takes place now, as then, in occasional large group sprees or drinking bouts in which intoxication is normal. Some similarities in socio-cultural situation are shared by all of these relatively loosely structured groups.

The few exceptions to the normal pattern of drinking behavior which were observed among the Camba must also be considered in the light of this interpretation. It was noted that the only Camba who never drink are the few Protestants. The fact that they are all members of fundamentalist sects (Assembly of God, Baptist, Free Brothers) for whom abstinence is an article of doctrine would not appear to be wholly adequate as an explanation of their deviance from the norms of the larger society. It is important to note that they have, in the church, the very kind of stable primary group which is lacking for the great majority. During meetings, three or four nights weekly, each individual plays an active role, and they call each other "brother." Between services, members of these churches often play volleyball and interact in other ways which differ markedly from the social isolation of Catholics who, by and large, take no active part in religious or extraceremonial activities together. It appears, in similar manner, that the presence of a prevailing atmosphere of genuine camaraderie stemming from a past of significant shared experiences and a common chauvinistic pride may be sufficient basis to unite the veterans, during their reunion, in a way which allows warm and easy fellowship without dependence on alcohol to overcome initial reserve.

The pattern of drinking at a wake is not the usual excessive drinking to oblivion which is normal for the Camba and which has often been described in other societies as serving to overcome the effects of grief. On the contrary, it is a sedate rite in which the drinker silently pledges to all present, and it has been said that it is precisely those who grieve the most (women) who "have no need" of alcohol in this context. It may be that on such an occasion the impact of grief is itself a unifying force for most mourners, and that those who need something more to bring them out of their introversion find in alcohol a means, symbolic or physiological, of achieving rapport with others in a situation where social reinforcement is especially important.

This discussion has emphasized the importance of the drinking group as a primary reference group. But this is by implication a relational conception—the focusing of emotion on an ingroup implies awareness of an outgroup. That such an awareness does prevail among the Camba, despite the ephemeral nature of their associations in drinking, is suggested by their confiding that they are "putting one over" on the priest whenever they have a party, in their ridiculing the alcoholic beverages of other peoples, and in the investigator's becoming "very much a Camba" in large part because he drank with them.[*]

Another striking feature of Camba drinking is the high alcohol concentration of the common beverage. It is difficult to understand why a people should consistently drink so strong a beverage, especially when they themselves frankly admit it is distasteful and even painful to do so. The presence of a constant and plentiful supply, together with ease of acquisition, are not sufficient explanations, especially in the light of the expense involved. It is possible that desire for immediacy or certainty of effect is involved here. Related to this problem is the curious fact that the Camba make no use of the several wild crops plentiful in the environment which could be rendered into beers or wines at no expense and with little effort, and which are so used by the very tribes from which they are descended.

It is generally agreed that distillation is a technological refinement which was unknown throughout the New World in pre-Columbian times. Certainly it was the Spanish colonists who introduced cane alcohol to the nomadic hunting tribes who occupied this area. Alcohol was an important commodity in the seventeenth-century South American slave trade, and some historians suggest that the Jesuits and Franciscans used it to lure Indians to their missions and to keep them in controlled settlements there.

Still another problem of interpretation is raised by the Camba custom of

[*] In like manner, Lemert (9) has noted an implicit conflict between Catholicism and drinking parties among the Salish Indians of northwestern North America.

drinking to the point of gross inebriation. The fact that they consistently cite the quest of drunkenness as their reason for drinking may be no more explanatory than the usual middle-class American cliché that one drinks "just to be sociable." Discrepancy between stated reasons and actual objectives is a commonplace in all phases of human behavior. However, the frequent occurrence of complete intoxication, even to the point of "passing out," would be inconsistent with the use of alcohol as a stimulus to general sociability. The Camba do not long retain the manic euphoria which would give grounds for the sociability rationale, but almost invariably drink beyond it to a stage of increased introversion and subsequent oblivion before regaining the easy rapport which so contrasts with their usual reserve. This may result simply from faulty judgment—miscalculation of the effects of *alcohol* and subsequent excess. Quite apart from the momentum of social drinking and toasting, and from the progressive effects of *alcohol* in distorting the powers of discrimination, it must be kept in mind that small amounts of so strong a beverage can appreciably change the concentration of alcohol in the organism of relatively small, light-weight people. Consequently, a single toast (comprising about 300 cc of 178-proof alcohol) could easily mean the difference between exhilaration and oblivion.

In summary, it is suggested that alcohol plays a predominantly integrative role in Camba society, where drinking is an elaborately ritualized group activity and alcoholism is unknown. The anxieties which are often cited as bases for common group drinking are not present, but fiestas constitute virtually the only corporate form of social expression. Drinking parties predominate among rare social activities, and alcohol serves to facilitate rapport between individuals who are normally isolated and introverted.

References

1. Berreman, Gerald D., "Drinking Patterns of the Aleuts," *Quart. J. Stud. Alc.,* 17:503–514, 1956.

2. Bunzel, Ruth, "The Role of Alcoholism in Two Central American Cultures," *Psychiatry,* 3:361–387, 1940.

3. Devereux, George, "The Function of Alcohol in Mohave Society," *Quart. J. Stud. Alc.,* 9:207–251, 1948.

4. Geertz, Clifford, "Drought, Death, and Alcoholism in Five Southwestern Cultures," unpublished manuscript, Harvard University Values Study, 1951.

5. Heath, Dwight B., *Alcohol in a Navajo Community,* unpublished Harvard College thesis, 1952.

6. Honigmann, John J., and Irma Honigmann, "Drinking in an Indian-White Community," *Quart. J. Stud. Alc.,* 5:575–619, 1945.

7. Horton, Donald, "The Functions of Alcohol in Primitive Societies: A Cross-Cultural Study," *Quart. J. Stud. Alc.,* 4:199–320, 1943.

8. Lemert, Edwin M., "Alcohol and the Northwest Coast Indians," *Univ. Calif. Publ. in Culture and Society,* 2:303–406, 1954.

9. ———, "The Use of Alcohol in Three Salish Indian Tribes," *Quart. J. Stud. Alc.,* 19:90–107, 1958.

10. Mangin, William, "Drinking among Andean Indians," *Quart. J. Stud. Alc.,* **18**:55–66, 1957.

11. Marroquín, J., "Alcohol entre los Aborígenes Peruanos," *Crónica méd.* (*Lima*), **60**:226–231, 1943.

12. Platt, B. S., "Some Traditional Alcoholic Beverages and Their Importance in Indigenous African Communities," *Proc. Nutrition Soc.* (*Engl. and Scot.*), **14**:115–124, 1955.

13. Rodriguez Sandoval, Rev. Leonidas, "Drinking Motivations among the Indians of the Ecuadorian Sierra," *Prim. Man,* **18**:39–46, 1945.

14. Sariola, Sakari, "Indianer och Alkohol," *Alkoholpolitic,* **2**:39–43, 1956.

15. Sayres, William C., "Ritual Drinking, Ethnic Status and Inebriety in Rural Colombia," *Quart. J. Stud. Alc.,* **17**:53–62, 1956.

16. Straus, Robert, and Raymond G. McCarthy, "Nonaddictive Pathological Drinking Patterns of Homeless Men," *Quart. J. Stud. Alc.,* **12**:601–611, 1951.

17. Viqueira, Carmen, and Angel Palerm, "Alcoholismo, Brujería, y Homicidio en dos Comunidades Rurales de México," *Amér. Indíg.,* **14**:7–36, 1954.

chapter 3

Ambivalence and the learning of drinking behavior in a Peruvian community [*]

Ozzie G. Simmons

Drinking and drunkenness are virtually universal among adult males in the Peruvian community of Lunahuaná. Drinking has a prominent integrative role to play in the functioning of the society, while drunkenness is culturally accepted within an extremely wide range of occasions and situations. Despite the frequency of drinking and drunkenness, alcohol addiction appears to be only minimally present in Lunahuaná. This must be attributed in large part to the fact that all drinking is limited to social contexts, that this provides vast latitude within which drinking is accepted, and that drinking is defined mainly as an integral part of the culture and only minimally as a response to the needs of the individual.[†]

[*] This chapter first appeared as an article in the *American Anthropologist*, 62, December 1960. The original article has been reprinted here with only slight modification. It is a revision of a paper read at the 1959 meetings of the American Anthropological Association in Mexico City. The data were collected during the writer's residence in Peru from 1949 to 1952 as field representative of the Smithsonian Institution's Institute of Social Anthropology.

[†] The last census taken in Peru was in 1940 (the previous one was in 1876), and the research in Lunahuaná was done in 1950 to 1952. According to the census (6), the municipal district of Lunahuaná had a population of 5,216 in 1940. There is every reason to believe, from evidence available as to how the census was conducted, that this figure represented a substantial underenumeration of the population of Lunahuaná, and the writer's best guess is that the population was between eight and ten thousand in 1950. The statement that alcohol addiction is minimally present in Lunahuaná is based on the fact that the writer could find no more than a dozen or so individuals in the entire community who might possibly qualify as addicts according to the criteria for alcoholism defined by Jellinek (see Chapter 20).

In a recent discussion of the literature on the socio-cultural aspects of drinking, Ullman (11) makes the point that in any group or society where drinking customs are well established and consistent with the rest of the culture the rate of alcoholism will be low; whereas in societies in which drinking customs are not well integrated (the Yankees of the northeastern United States and Irish-Americans are offered as examples) alcoholism rates are likely to be high. Ullman goes on to say that members of societies of the first type are free from ambivalence about drinking because their culture is so consistent in this regard, whereas it can be assumed that individuals in the second type of society will have ambivalent feelings about drinking since ambivalence is the psychological product of unintegrated drinking customs.

The case of Lunahuaná offers unequivocal support for the first part of Ullman's proposition, but it is in direct opposition to the second part in that Lunahuaneños are by no means free from ambivalence about drinking. In a previous analysis of drinking patterns in Lunahuaná (9) the present writer described this ambivalence as deriving from feelings of shame rather than from feelings of guilt and sinfulness. This relationship between integrated drinking customs, low addiction, and the attitude that drinking in itself is good but may bring shameful consequences in its wake is comparable to Lemert's (4) findings with regard to the Salish Indians of the Northwest Coast.

This paper considers the relationship between the learning of drinking behavior and the ambivalence in attitudes toward drinking in Lunahuaná, and is thus concerned with the process by which Lunahuaneños take on both attitude and behavior patterns with regard to drinking that are characteristic of the society. This discussion is intended as a contribution to an understanding of the teaching and learning of drinking behavior, which Bacon (1) has called "an essential field of research for the student of the problems of alcohol." No attempt can be made within the brief compass of this paper to portray in any comprehensive way the process by which drinking is learned in Lunahuaná, but only to touch on some of its characteristics as these appear to be related to the dominant attitudes toward drinking.

The Setting

The community of Lunahuaná is located 125 miles south of Lima in one of the river valleys that periodically interrupt the Peruvian coastal desert. It is situated 35 miles inland in a narrow river canyon, among the Andean foothills, and consists of a village and ten outlying barrios, or named locality divisions, with an estimated population of about ten thousand. The barrios form a chain of agricultural settlements about 13 miles long, in which each family lives on its own holdings. The village, which lies at the mid-point of the chain, is simply a center for goods and services and is inhabited largely by officials and merchants. Although predominantly Indian in physical type, the Lunahuaneños in no way identify with Indian culture.

They are of mestizo culture, a fusion of Indian and Spanish elements with an overlay of contemporary European and American influences. Among the most prominent differences between Indian and mestizo cultures are those in the areas of diet, drinking, dancing, music, humor, fiesta celebration, and leisure activities in general. More subtle differences are to be found in other aspects of culture and social structure, such as courtship and the perform-ance of political and occupational roles (3, 7, 8).

The principal cash crops of Lunahuaná are grapes and cotton, although a great many fruits and vegetables are cultivated in varying quantities. The production of wine and brandy was once the principal basis of the economy but since the advent of a highway from the coast in 1921 more and more of the grape harvest has been transported to Lima for sale there as fresh fruit. Fifty years ago, there were about a hundred distilleries in the com-munity; forty are still active but many of them produce small quantities. Lunahuaná has a long history of emigration as a consequence of chronic problems of land scarcity but every family that stayed has managed to hold on to some small piece. It is popularly believed that owning even a bit of land makes one independent, although in fact the vast majority must sup-plement this by wage work or share farming for the thirty-odd large land-owners, who also own most of the distilleries.

Adult Drinking and Ambivalence

Among adult males, frequent drinking and drunkenness are virtually uni-versal in Lunahuaná. Women may occasionally take a few drinks at a fiesta but in general they do not drink and in only exceptional cases do they participate significantly in the male drinking pattern. Drinking may occur on any occasion when two or more men get together, at any time of the day or night, and anywhere except in the church. Other than fiestas, celebra-tions of *rites de passage*, weekends, and special seasons on the job, drinking is not characterized by any daily or other periodic regularity. Drinking may stop short of drunkenness, and some who drink frequently may actually get drunk only once a month or less often. In order of popularity, Lunahuaneños drink *cachina* (12 to 14 per cent alcohol), essentially a home-made wine; *pisco* (47 to 50 per cent alcohol), a colorless grape brandy; and wine (about 12 per cent alcohol). Access to alcohol seems to present no serious economic problem even for the poorest in the community.

In part, the adult male Lunahuaneño may be characterized as timid, evasive, retiring, shy, indirect, at a loss for words, and uncertain as to his behavior when in the company of others. There is an inordinate emphasis on being a "correct" person, and the Lunahuaneño is always preoccupied with what others may think of him and always timorous lest there be un-favorable criticism. There are, however, many local sayings which ex-plicitly acknowledge that the Lunahuaneño becomes "another person" when he is drunk. As one informant put it:

A man passes through four "apparitions" when drinking that represent the following "bloods." Blood of the turkey, when a man is sober and cold. Blood of the monkey, which comes to pass after a man has drunk a little. This is the best state because the body warms up, and one becomes talkative, makes jokes, forgets his worries, and is in condition to make love to a girl. Blood of the lion, which occurs when a man has drunk even more. Now he loses his head, looks for arguments, is easily offended, thinks of the people who owe him money and has the courage to go and ask them for it. Blood of the pig, which comes to pass if a man has drunk too much. He cannot stand up and control himself, but can only fall down and sleep like a pig.

Attitudes toward drinking are predominantly permissive; there is a rich folklore that expresses a high positive evaluation of drinking. No one hides the fact that he has been drunk, nor has he any hesitation about excusing some defection by saying he was drunk. All the evidence indicates that Lunahuaneños attach little, if any, moral significance to drinking and drunkenness and have no guilt feelings to contend with in relation to drinking.

On the other hand, many Lunahuaneños said that they sometimes felt shame after a drunken episode if they had engaged in "incorrect" behavior and created a "scandal," defined as insulting others, fighting with friends, or—most frequently cited—mistreating wives, children, and relatives. One informant said that he usually felt shame after getting drunk because he was sure to have intruded somewhere, thrust himself into someone's house or elsewhere that he should not have gone, and made a lot of noise or engaged in insults. Another said he felt shame the day after a drunk because "with liquor the mute person speaks, like the parrot who talks when given wine. Sometimes when one is drunk he says things in a gathering that he should not say, that make his person ugly." In this regard, then, there is ambivalence in attitudes toward drinking, namely, that drinking in itself is good but it may bring shameful consequences in its wake.

The Charter for Youth

In Lunahuaná it is believed that there is no joy in life without drinking, that liquor was invented for the purpose of animating people and giving them pleasure, that it gives a person strength and will for his work, and that the grapevine will not produce unless its cultivators drink. Consistent with these notions, the "charter" of drinking also specifies that liquor is healthful not only for adults but for children as well. *Cachina* and wine are good for children because they "open the appetite," "clear the head," "kill the microbes," "relieve constipation," and "heat the nerves, which are cold." Moreover, liquor is good for their blood and prevents them from getting sick. As most frequently stated, minute quantities of liquor may be served to young children, girls as well as boys, particularly after lunch, in order to *tonificar* them; that is, it is used as a tonic for health reasons. For drinking that is defined as "moderate," the earliest age limit is usually specified as 10 to 12, and is permitted only to boys. The charter makes a sharp distinction, however, between such moderate drinking, defined as a "few glasses," and drinking "like a man" (to the point of drunkenness). It is all right for adolescents to drink moderately when they are "socially obligated," but the minimum age for adopting the drinking behavior of adult males is set at 18 to 20. The people say that it is "very ugly" to see boys under 18 drinking heavily or to the point of drunkenness.

There are two principal reasons offered to justify the disapproval of heavy drinking and drunkenness among adolescents: (a) they are too vulnerable to the effects of excessive alcohol intake, and (b) by virtue of this vulnerability they are much more likely than adults to engage in "incorrect" behavior. With respect to the first reason, there is a pervasive belief among Lunahuaneños that the period of later adolescence, from about 15 to 18, termed the "epoch of development," is critical and decisive for the life of the individual. Once he passes these years, he no longer is so vulnerable to illness. The consequences of heavy drinking under 18 are that a boy "will ruin his brain so that it will never be the same," "may ruin his blood so that he cannot beget sons," and may become so habituated to drinking that he will become a *vicioso* (an addict). If one is over 18, liquor is not likely to "get hold" of one so quickly; resistance to alcohol is greater because the "nervous system" gets stronger the older one becomes. Coupled with this belief that maximum physical strength and resistance are attained only at the end of adolescence is another notion to the effect that the age of "reason and responsibility" begins at 18 to 20 years. After this age boys can do "whatever they like because they can realize what they are doing," no longer need their parents' permission for what they do, and can drink as they like because they are able to "dominate" themselves.

The other reason advanced to justify disapproval of heavy drinking in adolescence, namely, that it will precipitate "incorrect" behavior, appears to be a direct consequence of the negative side of the ambivalence about drinking. If an adult may engage in behavior as a consequence of drinking that will arouse feelings of shame, then an adolescent is much more likely to do so. An adolescent should not drink like an adult because he is still "weak in the head and may commit many bad things." From an early age there is heavy emphasis in child training on behaving "correctly"; this emphasis tends to focus mainly on proper observance of respect relationships with parents and one's elders in general. Observance of proper respect is a continual preoccupation of Lunahuaneños in all interpersonal relations, but it is of particular concern in parent-youth relations. Prohibitions about adolescent drinking are most explicit in this area. Heavy drinking by adolescents in any situation is said to signify a lack of respect for parents, but it constitutes the most serious violation of respect rules if it is actually performed in their presence.

Thus the charter of adolescent drinking aims primarily to set limits to premature adoption of the patterns of drinking behavior that are considered normal for the society once its members have attained man's estate. Lunahuaneños do not say that the young should never adopt this pattern—

only that they should wait until they are adults before they do so. If the young take on adult patterns of continual and excessive drinking, their particular vulnerability to alcohol may lead them to commit indiscretions more readily than will adults, which will have even graver consequences than in the case of adults.

Learning Contexts and Pressures

Learning to drink begins at an early age in Lunahuaná. Most informants said they had their first drink of *cachina,* wine, or *pisco* between the ages of 9 and 13, and many said that children as young as 5 regularly receive their *copita* (little cup) of sweet wine. Children of all ages certainly have many opportunities to learn about drinking by example. They accompany parents to fiesta celebrations and other social occasions and are often present at work activities in the fields and distilleries, all of which are among the principal drinking situations to be found in the society. The writer observed women and children present as onlookers in a wide variety of such drinking situations, some of which terminated in complete drunkenness on the part of the adult male participants. Familial celebration of birthdays was most frequently reported as the situation in which one received his first drink and was initiated into moderate drinking. Some said they were "obliged" to take two or three drinks as early as their ninth or tenth birthdays and recalled becoming dizzy or sick as a consequence.

Perhaps the single most important drinking rule that obtains among adults is that one cannot refuse a drink if invited to partake. Those who attempt to refuse are subjected to intolerable pressure by means of a wide variety of devices. As one informant said, "if a man does not wish to drink, he has to go away from the place where the drinking is taking place and must avoid places where men are drinking." Another informant said:

You may be having a drink or two in a *tambo* [bar] with some friends, and someone fills your glass when you're ready to leave. Then there is no longer any measure to your drinking. If you do not drink, he says, "It seems as though we are not friends, that you have no good will, that you wish to be pretentious and and not associate with the poor." So that he may not be resentful, you have to drink. And if you do not drink, he spills out your *pisco* and says, "You don't like my liquor." Then the quarrels begin.

The constant attempt to make one's drinking partners drunk is characteristic of all drinking situations in Lunahuaná, but is particularly evident in work activities dedicated to the several phases of cultivation of grapevines and production of alcohol. The most important phases of cultivation, namely, the harvest, in April and May, and the pruning of the vines, in September, are times of very heavy drinking implemented through a series of elaborate drinking rituals traditionally performed in conjunction with the work. Boys of 15 and over are considered old enough to work along with the men, and, on the many occasions when the writer has observed adolescents in these work crews, these boys have been subjected to the same relentless pressure to drink that adults impose on one another. Most informants reported that they had first experienced being drunk between 15 and 17 years of age, and that it occurred either in one of these work situations or in family celebrations of *rites de passage*. In all of these accounts, the introduction to heavy drinking was under the tutelage of older persons, who usually included the boy's father or other male relatives. It appears, then, that the charter for adolescent drinking is somewhat at odds with the practice, in that those who verbally disapprove of adolescent drunkenness are often the very ones who promote it. Nevertheless, the charter has a discernible influence on the attitudes and drinking behavior of adolescents.

Despite the fact that initiation of adolescents into heavy drinking is usually accomplished by adults and during an age period forbidden by the charter, the evidence indicates that the frequency of heavy drinking and drunkenness among boys under 18 does not begin to compare with that characteristic of adult males. In part this is due to the fact that a substantial part of adult drinking occurs among peer groups in bars and at such times as before or after working hours or on weekends. Adolescents are ordinarily excluded from these drinking situations, and do not appear to engage in drinking on any significant scale when participating in their own peer group relationships. Even if the young were included in all the drinking sessions that occur on fiestas or in work activities, which is not the case, they would still have far fewer opportunities for drinking, and particularly for drinking heavily, than those ordinarily available to the adult male in Lunahuaná.

More important, however, the difference in drinking behavior of adolescents and adults seems to be largely due to differences in motivation to drink and in definitions of drinking as a means to social participation and status. The most characteristic pattern of adolescent drinking observed by the writer, whether in family or public fiestas or on the job, was one of reluctance and even outright refusal to drink the way adults were drinking. They would indicate a preference for the less potent beverage if a choice were available, and employ various devices to conceal their lack of wholehearted participation. These boys were not always allowed to have their way, but when they were they did not usually drink nearly as much as did the adults. Understanding of this reluctance on the part of adolescents requires consideration of the personal and social functions of drinking in Lunahuaná in relation to both adolescents and adults.

Adolescent Inhibitions

In a previous paper by the present writer (9), the interpersonal performance of the adult Lunahuaneño was described as being marked by a profound sense of distrust of others and a lack of confidence in his own ability to control the outcome of a given episode of interaction. For the Lunahuaneño, drinking reduces tensions and anxieties in interpersonal relations by serving as a catalyst in overcoming and dissolving his initial expectations that most interaction episodes will result in outcomes somehow unfavorable or disadvantageous for him. Although drinking is limited to social contexts (the few solitary drinkers are regarded as deviants) and is essentially a response to the expectations of the group, it must also meet these felt interpersonal needs of the individual.

In Yankee American culture, as Straus and Bacon (10) have pointed out, young people between the ages of 17 and 23 are faced with the difficult question, among others, of whether or not to drink alcoholic beverages, and for many this is by no means an easy matter to decide. In Lunahuaná, this question never arises, since the idea and act of drinking are learned early in the process of socialization and identified with those persons who have emotional significance for the individual. Thus internalized, drinking—like any other cultural pattern—can only be taken for granted as good in itself, and there can be no issue of whether or not to drink. Moreover, as the people say, "liquor is in everything, just like religion." It is commonly said that drinking goes on "from the time of birth until the time of death," a reference to the fact that drinking occurs when a child is born and when a person dies. To drink is to conform to a normal pattern of the group's culture.

The Lunahuaneño's view of others as potentially dangerous and his characteristic reaction—even to people he knows well—of suspicion and distrust are instilled into children at an early age. The model that is held up to children is one of keeping constantly to oneself and one's family. Children are kept close to home, unless on an errand or out with their parents, until they are 10 or 12, and are punished if they go into neighbors' houses. They are not allowed to appear when visitors are present for fear they will not exhibit the proper decorum and restraint. The imposition of such limited social horizons and restriction of opportunities for social interaction is reflected in the difficulties that Lunahuaneño males have in relating to others when they reach maturity.

Given these considerations of the normality and pervasiveness of drinking and of internalization of interpersonal fear, we may well ask why adolescents do not drink the way adults do, especially since they are sometimes encouraged to disregard the charter. In the first place, it is the writer's impression that the young are more directly and consistently oriented to the normative prescriptions of the charter than are the sanctioning agents themselves. They accept adult notions of physical vulnerability in adolescence, but, more important, they have effectively internalized the prescriptions, embodied not only in the rationale of drinking but in the other sets of norms and standards characteristic of the culture, regarding proper observance of respect relationships with parents and other adults. Adult Lunahuaneños are inconsistent in the application of the charter for adolescent drinking, not only because they encourage its violation in certain situations but because they usually fail to respond with negative sanctions even when violations are committed independently by adolescents. However, if drunkenness of adolescents leads to transgression of respect rules, this is another matter—one that calls for punitive action.

Secondly, despite the fact that adolescents share the characteristic difficulties of adult Lunahuaneños in interpersonal performance, the nature and range of interpersonal situations in which they are called upon to participate do not impose the strains and pressures upon them to which adults are subjected. Adolescence in Lunahuaná is a period of indeterminate status; one is no longer a child but neither is he permitted access to any of the symbols or rewards of adult status. Schooling terminates when one is around 14 years of age, and the subsequent years, until one is accorded adult status, are essentially a period of waiting and being held in abeyance. Boys will be called upon to do man's work in helping their fathers in the fields but receive no remuneration for this, and if they go out to do wage labor, they are expected to turn over the bulk of their earnings to their parents. This pattern may build up considerable aggression in adolescents, but indirect recourses for its release are available in the competitive activities of the ubiquitous soccer matches and of seeking to outwit each other as well as watchful mothers in sexual conquests of girls.

As adulthood is approached, however, problems of status become acute, and adolescent outlets for aggression are no longer appropriate. Chronic dissension comes to pervade the relationship between parents and adult children as a consequence of the reluctance of parents to retire and relinquish land holdings. The inhibitions to adoption of adult drinking patterns during adolescence lose their effectiveness and interpersonal demands become more stressful. The adolescent reluctance to engage in frequent drinking and drunkenness cannot persist in view of the fact that this pattern of drinking behavior is so thoroughly integrated with adult status. Since these patterns of drinking are actually a prerequisite for the majority of important social roles performed by adult Lunahuaneños, there are no satisfactory alternative channels to acquisition of adult status in the community. On the personal level, drinking now becomes the symbolically most appropriate means for reducing interpersonal anxiety and recourse for releasing aggression indirectly or for providing an adequate substitute for it.

General Implications

This discussion has provided a basis for understanding, at least in its broader aspects, the relationship between the learning of drinking behavior and attitudes toward drinking in Lunahuaná through examination of the process whereby both positive and negative attitudes toward drinking become incorporated during adolescence. From early childhood on, the act of drinking is symbolically and emotionally identified with the significant persons and the important situations in the community so that the idea of drinking itself becomes internalized as a normal culture pattern in which all males should participate. But Lunahuaneños are apprehensive about engaging in "incorrect" behavior as a consequence of drinking and are likely to feel ashamed if they actually do so. Hence the charter attempts to set limits to the frequency and amount of adolescent drinking so as to minimize the threat such drinking would pose to the proper observance of respect relationships that are highly valued in the society. Once adults begin to drink, however, they themselves take the lead in violating the charter. The consequent inconsistency between attitude and action may contribute to the development of the same ambivalent feelings about drinking in the new generation of drinkers.

In this paper, a direct relationship is presumed between ambivalence in adult attitudes toward drinking and prohibitions against adoption of adult drinking behavior by adolescents. Although the present analysis by itself cannot, of course, provide adequate documentation of this, the limited evidence available from other studies is consistent with the presumed relationship. In the case of the Salish Indians of the Northwest Coast, Lemert (4) reports the presence of both ambivalence about drinking and adult injunctions against drinking by the young. On the other side, the clearest instance is that provided by Mangin (5) in his study of drinking among Indians in highland Peru. In Vicos, there is no ambivalence in attitudes toward drinking and apparently no age restrictions against adoption of adult drinking behavior by the young or against joint drinking by young and old. Similarly, Bunzel (2) found neither ambivalence about drinking nor age prohibitions among the Indians of Chamula, in Chiapas, Mexico. These few instances hardly constitute definitive documentation, however.* Further empirical investigations in a variety of cultural contexts, including our own, are necessary in order to provide more satisfactory comparative evidence than is presently available.

References

1. Bacon, Selden D., *Sociology and the Problems of Alcohol: Foundations for a Sociological Study of Drinking Behavior*, New Haven: Hillhouse Press, 1944.
2. Bunzel, Ruth, "The Role of Alcoholism in Two Central American Cultures," *Psychiatry*, 3:361–387, 1940.
3. Gillin, John P., "Mestizo America," *in* Ralph Linton (Ed.), *Most of the World*, New York: Columbia University Press, 1949.
4. Lemert, Edwin M., "Alcohol and the Northwest Coast Indians," *Univ. Calif. Publ. in Culture and Society*, 2:303–406, 1954.
5. Mangin, William, "Drinking among Andean Indians," *Quart. J. Stud. Alc.*, 18:55–66, 1957.

* Bunzel's study of drinking in Chichicastenango, an Indian community in Guatemala, is also reported in this paper (2). In this case, she found considerable ambivalence about drinking, but gives no indication of adult attitudes toward adolescent drinking. One other instance of relevance here is Heath's study of the Bolivian Camba reported in Chapter 2. Although Heath clearly states that there is no ambivalence about drinking among the Camba, he makes no specific reference to attitudes toward adolescent drinking. He does say that drinkers "show no marked stratification by age, apart from the exclusion of children," and that "the youngest drinker encountered was 12."

6. Republica Del Peru, *Censo Nacional de Población de 1940,* Vol. 5, Lima: Ministerio de Hacienda y Comercio, Dirección Nacional de Estadística, 1944.

7. Simmons, Ozzie G., "El Use de los Conceptos de Aculturación y Asimilación en el Estúdio del Cambio Cultural en el Perú," *Perú Indíg.,* 2:40–45, 1952.

8. ———, "The *Criollo* Outlook in the Mestizo Culture of Costal Peru," *Amer. Anthrop.,* 57:107–117, 1955.

9. ———, "Drinking Patterns and Interpersonal Performance in a Peruvian Mestizo Community," *Quart. J. Stud. Alc.,* 20:103–111, 1959.

10. Straus, Robert, and Selden D. Bacon, "To Drink or Not to Drink," *in* Raymond G. McCarthy (Ed.) *Drinking and Intoxication,* Glencoe, Ill.: Free Press, 1959.

11. Ullman, Albert D., "Sociocultural Backgrounds of Alcoholism," *Ann. Amer. Acad. Pol. Soc. Sci.,* 351:48–54, 1958.

chapter 4

A new
cross-cultural study
of drunkenness[*]

Peter B. Field

The cross-cultural method has several important potential advantages for extending our knowledge of drinking behavior. First, this technique examines relations between variables across a number of tribes at once, while the typical anthropological report is restricted to just a single tribe. Furthermore, the method deals simultaneously with a great range of modal drinking patterns—from abstention in some tribes to periodic bouts of extreme drunkenness in others. Finally, the tribes that are included are separated from each other and also from Western industrial society, so that relationships emerging across a sample of tribes cannot be attributed to the widespread influence of a small number of cultural heritages. This method is therefore a potentially valuable tool in the development of general explanations of wide scope and applicability concerning drunkenness. These generalizations may in turn advance our knowledge of alcoholism in modern society.

Previous Cross-Cultural Research on Drunkenness

Cross-cultural research of this kind depends upon the development of valid rating categories for assessing the extent of drunkenness and their suc-

[*] This chapter was written especially for this book. The present writer is greatly indebted to John W. M. Whiting and David C. McClelland for research guidance, to George P. Murdock and Herbert Barry for suggestions and unpublished ratings, and to the National Science Foundation and the U.S. Public Health Service for pre-doctoral fellowship support. A short version of this chapter was read at the August, 1960 meeting of the Society for the Study of Social Problems. This chapter is based on an unpublished doctoral dissertation, *Social and Psychological Correlates of Drunkenness in Primitive Tribes*, Harvard University, 1961.

cessful application to the available anthropological literature on primitive societies. After this, the anthropological reports for each society must also be scored on other theoretically relevant variables which may then be related to the index of drunkenness. This has been done only once in the past —in the classic cross-cultural research of Horton (13).

To explain his results, Horton presented an anxiety theory of drunkenness. He proposed that a major factor determining the degree of drunkenness in a society is the level of anxiety or fear among the individual members. Drunkenness, however, can be inhibited as well as produced by anxiety. Consequently, according to Horton, the level of drunkenness in a society is a resultant of a complex interaction of anxiety-reduction and anxiety-induction. He states, for instance, that the ". . . strength of the drinking response in any society tends to vary directly with the level of anxiety in that society." However, since the ". . . drinking of alcohol tends to be accompanied by the release of sexual and aggressive impulses," and since sexual and aggressive impulses are often punished, drinking will be weaker where these responses lead to anxiety about punishment—that is, the ". . . strength of the drinking response tends to vary inversely with the strength of the counteranxiety elicited by painful experiences during and after drinking" (13, p. 230).

Horton's study was one of a series of research reports directly influenced by the efforts of Hull and his collaborators to integrate behavior theory and psychoanalysis. A hallmark of this approach was the explanation of complex socio-cultural phenomena in terms of individual drives—especially frustration or anxiety. Prior to Horton's work, for example, two members of Hull's school of thought reported an inverse relation between the price of cotton and the number of lynchings per year in the Deep South, and explained this in terms of frustration and aggression (14). In view of theoretical precedents of this kind, it is not surprising that Horton should have interpreted the level of drunkenness in a society as an expression of the level of fear or anxiety in the society. His research is, however, one of the very few reporting an important relation of any kind between the level of anxiety in a society and any aspect of alcohol use. Indeed, it is the only social research cited in a recent review of the most important research evidence that alcohol reduces fear (5).

Not all of Horton's results support his own theory unequivocally, and those which appear to do so vary greatly in quality. The most convincing support comes from his finding that aggressive and sexual responses are often released at drinking bouts, suggesting that there is ordinarily an inhibiting force which holds these responses in check. This fear-like force is temporarily weakened at drinking bouts. However, his two major indices of the social anxiety level—that is, an insecure food supply and acculturation by contact with Western civilization—are very indirect and questionable measures of fear. Furthermore, as Lemert (15, p. 370) has pointed out, Horton failed ". . . to include a well-defined variable of social organization. Correlating such things as the technological level of a society or the amount of its wealth or the death rate of its population with a psychological reaction such as anxiety can only partially reveal the dynamics behind primitive drinking, because these non-sociological facts always take on variable meaning and impact for the members of societies through the media of social organization." Several authors have also made the very important point that a simple anxiety theory of alcoholism and drunkenness is inadequate because it does not explain why other modes of reducing anxiety instead of drinking are not used (e.g., 16). Why does a society develop drunkenness in response to food shortages rather than, say, ritual magic aimed at inducing a reluctant god to supply food? Why, moreover, does a psychoneurotic become an alcoholic instead of developing a different form of anxiety-reducing personality disorder?

Since Horton wrote the above-cited paper, a number of studies of primitive drinking have been reported, but these have not unequivocally supported his position. As a case in point, Lemert (15) found that the greatest drunkenness among the Indians of the American Northwest occurred when they were enriched by the fur trade; it is hard to understand why this might have been associated with fear. For his part, Lemert identified a number of other factors—including cultural conservatism, anomie, and interclan rivalry—affecting drunkenness on the Northwest Coast. Other studies of individual tribes, such as Heath's study of the Camba in Chapter 2, have suggested social disorganization or social isolation as important causal variables in drunkenness.

Methods and Procedures

The re-examination of Horton's theory which is an integral part of the present study was made possible by the development of new cross-cultural scales which were not available to him. This re-examination was begun by assembling a group of scales on the basis of their theoretical relevance to alcohol problems.* These scales were originally developed by many different raters for a wide variety of purposes and vary widely in degree of reliability. Some, such as Horton's drunkenness measure or Murdock's (23) social structure ratings, have been scored by only one judge so that their interscorer reliability cannot be directly estimated (although we know from the magnitude of the correlations with other variables that it must be substantial). In certain other instances where reliability can be estimated, the measures are reliable enough to indicate the presence of a non-chance relationship but are too crude for more accurate prediction.

The most important scale in the tables to follow is Horton's measure of "strong vs. moderate and slight degrees of insobriety" (13, pp. 265–266). Tribes with "strong" insobriety were described by ethnographers as drinking to unconsciousness, drinking for many hours or days, or getting "excessively" drunk. The last category probably indicates extreme functional im-

* The source of each scale used in the tables to follow is given in the reference list at the end of this chapter.

pairment. Tribes with "slight" or "moderate" insobriety either did not get drunk, or, if they did, did not drink for days and did not drink to unconsciousness. This scale measures degree of drunkenness at periodic drinking bouts and not, of course, the number of alcoholics in the society or the death rate from alcoholism.*

After the scales were assembled, Horton's fifty-six tribes were divided into two subsamples of roughly equal size. The first subsample consisted of all of Horton's tribes that had also been rated by Whiting and Child (40). Preliminary correlations were examined using only this subsample. While only a few of the Whiting and Child child-rearing ratings showed promising relationships, a group of highly suggestive relationships appeared using Murdock's social structure ratings (23). These relationships were checked in the second subsample. As a rule, the preliminary relationships emerged just as clearly in the second sample, and for no important relation did an association reverse or change markedly between the samples. This strongly indicates that the relations found between drunkenness and social structure are not the result of capitalization upon chance associations. For this reason the subsamples were combined for ease of presentation. Finally, unpublished social-structure ratings on six additional tribes were kindly provided by George P. Murdock in a personal communication, and were added to the two subsamples to complete the final sample.

Unless otherwise indicated, scales were dichotomized at the median. Associations were tested for statistical significance by chi-square corrected for continuity with one degree of freedom. Tetrachoric correlation coefficients for each association were estimated by the method given in (38). All probability values reported in this chapter are based on a conservative two-tailed criterion. Any association based on less than fifty-six cases indicates that either an ethnographer or a rater omitted relevant information on one or more of Horton's tribes.

Results and Discussion

1. Drunkenness, fear, and subsistence insecurity

The first section of Table 1 shows the relations between Horton's measure of drunkenness and the best available measures of fear (10, 40). None of these relationships is statistically significant and no clear positive or negative trend appears. The first five measures of fear are drawn from beliefs concerning the causation of illness. Fear of spirits, for example, means that

---

* The scale also excludes solitary drinking and drinking by women. The few societies without available alcohol were excluded, and so were the societies with no satisfactory ethnographic information about drunkenness. Societies similar to a neighboring society already in the sample were excluded. The societies that were included come from all over the world, with a number of representatives in each major culture area. Horton excluded the Moslem societies of North Africa, since they have a religious taboo on alcohol; this was a questionable decision, but it probably affects neither his general conclusions nor mine.

the society attributes illness to malevolent spirits. The last rating is an even more direct measure of fear based on records of direct statements of fear of ghosts at funerals. All of these scales of fear have shown significant relations to other measures such as sex anxiety or severe child rearing (39, 40), *which suggests that they are genuine measures of fear.*[*] They are all reliable enough to show significant relations to Horton's drunkenness score, if they existed. Horton himself was unable to find a relation between degree of drunkenness and sorcery, but the reason for this was not clear. The consistent negative evidence in Table 1 suggests that, *within the limits of these measures,* variation in the level of fear is not related to the extent of drunkenness in primitive tribes.

TABLE 1

The Relations of Degree of Drunkenness to Indices of Fear

	χ^2	r_{tet}
Fear of sorcerers	0.00	−.06
Fear of spirits	0.00	.07
Fear of others (sorcerers and spirits combined)	0.00	.06
Fear of ghosts	0.34	.29
Fear of animal spirits	0.91	−.39
Fear of ghosts at funerals [a]	0.00	.08

[a] $N = 30$; 27 for the other measures.

The data in the first column of Table 2 clearly confirm Horton's finding that tribes with very primitive hunting and gathering economies tend to have more drunkenness than tribes with more advanced herding and agricultural economies. The second column in Table 2 shows a very strong relation between Horton's measure of an insecure food supply and the absence of agriculture; indeed, this relation is so strong that it is perhaps justifiable to assume that Horton's "subsistence insecurity" is more of an indication of the lack of a stable agricultural basis for society than of the level of fear.

The implications of this latter, alternative assumption are far reaching. We know that the social organization of a hunting tribe is quite different in some ways from the social organization of a tribe with an advanced herding and agricultural subsistence economy. Tribes that live by hunting are frequently nomadic but agriculture requires a settled, stable community. With the development of agriculture and herding, it is also possible to support larger concentrated populations which would starve under a hunting

[*] A few other measures of anxiety given by Whiting and Child also showed no significant relation to drunkenness, but these either were based on such small numbers or were so unclear, theoretically, that they are not presented here.

TABLE 2

The Relations of Type of Subsistence Economy to Degree of Drunkenness and Insecure Food Supply [a]

Subsistence Economy	Drunkenness		Insecure Food Supply	
	χ^2	r_{tet}	χ^2	r_{tet}
Predominance of herding and agriculture over hunting and fishing (4)	4.14 [b]	−.50	1.45	−.41
Agriculture	3.24	−.47	12.32 [c]	−.85
Animal husbandry	1.34	−.32	0.02	−.13
Fishing and marine hunting	3.86 [b]	.49	2.64	.49
Hunting and gathering	5.71 [b]	.57	2.42	.48

[a] For all insecure food supply correlations, $N = 37$; N is either 49 or 50 for the other correlations. The Murdock (23) scales on economy were divided at "important" versus "present but unimportant."

[b] $P < .05$.

[c] $P < .001$.

economy (22, pp. 80–81). When such a population is present in one place over several generations, community divisions will be formed, occupational specialization will be more obvious, and social stratification and centralized political authority become possible. At the same time complex corporate-kin structures may emerge with the addition of a unilocal rule of marital residence and the development of unilinear descent. Thus with the transition from the hunting band to the compact village, formalized social control over the individual's behavior may well become more diffuse and pervasive. Parallel psychological differences may also appear. For instance, Barry, Child, and Bacon (4) have shown that herding and agricultural tribes expect obedience and responsibility from their children, while hunting and fishing societies demand independence, achievement, and self-assertion instead.

2. Drunkenness and social organization

These results and speculations suggest that something other than fear, perhaps a social variable, explains primitive drunkenness. Perhaps this variable can be detected by examining the primitive drinking bout.

Horton has described the sequence of behavior in drinking bouts in this way: first there is gaiety, laughter, friendliness, lewd jokes, jollity, and loquacity. After this, sexual behavior, verbal quarrels, and fights are often observed. In the tribes Horton classifies as extremely drunken, this goes on for many hours or days, extreme functional impairment is usual, and the bouts end with most of the participants unconscious.

Although anxiety is certainly being reduced, something more important is happening. Respect and reserve are giving way to friendly equality. Usually inhibited aggressive and sexual impulses are emerging. Behavior is directed at momentary personal pleasure and self-indulgence rather than duty, responsibility, and task performance. There is loosely organized companionship rather than formal execution of institutionalized obligations. In one sense the group is clearly becoming disorganized, since its members eventually withdraw into unconsciousness; but this disorganization is the final outcome of informal tension release in a companionship setting. In summary, a personal, informal organization has replaced a formal, well-structured organization: alcohol has facilitated informal, personal interaction by temporary removal of social inhibitions; and it has disorganized precisely controlled behavior, making difficult the performance of duties, labor, respect and avoidance, ceremonials and rituals, and other legalized obligations requiring inhibition of impulses.

In tribes with a great deal of this kind of informal, friendly, loosely controlled behavior at drinking bouts, there is a strong possibility that ordinary social relationships are also informal, personally organized, and based on friendly equality. Marriages may be primarily unions of individuals for companionship and mutual support, rather than socially extended alliances designed to fulfill broader economic or social functions, such as inheritance and lineage continuity. Formal alignments of kinsmen with clearly formulated mutual rights and obligations may be weak or absent. Social solidarity may be stronger between individuals of the same generation than between adjacent generations—that is, the drunken tribes may have a wide-ranging kinship system emphasizing friendly solidarity among siblings, cousins, and spouses, rather than hierarchical, lineal solidarity between parents and children. This in turn might mean that the drunken tribes place less importance on the conservation and transmission across generations of an elaborate social tradition.

In these tribes the organization of tribesmen to attain common objectives may be weak and informal. That is, in these tribes functions such as ceremonials, military operations, and transmission of property from one generation to another may be carried on by individuals or informal groups rather than assigned to specialists such as priests, a warrior caste, or a land-owning group. In the informally-structured tribes with primitive hunting and gathering economies there may be few differentiated structures serving well-defined social purposes.

Another possibility suggested by this line of reasoning is that there may be a general weakness of extreme power, respect, or reserve differentials between individuals in the extremely drunken tribes. If a society is highly organized, prestige and power will be vested in a few individuals rather than diffused throughout the tribe. This may happen both in political organization and in the family. The leader of a South American band of hunters has little power, but an African monarch wields a great deal. Similarly, in the drunken tribes there should be no great differences between husband and wife in centralized power and in control of the family, and therefore polygyny should not be important. This informal equality may be reflected in the child-rearing practices: we would not expect a great deal of pressure for submission and obedience on the part of children in the drunken tribes.

Form of Kin Group. Preliminary evidence for the relevance of social organization in explaining drunkenness among primitive peoples is presented in Table 3. The following facts will help to clarify the meaning of this table. Tribes with kin groups organized into units tracing descent through males are called "patrilineal"; those organized into units tracing descent through females are called "matrilineal"; while tribes with both these forms of kin group are referred to as having "double" descent. In contrast, tribes lacking kin groups organized into special corporate units (tribes which, for this reason, are more loosely organized and might be expected to exhibit more drunkenness) are referred to as "bilateral," which means that kinship is traced through males and females without formal distinction.

TABLE 3

The Relation of Degree of Drunkenness to Type of Kin Group

Degree	Type of Kin Group			
of Drunkenness	Bilateral	Matrilineal	Patrilineal	Double
Extreme	19	5	9	1
Moderate or slight	2	3	12	4

Thus in Table 3, although patrilineal tribes appear to have somewhat less drunkenness than matrilineal tribes, the outstanding fact is the striking association of drunkenness with bilateral descent—in other words, its association with the absence of patrilineal or matrilineal kin groups of a corporate nature. Since, according to Murdock (22), kin groups based upon patrilineal and matrilineal descent parallel one another almost exactly, it seems permissible for statistical purposes to classify these together with double descent groups in a single category of "unilineal" groups. Viewed in relation to the presence or absence of unilineal kin groups so defined, degree of drunkenness yields a strong negative correlation of —.67 which is highly significant.*

A major distinction between the bilateral kindred, the most widespread and characteristic form of arrangement of kin in a bilateral society, and unilineal kin group is this: a unilineal kin group is a "corporate" group while the bilateral kindred is not. The term "corporate" means that unilineal kin

* $x^2 = 9.94$, 1 *df*; $P < .01$; $N = 55$. The degree of drunkenness was dichotomized at "extreme" versus "moderate or slight" in accordance with Horton's definitions noted above.

groups are structured groups with ". . . perpetuity through time, collective ownership of property, and unified activity as a legal individual" (28, p. 200). An individual and his kindred die, but unilineal kin groups, like tribes, extend indefinitely into the past and the future.

Murdock (22, p. 61) points out that since the kindred is not a group except from the point of view of one individual and since it has no temporal continuity, it ". . . can rarely act as a collectivity. One kindred cannot, for example, take blood vengeance against another if the two happen to have members in common. Moreover, a kindred cannot hold land or other property. . . ." Murdock notes further that a member of a bilateral kindred may be involved in conflicting or incompatible obligations, while these conflicts cannot arise under unilineal descent. He also states that unilineal kin groups are discrete social units, automatically defining the role of every participant in a ceremonial activity or every bystander in a dispute (22, p. 62). By contrast, according to Pehrson (28), bilateral societies have often been called "amorphous," "unstructured," "loosely organized," or "infinitely complex"—the latter term being synonymous with fragmented. He suggests, however, that bilateral tribes are not truly disorganized; they have a flexible, noncorporate organization featuring a network of horizontal ties uniting individuals of the same generation.

Similarly Davenport (6, p. 569) concludes that the kindred structure ". . . occurs where collective and corporate control is absent or minimal." Davenport also points out that in addition to kindreds, some bilateral tribes have nonunilineal descent groups which have some corporate functions. However, affiliation with them is not as well institutionalized as it is in unilineal societies: an individual's affiliation is usually determined by choice, not by birth as it is in unilineal tribes; he may move from one group to another during his lifetime; and his claim to membership in a group may depend on his decision to perform actions maintaining reciprocal ties with the group, or on performance of some specialized technique for validating membership, such as giving a potlatch.

In a later article Pehrson (29) points out that the bilateral Lappish band has a flexible, variable structure permitting the individual a wide range of alternative courses of action. The structure of the band, he reports, is a wide-ranging alliance of sibling groups held together—sometimes loosely —by conjugal ties. Devices such as the extension of sibling terminology to cousins increase the solidarity between members of the same generation. Sahlins (31) points out that in other bilateral tribes friendly relations between tribesmen may be secured at the expense of marital ties, as in Eskimo wife lending; in the most primitive tribes similar friendly relations are secured by the continuous circulation of food and other goods among individuals—a kind of mutual sharing that has also been noted in drinking groups. Finally, Wolf (42) reports that in open or non-corporate peasant communities, social, economic, and political arrangements are based on informal, personal ties between individuals and families.

Since there are several different kinds of unilinear kin groups, the non-bilateral societies in Table 3 were re-examined for evidence of possible differences in drunkenness in each type of group. The association of uni-linearity with little drunkenness was most marked for societies segmented into unilineal sibs: only seven of the twenty-one societies below the median on drunkenness did not have sibs. Of the twenty-two societies with this structure, fourteen were below the median on drunkenness. (Societies that had more inclusive structures—moieties or phratries—in addition to sibs were excluded from this tabulation and considered below.) According to Murdock (22, p. 73), ". . . the sib is associated with totemism and cere-monial, acts as a unit in life crisis situations, and regulates marriage and inheritance." In other words, it is associated with the most central symbols of formal solidarity, and regulates the individual's most important links to other individuals. Normally a sib is composed of several lineages, differen-tiating it internally. With sib exogamy, members of one sex marry into other sibs, thus forming collateral ties in the community. These tribes, then, have complex webs of formal kin affiliations spreading temporally and spatially throughout the entire society.

There were four tribes divided into unilineal moieties, or half-tribes, and all were above the median on drunkenness. Lowie (18, p. 247) points out that such moiety divisions are "fluid" and are not often found in tribes with large populations (p. 245). These indirect relations may well explain this result. On the other hand, there may be a failure to create strong soli-darity by overinclusion of members, since the solidarity of all kin groups necessitates the exclusion of some tribesmen. In any event, if these four tribes with moiety divisions had been classified empirically with the bi-lateral groups, the already high correlation between drunkenness and form of kin group would have been still higher ($r = -.78$, $P < .001$). (There were only two tribes with phratries—one drunk and one sober—so no gen-eralization is possible here.)

These results indicating the importance of social disorganization in primi-tive drunkenness also suggest a new explanation of Horton's findings on acculturation. His best predictor of drunkenness was severity of accultura-tion by contact with Western civilization. He examined the possibility that this might have been caused simply by the introduction of distilled liquors, and concluded that while there was some relationship, it was not an impor-tant one. He concluded that anxiety was produced during acculturation, and this caused drunkenness. However, it is not obvious that acculturation always increases anxiety, although it certainly may do so in special instances. Acculturation may in fact reduce anxiety by diminishing supernatural fears, or by providing rational solutions for anxiety-arousing cultural problems. It is very clear, however, that prolonged, intensive contact with Western civilization eventually disorganizes and destroys the social structure of a tribe. It also seems likely that rapid, far-reaching acculturative changes will be facilitated by an originally loose tribal social organization. For these reasons, it seems reasonable to suppose that Horton's relation between drunkenness and acculturation indicates an underlying process of loosening of a traditional social organization, not increased anxiety.

The general conclusion indicated by the findings to this point is: drunkenness in primitive societies is determined less by the level of fear in a society than by the absence of corporate kin groups with stability, permanence, formal structure, and well-defined functions.

Marital Residence. Table 4 shows that there is a strong relation between degree of drunkenness and the form of marital residence. "Bilocal" residence means that the newlyweds customarily make a decision at marriage as to whether they will reside near the bridegroom's parents or near the bride's parents; "neolocal" residence means that they reside in a new location. All 11 tribes with bilocal or neolocal residence are above the median on degree of drunkenness. The five tribes with "uxoripatrilocal" residence, in which residence with the bridegroom's family follows a period of residence with the bride's family, are also uniformly above the median of drunkenness. The large number of societies in which the bride leaves her home and lives with the groom near his family, which is called "patrilocal" residence, includes, on the other hand, most of the tribes below the median on drunkenness. Tribes with "matrilocal" or "avunculocal" residence (in which the newlyweds live in the first case with the wife's family, and in the second with the groom's mother's brother) are harder to place. The former seems to show the extreme drunkenness pattern while the latter seems to be much closer to the sober patrilocal pattern.

Since two of the avunculocal tribes have residence shifts partially similar to the uxoripatrilocal tribes, they have been classified with the non-patrilocal tribes, following conservative procedure. If, on the other hand, the crucial variable here is immediate residence with a male exercising authority over the groom, and if avunculocal tribes are therefore grouped with patrilocal tribes, the relation between residence and drunkenness will be still stronger $(r = .71,\ \chi^2 = 11.81,\ P < .001,\ N = 55)$.

TABLE 4

The Relation of Degree of Drunkenness to Form of Marital Residence

Degree of Drunkenness	Form of Residence				
	Bilocal or Neolocal	Uxoripatri-local	Matri-local	Avuncu-local	Patri-local
Extreme	11	5	8	1	9
Moderate or slight	0	0	4	2	15

The correlation between non-patrilocal residence and drunkenness $(r = .64)$ is almost as high as the correlation between bilateral descent and drunkenness.* There is a correlation of .67 between non-patrilocal residence and bilateral descent. While these two predictor variables are importantly related to each other, each predicts some independent portion of the total variance in drunkenness scores. The multiple correlation using these two variables as joint predictors of drunkenness is .72. This means that the degree of dependence of drunkenness on form of residence and kin group is so strong that its level can be predicted with moderate accuracy in individual tribes from just these two variables alone. If the tribes with unilineal moieties had been grouped with the bilateral tribes, and the avunculocal with the patrilocal tribes, the multiple correlation would have been considerably higher.

The extreme drunkenness of the neolocal and bilocal tribes appears to reflect the fact that it is difficult for a society to develop extended lineal kinship structures if independent choice of residence is permitted the newlyweds. It is also probable that if the married couple is permitted to choose its residence, it will not be constrained by lineal and corporate rules in many other areas. There seems to be an intimate relationship between drunkenness and personal choice, absence of institutionalized constraints, and isolation of both the nuclear family and the individual from corporate kin structures.

Absence of drunkenness, on the other hand, appears to be associated with male dominance reflected in patrilocal and perhaps avunculocal residence. We know that the father or the paternal grandfather usually wields authority in the household (22, p. 39) but we also know that he loses some of his power to his wife in matrilocal societies (33, pp. 507–508; 37). There are several reasons for this. In husband-wife conflicts, the wife will be supported by her own kinsmen, who are close at hand under matrilocal residence. Furthermore, since the man does not own land or the household in these tribes, his ties to his wife's home are weaker. Moreover, since the mother's brother can take on child-rearing duties, the father will be loosely attached to the nuclear family. He may divide his time between his sister's household and his wife's household, with both his authority and his obligations divided between them. For reasons such as these, Linton (17) concludes that marriage is particularly unstable in matrilineal societies.

By contrast, according to Linton, in patrilineal societies the woman is integrated into her husband's lineage by a series of marriage-stabilizing devices motivated by the interest of the husband's family in the children. With patrilocal residence, which means that the wife's kinsmen are at a distance and cannot support her, the father's formal and de facto authority grow. With increased centralization of familial power and the formation of hierarchical chains of command in the family, extreme drunkenness diminishes.

The tribes with uxoripatrilocal residence are significantly more drunken than the patrilocal tribes. In these five tribes, as in many of the matrilocal tribes, the bridegroom is required to serve as a hired hand for his wife's family, and must often undergo trials to determine his suitability for the

* For patrilocal versus all other rules of residence, $\chi^2 = 8.92$, 1 df; $P < .01$; $N = 55$.

marriage. It is only after this that he acquires full marital rights or, with uxoripatrilocal residence, permission to remove the bride from her own family. One implication of this custom is that the husband's authority over his wife develops only gradually and is not clearly reinforced by external social influences. A second implication follows from the fact that there are at least two shifts of marital residence in these tribes, and that authority over a man is not consistently held by a single person, but is successively taken by his father and father-in-law. This means the attenuation of lineal structures and so, perhaps, more drunkenness.

While sobriety is obviously associated with a father-centered family, the crucial factors mediating this relationship are not entirely clear. One possibility is that there is a general increase in respect, reserve, and self-control in these tribesmen, because most of their interpersonal relations are organized hierarchically. Another possibility is that with patrilocal residence there is decreased mobility on the part of the heads of the households; therefore there will be a greater opportunity for the formation of formalized social ties in the community, and this in turn implies that there will be strong pressure exerted against interpersonal aggression, informal self-indulgence, and related individualistic behavior prominent at drinking bouts.

Still another possibility is that there may be a general stabilization of the society's interpersonal relationships when the authority of the father in any society is legitimized and extended by supporting rules of residence and descent; that is, in societies where internal power struggles by individuals or groups are minimized in normal interpersonal relationships, prolonged drinking bouts with their inevitable changing, transient coalitions, and conflicts will also be minimized. Certainly these factors are not mutually exclusive. In fact, each to some extent implies the other.

One further possible stabilizing influence might be role differentiation and specialization within the family; with a highly stable power structure it would often be possible for the father to delegate increased authority to his wife in defined areas such as child rearing and routine household management, while he specializes for example in ceremonial or political activities. This role differentiation would in turn make husband and wife more interdependent, minimize conflicts over allocation of rights and privileges, make the family a more closely cooperating unit pursuing mutually accepted goals, and therefore suppress highly personal, individualistic drinking behavior. Quite a different result would be expected, on the other hand, in modern urban society where corporate division of labor means that the average worker is minimally involved in company goals, has relatively little commitment to his co-workers and supervisor, is free after work hours, and can change jobs at will (cf. Chapter 5). These conditions have little in common with those just discussed as prevailing in father-centered tribes, and may have opposite effects on drunkenness.

To summarize, drunkenness increases markedly if the authority of the man in the household is lessened or diffused, and if the nuclear family is less integrated into larger kin structures through bilocal or neolocal residence.

The Clan-Community. A clan has been defined by Murdock (22) in terms of three criteria: (*a*) it is a kin group based on a unilinear rule of descent uniting its central core of members; (*b*) it has residential unity; and (*c*) it shows clear evidences of social integration, such as positive group sentiment and recognition of in-marrying spouses as an integral part of the membership. Our data show that as the community approaches an exogamous clan organization, drunkenness decreases. More precisely, there is a significant correlation of —.59 between drunkenness and approach to a clan system in community organization (see Table 5).

TABLE 5

The Relation Between Drunkenness and Additional Measures of Social Structure

	χ^2	$r$tet	N
Approach to an exogamous clan-community	6.67 [a]	—.59	51
Presence of a bride-price (versus bride-service or no material consideration)	4.64 [a]	—.51	52
Non-sororal polygyny (versus monogamy and sororal polygyny)	3.26	—.46	46
Patrilineal extension of exogamy	7.24 [b]	—.65	45
Matrilineal extension of exogamy	2.32	—.44	43
Bilateral extension of exogamy	0.00	—.02	46
Degree of political integration	2.88	—.41	55
Degree of social stratification	0.54	—.22	52
Presence of slavery	1.49	—.35	46
Nuclear household (versus extended, mother-child, or polygynous household)	0.56	.25	49

[a] $P < .05$. "Approach to a clan community" compares societies with exogamous clan communities, exogamous communities, and exogamous divisions within the community against societies without reported clans or with demes (communities without localized exogamous units and with a marked tendency toward local endogamy). "Degree of political integration" compares politically independent local communities of less than fifteen hundred average population and societies where family heads acknowledge no higher political authority, against minimal states, little states, dependent societies, and societies with peace groups transcending the local community. "Slavery" compares societies with hereditary and non-hereditary slavery with societies with absence or near absence of slavery.
[b] $P < .01$.

The development of clan segmentation within a tribe implies both increased internal solidarity and increased separation or cleavage within the community. In other words, an individual is more strongly integrated within his own clan, but at the same time he is probably more isolated from individuals belonging to other clans. Seen from the outside, clans are exclusive corporations; this clannishness probably militates against the diffuse friendliness and broadly inclusive brotherhood that is an integral part of social drunkenness.

The clan differs from sibs and lineages by excluding as members siblings who have married out of the group. With the clan structure, then, the legal ties of mutual obligation linking siblings are not as close as with sib and lineage structures, and dispersed families are not unified by these sibling relations. Community integration, therefore, may well be weaker with the clan than with the sib structure, although household integration localized around the residentially unified clan should be at least as strong. If the extension of impersonal ties of obligation and control throughout the community helps diminish drunkenness, the negative relationship between the clan and drunkenness should not be as strong as that between drunkenness and sib-like structures. This is, in fact, what is found: approach to the clan community correlates —.59 with drunkenness, while sibs and segmentary lineage organizations correlate —.76 with drunkenness.*

Approach to a clan-community is correlated .74 with unilineal descent and .60 with patrilocal residence, with both relations significant at the .01 level of confidence. Since these three predictors of drunkenness are all positively intercorrelated to a moderate or strong degree, they appear to be variations on a single theme, such as corporate, formal social organization or traditional, hierarchical social solidarity. While the intercorrelation matrix was not computed, many of the predictors of drunkenness reported here may well be positively intercorrelated. If this is true, both the predictors and the drunkenness score could be conceived as loading highly on a general factor of corporate (formal) versus personal (informal) social organization.

Bride-Price and Form of Marriage. In primitive tribes there are several forms of exchange of services, goods, and gifts at marriage. One form previously discussed is bride-service, which is associated with lessened paternal authority and with extreme drunkenness. However, there is another form of payment for the bride that is more likely to reinforce the husband's authority over his wife, namely, the bride-price.† As might be anticipated, there is a moderate but statistically significant relation between the presence of a bride-price and the absence of extreme drunkenness (Table 5).

---

* This last correlation was derived by grouping societies with lineages, moieties, and phratries together with bilateral societies and comparing them to societies with sibs and segmentary lineage organizations.

† This is quite different from the familiar European dowry; it is a payment by the bridegroom to his wife's family compensating them for the loss of an economically productive member and giving the groom the right to remove his bride from her parents' home.

Undoubtedly this reflects some of the previous factors shown to be associated with little drunkenness, since the bride-price is highly correlated, for example, with patrilocal residence.

There are, however, certain important functions of the bride-price which suggest that it may have some independent influence. One such function suggested by Linton (17) and Gluckman (11) is the stabilization of marriage.* If the husband mistreats his wife, she may return to her parents' home and the husband must forfeit the goods he has paid for his bride. If, on the other hand, the bride is lazy or shrewish, she may be returned to her parents' home, and they must return the bride-price. Payment of a bride-price may also stabilize marriage by vesting in the father legal rights over his wife's children; if the wife returns to her parental home, she must abandon them. Moreover, the bride-price also creates ties between separated lineages. Malinowski (19) points out that the presents given at marriage by the husband have often been contributed in part by his kinsmen, and are often shared by the bride's relatives and clansmen as well as her parents. He concludes that these transactions bind two groups rather than two individuals. All such legalized, impersonal ties between individuals and groups may be an important factor in diminishing loosely structured, informal behavior in ordinary social relations, including drinking bouts.

With regard to the actual form of marriage, extreme drunkenness appears to be slightly more extensive in societies with monogamy or sororal polygyny than in societies with non-sororal polygyny (Table 5). (This correlation, of borderline significance, reaches the 5 per cent significance level by comparing only societies having more than 20 per cent of the marriages non-sororally polygynous with monogamous societies: $\chi^2 = 3.87$, 1 df; $P < .05$, $r = -.66$, $N = 27$.) This correlation is probably an indirect one. Societies with non-sororal polygyny usually have patrilocal residence, while sororal polygyny is more frequent and technically more feasible under matrilocal residence. Furthermore, it is doubtful if non-sororal polygyny itself plays a direct causal part in diminishing drunkenness. In these societies plural marriages are limited to the wealthy. The poorer tribesmen are usually monogamous and would be expected to exhibit the tendency toward more extreme drunkenness evident for other monogamous groups.

Rules of Exogamy. While all societies forbid marriage with a small number of close relatives, societies differ in the extent to which rules of exogamy

---

* Gluckman (11) notes, however, that there is no simple relation between the presence of a bride-price and the frequency of divorce in a society. Ratings on frequency of divorce (21) are available for only fifteen of Horton's tribes. A statistically unreliable correlation of —.11 ($\chi^2 = 0.00$) between drunkenness and the divorce rate was obtained. Because of the small number of cases little confidence can be placed in this relationship. The bride-price may well stabilize the jural (contractual-obligatory) aspects of marriage more than the affectional-companionship aspects; for information on the complex issues involved, see (21) and (32).

are extended to more distant kinsmen. Patrilineal extension of rules of exogamy, prohibiting marriage between individuals tracing descent through males to a common ancestor, is associated with the presence of patrilineal kin groups and should therefore be negatively correlated with drunkenness. Matrilineal extension of exogamy should also be negatively related to drunkenness for similar reasons, but since there are fewer matrilineal than patrilineal societies in the sample, the relationship should be a good deal weaker. The results in Table 5 confirm this expectation.

The expected relationship between drunkenness and degree of bilateral extension of exogamy, that is, to kinsmen traced through both sexes, is not so obvious. If extended rules of exogamy reflect a stable society, or by themselves create structure in a society, they might be related negatively to drunkenness. If, on the other hand, they indicate the absence of a corporate unilineal group, they might be related positively to drunkenness. The relationship actually found in Table 5 shows no important trend in any direction and is difficult to interpret.

Household Type and Settlement Pattern. The absence in our data of any important relation between household type and drunkenness was unexpected, especially since household type tends to predict a number of important psychological phenomena, including child-rearing practices (24, 39). The correlation between household type and drunkenness is empirically maximized by testing nuclear and polygynous households against extended and mother-child households. Even so, it is still an insignificant and unimpressive .36, and this combination of household types is hard to rationalize theoretically. No other combinations of household type yield a significant or nearly significant relation to drunkenness. Nuclear household tested alone against other household types (Table 5) correlates only .25.

There is, however, a significant relation between drunkenness and patterns of settlement, as rated by Murdock (23).* Since it was not possible to order his categories confidently with respect to degree of community organization, a correlation coefficient based upon a dichotomization would not be very meaningful. However, Murdock's two extreme categories— "nomadic bands" versus "complex villages and towns"—show a significant difference in degree of insobriety. All nine nomadic tribes are characterized by extreme drunkenness, while thirteen of twenty-seven tribes with compact villages or towns exhibit this pattern. It seems likely that factors of the sort already mentioned explain these relations, since tribes with very small population wandering over an extensive territory would have little chance of elaborating the kind of social organization apparently conducive to sobriety. There may well be an independent stabilizing influence exerted by the small village, however. The only two bilateral tribes that were relatively sober (Macusi and Taulipang) had a village settlement pattern.

Social Stratification and Political Integration. The final aspects of social organization investigated in this study in relation to degree of drunkenness

* $\chi^2 = 11.03$, 4 df; $P < .05$, $N = 55$.

were extent of social stratification (including the presence of slavery) and degree of political integration into units transcending the local community. While the elaboration of these aspects of social organization signifies population growth and complexity in social arrangements relative to small nomadic tribes, they are not of the same order in the structuring of social relations as is the development of corporate kin groups. Indeed, stratification and political integration may, in the course of social evolution, proceed at the expense of corporate kin groups and with consequences other than sobriety, as Bacon's discussion in the next section of this book so clearly suggests.

Hence it is not surprising, but nevertheless important, that none of the measures considered in this connection yielded a significant relation with degree of drunkenness. Within the range of complexity of social organization represented by our sample, there was a tendency for political integration and, to a lesser extent, stratification to be negatively correlated with drunkenness, but not significantly so. The lack of very strong relationships using these variables implies that kin group and residence factors may be the important causal elements, since they do not appear to influence drunkenness indirectly by mutual correlation with stratification or political factors.

3. Tests of some social-psychological variables

In a study of this kind it is important to explore variables other than those which obviously reflect social organization. Since this study is re-examining many of the hypotheses of Horton—hypotheses which were essentially psychological in conception—it is necessary to pursue their implications in the light of all available new evidence. Moreover, the social-psychological and clinical literature contains a number of points of view on drunkenness and alcoholism testable by the cross-cultural method. The recent proliferation of cross-cultural indices not only makes tests of alternative hypotheses possible, but also permits a crude comparison of the power of variables of social organization with other kinds of variables in explaining drunkenness in primitive societies.

Aggression Anxiety. An important feature of Horton's theory attributes the relative absence of drunkenness to fear concerning the expression of previously punished aggressive impulses. Yet in point of fact, all but one of Whiting and Child's (40) measures of aggression training or aggression in fantasy failed to relate significantly to Horton's drunkenness score. The single exception is shown in Table 6: there is a barely significant inverse relation between drunkenness and punishment for aggression in childhood, supporting this aspect of Horton's theory. However, the inverse relation between drunkenness and general pressure for responsible performance of duties and obedience is slightly stronger, suggesting that drunkenness is correlated with generalized lack of discipline instead of with permissive aggression training alone.

This interpretation seems to be supported by the other results in Table 6

TABLE 6

The Relation of Degree of Drunkenness to Selected Child-rearing Measures [a]

Child-rearing Measures	N	χ^2	z	$r$tet
Aggression socialization anxiety	26	1.39	1.97 [b]	−.47
Pressure for obedience and responsibility rather than self-reliance and achievement (from 5 to 12 years) (4)	20	3.23	2.76 [c]	−.71
Indulgence during childhood (from 5 to 12 years)	25	6.74 [c]	1.66	.81
Indulgence of the infant	25	2.06	1.00	.55

[a] χ^2 was computed at 1 df; z was estimated by the Mann-Whitney test for rank-ordered data.
[b] $P < .05$.
[c] $P < .01$.

which show that indulgence during childhood correlates significantly with drunkenness. Childhood indulgence is defined as a function of: protection from environmental discomforts; amount of overt affection shown the child; degree, immediacy, and consistency of drive reduction; constancy of presence and absence of pain inflicted by the nurturant agent; and lowness of degree of socialization demanded (Barry, Bacon, and Child, unpublished). (There were only a few tribes that were exceptions to this relationship—that is, that were both sober and indulgent to their children, or drunken and severe to their children—but these exceptions were quite marked. Since a rank test reflects the degree of exception as well as the presence of an exception, the association drops from high significance with a median division to borderline significance using a rank test.) Indulgence of the infant shows a similar trend to indulgence of the child, but is not statistically reliable.*

Wright (43) has previously shown that societies which punish aggression severely do not thereby eliminate aggressive responses; instead the object of aggression is changed. In societies with high aggression socialization anxiety, agents and objects of aggression in folktales are likely to be strangers, signifying displacement along a scale of similarity-dissimilarity to the hero and his family. My interpretation of these results is that in the sober societies aggression is displaced toward, and expected from, an outgroup, which is a logical corollary of the proposition that little drunkenness is found in societies segmented into a number of internally solidary lineal

* It is probably relevant in this connection that Parker (27) has found fifteen articles reporting a close mother-son attachment in alcoholics; and several authors have reported that youngest children in a family are both relatively indulged and overrepresented among alcoholics (25).

units. A reasonable general conclusion suggested by these facts is that fear of aggression directed against close relatives at drinking bouts is a more genuine causal influence diminishing drunkenness than is generalized fear of aggression, and that generalized pressure for strict obedience and self-control is still more important.

Wright (43) has also shown that acts of fantasy aggression are *less* intense in tribes which allow their children freedom to express aggression—that is, in the drunken tribes. This suggests, on the one hand, that the drunken tribes do not express aggression against distant or inappropriate objects; in other words, they are neither unusually conflicted about aggression nor "unconsciously hostile" in the psychiatric sense. On the other hand, the aggression of the drunken tribes will be much more obvious against family members and friends, because the psychological mechanisms enforcing submissiveness and respect are weak. While interpersonal relations seem to be stronger and more lasting in the sober tribes, this is achieved only at the cost of repression of aggression. The superficially strong interpersonal ties in the sober tribes are much more ambivalent than the loose, informal relations in the drunken tribes. This tentative formulation of drunken aggression needs further testing, on the other hand, in view of the lack of relation between drunkenness and the indices of projected aggression in Table 1.

Sex Anxiety. In his earlier study, Horton reported an association between premarital sex freedom and drunkenness, and in this chapter we have noted an inverse relation between degree of drunkenness and the extension of certain rules of exogamy. There are two major possible interpretations of these findings. Horton's explanation is that they both simply reflect sex anxiety, which is strong in the tribes that have little drunkenness. A more logical possibility, however, is that they both reflect hierarchical control of a variety of marital choices which might disrupt a corporate social organization.

As a further test of the sex anxiety hypothesis, drunkenness was correlated with the five best currently available measures of sex anxiety—measures based on the content of fantasy as well as actual punishment for sex play in childhood. More specifically, the measures used were: (*a*) sex socialization anxiety; (*b*) sex explanations of illness; (*c*) sex avoidance therapy; (*d*) duration of sex taboo during pregnancy; and (*e*) duration of sex taboo after childbirth.* None of these measures is related significantly to degree of drunkenness, nor is any trend apparent. The most promising non-significant negative relationship—with sex socialization anxiety—was not improved by use of a more powerful statistical test. The scale with the best reliability, as determined by its correlations with other measures, is the duration of the taboo on sexual intercourse following childbirth (2). While there are very few cases, there does not appear to be a better correla-

* The N's for the tests of significance and correlations utilizing these measures were, respectively: 21, 27, 23, 16, and 14. The scales were taken from (2) and (40).

tion with this measure than with others. The correlations between sex anxiety and drunkenness prove to be so generally weak that if a larger sample shows a genuine negative relation, it will probably be merely an indirect reflection of other factors. Factors that might produce such an indirect relation include generally restrictive social control, extended rules of exogamy, or incest fears generated in a tightly knit community.

In addition to the above, three more sets of tests bearing upon the relations of drunkenness and sex anxiety were made which involved the use of indices suggested by the frequent assertion that a major conflict in the lives of alcoholics centers around latent homosexuality.*

The first of these made use of Ford and Beach's (8) list of societies in which homosexual activities are normal and permitted for some members, frequently a *berdache* (male transvestite) who assumes a female role in life. This scale, however, is probably a much better index of overt than latent homosexuality. When societies permitting homosexual activities on the part of some members are compared with those in which such activities are reportedly absent, rare, or secret, the findings indicate that there is no correlation whatsoever, positive or negative, with degree of drunkenness.

The second set of tests made use, in contrast, of a very indirect measure, namely, Stephens' (35, 36) ingenious Guttman scale of taboos on menstruating women. Stephens noted that societies which isolate menstruating women in special huts or forbid them to cook believe that at this time they are dangerous to men, although not to themselves, other women, or children. In these societies there is also severe sex training, and the father is the main disciplinarian. These facts suggested to Stephens that menstrual taboos might be an indirect index of the psychoanalytic concept of castration anxiety, which has been claimed to be a factor in the causation of homosexuality. There are, of course, other logical interpretations of this scale; it may quite possibly indicate just sex anxiety, without any necessary implication for the development of homosexuality. However, there is no significant relation between Stephens' scale and the extent of drunkenness in the primitive societies sampled in this study.

Finally, consideration was given to the possibility of a correlation between drunkenness and male initiation rites at puberty, since Whiting and his collaborators (41) have contended that one of the several functions of these rites is the attempted removal of a latent female identification in males. Once again, however, the findings show no significant relation using the ratings in (1).

Although none of these latter variables is significantly related to drunkenness, there is a hint of a moderate negative relation with menstrual taboos sufficient to suggest that a significant correlation might be established with a larger sample. Yet if there is a genuine relation of this kind, it may reflect structural factors; periodic isolation of women demands a variety of

---

* N ranges from 20 to 24 in these three cases. On the theme of alcoholic conflict over latent homosexuality, see, for example, (27) and (7).

special and relatively complex social arrangements, including provision for non-menstruating women to assume the duties of the isolated woman, which may be technically difficult for a small band of hunters to maintain. In any event, we are forced in the light of the present evidence to conclude that however important they may be in individual cases of alcoholism, latent or overt homosexuality or sex anxiety are not important causal variables in extreme drunkenness in primitive societies.

It is impossible to rule out an indirect association between drunkenness and one possible kind of surface femininity. The personal, friendly behavior of the drunken tribes seems to have something in common with the traditional female sentimental, expressive role, while the impersonal, self-controlled behavior of the sober tribes shows similarities to the instrumental, command behavior associated with the traditional male role. At the same time, the emphasis upon diffuse brotherhood in the drunken tribes may produce friendly, companionate behavior among men. This possible surface femininity, however, seems to be quite different from the paranoid fear and hostility that has been claimed to be associated with unconscious homosexual impulses.

Orality and Self-Injury. Many psychoanalysts and psychiatrists (7) have identified oral fixations or frustrations as important causes of inebriety and alcoholism, following Freud's opinions concerning the relation between oral-erogenous sensitivity and drinking (9, p. 182). Without implying an equation between drunkenness and alcoholism, it seems pertinent in these circumstances to explore the relations between drunkenness and the best available measures of oral fixations and frustrations in primitive societies. Tests of significance and correlations were therefore computed for degree of drunkenness in relation to the following measures taken from (2, 10, 40): (*a*) age of weaning; (*b*) oral socialization anxiety; (*c*) oral satisfaction potential; (*d*) oral explanations of illness; (*e*) oral performance therapies (eating herbs or medicine to cure illness); (*f*) oral avoidance therapies (spitting, vomiting, adherence to food taboos to cure illness); (*g*) number of foods taboo during pregnancy; (*h*) feasts during mourning; and (*i*) food taboos during mourning.

The results indicate no important relation between drunkenness and any of these measures. Nor do the variables with the highest reliability (oral socialization anxiety and oral explanations of illness) appear to show stronger relations than the other variables. Thus, while oral fixations may play a role in particular instances of alcoholism, they do not appear to explain variations in drunkenness among primitive peoples insofar as they are adequately indexed by these measures.

Because psychoanalysts and psychiatrists have often singled out self-destructive motives as important factors in alcoholism,* an attempt was

---

* The work of Karl Menninger (20) is an outstanding example. A similar relation is suggested by anomie theories of suicide. For a discussion of various theories and new evidence on the relations of alcoholism and suicide, see Chapter 29.

made to determine what bearing measurable cultural tendencies toward self-injury have upon drunkenness in primitive societies. For an index of self-injury, reliance was placed on the work of Friendly (10), who has measured a number of variables of ascetic mourning. Friendly found that many of these (including vigils by the mourner, change in appearance, property destruction, purification, etc.) were positively interrelated, and she consequently developed, by summation, an over-all scale of ascetic mourning which proved to be positively related to severe child training practices.

One important variable of ascetic mourning, namely, degree of self-inflicted bodily injury, did not correlate positively with Friendly's other measures and was therefore treated separately in this analysis. The results show, however, that neither this latter measure nor the scale of ascetic mourning are significantly related to drunkenness in the societies considered in this study. Hence, the limited cross-cultural evidence suggests that there is no important general association between drunkenness and self-injury.*

4. A note on ethnic differences in rates of alcoholism

Caution is necessary in applying these results on primitive drunkenness directly to national or ethnic variations in alcoholism, since these phenomena have important differences as well as similarities. But it is a fact that some father-centered ethnic groups with a high degree of lineal social solidarity—such as the Jews and Chinese (34)—have very low rates of alcoholism and drunkenness, as the conclusions reported in this chapter would predict. These cross-cultural findings also suggest a highly speculative possibility that might be worth checking: that some patri-centered Western countries with a highly traditional, lineal social organization (such as Italy) have developed preferences for wine or beer rather than distilled liquors in part *because* of their social structure, which should discourage extreme drunkenness.

The Irish present a different problem. They are the group most over-represented among American alcoholics, and yet they seem on the surface to be a traditional father-dominated group. The most prominent current hypothesis concerning Irish drunkenness was proposed by Bales (3), based in part on Horton's anxiety theory. Bales noted instances of anxiety in Irish life and, following Horton, suggested that high anxiety played a causal role in Irish drunkenness. However, some of the anxiety-arousing conditions he mentioned, such as absentee landlordship and penal restrictions on Irish industry, can be explained just as well as indices of the alienation of the Catholic majority from the controlling jural, formal aspects of their own society (the imposed legal, governmental, and economic systems, and the established Protestant church).

* This does not preclude the possibility of a positive relation between drunkenness and other forms of guilt. However, the available measures of guilt (40) were based on too few tribes to permit an estimate of such a relation.

One writer on Ireland, in fact, uses the phrase "disorganized social system" (30, p. 46) to describe the wholesale evictions and the general loosening of ties to the land in the 18th and 19th Centuries. Furthermore, the authority of the Irish father in the home does not seem to be as impressive as paternal authority in southern Europe. Bales, for example, comments that the Irish-American father ". . . in many cases seems to have dropped into a role of impotence and insignificance . . ." Bales also noted a close mother-son attachment in many of his Irish alcoholics, and Opler and Singer (26) found a very close, dependent relation of the Irish son to his mother, who keeps him a "boy and a burden." These authors also call the Irish father "shadowy and evanescent." Factors such as these have been shown to be associated with drunkenness in primitive tribes in the present study. These suggestions underscore the need for a more extensive treatment of Irish drinking patterns in the light of these new cross-cultural findings.

5. Methodological check

By way of a methodological check on the findings and conclusions of this chapter, degree of drunkenness was examined in relation to Horton's five culture areas, and a significant relation between these variables was found *—the African tribes being the least drunken, the South American the most drunken tribes. This raises the possibility that the associations found might be explained on the basis of historical accident and parallel diffusion to contiguous tribes, rather than on the basis of cause-and-effect.

An unpublished technique to deal with questions of this kind has recently been invented by Roy D'Andrade of the Harvard Laboratory of Human Development and is summarized here with his permission. He reasons that the diffusion hypothesis would be supported if an expected relationship generally failed to occur in each of a pair of neighboring tribes, while the causal hypothesis would be supported if diffusion of both the antecedent and consequent had not usually occurred from one to another of a pair of neighboring tribes—between which diffusion might easily take place. He therefore divides the sample of tribes into the geographically closest possible pairs, excluding societies that do not form close pairs, and examines the patterns of relationship within these pairs.

D'Andrade examines the few cases in which the expected relationship fails to occur in each of a pair of geographically contiguous societies—that is, the usual antecedent does not produce the expected consequent in either tribe. Each of these cases he calls a victory for the historical-diffusion hypothesis. He then examines the few cases in which the predicted relation occurs in only one of a pair of geographically contiguous societies—that is, in which only one tribe has both the predicted antecedent and consequent, while the other tribe has neither. Each of these cases is a victory for the causal-functional hypothesis. D'Andrade's method was usable with Horton's

* $x^2 = 9.66$, 4 df; $P < .05$, $N = 56$.

sample even though Horton had excluded close pairs of similar tribes, since relatively close and relatively distant tribes could be distinguished.

Application of D'Andrade's technique to the relation between drunkenness and form of kin group, residence, and clan-community organization indicated victories for the causal-functional hypothesis by five to one, four to one, and three to one, respectively. Two of the three apparent victories for the historical-diffusion hypothesis were accounted for by the Hopi-Zuni pair. These tribes have a strong degree of traditional community solidarity, unilinear sibs, and little drunkenness, but matrilocal residence and agamous or deme community organization. This is probably not a genuine case of diffusion. It seems rather to signify two independent examples of the dominant influence of sib solidarity over opposed factors (such as marital weakness) in reducing drunkenness. The available evidence, then, does not support a diffusionist interpretation of the correlations reported in this chapter.

Summary

This chapter has reported an extensive re-examination of Horton's cross-cultural study of the functions of alcohol in primitive tribes. The most important single conclusion was that the degree of drunkenness at periodic communal drinking bouts is related to variables indicating a personal (or informal) rather than a corporate (or formal) organization, but is substantially unrelated to the level of anxiety in the society.

Following are some of the variables found to be positively correlated with relative *sobriety* in primitive tribes: (a) corporate kin groups with continuity over time, collective ownership of property, and unified action as a legal individual; (b) patrilocal residence at marriage; (c) approach to a clan-community organization; (d) presence of a bride-price; (e) a village settlement pattern (rather than nomadism). It was suggested that societies with these features are likely to be well organized, to have a high degree of lineal social solidarity, and to have interpersonal relationships structured along hierarchical or respect lines. It was hypothesized that these factors in turn controlled extremely informal, friendly, and loosely structured behavior at drinking bouts. This interpretation was supported by the fact that the sober tribes were shown to control aggression severely in their children, while the drunken tribes are relatively indulgent with their children and permit disobedience and self-assertion.

No indices of fear were found that correlated significantly with drunkenness, and it was concluded that Horton's measures of an insecure food supply and acculturation indicated a loose social organization rather than fear. Indices suggested by psychoanalytic hypotheses about alcoholism (oral fixations, latent homosexuality, and drives toward self-injury) did not predict primitive drunkenness. Suggestions about Irish alcoholism in the light of these results were made.

References

1. Anthony, Albert S., *A Cross-Cultural Study of Factors Relating to Male Initiation Rites and Genital Operations,* unpublished doctoral dissertation, Harvard University, 1956.

2. Ayres, Barbara C., *A Cross-Cultural Study of Factors Relating to Pregnancy Taboos,* unpublished doctoral dissertation, Radcliffe College, 1954.

3. Bales, Robert Freed, "Cultural Differences in Rates of Alcoholism," *Quart. J. Stud. Alc.,* **6**:480–499, 1946.

4. Barry, Herbert, III, Irvin L. Child, and Margaret K. Bacon, "Relation of Child Training to Subsistence Economy," *Amer. Anthrop.,* **61**:51–63, 1959.

5. Conger, John J., "Alcoholism: Theory, Problem, and Challenge, II: Reinforcement Theory and the Dynamics of Alcoholism," *Quart. J. Stud. Alc.,* **17**:296–305, 1956.

6. Davenport, William, "Nonunilinear Descent and Descent Groups," *Amer. Anthrop.,* **61**:557–572, 1959.

7. Fenichel, Otto, *The Psychoanalytic Theory of Neurosis,* New York: W. W. Norton and Company, 1945.

8. Ford, Clellan S., and Frank A. Beach, *Patterns of Sexual Behavior,* New York: Harper and Brothers, 1951.

9. Freud, Sigmund, "Three Essays on the Theory of Sexuality," *in* James Strachey (Ed.), *Standard Edition of the Complete Psychological Works of Sigmund Freud,* Vol. 7, London: The Hogarth Press, 1953.

10. Friendly, Joan P., *A Cross-Cultural Study of Ascetic Mourning Behavior,* unpublished undergraduate honors thesis, Radcliffe College, 1956.

11. Gluckman, Max, "Kinship and Marriage among the Lozi of Northern Rhodesia and the Zulu of Natal," *in* A. R. Radcliffe-Brown and Daryll Forde (Eds.), *African Systems of Kinship and Marriage,* London: Oxford University Press, 1950.

12. Heath, Dwight B., "Drinking Patterns of the Bolivian Camba," *Quart. J. Stud. Alc.,* **19**:491–508, 1958.

13. Horton, Donald, "The Functions of Alcohol in Primitive Societies: A Cross-Cultural Study," *Quart. J. Stud. Alc.,* **4**:199–320, 1943.

14. Hovland, Carl Iver, and Robert R. Sears, "Minor Studies of Aggression, VI: Correlation of Lynchings With Economic Indices," *J. Psychol.,* **9**:301–310, 1940.

15. Lemert, Edwin M., "Alcohol and the Northwest Coast Indians," *Univ. Calif. Publ. in Culture and Society,* **2**:303–406, 1954.

16. ———, "Alcoholism: Theory, Problem, and Challenge, III. Alcoholism and the Sociocultural Situation," *Quart. J. Stud. Alc.,* **17**:306–317, 1956.

17. Linton, Ralph, "The Natural History of the Family," *in* Ruth Nanda Anshen (Ed.), *The Family: Its Function and Destiny,* New York: Harper and Brothers, 1949.

18. Lowie, Robert H., *Social Organization,* New York: Holt, Rinehart, and Winston, 1948.

19. Malinowski, Bronislaw, "Marriage," in *Encyclopaedia Britannica,* (*14th ed.*), Vol. 14, 1929.

20. Menninger, Karl A., *Man Against Himself,* New York: Harcourt, Brace and World, 1938.

21. Murdock, George Peter, "Family Stability in Non-European Cultures," *Ann. Amer. Acad. Pol. Soc. Sci.,* **272**:195–201, 1950.

22. ———, *Social Structure,* New York: The MacMillan Company, 1949.

23. ———, "World Ethnographic Sample," *Amer. Anthrop.* **59**:664–687, 1957.

24. ———, and John W. M. Whiting, "Cultural Determination of Parental Attitudes: The Relationship Between the Social Structure, Particularly Family Structure, and Parental Behavior," *in* M. J. E. Senn (Ed.), *Problems of Infancy and Childhood*, New York: Josiah Macy Foundation, 1951.

25. Navratil, L. "On the Etiology of Alcoholism," *Quart. J. Stud. Alc.*, **20**:236–244, 1959.

26. Opler, Marvin K., and Jerome L. Singer, "Ethnic Differences in Behavior and Psychopathology: Italian and Irish," *Int. J. Soc. Psychiat.*, **2**:11–23, 1956.

27. Parker, Frederick B., "A Comparison of the Sex Temperament of Alcoholics and Moderate Drinkers," *Amer. Sociol. Rev.*, **24**:366–374, 1959.

28. Pehrson, Robert N., "Bilateral Kin Groupings as a Structural Type: A Preliminary Statement," *J. East Asiatic Studies*, **3**:199–202, 1954.

29. ———, "The Bilateral Network of Social Relations in Könkämä Lapp District," (Publication Three of the Indiana University Research Center in Anthropology, Folklore, and Linguistics), *Int. J. Amer. Linguist.*, **23**:(Part) 2, 1957.

30. Potter, George, *To the Golden Door: The Story of the Irish in Ireland and America*, Boston: Little, Brown and Company, 1960.

31. Sahlins, Marshall D., "The Origin of Society," *Sci. American*, **203**:76–87, 1960.

32. Schneider, David M., "A Note on Bridewealth and the Stability of Marriage," *Man*, **53**:55–57, 1953.

33. Simmons, Leo W., "Statistical Correlations in the Science of Society," *in* George Peter Murdock (Ed.), *Studies in the Science of Society*, New Haven: Yale University Press, 1937.

34. Snyder, Charles R., *Alcohol and the Jews*, Glencoe, Ill.: The Free Press, 1958.

35. Stephens, William N., *Child Rearing and Oedipal Fears: A Cross-Cultural Study*, unpublished thesis in education, Harvard University, 1959.

36. ———, "A Cross-Cultural Study of Menstrual Taboos," *Genet. Psychol. Monogr.*, in press.

37. Strodtbeck, Fred L., "Husband-Wife Interaction Over Revealed Differences," *Amer. Sociol. Rev.*, **16**:468–473, 1951.

38. Wert, James E., Charles O. Neidt, and J. Stanley Ahmann, *Statistical Methods in Educational and Psychological Research*, New York: Appleton-Century-Crofts, 1954.

39. Whiting, John W. M., "Sorcery, Sin, and the Superego: A Cross-Cultural Study of Some Mechanisms of Social Control," *in* M. R. Jones (Ed.), *Nebraska Symposium on Motivation*, Lincoln: University of Nebraska Press, 1959.

40. ———, and Irvin L. Child, *Child Training and Personality: A Cross-Cultural Study*, New Haven: Yale University Press, 1953.

41. ———, Richard Kluckhohn, and Albert Anthony, "The Function of Male Initiation Ceremonies at Puberty," *in* Eleanor E. Maccoby, Theodore M. Newcomb, and Eugene L. Hartley (Eds.), *Readings in Social Psychology* (3rd ed.), New York: Holt, Rinehart and Winston, 1958.

42. Wolf, Eric R., "Types of Latin American Peasantry: A Preliminary Discussion," *Amer. Anthrop.*, **57**:452–471, 1955.

43. Wright, George O., "Projection and Displacement: A Cross-Cultural Study of Folk-Tale Aggression," *J. Abnorm. Soc. Psychol.*, **49**:523–528, 1954.

GENERAL
OBSERVATIONS
ON THE MODERN
SETTING

Introductory Note. From this point on, the focus of this book shifts from the drinking patterns of simpler societies to drinking in complex society. Before proceeding to more detailed studies, however, it seems appropriate to consider in a general way what is meant by complex society and how complex society differs from simpler societies—either historic or primitive, such as those just reviewed. Moreover, it is imperative that we consider the broad implications of societal complexity for the social use and evaluation of alcoholic beverages.

To these ends we have chosen to republish, with only slight modification, an essay on alcohol and complex society by Seldon Bacon, which was delivered as a lecture at the Yale Summer School of Alcohol Studies in 1944. Prepared as it was some years ago, Bacon's essay suffers in the treatment of certain major trends in modern society which are much in the foreground of sociological discussion. One could wish, for instance, that the impact of the growing bureaucratization of life and related changes in social ethic, character structure, and modes of control were delineated in relation to drinking behavior and attitude. Moreover, since it was prepared for a popular audience, parts of Bacon's discussion will perhaps seem labored or oversimplified to the professional social scientist. Still, it remains, in our judgment, the best single effort to explore the meaning of societal complexity in relation to beverage alcohol.

On a more fundamental level certain objections might be raised to the kind of analysis Bacon offers—objections which it would be well to anticipate briefly. Societal complexity may, in the first place, be approached along lines other than the economic specialization which he emphasizes.

75

Anthropologists, for example, are fond of pointing to the elaborate kinship systems of certain economically simple groups as an illustration of the futility of comparisons couched in terms of the "simple" and the "complex." Bacon recognizes this problem, albeit cursorily, but has chosen nonetheless to forge ahead using economic specialization as the basic attribute of complexity and the point of departure for his essay.

Secondly, the contrast drawn between complex and simple societies pre-supposes a conception of the simpler systems which fails to encompass the full range of social organization in relatively unspecialized societies, not to mention their variable psychological stresses or the drinking patterns as-sociated therewith.* The important question from our standpoint, however, is not the inclusiveness of Bacon's conception of the small, undifferentiated, and tightly knit society as a generalization about social realities, primitive or historic. Rather, it is whether or not the contrasting conception of the simple society provides a useful antithesis for deducing consequences of specialization which, considered in conjunction with certain known effects of alcohol, illuminate the functions of alcohol in complex society. In the case of Bacon's essay, we believe that it does.

Several, though by no means all, of the themes touched upon by Bacon will be developed in various ways in later chapters, and it would be re-dundant to comment upon them here. Yet there is one theme of such im-portance to the later interests of this book that it bears special mention. This is the relation of societal complexity to alcoholism. Leaving aside for the moment the difficult question of definition, which will be considered later, we may note the relative absence of alcoholism reported for the primitive societies just reviewed. Drunkenness there may be in many of these societies, and often on a grand scale. Indeed, it may be that a broad-ened conception of types of alcoholism—say, as suggested by E. M. Jellinek in Chapter 22—might encompass considerable drinking in simpler so-cieties. Yet one senses from these studies, and from the larger body of anthropological literature as well, that the pattern of alcoholism which Jellinek (Chapter 20) and others have depicted as predominant in our own society is a rarity among culturally intact primitive peoples. Admittedly, this is a moot question and greatly in need of systematic investigation. Still, Bacon's attempt to analyze the context of complex society, while not of-fering a complete picture of the etiology of alcoholism, suggests how the very structure of social relationships and pressures of complex society

---

* To appreciate that certain types of simpler societies may exhibit some of the char-acteristics which Bacon associates with the enhanced significance of beverage alcohol in complex society, one need only recall such statements of Field (Chapter 4) as: "There seems to be an intimate relationship between drunkenness (in primitive societies) and personal choice, absence of institutionalized constraints, and isolation of both the nuclear family and the individual from corporate kin structures." Yet it seems equally clear that Field has shown sobriety to be correlated with a type of primitive society which quite closely approximates the model of simpler societies stated or implied by Bacon.

might precipitate a relatively total deterioration and isolation of the person prone to excessive drinking and lend cumulative, individualistic significance to drinking in a manner which seems unlikely on a proportionate scale in simpler societies. In any event, certain aspects of this whole problem will be dealt with later on, particularly in the chapters by Peter Park and Ralph Connor in Section IV.

chapter 5

Alcohol
and complex society [*]

Selden D. Bacon

One of the foundations for a more penetrating insight into the problems of alcohol is an appreciation of the many diverse origins from which the problems arise and of the many diverse channels in which they make themselves felt. It is my purpose to present one view of the nature and functions of alcohol from a broad, sociological framework. I say "one" view since there are many sociological approaches and I am not pretending to touch them all.

Alcohol has certain effects on the individual and certain effects on the over-all group of individuals. Some of these effects seem to have value for the individual and for society, a conclusion buttressed by the observed fact that, as a custom, the drinking of alcoholic beverages has spread to almost all groups of men ever known, and has enjoyed a long life in almost every society of which we have knowledge. It is equally clear that some of the effects of alcohol on individuals and on groups have been disadvantageous.

Let me mention very briefly some of the outstanding effects. For the individual, alcohol can reduce tension, guilt, anxiety, and frustration; it also can reduce operational efficiency below the minimum necessary for social existence, or even for existence at all. In relation to the total society, alcohol can make possible association and interpersonal activity which may ordinarily be barred; it can permit variations in ideas and activities also, although this is a minor point; and it can allow an escape valve for socially frustrated individuals, an escape which can be relatively safe. Alcohol can also break down individual participation in associations, thus weakening

[*] This chapter is a revised and somewhat shortened version of Chapter 14 in *Alcohol, Science, and Society*, New Haven, Conn., Journal of Studies on Alcohol, 1945.

them. It can impair the exactitude and rhythm of behavior patterns and socially valuable ideas, and it can impair foresight and the results of previous foresight.

The relationship of social structure to the functions—to the potentialities —of alcohol will be discussed here. You have read discussions of alcohol and simple societies. What is the effect of social complexity on the functions of this phenomenon?

Simplicity and Complexity in Social Structure

Simplicity and complexity as characteristics of a society are generally related not to end goals or final purposes but to the means of attaining those goals, the numbers and divisions of society and their interrelations. The end goals of the Trobriand Islanders are not basically different from those of the Manhattan Islanders. All these individuals want food, shelter, and clothing; they all want protection from enemies within and without their groups and from the unknown which is potentially dangerous; they all want pleasurable interaction with others—love, affection, prestige; they all want a certain degree of control over themselves and over their situation, both current and future. The way in which these wishes are concretely expressed or attained will vary, of course, in different societies, although there will be for all a minimum core of similarity determined by the biological similarity of all mankind.

The needs of the societies are: (*a*) a minimum satisfaction of the individual needs; (*b*) perpetuation of the species; (*c*) internal unity and order; and (*d*) protection from outside groups. The achievement of these ends can be relatively simple or relatively complex. For example, a group of fifty families, comprising perhaps three hundred people, can maintain itself by what we could call simple social processes. The members of each family could serve as a unit for production and consumption, grow their own crops, store them, prepare them, and eat them; they could build their own dwellings and make their own clothes, utensils, and weapons. They would worship their ancestral spirits through avoidance, sacrifice, prayer, and other ritual at their home.

Division of labor could be based on sex, age, and talent, but the latter would be only occasional; that is, on a hunt or in constructing a dwelling, one function might invariably be activated by a given individual, but the others would be capable of doing it. Except for age and sex differences, almost any member of the group could fulfill almost any of the activities of the group. Property ownership would vary with talent, application, and luck, but would not vary in as great a degree as in our society, since the possibility of exchange, the range of types of production, and the quantity of durable goods would be limited. Defense of one's physical self and of one's social prestige would be largely a familial and individual matter.

In contrast to this picture, consider the industrial, commercial, service, or professional worker in the large contemporary city. He does not produce his own food, shelter, clothing, or utensils. He does not distribute or store them. He may, in the case of food, do something about final or immediate preparation. Yet he must obtain food, clothing, and shelter, and he does so, but by totally different life activities. The steps by which this social revolution occurred are highly complex and cannot be detailed here. In the main, however, specialization had the result of allowing more and a greater variety of production and finer output—a result of great value for group survival. Its incidence continued to increase—in the areas of both the production of goods and the rendering of services—to an extent, in contemporary society, that almost defies description. Specialization has occurred, moreover, not only in the realm of mechanical acts but also in the realms of foresight and imagination, organization, responsibility, and the giving of orders. There are all manner of gradations and specialties along these lines within the specialized economic categories.

Not that specialization is limited to the economic sphere. Recreation, education, medication, religious activities, and protection from personal attack, from disease, from poverty in old age, and from fire, to mention the most obvious, have, to a very large extent, been taken over by specialists. Once these functions were activated in the home by a member of the family or by the person involved. Now we have professions, businesses, industries, services, and institutions to do these things for us. The same values of specialization apply here as in the economic sphere. Variety, quality, quantity, and speed are mightily enhanced. This specialization process has been speeded, refined, and enlarged by the development of a machine technology.

Results of Specialization

From this extraordinary specialization has sprung the greatest amount and variety of food, shelter, and clothing the world has ever experienced. There is protection against sickness, there are facilities for recreation, and there are many other values which go beyond anything even imagined by the sages of primitive groups. There are also some other results or concomitants from this process which have not been an unmixed blessing. These have been placed under several headings and will first be described and then related to the functions of alcoholic beverage consumption.

1. Social stratification

One result of specialization has been the appearance of a social stratification system. Without stating the reasons for it, let me merely postulate the process that like tends to cluster with like. Carpenters mix with carpenters, college professors with college professors, the unemployed with the unemployed, hobos with hobos, and actors with actors. Furthermore, this clustering of people according to one interest tends to make all of them more similar in other aspects and, consequently, more different from members of other clusters.

A second concomitant of this specialization is a hierarchical form of stratification. What we may call the horizontal stratification, just discussed, is accompanied by varying degrees of prestige, responsibility, training, and monetary reward. Since the amount of money determines the variety, amount, and quality of goods and services, and since, because of the efficiency of the specialized society, there are enormous amounts of goods and services, the wealthier groups become more and more different from the less-wealthy groups—a process enhanced, as in the other instance, by the process of like clustering with like. Further vertical stratification occurs because of conquest, immigration, and lesser processes.

2. *Interdependence*

Another result of specialization is that persons are equipped with only a vague perception of the interests, ideas, habits, problems, likes, and dislikes of those not in their group. Specialization is commonly related to ignorance. Few factory workers know anything about farm work, dentistry, international relations, wholesale distribution, geology, or soap making, nor do persons working in these other areas know much about factory work. This is not true in the simpler societies. The economic activities, recreations, and religious activities and beliefs of all are fairly common knowledge. There are those who are more skillful, more energetic, or luckier, but the difference is of degree rather than of kind. The smith and the priest may be exceptions, and there are certain activities limited to only one sex, but that is about all.

A further result of stratification, and of the consequent ignorance, is extreme interdependence. This may seem almost paradoxical: the more independent people become, the more dependent they become. However, this is just a loose use of the word "independent"; there is a difference between independence and specialization. Each one of these specialists needs the goods and services of many others and wishes for the goods and services of most of them. Thus, all the specialists are mutually dependent.

Many groups, if not most, deplore this idea of dependence and either deny its reality or state that it is a very bad thing. They are able to push its existence further from consciousness by utilizing their symbolic translation of goods and services, money.

3. *Role of money*

Money is a very important concomitant of increased specialization; it is needed because of the great differences between the specialists and because all the specialists need the goods and services of the others. This problem is *immediately*, but *only* immediately, settled by two steps: (*a*) the translation of every object and service into terms of a common denominator, an invention in the realm of ideas; and (*b*) a material invention, the representation of that symbolic denominator by tangible objects. In other words, running an elevator, preparing a person to meet death, growing corn, telling jokes, and organizing public health measures must all have a common denominator, and that denominator must be represented by a tangible, transferable, and carefully trademarked object. The immediate answer is money, but although this is a brilliant adjustment, it carries problems in its wake—problems unknown to less specialized societies and, also, problems known of old but enhanced and complicated because of money.

One use made of money is the denial of intergroup dependence. People refuse to admit they are dependent on other groups and individuals and on nature. The only thing they depend on is money. Rather than organize their lives and their efforts to satisfy their needs around activities and interpersonal relationships, many individuals attempt to organize their lives around an adjustment between themselves and money.

Another important value of money to the individual relates to his desire to maintain some degree of control over his own existence and over the situation immediately pressing him. That money has influenced the satisfaction of this desire is obvious, but what is the degree of its influence? The answer is that it exerts a controlling influence. Many persons in our commercial, industrial, and personal-service life can exert control over their own lives only through a weekly or daily wage. Whether or not they will receive that wage is dependent upon forces beyond their understanding and control. Effort and ability are important, but they are not controlling.

For the member of the less specialized society, this situation does not exist. Food and shelter and respect of others are subject, of course, to outside, uncontrollable factors (weather, fire, insects, personal and group enemies, disappearance or diminution of species of food animals and fish, and the like), but there is no danger of having perfectly satisfactory environmental conditions plus willingness and ability to work accompanied by the inability to get food, shelter, and protection. The complexities of the flow of money need only be recognized by us as existing. The relevant point now is that, in the specialized world, the worker's control of his life is, to a great extent, controlled by money, and he cannot control money. Moreover, he faces this problem every week, every day. It can control his whole life continuously. He cannot plan ahead without it, and he cannot be assured of what he will have.

This utilization of money in the specialized society has two important aspects for our consideration. The first is that different groups of persons who are heavily dependent on each other are enabled to avoid contact and to avoid mutual understanding and cooperation. To put it conversely, it allows mutually dependent groups to fight each other bitterly in a completely impersonal way. To dramatize this possibility, let us note how money can allow persons to hold utterly incompatible ideas. The example is purposefully extreme. If one man should go to another man's house—a member of the group but a stranger and an inoffensive one to him—and take away his food and furnishings, ruin his friendships, force his children to stop school, and prevent his family from having medical care and recreation, we would violently disapprove, no matter how the story was told. If this one man, by manipulating prices, credit, and wages, achieves the same result on many other men—strangers and inoffensive to him—but makes money for himself and for some others, then, depending on how the story was told, we might feel he was a very able person.

This incompatibility of ideas is one of the great questions in American life today. Note that the interposition of the idea of money between the two parties makes an extraordinary difference. This magic symbol is able to take away the viciousness and aggressiveness which otherwise would be observed. Many writers have pointed this out in contemporary literature. When the farmer is pushed off his land, when the city tenant is evicted, when the borrower of small loans is forced to pay three to four times the amount he received, it always appears that no one is being aggressive or unpleasant; it is just fate, the magical turn of the financial wheel. Nor can the aggrieved party find out who hurt him. The sheriff points to the finance company, the finance company to the bank, the bank to financial holding companies, the latter to stockholders, and all of them are terribly sorry if they happen to hear about it.

This brings us to the second point, which is that money is an artificial—that is, a humanly invented—idea, represented by paper and metal objects. Like all powerful and brilliant ideas or inventions—dynamite, political parties, electricity, unions, the family—it is both *useful* and *dangerous*. Instead of always insuring that specialized effort will be possible and that all the specialists will get all the specialized goods and services, it sometimes happens that it has very different results. It gets completely out of control. A lot of people can have no money at all and no prospect of getting any. A much larger number suddenly may have a great deal less than usual. And nobody knows what to do about it, although many are certain that the other fellow's ideas are crazy.

4. *Individualism*

For the present purposes, the final concomitant of the process of specialization is individualism. To describe this aspect we must consider another facet of complexity, namely, mobility. The physical possibility of mobility was enormously increased by the technological revolution of the last one hundred and fifty years. The need for such mobility rose from the specialization process and its concomitants.

Individualism refers, first, to the increased value of each individual to other individuals. Association is always of great value to every human being, and so other persons are always valuable, but in a world of specialists the value is extended and enhanced. For example, when bakeries first emerged in the colonies, the specialist baker was hardly an indispensable person. If one did not have cash or did not like shopmade products, one made one's own bread at home. This was possible because one had flour and other ingredients sufficient for the purpose at hand, one had utensils, basic equipment, oven space, and a kitchen; one had the skill, the time, and the feeling that it was right, proper, and natural to bake one's own bread. Specialization has its values, however, and bakeries became integrated into the way of life.

The baker has become indispensable if you want breadstuffs. If you have no money, you get no bread. If you do not like the baker, you can only go to another baker. You may not know the baker personally, but he is very important to you. So are the telephone linesman, the shoemaker, the laundryman, and the bus driver. This means that power adheres to individuals which was not present in the simpler society. If, in the more primitive group, John Jones decided to quit work, it was not just a matter of his starving to death; it did break up the pattern of life considerably, especially for John's family, but it did not directly and immediately threaten a large percentage of the group, and it was possible, although irritating, for someone else to take up the slack. John's work was as hard and as easy, as dignified and as undignified, as most other persons' work. Not many of us, however, could take on someone else's job today.

Nowadays the Jack-of-all-trades is characterized as being master of none. Furthermore, there are many jobs we would consider as below our respective dignities. More and more individuals have become clothed with a type of power unknown before. This aspect has a reverse side also. If the speciality becomes outmoded or requires almost no skill or training at all, then the person seems to have less power than any individual in the more primitive group. For the most part, however, the individual's social power has been increased by specialization just as the individual's physical power has been increased by the automobile and the gun.

A second consideration on this score is that the individual specialists or participants in a particular specialty have worked hard to extend this automatic importance and power. The bakers, the doctors, the tool-and-dye workers, the teachers, the shoemakers, and so on have endeavored to enhance and to guarantee their positions. They have a private stake in this process.

Another aspect of individualism is the person's lessened need for close social participation. The rise of money and mobility has had a great deal to do with the emancipation of individuals from tight, all-encompassing social organizations. Not having to depend on parents, priests, or neighbors, as did the member of the simpler society, the individual can withdraw from their control. He can look forward to making money, living in another place, having radically different ideas, and doing what he wants without their meddling. For the member of the primitive society such attitudes or actions meant death. Without father, brothers, cousins, or children, who would do business with you, who would back your side of an argument, who would protect you? The answer was clarion clear—"no one!" That was why banishment was such a terrible sentence. It meant some form of death, not quite determined how, when, or where, but fairly soon and very sure.

Today the young man leaves his home town "to make something of himself." He will adjust to strangers through money, through his drive and skill, and through luck in his specialty. He is "on his own," a great value in our society, although a death penalty among primitive groups. Not that he stays "on his own" very long. He joins groups, but more and more they tend to be specialized groups. Whereas the person in the simpler society worked, played, worshiped, gossiped, and, in general, lived with about the same group of persons, the individual in the complex society may belong to several groups with different personnel. The church group, the school group, the neighbors, the men at the shop, office, or store, the three or four close friends, may form half a dozen groups with varying personnel. These, in turn, may have slightly, even greatly, different ideas of what is proper, permissible, interesting, or desirable. Most important, the individual can shift from one group to another. This means that a wider range of behavior is open to him. The sanctioning power of any one group is, of course, potentially weakened by the varying norms of the others. What is of greater importance are the facts that these are specialized organizations and that a group having over-all societal interests does not command the individual's loyalty, as it could in a simple society.

One result of this situation is the commonly observed fact of a single individual following incompatible moral codes. A man can show aggressiveness, slyness, or laziness in his occupational morality which he would bitterly reject in his home circle. He can pray in one direction and vote in another. His life being somewhat compartmentalized, such relative variety of behavior is possible. This emancipation from a solid, unified, omnipresent group sanction has many assets for both the individual and society. It also has many liabilities. There is a loss of security in personal relationships. A wide field is opened up for fraud. Many groups are exceedingly shortlived, and competition between them is continuous, often bitter. A strong, widespread morality is more difficult to maintain. The greater freedom of action for the individual puts a heavy burden upon him; he has to face questions and problems that hardly exist in a simpler, uniform, less specialized society.

5. Major needs

I have sketched certain major attributes of a complex society which distinguish it from a simpler society. Let me now repeat my introductory statement. The end goals, the major needs of both individuals and of total societies, are not much changed by a greater or lesser complexity of society. The difference is in means, subgoals, organization, and numbers. The major aspect of complexity has been defined as a specialization of form and function. For modern Western civilization this specialization has been primarily economic. That is, changes in the economic structure have forced adjustment on other major institutions—family, church, government, caste—while changes by those institutions were not necessarily adjusted to by the economic structure. Do not think that ours is the only complex social structure or that the economic institution must always dominate in a complex world. The religious or the familial can be the dominant interest and can involve tremendous specialization.

The specialization was seen to result in the greatest production of goods and services yet attained by any society. It had also the following effects, although it alone may not have been responsible: (a) horizontal stratification; (b) vertical stratification; (c) less and less knowledge of the whole society, its ways, subgroups, and ideas; (d) extreme mutual dependence of subgroups and individuals; (e) a utilization of money which allowed impersonal contact between individuals and resulted in a new life orientation of all individuals, but which defied human control and resulted at times in the inability of masses of people to avail themselves even of the extraordinary amount of goods and services at hand; and (f) a great increase in the social potentiality of the individual and a decrease both in the unity of the society as a whole and in the enduring strength of any of its subgroups.

Social Complexity and Alcohol

We may next consider the significance of social complexity for the part played by alcohol both in relation to society as a whole and in relation to the life of the individual.

Donald Horton, in his description of primitive societies, has pointed out certain individual needs which are answered, more or less, by alcohol. One of these is the satisfaction of hunger and thirst, a very minor factor; another is a medicinal need, also very minor. Let us consider the effect of our complex societies on these two needs. In the society where increased complexity is dominated by the economic institution, beverage alcohol is not used for these needs. Goods and services have become so refined, have been so tested in competition, and are so plentiful, that such a second-rate food and fourth-rate medicine as beverage alcohol will tend in these regards to die out or be limited to those rare instances where alcohol has some special value. There will be a lag in ideas, however. Old ideas of the nutritional and medicinal values of alcohol will persist long after the best knowledge and experience will have shown them to be mistaken.

Another function of alcohol mentioned by Horton was its use in attaining religious ecstasy. Here alcohol must compete with fasting, purposefully induced exhaustion, self-laceration, drugs, and autohypnosis. Religious ecstasy, however, must be a generally approved and prestigeful affair before any of these techniques will be utilized. In our highly specialized economic life there is small place for religious ecstasy. Moreover, the mental state achieved by alcohol intake has been considered for many generations as ludicrous or disgusting rather than mysterious. Catalepsy, automatic writing, and conversion hysteria may still inspire some awe in the more superstitious, but even the most confirmed crystal gazers are scornful of alcohol-induced spiritual experiences. In this complex society, these functions of alcohol may safely be forgotten.

Another function of alcohol has been its use in <u>social jollification</u>. Although the distinction between the needs of the society as separate from those of the individual is occasionally difficult to perceive, in this instance a fairly clear discrimination can be made. The maintenance of order and of unity within the society is imperative for the survival of the society. The feeling that the individuals are a "we-group" as opposed to "others," the feeling that it is pleasurable to be one of "us," the restatement of the fundamental mutuality of the members—these values are attained by meetings of pleasurable purpose. In any society there will be stresses and strains which tend to break the unity; certain individuals will be unsatisfied, will be more ambitious than achieving; certain groups will be antagonistic. Meetings in which such ambitions, frustrations, and resentments are irrelevant, in which purely rewarding pursuits are at hand, will help restore or enhance the integrating principles.

As we have seen, one of the concomitants of complexity is stratification, another is ignorance of other subgroups, a third is the increased aggression allowed by the widespread utilization of money, and a fourth is increased individualism. The need for integrating mechanisms in a more and more complex society is a phenomenon whose existence can hardly be challenged. The difficulty of effecting such mechanisms is apparent. One of the best ways, aside from great external danger, is through amusements. They present an activity or interest which can be neutral to conflicting interests and personalities; they can be stimulating, they can be rewarding, and they hold small threat of punishment.

Theoretically we would expect an increase of pleasure meetings in a complex, competitive, individualistic civilization, and in our society this theoretical expectancy is fully met. There has been a development of both commercialized and non-commercialized pleasure rituals which would seem extraordinary to the members of the simpler society. From organized spectacles which operate 8 to 16 hours a day every day to the informal tea, cocktail, and card-game gatherings, the members of our society are almost surfeited with recreational association. As would be expected, activities connected with occupational specialty are generally held taboo at these meetings. Specialization and specialists, however, have infiltrated this area of behavior as they have almost all others.

With this extension and elaboration of recreation, alcohol's part in jollification or in pleasure association has become enhanced. Note the role of alcohol in these situations. We have, on the one hand, a society whose individuals are often (a) more self-contained and independent, (b) more ignorant of each other's interests and activities, (c) more separate from each other, and (d) more prone to aggressive and competitive relationships; on the other hand, there is a need for unsuspicious, pleasant, relatively effortless joint activity. How can one put these together? One way is to transfer the ordinary, diverse, specialized attentions of the individuals to one neutral object interesting to all—a spectacle, for example, or a chess game.

The trouble with this adjustment is that it does not allow much interpersonal activity.

Another way is to relax all the people. All of us here have undoubtedly experienced meetings intended to be recreational and found them stiff, uncertain, and tense. Intermixture does not take place. Despite the need to spread interaction, individuals remain aloof, or little groups of previous acquaintance maintain their own safe little cliques. The organizers have to break down the hostilities, the indifference, the ignorance, and the suspicions. To do this they try to get the individuals to relax. Alcohol is a quick, easy, fairly sure means of accomplishing this end. It may have other, less desirable effects; at the moment, that is irrelevant.

The conclusion on this point, whether reached by deduction from principles or by observation of our own society, is that the stratification, individualism, intergroup ignorance, and internal competitive tradition—all engendered by the complexity of society—enhance the function of alcohol. Complexity results in a need for greater integrative functioning; lessening of tension, uncertainty, and suspicion is necessary for this function; alcohol has been found useful in its accomplishment.

In addition to the need of the society for greater integration, there is also the need of the individual to make contacts, both occupational and recreational. In a mobile, multistratified world, this is more difficult than in a stable, less-stratified world. In a specialized, competitive world, recreational devices for the individual seem more essential. Yet the factors just discussed make difficult the attainment of that easy, trustworthy, non-competitive friendship situation which is requisite for interpersonal relaxation. Alcohol is obviously functional for achieving the lessening of suspicion, of competitive tension, of the barriers usually present between strangers in our society.

In contrast, then, to the effect of a complex society on the medical, food, and religious-exaltation functions of alcohol is the effect of the complex society on alcohol's function of promoting recreational and other association. This function is definitely enhanced.

Alcohol and Tension

We now approach the more important, perhaps the fundamental, function of alcohol for individuals. As you are all aware, alcohol is a depressant. It allows, through its depressing function, a relaxation of tension, of inhibition, of anxiety, of guilt. There is no need to define narrowly the meanings incorporated in these words. I will consider, however, the areas of behavior and attitude which are most commonly colored with these emotional characteristics. The listing I shall present is quite arbitrary. Around what personal problems of adjustment do anxiety, tension, guilt, and the like arise?

I would suggest the following: (a) the individual's opinion of himself; (b) gaining and holding the respect and the affections of others; (c) conflicting with others, through self-assertion, through criticism, through out-

and-out aggressions; (d) over-all security in ownership, prestige, and personal safety, as they are tied up with money; (e) responsibilities accepted in the achievement of specific goals; and (f) sexual matters.

This is a purely descriptive listing. It may seem to imply that these six are totally separate matters. They are not! The list is merely a convenient set of handles by which one can pick up and examine the package labeled "one human being." The handles alone are meaningless.

In a complex society these areas of behavior and attitude are more greatly challenged, are more difficult to live through or adjust to, than they are in a simpler society. For a very simple example, take the matter of self-assertion or the exhibition of aggression. In a world of extraordinary dependence on others, aggression is very dangerous. In a complex, specialized, stratified society we are continually in situations where we are dependent on others, and the others do not seem to care much about us. Elevator operators, waiters, salespeople, clients, partners—all of them have it in their power to frustrate us. By the very nature of the system they must frustrate us somewhat, since they serve fifty or five hundred other people in addition to us, and we must take our turn; that is ineradicable in association. So we get angry. But we cover it up. The complexity of society increases the incidence of aggression-provoking situations. The complexity of society renders the expression of aggression ever more dangerous.

Consider the matter of prestige, or recognition from others. In a society in which there is great homogeneity of activity, where most people do about the same things in the same way, the range of prestige is smaller. You are a good, a mediocre, or a bad workman. Furthermore, in a simple society the tangible marks of success, such as conspicuous consumption or ownership, are also limited in variety and quantity. In a complex society, however, the situation is dramatically different. There is an extraordinarily refined hierarchy of prestige. Much of the prestige goes with the position rather than with the individual's talent or exertion of effort or pleasing personality.

Furthermore, recognition and prestige depend more and more on obvious, often tangible, symbols. In the simple society, it is easy to tell who is an efficient, pleasant person. In the stratified, specialized society, it is not easy. People are more and more inclined to give recognition according to conspicuousness and wealth. There is not the time, there is not the knowledge, there is not the personal interaction on a variety of levels of experience, for people to judge. Yet, despite this weakness, the need to get good persons for specialized positions is pressing, and the goal of gaining prestige is enhanced. The result, of course, is increased apprehension, increased sensitivity, increased tension.

In a complex society where personal relationships are more and more specialized, impersonal, and competitive, and where various specialties are not understood by others, recognition, respect, and prestige are more intensely desired, are more difficult to attain, and are, perhaps, more suspect, than in simpler societies. This results in frustration, envy, aggression, and anxiety which do not appear in such marked form from this source in simpler societies.

The increased complexity of our social existence has increased social responsibilities. One of the outstanding characteristics of high position in any of our ways of life is increase in responsibilities. For many hierarchies we may say that the assumption of higher office is matched by an increase in the anxieties a person carries. One of the earmarks of the executive is his ability to assume anxiety with understanding and with poise. The person in the lowest rank carries very little anxiety about the function of the organization. At 5 P.M. he quits work and forgets about it, although he still carries personal anxieties. The high-ranking man carries his anxiety concerning the whole organization all the time. The one has little or no prestige and little or no anxiety on this account; the other has much prestige and much anxiety.

The general over-all security represented by money in a complex society has already been discussed. The increased anxiety from this source reflects through all of the significant emotional areas that were listed, in addition to possessing a ranking of its own. Although it weighs most obviously on the people in the lowest economic ranks or in marginal positions, it can be equally oppressive to people who, while not threatened with starvation, are threatened as to their social position and prestige.

Time forbids dealing with the other emotional areas. It is, or should be, sufficiently clear that interpersonal relationships and personal satisfactions are more difficult, are more anxiety provoking, are more exhausting, in a complex society.

The advantages of a complex society are manifest, but there is a price to pay. That price is intangible, difficult to measure or define. It can roughly be labeled as emotional insecurity for the individual. Since alcohol can reduce the impact, can allow escape from the tensions, fears, sensitivities, and feelings of frustration which constitute this insecurity, its role will be more highly valued.

I shall mention one more view of the enhanced importance or power of the alcohol-drinking custom that results from social complexity. The most obvious aspect of complexity has been described as specialization. Specialization occurred in the activation of this custom as in all the others. Specialized crops, specialized industries, specialized distribution, advertising, and financing, specialized retailing, all occur in the realm of alcoholic beverages just as in that of railroading, of dairy products, of education, or of men's clothing. Just as the function of clothing is extraordinarily expanded and enmeshed in other social organizations, beliefs, and activities because of specialized institutionalization, so is that of alcohol production, distribution, and consumption. For example, when one makes one's own clothes or one's own wine or whisky, there is a great deal of pressure, of anxiety, about not using the product unless it is really needed. Under conditions of specialized production, where there is competition, a monetary basis, and impersonal relations between producer, distributor, retailer, and consumer, this pressure is completely reversed. The more consumption, the more success. This process is heavily reinforced by the fact that unit costs tend to go down as the number of units produced goes up.

The effect of this concomitant of social complexity is to equip the whole constellation of alcoholic beverage activities, ideas, material objects, and organizations with motives, mechanisms, and functions which are utterly disconnected with the physiological and psychological functions of alcohol. The same distinction, of course, is true for all other specialized institutions.

Dysfunctional Aspects

Now we come to the effects of societal complexity on what might be called the socially and individually dysfunctional aspects of alcohol. The potentialities of alcoholic beverage consumption remain the same but are to be viewed in a different light. We could speak of dynamite in the same way; its properties do not change, but its effects on human beings can be of a tremendously constructive or tremendously destructive nature.

The complex society presents great rewards to individuals; two factors balance these rewards and are a sort of fixed charge: (1) breakdown of any part is far more dangerous than in the simple society; (2) there must be a more exact fulfillment of function than was previously necessary on the part of every subgroup and every individual. To put this in a more general way: the need for imagination and perception, for control over responses, for timing and balance, is greatly increased by the complex culture; just to get things done is a more delicate task, and the penalty for not getting things done has far greater social implications than in the simpler society. Do not illustrate this in your minds solely by the picture of a person driving a car or tending a machine. One tendency of our material culture has been to dominate our thinking in just such a narrow way. Think rather of relations between groups of people, employer and employee, principal and agent, people of different social classes; think rather of the foresight necessary in a production schedule, in bringing up children, in establishing governmental procedures. These activities in a complex society demand greater sensitivity, greater efficiency in action, greater imagination, and greater caution than in a simpler society.

Alcohol lowers sensitivity, efficiency, and caution. It deteriorates balance and timing. Personal aggression and irresponsibility are far more dangerous in a complex society, and, as an adjustment to this, child-training in complex society lays heavy emphasis on self-control—on inhibitions and repressions of aggression and irresponsibility; alcohol releases these inhibitions. Regularity of behavior is as essential in a complex society as in a complex machine. Alcohol can wreck regularity of behavior. I need not expand on this point; the conclusion is apparent. The need of the society for regularity, precision, individual responsibility, and integration, through self-control and cooperation, is increased by complexity. The achievement of these values is directly threatened by alcohol in proportion to its depressant action.

A further societal complication is to be seen in the means of control. It has been pointed out that specialized and formal groups have become more powerful and have extended their functions while all-purpose and intimate groups have been weakened. If the drinking of alcohol and its effects were limited to the area of one of these specialized groups, sanctions could be efficient; or if the society were simpler, more homogeneous, more dominated by some all-purpose, personally intimate and significant association, sanctions could be significant. The drinking of alcohol and its effects, however, infiltrate all manner of acts, associations, and ideas. The attempt to exert sanctions over this wide, loosely organized area will be met with opposition, argument, and relatively unabashed violation. The sanctioning authority will not be recognized. The ideology behind the attempt will be challenged. Social classes, minority groups, religious groups, locality groups, and other categories will not have the identity of purpose, understanding, and experience which would allow such action to proceed smoothly. The complexity of society is of manifest significance with regard to this point. Furthermore, the question of control can itself create further disorganization in the society. This, of course, is quite irrelevant to the physical and psychological properties of alcohol.

In a society already impersonal, competitive, individualistic, and stratified, the effect of excessive drinking on the individual is dramatic. I would only draw attention to the fact that the complexity of the society, and the concomitants of that complexity as here described, exaggerate and speed the deterioration process in the maladjusted person.

Summary

Now let us recapitulate the particular sociological viewpoint on alcohol here presented: Social complexity, in the case of Western civilization dominated by economic specialization, has enormously increased the number and variety of goods and services, has improved quality beyond measurement, and can produce with unparalleled speed. This is as true of alcoholic goods and services as of others. Complexity has also resulted in horizontal and vertical stratification, in mutual ignorance and disinterest of societal subgroups, in extreme interdependence of subgroups and of individuals, in the emergence of money as a controlling factor in human life, and in an individualism marked by the increased power of each person and the decreased power of such all-purpose, intimate groups as the family and the small neighborhood.

In relation to alcohol, these concomitants of social complexity have had the following seven effects:

1. They have practically eliminated three functions of alcohol which were of minor importance in primitive society, namely, food value, medicinal value, and religious-ecstasy value.

2. They have enhanced the need for integrative mechanisms in the society which are personally significant. The pleasure group is important here, but other meetings are not excluded. The function of alcohol in depressing certain inhibitions, anxieties, aggressions, and tensions, thus allowing relaxation, has increasing significance, since it can help in this process.

3. These concomitants of complex society have increased, compared with simpler societies, the weight of the anxieties of most individuals, and have added new anxieties. The depressant function of alcohol thus becomes more significant, especially since these anxieties are directly related to the most basic human drives.

4. The very nature of the specialization process has created a network of relationships, activities, wealth, social position, and so on, which revolve around the business of alcohol, thus bringing into existence a set of factors not present in the simpler society, a set of factors unrelated to the physiological or psychological properties of alcohol.

5. The complexity of society increases the need, if the society is to exist, for sharp discrimination, caution, accurate responses, timing, cooperation, and the acceptance of responsibilities. Alcohol, taken excessively, can deteriorate all of these.

6. The nature of the complex society makes social control over behavior that is not strictly compartmentalized into one or another institution an extremely difficult task. The drinking of alcohol and its effects are not present in only one institution or pattern of behavior but infiltrate throughout; the drinking itself is largely in the loosely organized area of individual recreation. Control of drinking behavior in the complex society is therefore a more difficult problem than in the simpler society.

7. The individual in the complex society has a far more formidable task in integrating himself to groups and ideas in a satisfying way, is equipped with more personal choice, and belongs to looser, more specialized, less personally satisfying associations. The excessive use of alcohol can more rapidly and thoroughly destroy such participation in complex societies than it can in the simpler, more general, more intimate groups of primitive societies. The power of alcohol to deteriorate personality is thus enhanced in complex society.

It can be seen, thus, that the complexity of society is a significant factor in the relations of alcohol and man. It obviously enhances the uses of alcohol for man. It obviously increases the dangers of alcohol for man. Social complexity has added new forces and motivations for the production and distribution of alcohol. It has diminished the power of agencies of control which could once be efficiently used.

SOCIAL STRUCTURE, SUBCULTURES, AND DRINKING PATTERNS

A.

CLASS AND STATUS

Introductory Note. It is a remarkable fact, in view of the proliferation of studies of social class and the obvious significance of alcohol in our culture, that no concerted effort has been made, heretofore, to chart the distribution and implications of drinking patterns in the stratification system. To be sure, allusions to drinking are scattered through community studies of class structure, but these allusions are uniformly of an incidental nature, not matters of primary concern. In survey work transcending the plane of the local community, categories of stratification are either too broad or questions pertaining to drinking too thin to be other than suggestive of "socio-economic differences," the interpretation of which is customarily left to the reader. It bears mention that this dearth of knowledge applies almost equally to pathological drinking, despite recent efforts to examine systematically the relations of drinking pathologies to social and economic class structure.[*]

An attempt to bring some order out of these scattered observations was made by John Dollard nearly two decades ago in a lecture on "Drinking Mores of the Social Classes," which was later published and widely disseminated (2). Dollard's analysis was frankly provisional and speculative,

[*] Cf. Hollingshead and Redlich (4), and Malzberg (5). In the first of these studies, the nature of social-class differentials in drinking pathologies is obscured because these pathologies were combined, for purposes of statistical analysis, with drug addiction. The second study points to a marked inverse relation between economic status and the prevalence of alcoholic psychoses. Suggestive as this finding is, however, the important question of the differential genesis of the alcoholic psychoses by economic stratum remains unanswered.

resting on no particular study of drinking behavior but upon general impressions gleaned from a series of community studies of social class conducted by W. Lloyd Warner and his associates, and Dollard himself. Perhaps because of the clarity of his presentation and the simplicity of the scheme, or because of the intellectual vacuum which his suggestions filled, Dollard's ideas became widely accepted as authoritative, even penetrating to elementary textbooks in sociology (3). His characterization of class styles of drinking has served as a standard for comparison, or as a point of departure, for virtually all subsequent discussions of class and drinking patterns, including the selections presented in this volume.

In these circumstances, it seems wise to outline the main features of Dollard's portrayal of class differences in drinking patterns even at the risk of excerpting too little from an already summary presentation. Here, as Dollard (2, pp. 99–100) presented it, is the nub of the matter:

In the Upper classes, drinking is not a moral issue. People at the top of our social structure drink a good deal; both sexes drink. Men and women drink in the same groups, in party style. There are, however, certain stiff controls here which do not exist in some of the lower classes. One is condemned in the Upper classes, not for drinking, nor for drunkenness, but for antisocial behavior while drunk. Fighting is taboo; aggressive behavior is heavily penalized even when expressed only in verbal assaults.

It is crucial to recognize the attitude of the Upper classes toward drinking because behavior patterns tend to sift downward in our society. Middle groups are likely to become tolerant and, perhaps, ultimately imitative of the customs of the topmost groups into which they, as individuals, would like to move. It might be said that the failure of Prohibition legislation lay in our social class system, for the highest people socially did not taboo drinking and their social customs were stronger than legislative controls.

In the Lower-Upper class we have the "cocktail set" who drink a good bit more recklessly than the people in the old families in the Upper-Upper class. The new families of wealth are in a rather insecure, frustrating position. They are constantly comparing themselves with the families who socially "own" the territory in which they live. The wealthy newcomers want to have an old homestead of their own; they want to have the prestige of lineage. Realizing that their great-grandfather was "just a butcher," rather than a powerful landowner, they suffer from a helpless feeling of inadequacy. Parental controls are weak and the scars from social competition painful, so Lower-Upper young people may try to escape from their social discomforts by drunkenness. There are case studies in several towns which lead us to suppose that there is some excessive, destructive drinking in this particular class group.

In the Upper-Middle class we have a strong evaluation of wealth and talent, and, ordinarily, moral values have restraint. However, the apparent nearness to the Upper classes and partial identification with this group have some effect on the drinking habits in the Upper-Middle class. In general, the men drink on social occasions, at their poker games and at casual gatherings in friends' houses, but Upper-Middle class women rarely drink. Drinking is not customary in mixed groups. Evidently, Upper-Middles have a neutral attitude toward drinking.

In the Lower-Middle class we would expect to find, with both sexes, a very strong taboo on drinking. Lower-Middle people value highly the traits of respectability which differentiate them from the Lower group. They emphasize this by rejecting the customs found in Lower classes. (Negroes in the Middle classes, for instance, will reject the spirituals and songs characteristic of Lower-class churches. In this way they emphasize their difference in the social scale from the Lower-class individuals of their own race.) Lower-Middle men and women are the most stringent in exerting social control over drinking.

In the Upper-Lower class, which is the chief labor group, there is much more drinking. The Upper-Lowers do not have the same taboos as the Lower Middles, but they do have some occupational restraints. A railway workman, for example, will tend to have an occupational taboo on drinking in some situations. In general, the Upper-Lowers drink at home and in the taverns, which provide a kind of club for Lower-class people. But if they are to be mobile into Lower-Middle class they have to change such habits.

Lower-class persons usually become openly aggressive when drinking because they have not been trained to exercise the control of aggression that is demanded of those at the top. In the Lower class, it is not a disgrace to get drunk and fight even if this behavior has dangerous consequences. A Lower-class man may be aggressive in the family toward wife and children. This group does not have the "drink like a gentleman" taboo. Differences in ethnic backgrounds are also conspicuous in the drinking customs of the Upper-Lower class—Irish, Jewish and Italian immigrants, for instance, retain customs that still have a "home color" when they settle in this country. There are differences as to beverages and controls of behavior. In the City of New Haven there are about 40,000 Italians; they drink wine with their meals. Some other ethnic groups, including the Jewish, have apparently a rather strong internal taboo on excessive drinking.

In the Lower-Lower class, drinking is socially unrestrained. There is the Saturday-night-to-Monday-morning binge, without much social control. Both men and women drink, although usually not in mixed groups. In the Lower-Lower class there is overt aggression; people are arrested for drunkenness, breaking the peace. There is much chronic drunkenness in this class.

In Chapter 6, Joseph Gusfield breaks out of the boundaries of commitment to the Warner framework in favor of a more flexible status-group analysis in the tradition of Max Weber. He also introduces a historical dimension into the discussion of drinking and stratification which is lacking in Dollard's presentation. Gusfield is not concerned to characterize the varieties of drinking patterns in their totality; his emphasis is on the temperance movement. Yet, in the editors' judgment, he rings down the curtain on efforts to comprehend the historic divergence and polarization of attitudes toward drinking in America apart from an appreciation of the struggles of status groups for preferential positions.

The rise to dominance of the abstinence and prohibition orientation, for instance, was bound up with the ascendance of a middle class whose ethic was tailored to the requirements of small-scale capitalism. Abstinence was not only intrinsically compatible with the core values and personality ideals of this stratum—values and ideals which were fundamentally hostile to the spontaneous expressions of emotional impulses (6)—it became, as well, a diffuse social symbol expressive of unity in style of life, functioned as a basic point of reference for status evaluations, and served as a major criterion for the assimilation of culturally diverse elements into the newly ascendant middle-class way of life. Gusfield's study shows clearly that the recent decline in this orientation and its entrenchment in certain narrow sectors of society are to be understood in terms of changes in the total social and economic structure, involving status struggles and realignments and the emergence of new status groups.

This kind of analysis is of interest not alone for the light it sheds on the social bases of drinking attitudes and the ideologies of amelioration and control of alcohol problems. It should prove of interest also to students of social stratification, for, if the analysis is sound, the distribution, rise, and fall of particular complexes of drinking attitudes and ideologies provide a valuable clue to the dynamics of the social order.

The selection which follows, by Gregory Stone, continues at the level of community study the same kind of general concern for the status significance of drinking which is evident in Gusfield's broad social-historical analysis. Stone, in contrast to Dollard, conceives of the structure of the community in terms of complex and shifting status arrangements, as opposed to an overarching system of discrete and hierarchically ordered classes. In the larger study from which his report derives, Stone and his associates made use of Warner's index of status characteristics (without commitment to his concept of the class system) in establishing status rankings and, particularly, in depicting the styles of life of those members of the community whose lives are most firmly anchored in the local community itself. They found it essential, however, to introduce into their discussion a new axis of status, involving a distinction between "localites" and "cosmopolites."

The addition of this dimension considerably enriches the analysis of the status structure and the dynamics of life styles, and it paves the way for a better understanding of the factors underlying changing drinking patterns. (Surely the status competition between localites and cosmopolites which Stone describes echoes the split between old and new middle classes to which Gusfield makes reference in discussing the decline of the temperance movement.) While several of the inferences which Stone draws from his data provide important clues for research on alcohol problems, his major contribution undoubtedly lies in his original and systematic exploration of the far-reaching status implications which surround the use of beverage alcohol in our culture.

The reader will note that there are several points at which Stone's findings lend qualified support to Dollard's earlier observations. This is true, for example, in the tendency of the lower-middle stratum to deprecate drinking. Yet there are other points at which discrepancies appear, as, for instance, in the indication of marked sex differences in the lowest stratum with regard to certain aspects of drinking pattern. To further clarify the questions of fact which such discrepancies raise—and in recognition of the dangers of generalizing from a single community study—we present in the next chapter a brief selection from a survey of drinking patterns by Joseph Lawrence and Milton Maxwell. As the authors are at pains to explain, the design of their study permits only limited comparisons with Dollard's material. Yet, on the basis of their findings, Lawrence and Maxwell have made a strong case for drastically revising the conception of lower-class drinking put forth by Dollard.

No sociological discussion of drinking among the lower strata of our complex society would be complete, however, apart from systematic consideration of the milieu of Skid Row which envelopes and expresses the way of life of a substantial part of the declassé segment of the populace. It is to this task that this subsection's final selection, by Earl Rubington, is concerned. Drawing upon many years of disciplined first-hand observation, Rubington has, we believe, considerably advanced the conception of Skid Row by viewing it essentially as a retreatist subculture—although he does not specifically use the term—characterized by a definite though elementary social organization and in symbiotic relations with the larger society. In the discussion which follows, Rubington proposes a general conception of the functions of Skid Row vis-à-vis the maintenance of the larger society and its value system, in addition to introducing new material on the organization of Skid-Row drinking groups. In the latter connection, the rank system among drinkers and the variables conducing to a general downward mobility trend on Skid Row are analyzed in detail.

With regard to the determinants of the selection of the Skid-Row alternative which Rubington discusses, we would certainly agree with his rejection of highly individualistic approaches to this problem. It may well be, however, that the kind of sociological formulation recently proposed by Richard Cloward (1), and briefly discussed in the introductory note to a later section of this volume, holds promise for supplementing Rubington's stress on differential associations at the primary group level as the major selective mechanism. In any event, the reader is urged to consider Rubington's study in conjunction with our mention of Cloward's work and the related report of research by David Pittman and Wayne Gordon in Section IV.

References

1. Cloward, Richard A., "Illegitimate Means, Anomie, and Deviant Behavior," *Amer. Sociol. Rev.*, 24:164–176, 1959.
2. Dollard, John, "Drinking Mores of the Social Classes," in *Alcohol, Science and Society*, New Haven: Journal of Studies on Alcohol, 1945.
3. Freedman, Ronald, et al., *Principles of Sociology: A Text with Readings (rev. ed.)*, New York: Holt, Rinehart, and Winston, 1956.
4. Hollingshead, August B., and Frederick C. Redlich, *Social Class and Mental Illness*, New York: John Wiley and Sons, 1958.
5. Malzberg, Benjamin, *The Alcoholic Psychoses: Demographic Aspects at Midcentury in New York State*, New Haven: Journal of Studies on Alcohol, 1960.
6. Thorner, Isidor, "Ascetic Protestantism and Alcoholism," *Psychiatry*, 16:167–176, 1953.

chapter 6

Status conflicts
and the changing ideologies
of the American temperance
movement *

Joseph R. Gusfield

Studies of American social movements have devoted most attention to organized attempts to improve or maintain the economic or political position of specific parts of the social structure. The temperance movement, however, has often seemed on the periphery of major political events. Despite its 130-year record of vitality and significance, and despite the achievement of a Constitutional amendment, the temperance movement has been little studied by American scholars (26, 29). Not clearly related to economic or political aims of classes in the economy, it has been difficult to subsume under traditional views of political life.

Recently, Richard Hofstadter has proposed a useful distinction between "interest politics" and "status politics" (21, p. 43 ff.). Groups which use political agencies to achieve concrete economic aims are engaged in "interest politics." Such interest-oriented activities have formed the bulk of historical analyses in the United States. Sometimes, however, movements arise which display no clear-cut economic goals. The adherents are concerned with improving or maintaining their deference or prestige in the society. Such movements are likely to pursue symbolic goals, not readily explainable by a theory of group interests. The economic position of the adherents is not touched by the movement. At stake is the place of the group in the status order, in the distribution of honor or prestige.

The American temperance movement may best be understood as an ex-

* This chapter was written especially for this book. The chapter is based upon the author's *Middle Class Reform: A Study in the American Temperance Movement* (a monograph in preparation). The project has been partially supported by a Summer Faculty Fellowship granted by the University of Illinois Graduate Research Board.

ample of a status movement. Through its social base and through its central concern, drinking, the movement has been linked to major distinctions in the American status order. Both as a means to consolidate new status and as a means to defend positions now threatened, the temperance movement has reflected status struggles of the nineteenth and twentieth centuries. As these changed, the commanding doctrines and images of the movement and its ideological structure have correspondingly changed.

Temperance and the American Middle Class

1. *The status significance of alcohol consumption*

Organized efforts to control and limit drinking or the sale of alcoholic beverages have been persistent in the United States since the early nineteenth century. Although alcohol has not been the only item of consumption with which reformers have been concerned, it has been the one most provocative of controversy. The prohibition of narcotics has met little organized opposition. The prohibition of cigarettes, coffee, or cola beverages has not aroused a strong or vibrant movement. Why has alcohol been so significant an issue?

Drinking (we use this word to include alcoholic consumption, including liquors, wines, beer, and hard cider) performs several functions at an individual and societal level. We shall focus our attention on its use as a symbol of status in American life. The use, or the abstinence from, alcohol has appeared in American life as one means for the validation of the social position of its users or non-users. In prescribed forms or in conspicuous non-consumption, it is one of the ways by which people indicate to others the "place" they hold in the status order. Proper drinking habits are one of the necessary behavior patterns for maintaining membership in specific status-bearing groups.

In American society, drinking is often one important sign which differentiates age groups and sexes. In many groups, the young man symbolizes his entry into adulthood by being permitted to use alcohol. One of the legal privileges of adulthood in American communities is that of buying liquor in taverns. Although there has been much change, the American male still defines the use and abuse of alcohol as a male privilege, a symbol of his power and prestige when compared to the female. The disapproval of female drunkenness is greater than the disapproval of male drunkenness.

The kinds of beverages used, the amount and frequency of drinking and the permissiveness shown toward insobriety vary among human cultures (23). Recent studies of American life (many of which are summarized or presented in this volume) have examined the drinking patterns of ethnic groups and social classes. Similar variation has been found. An example of this variation is the finding that upper socio-economic groups are more permissive in their acceptance of drinking than are the lower middle classes (1, 10, 33).

Alcohol consumption has often appeared as a negative status symbol in American life. Sobriety and abstinence have often been part of the style of life necessary for members of the middle class. The opposite has often been seen as the mark of lower class life. Drinking has been part of the negative reference group—the group whose behavior patterns are to be avoided (28). Whatever the rejected behavior is, the fact that it is associated with negative reference models heightens the avoidance of it and makes it a fit symbol of status. It becomes a clearer sign of membership in one group and of exclusion from the other. We can see an example of this in religious sects which have split off from some parent church. Frequently, such sects enjoin areas of behavior which have become associated with the parent. Prohibitions against dancing, gambling, wearing of ties, drinking, or engaging in sports serve to distinguish the life style of the sect from that of the parent (14, 17, 32).

2. Temperance and middle class ethics

While most symbols of group differentiation have some moral connotation, temperance has carried a heavy load of ethical content. Its role as a status symbol has been especially important because it has been related to styles of ethical behavior obligatory in the value system of American middle classes of the nineteenth century. A moral quality has adhered to abstinence and sobriety. One of the early temperance tracts (35) put it this way:

The Holy Spirit will not visit, much less will He dwell with him who is under the polluting, debasing effects of intoxicating drink. The state of heart and mind which this occasions is to Him loathsome and an abomination.

In the complex of values which has characterized the American middle classes, self-mastery, industry, thrift, and moral conduct have been signs of attainment of prized character traits. Adherence to self-denial has been viewed as a necessary step to the achievement of social and economic success. Recreation, sermonized a Protestant minister of the 1850's, makes us fit for the work of the world. Amusement is pleasure for its own sake and is rejected because it has no utility for the economic and industrial life (9). Drunkenness and indulgence are signs of the value-orientation of the person and hence possess status meaning.

The ethic which supported temperance and the temperance movement was associated with the rise to dominance of the middle classes in American life. Temperance became obligatory behavior for all who sought to operate within the major social institutions. If sobriety in all areas of life is demanded by family, employer, and friend, then the young man should at least preserve his reputation if he wishes to "strive and succeed." The character valued by a dominant class is supported by the rewards which it obtains and the punishment which its presence entails.

As social classes rise and fall, as new classes emerge and contend for power and status, the status value of styles of life are called into question. Because it has been a significant status symbol, drinking has been an issue through which status struggles have been manifested. As the fortunes and the honor of the old middle class have risen and fallen, the temperance movement has shifted and changed its characteristics.

Temperance: Federalist Aristocracy and Jacksonian Common Man

In postcolonial America political and social power were largely in the hands of an aristocracy of wealth, based on the commercial capitalism of the East and the semi-feudal plantations of the South. American social structure was deeply and rigidly divided into discrete classes. ". . . Democracy was new; men were still described as gentlemen and simplemen . . . disparities of rank were still sustained by those of property" (13, p. v). As this social system gave way to equalitarian attack, the temperance movement emerged. At first, it was an attempt to control the new upsurge of democracy by defenders of the old order. Later it changed into an expression of the growing and now dominant middle classes in their efforts to reform and control their communities.

1. Drinking in colonial America

In the colonial period, drinking took place within a social system in which it was limited and controlled. Drunkenness occurred and was punished, but it was seldom frequent or widespread. Taverns were licensed, less to reform the habits of customers than to regulate inns for the benefit of the traveler. Beers and wines were often used with meals and innkeepers were respected members of the community. The moderate use of alcohol was approved and the tavern was one of the major social centers. Even though drunkenness increased with the development of towns in the eighteenth century, conditions were well confined within the boundaries of propriety (26).

2. The break-up of the old order

The appearance of a "drinking problem" was symptomatic of the breakdown in the system of social controls which had characterized colonial America. After the Revolution, the United States entered a period in which the small farmer and the artisan pressed for a greater degree of participation in the affairs of the nation. Clearly, the old order of status and political power based on wealth and breeding was under attack. This change in the social atmosphere was paralleled by a decline in religious devotion and a great upsurge in drinking. During the late eighteenth century, religious controls were less effective as instruments of social control over the farmer and the townsman. Drinking was far more common and drunkenness more acceptable. Apparently the experiences of camp and battlefield had been carried over into civilian life.

In New England, the political leadership of the aristocracy of wealth and the moral leadership of the established churches worked hand in hand. A threat to one was also a threat to the other. Both the clergy and the judiciary were viewed as stabilizing influences in society. Coming in a period of political conflict, the increase in drinking and in religious infidelity had a special meaning for those who were committed to the old order.

3. The temperance movement before 1840: outer-directed reform

In its earliest phase, from the late eighteenth century to about 1840, the temperance movement was dominated by the effort of the old order to maintain the status of the New England aristocracy through reform of the now advancing "common man." In the programs of the earliest known local temperance organizations, the reform of the employee by the employer is given an important position (11). The Litchfield, Connecticut, organization in 1789 pledged discontinuance of distilled spirits for both members and their employees (26). The Moreau, New York, Temperance Society (founded in 1808), made the increased efficiency of labor the central point in its argument for limited drinking (24, 26).

While both of these organizations proved to have a short life, they revealed the tone of the more stable associations which developed later. These were politically Federalist and religiously orthodox Calvinist in composition. In their doctrines and principles they expressed fear of the common man as an underlying source of concern with drinking. In their efforts at reform they were oriented to reforming others—the classes below them and outside the movement. While they included themselves, their major orientation was outer-directed.

This is seen in the career of the Reverend Lyman Beecher, the leading voice of the early temperance movement, as well as the leader of Neo-orthodoxy in New England. In religion, he inherited the leadership of the moral regeneration movement among the New England Calvinists. In politics he was a staunch Federalist. It was Beecher who headed the attack on republicanism and infidelity. In 1811 he surprised the faithful by a demand for prohibitions against ministerial drinking. In 1813 he was responsible for the development of the Connecticut Society for the Reformation of Morals. In a speech at Yale College, in 1812, he revealed the relationship between Federalism, orthodox religion, and temperance:

Our institutions, civil and religious, have outlived that domestic discipline and official vigilance in magistrates which rendered obedience easy and habitual. The laws are now beginning to operate extensively on necks unaccustomed to the yoke, and when they shall become irksome to the majority, their execution will become impracticable. . . . To this situation we are already reduced in some districts of the land. Drunkards reel through the streets day after day . . . with entire impunity. Profane swearing is heard . . . (2, Vol. 1, pp. 255–256).

During the 1820's and the early 1830's the temperance movement developed as a well-organized force. Its prevalent tone was anti-Jacksonian and its officers generally men of wealth, prominence, and Federalist persuasion. This was true of the Massachusetts Society for the Suppression of Intemperance, founded in 1813. It was also true of the early period of the first temperance association (1826), the American Temperance Society. Congregational and Presbyterian ministers formed a very large portion of the leadership. The same religions predominated among the secular leadership. New England, and especially eastern Massachusetts, was the major source of members of the executive committee (4, 6). In its use of persuasive materials, the temperance movement made Beecher's *Six Sermons on Intemperance* the leading statement of the temperance cause. These sermons, written in 1826, presented the same tone of a defense of the old order already exemplified above. Despite the fact that the Methodists had strongly endorsed temperance positions, they had almost no representation in the organized movement during this period. In western Massachusetts, where the Methodists were strong, they were also fiercely pro-Jackson. The dividing lines, it is clear, were those of class and status.

4. The entry of the common man: self-directed reform

As aristocratic dominance gave way, so did the power of the orthodox churches. Religion was not shoved aside in a wave of equalitarian secularism, somewhat as the French Revolution developed anticlericalism. Instead, evangelical and revivalistic religions emerged as new sources of social control and as effective agencies in promoting the temperance ethic. The Methodists had condemned the sale of liquor as early as John Wesley's visit to the United States in the late eighteenth century. Frontier communities depended on the church as a major source of order and morality. The revivalism of the Great Awakening in 1815 and the many similar events afterwards were partly responsible for the spread of temperance attitudes among the mass of middle- and lower-class citizens. Their appearance in the organized temperance movement changed its character, doctrines, and composition.

The loss of control by the "rich, the well-born and the able" (26, p. 92) is evident in the appearance of new movements, tactics, and organizations. These newer aspects of the temperance movement made an appeal to the average man through emotional and dramatic means. Unlike the earlier movement, they were usually led by secular persons.

Within the temperance movement of the 1830's the chief issues were those of the scope and the methods of temperance. New demands had arisen for a more direct political attack on the sale of liquor. Demands had emerged for a position of total abstinence rather than the previous positions of limited and moderate drinking. The social basis of the abstinence issue is suggested by the heavier strength of total abstinence supporters in the West than in the East. Endorsement of total abstinence lost wealthy supporters in New York State. Two changes occurred to the movement in this period: It became more extremist as it became more equalitarian, and it was more directly drawn into political controversies.

The increased extremism of the movement may be due to the fact that it was increasingly oriented toward the same group that constituted its membership. It was more and more self-oriented, seeking to develop and maintain the reform of its membership and the social classes in which they were affiliated. By 1840, the development of temperance as a sign of religious and social acceptance had been accomplished. The new temperance organizations made their appeal to reformed drunkards, to artisans, and to a social segment with experience in the revivalistic meetings of the times. Temperance programs were conducted with the style and the techniques of Methodist, Baptist, and non-orthodox Presbyterian camp meetings. Emphasis in meetings was on the confession, the pledge, and the flamboyant oratory of a secular leadership, often composed of reformed drunkards. Often, the temperance organization also functioned as insurance society and lodge for the city or town workers. Such groups had a popularity which the more staid and conservative organizations could not capture. To the vivid appeals of the newer associations there were added the highly emotional and dramatic qualities of the temperance story, such as *Ten Nights in a Barroom* or *The Drunkard*.

Abstinence was thus becoming a potent sign of middle-class status, distinguishing the abstainer from the lower levels of the ne'er-do-wells, the unambitious and the irreligious. Abstinence displayed one's religious adherence and showed that the abstainer had the character which both sought and merited the fruits of ambition. Temperance fiction repeatedly told a story in which the fruit of the vine is laziness, poverty and disgrace. The convert to abstinence achieves prosperity through his industriousness. In L. M. Sargent's *Wild Dick and Good Little Robin* we find the typical denouement:

Richard (having reformed) continued to grow in favor with God and man. He gave Farmer Little complete satisfaction by his obedience, industry and sobriety. He was permitted to cultivate a small patch of ground, on his own account. . . (34, p. 33).

Two other social conflicts contributed to the new context of the temperance movement. The first of these was the clash between native and immigrant which emerged during the 1840's and 1850's. Immigrants from Ireland and Germany were heavy additions to the American labor force in this period. There was little institutionalized opposition to drinking among either the Irish or the Germans. Catholic or Lutheran, they brought a non-Calvinist culture into puritan America. Generally at the bottom of the American social and economic scale, they enhanced the negative reference of alcohol consumption (19). One important source of the Know-Nothing vote was in temperance adherents. The area and period of greatest legislative triumphs for the temperance movement was also the area and period of greatest Know-Nothing dominance (3, 18).

The second social conflict united classes in the North against the South. By 1840 the struggle between Federalist and Republican was over. Early in its career temperance had found political allies in the struggles for religious reforms, such as the Sabbatarian movement and the promotion of foreign missions. After 1840 it was part of the complex of antislavery, nativism, and political Republicanism. Both the prairies and the East were attracted to temperance. So strong was the alliance between Abolition and temperance that the temperance movement was unable to develop in the South. Despite a promising beginning in the 1820's the South remained virtually closed to temperance organizations until after 1900.

The life of Neal Dow, temperance leader and founder of the Maine prohibition law, illustrates the complex of alliances which came to provide the foundations of the temperance movement before the Civil War. He was intensely anti-Jackson in the 1820's. In 1832 he found a place in the nativist anti-Masonry movement. In 1848 he became a Free Soiler and in 1856 staunchly supported the new Republican ticket. At all times he was a devout adherent of the antislavery cause. His political life expresses the changing national issues manifested in the temperance movement (12).

By the outbreak of the Civil War, temperance was dominant in the moral code of American drinking. The middle class had come to supremacy in American values and politics. This class consisted of the small retailer, the independent farmer, the local professional and the owner of the small factory. During much of the nineteenth century, American education, politics, religion, economic virtues, and social movements reflected the characteristic perspectives of this class. In experience they were rural; in religion they were Protestant. Whether they lived in small town, city or farm their background reflected the virtues of agricultural life. Common experiences in a world of economic expansion based on individual mastery supported a value system. Industry, thrift, self-discipline, foresight, and sobriety were clearly understood to be the virtues of the good and the successful.

Temperance: The Unity of Progressivism

The temperance movement before the Civil War had been a movement to reform the middle classes. From the post-Civil War period to about 1900, two streams are found in temperance: an ameliorative movement to convert the urban lower class to the virtues of American middle-class life and a movement against the sophisticated easterner and the urban upper classes. Each stream was related to larger movements in American politics. Dual streams of urban Progressivism and rural Populism coursed through the riverbeds of temperance.

1. *Progressive social Christianity: response to the urban challenge*

The bundle of social problems wrapped up in the terms urbanization and industrialization took form in the last 25 years of the nineteenth century. In the wake of an industrial and immigrant proletariat, many reform movements emerged, attempting to reconcile the realities of the city with the ideals of middle class small town society. Religion was one major source of the impulse to improve man's lot and to enable him to reach perfection, or the closest to perfection—middle-class respectability and success.

Henry May (27) has distinguished three forms of the movement called Social Christianity: (a) a conservative form, accepting the principle of a laissez-faire individualism in economic affairs but seeking to soften its harsher consequences through individualistic, voluntary, and philanthropic means; (b) a Progressive Christianity, searching to improve the form of present institutions but accepting the general outlines of the political and economic order; (c) a radical Christianity which rejected the capitalist framework and sought to fashion a new order. All three forms are discoverable in the temperance movement of this period, often in the same organization. Of the three forms, however, it was the Progressivist which exerted the most influence. The Social Gospel, an essentially Progressivist movement, had its source in the educated and pious middle classes, not in the ranks of the urban disinherited or the rural disaffected.

The activities of the Woman's Christian Temperance Union can be used to illustrate the reformist and Progressivist temper during the 1880's and 1890's. Its actions manifested the concerns of a dominant social group for the urban problems arising in an industrial society.

One response of this temperance organization was an orientation which viewed temperance as a solution to the problems of the urban worker. As in the early period of temperance history, the movement was not addressed to its members or to their social groups. Instead it was addressed to the outsider, the urban lower classes. Committees existed to carry the temperance message to miners, railroad men, lumbermen, and to the newly arrived immigrants. The object of reform is in the status level below the membership. To the workingman the message was clear: sober workers are the answer to problems of mass poverty. Abstinence is the route to success and acceptance in the middle class. An assimilationist solution is offered: embrace the character traits of the middle class. The use of abstinence as a symbol and a price is central to this appeal.

A second response of the W.C.T.U. was support of movements aimed at amelioration of the inequities suffered by the urban poor. The "temptations" of the working girl in the city, the intemperance of the working classes, the effort to reform prison life, the fight for limits on child labor—all these were objects of W.C.T.U. support. Despite their view of temperance as a solution to problems of the business cycle, the W.C.T.U. showed great sympathy with the struggles of labor during the 1890's. They applauded the Supreme Court decisions favoring a right to strike and chided employers to refrain from "kindling the spirit of animosity among those struggling under the iron heel of oppression" (36, p. 447).

The Progressivist motif in the temperance movement was not the ideology of a group under threat of the deprivation of power or status. They did not fear the underprivileged. They could afford a reformist and ameliorative spirit. While an aggressive nativist strain certainly appears in early W.C.T.U. documents (the 1870's), during the 1880's and 1890's the dominant attitude toward the immigrant was that of an effort to Americanize and "Christianize" the stranger. In the descriptions of immigrants and in the work of W.C.T.U. committees emphasis is placed on missionizing rather than on rejection. Despite the existence of an intensive and aggressive nativist movement in the United States during the 1890's, the W.C.T.U. formed no linkage with any organized aggressive nativist groups. As in its temperance ideology, it looked downward at the urban poor and upward to their ascendance into the middle class under the sponsorship of the native, rural Protestant.

2. Temperance and Populism

The Populist strain in the temperance movement was a decidedly different motivational force from that of Progressivism. Nineteenth century Populism was the political movement of a social segment, the American farmer, under strong threat of loss of power, status, and income. It did not seek to uplift the downtrodden. Its adherents were one form of the downtrodden. Temperance played a role within the movement. It was manifested in the development and growth of the Prohibitionist party and in the pro-temperance positions of such Populist organizations as the Grangers, the Greenbackers, the Non-Partisan League and the People's party, in its earlier stage.

The affinity between Populism and temperance was more historical than meaningful and logical. Agrarian radicalism was rife in the areas in which temperance had become dominant. The roots of the radicalism lay in the nature of crops and in the economic relationships between farmer, small town, and city. Temperance came along for the ride. Nevertheless, one stream of the temperance movement was accordingly couched in the language and in the perspective of the Populists. In their effort to gain adherents, each appealed to the aims of the other.

The Prohibitionist party platforms of the 1870's and 1880's are one source of evidence for a Populist stream in the temperance movement. Along with prohibition, female suffrage, and an antipolygamy amendment, these platforms recommended such Populist items as the graduated income tax, direct election of senators, abolition of stock exchanges, and governmental control of railroads (7). The Prohibitionist party found its strongest support in the areas of Populist sympathies, in the midwestern states of Iowa, Kansas, Nebraska, Indiana, and North Dakota.

Where Progressivists aimed at converting sinners, the Populists aimed at controlling power. Prohibition was congruent with the political emphasis of the Populists. Further, the perspective of the Populist saw big business as arch-villain. Involved in the opposition to Eastern financial and industrial capitalism, the Populist was quick to emphasize the liquor industry as the source of intemperance. While all wings of the temperance movement opposed the sale of liquor, the Prohibitionist party made this the central plank. The title of the collected addresses of the Prohibitionist orator, John B. Finch, suggests the Populist strain in temperance. It was called *The People versus the Liquor Traffic.*

The relation of temperance to Populism further enhanced the antiurban and nativistic strains in temperance circles. Among the agrarian circles, where temperance was a widely held norm, Populism and temperance formed a single unit. One delegate to the People's party convention of 1892 remarked that a "logical Populist" was one who had been first a Granger, then a Greenbacker, then a Prohibitionist, and then a Populist (20, p. 305). The agrarianism of the Populist was one important source of temperance strength and represented a fear of urban life in contrast to the urban reformism of the W.C.T.U.

3. *The unity of the temperance movement*

There were decided limits to the influence of the Populist spirit in the temperance movement of the nineteenth century. Temperance was only one string on the Populist fiddle and Populism only one stop on the temperance flute. When the People's party drew up their platform of 1892, they refused to endorse prohibition. The fear of antagonizing the German vote was too strong. Although Frances Willard, then president of the W.C.T.U., chaired that convention and was a leading spokesman of the Populists, she was unable to enlist the state W.C.T.U. organizations to support them. These movements touched and influenced each other. They did not absorb each other.

It is the breadth of the temperance movement in the late nineteenth century which is so impressive. Almost every progressive, radical, or conservative movement had some alliance with it. Populists and Progressives, labor and farmer, urban and rural, male and female, Christian and secularist had for some reason or opportunity to be an adherent or a sympathizer in the temperance movement. To belong to one was not to be disloyal to the other. The overlapping of conservative, progressive, and radical is the outstanding quality of the movement in this period of history.

Nowhere can the unifying character of the temperance movement be better observed than in the career of the famous National W.C.T.U. president, Frances Willard. She was one of those Reformers with a capital "R" who fill the pages of nineteenth century American history. Her motto might well have been, "Nothing new shall be alien unto me." She threw herself into the suffrage movement, the dress reform crusade, the spread of cremation, the vegetarian cause, the kindergarten campaign, and a multitude of other reform interests. After 1890 she added Populism, Fabianism and Christian Socialism to her major concerns. Sparking the campaign for equal rights for women, she learned to ride a bicycle in order to popularize the freer and healthier costume which permitted this form of exercise. Willard attempted to unite the W.C.T.U., the Populists, and the Prohibitionist party.

She used her influence to throw W.C.T.U. support behind female suffrage and the labor movement.

The attempt of Frances Willard to convert a humanitarian, middle-class organization into an arm of political and economic radicalism was not successful. Yet the fact that she was able to forge links of understanding and aid between conservative and radical social Christianity, between urban and rural interests, and between the needs and aims of immigrant labor and native middle class demonstrates the unifying impact of the temperance movement in its Progressive phase. While church circles condemned the strikes of the 1890's, the W.C.T.U. defended the rights of labor unions. When Populism was viewed as a political terror by respectable members of the middle class, at least the W.C.T.U. listened to criticism of the social order.

The Polarization of Forces

With the tremendous increase in immigration after 1890, large numbers of Catholics and Jews entered the American population. With the development of industry and the growth of cities, the dominance of the rural, agricultural segments of the society appeared to be waning. As America entered the twentieth century, the bonds of unity were again under great strain. During a 20-year period of relative prosperity, the struggle for status was marked. While the temperance issue had been peripheral to political concerns in the past, in the twentieth century it became a dominant political question. One consequence of this dominance was the decrease in the unifying functions the temperance movement had performed in the past.

The Populist strain in temperance had been aggressively antiurban and antialien. It had seen the goal of the movement to lie in the abolition of the liquor industry. Humanitarian aims of reform and conversion were decidedly secondary concerns. After 1900, this strain in the movement increased and spread to the church-going, middle-class citizens. The humanitarian strain which sparked Progressive Christianity lessened, although it remained as one source of temperance activity.

After 1900, leadership of the temperance movement shifted to the Anti-Saloon League and the Methodist Board of Temperance and Morality. Both of these organizations gave supreme importance to the political aim of state, local and national prohibition. While the W.C.T.U. continued its humanitarian and conversionary activities they were decidedly secondary to its support of prohibition. Thus the movement underwent two radical changes:

In the first place, actions were oriented to a specific concern with temperance legislation. The Protestant churches were mobilized as political pressure groups (29). With the work of the League and the Board, the South became a vital part of the temperance movement, adding to the Populist strain in temperance. Unlike the Prohibitionist party, no alliance between temperance and other organized movements was formed or desired. Temperance became an issue divorced from other political programs and ideologies.

Secondly, the Social Gospel ceased to be a source of temperance sentiment. Despite the fact that the Social Gospel increased its influence in American churches after 1900, in the temperance movement the opposite was the case. Even the movement for female suffrage was less actively sponsored by the W.C.T.U. after 1900 than it had been in earlier years. Within the W.C.T.U., the urban worker is less often viewed as an object of reform and more often approached as a possible voter in the Prohibitionist cause. Work of W.C.T.U. committees indicated decline in general reformist interests.

The segregation of temperance from other movements, at the same time as it became a dominant issue in politics, fostered the polarization of status groups in American life. That segregation was both a manifestation and an enhancing force in pitting the urban, secular, immigrant groups against the rural, Protestant, and native middle classes. As the power of the church member led to victory after victory for prohibition in state and local campaigns, the wets were pushed into greater organization. After the Eighteenth Amendment was passed, the status struggle was in full force. The dominance of the middle-class style of life was symbolized in Prohibition. It became the focal point for the political and social ambitions of American status groups.

The polarization of forces and the central position of the temperance issue helped explain why the temperance movement in the 1920's became linked to aggressive nativism, agrarian defense, and a conservative economic order. The very success of political pressure made the temperance movement wary of change. The prosperity of the 1920's was attributed to Prohibition. The Ku Klux Klan and aggressive nativism were one strong source of temperance support. The humanitarian impulse was still there, as in the W.C.T.U., but it was enfeebled beside the louder voices.

The nomination of Al Smith was the climax. Seldom has there been an American election in which economic issues were less important. Smith forced the commitments and loyalties of the American public to the status groups ranged against each other. Catholic and Protestant, urban and rural, agriculture and industry, wet and dry—in these dichotomies, the Progressivist strain was lost. The urban, northern middle class, once a strong temperance support, was weakened in the struggle.

Middle Class Decline and Moral Indignation

1. The post-Repeal change in drinking habits

Two quotations sum up much of the shift in American drinking habits since the repeal of the Eighteenth Amendment. The first is from the W.C.T.U. journal, *The Union Signal*, and was written in 1889:

The class least touched by the evil thus far is that which here, as elsewhere in the land, forms its bone and sinew—the self-respecting and self-supporting class whose chief pleasures in life center in and about the home (37, p. 3).

The second quotation is from an interview with a member of the National W.C.T.U. staff in 1953:

There has been a breakdown in the middle classes. The upper classes have always used liquor. The lower classes have always used liquor. Now the middle class has taken it over. The thing is slopping over from both sides.

After Repeal, total abstinence became less acceptable than it had been before Prohibition. Added to the upsurge of the non-Protestant and secular groups was an increased permissiveness toward drinking among the middle classes. The change in drinking norms is itself a reflection of deeper shifts in life styles and social structure. Many observers have called attention to the development of a new segment in the middle class. With the rise of a corporate economy of large-scale organizations, a new middle class of salaried white-collar workers, managerial employees, and professionals has developed. The styles of life of such groups contrast with those of the old middle class of small enterprisers, independent farmers, and free professionals. The new middle class is less likely to adhere to old middle class values. In an economy of surplus and in an atmosphere of organizations, mastery over other men supplants mastery over things and over the self as character virtues. Ability to "get along with others," to be tolerant, and to express solidarity are prized to the detriment of the complex of old middle class virtues. As the new class increases in size, a split has occurred within the middle classes between the old and the new sectors.

The cosmopolitanism of the new middle class supports the norms of permissive drinking. Unlike earlier periods, the aspirant to middle class status may now find that abstinence has become a negative symbol. The advocacy of moderate drinking has become widely held among church-going, respectable members of the middle classes in America. As one temperance writer has put it:

Cocktails or Scotch and soda have become a badge of membership in the upper middle class to which every college student aspires (25, p. 864).

2. The alienation of the temperance movement

One result of the change in middle class drinking habits has been the development of a posture of alienation within the temperance movement. This has arisen as church, school, community, and government have assumed a more hostile attitude toward temperance and toward the temperance adherent.

An area in which the change has been most crucial is that of the church. The Protestant church-goer and the Protestant clergy are less likely today to support a policy of total abstinence than before Repeal. The churches are reluctant to aid temperance organizations, in many cases. Ministers are less willing to preach and teach temperance doctrines. A neutral or moderationist stand has greater acceptance in church circles than it had in the earlier period.

Faced with a hostile environment, the temperance adherent feels ostracized, shunned, and ridiculed even among the circles in which he or she was formerly welcomed. One W.C.T.U. member in a rural town expressed this common sentiment in the following interview excerpt:

Well, as you have probably learned, this isn't the organization it used to be. It isn't popular you know. The public thinks of us—let's face it—as a bunch of old women, as frowzy fanatics. I've been viewed as queer, as an old fogey for belonging to the W.C.T.U. . . . This attitude was not true thirty years ago.

3. *Temperance and the middle-class status struggle*

In its contemporary form, the temperance movement is embedded in the struggle between old and new segments of the middle classes to enunciate the dominant life styles in America. Temperance has emerged as a symbol of the defense of an old status order against the rise of a new one. The negative reference symbol is no longer the urban underprivileged. The Populist element has widened to include the middle class as well as the upper class as objects of reform and opposition. The linkage between temperance and other movements appears in the complex of social, political, and economic programs expressing the defense of traditionalist values.

The figure now appearing as a central target of both reform effort and righteous disapproval is that of the moderate drinker. This doctrine of moderate drinking is most likely to be found in the upper-middle-class circles where temperance was formerly accepted. The resentment and indignation of the temperance movement has been directed toward this group. A W.C.T.U. journal editorial presents a typical attitude:

Once the drinker and the drunkard were frowned upon. One who was drinking was not welcome at a party; he was not entrusted with an office in his or her church. . . . Drinking has now become so prevalent that one who would cry out against it is regarded as a fanatic. Even the preacher who dares to speak out boldly is sometimes regarded as exceedingly narrow and such narrowness would make that preacher unacceptable to some churches (38, p. 9).

In editorials, articles, and fiction, temperance organizations reflect the belief that total abstinence is now a negative reference symbol among the upper-middle classes. The argument of social pressure—everybody drinks and drinking is socially necessary—is constantly attacked in temperance literature. The context of the drinker is now set in respectable, church-going, middle-class circles. The conflict is posed as one between moderate drinkers as prestige figures and the old-fashioned total abstainer. In one fiction story in the W.C.T.U. journal, the heroine, Jane, reveres her "old-fashioned Christian grandmother." Jane's mother ridicules the daughter's temperance pledge as prudishness and as a hindrance to her social position (39).

This defection of the upper-middle class from the temperance movement is further indicated by shifts in the social composition of local leaders in the

W.C.T.U. In a previous study (15) we have shown that wives with husbands in upper-middle class and upper class occupations are less often found in local officer positions in the W.C.T.U. since Repeal than they were in the previous periods. The local professional and the businessman is less likely to support temperance today than he was in an earlier era.

4. The fundamentalist response

As temperance is a symbol of the status conflict between old and new middle classes, it is embedded in a general defense of traditional values. This more general clash is a source of temperance enthusiasm and a possible area for alliances between the temperance movement and other organizations.

We refer to this more generalized defense movement as the "fundamentalist response." It involves an intense and positive affirmation of traditional values and an intense rejection of values associated with modernism (30, 31). Forces of science, secularism, urbanization, and political change are viewed as detrimental to the value system embodied in traditional nineteenth century ideals. The clash is then defined as that of old against new.

The prime motive for this general movement is indignation at lost status —the decline in power and prestige attendant upon transitions in the American economy, government, and social structure. As a general movement it is identified as one element in right-wing conservatism—fundamentalist in religion, nativist in domestic issues, nationalist in foreign policy, and right-wing in politics.

Evidence for sentiments of fundamentalism appear in shifting concerns of the W.C.T.U., in committee activities, toward greater emphasis on the re-establishment of religious ritual in families, in traditionalist systems of character training for children, in a rejection of past internationalist foreign policy positions and in the espousal of opposition to the United Nations. In speeches during the 1930's, W.C.T.U. officials displayed a defensive conservatism on political and economic questions.

The central concept in this conservatism is that of "character." We have seen that this was also central in the value system supporting temperance. The argument is now set forth that the evils of the present day are the result of the decline in positive supports to the development of adequate character traits. The ills of society are then the consequence of intemperance produced through the decline in religious values:

A good *old-fashioned* revival would greatly correct what ails us by getting people out of such things as saloons, race-tracks and gambling places and into the churches. People have changed, not God. . . . More parents than children are delinquent. Religion, in terms of sincerity, weekly church-going and grace before meals is the best form of juvenile protection (8).

This form of middle-class conservatism is not based on direct economic interest. In religion and politics, change is rejected where it threatens the status of the old values around which the life style of the old middle class had been organized. It is the decline in importance of these symbols and the values they symbolize which is experienced as deprivation. It is the supplanting symbols which are objects of indignation.

The Dilemma of the Temperance Movement

Efforts to link the temperance movement to extremist forms of neo-Populist indignation have not been successful. There are many instances of the existence of such sentiments in temperance adherents. Statements of officers on political issues, testimony before congressional committees, and interviews reveal a strain of aggressive nativism, of right-wing political positions, and of nationalistic xenophobia. During the nineteenth century the temperance movement gained much zeal and enthusiastic support from the linkage to major social movements in other spheres. The possibility does exist today of moving the temperance effort even closer to the fundamentalist response. In general, temperance organizations have not done so. They have sought to temper neo-Populism with the sweeter waters of a humanitarian Progressivism. The dilemma of the movement lies in the difficulties this entails in the current society.

The problem of current temperance ideology has been sketched in the section above. That problem arises from the changed status of total abstinence as a symbol of social position. Drinking is more acceptable within middle-class circles than it was in earlier periods. This change has converted temperance adherence into a rejected and minority position in American life. Especially significant both for prestige and for organizational effectiveness, this change has undermined the role of the churches and the schools as active agents in the training and mobilization of temperance support. The temperance movement can no longer depend on school, church, and family to produce a generation of adherents and sympathizers.

The issue is thus posed as one of choice between alternative social bases. Sentiments supporting temperance are an element in the neo-Populist and aggressive extremism of some forces in the fundamentalist response. However, this movement, with its xenophobia, nativism, and ultraconservative politics, is a minority position unacceptable within the mainstream of contemporary middle-class respectability. "Somewhere along the way the Populist-Progressive tradition has become sour, become ill-liberal and ill-tempered" (22, p. 19). The churches will no longer support the polarization of social forces which they were willing to support in the prohibition conflict of the early twentieth century. To secure this social base of prestige the temperance movement finds it necessary to link its ideology to a humanitarian progressivism, emphasizing the prevention of chronic alcoholism, as well as subsidiary concerns such as juvenile delinquency and drug addiction. Political and social issues beyond this narrowed approach run the risk of alienating the movement by identifying it with the social base of the extremist, the "right-wing radical."

The sources of zeal and enthusiasm lie in the sentiments of indignation nourished by loss of old middle-class status. The sources of prestige and acceptance lie in the middle-class groups now heavily exposed to doctrines of moderation in drinking and less moved by the fundamentalist response. To win support here the movement must blunt the edges of sharper conflicts, raging around the status split in the middle classes. Concern with the chronic alcoholic and other popular social problems may greatly change the character of the movement.

In the past the temperance movement has been an attack upon immorality. For the old middle class in American life, drinking has been preeminently a moral issue and a status divider. It was a threat to the character and values which they prized. Abstinence was a ticket of admission into respectability. As the guardians of the dominant values, the old middle class could function as prize specimens of the efficacy of those values. This moral and valuational base is no longer the root of humanitarian sentiment in alcohol problems. When temperance becomes linked to movements of health, then the professionals—the doctors, psychiatrists, sociologists, and other scientific personnel—lay greater claim to a public hearing than can the temperance movement.

A cloud of alienation and rejection hangs over the American temperance movement. Whether to seek its removal or to use it as a source of organized zeal is the basic dilemma of the contemporary movement. Through much of its history the temperance movement has remained a remarkably diffuse movement. It has been open to adherents of many other organized movements, many of which opposed and contradicted each other. While events of the past 40 years have diminished its diffuse quality, the movement has not yet embraced a highly polarized position. In the past it was a meeting point for seemingly diverse elements in the American society. Each successive wave of conflict, defeat, and rejection accentuated the alienation of the movement from its past base in a dominant middle class. During the twentieth century the middle-class ideology of Progressivist welfare for the downtrodden has played less and less of a role. Many forces, however, pull the movement back toward less extreme and more accommodative functions. There are important aspects of the temperance movement which function as mechanisms of social cohesion, stressing common interests and sentiments in American life. The more diffuse the movement, the more it is capable of gaining a less zealous but higher status base, closer to centers of institutional control. It is when social movements are ideologically closed to all but the most deeply committed that they most accentuate the schisms and conflicts of the society.

References

1. Bacon, Selden D., and Robert Straus, *Drinking in College,* New Haven: Yale University Press, 1953.
2. Beecher, Charles (Ed.), *Autobiography of Lyman Beecher,* New York: Harper and Brothers, 1864.

3. Billington, Ray, *The Protestant Crusade, 1800–1860,* New York: The MacMillan Company, 1938.

4. Bodo, J. R., *The Protestant Clergy and Public Issues,* Princeton, N.J.: Princeton University Press, 1954.

5. Bridenbaugh, C., *Cities in the Wilderness,* New York: Ronald Press, 1938.

6. Clark, George, *History of Temperance Reform in Massachusetts, 1813–1883,* Boston: Clarke and Carruth, 1888.

7. Colvin, D. L., *Prohibition in the United States,* New York: George H. Doran Company, 1926.

8. Colvin, Mrs. D. L., Address by the President of the National W.C.T.U., quoted in *The Chicago Daily News,* Sept. 10, 1951.

9. Cuyler, T. L., "Christian Recreation and Unchristian Amusements," sermon delivered at Cooper Institute, New York, Oct. 24, 1858. Reprinted in pamphlet form and contained in the Fahnstock Collection of pre-Civil War pamphlets, Vol. 6, Champaign, Ill.: University of Illinois Library.

10. Dollard, John, "Drinking Mores of the Social Classes," in *Alcohol, Science and Society,* New Haven, Conn.: Journal of Studies on Alcohol, 1945.

11. Dorchester, D., *The Liquor Problem in All Ages,* New York: Phillips and Hunt, 1887.

12. Dow, Neal, *Reminiscences,* Portland, Me.: Express Publishing Company, 1898.

13. Fox, D. R., *The Decline of Aristocracy in the Politics of New York,* New York: Columbia University Press, 1919.

14. Goldschmidt, Walter, "Class Denominationalism in Rural California Churches," *Amer. J. Sociol.,* 49:348–355, 1944.

15. Gusfield, Joseph R., "Social Structure and Moral Reform: A Study of the Women's Christian Temperance Union," *Amer. J. Sociol.,* 61:221–232, 1955.

16. ———, "The Problem of Generations in an Organizational Structure," *Social Forces,* 35:323–330, 1957.

17. Hall, Thomas, *The Religious Background of American Culture,* Boston: Little, Brown and Company, 1940.

18. Handlin, Oscar, *Boston's Immigrants,* Cambridge, Mass.: Harvard University Press, 1941.

19. Hansen, Marcus, *The Immigrant in American History,* Cambridge, Mass.: Harvard University Press, 1940.

20. Haynes, F., *Third Party Movements,* Iowa City: State Historical Society of Iowa, 1916.

21. Hofstadter, R., "The Pseudo-Conservative Revolt," *in* D. Bell (Ed.), *The New American Right,* New York: Criterion Press, 1955.

22. ———, *The Age of Reform,* New York: Alfred A. Knopf, 1955.

23. Horton, Donald, "The Functions of Alcohol in Primitive Societies," *Quart. J. Stud. Alc.,* 4:199–319, 1943.

24. Ingraham, W., "The Birth at Moreau of the Temperance Reformation," *Proceedings,* VI, 115–133, New York State Historical Association.

25. King, Albion Roy, "Drinking and College Discipline," *Christian Century,* July 25, 1951, 864–866.

26. Krout, John Allen, *The Origins of Prohibition,* New York: Alfred A. Knopf, 1925.

27. May, Henry, *Protestant Churches and Industrial America,* New York: Harper and Brothers, 1949.

28. Merton, Robert, "Continuities in Reference Group Theory," *in* Robert Merton, *Social Theory and Social Structure,* Glencoe, Ill.: The Free Press, 1957.

29. Odegard, P., *Pressure Politics,* New York: Columbia University Press, 1928.

30. Parsons, Talcott, "Certain Primary Sources and Patterns of Aggression in the Social Structure of the Western World," *Psychiatry,* **10**:167–182, 1947.

31. ———, "Some Sociological Aspects of Fascist Movements," *Social Forces,* **21**:138–147, 1942–43.

32. Pope, Liston, *Millhands and Preachers,* New Haven, Conn.: Yale University Press, 1943.

33. Riley, John W. Jr., and Charles F. Marden, "The Social Pattern of Alcoholic Drinking," *Quart. J. Stud. Alc.,* **8**:265–273, 1947.

34. Sargent, L. M., "Wild Dick and Good Little Robin," in *Temperance Tales,* Boston: Whipple and Damrell, 1836.

35. *Temperance Manual,* no publisher, 1836.

36. Woman's Christian Temperance Union, *Annual Report,* 1894.

37. ———, *The Union Signal,* May 16, 1889.

38. ———, *The Union Signal,* Feb. 21, 1953.

39. ———, *The Union Signal,* June 3–July 29, 1939.

chapter 7

Drinking styles
and status arrangements[*]

Gregory P. Stone

Every human transaction is accomplished in a matrix of appearances or a shifting amalgamation of locales, settings, scenery, dress, posture, and gesture.[†] Appearances assist those involved in transactions to maintain continuing identifications of one another, enabling mutual empathy and underwriting the meaning of the transaction. The identifications mobilized by appearances include status assignments and appraisals,[‡] and it is our contention that the drinking of beverage alcohol may be apprehended as an appearance which has overriding status implications. Drinking may often have the effect of changing or consolidating the drinker's place in some larger status arrangement. Such drinking appearances are distinctive and, as such, are conceptualized as styles. Drinking styles extend beyond the conventional behavioral characteristics of drinking—amount and kind of beverage consumed, frequency of drinking, or incidence of inebriation—to include drinking locales, their decor, and the drinkers' decorum.

Drinking styles, then, are viewed as affecting the drinker's place in some larger status arrangement—a phrase that is more precise and accurate than

[*] This chapter was written especially for this book. The writer is indebted to Jack Munro, graduate student at Washington University, for his assistance in the content analysis of these interview materials and to Keith Miller, a colleague, for aid in classifying the interview materials that deal with status relevance of drinking styles.

[†] The notion of drinking as an appearance has been suggested by Erving Goffman (4).

[‡] Status is used in this article after the fashion of Max Weber (12). An exception is provided by our contention that those sharing the same honorific or respectable life styles may or may not, on that basis, constitute themselves as a social group. When they do, we shall speak of a social circle; when they do not, a status stratum.

the more frequently employed "social class system" which easily leads the analyst to preconceive the distribution of status as an hierarchical phenomenon and to confuse status with other dimensions of stratification such as economic class or political power. Both of these contentions are illustrated by the case of Vansburg, Michigan, the setting for this analysis of alcoholic drinking.*

Vansburg has many of the characteristics of "Elmtown," and it was originally assumed that the status order of the town would approximate the model of a "social class system." Therefore, Warner's well-known Index of Status Characteristics (11) was used to stratify the community into five social classes or, as we prefer, status strata. This was accomplished, although the adaptation of the Index of Status Characteristics to local community conditions was disturbed by certain anomalies. Specifically, the status order was not clearly reflected in community ecology, the local judges of status disagreed on status ratings for occupations in the middle range of a presumed continuum of occupational status, and a high proportion of truckers in the labor force meant that the heads of many households were more often out of town than in town so that the status reputations of their families were somewhat blurred (10, pp. 153–154). The chief difficulty, however, arose from what we have called an "invasion of the cosmopolites" which resulted in a Y-shaped arrangement of social circles and aggregations in Vansburg, rather than the conventionally assumed truncated pyramid.

At the higher levels of status, as measured by the Index of Status Characteristics, the "cosmopolites" were engaged in a contest with the indigenous "old families" for the respect of the other community residents:

Certain national manufacturers had singled out Vansburg—a source of low-cost labor—as a site for the location of decentralized assembly plants and warehouses. Managerial personnel employed by these concerns and by various state departments and agencies which had located their offices in Vansburg, the county seat, had taken up residence in the city. Thus, managerial personnel in significant numbers had been recruited into the community. They came principally from outlying metropolises and other large urban centers. Other persons had also come into the community from larger cities. . . . A wealthy urbanite had purchased the local newspaper and established his residence in town. These people did not accept either the conventional symbols or the conventional norms of status held by the members of the community prior to their arrival (10, p. 155).

The ensuing refusal of these cosmopolites to establish their local status by emulating the life styles of the old families resulted in a cleavage in the status order of Vansburg, reaching down to what Warner speaks of as the "upper-lower class" and enlisting the respect of the younger adults for the cosmopolites. Older adults more often continued to demonstrate their status allegiances to the old families.

* Vansburg, Michigan is a county seat with a population of about ten thousand. For 6 years, beginning in 1950, it was the site of an extensive study of clothing sponsored by the Michigan State University Agricultural Experiment Station. The writer served as field director of this study.

That the cleavage was conceptualized by many members of the community as a difference between "drinkers" and "non-drinkers" is of obvious relevance:

This was merely the way the townspeople conceptualized the schism. It had little to do with whether or not the people referred to drank. Rather, it was *how* they drank—the difference between the "standing drinkers" and the "sitting drinkers" (10, p. 155).

Moreover, drinking was apparently a way of entering a status claim which could challenge the status of the old families.

The Country Club, for example, has undergone a complete alteration of character. Once the scene of relatively staid dinners, polite drinking, and occasional dignified balls, the Country Club is now the setting for the "businessman's lunch," intimate drinking, and frequent parties where the former standards of moral propriety are often somewhat relaxed for the evening. Most "old families" have let their memberships in the club lapse (10, p. 155).

Or, where they have not let their memberships lapse, they have not maintained active participation. As one member of an old family put it, "I know, before the war, we used to dress up in formals for dinner parties and dances. Now we don't dress up. In fact, we don't have much in the social life way."

The present report provides a secondary analysis of the interviews gathered in the Vansburg study of clothing in the effort to discern the relevance of alcoholic drinking for the drinkers' positions in the status arrangements of the community. As such, the inquiry seeks to check out and extend the impressions just reviewed which were reported before the larger research was completed.

The Saliency of Drinking in Vansburg

Two hundred and twenty adult men and women, constituting a stratified random sample of married couples resident in Vansburg in 1950, participated in this study.* Of these, 181 completed four interview schedules and a modified *Thematic Apperception Test*, while the rest completed two schedules before refusing to continue the interviewing. Normally, two visits were made to each subject. Modal interviewing time was 3 hours per person. The interview questions were mostly open-ended and, of all the questions asked, only a part of one explicitly suggested drinking alcoholic beverages. The context of this instance was an effort to probe recreational behavior by presenting a check list of twelve common recreational activities

---

* The strata were defined by the seven-point occupational status scale which is an important component of Warner's Index of Status Characteristics. Since the number of married couples selected for interviewing was in direct proportion to the total number of married men employed in occupations receiving the seven different ratings, the "very high" and "very low" status occupations contain fewer informants than the less extreme ratings. As a consequence, less information is available on drinking styles at the extremes of status than in the middle ranges.

to each subject. Among the activities listed was "visiting a tavern." Nowhere else in the schedules was the drinking of beverage alcohol explicated or suggested.

Given this very minor reference to drinking in an inquiry devoted to a lengthy consideration of clothes, it is interesting, indeed, to note that 106 subjects (48 per cent of the total interviewed) made one or more references to alcoholic drinking.* Of these, only fourteen subjects made simple acknowledgments of tavern visits in response to the check-list item mentioned above. Fourteen other subjects acknowledged tavern visits but made additional spontaneous comments about drinking. However, 78 subjects made spontaneous comments about drinking without acknowledging tavern visiting. In short, just under three-fourths of the references to alcoholic drinking were not prompted at all by the check-list item suggesting such drinking. On the contrary, they were prompted by other questions dealing largely with matters of social status.

1. *References to alcoholic drinking*

Before turning to the substantive significance of these references, their distribution will be briefly discussed. The references were not differentiated by sex of respondent, nor did the Index of Status Characteristics discriminate directly among the references. There was, however, some tendency for cosmopolites to refer more frequently than localites to alcoholic drinking (57 per cent of the cosmopolites, 46 per cent of the localites).† However, closer examination of these differences revealed that the preponderance of the references by cosmopolites was provided by women. Over two-thirds of the cosmopolite mentions of drinking were by women, while this was true of less than half of the localite mentions. When the women were considered separately, we found that of the twenty-eight cosmopolite women in the total sample, nineteen (68 per cent) referred to drinking; of the eighty-four localite women, thirty-five (42 per cent) made such references. Finally, in every classification of the Index of Status Characteristics in which cosmopolitan women were found (none appeared in the "lower-lower" category), those mentioning drinking exceeded those who did not. However, the opposite was the case for localite women, since those mentioning drinking were in the minority at each status level.

2. *Valence of references*

Each reference to alcoholic drinking was classified as disapproving, ap-

* The phrase "alcoholic drinking" is used as a shorthand for the drinking of beverage alcohol, without any necessary connotation of alcoholism.

† Since the cosmopolite-localite schism was not anticipated in the study design, localites were differentiated from cosmopolites by intensive scrutiny of the interview materials to determine whether or not the "life-space" of each informant more or less coincided with the boundaries of Vansburg—whether the world of Vansburg was or was not the informant's personal world. Recently, of course, techniques have been developed to determine the difference much more precisely. On this point, see Gouldner (6). Incidentally, Gouldner also reports the greater saliency of drinking in the cosmopolitan life style as contrasted with the local life style.

proving, mixed approval and disapproval, or non-evaluative. There were no overall sex differences in these "valences" but some status differences were disclosed. Using the Index of Status Characteristics, we found that non-evaluative comments were concentrated in the "upper" and "upper-middle" strata. These strata were also underrepresented among those making disapproving comments on drinking. "Upper-lower" and "lower-middle" strata, in contrast, were overrepresented among those making disapproving remarks about drinking. Within all these strata, sex differences emerged, and the stratum differences observed seemed, in fact, to be differences among the women rather than for the total sample. Table 1 shows that the preponderance of disapprovals is found among women of "lower-middle" status and below. The data provide some qualified support for the observations of Dollard (1). In-stratum sex differences appear in each stratum except the "upper-lower." In the "upper" and "upper-middle" strata, males are relatively more disapproving than women, while in the "lower-middle" and "lower-lower" strata the differences are reversed.*

TABLE 1

Social Status Differences in the Valence of Spontaneous Remarks About Alcoholic Drinking Made by Fifty-four Vansburg Women

| | Status Strata | | | | | Total | |
| | Upper N | Upper-Middle N | Lower-Middle N | Upper-Lower N | Lower-Lower N | | |
Valence of Remark						N	Per Cent
Non-evaluative	4	2	1	1	3	11	20
Approval	1	4	2	7	1	15	28
Mixed approval and disapproval	—	1	2	4	—	7	13
Disapproval	—	1	8	8	4	21	39
Totals	5	8	13	20	8	54	100

$$\chi^2 = 11.30 \text{ [a]} \qquad P < .01 \text{ [b]}$$

[a] In the computation of the chi-square, the first three rows, the first two columns, and the last two columns were combined so that the chi-square is for a sixfold table with 2 degrees of freedom.

[b] A P value of .01 or less has been chosen as the level of significance for this study.

* Only the "lower-middle" stratum provided sufficient references for a test of significance. For these subjects, a chi-square test showed that disapproving comments made by women are proportionately greater than those made by men (P < .05). In the upper stratum, two of four men disapproved, contrasted with none of five women; in the upper-middle stratum, three of seven males disapproved, contrasted with one of eight females; and in the lower-lower stratum, one of five men disapproved of drinking, contrasted with four of eight women.

Cosmopolites referred to alcoholic drinking in greater proportion than did localites, as we have seen, and this may have been a consequence of their relatively greater approval of drinking. Nearly 40 per cent of the cosmopolites approved, as compared to about a fourth of the localites making references to drinking. Disapproval not unexpectedly showed a reciprocal pattern, with 29 per cent of the cosmopolites and 40 per cent of the localites expressing disapproval in their comments. The mixed and non-evaluative responses to drinking were made by equal proportions of both groupings. Again we found that the localite-cosmopolite differences were more pronounced for the women who referred to drinking than for the men. Twice the proportion of localite women disapproved as approved of drinking—just over two-fifths as compared to one-fifth. Cosmopolitan women, however, approved in about the same proportion as cosmopolitan men and disapproved in roughly the same proportion, providing a sharp contrast with the localite women.*

Drinking Locales: Taverns and Clubs

When these interviews were taken, Vansburg was a "3.2 town," that is, only 3.2 per cent beer was sold over public bars. Beverages of greater alcoholic content could be purchased for immediate consumption only in private clubs. The status relevance of alcoholic drinking can be detected through an examination of attitudes mobilized by these private drinking clubs, but first some attention must be given to tavern drinking among the Vansburg citizens in our study.

1. *Tavern drinking*

A total of 28 † of the 106 subjects who referred to drinking in the interviews also mentioned that they visited taverns as a form of recreation. However, tavern drinking for this sample was not grossly differentiated according to sex, status stratum, or local-cosmopolitan orientation. There was some tendency for the upper stratum to be underrepresented among tavern-goers (1 of 16) and for the lower-lower stratum to be overrepresented (7 of 31).

---

* Among the nineteen cosmopolitan women commenting on drinking, all disapproving responses (six in number) occurred in the lower-middle and upper-lower strata, as did both mixed responses (two cases). Non-evaluative or objective responses (three) were made by higher status cosmopolitan women. These data may be referred to our earlier comments on the character of the "cosmopolitan invasion." The "invaders" were primarily upper- and upper-middle-stratum families. Lower-stratum families who manifested cosmopolitan styles were, for the most part, localites whose deference had been won by the cosmopolites in the status contest. It is quite possible that the "victory" in these cases was not complete at the time of interviewing, with local lower-middle and upper-lower attitudes toward drinking still persisting among the converts, while still other converts in these strata looked upon cosmopolitan drinking with some ambivalence.

† Of these, there were two instances of obvious confusion between taverns and clubs: two upper-middle stratum subjects referred to the Buffalo Club bar as a tavern. These two cases were therefore eliminated from the analysis of tavern drinking.

Also, cosmopolitans were somewhat overrepresented among respondents who acknowledged tavern visits.

Yet analysis of tavern drinking within each sex category did disclose significant status and localite-cosmopolite differences. Specifically, lower-lower status men were significantly overrepresented among tavern-goers (6 of 19), while men in all other strata combined were underrepresented (8 of 89). On the other hand, cosmopolitan women were significantly over-represented among tavern-goers (6 of 29); localite women, underrepre-sented (6 of 83). It may be noted, too, that only one of 19 lower-lower stratum women acknowledged tavern visits, compared to 12 of 93 in other strata. Seen in conjunction with the data on men, this finding offers some support to an earlier suggestion of the writer (9) to the effect that leisure activity is most extensively differentiated according to sex in the lowest socio-economic stratum.

We also found that over-all status differences in tavern-going char-acterized the local men, but not the cosmopolitan men. About a third of the lower-lower status localite husbands visited taverns, compared to less than a tenth of the localite men in other strata. This tendency for drinking pat-terns to show more consistent status differences among locals than among cosmopolitans may be seen clearly in the analysis of drinking clubs and may reflect a characteristic of behavior in general, namely that status *ranking* is a more salient determinant of behavior for those who live in communities (the localites) than for those who live in the society at large (the cosmo-polites).*

2. Drinking clubs

In our broader analysis we have shown how cosmopolites impose the styles of the metropolis on the status arrangements of the town as they contest with indigenous status groups for the deference of community members. This may result in anomalous status patterns as far as drinking behavior is concerned. For example, the status range of public drinking places in the metropolis is normally much greater than the status range of such places in Vansburg, where taverns largely cater to the drinking tastes of those in the lower reaches of the status range. Yet, some cosmopolites "carried" public-drinking patterns adopted elsewhere to Vansburg, momen-tarily upsetting the status distributions of tavern patronage. The only public place where the writer observed upper- and upper-middle-status persons drinking beer was in a local hotel. The majority of these people (all men) were, significantly, cosmopolites who had recently entered the town, but, interestingly, the informal circle was referred to by themselves and by others as the "Kaffee Klatsch."

With the exception of the *Gute Freunden*, a predominantly localite high status club, all private drinking clubs were local chapters of national as-sociations, and chapters of the same national organization recruit members

---

* For the same phenomenon in another area of behavior, see Gray (7).

from different status strata and social circles in different towns and cities. Thus, members of high status chapters in some cities, moving to still other cities and towns, may find themselves in lower status associations in their new places of residence, or vice versa. (Compare the status distribution of local and cosmopolitan members of Vansburg private drinking clubs shown in Tables 2 and 3.)

TABLE 2

Frequency Distribution of Localite Membership in Vansburg Drinking Clubs by Status Stratum

Status Stratum	Gute Freunden	Country Club	Buffaloes	Veterans	Falcons	Leopards
		Vansburg Drinking Clubs				
Upper	2	2	2	3	—	—
Upper-middle	2	4	7	1	2	—
Lower-middle	—	2	6	21	2	—
Upper-lower	—	—	1	12	6	7
Lower-lower	—	—	—	1	2	3

TABLE 3

Frequency Distribution of Cosmopolitan Membership in Vansburg Drinking Clubs by Status Stratum

Status Stratum	Gute Freunden	Country Club	Buffaloes	Veterans	Falcons	Leopards
		Vansburg Drinking Clubs				
Upper	1	2	4	3	3	1
Upper-middle	1	3	4	3	—	—
Lower-middle	1	2	4	6	—	—
Upper-lower	—	—	—	3	2	2
Lower-lower	—	—	—	—	—	—

Table 2 presents the established status ordering of drinking clubs in Vansburg at the time of the interviewing. That this distribution is not merely an artifact of our statistics and the very small number of cases but is rooted in the status awareness of community residents is clear from many interview excerpts. For example, an upper-middle-stratum localite, asked whether there were any different "social classes of people" in Vansburg, demonstrated the tight interrelationship among status, drinking styles, and drinking clubs in his reply:

Yes there are. There is the one that consists of practically all laboring folks, almost all working folk—not all of them. I'm thinking of the Falcons Lodge. They have lots of parties; most of their time is spent drinking, playing cards, and playing slot machines. One class of the same people is the working class. They spend most of their time drinking in the taverns and gambling. Then, there are the Buffaloes. Some of them are in the money. They gamble. It got so bad they had to try to stop them. The pot got to two thousand bucks. There are some "working boys" in there; some won; some dropped money over and over again. They put a stop to it. You know, when you play for money like that, there can be trouble. The rest of them are climbers. They are minor administrative people in the factories and stores. They do drinking, but not as much as the Falcons. Then, there is the solid business man. Sure, they drink, but at home—just a social drink. They play cards, but don't gamble as much.

Less comprehensive, but still illustrative, are the remarks of a lower-middle-stratum cosmopolite woman prompted by a question asking whether any people in town dressed below average most of the time:

Those would be the ones who go to the Leopard's Club—the lower element in town. They might dress flashily, but not right. They go on drunken brawls right in the lodge hall. The Buffaloes are the opposite.

Referring to those who, in her estimation, dressed above average most of the time, she continued in the same vein:

The Country Club set. They're just as high rollers, when it comes to booze, but they have clothes and cars, whether they're paid for or not. They consider themselves the ones to set the fashion.

Thus, we can see how participation in the various drinking clubs of Vansburg affects the status of the drinker. Membership in a drinking club wins for him a certain respect or disrespect from others in the community, and this is often ascribed in terms of some imputed drinking style.

Over half of the 106 respondents making reference to alcoholic drinking referred to these drinking clubs in their comments. Most of these comments were derogatory, and the derogations were directed for the most part to clubs with status ratings different from those of the derogators. We shall infer from these materials that the derogation of a drinking club symbolizing a status stratum or social circle different from the stratum or circle to which the derogator belongs often has the consequence of heightening or reinforcing the status of the derogator. In short, the derogation of others' drinking styles is often an invidious comparison. The interview materials illustrate this. For example, an upper-middle cosmopolite woman explained why she would not wish to join the Falcons: "The Falcons—they have pretty wild times—drink a lot to excess. At the nicer clubs, they drink, but not like that."

An upper-lower localite woman explained why she would not consider joining either the Falcons or the Leopards:

I like to drink, but I don't like this heavy drinking. I don't want anyone else fooling around with my husband. The Leopards is not as bad as the Falcons. Now, I belong to the Sisterhood. They're not a drinking lodge. They're pretty fussy —won't let everybody in, but most that want to belong are ones who amount to something. We wouldn't want heavy drinkers or cheap women.

An upper-lower class cosmopolitan trucker, a member of the Falcons, realizes the increment of self-esteem in a somewhat different way: "Some of those guys in the Buffaloes, when they want to really have a good time, go to the Falcons."

Appraising responses to drinking, therefore, may sometimes act to "firm up" the value of the drinking styles of status peers and "put down" the value of the drinking styles representative of different status strata and social circles. In this way the appearance of drinking, mobilizing, as it does, the status appraisals of "outside" audiences, may be an important mechanism of status consolidation both for the appraising audience and the circle or stratum appraised. There is, however, a risk, aggravated by the transiency of cosmopolitanism; that is, to drink in an "alien" style may be to lose status parity with the members of one's own status stratum.

Drinking Styles and Status Arrangements

About a fifth (19 per cent) of the 106 references to alcoholic drinking were implicated directly with the status arrangements of Vansburg since that many comments were elicited by the question: "Are there any different social classes of people in this town?" Responses to this question in terms of drinking styles were made in the vast majority of cases by localites (nineteen of twenty relevant responses), and these were usually gross characterizations of strata. For instance, a lower-lower localite husband answered the question in this manner: "I suppose lots like to go to beer parlors, bowling alleys, and places like that, and others don't." * One lower-middle localite distinguished "the night club class and the classical class"; another differentiated "the ones who hang around the taverns and the people who stay away from them."

Not all responses were this gross, however. An upper-lower localite discerned three status strata: "There's the middle class, the groups that frequent the taverns and things of that kind, then, the groups that attend the Country Club. We never felt we could afford that—don't care about golf."

A final example will show that some responses to this question were even more subtle. In the words of a lower-middle-stratum localite husband:

> There are those that drink beer in taverns and those that have their Scotch whiskey at home and those that don't drink. Then, there are those that believe they are no part of a social group, but yet are on speaking terms with the various groups.

These excerpts show, then, that the entire status configuration of a community may be apprehended by some residents in terms of drinking styles.

---

* Bowlers, of course, are very conscious of the frequent stereotyped disesteem their sport incurs. For example, a lower-middle-stratum couple, mentioning that their bowling team was their favorite organization, were working actively to maintain the dignity of the sport. The husband would not permit "so-called roughnecks and drunks" in his bowling league, for, in his view, "Bowling alleys are not a place where the lower element meets." His wife concurred: "We want to keep bowling a refined sport, and not let the lower element in."

Not only were status strata differentiated in terms of drinking but local and cosmopolitan styles which cut across strata were similarly distinguished. A localite furniture dealer distinguished his own "conservative" (or localite) circle from the "tin-horn millionaires" (the cosmopolite circle), and the drinking style of the latter circle entered into his assessment:

"You'll find that, generally speaking, the crowd we run with are conservative. I travel with the conservative crowd. We don't try to outdo each other. Associations have some effect on everything you do. Our crowd has money, but it doesn't show much. They are all business folks, but nobody can crap anybody. You can look 'em up in D and B. There is no object to fooling around. [*Interviewer: Do any people in town fool around that way?*] The "tin-horn millionaire" crowd: they are dressed to beat hell. They owe about three-quarters of the amount for their clothes. They have everything but the money. They aren't crapping anyone but themselves and some half-ass people. A lot of 'em have minor administrative jobs in the plants. You don't find many professional people in that group. That crowd spends a lot of time at the Buffalo Club. They hate to go to the Chamber of Commerce, but they do. They do more partying; we spend more time at home. They go to the dance halls and taverns. Their organizations are the Buffaloes, the Country Club, the Lions, and the Rotary; ours are Kiwanis (there's not much money there, but they're all swell), the Generals rather than the Buffaloes, because it's not a drinking crowd, and the Chamber of Commerce. It shows up in clothes and clubs. We go to the good shows and good places to eat. They go to burlesques. There is no clash between the two, but they are two different types. . . . There have to be a few lines drawn. You can't help it. It's just normal that you have to associate with people in your station."

There are, of course, many comments to be made on the above excerpt—the fact that "our crowd has money," but "there's not much money" in "our" organization, or the whole tenor of invidious comparison—but the reader can make his own interpretations. Our point is that the two predominant axes of status in Vansburg—status rank and localism-cosmopolitanism—were apprehended by some residents of the community in greater or lesser extent as manifested by drinking styles.

1. *Status placements, disrespect, and irrelevancies*

Although only a fifth of our respondents reconstructed the total status configuration of Vansburg by referring to drinking styles, almost three-fourths made comments about drinking that were status relevant in one way or another. Such statements were classified according to whether they consisted *predominantly* of status assignments that were not explicitly evaluative * or of negative status appraisals (disrespectful remarks). Status assignments consisted either of (*a*) the imputation of some named social circle or status stratum on the basis of observed drinking behavior, or of (*b*) inferences about drinking behavior on the basis of imputed membership in a social circle or status stratum. Examples of this kind of response to alcoholic drinking have already been provided by the cited comments of

---

* The term, "status assignment" is derived from Warner's notion of "Rating by Simple Assignment to a Class." See Warner, Meeker, and Eels (11, p. 80). It is recognized that all status comments are implicitly evaluative.

those who delineate the status configuration of the community in drinking terms. In a similar manner, an upper-lower-stratum localite woman agreed in relatively non-evaluative terms, that there were social classes in Vansburg: "Morally yes—there are such classes. There are some of them who spend money and live in a tavern. At least that's the way I look at it."

A lower-middle cosmopolitan housewife made a direct status inference from imputed drinking behavior, when she acknowledged that she did not wish to join the Leopards: "It's a different element—drinking—the educational level is not in our class."

Observing a drawing depicting a man in a work shirt with rolled-up sleeves, an upper-middle cosmopolitan man commented: "He's in the working class. By the looks, he'll probably go out and buy a bottle of whiskey or else a pint of gin."

A localite wife of an upper-middle stratum druggist mentioned drinking in an aside to the interviewer by referring to the way in which her local community status as a minister's daughter precluded her drinking socially and playing cards, even though her father had passed away many years before. Such comments as these implied a kind of one-to-one relationship between drinking and status. Drinking and status were conceived, in effect, as signals of one another.

Negative appraisals of drinking styles comprised the largest category of status-relevant responses, including more than two-fifths of the respondents making comments about alcoholic drinking. A few examples embrace the range of negative status appraisals:

The Falcons—that's a drunken brawl of a place. A lot of trash belong to the Falcons.

[*Observing a drawing of an older woman dressed in a sweater and skirt and wearing bobby-sox.*] Well, actually that could be a saloon or something that she just came out of, and he doesn't approve of, and he is giving her the look. . . . I mean she looks squelchy. She's dressed like somebody who would hang in a saloon.

The Black family is completely disintegrated. There's one surviving member. He's drunk most of the time.

Yes, there are social classes in this town. You have your club members that attend all their social functions. You have a type that's interested in church or educational affairs. And you have a type that just like to hang around home like me. [*Interviewer: Anything else?*] Well, the barflies, but that's not a class of people.

Note that the final comment amounts to total disqualification of those who adopt a particular drinking style from any claim to community status— "that's not a class of people."

Comments that had no relevance for social status were made by about a fourth of the respondents referring to drinking. We shall refer to them cursorily later, since they are not in the focal center of this report.

Although the frequencies of these categories are not significantly differentiated, some interesting directional trends were observed. They are detailed here because they find some corroboration in other researches on social status. Table 4 presents the social status distribution of respondents mentioning alcoholic drinking in the categories of status implication. With the exception of the upper stratum (where numbers are very small and sampling variation probably large), the table shows that the relative frequency of status assignments decreases with decreasing social status. So far as we know investigation of this phenomenon has not been reported in the literature, but the curvilinear association (again, excepting the upper stratum) between negative appraisals and social status, showing increasing frequencies of disrespect for drinking in the middle range, does provide some confirmation for Dollard's (1) earlier qualitative observations. Finally, the increase in the relative frequency of comments about drinking that seem to have no status relevance with the decreasing social status of the respondents would seem to support findings made elsewhere (2) to the effect that the status dimension of stratification has its lowest saliency among those classified in lower socio-economic strata by sociologists.

TABLE 4

Status Implications of Responses to Alcoholic Drinking by Frequency of the Status Stratum of Respondents

| Status Implications [a] | Social Strata | | | | | |
	Upper	Upper-Middle	Lower-Middle	Upper-Lower	Lower-Lower	Total
Status Assignments	2	9	8	9	4	32
Negative Appraisals	6	3	13	17	7	46
Irrelevant for Status	1	4	5	11	7	28
Total	9	16	26	37	18	106

[a] The distributions in this table appear to be inconsistent with the distributions in Table 1 for three reasons: (a) they include the responses of both men and women; (b) most status references have some "valence"; and (c) not all statements with "valence" are status relevant.

Localism-cosmopolitanism more sharply differentiates the distribution of respondents within these categories bearing on status relevance. Table 5 shows cosmopolites underrepresented among respondents whose comments have no seeming status relevance and among those responding to observations of drinking with negative appraisals. Cosmopolites tend, therefore, to be less obviously evaluative in their responses to drinking behavior than locals, although they respond more frequently in terms of its status implications. Since their responses are often in the nature of status assignments, drinking may be used by cosmopolitans as an index of membership in specified social circles or status strata. It may be seen as a distinctive expectation of prevailing social circles but not judged harshly or referred to other contexts of social relations by these people.

TABLE 5

Status Implications of Responses to Alcoholic Drinking by Frequency among Localites and Cosmopolites

	Localite-Cosmopolite Status		
Status Implications	Localite	Cosmopolite	Total
Status Assignments	19	13	32
Negative Appraisals	37	9	46
Irrelevant for Status	22	6	28
Total	78	28	106

$$\chi^2 = 4.775 \qquad .01 < P < .10$$

Probably because their response to drinking styles is less overtly evaluative, we find few invidious comparisons entered by cosmopolitans. One consequence may well be that they are denied the same reflected sense of self-esteem that typically accrues to those localities who disvalue the drinking of others. For instance, the negative appraisal of high status drinkers in Vansburg made by this lower-lower-stratum localite woman undoubtedly made her own local status more tolerable:

I've seen some of these people dress up. Oh, lovely! Then they go in and start to drink and, when they're out, their hair is a mess. There *is* a mess! Drink does a lot! [*Interviewer: What people did you have in mind?*] Mostly big names in the community.

Highly sensitized to matters of status, cosmopolites may, at the same time, be less able to take advantage of its comforts and reassurances.

2. Styles of drinking

Negative appraisals of drinking behavior were closely tied to its stylization. The status significance of drinking ordinarily extends beyond the fact that a particular kind of beverage is typically consumed by some given social circle, as the "highbrow" is said to be identified by his "perfectly adequate little red wine" (8, p. 101). It considers, instead, the way in which the beverage is consumed. The vast majority of disrespectful remarks about drinking was incurred by *expressive drinking*—that is, drinking accompanied by spontaneous affective behavior offensive to the norms of various community audiences (usually lower-middle-stratum localites). When drinking was accompanied by fighting or sexual promiscuity, localite tongues were set wagging. If respondents did not stylize drinking behavior by putting it in a context of related postures and gestures, fewer negative appraisals ensued. Finally, if drinking was construed as *impressive* in style, as it was by two respondents, i.e., if it was perceived as self-controlled in the interest of winning the esteem of others, no negative appraisals were elicited. The relationship between the stylization of drinking and the character of elicited appraisals is shown in Table 6.

TABLE 6

Stylization of Drinking and the Frequency of the Character of Appraising Responses

Appraisal Responses	Styles of Drinking			
	Impressive	Expressive	None	Total
Tolerant or favorable	2	4	7	13
Negative appraisal	—	41	13	54
Total	2	45	20	67

$$\chi^2 = 6.64 \text{ [a]} \qquad P < .01$$

[a] The first column is omitted from the computation of chi-square; therefore, the chi-square is for a fourfold table with one degree of freedom.

Primarily, then, the expressive stylization of alcoholic drinking is what incurs the negative appraisals of others. In Vansburg, this style is also represented by particular locales. Some taverns, for example, represent expressive drinking, as this respondent's comments indicate: "I think water seeks its own level. The ones I don't want in my club are the kind you find down at Ken's Bar—fellows that get drunk and disorderly."

The most frequent symbolic settings for expressive drinking, however, are the private drinking clubs. The Country Club, newly won home of the cosmopolites, was looked upon by each of three respondents making reference to it as a scene of frequent expressive drinking, while a majority (fourteen of twenty-three) of respondents who mentioned the Falcons referred to it as such a setting. In this connection, it was previously shown in Tables 2 and 3 that upper-stratum cosmopolites held three of five cosmopolitan memberships in the Falcons, while upper-stratum localites held none. Thus, it may be that any given transient circle in a community may win a reputation for expressive drinking inadvertently by holding a membership in a national organization whose local chapter has come to represent that particular drinking style.* This could have a self-confirming consequence in some cases: cosmopolites come to town, resume earlier affiliations, take on the reputation of the local organization and act in terms of local expectations. It seems more likely, however, that expressive styles are emerging as the predominant styles for those who live in the consumer society at large. Thus, they replace the restrained impressive styles of local communities as mass media and rapid means of transportation extend the

* I am reminded of the new residents of Park Forest who often inherit the reputations of their predecessors. See Whyte (13, p. 384).

horizons of Americans beyond the bounds of town and province. In any event, all four approvals of expressive drinking in our sample were set forth by cosmopolitan respondents.

Other Styles of Drinking

Drinking may not always have implications for the consolidation or change of the drinker's status. There are other styles. Some of these may have ultimate consequences for the status of the drinker, since drinking together is a way of joining together, and joining together at a table or a bar ordinarily signifies the status parity of the drinkers. Yet, there may be other ramifications that extend beyond the realm of mere respectability. A cosmopolitan executive of a national corporation which had recently opened a packaging plant in Vansburg, for example, implied that problems other than status problems might arise, were he to join the Falcons or the Leopards:

> In my particular case—I have the largest plant in town, and my employees belong to those organizations—the minute I'd walk in there, there would be at least twenty-five bottles of beer on my table. There's no stopping it. You know what I mean. I'm the employer, and it would be a funny situation.

Probably the problems posed by drinking with his employees include those of administering authority. The intimacy of commensal drinking in the lodge would undoubtedly disturb the execution of authority in the plant.

This point is made more obvious in the statement of a county judge. This judge must maintain impartiality in his administration of legal decisions, and membership in the private drinking clubs of Vansburg could seriously undermine the requisite judicial stance of aloofness:

> There are no clubs I want to belong to now. I used to belong to Kiwanis. I used to belong to the Veterans. When they put the bar in, I got out. I was invited to join the *Gute Freunden* club. It's social. I didn't think I'd like to join. I don't want to be influenced because I belong to a certain group. They say so-and-so won't do anything to such-and-such, because they belong to the same club. This way no one can pull strings on me. I thought it would be a financial burden, and time. Sometimes you have to choose between family and club.

Or, drinking may be looked upon as a starting point on the road to general personal immorality. Once drinking is taken up, so to speak, psychological barriers to immoral behavior are let down. A lower-middle-stratum local housewife presented this point of view:

> You see young and older ones who drink a lot. They don't go with the religious classes. There are bars at the Country Club, Buffaloes, and Leopards. I don't believe in bars. When liquor goes in, sense goes out.

In this vein, drinking may suggest an incipient seduction to be resisted by all "nice girls," as it did to this upper-stratum localite woman, responding to a drawing depicting a group of adolescents standing in front of a building:

And one of the girls looks much overdressed, and it looks as though a boy had come up, or a young man had come up and made some remark to her that she didn't care for, and she looks at him very scornfully. . . . I think he might have said, "Hiya, Babe. How about coming over and having a drink or something?" . . . Well, she looks as though she were not going to do it.

In response to the same drawing, an upper-stratum cosmopolitan woman infers that the edge of drinking is the edge of violence and general disorder:

Well, I think—it looks to me that it's outside of a bar, or outside the back of a building where they've all been—it's very evident that this gentleman wants the girl to do something or go somewhere she doesn't want to go, or she's angry about something, maybe because he made her come out at the time. This girl is very interested, because she has not been there long. She's not associated with those kind of people very long, and her expression is almost one of wonder. Her escort is staying back. He's been there, but he doesn't want to get mixed into anything like a street brawl or fight.

An upper-lower-stratum localite housewife linked drinking to the deterioration of family life in her response to a drawing showing three people in a large luxuriously furnished living room:

Well, that lady there looks like she was on the witness stand, don't she? Maybe she's getting a divorce from that man sitting on the seat. Anyway, he looks like he's kind of a bum. Maybe he doesn't support her very good. . . . Looks like he may be drunk, and drinking leads to a lot of divorce and trouble.

In each of these excerpts linking drinking with the deterioration of personal life and social relations, there is of course a status implication, since morality is so closely linked with respect.

Drinking may also be stylized as a "removal activity,"—a way of obliterating the oppressive experiences and "realities" of the daily life (5, p. 464). This appears in the response of a lower-lower-stratum localite to one of the modified *TAT* drawings: "Well, it looks like the old lady told him off or something, and he's going to the beer garden or somewhere like that. . . . Looks like a beer garden to me." By facilitating reverie, drinking may facilitate such "removals." An upper-stratum localite woman interprets the same drawing in this way:

Well, she looks like she might go in for a glass of beer. . . . Well, she—it's because there's such a desire to be young, and I don't think that she could fool herself about being young, unless she had some liquor.

The fact that drinking may "remove" the drinker from cares and oppressions of everyday life may have the consequence of absolving drinkers from responsibility for violations of social conventions. Metaphorically, the drinking violator isn't "there." This possibility was suggested in other responses to the modified *TAT* drawings:

That fellow in the center looks like he might be a bartender. He's got a pretty good stomach on him, ain't he? . . . Baldheaded, and he looks like he was a bartender. . . . It's a woman. . . . Oh, probably they got in a row in a beer garden, and this fellow's got after his wife, and he's mad about it. He's kind of taking hold of his arm. He's got his arm on the lady, though—the fat fellow. I expect he's trying to get her. He's probably after that man's wife. . . . Yes, the man on the left's her husband. . . . The fellow in the center—he's trying to get her. . . . Well, when he comes out of his drunk, he won't remember it. Probably then it will be all settled up.

In response to the same drawing, an upper-lower-class localite suggests the same function of drinking:

That could be a neighbor's, and that guy in the middle has come home drunk and threw a tin can over the other side of the fence on these other people's property, and they've evidently come over after him, and he's trying to tell them that it won't happen again, and have them go on home, and he'll promise that he won't do that any more, or anything like that, and they won't hold it against him.

Closely related to drinking as a removal activity is its use as a means of "cooling out" a disgruntled other (3). Drinking may be employed to remove the disgruntled other from the disturbing situation, enabling him to recoup his perspective and self control. Again, *TAT* responses provide instances of this stylization of alcoholic drinking:

Like I say, it could end up in a fist fight. . . . It could end up in going out and having a few beers. [*Interviewer: What do you think the outcome might be, though?*] Let's let 'em have a couple beers, huh?

An upper-lower-stratum cosmopolite provided another pertinent example in his response to a *TAT* drawing:

Two girls—very unhappy. . . . Well, I think they should have a hair-pulling contest, and I'll take the one on the right against the one on the left. [*Interviewer: What do you think will finally happen there?*] They'll go down the street arm in arm, like two good looking girls should. Probably head right for the saloon —I mean, the soda bar.

All male informants were presented with a story in which a foreman, promoted to division head, had failed to change his dress, and, as a result, was shunned by those with whom he had been promoted. An upper-lower-stratum localite commented on the story in this way:

In that particular case, if I was acquainted with him, I'd have taken him aside and had a drink with him. I'd have said, "Look here, John, you've gotta wear different clothes." I'd have allayed his fears that, if he dressed up, the other foreman would have thought he was stuck up.

Thus, drinking may serve as a way of smoothing over ruffled feelings by promoting an atmosphere of easy conviviality in which disturbing events may be discussed.

These various modes of drinking—drinking as a way of developing social ties and obligations, as an enticement into immoral activity and social disorder, as a removal activity, and as a "cooling out" mechanism—do not, of course, exhaust the ways in which alcoholic drinking is stylized in Vansburg. However, their presentation does indicate that status is variously linked up with drinking styles and that status may not always be at stake when alcoholic beverages are consumed. Yet the status implications of drinking, as revealed by this secondary analysis, were the overriding implications. As such, they may assist the student of drinking behavior better to understand the phenomenon in American society.

Some Implications

There is no way to assess the validity or reliability of a secondary analysis such as this. One might argue that, because the remarks we have analyzed were spontaneous, they were, in consequence, more revealing of "reality" than self-conscious attitudes toward drinking prompted by direct interrogation. Yet it might also be contended that the recording of such spontaneous remarks by the several interviewers who worked on the project would be extremely biased by the interviewers' own conceptions of alcoholic drinking, since they would mediate the informant's willingness to disclose his views and since such asides might easily be interpreted as irrelevant for the larger research. In any event, the issue is moot. Here we wish merely to draw out a few implications of our analysis, taken at face value.

One such implication concerns the treatment and recovery of alcoholics. It seems generally agreed that the most successful therapeutic program for the treatment of alcoholism has been formulated and established by Alcoholics Anonymous. Casual observation of the membership of this group suggests that most members would be classified, prior to their alcoholism, as lower-middle or upper-lower status. Here are the strata which presumably have the greatest "stake" in their social status. They have the most to lose. Our hunch is that those who have arrested their alcoholism through association with Alcoholics Anonymous are those who have fallen from these strata because of the disesteem their alcoholism incurred from their peers. Alcoholics Anonymous has provided a new social circle for such people within which they can recoup a sense of dignity, identity, and responsibility denied them by the circles and strata from which they have fallen.

Our data lead us to suggest, however, that the loss of dignity precipitated by disesteemed drinking behavior may be felt more acutely by the localite— the one whose life space is bounded by his community of residence. He is more dependent upon the appraisals of those around him for his status in life than is, for example, the cosmopolite, who may leave the community for some other residence at any moment, dependent upon the whim of "the organization." It is the localite, then, who may be more susceptible to the therapeutic program of Alcoholics Anonymous, since the rewards of the program are so meaningful to him. As cosmopolitanism pervades every corner of the society, might it not mean that Alcoholics Anonymous will meet with less enduring success in its treatment of alcoholism?

More broadly, if there is validity to the observations in this chapter, we would conclude that the most salient feature of alcoholic drinking in

American society is presented by the way in which that drinking bears on the social status of the drinker. We also suspect that the proliferation of cosmopolitan styles will result in an even greater extension of expressive drinking in the society, involving both more men and more women. Finally, the characteristically non-evaluative way in which cosmopolitans look upon alcoholic drinking poses some larger problems for the therapeutic treatment of the alcoholic.

References

1. Dollard, John, "Drinking Mores of the Social Classes," in *Alcohol, Science and Society*, New Haven, Conn.: Journal of Studies on Alcohol, 1945.

2. Form, William H., and Gregory P. Stone, "Urbanism, Anonymity, and Status Symbolism," *Amer. J. Sociol.*, **62**:507, 1957.

3. Goffman, Erving, "On Cooling the Mark Out: Some Aspects of Adaptation to Failure," *Psychiatry*, **15**:451–463, 1952.

4. ———, *The Presentation of Self in Everyday Life*, Edinburgh: Social Sciences Research Centre, 1956.

5. ———, "Total Institutions," *in* Maurice Stein, Arthur Vidich, and David White (Eds.), *Identity and Anxiety*, Glencoe, Ill.: Free Press, 1960.

6. Gouldner, Alvin, "Cosmopolitans and Locals: Toward an Analysis of Latent Social Roles," *Admin. Sci. Quart.*, **2**:281–306; 444–480, 1957–1958.

7. Gray, Corrine, *Orientations to Fashion*, unpublished master's thesis, Michigan State University, 1953.

8. Lynes, Russell, "Highbrow, Lowbrow, Middlebrow," in *Harper's Magazine Reader*, New York: Bantam Books, 1953.

9. Stone, Gregory P., "Some Meanings of American Sport," *College Physical Education Association—60th Annual Proceedings*, Columbus, Ohio, 1957, pp. 25, 27.

10. Stone, Gregory P., and William H. Form, "Instabilities in Status: The Problem of Hierarchy in the Community Study of Status Arrangements," *Amer. Sociol. Rev.*, **18**: 149–162, 1953.

11. Warner, W. Lloyd, Marchia Meeker, and Kenneth Eels, *Social Class in America*, Chicago: Science Research Associates, 1949.

12. Weber, Max, "Class, Status, Party," *in* Hans H. Gerth and C. Wright Mills (Eds.), *From Max Weber: Essays in Sociology*, New York: Oxford University Press, 1946, pp. 180–195.

13. Whyte, William H., *The Organization Man*, Garden City, N.Y.: Doubleday Anchor Books, 1957.

chapter 8

Drinking and socio-economic status [*]

Joseph J. Lawrence and Milton A. Maxwell

In connection with a recent poll of drinking behavior in the State of Washington, the senior author undertook a study of attitudes and behavior by socio-economic status (3) which provides the basis for this report. Four status categories were developed. The respondents were scaled according to the Guttman technique, using the three variables of occupation, education, and family income. In the scaling process, each of these variables was dichotomized. Occupations were divided into manual and non-manual; the educational achievement was divided at the point of having or not having completed 12 years of formal schooling; and family income was dichotomized at the point of receiving $3,000 or more per year.[†] The resulting scale yielded a coefficient of reproducibility of .934, indicating an acceptable scale. The distribution of respondents in the four socio-economic status categories resulting from the scale analysis is presented in Table 1.

Before reporting the findings on drinking patterns, the question of the comparability of these four status categories with other, more familiar

[*] This chapter was written especially for this book. The poll on which this study was based was conducted by the Washington State University division of the Washington Public Opinion Laboratory. Selected findings emerging from this "alcohol poll" have been previously reported by Haer (2) and Maxwell (4, 5).

[†] The dichotomizing of the respondents on each scale item yielded the following percentages: 36 per cent were non-manual; 51 per cent had completed 12 years or more of school; 69 per cent reported family incomes of $3,000 or more per year. It should be added that 65 of the original sample of 478 were dropped from consideration; 56 because they were retired and had not indicated their former occupations; 8 because they failed to respond to two of the three scale items; and 1 other who apparently was an alcoholic.

TABLE 1

Socio-Economic Status Categories

Status Level	Number of Respondents	Per Cent of Respondents
I	116	28.1
II	108	26.1
III	120	29.1
IV	69	16.7
Total	413	100.0

characterizations of class levels merits consideration. In his observations on the drinking mores of the social classes (excerpted in the introductory note), Dollard (1) made use of the six-fold class division developed by Warner and his colleagues. Moreover, he estimated the proportion of the populace in each class on the basis of the findings obtained in Warner and Lunt's Yankee City study (7). It would be ideal if the four status categories of the Washington State study matched four of Dollard's six class levels, or some combination thereof, but this cannot be assumed to be the case.

In the first place, no Warner type of analysis has been made in any Washington community. Furthermore, such an analysis would be impossible to carry out for the population of an entire state. So, we do not know what proportion of the Washington population would be found in each of the six class levels, nor can we assume that our four status categories reflect the same criteria for status placement used by Warner and Dollard. Even assuming the strata used by Dollard and those in this study are comparable, only status IV would have perfect correspondence with one of Dollard's classes—status IV would be 100 per cent lower-lower class. Correspondence would decrease rapidly in status III (72 per cent upper-lower) and status II (54 per cent lower-middle). Status I would be 50 per cent lower-middle, the residual half falling into the upper-middle and the two upper classes. These considerations suggest that only cautious comparisons can be made with the Dollard material, and then only at the lowest status levels.

Findings

The percentages of drinkers and abstainers in each status level are presented in Table 2. About three-fourths of the men in each of the four status levels drank beverage alcohol with no significant status differences in the per cent of drinkers and abstainers. In the case of the women, on the other hand, a very significant difference was found. Only about a fifth of the women in status IV drank at all, whereas 60 per cent or more of the women in the other three status levels drank. Although the data are not presented here, there was also a lack of significant difference for both male and female *drinkers* in terms of status level with regard to their quantity and frequency of drinking as measured by the Straus-Bacon Quantity-Frequency Index (6).

TABLE 2

Drinking Behavior by Sex and Status

	Men			Women [a]		
Status Level	N	Drank: Per Cent	Abstained: Per Cent	N	Drank: Per Cent	Abstained: Per Cent
I	47	74.5	25.5	66	63.6	36.4
II	51	76.5	23.5	56	67.9	32.1
III	62	83.9	16.1	57	59.6	40.4
IV	40	77.5	22.5	29	20.7	79.3

[a] $\chi^2 = 19.70, P < .001$.

Even though no secure comparisons can be made, these findings do have a bearing on Dollard's observations. He implied that the smallest percentage of drinkers would be found in the lower-middle class and that this would be true of both men and women. For the class below (upper-lower), Dollard indicated that there is much more drinking, and that in the lower-lower class socially unrestrained drinking for both males and females occurs. The present study, on the other hand, reveals no status level differences among men with regard to drinking and abstaining, or with regard to quantity and frequency of drinking. The significant differences found among women run counter to Dollard's descriptions. Actually the lowest percentage of women who drink (21 per cent) is found in the bottom status level, the proportion being substantially below the 60–68 per cent drinkers among women in the three upper status levels.

Findings on the extent of approval of moderate social drinking according to sex and status are presented in Table 3. The least approval was found in status IV; this was true of both men and women, although the status difference in attitude is significant only in the case of women. Only 34 per cent of the status-IV women expressed approval as compared to 61 to 72 per cent of the women in the three higher categories. This finding is counter to Dollard's observation that there is greater approval of drinking at the bottom of the scale.

The study also investigated tolerance toward drunkenness in men and women by the status level of the respondent. Tolerance toward drunkenness was defined to include attitudes of indifference, amusement, pity, and desire to help, while intolerance included attitudes of disgust, scorn, fear, and loss of respect. Both sexes at all status levels reported more intolerance toward

TABLE 3

Approval of Moderate Social Drinking by Sex and Status

	Men			Women [a]		
Status Level	N	Approve: Per Cent	Disapprove: Per Cent	N	Approve: Per Cent	Disapprove: Per Cent
I	46	76.1	23.9	64	60.9	39.1
II	51	82.4	17.6	54	68.5	31.5
III	59	67.8	32.2	55	70.9	29.1
IV	36	61.1	38.9	29	34.5	65.5

[a] $\chi^2 = 12.16, P < .01$.

drunkenness in women than in men. Furthermore, intolerance toward drunkenness in women was about equally high at all status levels.

Even though both sexes exhibited more tolerance of drunkenness in men, the majority reflected intolerance. There were, however, status differences. Intolerance was lowest in status I, highest in statuses II and III. Attitudes in status IV fell in between. These data provide limited support for Dollard's finding of greater tolerance of drunkenness in men at the top and the bottom of the scale; but the relatively low degree of tolerance at the bottom is inconsistent with Dollard's description.

Related drinking behaviors such as time and place of usual drinking and most used beverage were studied. Evening, defined as beginning at 6:00 P.M., was the usual time of drinking for all status levels, regardless of sex, and this pattern was most evident in status I. Drinking at all other times increased progressively with each status level in descending order, but the trend was not statistically significant.

Place of usual drinking was found to be predominantly the home, defined to include the homes of friends as well as one's own home. Two-thirds or more of the men and 77 per cent or more of the women usually drank in homes. No significant status differences were found.

Among men at all status levels, beer was the most used beverage, with a trend toward increased consumption of beer in descending status order (from 51 per cent in status I to 76 per cent in status IV). Women in statuses I and II more often used spirits (60 and 64 per cent) while there was almost equal use of spirits and beer in statuses III and IV. This reflects greater use of beer at lower-status levels, but there are not statistical differences in usage of beer and spirits by status levels.*

* Wine was not included in the analysis because no men and only 5 per cent of the women reported it as the most-used beverage.

Discussion

The comparability of this study with Dollard's oft-cited lecture on the drinking mores of the social classes is very limited indeed. No direct comparisons are possible at all at the upper-middle- and upper-class levels. Only at the bottom of the scale is a cautious comparison permissible. At that level, however, status IV presents a picture which is not congruent with Dollard's description of considerable and socially unrestrained drinking on the part of both men and women. This is not to claim that Dollard's observations at the lower-class levels were inaccurate with regard to the communities studied, but the present study does provide a caution against generalizing Dollard's description of lower-class drinking behavior. The impression that there is more drinking and more unrestrained drinking at the bottom of the social scale is, of course, held by others. The present writers have frequently encountered this view, which is a part of the stereotype of the lower class. It may well be that the lower-lower-class drinking pattern which Dollard described does exist among some members of this class in the State of Washington as well as in the communities to which Dollard referred. The present study suggests, however, that this kind of conspicuous behavior may not be the pattern of the majority in this class, especially of the women.

References

1. Dollard, John, "Drinking Mores of the Social Classes," in *Alcohol, Science and Society*, New Haven, Conn.: Journal of Studies on Alcohol, 1945.
2. Haer, John L., "Drinking Patterns and the Influence of Friends and Family," *Quart. J. Stud. Alc.*, 16:178–185, 1955.
3. Lawrence, Joseph J., *Alcohol and Socio-economic Status in the State of Washington*, unpublished master's thesis, Washington State College, 1955.
4. Maxwell, Milton A., "Drinking Behavior in the State of Washington," *Quart. J. Stud. Alc.*, 13:219–239, 1952.
5. ———, "A Quantity-Frequency Analysis of Drinking Behavior in the State of Washington," *Northwest Science*, 32:57–67, 1958.
6. Straus, Robert, and Selden D. Bacon, *Drinking in College*, New Haven: Yale University Press, 1953.
7. Warner, W. Lloyd, and Paul S. Lunt, *The Social Life of a Modern Community*, New Haven, Conn.: Yale University Press, 1949.

chapter 9

"Failure" as a heavy drinker: the case of the chronic-drunkenness offender on Skid Row *

Earl Rubington

Skid-Row Existence

Alienation from major value-patterns is one price a complex society must pay for ineffective socialization. Those alienated from basic cultural traditions fend for themselves in one way or another. A certain proportion of the alienated find it convenient to fend together, and they do so by banding together and expressing their alienation as part of a pattern of organized behavior. Denied status in respectable society, they develop or seek out a social organization in which a role more suitable to their own needs is possible. Skid Row, traditional haven for certain types of exiles, affords roles for several types of unattached adult males. If the needs of some deviants include *heavy* drinking, Skid Row, with its broad tolerance of deviant behavior, can likewise accommodate them. All sociological aliens do not make their way into Skid-Row subculture (3). Unless they establish some connections with people who can provide group support for the expression of their alienation, they are not likely to identify themselves with Skid-Row subculture.

Failure to account for the absence of some alienated individuals on Skid Row casts doubt on the individualistic literature on unattached heavy drinkers. The bulk of this literature stresses undersocialization, broken homes, low educational attainment, low occupational rank, high residential mobility,

* This chapter, written especially for this book, is a revision and extension of an earlier article (10). In addition, it includes new material based on the writer's field work in New Haven and a number of new sources on Skid Row which have come to his attention since publication of the earlier version (3, 4, 5, 7, 8, 9).

146

mental illness, psychopathic personalities, and physical defects as factors which cause persons to take up Skid-Row social life (11). Nevertheless, many other people with similar characteristics fail to select the Skid-Row alternative. If people with similar characteristics do not select the Skid-Row alternative, then theories which assign causality to these attributes are insufficient. The literature stressing individual attributes as the major determinants of behavior assumes that all people with these attributes will withdraw ultimately from society and become completely dependent upon alcohol.

In this view, the final stage of withdrawal from society takes place when the social isolate is alone on Skid Row with his bottle as a substitute for people. Since these attributes are necessary but not sufficient conditions of alienation, explanation for Skid-Row recruitment lies elsewhere. The position taken here is that these attributes are indices of disrupted social relationships. Where attribute theorists argue that absence of rewarding social relationships necessarily leads to further withdrawal and ultimate dependence on alcohol, the contention here is that absence of rewarding social relationships creates the search for a primary group. Ultimate dependence on alcohol is a possible consequence of this search, but it is neither the most likely nor the only consequence.

Under certain conditions, establishment of new primary group ties may result in abstinence, moderate drinking, or even alcoholism. It may also result in a host of entirely different patterns of behavior. Under certain other conditions, new primary group ties cause habituation to alcohol. For incipient offenders, dependence upon an alienated primary group sets in motion habituation to alcohol. Habituation, for chronic drunkenness offenders, is more likely to be the result of a new system of social relationships rather than the effect of no relationships at all.

Establishment of new primary group ties following a disruption of previous social ties would seem to be, then, the most satisfactory hypothesis to account for selection of subcultural alternatives (6). Given two individuals subjected to similar stress and strain in their social relationships, one avoids the Skid-Row alternative because a different system of interpersonal relations binds the prospective deviant to major value patterns. This suggests that the next primary group into which the person enters consequent to major stress determines subsequent conformity to dominant social norms. High rates of informal social participation of juvenile delinquents (2) and incipient alcoholics in their teens (12) lend strong support to this hypothesis.

Skid-Row Functions

An achievement-oriented society which gives status for effort requires negative reference groups to maintain striving. These groups are composed of "failures" and "social misfits" who collect in the "blighted areas" of many American cities. Residence in these areas, according to conventional imagery, is the result of inability to comply with the ethics of individual responsibility. Residence there symbolizes rejection of dominant emphases on upward social mobility. Upward social mobility requires downward social mobility as a condition of further status striving of some, validation of present status for others. Skid Row, an area in which recruits have descended from earlier statuses, provides strong support for out-group achievement norms.

For the Skid-Row in-group, functions are somewhat similar. Association with people who have undergone similar experiences compensates for alienation. Knowledge that one is no longer alone breaks the status fall. Social support, which the respectable world withdraws, comes from one's associates on Skid Row with less effort. Existence within the Skid-Row community of internal negative reference groups makes it possible for some even to deny the facts of status fall.

Recruitment Patterns

Selective drift accounts for replenishment of Skid-Row populations. Skid Row, not self-perpetuating as most societies, depends upon migration. Periodic migration of the several types of sociological aliens guarantees stability and continuity of Skid-Row subculture beyond the life cycle of any of its current members. Uprooted and alienated from the American value system and the social structure which supports and distributes those values, some unattached individuals find their way into the subculture once they have "hit the skids."

Despite popular stereotypes, the several social strata which make up American society do not contribute their equal share of Skid-Row recruits. These strata differ in the access they offer the alienated for orientation and induction into Skid-Row subculture. Because of these differences, Skid-Row homeless emerge mainly from the lower and lower-middle classes. These strata appear to be more vulnerable to physical and mental illness, economic insecurity, broken homes, and cultural inconsistencies. These are some of the social conditions which precipitate alienation. Under appropriate conditions, a certain number of the alienated become oriented towards and later inducted into Skid-Row life. The social strata from which recruits have been alienated shape orientation and induction into Skid-Row subculture. These differences bear heavily on the ways men participate once they have been introduced to it.

Skid-Row Drinking Groups

After recruitment, induction into Skid-Row subculture takes place. Once there, men classify themselves by whether or not they use alcohol. Among heavy drinkers, further sorting occurs leading to a pattern of differential association. Differential association makes for social organization, complete with "drinking culture" and types of heavy drinkers. The subculture sets drinking norms, and the organization distributes men by their conformity with these norms.

The drinking subculture defines moral rules of heavy drinking, and the social organization establishes modes of enforcement. Enforcement is necessary if heavy drinkers are to defend themselves against stigma and social punishment which attend heavy drinking, both on and off Skid Row. Containment of drinking deviance is the problem which the drinking subculture and social organization attempts to solve. Interaction between subculture and social organization creates a rank order of heavy drinkers. Ranking is in accordance with degree of containment of deviance. Drinking groups distinguish from each other by the type of personal and social controls they exercise. These distinctions create negative reference groups within the organization of heavy drinkers. Members of these groups are failures in containing deviance. Their failure, resulting from widespread deviance from moral rules of heavy drinking, makes them models to avoid.

Being able to point to some heavy drinkers who are "in worse shape" than oneself, to others whose deviance has become diffuse rather than specific in nature, cushions the status fall. All "drunks" consider themselves as "marks," suitable objects for indignities, punishments, and exploitation, both on and off Skid Row. To find others lower on the escalator of social mobility mitigates one's own punishment. Drinking culture is "easy" (1), and it sets standards of negative achievement. Those who suffer least rank higher.

The Rank Order of Heavy Drinkers

Ability to command a sufficient supply of alcohol and trusted drinking companions without working constitutes highest rank among social drinkers on Skid Row. Access to both a sufficient supply and safe drinking places guarantees high rank among solitary drinkers. High-ranking social drinkers are less visible to others, hence less exposed to social punishment. Better organized and with more means, they take precautions to ensure maximum reward from drinking with minimum punishment. They frequent the best Skid-Row bars, occupy more expensive rooms in hotels and rooming houses, observe more elaborate drinking ritual, and maintain more control over drinking occasions and partners. Both they and similarly situated solitary drinkers maintain anonymity on and off Skid Row and are "better" candidates for a return to respectability when they complete their drinking cycles.

Inability to procure a sufficient supply of alcohol and to choose one's drinking companions defines the lowest ranks of social drinkers. The social drinkers appear most often on the street, frequently as panhandlers, and are the most visible. Their counterparts are derelicts who drink non-beverage alcohol in solitude while deviating from minimal pedestrian decorum. These two groups, within the lowest rank, contribute the largest share of chronic-drunkenness offenders, far out of proportion to their numbers.

Panhandlers consort in the fleeting "bottle gang" relationship. Most gangs are short-lived, existing only as long as it takes to empty the bottle; others endure for longer periods. Even here, though, social organization exists, however minimal. Conditions of entry are fairly relaxed, but an etiquette of sharing, procuring, and drinking from the bottle governs "bottle gang" conduct. Reduced circumstances bring members together; they drink furtively in groups on the street. Their low standards of dress, personal cleanliness, and manners together with the fact that they so often "gang up" make them highly visible. They are excluded from most bars and all but the most miserable housing accommodations such as flophouse dormitories and missions. Their ability to contain deviance resulting from drinking, as well as in other areas, is minimal, though they make some attempt to avoid social punishment. The only control they appear to submit to is enforced sharing of inexpensive wine; it is this minimal degree of control which paradoxically exposes them to the highest degree of social punishment.

In between these two outermost ranks are regular workers who are either social or solitary drinkers, then casual laborers who drink in groups or privately. Regular workers, whether social or solitary drinkers, occupy rooms in inexpensive hotels or middle-range rooming houses. Both have their favorite bars and drinking companions; degree of control on drinking deviance is somewhat less than among the highest-ranking drinkers. This is because social drinkers among regular workers do not exclude others so rigorously. They feel less shameful about heavy drinking than do higher-ranked drinkers, hence, take less pains to conceal it. They have a wider range of drinking acquaintances, set barroom norms on drinking behavior, and frequently stand drinks for everyone in the house. Since they work regularly despite heavy drinking, they can maintain the fiction that drinking does not interfere with their work. Because they get up the next morning and go to work, they are held in high esteem by men in the lower ranks.

Men in the rank beneath regular workers finance drinking episodes by casual labor. So long as they cling to the norm of productive labor, they remain out of the ranks of derelicts and panhandlers whom they despise. They seek to establish friendship with regular workers as another means of obtaining alcohol. Although there are more social than solitary drinkers at this level of social organization, their style of life outside of drinking is about the same. They occupy the cheapest of rooms in flophouses, the cubicles, occasionally sleeping in flophouse dormitories when funds are low. Though they prefer whisky, they are forced very often to resort to drinking cheap, fortified wine; this sets them apart from the regular workers who look with disfavor on wine drinkers.

Social drinkers among casual laborers are less concerned about concealing heavy drinking, more concerned about avoiding social punishment. Though less ashamed of heavy drinking particularly when in a group, they make attempts to contain deviance to drinking and protect each other from punishment. Their measures for protection arise, however, from more experience with punishment than regular workers. Casual laborers who migrate a great deal are best informed in the facts of punishment. Despising "bums" the most because of the closeness of their own status with that of "bums," they report on the failure of "bums" to observe any standards. Casual laborers know best that social punishment does not come only from the police; in their own view, the lower one drops in the ranks, the greater the exposure to punishment and exploitation from within the ranks as the focus on drinking increases. While they contribute a fair share of chronic-drunkenness offenders, they attempt to minimize their contacts with the county jail. Many of them, after their first arrest, leave town and migrate to another Skid Row in the hope of protecting their anonymity from the police. Solitary drinkers in this category are more often solitary by necessity rather than by choice; others shun them because they become "performers" once intoxicated. The "performers" in the casual laborer-solitary drinking category, known as "jail bait," are more apt to become chronic-drunkenness offenders.

Because of the effects of heavy drinking on behavior, movement takes place within the organization of drinkers. Movement is generally of two kinds; either the heavy drinker departs from Skid Row entirely or he descends the escalator of mobility. Descent is contingent upon violation of moral rules on heavy drinking which each rank seeks to uphold. Under conditions of reward for drinking deviance, the ranks remain apart. Under conditions of social punishment, cross-rank contact takes place.

Though the drinking subculture sets restraints on social organization, heavy drinking induces tensions between the subculture and social organization. When supplies diminish, drinkers cross ranks, usually in a downward direction. Patterns of mutual aid exist within each rank; the lower the rank, the greater the number of people one is required to help out. Reciprocally, the greater movement in ranks, because of the contingencies of heavy drinking, constantly shifts relations from contract to status. One aspect of rank differences is that at higher levels men can dominate drinking situations by playing the role of the "givers." Conspicuous waste in the form of sharing one's good fortune, usually buying drinks for others less fortunate, marks one as an important person. At lower levels, "takers" predominate, particularly under conditions of cross-rank contact. Through these contacts in which givers dominate takers, acculturation takes place. Each rank learns something of the attitudes and behavior of the other. In these symbiotic relations, lower-ranked men aspire to move up into the next rank; higher-ranked men gain the respect of others, which helps them momentarily, at least, to deny the social facts of downward mobility.

Jail makes possible considerable cross-rank contact. Boundaries between ranks are relaxed considerably during incarceration. Exposure to common social punishment heightens awareness of the inordinate interest all share in heavy drinking regardless of outside rank. These contacts revitalize "drinking subculture." One consequence is a special case of anticipatory socialization in which higher-ranked men take on attitudes and behavior of lower-ranked men unwittingly. Through these contacts, motivation to some men, frequent jail contacts foster the self-image of the irreversible alcoholic; for others, jail contacts offer recuperation and time to plan the next drinking episode.

Arrest for public intoxication constitutes a failure to conceal drinking deviance adequately. Arising out of differential exposure to social punishment which defines the ranks, it has two major consequences. Offenders become marked men to the police and other agents of social punishment; perhaps, more important, they become marked for each other. Failure to contain deviance establishes an identity which affects social organization "on the outside." After discharge, each offender is not too surprised to find that his circle of acquaintances has increased. He knows more heavy drinkers, more heavy drinkers know him. Once identity becomes public because of arrest, veritable strangers approach each other either to ask for help or to suggest a common search for a bottle.

Heavy drinkers strive desperately to maintain differences in rank, denial of social failure being the main problem which Skid-Row subculture attempts to solve, if only on ideological grounds. Failure to avoid social punishments, however, causes a downward reshuffling of groups. Sober periods realign the ranks; once drinking resumes, those who lose control over their drinking pattern are expelled. Inability to maintain a supply of alcohol or exercise choice over drinking companions parallels a failure to comply with the moral rules of different drinking groups. At this point reliance upon other heavy drinkers similarly "marked" by exposure to social punishment increases. When men become almost as dependent upon peers as they are on alcohol, exposure to social punishment is at its greatest. Then conformity to drinking norms at least insulates them from punishment. These men constitute the hard core of chronic-drunkenness offenders, the most difficult to resocialize.

Summary

Men come to Skid Row by several routes. Some come to drink heavily and to avoid punishment. Others come by different routes but then become heavy drinkers through group pressure. Both kinds of men are able to gain some anonymity and engage in what respectable society calls uncontrolled drinking. Despite Skid-Row tolerance of deviant behavior, especially heavy drinking, social organization exists. Holding a license for petty deviation from respectable society, Skid-Row subcultures work to contain deviance within bounds and to keep social punishment down.

Complete avoidance of social punishment, however, is impossible among Skid-Row heavy drinkers. Hence, rank among these drinkers is apportioned by degree of avoidance, and failure to comply with moral rules on drinking makes for punishment. Although chronic-drunkenness offenders are drawn from all ranks, the number of offenders varies inversely with rank. Since the organization centers on heavy drinking, the emphasis on drinking controls is always being weakened. The result is a system always percolating in a downwardly mobile direction, always precipitating out men who join the ranks of offenders as they descend.

References

1. Arsenian, John, and Jean M. Arsenian, "Tough and Easy Cultures: A Conceptual Analysis," *Psychiatry*, 11:337–386, 1948.

2. Atwood, Bartlett S., and E. H. Shideler, "Social Participation and Juvenile Delinquency," *Sociology and Social Research*, 18:436–444, 1934.

3. Bain, Howard George, *A Sociological Analysis of the Chicago Skid-Row Lifeway*, unpublished master's thesis, University of Chicago, 1950.

4. Bogue, Donald, *The Homeless Man on Skid Row*, NORC Report 65-1, Chicago: University of Chicago Press, 1958.

5. Caplow, Theodore, Keith A. Lovald, and Samuel E. Wallace, *A General Report on the Problem of Relocating the Population of the Lower Loop Redevelopment Area*, Minneapolis: Minneapolis Housing and Redevelopment Authority, 1958.

6. Cohen, Albert K., *Delinquent Boys: The Culture of the Gang*, Glencoe, Ill.: Free Press, 1955.

7. Day, Beth, *No Hiding Place*, New York: Holt, Rinehart and Winston, 1957.

8. Peterson, William Jack, *The Culture of the Skid Road Wino*, unpublished master's thesis, State College of Washington, 1955.

9. Pittman, David J., and C. Wayne Gordon, *Revolving Door: A Study of the Chronic Police Case Inebriate*, Glencoe, Ill.: Free Press, 1958.

10. Rubington, Earl, "The Chronic Drunkenness Offender," *The Annals*, 315:65–72, 1958.

11. Straus, Robert, "Alcohol and the Homeless Man," *Quart. J. Stud. Alc.*, 7:360–404, 1946.

12. Wahl, Charles W., "Some Antecedent Factors in the Family Histories of 109 Alcoholics," *Quart. J. Stud. Alc.*, 17:643–654, 1956.

B.

RELIGION AND ETHNICITY

Introductory Note. It is now firmly established that different ethnic groups within the United States exhibit strikingly different rates of drinking pathologies, ranging from simple inebriety to the extremes of alcoholism and the alcoholic psychoses. There is evidence also that, despite a common core of opposition to drunkenness, the varieties of religious groups and traditions with which ethnicity is so often intertwined are differentially effective in thwarting drinking pathologies. One cannot say for certain what the *absolute* rates of alcoholism or other drinking pathologies are for particular ethnic or religio-ethnic groups. It is firmly established, nevertheless, that the Irish and Scandinavians, to take two clear-cut examples, have contributed disproportionately to the total fund of drinking pathologies in this country, while the yield from certain other groups such as the southern Italians and the Jews has been far below chance expectations. Moreover, relative differences among such groups persist with surprising tenacity over the generations. Collectively, these facts lend a special significance to the study of ethnic- and religious-group drinking patterns in the context of a concern to understand alcoholism. More broadly, they offer a challenge to sociological inquiry analogous to the challenge offered by Durkheim in connection with varying group rates of suicide.

We can only present illustrations of the growing body of research on religious- and ethnic-group drinking patterns. Elsewhere in this book, particularly in Chapter 6 by Gusfield and in Chapter 13 by Straus and Bacon, indications may be found of the significance of religious values and memberships in shaping drinking behavior and attitude. By way of reference to the literature at large, we would particularly like to call the reader's attention to the provocative essay of Thorner (6) and the more empirical work of Skolnick (7) which examine the implications of the relatively ascetic forms of Protestantism for drinking attitudes, behavior, and pathology. Among ethnic group studies, the work of Barnett (3) on the Cantonese and of Lolli and his associates (5) on the southern Italians deserve special mention. Here, however, we have chosen to present excerpts from studies of two groups that exemplify virtually an ideal-typical contrast insofar as drinking patterns and pathologies are concerned, namely, the Irish and the Jews.

Among sociologists, Robert Bales deserves credit for first recognizing and exploring systematically the implications of the Irish-Jewish contrast in the effort to further the understanding of alcoholism and related pathologies.* The theoretical scheme for explaining group rates of alcoholism which emerged from Bales' work is outlined in Chapter 11 by Charles Snyder. Yet is should be emphasized that group rates of alcoholism are, in Bales' view, resultants of the interaction of three major sets of variables or factors, and that in accounting for the *difference* in rates of alcoholism between the Irish and the Jews—not the absolute rates—Bales underscored the one factor of the strikingly different normative orientations toward drinking which are embedded in the cultural traditions of these two groups.

Bales' original study (1) comprises a tightly knit, logical whole, and it is therefore with some hesitation that we present a mere part of it. To date, however, his ideas have gained currency largely through a very summary article (2) which hardly does them justice, while his original work has remained unpublished. Given his own emphasis upon normative orientations toward drinking, together with the virtual absence of comprehensive published materials on the subject, we have chosen to include that portion of Bales' original study which treats of the normative attitudes toward drinking prevalent historically among the country Irish and which were presumably formative of the attitudes of Irish immigrants to this country during the latter part of the last century.

If we are to see Bales' work on the Irish in proper perspective, certain further considerations must be brought to the fore. That alcoholism has been quite prevalent in Ireland is beyond question, and Bales' assumption of relatively high rates during the period with which he is concerned seems plausible. Yet there is a gap, bridged only by inference, between the more convincing postimmigration statistics indicating extraordinarily high rates of alcoholism among the Irish in America and the old country situation which Bales describes. The fact is that possible traumata of the immigration and postimmigration experience which might have accentuated drinking pathologies have still to be investigated sociologically—as, indeed, have drinking patterns and pathologies in contemporary Ireland. Here, then, are im-

---

* At about the same time that Bales was conducting his research, a suggestive comparative study of attitudes toward drinking among Catholic-Irish, Protestant, and Jewish adolescents was being made by psychologist Donald Glad (4). Further reference to Glad's study is made in Chapter 11 by Snyder.

portant leads for future sociological and social-historical research. Against the background of Bales' study, their systematic pursuit might provide a greater sense of closure concerning the socio-cultural conditions which maximize group rates of alcoholism.

The material presented by Charles Snyder in Chapter 11 represents part of a logical extension of Bales' earlier work. Since it carries with it its own brief introduction, no extended remarks need be made here. It bears mention, however, that Snyder's report aims to broaden the conception of the content, sources, and vitality of the Jewish normative attitudes toward drinking beyond the nexus of the ritual drinking stressed by Bales, though not to the exclusion of it. Despite an emphasis upon cultural content which is shared with Bales, there are perhaps hints of a structural nature in Snyder's study which may well permit of generalization to other groups. A fundamental question which must be raised in relation to all such studies is whether we can generalize about the structural conditions under which different normative orientations toward drinking emerge and become effective, or whether we must continue to talk largely in terms of specific cultural traditions. We hope that future research which seeks to clarify and generalize the structural contexts in which various types of normative attitudes toward drinking are lodged will supply answers to this question and forge stronger links between such studies as Field's on the range of variation in drunkenness among primitive societies and the general studies of the drinking patterns of ethnic and religious groups in our own society.

References

1. Bales, Robert F., The "Fixation Factor" in Alcohol Addiction: An Hypothesis Derived from a Comparative Study of Irish and Jewish Social Norms, unpublished doctoral dissertation, Harvard University, 1944.

2. ———, "Cultural Differences in Rates of Alcoholism," Quart. J. Stud. Alc., 6:480–499, 1946.

3. Barnett, Milton L., "Alcoholism in the Cantonese of New York City: An Anthropological Study," in O. Diethelm (Ed.), Etiology of Chronic Alcoholism, Springfield, Ill.: Charles C. Thomas, 1955.

4. Glad, Donald D., "Attitudes and Experiences of American-Jewish and American-Irish Male Youth as Related to Differences in Adult Rates of Inebriety," Quart. J. Stud. Alc., 8:406–472, 1947.

5. Lolli, Giorgio, Emidio Serianni, Grace M. Golder, and Pierpaolo Luzzatto-Fegiz, Alcohol in Italian Culture, Glencoe, Ill.: Free Press, 1958.

6. Thorner, Isidor, "Ascetic Protestantism and Alcoholism," Psychiatry, 16:167–176, 1953.

7. Skolnick, Jerome H., "Religious Affiliation and Drinking Behavior," Quart. J. Stud. Alc., 19:452–470, 1958.

chapter 10

Attitudes toward drinking in the Irish culture[*]

Robert F. Bales

Ideas and Sentiments Toward Drinking

> Why, liquor of life, do I love you so,
> When in all our encounters you bring me low?
> You're my soul and my treasure, without and within,
> My sister, my cousin, and all my kin!
>
> O Usquebagh! I love its kiss—
> My guardian spirit I think it is;
> Had my christening bowl been filled with this,
> I had swallowed it, were it a fountain!
>
> Many's the quondam fight we've had,
> And many a time you made me mad,
> But while I've a heart it never can be sad
> When you smile at me, full on the table.
>
> Surely you are my wife and brother—
> My only child—my father and mother—
> My outside coat—I have no other—
> Oh! I'll stand by you, while I am able.[†]

It is difficult to know how much of the native Irish culture survived, as an influence, direct or indirect, upon the Irish immigrants to America and their sons, who actually became addicted to alcohol in such relatively

[*] This chapter is a revised and shortened version of Chapter IV, pp. 152–235, of the unpublished doctoral dissertation, *The "Fixation Factor" in Alcohol Addiction: An Hypothesis Derived from a Comparative Study of Irish and Jewish Social Norms*, by Robert F. Bales, Harvard University, 1944.

[†] An old Irish song by Turlogh O'Carolan. The first two verses are from McCarthy (34) and the last two verses are from Barrow (7).

large proportions. The Irish have had a long and picturesque history with alcohol—a history in which the use of alcohol has undergone major fluctuations and has penetrated deeply into nearly every aspect of their social life. A thorough historical treatment cannot be undertaken here; yet it is not possible to delineate the ideas and sentiments centering around the act of drinking as they may be presented to individuals now socialized in the culture without some dependence upon detailed historical materials.

Alcohol addiction rates for Irish males during the period between 1900 and 1940 were relatively high in comparison to other groups. Assuming a modal age of 35 or 40 for these addicts, the time of birth and socialization of many of these men fell in the last quarter of the 1800's, and, taking the socialization period of their parents into account as relevant, we may see that the usages in Ireland as early as the first part of the last century are germane. Fortunately, much historical material is available for this period. For these two reasons this period was made the "center of gravity," for the following analysis. The life cycle of the male of the small farmer class in southern Ireland, born around 1825 and living till around 1900 will thus form the central expository frame. Extensions into other classes and into the past will be made whenever it seems desirable, and into the present whenever possible.

Although there is no formal distinction of status between a male and female child at birth in the Irish small-farm class, it is desirable to have a male child "so that the father and mother may be assured both of an heir to the property and of protection in their old age" (18). The first *rite de passage* in the child's life is Baptism, a sacrament in the Roman Catholic Church, which ritually removes original sin and changes the possible destiny of the child's soul from Limbo to Heaven. After the Baptism, a "christening party" is in order, now as in the past, which is an informal gathering of relatives or "friends" as they are called in Ireland, and at a "good rousing christening" (12) whisky was liberally provided. The family's status was at stake in this matter, and niggardliness in the amount or quality of whisky provided was to be avoided. The drinking on these occasions was convivial, not a part of the ritual of Baptism, though it had a social meaning. He who offered liberally was regarded as a "good fellow," and his offering implied that he regarded the other as a "good fellow." The exchange was thus symbolic of social solidarity and acceptability on both sides, but was without explicit religious meaning.

Training in food habits is one of the first types of training that any child receives, and attitudes toward food may be important in the formation of attitudes toward drinking. Whatever else it may be, the act of drinking is an oral activity, mechanically, and eating and drinking stand in close relation to each other, both psychologically and socially. One activity may be substituted for the other, to a certain extent, with psychological satisfaction, and social definitions concerning either activity may carry over to the other, or force substitution of the one for the other, depending on the way in which the definitions are made.

The available evidence indicates that certain strictures on the eating of food have existed in the Irish culture, both situational and psychological, and that there is a tendency to substitute drinking for eating in response to certain situations.

The first type of stricture is the irregular and sometimes altogether inadequate food supply of Ireland in the past. Severe famines have occurred periodically in Ireland, and the food supply has always been somewhat uncertain. It might be difficult to prove conclusively that these conditions have had a direct influence on the national food habits, or attitudes toward food, but it seems quite logical to suppose that they have played some part, perhaps a very important part, in the formation of the "careless," somewhat depreciatory regard of food, the shame connected with it, the willingness to fast, and the tendency to neglect meals which have been variously reported as characteristic of the Irish. McCarthy, for example, says:

Allowing for exceptions, the Irish middle and lower classes have what the English would call very unpractical notions about food. If a stranger, even of their own class, discovers them eating, they are quite confused, especially the women, and hurry through the meal, or finish before they have taken as much as they had intended to take; while the children retire into the dark corners of the cottage. . . . This sensation of shame at being found eating, so general amongst the Irish labourers and small farmers, is partly due to a suspicion that the food and its mode of service are not good enough to do them credit; and partly to a feeling of pain that they cannot ask the visitor to join them; and also because the self-sacrificing Celtic spirit thinks it a weakness to be obliged to eat at all. Most Irishmen and Irishwomen are proud of being able to fast, and would be ashamed to complain to a stranger about shortness of food, or to admit that they were hungry (34, pp. 117–119).

It is hardly credible, however, that every Irishman who exhibited the shame association to food acquired it in this manner. The missing link in the chain of reasoning is supplied by the information which McCarthy gives about the socialization of the child:

The labourer's children, as a rule, never get a regular, sitdown meal, but take their food anyhow, in scraps given to them by the father when he is eating, and by the mother, after the father has gone to work. The Irish mother will see herself or her husband short rather than allow the children to go hungry, and usually does so in secret. How often have I seen a labourer, after a hard morning's work sit down uncomplainingly to a comfortless dinner of dry bread and black coffee, eagerly watched by his children and his dog. And, although there would not be enough set before him to make half a meal for an English workman, the poor man would give mouthfuls to his children as he broke the bread, and occasionally throw a piece to the faithful dog, which probably had never got, and would never get, a full meal in the whole course of its life, while the cat looked on with disapproval from the top of the dresser. When the man had left the house, the wife would produce more food and give the children a comparatively good meal! (34, p. 118.)

This, it would seem, is a situation for associating guilt with food in the mind of the child. The mother, acting unselfishly in the face of a real or feared shortage of food, denies the father in front of the children, and he in his turn, denies himself still further, in their interest. If the child understands this situation at all, he must feel that the father is being cheated, and that he, the child, is responsible. The food he receives after the father has gone then comes as undeserved, and the eating of it would be expected to create further guilt. This guilty consumption, when discovered by another, is felt as shame. This is a theoretical construction, of course, and goes somewhat beyond the bare facts which McCarthy reports, but it makes psychological sense of the facts.

One more situational factor which fits into the picture, as another source of the feeling of uncertainty about the food supply, lies in the nature of the yearly cycle of crops. In the past, if not now, the small farmer has had to contend not only with the periodic major famines, but with the likelihood of a month or perhaps more of partial hunger each year. Arensberg reports:

The first crop (of the spring planting) is cabbage, which was planted at odd times very early. It is practically the only green of the diet and old people remember June or July *an chabáiste*, "the hungry month," when a delayed potato crop might condemn them to a month or more of semi-starvation upon cabbage. Today new varieties of potatoes mature as early as June (3, p. 50).

It is an odd fact, for which there is no ready explanation, that more regular methods of coping with these situational uncertainties did not develop. A certain disorderliness, a "lack of foresight," a shifting from one extreme to another, has been noted time and again, as a generalized characteristic of the Irish, however it may be explained, and this has left its mark on children, in food habits as in other matters.

McCarthy regards the fasts imposed by the Church as one of the important factors in the "harm to the national character in Ireland" which drinking has produced:

The main difference between the drinking habits of Ireland and Great Britain is that Irishmen drink fasting, while Englishmen drink with and after food. . . . The fasting on one meal and a collation imposed by the Church in Lent, and the abstinence from meat, butter, and eggs on various days throughout the year, are largely responsible not only for the national love of drink but also for its singularly evil results among Irish Catholics. [*With regard to the priests:*] . . . the habit of taking wine twice fasting (first when communicating, then at the ablutions) when celebrating their daily mass, make them particularly prone to the peculiar influence which alcohol has wielded over the human mind from the beginning of history. The enforcement of the heavy fasts made the people careless about their meals. There was never any fast imposed on drink; and, when the people felt weak, they took drink instead of food (34, pp. 295–297).

The essential situation, as McCarthy sees it, seems to be this: although drinking is psychologically and perhaps physiologically in the same class with eating, so that one can be substituted for the other, the social defini-

tions, which place strictures on food and not on alcohol, pla
ferent classes of objects. As he puts it:

Amongst the Irish Catholics, drink is the synonym for hospit
alone and is not associated with food. . . . Drink is more idealised .   ᴜᴀn
in England, through not being kept in the home and taken there with meals as
it is in England (34, p. 293, 297).

The social separation of the two makes it possible for the strictures to apply
to the one and not to the other, thus facilitating their substitution.

It is no accident that whisky is so "easy" and "handy" at the fairs. It is
a result of the connection between drinking and the transaction of business
there, and the practice of "treating" friends, which will be described later.
McCarthy also comments on the same situation:

The middle-aged farmer or labourer in Ireland will start for fair or market at
four or five A.M., and, when his business is done, at, or soon after, noon, will go
straight to a public-house and stay drinking with his friends and relatives until
eight or nine in the evening, when he leaves for home helplessly drunk, not having taken a morsel of food all day. Nor does he take food when he gets home;
but throws himself into bed to sleep off his carouse. Not till the next day will he
taste food, after a thirty or even forty hours' fast (34, p. 300).

In the towns there was another custom, in the nineteenth century at least,
which tended to promote the substitution of drinking for eating. At that time
it was customary in Dublin, and in Ireland generally, to give domestic
servants money, called "weekly money," instead of breakfasts in the house,
as was done in England. The custom was so well established that servants
would not accept places without weekly money. One householder of Dublin
gives his opinion of this practice as follows:

I think a worse system could not possibly be introduced, inasmuch as the ser-
vant is too often induced to pocket the money and pilfer the master and mistress
of provisions as a substitute for it, and in the next place they too often carry this
money out, and go to public-houses or grocers' shops with it and spend it in drinking instead of eating; it also gives a pretext for going out . . . (44, pp. 301–
302).

All in all, the picture is coherent. In the Ireland of the last century certain situational factors—notably the periodic famines and the annual month
of hunger—together with a relative inability to relieve the uncertainty due
to poor transportation, an almost exclusive dependence upon a few types
of foods, and a general unexplained lack of provision for the future, seem
to have reacted with pride and hostility in such a way as to produce a
negativistic orientation toward food, which in turn, through the process of
socialization of children, gathered a freight of guilt and shame, which was
reinforced still further by the frequent fasts prescribed by the Church.
These were, and probably to some extent still are, the strictures on
food. On the other hand, the symbolic separation of food and alcohol on
the social level, with the various permissive and customary uses of alcohol,

have promoted a tendency to substitute drinking for eating as an equivalent psychological satisfaction.*

The tendency has been the precise opposite of that which appears to operate in the Jewish culture. Whereas in the Jewish culture the strictures tend to apply to the act of eating and the act of drinking alike—both are ritually controlled—in the Irish culture the ritual strictures and other situational strictures apply to the act of eating with considerable force, but hardly at all to the act of drinking. As a result, the act of drinking in the Irish culture is almost completely exposed to the influence and control of other ideas and sentiments—structured on the social level to be sure, but much less closely integrated with the central complex of deeply internalized, compelling, and untouchable ideas and sentiments about the sacred and the moral, upon which the individual's whole solidarity with the group, hence his basic security, depends. The following material will indicate what some of these ideas and sentiments were, and probably, to a significant extent, still are.

From infancy the Irish child of the nineteenth century saw a great deal of drinking, by both males and females, older and younger, and early began to participate himself. "Make your head while you are young was advice frequently given by elders to their juniors" (10, p. 152). A good deal has been written about the haphazard discipline of children in the Irish culture—the constant recourse to frightening and intimidation, the sudden and sometimes violent physical punishment, often followed, just as suddenly, by the lavishing of love, praise, and pity; the habit of misinforming and teasing or "codding" the children, and encouraging "scuffing" among the little boys for the amusement of the elders (34, pp. 93). In this process of discipline, whisky apparently played a part, as a reward or inducement to the child.

Kerr reports that during the wave of ether drinking which swept certain parts of Ireland in the middle of the last century the practice was general among both sexes, in all classes, especially the farmers and agricultural laborers, and among all ages in the affected areas:

The mother may be seen with her daughters, and maybe a neighbour-Irish-woman or two, at a friendly ether "bee." The habit has become so general that small shopkeepers treat the children who have been sent to purchase some article, with a small dose of ether, and school-masters have detected ether on the breaths of children from 10 to 14 (or even younger), on their arrival at school. . . . The small shopkeepers also supply the hawkers (who are very often women), who attend fairs and other festive gatherings to dispense the "draughts" of the liquid poison. These "draughts" are also to be had from the surgeries of some medical practitioners, and in cottages or ether shebeen, where the cottager keeps a pig or two, and sells ether, the country people frequently giving potatoes, meal, or other produce in exchange. The hawkers carry about a bottle of ether, and do not scruple at selling to any one, however young, bartering a little for one or

* It is significant in this connection that in one of the case records of alcohol addicts examined in the course of this study, an Irish patient, born in Ireland, is reported to have gone on a 10-day hunger strike before he came to this country, and at the time he was brought to the hospital, was threatening another.

two eggs. In this way the children may procure ether on their wa
pp. 131, 135).

What was true of attitudes toward ether intoxication in the affected area.
was true in general of attitudes toward alcoholic intoxication in other areas.
Le Fanu reports a letter written to him from a friend traveling to one of the
islands off the coast of Sligo. The friend writes:

> Most of the men were more or less drunk; the air seemed laden with fumes
> of poteen. We saw a couple of stills, one at work. The schoolmaster says that
> the children are getting quite dull and stupid from being constantly given tastes
> of whisky (30, pp. 291 ff.).

The distillation of "poteen," as the native mountain whisky was called,
was illegal at this time, and the children came in very handy, here as in all
parts of Ireland, as sentries, barefooted, fleet, and elusive, who gave the
alarm at the approach of any strangers (32). Some of them are reputed to
be exceedingly canny in confusing and misleading the revenue officers (12).
The children also brought turf for the fire and helped in various other ways.
Long reports having visited one isolated village, "a famous village entirely,
as it was reputed to have produced more priests and 'poteen' than any
other village in the west of Ireland." When Long asked what the connection
was between priests and poteen, one old fellow explained, "Sure yer
honour's simple: doesn't 'poteen' make money, and doesn't it take money to
make a priest?" (31, p. 32.)

It was the ambition in most Irish families to have at least one son become
a priest. Not only was this a great honour, and the fulfillment of every pious
mother's desire, but it helped solve the problem of what to do with all of
the boys, since only one could marry and take over the family farm, and this
only when the father was ready to abdicate and sign it over. The grooming
of the boy who showed any inclinations in the direction of the priesthood
was begun early.

The Irish clergy as a whole have always been inclined to be tolerant about
drinking. The few notable exceptions have only sharpened this fact, and
the numbers who have given factual grounds in their own behavior for later
exaggerations and enlargements, if such they be, have been greater, without doubt, than the number of abstainers and temperance enthusiasts.* The

---

* For example, see Joyce (26, pp. 118–121). MacLysaght (33) says referring to
the period 1660–1689: "It cannot be doubted . . . that the clergy were somewhat
given to this failing (drunkenness). Not only was this true of the Catholic priests
who had fallen away from Rome, and of the Protestant clergy, most of whom,
especially in rural districts, were little ornament to the Church, though no doubt
hardly meriting J. P. Mahaffy's description of their predecessors of a generation or
two earlier as 'a set of very profane and drunken fellows,' . . . it was true also of the
otherwise exemplary priests who were under the control of the Bishops. . . . Speaking
generally Cardinal Moran expresses the opinion that, considering the circumstances
of the time, abuses were few. Drunkenness must have been deeply rooted in some districts, for Arch-Bishop Plunket became an abstainer as an example to his clergy: 'Give
me an Irish priest without this vice,' said Blessed Oliver, 'and he is assuredly a saint.' "

rural Irish clergy, however, were recruited from the people, they were supported by the people, and it would be strange indeed if their attitudes toward drinking were sharply at variance with those of the devout peasantry to whom they ministered. Especially is this true in view of the formal position of the Roman Catholic Church, which Father Ireland described as follows:

The Catholic Church does not assert that the moderate and legitimate use of intoxicating drinks is a moral evil, or sin. Neither does she assert that the manufacture and the sale of intoxicating liquors are of themselves moral evils, or sins. All this is clear and undoubted. But there are other and important aspects of her teaching which the Catholic Church will not, and cannot overlook. In her eyes intemperance is a sin, heinous and soul-wrecking, whose victims shall not possess the Kingdom of Heaven (25, p. 502).

The important things about which both clerics and anticlerics seem to agree are that the Church erects no formal barriers to drinking as such, that the prerogatives of drinking were fiercely guarded by the people, and that in the face of strong pressures from the latter side, the practical attitude of the Irish clergy generally was tolerant and permissive, occasionally interrupted with protests, but just as often veering into a more or less complete participation in the drinking customs of the people. There is no question about whether or not the clergy in general drank other than in the rituals—they did. The problematic thing is the extent, and evidence here indicates a considerable fluctuation from individual to individual, section to section, and from one period to another.

The boy starts to school at the age of 6 or 7, and he goes to his first confession soon after. After going to confession for some time he is prepared for his first Communion by special religious instruction. In all likelihood he has witnessed the act of communion before, perhaps as an altar boy, has observed and perhaps felt himself the attitudes of reverence and awe for the Host and the Chalice. The child probably does not have a learned understanding of the act, so heavily freighted with mystic and transcendental meanings in the formal theology of the Church, but he probably understands the elements of the Eucharist, appearing as the consecrated Bread and Wine, to be the Body and Blood of Christ, as defined in the words of the ritual, and that in taking the Host into his own body he is coming into contact with the sacred.

For present purposes, the symbolism of this act, which Catholic theologians would probably not call "symbolism" at all (41), is the virtual equivalent of the Hebrew Kiddush at Passover (to which both the rabbi and the Catholic theologian might object) in that it signifies a union with the sacred. The notable difference between the participation of the Irish-Catholic child and the Jewish child in these cognate rituals, however, is that the Irish child does not partake of the wine, either as a child or as an adult, unless he becomes a priest. Since 1099, by papal decree, the wine has been omitted from the child's communion, and the communion of the adult laity in the bread alone was enjoined by the Council of Constance in 1415 and again by the Council of Trent in 1562 (15). In the Roman Catholic Communion, the priest partakes of the wine, the laity of the bread only. Thus the communicant sees the priest partake of the wine, and recognizes it as part of the ritual, but does not himself drink as part of the ritual act.

For several reasons the relation of this particular act of drinking, and the sacred meanings attached to it, to other familiar and usual acts of drinking would be expected to be much less intimate in the Irish culture than in the Jewish. First, the laity does not participate in the sacred act of drinking in the Irish culture, as it does in the Jewish. Second, the Jewish child is introduced to the relevant sacred ideas and sentiments at an earlier age and in more familiar surroundings than is the Irish child. Third, the Irish child is intimately acquainted with other, non-ritual uses of drinking as a matter of personal participation, earlier and in much greater number than is the Jewish child. Fourth, the sacramental wine is in a class by itself in the Irish-Catholic culture, since wine is the only acceptable liquid for the ritual (15); whereas in the Jewish culture wine is the most appropriate beverage, but where wine is not accessible, "strong drink," "i.e., beer or mead, and later on, spirits, under the name of 'wine of the country'—or any beverage other than water, such as sirup of the juice of fruits" (16, 29), have been used, and are deemed fit substitutes for wine in the rituals. Thus, by cultural definitions, the attitudes applying to the wine used in the ritual are also expected to apply to other alcoholic beverages in the Jewish culture, whereas in the Irish culture they are not.

With regard to the generalization of attitude on the part of the priest himself, who, unlike the laity, does drink the wine in the sacred context, the investigator wrote to a priest interested in the incidence of alcoholic disorders in the priesthood, suggesting that such an attitude might tend to constitute a sort of protection against addictive drinking. The following answer was received:

I doubt very much that what you term "ritual drinking" can be conceived of as "a protective attitude tending to prevent the development of a type of attitude toward drinking which is found in addicted drinkers." It would be very difficult I think to show that drinking wine in the Holy Sacrifice of the Mass is conceived of in any way as drinking by the average priest. The amount taken is quite small. The ordinary cruet holds perhaps three ounces. Sometimes it is sour or unpleasant wine, but more commonly one of the sweet types of wine. So far as I can see, the taking of wine at Mass would have very little influence on a priest's concept of drinking outside of Mass (40).

If the attitude toward the consecrated wine is quite isolated from other attitudes about drinking in the mind of the priest, such an isolation would surely be even more pronounced in those who merely witness the act.

The use of wine in the Holy Communion is the only strictly ritual use of alcohol in the Irish-Catholic culture, so far as can be determined. This does not mean that alcohol is not used in connection with other social events and *rites de passage* of which rituals are also a part—on the contrary, in practically all of these alcohol is used, but it is used before or after the ritual, and is decidedly not a part of the ritual. In these events its use is convivial.

Morewood, an Irish historian of sorts, writing in 1826 mentions as one important factor in the "influence and hold which the use of intoxicating liquors has obtained over lower orders of the Irish," the number of "festive and saints' days appropriated to religious observances, marriages, christenings, patterns, fairs, and wakes" which as he says, were "all so many scenes of festivity and joy" (37, p. 363), and later calls "all so many scenes of revelry and intemperance" (38, p. 706).

The carousing on pilgrimages has been noted a number of times, probably most frequently by anticlerical writers, but there is no substantial reason to doubt that aside from their more or less inflammatory language and possible exaggeration, their reports are based on fact, and that the custom was a comparatively old one. MacLysaght, a careful and scholarly historian, in speaking of conditions in the seventeenth century says:

The allegation that pilgrimages were made the occasion for a popular outing of the modern bank-holiday type is not general. I will quote one, for what it is worth, my authority being Sir Henry Pierse, who, I may observe, shows throughout his writings a pronounced anti-Catholic bias. Having described the pilgrimage itself, which took place to a spot of great natural beauty and involved much physical hardship on the pilgrims, who completed the journey over a stoney path at the edge of a precipice on their naked knees, he goes on: "their devotions done, they return, shod and merry, no longer concerned for the sins that were the cause of that so severe penance but as if they now having paid the score longed to go on in them again they return with speed to a certain green spot of ground and here fall to dancing and carousing, for ale sellers in great numbers on these days have their booths as in a fair and to be sure the bagpipes fail not to pay their attendance. Thus in lewd and obscene dances with excess of drinking the day of their devotion is ended, so as now one who should see them would think they had been celebrating a feast of Bacchus, or oftentimes it falleth out that more blood falls on the grass from their drunken pates when the pilgrimage is ended than was before shed on the stones from their bare feet and knees during their devotions." (33, p. 169.)

The brawling and broken pates referred to seem exceedingly bizarre at first mention, but they undoubtedly were the "faction fights" for which the Irish have been notable. The "faction fight" differed from the "party fight" between the Catholic and Protestant groups, which were more bitter and lethal, in that the participants in the "faction fight" were all Catholic Irishmen, who were basically solidary, and who would stand together in the face of any outer opposition, from the Protestant Irish or the English. The factions were extended kinship groups, augmented by tradesmen and allied kinship groups, who feuded over incidents, often land disputes, or "law shoots" generations back. The original incident might have been trivial, but the feud was perpetuated by the injuries and even deaths which resulted from each new fight.

The boys at school, in Carleton's time, were forced to line up with one faction or another, if their family allegiance was not already clear, cudgels or "shillelaghs" were lovingly prepared, and the boys enacted the faction fights. Many of these took place at the village fairs, sometimes after weddings and funerals, or any other social event, such as the pilgrimages, where leading members of the factions and a sufficient number of supporters were likely to meet.

Drinking was the invariable prelude. The fights were regarded, curiously enough, as a sort of recreation; they were relished and sought; and were initiated, as the drinking got well under way, with shouted insults and challenges. The leader of one faction might proceed down the street, dragging his coat behind him, daring whoever had the courage to step on it, capering and shouting in high humor. The battle grew more deadly in intention as the shillelaghs drew blood, as men were killed, and the women were drawn in. All sorts of household furnishings were used, especially by the women, but cudgels were regarded as proper, while knives, cutting instruments, guns, etc., were not, although they were sometimes used. The final victory of one side, of course, was celebrated by a triumphal carouse (11).

Besides the pilgrimages to sacred spots, in Carleton's time there were so-called "stations" which simply meant the "coming of the parish priest and his curate to some house in the townland, on a day publicly announced from the altar for that purpose, on the preceding Sabbath." Neighbors and friends in the vicinity gathered in to make their confessions, to communicate, and later participate in the festivities. The food and drink for the accompanying festivities were provided by the host to whom the honor of entertaining the priest and curate had been extended.

When a boy is somewhere between the ages of 12 and 15, the rite of Confirmation marks his transition from a passive to a supposedly active religious status as "a soldier of Christ and heir to the kingdom of heaven," a member of the church militant (18). Socially, Confirmation roughly marks the end of schooling, unless the boy is to become a priest, and the taking on of a semi-adult role, with increasing work and greater responsibility. Drinking plays no part in this *rite de passage*, ritually at least, and no mention of convivial drinking at this transition point has been found in the present investigation, though it may exist.

Confirmation does not bring full adult status to the boy, and cannot, in view of the family system and the relation of that system to the limited land resources. The situation at present, as described in detail by Arensberg and Kimball (4) in an anthropological study, is apparently very similar to what it was in the past century. The small farms are tilled by single families. The father and his sons work in the fields, the mother and daughters in the house and around the "haggard" or farm yard. The parents of the father live in the "West Room," to which they retire in semi-sacred isolation upon relinquishing their farm to their son. A son cannot marry until his father is ready to sign the farm over to him and relinquish control. Until that time the son is called a "boy," and has the social status of a boy, no matter how old he may be.

In the countryside this subordination of the sons does not gradually come to an end. It is a constant. Even at forty-five and fifty, if the old couple have not yet made over the farm, the countryman remains a "boy," both in farm work and in the rural vocabulary. In 1933, a deputy to the Dail raised considerable laughter in the sophisticated Dublin papers when he inadvertently used the country idiom in expressing country realities. He pleaded for special treatment in land division for "boys of forty-five and older"—boys who have nothing in prospect but to wait for their father's farm. For "boyhood" in this instance is a social status rather than a physiological state. A countryman complained to me in words which tell the whole story. "You can be a boy forever," he said, "as long as the old fellow is alive." (3, p. 59.)

Fathers of "boys" of 45 and 50 collect any wages they may earn at day labor elsewhere, and the "boy" must look to his father for direction, advice, and even spending money. The "boy" is not regarded as capable of bargaining in the market as his father does.

Added to this enforced submission to the authority of the father, there is strict separation of the sexes and minimization of intimate contact which begins at an early age and continues until marriage and beyond.

The boys are taught to look upon themselves as superior to the girls at a very early age and soon cease to associate with them; the average boy of nine or ten being ashamed to be seen in the company of his sisters, lest he should be called a Sheelah. The peasants' cottages, especially of the old mudwalled type, are so small, and the families are so large, that the boys and girls are of necessity very much together indoors. But their modesty is exemplary; and, though sleeping, perhaps in the same apartment, the boys are as separate from the girls as if they were in the different bedrooms of a large mansion (34, p. 110).

Even after marriage the tendency to separation persists in the spheres of work, responsibilities, interests, and recreation. To this it is only necessary to add the severe sanction placed upon the expression of sexuality by the Irish Catholic Church, and those conditions which result in a fairly persistent fund of unresolved rebellious and sexual tensions in the "boys" become clear.

As a corollary of this complex of conditions in the primary family structure, there has been a pronounced development of solidary groups of "boys" and married males up to the "old fellows," graded according to age levels, marital status, and other criteria (3). In their meetings at designated houses and pubs, drinking performs complex social and psychological functions.

One of the most important of these functions, apparently, is in the relief of sexual tension. The conditions which perpetuate the tension lie in the family system, and its control is functionally necessary if the family system is to be preserved. That drinking and male companionship function as a sort of safety valve in the release of sexual tensions is indicated by a rather unusual attitude toward the "teetotaler" which Arensberg heard several times expressed by lower-middle-class men, a feeling that the teetotaler is a menace to society, because he is the man who is likely to prowl around the streets getting girls into trouble and destroying their characters (39). Elise de la Fontaine states:

We must remember that the norms of the community require the repression of sex and the rigid segregation of the young unmarried of the sexes except at stated times, although recently dances in the home to the music of a gramophone have been accepted. I have heard from responsible Irish people that the danger to society lies not in the drunkard or the young man who frequents the public house with his companions of his own age and class, but with the teetotaler. The latter is a lone young man, in a sense outcast by his age group, and the argument is that he will be a menace to the sexual standards, which, in the country districts are also standards of farm prestige and economic unity. Drinking is thus a socially approved reaction (17, p. 32).

McCarthy mentions, in another connection, the tendency to substitute drinking for the active pursuit of a mate, perhaps partially ignoring the difficulties which actually stand in the way in so many cases. "Is a girl beautiful and does a young man feel that he ought to exert himself to win her as his wife?," he asks, rhetorically, and replies: "Instead of doing so, he takes a drink and thinks and talks about her, and never woos her." (34, pp. 297–298.) It may be that the words of the "Cruiskeen Lawn," an old song sung by Irishmen all over the world, are an actual reflection of the function of drinking as a sexual substitute. The words of the chorus, translated into English are, "The love of my heart is my little full jug, here's health to my darling girl!" (34, p. 290.)

There is no need to depend upon indirect symbolism; the function of drinking as a sexual substitute is indicated quite clearly by the attitude toward the teetotaler. Arensberg observes further:

. . . any emotional difficulty of young men is believed best treated by advising them to "drink it off." Drowning one's sorrows becomes the expected means of relief, much as prayer among women and young children, or among the older people (39).

There is little doubt that the essential attitude as to the proper relation between young men and women, at least, if not the prescription of drinking as the proper mode of meeting the difficulty, has been preserved in Irish-American culture.* For example, one 39-year-old Irish alcoholic, who lived with his parents and supported them, was praised by the neighbors, who said, "He is a fine fellow, ignoring girls, so that he can do everything for his parents." His mother said virtually the same thing: ". . . her son has no interest in girls or other things because he is working long hours and thinking of his parents. However, she says, she has always hoped he would marry and live with them." † A number of cases indicated that the patient

---

* For a literary example see Farrell's (19) account of Studs' first love affair.

† In the course of this study, the author examined a number of case records of alcoholic patients. Further information about these cases may be found in the doctoral dissertation from which this chapter is derived.

had "no interest in girls," but was interested in "athletics" and other activities with the boys.

On the other hand, the drunkard in Ireland is not condemned, unless he is married and his drinking threatens the family's cash resources or tenure on the land, when he is said to "go to town and drink the money," or "drink the land up," leaving nothing for his parents, siblings, or children (39). Where drunkenness begins to interfere with the primary family system and its economic base, rather than facilitate its preservation, it is condemned. Short of that, drunkenness, as Arensberg says, is "laughable, pleasurable, somewhat exciting, a punctuation of dull routine to be watched and applauded, and drunken men are handled with care and affection" (39). The drunkard is handled with maternal affection, often referred to as "the poor boy," with a special connotation of sympathy, love, pity, and sorrow. If married, the drunkard is compassionately classed by his wife with "the min, God help us!" (45, p. 87.) The man who is drunk is sometimes regarded with envy by the man who is sober.

With these role definitions, the drunkard is provided with ready justification, indeed, he may even build up a sort of fictional idealization of himself, on the basis of the success he might have had. The drunkard role relates to the actual frustrations imposed upon the "boy" by the family and land tenure systems. In this context, the role of the drunkard can be interpreted as having a functional value, not only in the adjustment of the individuals caught in the "boy" role, but also in the protection and preservation of the larger system in which the suppression of advancement on the basis of functional achievement for certain members is a "necessary evil."

When marriage finally comes, complex readjustments must take place in the family. In rural Ireland, the marriage is often arranged through a "speaker" and involves the signing over of the farm to the son and agreement with the father of the bride as to her "fortune" or dowry. The amount of the fortune depends upon the worth of the farm to which she is going, and the land, stock, and other facilities are carefully inspected by the bride's father before any agreement is concluded. The process of bargaining is conducted at the public house, with the liberal aid of whisky. The first drink is "called" by the young man, the second by the young lady's father, and so on, back and forth as they near agreement, until the whole party is well on the way to intoxication. Finally, the whole series of agreements is written up in a single document and signed (3). Customs were apparently much the same in the nineteenth century, though perhaps drinking played a larger part. Carleton in "Shane Fadh's Wedding" (11) gives a detailed description of a marriage, which can virtually be chronicled in terms of the references to drinking.

The use of whisky on the occasion of marriage is clearly convivial. One example will serve for many. Another writer tells of a wedding in Dublin in the nineteenth century. "In Ireland," he says, "we have a snug little thing in the corner called 'the priest's bottle,' and after undergoing the mighty fatiguing ceremony of marriage, a drop of it sets the nerves straight, and bothers the senses beyond all comparishment." (1, pp. 128–129.) Further, it is clear in this example that the convivial use of alcohol, with its symbolism of solidarity, acceptability, and "dacency" of the participants to each other, merges almost imperceptibly into what may be called a utilitarian attitude, as drinking is used in a way calculated to manipulate the sentiments of others (as in the persuasion to marriage) or the hedonic state of the self (as in "drinking off" emotional difficulties and "setting the nerves straight"). This merging of utilitarian elements with convivial elements will be more clearly seen later, and, many usages can be classed as almost purely utilitarian.

Marriage may solve the problem of specific sexual tension for most of those who finally marry, but it does not resolve the tensions of rebelliousness and resentment so effectively, in fact new antagonisms are often involved. Typical conflicts in the new family constellation are those between the wife, who is likely to be determined to establish her new role as mistress of the household, and the mother, who is apt to resent the relinquishing of her role as unquestioned mistress of the household to the strange girl brought into the house "on top of her" (8, pp. 125–126), a conflict which involves the allegiance of the husband to both; between the son-husband, who takes over active management of the farm work, and the "old fellow," who still wishes to retain control and direction in spite of his retirement; and finally between the wife, who has broken her former ties, and the husband, who finds it difficult to decrease his association with "the boys," who still provide him with a refuge when the situation at home grows too tense.

Elise de la Fontaine points out that "drinking in clubs, hotels, and saloons affords the chief social life of the men and the chief means of getting them out of homes dominated by their women" (17, p. 32). Arensberg comments on the sharp division between men's and women's spheres and the dominance of the wife in the household, so that "in the towns where the men have no field and meadow to retire into, any dispute necessitates the men's flouncing out of the house to the screamed recriminations of the wife, who remains in possession" (39). The husband, in these cases, goes to the boys, and the division between his long standing allegiance to the boys, and his new one to his wife is likely to remain a point of conflict between husband and wife for some time after their marriage.

In the gatherings of the boys of his own age and social position, the male finds a place where his status is secure, and this security and solidarity is manifested and strengthened by the ubiquitous practice of "treating." In McCarthy's description of the practice the symbolic elements, that is, the meanings attached to the act, come out very clearly:

The habit of "treating," which prevails to some extent in Great Britain, is a social law in Catholic Ireland enforced with all the vigour of a Coercion Act. If a man happens to be in an inn or public-house alone, and if any of his acquaintances come in, no matter how many, it is his duty to "stand," that is, to invite them to drink and pay for all they take. Then, when the drinks are consumed, another member of the company is expected to "stand," and invariably does so. Then if there are half a dozen men in the company, each insists on "standing" drinks all around. There is usually a dispute, as some of the men do not want to take so many drinks; but, if the majority are in favour of letting each man pay for a round, the minority have to give in. It is a deadly insult to refuse to take a drink from a man, unless an elaborate explanation and apology be given and accepted (34, pp. 308–309).

To refuse a drink from an equal is "a quair way o' showing frinship," and brings the suspicion that some offence has been given.

The treating customs of Ireland have persisted, at least to a certain extent, in this country. One alcoholic patient, an Irish bartender, when asked what he thought to be the reason for his drinking answered:

There should be a law that nobody should be allowed in a bar room to invite another person to drink and then to pay for this person. As things are at present, one invites the other, the other then pays for the first, a third come in and invites the first two, and so it goes.

As Arensberg puts it, "drinking together is the traditional reaffirmation of solidarity and equality among males."

For that reason there is no paying Dutch treat and in any group of young or older men each must stand his round in turn under pain of giving offense and under pain of losing caste. Thus "friends" (cousins of the same generation—the chief agricultural cooperators—and in-laws of the same generation) must stand one another drinks on meeting; farmers intent on proving their equality with townsfolk must drink with them, standing them their rounds; and a sure way to cause resentment, because it is a mark of refusal to grant equality, is to refuse to accept or return an offer to drink with another man. Shopkeepers thus give as their chief reason for not admitting shopclerks ("assistants") to their clubs or for trying to avoid them on the streets is that "they would have to drink with them." A politician in providing rounds of drinks for his constituents or standing them drinks individually is thus taking advantage of the usual ritual of male recognition and companionship (39).

In the manipulation of these symbols by the politician the utilitarian element mentioned earlier can be seen to be creeping in.

It is interesting to note that the custom of treating has its obverse form in the "round of rascals," used as a symbolic aggression against whoever may be chosen as the object of attack. Grattan reports such an incident at a gathering of Irish gentlemen in the nineteenth century:

"Now, gentlemen, a bumper toast, if you please. Fill with your left hands and pass the bottles the wrong way. I am going to give you a round of rascals," exclaimed the Squire with an air of mock gravity, which produced the desired effect of making every one laugh. Every one filled as desired, pushed the bottle backwards, and raised his glass to his head. "Here's to Lord _____, with all dishonour—let everyone drink the toast as he likes it." The name of a leading Irish politician, very unpopular with all parties, was mentioned, and everyone laughed, but no one was angry, for they all neither loved nor hated, they only despised him (23, p. 102).

Drinking is inextricably tied up with the expression of aggression in the Irish culture, not only covert aggression against the elders, or more open aggression against persons disliked in the community (as in the "round of rascals"), but most importantly, overt and active and persistent aggression against the English. The English tried for centuries to control the manufacture, sale, and consumption of alcoholic beverages in Ireland—mostly for the sake of revenues, as authorities seem to agree—and always without success (13, 38, 44).

It was quite easy for an Irish patriot, sincere or otherwise, to gain an audience at the gatherings of the boys, or men, at some hidden "shibbeen" and stir up a minor rebellion. A nineteenth-century writer tells of such a meeting at the secluded house of a farmer, who got enough money from the sale of illicit ale to pay his rent and buy seed for the next year's crop.

The conspirators knew that . . . [the shibbeen] . . . would be well attended —as such places are—and that Irishmen are never more inclined for mischief than when under the influence of liquor, which would be the case with them on this night, being always eager to deceive the revenue, even at their own expense . . . the youthful peasantry of the surrounding country had this night assembled, intent upon no other design than that of defrauding his Majesty's revenue, assisting a poor man, and making themselves *mellow.* . . . Amorous ditties were the first essays of the night; but as they became more foolish they became also more wicked: the old sang the "tales of other days" in melancholy verse, and treasonable songs began to prevail (2, pp. 64–65, 68, 69).

The expression of both sexuality and aggression appears clearly here. Whisky was also used to instigate overt acts of aggression. Attacks on "informers," on newcomers who took over the farms of community members who had been evicted for failure to pay their rents, and others, in which the man was often killed and his house burned, were prepared for by a liberal dosage of whisky for those in the attacking party (44).

In the folk songs and folklore of Ireland, whisky has for centuries had the connotation of bringing power and victory—perhaps simply as a reflection of its obvious advantages of releasing inhibitions and "raising courage," perhaps through some more devious symbolic development from its designation as the "water of life" (38, p. 618).

In no context, with the possible exception of party and faction fights, has the connection between drinking and aggression been shown so clearly as in the opposition to English laws and law-enforcement officers. Sir Jonah Barrington remarks that the Irish make no very strong objection to being shot at by a regular army, since they may have given a legitimate reason for it—and anyway, as they said, their "fathers and forefathers before them were always used to *that same*"—

But those manslaughters which occur through the activity of the revenue officers in prevention of distillation, they can never reconcile themselves to, and never forgive. They can not understand the *reason* for this at all, and treasure up a spirit of savage revenge to the last day of their lives (6, p. 358).

Barrington laments that something cannot be done to "prevent perpetual resort to that erroneous system of mountain warfare and revenue bloodshed, which ever has kept, and ever will keep, whole districts of Ireland in a state of excitement and distraction" (6, p. 358).

The exciseman or "guager" was hated with venom and a prodigal amount of ingenuity was expended in tricking him. Apparently the magistrates, as well as the excisemen, could be and were bribed, a fact which only increased the contempt of the people for them and for the law. Sometimes whole districts were virtually given over to illicit distillation (13), with the collusion of magistrates who were able to gain by the purchase of cheap smuggled spirits which they could sell at a profit (13). In other cases there was collusion with the local gentry who stood to gain by the higher rents which they were able to extort from their poteen-making tenants (13). Such districts were protected by an elaborate guard system, in which the boys often played an important part, because, in their bare feet, they could outrun and often outsmart the "guager" (30).

Sometimes the exciseman was kidnapped and held until a big "run" was completed or until the traveling court moved on (38). Sometimes a riot was started in another district to draw the soldiery away (30). The farmers often built secret chambers in their outhouses for storing the requisite materials, and "many of them had what were called Malt-steeps sunk in hidden recesses and hollow gables, for the purpose of steeping the barley, and afterwards of turning and airing it, until it was sufficiently hard to be kiln-dried and ground" (11, pp. 52–53), or sometimes "treacle" or brown sugar, which could be purchased without suspicion, was used (31). Special "slipes, . . . a kind of car that was made without wheels" were used to transport the materials over morasses and bogs to the still-houses in places which could not be reached by wheeled vehicles (11).

In brief, it is quite clear that drinking and the activities closely related to it were, and to some extent, still are, instruments of political aggression and resistance in Ireland. The activities were important because they provided an outlet for the expression of a fund of tensions centering around the political relation to England. As a mode of expression for this range of strong sentiments of solidarity and antagonism, drinking and the activities related to it also became a means of utilitarian manipulation and exploitation which the unscrupulous used to suit their own purposes.

Drinking played a very similar part in the economic life. The symbolism of solidarity implicit in treating played an important part in facilitating economic transactions, and here also, as in political activity, it tended to break down into a sort of utilitarian manipulation.

Among the small farm class the great bulk of economic exchange, whether of labor, tools, or products, tends, even at present, to be non-monetary in nature. "Boys" are "lent out" to "friends," that is, to kinsmen, and they give labor in return, a practice which is known as "cooring" (3).

The exchange of tools and products takes place along the same lines of mutual rights and obligations implicit in "friendliness." No formal account is kept (34). At one time it was the custom for the people of the countryside who wanted to show any special appreciation to one of the local gentry to gather at his place one morning and spend the day harvesting his crop, an event known as a *Mehill*. In this display of solidarity, as in the mutual aid of the farmers themselves, the exchange of money was out of the question.

At such a time nothing could be more offensive than any offer of monetary recompense, but it was the invariable custom to entertain the welcome guests with the utmost hospitality. A plenteous feast was spread at due season, under the trees, and great was the good humor and goodwill that prevailed. Nor could any form of Local Veto prevent the circulation at frequent intervals through the day of that form of refreshment which has been the traditional meed of the reaper ever since the Heroic Age (14, p. 28).

A plentiful supply of whisky in this context, as among the farmers themselves (14) was an acceptable form of "payment," because it had no utilitarian taint, but indicated good will and friendship, and because it was not in any exact sense "payment in full," but implied a continued state of mutual obligation.

The main cash transactions of the small farmers are with townsfolk or "strangers," but even here the symbolism of solidarity implicit in treating tends to be retained as a part of the transaction. Perhaps the farmer feels uncomfortable unless he can leave feeling that the man with whom he has exchanged is in some sense a "friend." It seems most likely that treating did not at all originate in the economic transactions at fairs and markets, as Mooney (36) suggests, but rather persisted as a part of such transactions after they began to lose their original Gemeinschaft character, with the development of fairs, markets, and villages.

In Mooney's account, however, the breakdown toward utilitarian manipulation can be more clearly observed:

[The custom of treating] . . . grew from the ancient usage observed in buying and selling in fairs and markets in Ireland. The seller of a horse, cow, or pig, would *treat* the buyer with a sort of "luck penny:" that is, having agreed about the price of the animal, the seller was to return something to the buyer from the money received, which something was spent in liquor. It not unfrequently occurred that a cunning seller of an animal, took his customer into a public house before the bargain was struck, to treat him—that is, to *soften* him; in other words, to deprive him of his right judgment, that he might the more easily get a high price for the animal offered; and often has it occurred that both parties remained drinking during the entire week, until the whole price of the cow, horse, or pig was spent! (36, pp. 65–70.)

At the fairs the breakdown toward the display of aggression also tended to occur. There one was likely to meet his friends, of course, and he must treat them: "it's always an unpleasant thing for a body to go to a fair or market without anything in their pocket . . . for fraid that any friend or acquaintance might thrate him; and then it would be a poor, mane-spirited thing . . . to take another man's thrate, without giving one for it." (11, p. 93.) As the whole day was usually spent at the fair, selling the stock or meeting friends, an advanced stage of intoxication was likely to be reached, and the situation was ripe for a round with the shillelaghs, or perhaps a faction fight (9).

In the town economy the practice of treating was an adjunct of practically every business transaction, at least in the nineteenth century, and probably still is to a considerable extent. McCarthy, writing in 1911, says:

> The tippling habits of the better-class Catholics in the cities and towns are worse than those of the farmers. To one who has lived for some time in England, the mixture of tippling and business seems like some incredible dream. Little bits of business get in, as if by stealth, between the drinks during the day! Few, indeed, are the men of business to be found invariably at their places of business. One has to seek out most of them elsewhere, usually in the drinking bars. Such men never seem to do anything for itself alone, except drinking. If they go to fish or hunt, it is to fish or hunt and drink; if to visit a sick friend, it is to see the friend and drink; if to walk or ride, it is to walk or ride and drink; if to buy or sell, it is to buy or sell and drink (34, p. 303).

Among the working classes in the towns of Ireland at the time of the inquiry of the House of Commons (1834) the practice of treating was tied up with the method of payment of the workmen. In some cases the paymasters were in collusion with the keepers of houses, and either paid the workmen at the public houses, or sent a number of them with a four- or five-pound note, larger than the pay of any of them, to get change at the public house, and "although there is no absolute law upon the subject, it is expected as a matter of course that each will drink a glass of spirituous liquor as a compensation to the master of the house for the change" (44, p. 98). In other cases (44) the foreman was allowed to drink without cost at the public house to which he brought his men, or often enough, the employer or foreman himself was a spirits seller. In still other cases the paymaster paid the men so late on Saturday night that it was impossible for them to buy groceries and other provisions for their families before they started drinking.

In the Irish culture there are many practices involving the drinking of alcoholic beverages in which the intent and meaning are almost purely utilitarian and these usages apparently antedate the convivial uses. There are indications that medicinal uses of alcohol, preventive, palliative, and curative, were prominent in the Irish culture from very early times. It is not known when *aqua vitae*, that is, distilled spirits, was first introduced or manufactured in Ireland, but it was in use at the time of the English invasion under Henry II, 1171. Morewood suggests, on the basis of etymological evidence, that the art of distillation may have been introduced directly from India, but thinks it more likely that distilled spirit came from Spain or Italy (38).

Whatever the reason, whether the associations of its name, or its association with the repositories of medical knowledge at the time,

Aqua vitae was first used in [Ireland] only as a medicine, considered a panacea for all disorders, and the physicians recommended it to patients indiscriminately for preserving health, dissipating humours, strengthening the heart, curing colic, dropsy, palsy, quartan fever, stone, and even prolonging existence itself beyond the common limits. Hence it was eagerly sought for, and the taste, thus formed, has been transmitted from generation to generation, with an attachment which time seems rather to strengthen than to diminish (38, p. 616).

In keeping with its earlier medical use, spirituous liquors were sold in apothecaries' shops. It is hard to say just when they began to be used extensively in a convivial way, but we are provided with a small clue by an exhortation of an Irish gentleman to his peers on their "excessive and destructive consumption of Foreign Wines and Brandies," a fashion among the landed gentry of his time which he disapproves apparently not least on the basis of its economic effects, since it led to a neglect of alcoholic drinks which could be manufactured in Ireland:

. . . as debauched as we are grown, many men can remember when we were as remarkable for our sobriety, as we are now for rioting and drunkenness; when our ancestors, of the best families of the nation, used to have their wines brought in by the dozens (instead of much larger amounts), and when sack and spirituous liquors were sold at the apothecaries shops for cordials to the sick. The taverns indeed have long since taken that trade out of their hands, but in return they have brought them in ten fold, a greater one, for their drugs, by increasing the number of patients, and what is worse, of distempers too . . . (35, p. 40).

Madden's exhortation was first printed in 1738, and from his reference to the "many men" who could remember, it may be inferred that the selling of spirits primarily in apothecaries' shops may have been the practice perhaps as late as 1660 or thereabouts.

Change in the place of sale did not obliterate the medicinal use of alcohol, however. There are numerous evidences that medicinal uses were widespread in Ireland and have existed to the present day there as well as among the Irish immigrants to America. Many of the allusions, anecdotes, and observations, which form the bulk of the evidence are preserved in the accounts of travelers in Ireland, or in the writings of native Irishmen who, either in semi-fictional form, or in memoirs and reminiscences, have tried to convey a faithful picture of life in Ireland as it existed in their time.

One of the most frequently reported usages is the drinking of whisky as a preventive and palliative measure against the damp and cold. John Gamble, a traveler in Ireland in 1810, relates several instances of this kind. One morning, after a hard journey by coach, he is invited by one of his drunken traveling companions of the night before to come into his house and " . . . have a drop of something warm, just to keep the damp out of [your] stomach this cold morning" (22, p. 146). The author refused, on the ground that he never drank in the morning.

Gamble reports it as a universal custom in the country parts of North Ireland for the guest who arrives from a long and generally wet ride, to be

provided with a large pail full of warm water, in which his feet are washed
by "his fair attendant":

> In this very damp climate, to guard against the effects of cold is of peculiar
> importance. Irish kindness is, therefore, exerted in restoring checked perspira-
> tion; and in addition to (the warm footbath), warm whisky punch, which is lib-
> erally prescribed and freely taken, proves a powerful auxiliary (21, p. 346).

Two circumstances seem to have been intimately connected with the
prevalent use of whisky as an antidote to the damp and cold. The first is
the weather in Ireland, which is noted for its sudden changes from sunshine
to rain, for its dampness and coldness, so that it was common for travelers
and workers to come home at night, or to an inn, drenched to the skin, or
to have to begin their day in the rain. Gamble, indeed, takes it as self
evident that this circumstance is largely responsible for the Irishman's
"great tendency to drunkenness" (21, p. 159).

The second circumstance is the prevailing neglect or lack of proper
clothing among the Irish working men:

> They do not study their comfort in clothes, and will go out on a cold winter's
> day in the same apparel as they wear in summer, thinking it as natural to be cold
> as hungry. Whenever I see a procession of the unemployed in England, what
> strikes me most, as an Irishman, is the comfort and soundness of their clothes,
> as compared with Irish labourers in the best of times on a working day (34,
> p. 299).

This comment was made in the early twentieth century, but the condition
to which it refers must have existed from some time earlier. The song which
praises whisky as "my outside coat, I have no other," is very old at any
rate.

The idea that spirits had a genuine medicinal value in cold and damp
climates was not merely a popular fancy based on the subjective feeling of
warmth which alcohol undeniably produces, but apparently at one time
was held seriously by at least a portion of the medical profession, and by
others in responsible positions. In the inquiry of the House of Commons on
drunkenness in 1834, several witnesses were asked "whether, in such a moist
climate as Ireland, whisky is at all necessary to health" (44, p. 97), and
several complaints were made to the committee against the practice, in the
British Army and Navy, of giving, and in some cases forcing, rations of
spirits (44). In brief, the impression that the use of alcohol is more or less
inevitably linked to the climate seems to have been quite general in the
nineteenth century.

Another use of whisky in Ireland, in no way novel, and yet distinctly
worth noticing as part of the general medicinal use of alcohol which existed there, is its use as a stimulant or reviver in cases of fainting, unconsciousness, or shock. An example will be ample to illustrate this common use.
A man has been hanged, and by chance the job has been clumsily done:

After hanging the limited time he was cut down and given to his friends; he was carried to the nearest cabin, and as is almost always done in Ireland, all the vulgar methods in use were practiced to recover him; his feet were put into warm water, he was blooded by a countryman with a rusty lancet, and rubbed with spirits, which were likewise applied to his nostrils and lips and poured down his throat. He opened at length his eyes, and milk was given him from a woman's breast, which in Ireland is supposed to be a medicine of great efficacy (21, p. 235).

One of the most striking instances of the medicinal use of alcohol is its connection with the several epidemics of cholera in Ireland. On March 14, 1831, the dreaded plague made its first appearance in Belfast. When it was first discovered in the town, many of the inhabitants fled to the country, but it spread rapidly and, before it was over, proved to be nearly as fatal as the Black Death which had preceded it (20). Perhaps the idea that brandy or whisky was an effective preventive of cholera traces in some way to its early use to prevent "fluxes" (diarrhea), as persistent diarrhea is among the first warning symptoms of impending cholera. Actually, the official medical instructions published by the English government 20 years later strongly recommend temperance at this stage, and cite instances where brandy appears to have precipitated a fatal outcome of the impending attack. Whatever the origin of the idea, it was widespread in 1831, as indicated in the testimony of Mr. G. W. Carr, of New Ross, before the House of Commons Committee in 1834:

Connected with the mischief and erring opinions on this subject, I wish to state, that the plague of the cholera was rendered a thousand-fold more fatal in Ireland from false opinions; an additional door was opened for drunkenness. Independent of the destructive effects of spirits on cholera patients, multitudes began for the first time to drink them as a preservative from infection, and have thereby become drunkards; and very many, who had totally renounced the drink, company, and habits of drunkards, were induced to take a little spirits by way of precaution, and have been thereby again entangled in drunkenness. Some have died of the disease which they thus fed, and others have not yet been recovered from their secondary slavery and disgrace (44, p. 302).

In April 1849 the cholera appeared again, this time in Dublin, and though the epidemic was not so widespread as in 1831, the people again showed their abundant faith in spirits, as reported by Mr. F. T. Porter, a barrister in that city:

In the great majority of cases ardent spirits were administered; and the police were frequently complained to by officers of health and other sanitary officials who had been called on to relieve pretended sufferings, in the expectation of brandy or whisky being promptly afforded. Occasionally, on being refused the coveted dram, the mock sufferer became at once invigorated, and addressed abusive language and threats of personal violence to "the cholera fellow." Some instances of approbrious and menacing expressions were brought by summons under my cognizance . . . (42, pp. 228–229).

Facilities for medical care, even of the crude and faulty type which the dispensary doctors were able to provide, were all but entirely lacking in some sections and for the poorer parts of the population in the first half of the nineteenth century. It seems likely that this condition was one of the factors which contributed to the continued reliance in the supposed medicinal virtues of whisky. The people's attitude toward medical treatment in general, uncomplicated by knowledge of its intrinsic workings, was largely based on simple faith—faith in Divine Providence, in the superior knowledge and power of the doctor or apothecary who prescribed, or in the generalized virtue of "a bottle," as they tended to call any medicine, for any ailment (43).

The Irish dispensary doctors, whose lives without doubt were bleak and full of frustration, were prone to occasional lapses in temperance and in some cases to continual drinking, in spite of the disapproval of the local government boards. The dependence of a doctor upon alcohol apparently did not disturb the faith of the peasantry in his powers. The drunken Irish doctor has become almost a literary stereotype, portrayed sometimes humorously, sometimes with pathos. Robinson tells of one old toper who, having once mixed a potion of almost miraculous effectiveness while thoroughly befuddled (a potion which he has never been able to duplicate), now defends his drinking to a member of the Local Government Board:

"Man dear," he said, "ye don't understand. If the Local Government Board had any notion of the knowledge and wisdom that takes a hould of me when I have the drink taken, d'ye know what they'd do? Instead of sending you down to be spying on me and lecturing me—mind ye I'm not blaming ye; I quite see your point of view—they'd send me up a barrel of whisky onct a week, so they would, with a sealed order directing me to drink my fill before ever I attended on a red ticket at all!" (43, pp. 32–33.)

One specific medicinal use of alcohol which is of particular importance is and has been current in Ireland—that of a drink or two on the "morning after" as an antidote to the symptoms of a hangover. Indeed, the popular designation of this drink as "a hair of the dog that bit you" may likely be Irish in origin. Birmingham writes that ". . . the belief in the curative value of a hair of the dog that bit you is still held quite literally in some parts of Ireland." He tells an amusing story of a gentleman in Connacht who received a terrier as a present. This dog had a peculiarity of biting the bare legs of boys. The unfortunate owner of the dog expected the father of one injured boy to demand a huge sum, but to his great relief, the father ended his account of the incident with the modest request of "a hair out of the dog's tail."

"Take the hair," said the owner. "Take all the hairs there are. Take the tail itself if you like." "Sure, that'd be too much altogether," said the father. "All I want is a hair to lay on the bite in the young lad's leg the way no harm would come of it." (9, pp. 201–202.)

It would be difficult to find out when the phrase came to be used to refer to the morning-after drink, but its aptness is obvious, and it was probably current among the peasantry in the nineteenth century, as indicated in McCarthy's reference to it as "the old saying." McCarthy is giving an account of a certain case of matchmaking which he considered typical. The matchmaker is trying to persuade Patrick, a bashful, clumsy young farmer, that a certain young girl would make an excellent wife for him. As a final cap to the long recital of her virtues, the matchmaker adds:

". . . and I have it for a fact, that when her father and brother comes home after the fair a little elevated, as 'tis often a good man's case, she helps 'em upstairs; and the next morning she always cures them with a hair of the dog that bit 'em, as the old saying is." " 'Tis a great wonder that she's not picked up," said Patrick contemplatively . . . (34, p. 246).

It seems likely that the practice of drinking on the morning after has varied in different classes, and in different times, though indications (38) are that it has existed for at least a century. McCarthy, speaking of conditions in 1911 says that many of the middle-aged farmers keep on drinking for several days after the fair, while others do not stop at all; however, he believes that the majority of them do not resume drinking on the day after, but keep sober until the next fair or market, when they again get "gloriously drunk" (34, p. 300–301).

Some of the sketches of Sir Jonah Barrington (6) leave no doubt that bouts of several days were by no means unknown among the gentry of Ireland of the middle of the nineteenth century. Rev. John Edgar, speaking of the period around 1834, says:

It is customary among many tradesmen to take a "morning" as it is called, one glass of spiritous liquor early every morning. . . . It is a very general complaint in reference to whole classes of tradesmen that they spend in idleness and dissipation . . . [not only the Saturday night and Sunday, but also] . . . the Monday and very frequently the Tuesday . . . [of every week. This extended drinking they call] . . . the run, the spree, the tipple . . . (44, pp. 87, 92).

Indications are that the "morning" existed in some places and to some extent as a practice not necessarily connected with previous heavy indulgence, as a sort of general stimulant. John Gamble speaks of one of his hosts, a Presbyterian, who has taken a limited pledge:

He is sworn to drink but one glass in the day, which he tells me he takes as soon as he rises in the morning, and feels no more inclination for it till the same hour of the following day (21, pp. 262–263).

In the nineteenth century, the Irish began to emigrate to America in large numbers. One of their customs was to hold a sort of wake on the evening before the departure of the emigrant. A certain Dr. Atthill recalls a part of a ballad someone had written describing the festive scene, the mighty consumption of food, and the aftereffects on guests who "Eat scones of Boxty bread, and oceans drank of tea." The doctor goes on to explain:

Boxty bread was made up of equal parts of raw potatoes grated, and flour; was baked on a griddle; was heavy and indigestible. Each scone would weigh quite one pound. The ballad described the subsequent suffering and the cure, which consisted of rolling and rubbing, and whiskey administered freely (5, p. 59).

In short, it is hard to think of medicinal use of alcohol which has not been current, at one time or another, in the Irish culture.* Its use as a medicine was strongly established in the nineteenth century, when so many of our immigrants came from Ireland—even in the first enthusiasm of the temperance movement which had its beginnings in 1829, the pledges of temperance apparently quite often contained the provision that whisky might be taken medicinally (7).

There are many indications that when the Irish came to America, they brought these ideas and practices along with them. Hansen, in speaking of the drinking habits of the Irish immigrants, says: "The fatigue of heavy labor demanded a stimulant; fever and ague required an antidote; homesickness had to be dispelled. For all these ailments whisky provided a universal remedy . . ." (24, p. 109).

The medicinal use of alcohol persisted among the Irish who came to America, from all indications. The wife of one Irish patient whose record was examined "gives him whisky and hot milk to sober him off." This patient did not drink much during prohibition, "except during the flu epidemic, when he took three drinks of whiskey every day." He is puzzled because drinking did not seem to have a bad effect on his father. "He believes that the weather in Ireland has something to do with it—people felt all right the next morning." The wife of another Irish patient wishes that her husband were "the type of man who could spend a few hours with friends over a bottle, and quit, this as a social recreation." He cannot do this however. "His stomach is not strong, and he continues drinking to cure his sickness. His last visit to the hospital was the result of a spree developing from his having been given a few spoonfuls of alcohol for a cold." The stereotype of the drunken Irish doctor has not disappeared. One patient, himself a doctor and Irish, testifies that he knows "a great many Irish doctors who drink heavily," and another Irish patient, a fireman, contends that no patient is ever "cured" of drinking, on the evidence that it is "common knowledge" that doctors drink.

To return from the everyday use of alcohol in the Irish culture to the usages connected with the principal points in the life cycle: the final *rite de passage* is the funeral. The funeral proper, a Mass just before burial, is administered by the Church. The wake is a social adjunct—not an integral part of the religious ritual. Usually it takes place on the night before the Mass and burial. At one time "wakes" were held at night in churchyards in remembrance of saints, and the occasion came to be a sort of fair, with peddlers

---

* Alcohol was also used in a concoction with boiled nettles in the treatment of measles. See Kavanagh (27, p. 19).

and entertainers. Not infrequently such a wake was the scene of singing, dancing, drinking, and other merrymaking, which often enough ended up in a faction fight. These "wakes" are to be distinguished from the death wake, although there are historical connections between the two, and a high degree of similarity in certain respects.

According to MacLysaght (33, p. 168), "the idea of regarding wakes as a source of entertainment . . . was [probably] . . . not common until the very end of the seventeenth century, and the scenes so graphically described by eighteenth and nineteenth century writers were a subsequent development." At the present time the wake is a "pale reflection, a bewildered memory" (32, pp. 113–114) of the eighteenth and nineteenth century ceremonies.

Wakes are sufficiently common both in Catholic and Protestant Ireland today, but they are fast becoming a discredited institution. In many dioceses the Catholic Bishops have absolutely forbidden them. The priests sometimes go so far as to threaten to withhold the rites of Christian burial if the wake is not dispensed with. The reason of this, of course, is not that the wake is a relic of paganism, but that it is apt to cause an excessive amount of drinking and extravagance (32, p. 112).

As to the wakes of the eighteenth and nineteenth centuries, which have caused so much comment, there is little doubt that factual grounds existed for the types of criticism which were made:

. . . the abuses connected with wakes were more serious than the mere indecorum of merrymaking on a solemn occasion; the merrymaking was frequently not of an innocent kind, for it involved not only excessive drinking but also practices which were always coarse and very often actually licentious. A great deal of evidence of this has already been collected in print, all pointing in the same direction. While some writers charitably designate as "this jovial crew," or as "revellers as if at one of the feasts of Bacchus," the participants in what others describe as orgies, that abuses existed is denied by none (33, pp. 167–168).

Summary

Among the Irish, in contrast to the Jews, there is virtually no *ritual drinking* in the religious sense. The only exception is the drinking of the wine by the priest in the Mass, and there are ample reasons to minimize the importance of this ritual act for the laity so far as its functional relation to other types of drinking is concerned: first, consecrated wine, by social definition, is in a class by itself, and is not identified with other types of alcoholic beverages, nor interchangeable with them; second, by reason of its extremely loose coupling to the socialization process in that a host of other non-sacred ideas and sentiments regarding drinking are presented to the child as his earliest introduction to drinking, the sacred ideas and sentiments are not introduced until comparatively late in the process, and even then, not as elements in his activity.

A great part of the drinking in which the individual participates, from the beginning to the end of his life cycle in the Irish culture, is *convivial drinking,* which has symbolic elements, to be sure, but symbolic elements which are different in two important ways from those which are a part of ritual drinking in the religious sense as practiced in the Jewish culture.

First, those symbolic elements which are essentially "communicative" in function, that is, which are used by the individual primarily to convey certain meanings to others in terms of the arbitrary social meanings attached to the act, do not refer to the central core of sacred ideas and sentiments of the Irish Catholic culture, as they do in the Jewish culture. In the Irish culture the individual does not express anything about his relation to the sacred in drinking; his drinking or not drinking has no determinate relation to religious ideas and sentiments which are a part of his own and others' orientation.

What the individual does express and communicate to others by acts of convivial drinking in the Irish culture is his solidarity with certain groups within the social system. Thus, drinking together is a symbolic certification or manifestation of the solidarity of "friends" or kinship groups, of the acceptance of the individual male as a "man among men," as an equal in his own solidary age group; drinking together is a manifestation of the equality and solidarity of town and country folk, of the guest and the host, the politician and his constituents, the seller and the buyer. Refusal of men of different classes to drink with one another indicates a lack of solidarity, but as the lack of solidarity passes into hostility, drinking, rather than abstention, again becomes the vehicle for expressing hostility—the covert aggression of the "boys" toward the "old fellows," covert and open aggression against disliked members of the community. Finally, drinking is both a manifestation of, and an actual utilitarian preparation for, faction and party fights, attacks on informers, and the perpetual rebellion against the age-old enemy, England.

Thus, the second way in which the symbolic elements centering around the act of drinking in the Irish culture differ from those around ritual drinking in the Jewish culture, is that they are not exhausted by those with essentially "communicative" functions which are implicit and complete in a single act of drinking. A large part of them consist of knowledge, socially current, approved, and recommended to the individual, of the ways in which *intoxication* (not simply the single act of drinking) can be used or utilized as a means of attaining perfectly empirical ends. These ends, in turn, are not exhausted by common social ends or joint social purposes, but include the satisfaction or relief of all sorts of individualized, self-oriented, self-contained needs of the personality and the physical body—ends which may exist apart from, or be in conflict with, the interests of others.

The use of intoxication, or drinking leading to it, whether of the self or of others, in order to gain some personal advantage over the other, or to bring relief or satisfaction of self-oriented, self-contained needs, may be called *utilitarian drinking.* The distinction is *not* that ritual and convivial drinking contain symbolic elements, whereas utilitarian drinking does not, but that the content of the ideas and sentiments, their relation to other internalized orienting factors of the personality, and consequently their function for the individual, is quite different in each type of drinking.

Besides the use of drinking and intoxication in political and economic contexts, which involves both convivial and utilitarian aspects, it has been shown that there is a large body of usages in Ireland which can be classed as almost purely utilitarian, and historical evidence seems to show that whisky has had this character from the time of its first incorporation in the Irish culture. Its uses as a medicine for practically all the miscellaneous antique ills to which man is subject need not be repeated in full—among those which have been the more prominent are colds, fevers, diarrhea, flu, and cholera. Its everyday use to begin the day, to get rid of a "hangover," to quiet hunger, to relieve stomach disorders, to get warm, to keep warm, to reward the child, to release sexual and aggressive tensions, to relieve emotional difficulties ranging from minor upsets and disappointments to deep grief, to restore consciousness in case of fainting and shock, to improve the physician's skill, to dispel fatigue and to promote sleep—all of these and more are utilitarian uses, prominently structured and sanctioned in the Irish culture.

The second major conclusion is that it is this complex of utilitarian ideas and sentiments, deeply internalized through repeated overt actions in which the ideas and sentiments are objectively represented, that "sets the stage" as it were, for certain further articulation and reinforcement on the individual level, and that is thus primarily responsible for the notably higher rate of alcohol addiction among the Irish, as compared to the Orthodox Jews.

References

1. Anonymous, *Real Life in Ireland by a Real Paddy* (4th ed.), London: Methuen and Company, 1904.

2. Anonymous, *Tales of Irish Life, Illustrative of the Manners, Customs, and Condition of the People,* London: J. Robbins and Company, 1824.

3. Arensberg, Conrad M., *The Irish Countryman,* New York: The Macmillan Company, 1937.

4. ———, and Kimball, S. T., *Family and Community in Ireland,* Cambridge, Mass.: Harvard University Press, 1940.

5. Atthill, Lombe, *Recollections of an Irish Doctor,* London: The Religious Tract Society, 1911.

6. Barrington, Sir Jonah, *Personal Sketches of His Own Time,* New York: Redfield, 1853.

7. Barrow, John, *A Tour Round Ireland, Through the Sea-Coast Counties, in the Autumn of 1835,* London: John Murray, 1836.

8. Birmingham, George A., *Irishmen All,* New York: Frederick A. Stokes Company, 1913.

9. ———, *The Lighter Side of Irish Life,* New York: Frederick A. Stokes Company, 1912.

10. Callwell, J. M., *Old Irish Life,* Edinburgh and London: William Blackwood and Sons, 1912.

11. Carleton, William, *Tales and Stories of the Irish Peasants,* Dublin: James Duffy, 1846.

12. ———, *Traits and Stories of the Irish Peasantry* (9th ed.), London: William Tegg, 1869.

13. Chart, D. A., *Ireland, From the Union to the Catholic Emancipation, A Study of Social, Economic and Administrative Conditions, 1800–1829,* London: J. M. Dent and Sons, 1910.

14. Conmee, Rev. John S., *Old Times in the Barony,* Dublin: Catholic Truth Society, no date.

15. Conybeare, F. C., "Eucharist," *The Encyclopedia Britannica* (11th ed.), Cambridge: University Press, 1910.

16. "Cup of Benediction," *Jewish Encyclopedia,* Vol. IV.

17. de la Fontaine, Elise, "Cultural and Psychological Implications in Case Work Treatment with Irish Clients," *Cultural Problems in Social Case Work,* New York: Family Welfare Assn. of America, 1940.

18. Donovan, John, "Age and Sex in the Social Structure of Ireland," unpublished notes.

19. Farrell, James T., *Studs Lonigan,* New York: Modern Library, 1938.

20. Foley, Patrick, *Irish Historical Allusions,* Tribune Publishing Company, 1916.

21. Gamble, John, *A View of Society and Manners in the North of Ireland, in the Summer and Autumn of 1812,* London: C. Cradock and W. Joy, 1813.

22. ———, *Sketches of History, Politics and Manners, Taken in Dublin, and the North of Ireland, in the Autumn of 1810,* London: C. Cradock and W. Joy, 1811.

23. Grattan, Thomas Colley, *Beaten Paths; and Those Who Trod Them* (2nd ed.), London: Chapman and Hall, 1862.

24. Hansen, M. L., *The Immigrant in American History,* Cambridge, Mass.: Harvard University Press, 1940.

25. Ireland, Father John, "The Catholic Church and the Saloon," *North American Review,* Vol. CLIX, 1894, p. 502.

26. Joyce, P. W., *A Social History of Ancient Ireland,* Vol. II, London: Longmans, Green, and Company, 1903.

27. Kavanagh, Patrick, *The Green Fool,* London: Michael Joseph, 1938.

28. Kerr, Norman, *Inebriety or Narcomania,* London: H. K. Lewis, 1894.

29. Koplowitz, Rabbi Isidore, *Midrash Yayin Veshechor, Talmudic and Midrashic Exegetics on Wine and Strong Drink,* Detroit, Mich.: No publisher indicated, 1923.

30. Le Fanu, W. R., *Seventy Years of Irish Life, Being Anecdotes and Reminiscences,* New York: The Macmillan Company, 1893.

31. Long, Major A. W., *Irish Sport of Yesterday,* London: Paternoster Row, 1922.

32. Lynd, Robert, *Home Life in Ireland,* London: Mills and Boon, 1909.

33. MacLysaght, Edward, *Irish Life in the Seventeenth Century: After Cromwell,* London: Longmans, Green, and Company, 1939.

34. McCarthy, M. J. F., *Irish Land and Irish Liberty,* London: Robert Scott, 1911.

35. Madden, Samuel, *Reflections and Resolutions Proper for the Gentlemen of Ireland, as to Their Conduct for the Service of the Country,* Dublin: R. Reilly, 1738, Reprinted, 1816.

36. Mooney, Thomas, *Nine Years in America, A Series of Letters to His Cousin, Patrick Mooney, A Farmer in Ireland,* Dublin: James McGlashan, 1850.

37. Morewood, Samuel, *An Essay on the Inventions and Customs of Both Ancients and*

Moderns in the Use of Inebriating Liquors, London: Longmans, Hurst, Rees, Orme, Brown and Green, 1824.

38. ———, *A Philosophical History . . . of Inebriating Liquors . . . and other Stimulants,* Dublin: W. Curry, Jr., and Company and W. Carson, 1838.

39. Personal communication, C. M. Arensberg.

40. Personal communication from Dom Thomas V. Moore, Graduate School, The Catholic University of America, Washington, D.C., Aug. 31, 1943.

41. Pohle, J., "Eucharist," *The Catholic Encyclopedia,* Vol. V, New York: Robert Appleton Company, 1909, pp. 572–590.

42. Porter, Frank Thorpe, *Gleanings and Reminiscences,* Dublin: Hodges, Forster and Company, 1875.

43. Robinson, Sir Henry A., *Further Memories of Irish Life,* London: Herbert Jenkins, 1924.

44. Select Committee on Drunkenness of the House of Commons, *Evidence on Drunkenness Presented to the House of Commons,* London: Samuel Bagster, Jr. (Printer), around 1834.

45. Somerville, E., *The Smile and the Tear,* London: Methuen and Company, 1933.

Culture and Jewish sobriety: the ingroup-outgroup factor[*]

Charles R. Snyder

Jewish experience with beverage alcohol poses some crucial questions for all who are concerned with the problems of alcohol which beset modern society. The drinking of alcoholic beverages is widespread among Jews and has been so since ancient times. In terms of percentages, there are probably more users of alcoholic beverages in the Jewish group than in any other major religio-ethnic group in America. Yet as has been shown repeatedly both in this country and abroad, rates of alcoholism and other drinking pathologies for Jews are very low.

Two further considerations must be added to this paradox in order to clarify its significance and to suggest the kind of research which might prove fruitful. First, there is no lack among Jews of acute psychic tensions of the sort which are popularly supposed to cause drinking pathologies. In comparison to certain groups exhibiting an excess of alcohol problems, perhaps it may be said that they have an undue share of anxieties which have their origin in broad social and historical circumstances. Hence, psychological explanations of drinking pathologies which are exclusively phrased in terms of disproportionate needs to relieve psychic distress seem patently contradicted by the facts of Jewish experience. Second, the heterogeneity of Jews in terms of physical or racial characteristics casts doubt upon any kind of bio-racial explanation. This doubt is considerably strengthened by the failure of science to uncover any specific hereditary mechanisms suf-

[*] This chapter represents part of a larger study reported in (31). The excerpts and special introduction presented here also appeared under the same title in Marshall Sklare (Ed.), *The Jews: Social Patterns of an American Group,* Glencoe, Ill.: The Free Press, 1958. They are reprinted here with only slight modification.

ficient to account for drinking pathologies. These considerations thus high-light the possibility that at least part of the explanation for Jewish sobriety may be found in the cultural tradition of the Jewish people. While there is no logical need to deny a conditional role to bio-psychic factors in the genesis of drinking pathologies, the facts augur well for the sociological approach in attempting to understand the Jewish experience and, by im-plication, alcohol problems in general.

The present study is part of a larger research plan designed to extend our knowledge of American Jewish drinking patterns and to test different explanations of the rarity of drinking pathologies in this group. To place this chapter in perspective, brief comment on the most promising line of ex-planation in the light of our over-all findings (31) seems warranted.

Of the various theories advanced, the one proposed by Bales (1, 2) ap-pears to have the greatest explanatory value. On the most general level, his theory holds that group rates of extreme drinking pathologies are re-sultants of the interaction of three major sets of contributing factors. The first of these may be called *dynamic factors,* referring to the group incidence of acute psychic tensions or needs for adjustment sufficient to provide the driving force in drinking pathologies. The second consists of *alternative factors,* that is, culturally defined possibilities of adopting behavior pat-terns other than excessive drinking which are nonetheless functional equiva-lents in channeling and relieving acute psychic tensions. The third set may be designated as *orienting factors,* or the kinds of normative attitudes to-ward drinking itself which are carried in the cultures of different groups. Obviously these factors are exceedingly difficult to weigh in a given empiri-cal situation. Nevertheless, in his specific discussion of the Jewish group, Bales emphasized the orienting factor of the particular normative attitudes toward drinking which are embedded in the rituals of Orthodox Judaism as being sufficient to account for the *difference* between Jewish rates of drinking pathologies and the rates for certain other groups with quite dif-ferent normative attitudes.

Those who are familiar with traditional Judaism will at once recognize how extensively and firmly drinking is woven into the traditional rituals of the annual cycle of holy days and festivals, the *rites de passage,* and the observances of the Sabbath. They will also be cognizant of the extension of religious symbolism to drinking situations apart from formal acts of sanctification. Indeed, normative Judaism generally locates the act of drink-ing squarely in the network of sacred ideas, sentiments, and activities. In the context of this tradition, drinking is defined as symbolic, expressive, and communicative rather than as convivial or hedonistic in character. It will perhaps not strain the imagination overly much to suppose, with Bales, that early training and continued participation in religious drinking rituals help structure in the character stable attitudes toward drinking, and that such attitudes are incorporated in the personality together with the most power-ful religious ideas and sentiments of the group and are renewed and vitalized in the ceremonies and rituals which best express and reinforce these ideas and sentiments later in life. In any event, it was Bales' view that this body of tradition develops drinking attitudes of a quality and intensity sufficient to counter the development of hedonistic or addictive drinking.

This line of reasoning clearly links the distinctive sobriety of the Jews with the Orthodox religious tradition and its corpus of ritual and ceremony. Our own research, utilizing present-day diversity in Jewish religious affiliation and practice, checked this point of view systematically. Our findings to date are supportive: intoxication and signs of more extreme drinking pathologies are conspicuous by their absence among the more Orthodox, despite their extensive use of wines, spirits, and beers. However, as religious affiliation shifts from Orthodox to Conservative to Reform and to Secular, signs of drinking pathologies show marked and systematic increase. Moreover, these changes cannot be attributed to the direct influence of social class or generational factors. This is important because a host of studies, including our own, have shown differentiation among Jews in this country in their religious affiliation and practice along class and generation lines.

Statistical analysis indicates, however, that continued sobriety is to be found wherever the Orthodox tradition is vital—albeit in attenuated form —regardless of social class or generation status. The earmarks of drinking pathologies become significantly evident where this tradition has been discarded, particularly if this is true in the earliest stages of socialization. All of this is not to say that Jews—other than the Orthodox—are debauching themselves with drink. Rather, there appears to be a trend toward convergence with wider societal drinking averages, normal or pathological—a trend which corresponds with a decline in the vitality and impact of the Orthodox Jewish religious tradition. It is data of this kind which lend plausibility to Bales' point of view.

There are, however, other possible explanations of our findings. Also, there are aspects of Jewish tradition other than ritual drinking which comprise relevant parts of the total cultural orientation toward beverage alcohol. In the material which follows, we will seek to evaluate theories which in various ways have sought the explanation of Jewish sobriety in the relations of Jews to the larger society. This will involve us in an analysis of those particular aspects of Jewish culture which, while bearing on drinking behavior, are intimately connected with the ingroup-outgroup situation, that is, with the status of Jewry as a minority group.

Some Theoretical Considerations

The theories of Kant (17), Fishberg (9),* and others emphasize the ingroup-outgroup situation as decisive for Jewish sobriety.† Kant wrote:

* Fishberg's views as relevant here are best expressed in Bernheimer (4).

† The Jewish group is designated as an "ingroup" so as to suggest consciousness of group identity vis-à-vis the larger Gentile society (the outgroup), and in recognition of a cultural tradition which embodies in many ways an ethnocentric view. However,

Women, ministers, and Jews do not get drunk, as a rule, at least they carefully avoid all appearance of it, because their civic position is weak and they need to be reserved. Their outward worth is based merely on the belief of others of their chastity, piousness and separatistic lore. All separatists, that is, those who subject themselves not only to the general laws of the country but also to a special sectarian law, are exposed through their eccentricity and alleged chosenness to the attention and criticism of the community, and thus cannot relax their self-control, for intoxication, which deprives one of cautiousness, would be a scandal for them (17, pp. 777–778).

Whatever the inadequacies of this point of view, the minority status of the Jew cannot be dismissed as of no consequence for Jewish sobriety. Nearly all students of Jewish drinking behavior have attributed significance to this situation in one way or another. Even Bales (1) suggests that the fear of retaliation from dominant groups may provide reinforcement to a norm of sobriety which he thinks derives ultimately from religious beliefs and practices. A survey of the literature on the influence of the ingroup-outgroup situation on Jewish drinking behavior, however, makes it especially clear that speculation has far outrun the accumulation of supporting evidence. By and large there has been cavalier indifference to the need for basing theories on firm factual foundations. Only Glad (11) attempted direct verification of Kant's type of theory which explains Jewish sobriety as a minority sect reaction to fear of censure from powerful majorities. Glad interprets his own evidence as non-supportive of the theory, but for reasons discussed elsewhere (31) Glad's findings are inconclusive.

There is some further indirect evidence bearing on this problem. Bales (2) made a painstaking analysis of what he calls the empirical adequacy of Kant's argument and, like Glad, concluded that the facts do not support the theory. However, the facts upon which Bales based his rejection of Kant's theory are not facts concerning ingroup-outgroup influences on Jewish drinking behavior. The facts which in Bales' opinion challenge the empirical adequacy of Kant's explanation are drawn from histories of alcoholics. Bales reasons that, in the last analysis, Kant's theory attributes sobriety and the absence of alcoholism among Jews to the operation of the cognitive faculties —that is, the Jews, although they drink frequently, avoid excess and addiction by rationally assessing the consequences. This presumed rational assessment is made in the context of the actual or potential censure to which members of the disadvantaged Jewish minority are exposed. But experience with alcoholics does not support an assumption that knowledge of the dangers and undesirable consequences of excessive drinking enables the exercise of good judgment or "will power" sufficient to prevent alcoholism. Accordingly, Bales concluded that Kant's explanation and the analogous explanations of others are empirically inadequate.

Bales' criticism of the "rationalist fallacy" in these arguments is astute and

these terms are intended only as ideal types. By no means do all nominal Jews experience an equivalent sense of "ingroupness," and distinctions in this respect have an important bearing on Jewish drinking behavior.

suggestive. It highlights the naïveté of trying to explain the consistent sobriety of the Jews without some disciplined understanding of the nature of
alcoholism. The critique also points to a body of facts which must be accounted for, at least by implication, in any adequate explanation of Jewish
sobriety. Bales' reasoning, however, tends to obscure the need for a thorough
analysis of the influence of the ingroup-outgroup situation on Jewish drinking behavior. This results from the implicit assumption that the nature of
that influence is of the sort which Bales imputes to Kant's brief description and that the Jewish response is actually a purely rational one. This
assumption, however, has no systematic evidence to support it.

In Bales' argument this assumption is connected by a chain of inferences
to facts on the etiology of alcoholism, and Kant's type of theory is accordingly found wanting. But Bales' (1, 2) readmission of Kant's explanation as
a secondary factor in Jewish sobriety testifies to his own reluctance to dis-
miss ingroup-outgroup relations as of no importance for the sober response
of Jews to beverage alcohol. We must therefore question whether the assumption of a rational response to imminent censure or danger exhausts
the significance of the ingroup-outgroup situation for Jewish sobriety. It
seems that the resolution of the problems engendered by Bales' criticism of
Kant's theory lies in further factual investigation of the influences on Jewish
drinking of the Jewish ingroup, the Gentile outgroup, and the relations between Jews and Gentiles.

Yet another facet of the ingroup-outgroup situation remains to be considered. The outgroup has been held by some observers to exercise a demoralizing influence on Jews in their use of alcoholic beverages. Fishberg
(9) and Myerson (24), for instance, assert that the assimilating Jew who
has increasing contacts with Gentiles is more prone to drunkenness and alcoholism than his compatriot of the ghetto.* The implications are clear:
relations with the outgroup, which have been seen by Kant, Fishberg, and
others as a major cause of Jewish sobriety, are seen also in an entirely
different light as the source of increasing intoxication and alcoholism among
Jews. The evidence supporting this latter view is sketchy. It consists largely
of clinical impressions and a few statistics which suggest greater inebriety

---

* The demoralizing influence of outsiders and the identification of hedonistic drinking with assimilation (more accurately, with idolatry) is not a new idea or simply an
observation of modern theorists but one that has long standing in Jewish culture, as
the following tradition indicates: " 'And they called the people unto the sacrifices of
their gods: and the people did eat, and bowed down to their gods' [Numbers 25:2].
They [the Midianites] followed his [Balaam's] advice. . . . They put up shops for them
and placed therein prostitutes and in their hands were all manner of attractive things.
. . . And a young woman issued forth bedecked and perfumed and lured him and
said, Why do we love you and you hate us? . . . Thereupon she gave him the wine
to drink, and Satan burned in him. . . . When he asked her for sexual intercourse
she said, I will not submit until you slaughter this to Peor and bow down to him.
And he replied, I will not bow down to an idol. She said to him, You are only un-
covering yourself. And he was mad with passion for her and did so." This tradition, with
variations and amplifications, occurs in numerous ancient Talmudic and Midrashic
sources.

among relatively assimilated Jews. However, little or nothing has been revealed of the conditions under which changes are induced in Jewish drinking behavior and attitude, or the actual role of ingroup-outgroup relations in the process.

It is apparent that several questions of fact must be answered before a general evaluation of the impact of the ingroup-outgroup situation on Jewish drinking behavior can be made. For example, can immediate social pressures from the outgroup be inferred from a difference in Jewish drinking behavior in ingroup and outgroup contexts? Are these pressures handled differently by various categories of Jews and, if so, why? Do Jews perceive social pressures regarding drinking in terms of ingroup and outgroup? Are these perceptions related to stereotypes of Jews and Gentiles which are part of the Jewish cultural tradition? If so, what is the nature of these stereotypes and what functions do they serve? Does the vitality of these stereotypes depend upon strong group identification and participation in other aspects of Jewish culture? Can the findings on these various points be woven together with evidence which indicates such a decided difference in the relative sobriety of Orthodox and non-Orthodox Jews? How then, is the significance of the ingroup-outgroup situation for Jewish drinking behavior to be assessed? These are the kinds of questions which we will attempt to answer, if only in a preliminary way.

Intoxication in Ingroup and Outgroup Contexts

The question has been raised whether or not there is a difference in response to alcohol when Jews drink with members of the ingroup or in outgroup contexts. A behavioral difference in this respect should be indicative of the nature of ingroup and outgroup influences on Jewish sobriety. Suggestive evidence is to be found in the reports of our sample of New Haven Jewish men * on the social contexts in which episodes of intoxication oc-

* The basic materials for this study were obtained from two sources. First, from interviews with a random sample of seventy-three New Haven Jewish men. Second, from questionnaires administered to a larger sample of male Jewish college students as part of the College Drinking Survey (34). Details of sampling procedures and conventions used in the analysis and presentation of data may be found in (31). Attention must be called, however, to the fact that Jewish students in the Survey were not drawn from any single locale or college setting. The sample of Jewish students represents an aggregate of Jewish youth scattered in eighteen different colleges in various parts of the United States. Moreover, some selection was introduced in the sampling procedures of the College Drinking Survey. Of outstanding importance to this study was the inclusion of Orthodox Jewish students in greater proportion than their probable proportion in the American Jewish population might warrant. Because of these sampling procedures and the intrinsic limits of the universe under study, findings from the Jewish student sample cannot be thought of as direct measures of the incidence of socio-cultural traits in the American Jewish population. Nor are findings from this sample directly indicative of characteristics of particular communities, as are the findings from our New Haven sample. Even generalizations about drinking and other characteristics of Jewish college students based on this sample must be asserted cautiously. Despite these qualifications, the sample of Jewish students is of decided value in studying *relations* among socio-cultural phenomena pertinent to this research.

curred. Of course, pinning down all these contexts is an impossible task when respondents have been intoxicated frequently. Descriptions were actually obtained for only 40 per cent of the instances of intoxication reported by men in this sample. Of these instances, however, 60 per cent took place either in military service or in college, with military service predominating. It is not certain that the social composition of the drinking group was preponderantly Gentile in all instances of intoxication in the service or in college. But the answers of several men questioned on this point indicate that the companions were frequently non-Jewish. Moreover, of the seventeen in this group who had been intoxicated more than five times in their lives, at least twelve experienced some or all of the episodes of intoxication in the service or in college. When it is borne in mind that drinking actually occurs more often in ingroup than outgroup contexts, the fact that a substantial proportion of intoxication occurs in outgroup contexts assumes considerable significance. Without obscuring occasional instances of intoxication in Jewish settings, as at a Bar Mitzvah or wedding, the evidence points to the influence of the larger Gentile society in modifying Jewish patterns of moderate drinking and sobriety.

Because many of the Jewish students in the College Drinking Survey (34) sample attended colleges where a plurality or substantial minority of the student body are Jews, military service probably represents a more extreme outgroup situation than does college for these students. Consequently, a comparison of the patterns of drinking and sobriety in veterans and non-veterans among the Jewish students should be indicative of ingroup-outgroup influence. A reflection of these influences is to be found in the fact that of those Jewish veterans who reported on the regularity or irregularity of their drinking patterns in military service, 65 per cent had had an irregular pattern as against 35 per cent with a regular pattern. Of course regularity or irregularity may mean many things, and there is no assurance from these data that Jewish students were more prone to intoxication while in the service.

Subsequent questions on differences between current civilian drinking and practices while in the service revealed that 49 per cent of the veterans now drink less, 37 per cent about the same, and only 14 per cent more than while in the service. Still there is possible ambiguity in statements concerning "drinking more" or "drinking less," which may refer to frequency of drinking rather than to quantities consumed. However, from what is known of Jewish interpretations of "drinking more" or "drinking less" there is little doubt that quantity was foremost in the minds of these students. Hence, a substantial proportion of Jewish veterans who reported drinking more in the service were almost certainly expressing an increase in the quantities of alcoholic beverages consumed in particular drinking situations and not just an increase in frequency of drinking.

The soundness of this interpretation is indicated by the fact that Jewish student veterans reported substantially higher frequencies of intoxication than non-veterans. On the one hand, only about a fourth of the non-veterans reported having been drunk twice or more, or tight more than five times. On the other hand, about half the veterans had exceeded these limits. Uncritical reliance on gross differences in intoxication between veterans and non-veterans, however, may be misleading. Veterans in college tend to be older than non-veterans and consequently have had more time to accumulate experiences of intoxication (3, 4). Age differences must therefore be taken into account before differences in intoxication among the Jewish students can be attributed to the service situation. To determine the effects of age differences, veterans and non-veterans were divided into two age classes (according to whether or not they were above or below the mean age for the sample of Jewish students) and were further classified by extent of intoxication. The resulting distribution is shown in Table 1 and it is clear that veterans in both age classes exceed non-veterans while differences by age are inconsequential.*

TABLE 1

Frequency of Mild Intoxication (Tight More than Five Times) in Veterans and Non-veterans among Jewish Students, by Age Classes (in Per Cent)

Age	Veterans	Number Reporting	Non-veterans	Number Reporting
21 or less	49	(29)	25	(336)
Over 21	54	(101)	24	(45)

The difference in extent of intoxication between the veterans and non-veterans is particularly noteworthy because it does not apply to college students as a whole. On the basis of their general study of drinking among college students, Straus and Bacon (34) concluded that there are no significant differences in intoxication between veterans and non-veterans when age differences are taken into account. This is not the case with Jewish students. Apparently military service is related to greater experience of intoxication while age difference is insignificant within the narrow age range of these students.

Social Pressures

More direct evidence of the differential influences of social environments on Jewish patterns of drinking and intoxication is contained in sections of the New Haven interviews. The seventy-three Jewish men in the New

* Chi-square of the difference by veteran status is 18.54, P (at 2 degrees of freedom) is less than .001. To simplify presentation, only data on milder intoxication are shown in Table 1. Data on more severe intoxication show an analogous difference by veteran status.

Haven sample were asked whether they had been criticized for their drinking practices, either for "not drinking enough" or for "drinking too much." In reply, forty-three said they had felt criticism for not drinking enough, while only sixteen reported criticism for drinking too much. Forty-seven respondents identified the sources of these pressures. Analysis of the results (Table 2) indicates that Jewish men perceive the Jewish group as exerting pressures in the direction of moderate drinking and sobriety, while the non-Jewish milieu is perceived as the primary source of pressures to drink to excess.

TABLE 2

Sources of Social Pressures on New Haven Jewish Men to Drink More or Less

Pressure	Jewish	Mixed	Non-Jewish
To drink more	2	11	18
To drink less	15	1	0

$$\chi^2 = 35, \ P < .01$$

The content and sources of the pressures summarized in Table 2 deserve further attention. With the exception of one case which is equivocal, all Jewish men who had been criticized for drinking too much reported the source of criticism as specifically Jewish and familial. "The folks used to think I drank a little too much," or "My wife doesn't like to drink at all," were typical comments. By contrast, criticism for not drinking enough was confined almost exclusively to the categories of friends, acquaintances and business associates. Also, several men who reported criticism from mixed sources for not drinking enough added qualifications such as "mostly non-Jewish." Of the two men who reported exclusively Jewish criticism for not drinking enough, one said he was teased on Passover for just touching the wine to his lips, whereas the traditional rule calls for drinking the better part of four cups. The other indicated a jocular form of criticism from relatives—"We need lots of schnapps 'cause old X is here," hardly to be interpreted as an expectation that the respondent should actually drink larger amounts. Reactions to this kind of ingroup criticism are essentially humorous, but outgroup criticism of not drinking enough may evoke responses of moral indignation, resentment, and resistance. Typical are reactions such as these: "They call me a sissy, but I don't care." "They try to get me to take more, but I never do." "It's just none of their business!"

These data are sufficiently unambiguous to permit some important inferences. In the first place, twice as much felt pressure to drink more was reported than to drink less. This suggests the covert nature of the social pressure on adults within the Jewish group and the implicit acceptance of the sobriety norm. However, should overt social pressure be brought to bear on the individual by other Jews, it will more than likely be in the direction of moderate drinking and sobriety. This does not mean that Jewish men never find themselves in the position of refusing a drink offered by a Jewish host. However, such a situation would not ordinarily generate sufficient tension to leave an emotional residue which would be expressed as a feeling of social criticism. In the second place, a substantial number of Jewish men feel that the social milieu does bring pressure on them to drink more than they ordinarily drink, but these pressures are perceived as emanating primarily from the outgroup. In sharp contrast, the outgroup is seldom or never perceived as exerting explicit pressure toward moderate drinking and sobriety.

Variations in Response to Outgroup Pressures

In the light of the facts on the social sources of pressures to drink less moderately, the more frequent intoxication among Jews in military service and college can perhaps be understood as a response to outgroup pressures. Our New Haven data, however, indicate a decided absence of intoxication in the course of daily contacts with non-Jews within the community. This raises the question as to why Jewish men often yield to outgroup pressures in the service and in college, but only rarely in the course of ordinary events. Certainly intracommunity contacts between Jewish men and Gentiles are frequent and there is evidence in our interviews that drinking is sometimes involved in these situations. The interview materials also confirm that in these latter situations social pressures are often brought to bear on Jewish men to drink beyond the limits to which they are accustomed. Our view is that the solution of this problem hinges on the different types of socially structured situations and relations which arise between Jews and non-Jews within the community, in military service, and in college.

1. Sobriety in intracommunity relationships

While supporting data cannot be presented in quantitative form, there is reason to believe that role and situation are more often instrumentally defined by Jewish men during intracommunity contacts with non-Jews than during military service or in college. There is also reason to believe that an instrumental definition of the situation helps to constrain the drinker from intoxication. If these assumptions are valid, constraints should be at a maximum where social pressures to drink more are experienced by Jews in the course of daily intracommunity relations with Gentiles.

The idea that an instrumental orientation exerts constraints in the drinking situation stems in part from Glad's (11) suggestions based on his comparative study of Jewish, Irish-Catholic, and Protestant attitudes toward drinking. Glad proposed that the Jews tend to be oriented toward long-range goals in contrast to the Irish who are more concerned with proximate goals. Among Jews, recognition, achievement, and understanding take precedence over proximate goals like warmth, friendliness, and concern for how people feel, which Glad believes are more valued by the Irish. Glad therefore suggested that in most situations Jews drink as an incidental means to the achievement of the long-range goals, and that heightened concern with those goals necessitates constraint in the drinking situation. However, since we lack more refined measures of value emphases in these two cultures, such generalizations seem hazardous. Also, in Glad's construction there is some implication of indifference on the part of Jews to proximate goals (such as warmth, friendliness, and concern for the feelings of others) for which there is no factual basis.

There would seem, however, to be factual justification for asserting a cleavage in Jewish life whereby the satisfaction of proximate goals is confined to relations with Jews while the satisfaction of goals giving rise to an instrumental orientation is more characteristic of relations with Gentiles. Certainly in the eastern Europe of a few generations ago the expressive and affective life of Jews was of necessity, as well as voluntarily, restricted to family, ghetto, and ethnic community. Relationships with Gentiles were largely defined by the Jews' precarious "middleman" role between nobility and peasant masses.* Concern with economic survival daily forced Jews out of the emotionally satisfying and protective ghetto, but in the capacity of "economic man." There was little approach to the cultivation of primary-group ties on the part of either Jews or Gentiles. Moreover, ethnic cleavage tends to persist in the modern American community, although in attenuated form (31). In daily community life the affective and expressive relations of Jews are still to a large extent confined within the boundaries of family and ethnic group. Our New Haven data suggest that, by contrast, relations with non-Jews tend to be instrumentally defined; in intra-community contacts with non-Jews, New Haven Jewish men are typically in business roles (sales and service and professional roles) characterized by functional specificity and affective neutrality. The situational goals are the contract, the sale, making a good impression, and the larger goals of money, recognition and status which these imply. In these situations, cognitive interests are given primacy. It is imperative "to be on one's toes" and "keep one's wits about one" in order to manipulate objects and persons in the situation to the desired end. Consequently, an element of renunciation and discipline is introduced (26); the individual feels pressure not to "give in" to modes of gratification like intoxication which disrupt cognitive processes and interfere with the achievement of larger objectives.

Evidence of an instrumental structuring of relations with non-Jews and the constraints which this definition exerts on drinking was spontaneously

* In describing contacts between Jews and non-Jews in the eastern European *shtetl*, Zborowski and Herzog (39) have this to say: "The market represents the chief contact between the Jew and the non-Jew, who for the shtetl is primarily the peasant. Aside from the market and scattered business associations, they inhabit different worlds. . . . The seeds of all their relations are in this marketplace contact." On the middleman role of the Jews in eastern Europe, see Dubnow (7).

given in the course of interviews with New Haven Jewish men. The following interview excerpts illustrate these points quite explicitly:

[*Mr. X, a salesman, 50 years old:*] I sell. I'm out on the road. I could get a drink in every home I go in. They're [non-Jews] always offering but I usually give them an excuse. I tell them I'm on doctor's orders not to drink. In that way I don't insult anyone. [*At a later point in the interview:*] I don't get to know my customers that well. You can't get too familiar with them or they start to take advantage of you. They want to treat you like one of the family but you have to draw the line.

[*Mr. Y, 47 years old, an executive in the transportation field in a capacity which brings him into personal contact with a wide range of the firm's customers largely non-Jewish:*] When I do drink nowadays it's a question of entertaining business-wise, and "occasions." . . . When I'm entertaining in business connections I feel you've got to keep a certain amount of decorum. You're doing it for a purpose!

[*Mr. Z, 60 years old, owner of a small building firm, states that he does a good deal of his drinking in "business" and with "business associates" who are predominantly non-Jewish. Under these circumstances, he says:*] I'll do what the rest are doing. If they're having high-balls, I'll sit in and hold on to that glass for sociability. . . . A man shouldn't drink, but there are times a man has to drink. But the less you drink, the better. People shouldn't take more than two drinks on any occasion. Two drinks should be the limit. . . . I entertain a lot but that's not any personal expense. We buy liquor at Christmas and other times but that's business, not personal. With business associates, I'll go wherever they take me. I try to make them feel as pleasant as possible.

It would be erroneous to suppose that the instrumental orientation expressed in these excerpts is something distinctively Jewish. Obviously this attitude is required by many roles in society, occupied by Jews and non-Jews alike. It would be equally erroneous to imply that all intracommunity relations between Jews and Gentiles are instrumentally defined by Jews. In the modern American community, social contacts frequently arise between Jews and Gentiles which fall within the range of primary-group relations. However, in choosing intimate non-Jewish friends, Jews may avoid those who drink excessively and who might put pressure on them to do likewise. The following excerpt illustrates this process of selection where friendship alternatives are open:

My closest friends are Jewish [but] . . . my friendships have spread out in recent years to include many non-Jews. [*He lives in a very mixed neighborhood, but he adds:*] None of my friends are excessive drinkers!

What is important, however, is that an instrumental orientation may exert a constraining influence on intoxication among Jews at precisely the point where they are likely to be urged and pressed to drink in a hedonistic fashion, namely, in contact with Gentiles. It is also important that, although anxiety about the loss of cognitive orientation is evidently a deterrent to intoxication in these situations, the cognitive emphasis is in the nature of a means to other ends rather than an end in itself. There is no obvious relation between this emphasis and the general valuation of mental faculties deriving from the Jewish tradition of learning and study.

In considering Jewish resistance to pressures to drink excessively in the course of intracommunity contacts with non-Jews, the proximity of the Jewish family and Jewish community should not be forgotten. These, presumably, act as negative sanctions on intoxication. Stable relations with family and ethnic community may also strengthen the Jewish man's personal sense of Jewishness with which, as we shall try to show later, the concept of sobriety is intertwined. Indeed, as long as family and community sanctions are imminent and the sense of ethnic identification strong, outgroup pressures to drink more may intensify adherence to the sobriety norm. A stubborn feeling that "they [Gentiles] cannot break me" seems to be reflected in the remarks of several respondents, and an instrumentally structured role relationship would simply reinforce this resistance. Changes from norms of moderate drinking and sobriety should occur where emotional investment is shifted to the non-Jewish outgroup, where ingroup sanctions are no longer imminent and where an instrumental orientation no longer constrains. In circumstances of this kind, resistance to outgroup pressures may be expected to weaken. Anticipated is a tendency toward conformity with patterns of drinking or intoxication characteristic of the particular group or stratum with which the individual identifies.

2. Intoxication in military service

These conditions for change are closely approximated in military service and to a lesser extent in college, and the facts suggest that Jews actually are more prone to intoxication in these contexts. However, data on the contexts of intoxication need to be supplemented by qualitative impressions before the impact on Jewish drinking behavior of situations like military service can be fully appreciated. In the service Jews are severed from the intimate milieus of family and community which support patterns of moderate drinking and sobriety. They are impelled by circumstances to make primary-group identification with non-Jews whose drinking patterns are at variance with their own. Conformity to norms of relatively heavy drinking is evidently often a condition of acceptance into those intimate, tightly knit primary groups which studies of army life (30) suggest are essential for the maintenance of individual morale. As one New Haven man expressed it:

I started in the Army like a lot of others. No one in my old gang drank. I started drinking more in the Army with the attitude of trying to be one of the boys. [*Actually this man drank frequently before entering the service. His reference is to hedonistic drinking.*]

Moreover, military service not only disrupts normal social relations and routines but apparently often undermines instrumental, goal-directed activities. This tendency is reflected time and again in the assertion by Jewish men that they drank more in the service because there was nothing else to do. The following comment is not at all atypical:

I drank more in the Army. There wasn't much else to do. When you were in town you went to bars with the Company. You'd sit and drink and listen to records. I usually get sick before I lose control but this completely excludes the Army. I guess I've passed out a few times, at that, in the Army.

Military service, too, is a context alien to the eastern European Jewish tradition and especially the Orthodox religious tradition.* A perusal of the reports of the New Haven Jewish men on their military experience often gives the impression that they were "fish out of water." General discomfiture, together with the disintegration of goal-directed activities and experience of social pressure, is clearly expressed in this case:

I did a fair amount of drinking in the Army. Every time we'd get a week-end pass we'd drink. Why? Didn't have a hell of a lot else to do. My buddies in the Army would criticize me [for not drinking enough]. You'd want to stay sober enough to get back to the truck and they wouldn't care. They weren't Jewish— damned uncomfortable I was in the Army!

Sometimes military service appears to be an acutely anxiety-producing situation for Jewish men. Cut off from emotionally supportive relations with family and ethnic community and from the community of values which give daily routines and instrumental activities their meaning, some Jewish men become extremely anxious and confused. In isolated instances, alcohol was sought as a means of escape from an alien and distressing situation, as the following excerpt testifies:

Two or three times in the Army I just went out, left camp, had a few drinks— from that point I don't remember until I got up the next morning. In the Army I was depressed and homesick. I went out and got drunk. They called it psychoneurosis. Then, I snapped out after [a medical discharge]. Didn't drink any more after that. [He means that he did not drink hedonistically subsequent to his military experience; he currently drinks alcohol about 125 times a year.]

However, acute loss of orientation and accompanying anxiety may be the exception rather than the rule. Perhaps more typically Jewish men drink heavily in military service to gain acceptance into Gentile primary groups toward which it is meaningless to assume an instrumental attitude and from which basic emotional supports are sought because there is no alternative.

3. Response of different religious categories

Is there a marked difference among Jews of different religious affiliation in response to the situational pressures to drink immoderately which arise in military service? Different responses to the same situational pressures might indicate varying intensities of inner sentiments supporting Jewish norms of moderate drinking and sobriety. Similarities, while not vitiating the

---

* There is a long history of Jewish protest against military service in eastern Europe, a protest which stemmed partly from pacific religious ideals and partly from reaction to the deliberate attempts of despotic governments, such as the regime of Nicholas I of Russia, to crush Judaism and assimilate the Jews through the imposition of long and harsh terms of military service. For evidence of this situation in nineteenth century Russia and Poland, see Dubnow (7). The traditional rejection of temporal power as a means of maintaining Jewish "moral hegemony" is discussed by Riesman (28).

role of inner attitudes, would certainly point to the importance of the social environment in sustaining or modifying these norms.

Unfortunately our New Haven data are insufficient to permit refined conclusions on these points, and the small number of Orthodox veterans in the student sample seriously limits the possibilities of generalization. Clues are nonetheless forthcoming from the data in Table 3 on the extent of intoxication of veterans and non-veterans among the Conservative and Orthodox combined in a single category, and the Reform and Secular, likewise combined. Although significant differences appear between these religious categories irrespective of veteran status, there is also significantly more intoxication among veterans when religion is held constant.* While insufficient to nullify differences between more and less Orthodox Jews, the service situation evidently exerts a powerful influence towards heavier drinking which is responded to by all the religious categories.

TABLE 3

Frequency of Intoxication (Drunk Twice or More) in Veterans and Non-veterans among Jewish Students, by Nominal Religious Affiliation (in Per Cent)

	Veterans	Number Reporting	Non-veterans	Number Reporting
Orthodox and Conservative	33	(15)	12	(125)
Reform and Secular	62	(21)	35	(89)

The burden of the evidence appears to be that the internalization of norms and ideas antithetical to hedonistic drinking is often insufficient to sustain patterns of moderate drinking and sobriety in the face of strong situational counterpressures, such as those which arise in military service. Evidently, conscience alone cannot guarantee conformity to behavioral patterns which are at variance with primary-group norms. The moral consensus of the primary group appears to be a potent factor determining the character of the individual's drinking behavior. The obverse implication of an increase in intoxication in the service is, of course, the overwhelming importance to Jewish sobriety of regular participation in a Jewish milieu which supports norms of moderate drinking and sobriety. Where the sober dictates of individual conscience and primary-group consensus are in harmony, as in the Orthodox religious community, the likelihood of continued sobriety would appear to be greatest despite extensive drinking.

* Chi-square of the difference in drunkenness along religious lines, holding veteran status constant, is 19.28, P (at 2 degrees of freedom) is less than .001. Chi-square of the difference by veteran status is 10.18, P (at 2 degrees of freedom) is less than .01. Data on milder intoxication have been omitted here but show a similar pattern.

4. *Insulation of Orthodox Jews from outgroup pressures*

The data in this section also point to an important latent f\
broader religious complex in sustaining Jewish norms of mo
ing and sobriety. Orthodox norms circumscribe the social life
Jews so as to minimize the emergence of close, primary-group re ...ons with
Gentiles. This is readily apparent in the prohibition on intermarriage, in
dietary restrictions, and the like. But no less important is the totality of
norms which channel the Jew's emotional and expressive life within the
confines of the Jewish community.* By curtailing the development of primary-group ties with non-Jews, Orthodox Judaism insulates its adherents
from outgroup pressures to drink immoderately. Orthodoxy does not do away
entirely with social contacts between Jews and Gentiles. Thus mere social
contact with Gentiles is hardly a cause of intoxication among Jews. But
Orthodox Judaism tends to narrow the bases of Jews' contacts with outsiders largely to the economic area where instrumental attitudes predominate. The effects of this circumscription are twofold. On the one hand, the
potential influence of primary-group relations with non-Jews in modifying
drinking behavior is mitigated. On the other hand, the structure of the
permitted role relationship may itself induce additional constraints in the
drinking situation.

The observant Jew is thus doubly protected from outside pressures to
drink hedonistically, while within the confines of the Orthodox community
consensus supports sobriety and the act of drinking is ritually controlled.
With the continuation of ethnic cleavage but a decline in religious motives
for drinking, the instrumental drinking described by Glad (11) is perhaps
becoming more important to Jews. Accordingly, continued separatism and
the value complex from which instrumental attitudes derive may represent
a second line of defense against intoxication. However, where the insulating
function of Judaism disintegrates and instrumental orientation is disrupted,
moderate drinking and sobriety apparently often give way to convivial and
hedonistic drinking.

Ethnocentrism and Jewish Sobriety

All of this leads us to juxtapose two sets of facts. First, as shown elsewhere (31), strong moral condemnation of intoxication is prevalent among
the more Orthodox Jews; second, as we have seen, Jews associate social
pressures toward moderate drinking with the ingroup and toward "more"
drinking with the outgroup. Actually, these ideas and sentiments are indicative of underlying cultural stereotypes of sober Jew and drunken Gentile
and of the incorporation of sobriety in the ethnocentrism of the Jewish
group. The exact character and prevalence of the stereotype, as well as the

---

* The insulating character of Orthodox Judaism has been discussed in the recent
sociological literature by Warner and Srole (38).

forces maintaining or modifying it all constitute subjects which are of some consequence in the study of Jewish sobriety.

1. *Stereotypes of sober Jew and drunken Gentile*

The elucidation of Jewish stereotypes can be started by considering the responses of Jewish men to questions pertaining to beliefs about Jewish and Gentile drinking practices. In the New Haven interviews, the Jewish respondents were directly asked whether they thought Jews drink more, less, or about the same as Gentiles. On the basis of responses to these questions, it may be concluded that the prevailing belief is that Jews drink less than non-Jews. Of the sample of seventy-three men, fifty-four asserted this to be the case. Not a single man asserted that Jews drink more than non-Jews and only seven felt that Jews and non-Jews drink about the same, while the remaining twelve refused to offer a definite opinion on this point. In questioning respondents, no attempt was made to specify whether "more" or "less" referred to the incidence of drinking, frequency of drinking, or amounts consumed. Where respondents made assertions about the simple incidence and frequency of drinking among Jews and Gentiles, these were usually consistent with their beliefs about drinking to excess. In other words, it was implied that the incidence and frequency of drinking among non-Jews is greater than among Jews, which is by no means necessarily the case.

It must be observed at once that questions about drinking among Jews and non-Jews induced considerable conflict in respect to particularistic and universalistic values. A few excerpts from the interview records will illustrate the nature of the competing values:

Definitely [Jews drink less], but I can't think in those terms.

I don't see any reason why they [the Jews] should be any different from anyone else.

I think everybody should drink less than they do.

I didn't study it. I'm not looking into it. There are all kinds of fish in the sea.

Give me half a minute to think. I'm an authority? Jews are a minority. There are fewer Jews. I think they're about the same. I think the Irish drink more than Italians. Poles drink. Jews are human. Jewish peddlers used to drink when they were cold. Jews shouldn't be an exception. They're no chosen people.

That may be just prejudice. I don't like to make general statements.

I'd hate to say. Most of my friends, Jews and non-Jews, drink about like I do.

Hard to tell, it's up to the individual.

There's an old saying among Jews of my class—my father has an old theory that Jews drink less than Christians. It's hard to say. It might be so. I don't mean this with a racial bias, it just might be that Jews drink less.

That's something I wouldn't say, I couldn't say, but I think they do [drink] less. There are very few drunkards among the Jewish race.

I don't think it has anything to do with nationality. I don't want to bring it in. If Christians were raised in a non-drinking environment they wouldn't either.

Well, I don't think necessarily less—they—I think you can base it on occupation, on per cent. There's more Gentiles patronizing taverns, grills, etc., than Jews.

These examples are sufficient to show that, while the prevailing Jewish belief is that excessive drinking is a Gentile characteristic, there are strong competing values which make it difficult for many Jews to admit discussion of the matter in these terms. The conflict between universalism and particularism is nothing new in Jewish culture. It has been the fundamental paradox of normative Judaism since ancient times (23). In all probability the protracted minority status of the Jews has sensitized them to this value conflict and current democratic ideologies have reinforced the universalistic side of the coin. Time and again the themes that "we're all human," and "it's up to the individual," and "these things are not racial or nationality matters" are to be found alongside statements of a highly particularistic and ethnocentric nature in the interviews.

In the historical experience of the Jews in Europe, there was probably considerable objective basis for Jewish beliefs about excessive drinking among Gentiles. At least historians of Jewish life in eastern Europe, such as Dubnow (7), relate that the Gentile peasantry became intoxicated with tiresome regularity. In America, where there are many millions of abstainers, the objectivity of these Jewish beliefs is open to some question, although abstinence sentiment is most apparent in rural areas (18) while American Jews are predominantly urban. What is sociologically significant, however, is not the objective truth or falsehood of these beliefs but whether or not they are believed. As Thomas and Thomas (36) observed, "If men define situations as real, they are real in their consequences." Of further significance is the question as to whether or not Jewish beliefs about drinking among Jews and Gentiles are linked with basic moral ideas and sentiments. The problem is whether or not these beliefs reflect concepts of ethnic virtue whose emotional importance is magnified by reference to opposite characteristics in outsiders.

In an effort to probe deeper into this problem, the New Haven Jewish men were asked whether they had the idea in childhood that sobriety was a Jewish virtue, drunkenness a Gentile vice. In response to this question, 27 of the 73 men answered yes, 38 answered no, and 8 said they did not remember or could not answer. Taken at face value, these findings seem partially to contradict the results and inferences from the more matter-of-fact question as to whether Jews drink more or less than non-Jews. However, in the face of further evidence the apparent contradiction fades away. Later in the interview, Jewish men were asked whether or not they were familiar in childhood with stories, songs, poems or sayings which suggested sobriety as a Jewish virtue, drunkenness as a Gentile vice. As an example the little ditty "Shikker iz a Goy" (Drunken is a Gentile) was frequently cited. Despite the logical inconsistency, responses to this question reversed the trend of answers to the previous question on sobriety as a Jewish virtue, drunkenness as a Gentile vice. A majority of forty-eight answered that they were familiar as children with such folk beliefs, only seventeen replied that they were not, while eight said either that they did not remember or could not answer.

The increase in affirmative answers to the second of these two questions is associated with the relinquishment by some Jewish men of universalistic attitudes in the interview situation. This turnabout accompanied the respondent's recognition that the interviewer knew the prevailing folk beliefs and that it was therefore no longer necessary to conceal ethnocentric ideas behind a universalistic front.* This process of relaxation in the interview situation may be illustrated by some examples. One elderly man who said that Jews and Gentiles drink "about the same" asserted later that drunkenness is "more a Gentile characteristic," although he felt obliged to qualify this by the phrase, "in a way." When the interviewer subsequently inquired whether he knew "Shikker iz a Goy," he was surprised and delighted, and insisted on singing the entire song, as well as some other ditties of similar import, for the interviewer's benefit. In another case the respondent tenaciously denied awareness of any differences between Jews and Gentiles. At the mention of the song "Shikker iz a Goy," however, he exclaimed, "Say, you must have really studied this!" and went on to say that he had long been familiar with these notions. Nevertheless, some Jewish men were either reluctant or refused to give up their universalistic attitude. Moreover, the insistent qualification that "they (the folk beliefs) didn't leave any impression on me" was often heard. In one interview, a relative of the respondent happened to be present when the interviewer mentioned "Shikker iz a Goy." The respondent, who had answered in the negative to the preceding question on the imputation of drunkenness to Gentiles, just shook his head: "Never heard of it!" At this his relative remarked, in amused astonishment, "Aw, come on—everybody knows that! Why, mother used to sing me to sleep with it when I was a baby!" The respondent smiled a bit sheepishly but continued shaking his head, indicating with a wave of his hand that he was ready for the next question.

The qualitative import of Jewish stereotypes could easily be lost among statistics and anecdotes. Thus it may be well to give the content of the little song, "Shikker iz a Goy," which has been translated from the Yiddish as follows:

> The Gentile goes into the saloon, the saloon,
> And drinks there a small glass of wine;
> he tosses it off—his glass of wine.
> Oh—the Gentile is a Drunkard—a drunkard he is,
> Drink he must,
> Because he is a Gentile!

* Interviewers were both Jewish and non-Jewish; the majority of the interviews were conducted by non-Jews. Whatever the interviewer's identity, this was only revealed if the interviewee specifically asked about it. Because the leading non-Jewish interviewer has a name which could be taken as "Jewish," many respondents tended to assume that he was a Jew.

> The Gentile comes into our alley, our little street,
> And breaks the windows of us poor Jews;
> > our windowpanes are broken out,
> For—the Gentile is a Drunkard—a drunkard he is,
> Drink he must,
> Because he is a Gentile!

> The Jew hurries into the place of prayer;
> An evening prayer, a short benediction he says,
> > and a prayer for his dead.
> For—the Jew is a sober man—sober is he,
> Pray he must,
> Because he is a Jew.*

It would be an exaggeration to impute great historical or educational significance to this song itself. It evidently originated in the Russian ghettos and is unquestionably not known to many Jews. However, the linkage of sobriety with Jewish identity, drunkenness with Gentile identity is so explicit that it seems doubtful that such a ditty could gain much currency unless it were congruent with generally held Jewish concepts and values. Moreover, the ideas expressed in "Shikker iz a Goy" are quite consistent with Clark's (5) recent satirical "Portrait of the Mythical Gentile," an attempt to depict the essence of current Jewish stereotypes of Gentiles. As his opening remark, under the heading "Gentile Appetites," Clark characterizes prevailing Jewish beliefs as follows:

All Gentiles are drunkards. They have not only debauched themselves, but have made drunkards of many Jews. The Gentile drinks enormously, but without savor, being insensitive to vintage and admixture (5, p. 548).

The substance of these findings is that sobriety has been incorporated into the ethnocentrism of the Jewish group. In his classic discussion Sumner (35) pointed out that the principal function of ethnocentrism is the clarification and intensification of a group's norms and sentiments through the magnification of their opposites as characteristic of disliked or hated outsiders. Following Sumner's reasoning, stereotypes among Jews of sobriety and drunkenness in terms of Jew and Gentile clarify sobriety as "our way" and intensify the emotional sentiments supporting it with broader feelings for things Jewish as opposed to things which are not.

Sumner, however, referred in his discussion of ethnocentrism to a relatively undifferentiated "primitive society" and probably presupposed a solidarity which cannot be taken for granted in the heterogeneous nominal Jewish group of today. The influence of Jewish stereotypes as a deterrent to intoxication may well depend upon the vitality of a larger network of

---

* Translated by Bales (1). While Bales cited this song and the "stigmatization of the Goyim as drunkards," he did not develop the possible reinforcing effects which this stereotyping may have on Jewish sobriety. Rather, he turned to a consideration of the menace which the drunken peasants constituted to the Jewish town dwellers in Czarist Russia, and to the question of whether or not Jewish sobriety was a response to this situation.

ethnocentric ideas and sentiments which are not equally distributed among nominal Jews.* However, in the minds of many Jews, the belief that Gentiles drink more than Jews may be a proposition which has little or no relevance apart from its objective status as true or false. Before such beliefs can regulate drinking behavior through the dictates of conscience and social sanction they must be imbued with emotional value and moral significance. Whether or not reinforcement for a norm of sobriety stems from Jewish stereotypes would seem to depend on the kinds of ideas and sentiments which are more generally mobilized by the symbols of ingroup and outgroup —Jew and Gentile. To touch on the implications of this problem requires more extended discussion of the probable role of ceremonial Judaism in giving definition and emotional support to Jewish group symbols, ethnocentric norms and ideas.

2. Significance of the Orthodox definition of the Jewish situation

The ceremonial observances of Orthodox Judaism are interlaced with a system of basic religious ideas which, while universal in much of their ethical import, are nevertheless ethnocentric in character. It is the basic ethnocentric ideas of traditional Judaism which in large measure define the situation of the religious Jew in society at large. These premises define the Orthodox Jew's position vis-à-vis the criticism and hostility of the wider society, which have been referred to extensively in the literature on Jewish drinking behavior, as well as toward its attractions. Our supposition is that stereotypes of sober Jew and drunken Gentile take on emotional connotations which reinforce a pattern of sobriety through association with these broader ethnocentric ideas and supporting sentiments.

While Orthodox Judaism has no monopoly on ethnocentrism, the ethnocentric concepts of traditional Judaism are not to be understood solely as a defensive reaction to discrimination and rejection by society. Orthodox Judaism has made capital of the ingroup-outgroup situation. The Orthodox view presupposes a special and sacred covenant of the Jews with God. Much of the message of the Scriptures is devoted to the ideas that Jews are chosen, separate and sacred, with a special mission and purpose in this world. Orthodox injunctions set apart and insulate Jews from profane contact with outsiders. Tradition exhorts the pious Jew to exemplify the superiority of Judaism and belief in the one true God by strict conformity to the Law (the Torah). Orthodox Jews know that there will be censure and retaliation from outsiders and catastrophe in this life. This is interpreted, in accordance with Biblical concepts, as the instrument of God's judgment for failure to live up to the dictates of the religion.† The traditional Jewish point of

---

* In fact, the writer has observed situations where references to the characteristic sobriety of Jews apparently motivated nominal Jews to drink immoderately.

† God's punishments for disobedience as well as the rewards for conformity to the Law are stated in no uncertain terms in Leviticus, and the role of outgroups in this process is very clear: "Ye shall be slain before your enemies: they that hate you shall reign over

view, together with its general social implications, is well expressed by Moore (23) as follows:

God "hallows his Name" (makes it holy), therefore, by doing things that lead or constrain men to acknowledge Him as God. And as it is God's supreme end that all mankind shall ultimately own and serve him as the true God, so it is the chief end of Israel, to whom he has in a unique manner revealed himself, to hallow His name by living so that men shall see that the God of Israel is the true God. This is the meaning of the kiddush-ha-shem, the hallowing of the Name. . . . The opposite of the hallowing of the Name is the profanation of the Name (hillul-ha-shem). It includes every act or word of a Jew which disgraces his religion and so reflects dishonor upon God. The world judges religions by the lives of those who profess them—the tree by its fruits. It was thus that the Jews judged other religions; the vices of the heathen prove the nullity of the religions which tolerated such behavior, and even encouraged it by the examples of their gods. A favorite topic of Jewish apologetics was the superiority of Jewish morals, not merely in precept but in practice, and they argued from it the superiority of their religion, thus inviting a retaliation which the heathen world let them experience in full measure. Individuals, sects, religions, which profess to be better than others must always expect to have their conduct observed with peculiar scrutiny and censured with peculiar severity. (Vol. 2, pp. 103, 108.)

The sociological significance of this passage is that in the total context of ingroup-outgroup relations the pious Jew feels a generalized pressure or motivation to live in accordance with the dictates of his religion—a pressure which arises in part from his own ethnocentric assumptions.

In some respects, Moore's conclusions as to the principal motive to moral conduct in Judaism parallel Kant's explanation of Jewish motives for sobriety. As between these eminent thinkers, however, there is a difference in emphasis which is pertinent here. Kant mentions the idea of "chosenness" but he stresses the "outward worth" of the Jew, based on the belief of others in his "separatistic lore." He seems to imply that it is simply a concern for status or worth in the eyes of outsiders which motivates Jews to reserve. Then Kant's argument takes an ambiguous turn. He writes of the Jews' fear of "intoxication which deprives one of caution" in apposition with outgroup censure and criticism. Kant's remarks thus become open to two kinds of dubious interpretation.

The first doubtful line of reasoning is that the individual Jew or the Jewish group has experienced, and consequently eschews (or, on the basis of experience realistically anticipates and therefore eschews), direct criticism, censure, or retaliation from Gentiles while in a state of intoxication or for achieving such a state.* The evidence that has been presented here on the

_____

you" (26:17); "And I will bring a sword upon you, that shall avenge the quarrel of my covenant" (26:25); "And I will scatter you among the heathen, and will draw out a sword after you: and your land shall be desolate" (26:33); "And ye shall perish among the heathen, and the land of your enemies shall eat you up" (26:38).

* This first line of reasoning is quite clearly exemplified by Fishberg in Bernheimer (4). At one point Glazer (12) also seems to favor this kind of argument, although he modifies it somewhat by saying: "It is not consciousness of the siege that prevents any individual Jew from taking one more drink—motivation is more complicated than

character and sources of direct ingroup and outgroup pressures in respect
to drinking, as well as on Jewish responses to and perception of these pressures, makes it difficult to sustain such an interpretation.

The second and subtler line of reasoning appears in the writings of Haggard and Jellinek as follows:

> The most reasonable of these explanations of Jewish sobriety seems to be the
> one given by Kant, who thought that the Jews, forming isolated groups within
> other nations and being exposed to constant censure, must avoid, in the interests
> of racial welfare, anything that would make them conspicuous. Their temperate
> use of alcohol is an unconscious defense against the censure of their race (13,
> p. 169).

How the avoidance of conspicuousness in the eyes of others could be a
criterion for the selection and perpetuation of Jewish norms, including the
temperate use of alcohol, is difficult to see. The bulk of Orthodox Jewish
observances are conspicuous to many Gentiles. Indeed, to staunch anti-Semites the totality of Judaism is conspicuous, and it is to be doubted that the
devout Jew who observes his Sabbath is blissfully unaware of the situation.
As for the standard of "interests of racial welfare" to which Haggard and
Jellinek allude, if this refers to individual or group wisdom of an essentially
prudential character or to a standard *ex post facto* imposed upon the group
by an observer, it is of doubtful value in explaining Jewish sobriety. But if
it means that ideas of welfare are associated with temperance in drinking
among Jews, we can only agree, with the proviso that they are probably
associated also with the "intemperate" use of alcohol by certain other groups.
The attachment of the idea of group welfare to particular ways is, of course,
exactly what Sumner (35) considered to be the common or defining characteristic of the mores. However, what is or is not imbued with the idea
of welfare by Orthodox Jews is not determined by the avoidance of con-

---

that. But it is the consequences of the siege, passed down from generation to generation . . ." The case of the American Negro is particularly instructive as a test of the
theory that simple avoidance of retaliation or censure can motivate the sobriety of
relatively defenseless minorities. Authorities agree that the Negro in America, occupying
an inferior social position, has been the butt of criticism from whites and often the
object of persecution. Individually and collectively Negroes are vulnerable to punitive
caste controls and occasional outrages against person and property. Yet, as Dollard (6)
points out in his discussion of the psychic compensations or "gains" which accrue to
Negro lower-class caste status, the behavior of lower-class Negroes in "Southern Town"
is quite permissive in respect to the expression of aggression and sexuality and, apparently, drunkenness. On the whole, the evidence at least indicates that in urban
areas, where Jews are also concentrated, intoxication is quite common among Negroes
and that subordinate minority status is of itself insufficient to induce a pattern of
sobriety. It is possible, however, that where the more ascetic forms of Protestantism
have gained strong adherence among Negroes, and where there is striving among
them to differentiate from the lower classes and emulate white middle-class "respectability," pressures to sobriety will be intense and enhanced by consciousness of race
difference.

spicuousness.* Jews might indeed have appeared less conspicuous to many Gentiles had they been more prone to drunkenness, their very sobriety being a point of differentiation, at least in their own eyes.† Nor does the fact that hedonistic drinking and intoxication are officially censured in Christianity, as well as in Judaism, mean that a striving to live up to Christian norms is the motive for Jewish sobriety. Adherence to traditional Judaism is certainly intimately bound up with ideas of group welfare, and in the Orthodox view welfare in turn is indicated by the status of relations with outsiders. However, that which is welfare to Orthodox Jews—that is, those ways of behavior that are imbued with the element of welfare—is primarily determined by the Law and the criterion of conformity to the Law, whose norms are defined as fixed and immutable, revealed by God and embodied in tradition.‡ Acts which are believed to threaten welfare are above all acts which deviate from and negate the ingroup religious code, the more so if they do so conspicuously in the eyes of both Jews and Gentiles. The im-

* For situationally or permanently assimilating Jews, however, what is or is not conspicuous in terms of wider societal norms may be of the utmost importance to perceived welfare and in determining behavior.

†The evidence on Jewish stereotypes suggests that this is very much the case. The thesis can even be entertained that non-Jewish criticism, far from being actually or potentially directed at intoxication and ensuing behavior, was directed at the uncompromising sobriety of the Jews. A recent comment by Glazer (12) is suggestive: "Something happened and it's hard to say whether it was that the Jews began drinking less or the rest of the world began drinking more. . . . In any case, sobriety was added to the catalogue of traits that annoyed the Gentiles." The tacit assumption of this statement is quite the opposite of Kant's. It implies that Jews might have been less the butt of criticism had they seen fit to "let their hair down" and get drunk now and then, although the "damned if you do, damned if you don't" principle might well have prevailed.

That the Jews early distinguished themselves and were distinguished by their sobriety among surrounding peoples is suggested by a variety of facts. For instance, the Hellenic society and culture which enveloped Judaism for centuries after the Macedonian conquest hardly looked on intoxication with disfavor, as McKinlay (21, 22) has demonstrated. Evidence on drunkenness among such peoples as the Persians, the Babylonians and certain Semitic peoples in the Mediterranean region has also been compiled by McKinlay (20). Of greater significance is historical evidence of excessive drinking in more recent times by European peoples among whom large numbers of Jews have lived in comparative sobriety. For example, according to Sebastian Franck (16), inebriety was common to both sexes and among all classes in sixteenth-century Germany, the prevailing attitude being one of indifference. Franck even noted the contrasting sobriety of the Jews and attributed their wealth to their "abstinence." The drunkenness of the eastern European Gentile peasantry has already been noted. Apparently, drunkenness often accompanied the most violent expressions of anti-Semitism in those countries, and it is constantly noted in this connection and derided by Jewish historians such as Dubnow (7).

‡ It is not intended to imply that Judaic norms have in no way been subject to modification, reinterpretation, and alteration, and that realistic adjustment to changing life conditions has had no role in this process. Our point is simply that the Orthodox emphasize the immutability of the religious system and associate individual and group welfare therewith.

portance of this emphasis, as opposed to a general Jewish need to avoid conspicuousness in the interests of racial welfare, is that it leads to different predictions as to the behavior of religious and irreligious Jews in the face of outgroup censure and criticism.

These considerations lead, then, to a third interpretation latent in Kant's argument, which becomes clear in conjunction with the passage from Moore, cited above. Moore in no way detracts from the importance of outsiders as a source and reference for the Jew's moral judgments of behavior and as a stimulus to conformity with ingroup norms. However, where Kant fails to be explicit, Moore emphasizes the basic idea of moral superiority in Judaism which gives the pious Jew a sense of inner worth or dignity in being Jewish. The principles of the hallowing and profaning of the Name derive their power to motivate moral conduct among Jews in a hostile environment from the initial premise of moral superiority. Theoretically, the enhanced motivation to conformity with Jewish norms is a resultant of the interaction of the fundamental ethnocentric idea together with the censure and hostility of outsiders. In this view, the Jew who is deeply committed to the premise of Jewish moral superiority simply intensifies conformity to his own distinctive cultural norms in the face of outgroup pressure and criticism. He intensifies also his scrutiny of the moral conduct of fellow Jews in the light of Jewish norms. In association with these ethnocentric ideas and relations of hostility with outsiders, cultural definitions of sobriety as a Jewish virtue, drunkenness as a Gentile vice, should enhance motivation to conform to Jewish norms of moderate drinking and sobriety.*

3. Ceremonial participation and the mobilization of sentiments in support of group symbols and ethnocentric ideas

The character of Jewish response to outgroup censure would seem, however, to be determined by the intensity of sentiments supporting basic ethnocentric ideas. Lacking belief and emotional conviction as to their own moral worth in being Jewish, many Jews may tend more toward conformity with wider societal norms when faced with outgroup criticism and censure. Evidently this is what Sartre (29) means when he says: "What stamps the inauthentic Jew is precisely this perpetual oscillation between pride and a sense of inferiority, between the voluntary and passionate negation of the traits of his race and the mystic and carnal participation in the Jewish reality." However, given the sense of inner worth and value in Jewishness, Jews may simply emphasize those aspects of behavior, including sobriety, which are culturally defined as distinctively Jewish. A basic problem is thus how the symbols of Jewishness come to command the moral sentiments

---

* Probably it was in this sense that two of the New Haven Jewish men asserted in an "off the record" manner, at the conclusion of their interviews, that the need to "keep up a good front" and "save face" before Gentiles was a basic motive in Jewish sobriety. These men did not, of course, go on to point out that what constitutes "good front" or "face" is determined by the values of the ingroup.

so as to sustain the sense of inner worth and motivate conformity to Jewish ideals.

It is our own hypothesis that, more than any other feature of Jewish life, participation in the ceremonials and rituals of Orthodox Judaism fosters the sense of inner worth together with ethnocentric ideas and moral sentiments. Theoretically, ceremonial and ritual are especially effective because of the particularly strong internalization of group symbols, norms, and ideas which take place through this kind of activity. As Durkheim (8) observed, the social functions of ceremonial and ritual have to do primarily with the maintenance of group solidarity and the integration of group symbols, norms, and ideas with supporting emotions or sentiments.* According to Durkheim, ceremonial and ritual are everywhere accompanied by sacred as opposed to utilitarian attitudes, and characteristic sentiments of reverence and respect. Durkheim ultimately identified these sentiments with veneration for the authority of society itself rather than with the intrinsic properties of the sacred symbols, objects, or states of nature they are assumed to represent, as had earlier writers. He perceived, however, that the connection of norms and ideas with supporting sentiments of solidarity and moral authority is achieved through the use of collective symbols (and particularly the major symbols of the authority of the group itself) in the context of ceremonial activity. In Orthodox Jewish ceremonial and ritual the sacred symbols of God are endlessly reiterated and so also are the various symbols of the Jewish group itself. Through ceremonial participation Jews reenact their solidarity with the group and renew their contact with the overwhelming symbols of its moral authority. The familistic character of many ceremonies also dramatizes and reinforces the system of authority in the family, integrating "concrete" or "real" authority with the "abstract" symbolism of the moral community (1). There is no need here for a detailed exposition of this symbolism. What is pertinent is simply that the symbols of the moral community are prominent and that the internalization of these symbols (that is, their connection with the sentiments of solidarity and moral authority) is enhanced through ceremonial and ritual activity.

From this point of view Jewish ceremonial and ritual patterns are conceived of as more than forms for the expression of religious ideas and sentiments. They are also a mechanism which transmits and sustains basic Jewish cultural values. Presumably ceremonial observance strengthens the value of Jewishness, as well as the moral sentiments which group symbols command. We believe, too, that ceremonial participation, or socialization within this tradition, facilitates the internalization of the Orthodox definition of the Jewish situation in relation to the larger society. Theoretically, then, stereotypes of sober Jew and drunken Gentile should elicit the most powerful moral sentiments supporting a norm of sobriety among more observant Jews, while participation in ceremonial and ritual should enhance

---

* A good summary of Durkheim's ideas, as they are pertinent here, is contained in Parsons (25).

motivation to conform to this norm in the context of tense ingroup-outgroup relations.

4. Effects of ceremonial participation on the intensity of sentiments supporting ethnocentric marriage norms

There are no data by which to test directly the extent to which stereotypes of sober Jew and drunken Gentile activate sentiments which support norms of moderate drinking and sobriety among Jews; nor can the precise relationships between ceremonial observance and the mobilization of these sentiments be determined. Actually, all the evidence on reduced condemnation of drunkenness and increased intoxication with declining Orthodoxy is consistent with the point of view set forth above. The problem is that declining Orthodoxy also correlates with changes in other aspects of Jewish culture—such as ceremonial drinking—aspects which may independently contribute emotional support to norms of moderate drinking and sobriety. Hence, it is exceedingly difficult to isolate the specific contribution of ethnocentric ideas and sentiments.

A partial resolution of this dilemma lies in the demonstration that sentiments supporting ethnocentric ideas are strongest among the more ceremonially Orthodox in respect to behaviors unrelated to drinking and intoxication. In this connection, data on marriage preferences from our New Haven study are highly suggestive. The intensity of sentiments opposing marriage between Jews and Gentiles is probably an especially good index of commitment to broader ethnocentric ideas because intermarriage so obviously threatens the integrity of the Jewish moral community (unless there is conversion to Judaism). Ordinarily, students of acculturation and assimilation pay particular attention to ethnic behaviors and attitudes regarding intermarriage on the assumption that these data reflect the continued solidarity or dissolution of the group. Available statistics (3) indicate a high rate of inmarriage among Jews, although the rate of intermarriage has fluctuated widely in different times and places, reaching a recent peak in pre-Nazi Germany, where Orthodox Judaism was in relative decline. Statistics gathered in New Haven (19) suggest that intermarriages are less than 10 per cent of all Jewish marriages. The data from the New Haven interviews show also that Jewish men, irrespective of ceremonial observance, share the belief that Jews should marry Jews rather than Gentiles. Our immediate concern, however, is not with intermarriage rates as such. It is rather with the strength or intensity of sentiments supporting the belief that inmarriage is desirable, as these may relate to ceremonial observance. Our hypothesis is simply that the intensity of sentiments supporting this ethnocentric belief among Jews diminishes with declining ceremonial observance.

In the New Haven interviews a series of questions put before the Jewish men were designed to elicit the relative intensity of sentiments supporting the inmarriage norm. The respondents were first asked to assume that they had a son of marriageable age who has met a congenial girl with whom he had common interests. They were then presented with five hypothetical situations and requested to indicate the degree of their preference for a girl of either Jewish or Protestant origin (although not necessarily religiously observant in either case). In each situation a value conflict was introduced by associating the Jewish girl with an undesirable personal or social characteristic while the Protestant girl was described as socially and personally desirable. Preferences in each situation were recorded on a four-point check list of intensity, as follows:

1. I would much prefer her to be Jewish even if she . . . (had the particular undesirable characteristic).
2. I probably would prefer her to be Jewish even if she . . . (had the particular undesirable characteristic).
3. I probably would prefer she not . . . (have the undesirable characteristic) than that she be Jewish.
4. I would much prefer she not . . . (have the undesirable characteristic) than that she be Jewish.

Responses to each question were scored 1, 2, 3, or 4 (a score of 1 being the strongest preference for Jewishness) and the scores on the five questions were summed into an index of intensity of sentiments.[*] The minimum score of 5, therefore, indicates the strongest preference for Jewishness. A maximum score of 20 would indicate strongest preference for a Protestant girl in the face of the undesirable characteristics associated with the Jewish girl. The mean and median scores of the fifty-eight men who gave adequate information on all five questions were 8.2 and 8.0, respectively. Theoretically, a neutral score would be 12.5. Thus the central tendency of the sample is in favor of marriage with the Jewish girl despite her undesirable characteristics.

The hypothesis that ethnocentric sentiments are strongest among the ceremonially more observant was tested by constructing two categories of strong and weak sentiments and comparing the distribution of the Jewish men in these categories according to degree of ceremonial Orthodoxy.[†] Men with index scores of 8 or less (i.e., below the mean) are considered to have "strong sentiments" favoring inmarriage, while those with scores above 8 are considered to have "weak sentiments" in support of this norm. It is clear from Table 4 that the intensity of sentiments supporting an ethnocentric marriage norm progressively weakens with declining ceremonial observance. Moreover, data presented elsewhere (31) suggest that this relation obtains at different social class levels.

[*] This index is not, properly speaking, a scale of intensity of sentiments. The supposition was that a simple summation of scores would sufficiently differentiate extremes of strong and weak sentiment. Confirmation of the present findings through the use of refined scale techniques is greatly to be desired. The writer is indebted to Dr. Jackson Toby, of Rutgers University, for the design of these questions.

[†] As defined in terms of ritual drinking experience. "Most Orthodox" men were those brought up in homes where the Kiddush was regularly observed.

TABLE 4

Intensity of Sentiments Supporting Ethnocentric Marriage Norms among
New Haven Jewish Men, by Degree of Ceremonial Orthodoxy

	Strong Sentiments	Weak Sentiments
Most Orthodox	9	3
Intermediate	18	11
Least Orthodox	3	12

$$\chi^2 = 10.10, P < .01$$

There is not a one to one correspondence between relatively high frequencies of intoxication and high scores on the index (indicating weak
ethnocentric sentiment). Some Jewish men with high scores have seldom
or never been intoxicated. However, of the men reporting on marriage
preferences who had been intoxicated more than five times in their lives,
seven had scores of 10 or more on the index while only four had scores below 10. These findings suggest that a weakening of ethnocentric sentiments, although not in itself productive of intoxication, may be among the
necessary conditions for increasing intoxication among Jews.

More generally, the findings suggest that the relative value of Jewishness
is enhanced by ceremonial observance and that the sentiments supporting
ethnocentric ideas are stronger among ceremonially Orthodox Jews. It is
plausible to infer from these facts that the imagery of sobriety as a Jewish
virtue, drunkenness as a Gentile vice, elicits strong moral sentiments in support of norms of moderate drinking and sobriety through association with
a broader network of ethnocentric ideas and sentiments which are deeply
internalized in the personalities of the more Orthodox Jews. As ceremonial
observance wanes, however, stereotypes of sober Jew and drunken Gentile
may lose their power to mobilize and reinforce emotions supporting these
norms because the symbols of Jewishness lose the inner emotional significance achieved through ceremonial participation. Just as the sentiments
supporting ethnocentric Jewish ideas about marriage lose their intensity, so,
we suggest, do sentiments elicited by stereotypes of sober Jew and drunken
Gentile, and for essentially the same reasons.

5. Evaluation of the role of group stereotypes

With these concepts in mind, we may essay a more general evaluation of
the role which stereotypes of sober Jew and drunken Gentile may play in
Jewish sobriety in conjunction with the Orthodox definition of the situation
and relations of hostility with outsiders.

To the religious Jew sobriety is a Jewish virtue. It is a measure of the
Jew's worth, not directly in the eyes of Gentiles, who are reputedly prone
to drunkenness, but in his own eyes and in the eyes of members of his

group. Sobriety is a standard, among others, by which the degree of fulfillment of obligations to God and to the Jewish religious community may be determined. To the pious Jew intoxication is antithetical to the dictates of his religion. It is incompatible with the performance of daily rituals which demand consciousness, caution, self-control, and discipline lest the Name be profaned. The religiously observant Jew has ritualized the use of beverage alcohol; he has brought drinking within the sphere of the most powerful social controls and moral sentiments. As Kant suggested, intoxication does deprive one of caution and it is linked in the mind of the devout Jew with loss of self-control and the commission of any number of acts which may be profane, unclean, aggressive, sexual, and otherwise improper in nature. For the religious Jew retaliation from the outgroup is inseparably connected, symbolically, with all relaxation of moral standards and religious discipline. Tensions between ingroup and outgroup therefore provide a tremendous rationale and motive for applying negative social sanctions to intoxication and for creating an atmosphere in which sobriety is expected of all.*

Beyond this, to the Jew who takes pride in his religion, intoxication and the drunkard are symbols of outgroup moral degeneracy and targets for scorn and derision. In the imagery of the group, to be a drunkard is to profane oneself, to become like the irresponsible Gentile. The hypothetical sanction is extirpation. Among the strictly observant, Jews who outmarry are considered dead. Funeral ceremonies are held and future contacts with the defectors are taboo. Similarly, in the symbolism of the group, intoxication and the drunkard are identified with ceasing to be a Jew. In this context the implications of a well-known Jewish folk saying become clear: "*A Yid a Shikker, zoll geharget veren!*" ["A Jew who's a drunkard, may he get killed!"] It is not just that the Jewish drunkard may expect to be or will be killed by a hostile outgroup; he deserves death!

The imagery of sobriety as a Jewish virtue, in sharp contrast to the sinful drunkenness of Gentiles, has further implications once the Orthodox Jewish

---

* There is some question as to whether or not beliefs about retaliation and catastrophe as instruments of God's judgment for Israel's failures actually gained a real foothold among the Jewish people until the powerlessness of the group was concretely experienced by several generations in the Diaspora. This is intimated in Moore (23). Thorner (37) suggests, however, that even prior to the Diaspora "Their [the Jews'] strategic position in the Fertile Crescent invited attack from the great warring empires, another situation which intensified the group solidarity and alertness to Yahweh and his Commandments. . . . Thus both prior to and during the Diaspora a gradually internalized value-system with its demand for a rationally controlled impulse-life subordinate to what were considered higher ends came under constant threat of attack and was thereby consolidated." The further working out of this aspect of Orthodox ideology so as to motivate and rationalize the solidarity of the Jews as God's chosen people in the Diaspora is alluded to by Riesman (28): "Occasionally, the group's 'nerve of failure' was supported by the notion that its very powerlessness proved the Jews to be in fact the Chosen of God. In this way, defeat itself could strengthen the faith of the 'saving remnant' of Jews."

definition of outgroup retaliation as punishment for the relaxation of religious discipline is taken into account. Through this system of ideas hedonistic drinking and intoxication become connected with all the realistic and imaginary anxieties and fears of extreme punishment from Gentiles which are so manifestly present in the Jewish group. Acute intoxication may thus symbolize more dramatically than other modes of deviant behavior a state of helplessness and vulnerability which cannot be offset through the exercise of that self-control and moral discipline which Judaism enjoins. The obverse of this situation is the fear of releasing all the aggressive and retaliatory impulses which are relentlessly checked by the Orthodox religion and the exigencies of a powerless minority status. Consequently, the counter-anxieties elicited by the very idea of intoxication may be extraordinarily powerful.

It may be suggested, however, that with declining ceremonial and ritual observance the sentiments associated with beliefs about sober Jews and drunken Gentiles tend to wane. Powerful group symbols lose emotional support. The "outer" moral authority of Jewishness and its correlate of inner worth lose significance, while anxieties about retaliation and the expression of aggression are lessened along with the relaxation of Jewish moral standards and religious discipline. To individual Jews the cognitive and emotional meaning of these ideas derives from a broader context of identification with Judaism. It is worth re-emphasizing that this identification is most clearly expressed, sustained, and transmitted through Orthodox religious ritual and ceremonial.

6. Persistence of group stereotypes beyond religious boundaries

There is, of course, an ethnic cleavage which persists beyond the boundaries of religion. In the process of socialization many Jewish children internalize and carry on traditional Jewish attitudes which parents still share despite the abandonment of ceremonial observances. Moreover, anti-Semites incessantly manage to discover or conjure up characteristics which set apart even secular Jews from their fellow citizens. Among Jews themselves there is recognition of a common descent and of an ethnic heritage, although many Jews are evidently in doubt as to the nature of this heritage.* Of late, considerable fanfare has been sounded over Jewish nationalism with the ascendance of the State of Israel to legitimate political status among the nations. For the more secular in the American Jewish community, philanthropic and political activities, in contrast to specifically religious activities, enhance the sense of Jewish group membership. In this connection it is pertinent to note that acknowledgment of stereotypes of Jewish and Gentile drinking appears to be related to continued sobriety despite the

---

* The confused state of conceptions of the Jewish cultural heritage is mirrored in Infield's (15) effort to define contemporary Jewish culture. Virtually the only substantive feature which Infield finds common to contemporary Jews is "the odium of defection," although he proposes some questions whose answers might yield more abstract common denominators.

abandonment of most ritual observances (31). However suggestive these facts may be of the influence of ethnic stereotypes on Jewish sobriety beyond the traditional community of religious participation, they should not obscure the likelihood that these stereotypes are most pervasive and powerful within the religious community. It is in terms of cultural continuity with the Orthodox religious tradition that these beliefs and their normative influence can be best understood.

General Effects of the Ingroup-Outgroup Situation

The tentative general conclusions to be drawn from the present research with respect to the influence of the ingroup-outgroup situation on Jewish drinking behavior and sobriety are these: It is not direct censure for intoxication from outsiders, or the realistic possibility of censure or retaliation while in a state of intoxication, which is most significant for Jewish sobriety. In the American cultural setting, direct social pressures from outsiders concerning drinking apparently work in the opposite direction. They tend to induce convivial and hedonistic drinking among Jews, rather than moderate drinking and sobriety. Jews actually conform to these outgroup pressures precisely where relations of solidarity with the Jewish community are situationally disrupted or permanently attenuated. By contrast, it is the Jewish group which exerts direct social pressures inducing moderate drinking and sobriety. The effectiveness of these ingroup pressures apparently varies directly with the solidarity of Jews with the Orthodox religious community.

However, none of these effects can be divorced from the more general context of tensions which exist between Jews and Gentiles in society as a whole. Intergroup tension may intensify Jewish ethnocentrism and heighten conformity to traditional norms among more religious Jews. When refracted through Orthodox ideology, the threat of conflict and anxieties about retaliation probably stimulate ingroup moral discipline. Acute intergroup tension may also reduce Jewish participation in Gentile society and motivate a return to the ingroup and a renaissance of traditionalism among the less religious, more assimilated Jews. As one New Haven Jewish respondent put it: "When times are good the Jew forgets his religion, but then the Goy gets his fur up and it's back to the old ways." Consequently, sobriety having the status of a Jewish virtue, adherence to this norm may be affected by the vicissitudes of tension and antagonism between the Jewish ingroup and the Gentile outgroup in society at large. It is our belief that in these terms Kant's explanation of Jewish sobriety makes sense. To be stressed, however, is the fact that the basic ideas and ceremonials of traditional Judaism have a certain autonomy or vitality which is not immediately contingent on ingroup-outgroup tension and it is with these ideas and practices that Jewish sobriety is most intimately associated. Before the response of Jews to the ingroup-outgroup situation can be understood in respect to the drinking of alcoholic beverages and other behaviors, the incidence and impact among Jews of these cultural patterns must be taken into account.

These tentative conclusions are compatible with broader sociological conceptions of the nature and consequences of relations between status groups in society at large. In their recent general discussion of this subject, Stone and Form (33) call attention to the fact that a group's self-respect is not always commensurate with the social honor which it is accorded by society. They reiterate Max Weber's observation that the sense of dignity experienced by a group may bear no correspondence to its objective position in the actual status hierarchy. As Weber says (10, p. 189): "But pariah peoples who are most despised are usually apt to continue cultivating in some manner that which is equally peculiar to ethnic and status communities: the belief in their own social 'honor.'" Following Weber's thought, Stone and Form go on to observe:

> The sense of dignity that transcends the negatively privileged position of a status group is anchored in the future, often contingent upon the fulfillment of a mission . . . . When the characteristic sense of dignity or personal worth of members of status groups and aggregates is examined with reference to their objective status, and gross intransigencies are disclosed, the conditions for what Hughes has termed "status protest" have been established. Where there are great disparities between dignity and objective status, a group may reject existing status arrangements and establish itself as a status group outside the ongoing status structure of the community (33, p. 152).*

The historical condition of the Jews in Western civilization might be characterized as one of chronic status protest in this sense. However, the disparity between inner worth or dignity and objective status (which is the condition for status protest) is not solely a consequence of the hostility and contempt of society. It is also a function of the ethnocentric ideas of the Jews themselves. These ideas are most clearly embodied and transmitted in the Orthodox religious tradition and internalized most effectively through Orthodox Jewish ceremonial and ritual observance. It is also possible that through the elaboration of ceremonial and ritual Jews have given expression to the need to reject existing status arrangements and to establish themselves in large measure outside the ongoing status structure of the wider society. Adherence to Jewish norms of moderate drinking and sobriety is, as we have shown (31), intricately bound up with Orthodox ceremonial and ritual observances. Deviation from these norms may thus be broadly conceived as a complex function of the vitality of ceremonial Judaism considered together with the objective position and subjective evaluation accorded to Jews by society.

Clarification of the Roles of Ritual Drinking and Other Factors

Our analysis would be seriously misleading if the imagery of sobriety as a Jewish virtue, together with broader ethnocentric ideas and sentiments and the pressures arising from ingroup-outgroup relations were conceived of

* The concept of "status protest" is developed by Hughes (14).

as causing the sobriety and virtual absence of drinking patholog̣ Jews in some ultimate or final sense. No such thought is intended. Under certain conditions these factors are assumed to provide strong motivation and reinforcement to a norm of sobriety and, accordingly, constitute part of a complex of socio-cultural variables which must be considered. However, other features of Jewish culture may certainly contribute to the effective social regulation of the use of beverage alcohol. In this connection we share Bales' belief that the extensive ritualization of drinking in Jewish religious ceremonial is of the utmost importance.* Especially to be noted is the fact that traditional Jewish religious symbolism quite explicitly links the major ethnocentric idea with the ritual drinking situation. Thus the Sabbath Kiddush concludes with these words (27): "For Thou hast chosen us and sanctified us above all nations, and in love and favor hast given us the holy Sabbath as our inheritance. Blessed art Thou, O Lord, who hallowest the Sabbath." Yet in focusing attention on ritual drinking there is a tendency to lose sight of other factors. It might easily be concluded from Bales' discussion that ritual drinking by itself creates all the powerful ideas and sentiments in traditional Jewish culture which are opposed to intoxication and hedonistic drinking. And at times Bales himself seems to advocate this narrow conception. However, he does mention secondary factors in Jewish sobriety and refers to the "underlying ideas and sentiments" associated with the ritual use of wine as providing the "primary emotional impetus" to the hatred of intoxication and barriers to the formation of addictive motives among Jews.

Actually, there is a twofold significance to ritual drinking in Bales' argument which is not always clear. On the one hand, ritual drinking may be conceived as giving form and expression to religious ideas and sentiments integral with a larger pattern of ceremonial and ritual observance. Because of his involvement in a wider pattern of ceremonial and ritual observances, the pious Jew approaches alcoholic beverages with a generalized ritual attitude. On the other hand, insofar as ritual drinking is experienced early and practiced continuously in life, this specific mode of drinking has the effect of reinforcing in the personality the ideational and emotional connections between the acts of drinking and the most powerful sentiments and symbols of social control in the Jewish group. In short, the traditional prescriptions to drink ceremonially reinforce the connections between the ideas and sentiments associated with the generalized ritual attitude and the act of drinking itself. A stable attitude toward the drinking of alcoholic beverages is consequently molded which does not leave the outcome of drinking to chance, individual experiment, fear, or ignorance.

Yet there is still the knotty problem of the generalization of a controlled attitude toward drinking. This problem is most broadly illustrated by the fact that human behavior is so flexible that patterns of ceremonial drinking

---

* Our reference here and in the ensuing discussion is to Bales' ideas as set forth in his dissertation (1) and reiterated in summary form (2).

can alternate with patterns of convivial and hedonistic drinking within the same cultural framework. Why, then, has there been no such alternation or dualism in Orthodox Jewish life?

Part of the solution to this problem probably lies in the fundamental idea of Orthodox Judaism as a "total way of life" through which all man's activities are to be sanctified. Orthodox Judaism presses for integration, for the permeation of all facets of life with sacred symbolism. The possibility of this kind of integration appears to be bound up with a pattern of close communal living. The hostility and discrimination of outsiders has contributed to this integration by forcing Jews to live under the compact social conditions congenial to it. The tendency toward permeation of all activities with religious values is clearly evident in the Orthodox requirement that the Jew must pronounce a benediction before drinking any beverage in any circumstance. This custom obviously facilitates the extension to the drinking situation of ideas and sentiments of reverence and respect and the larger moral meanings associated with being a religious Jew, even though the situation is not otherwise of an essentially religious character. However, reinforcing the tendency toward a controlled use of alcoholic beverages, which is immanent in the extension of a ritual attitude, are the ethnocentric ideas and sentiments and pressures arising from the ingroup-outgroup situation.

Through the network of ethnocentric symbolism and sentiments the idea of sobriety becomes integrated with the feeling of moral superiority in being Jewish. Orthodox Jews have claimed legitimacy for their religion and defended Judaism through the cultivation of and adherence to what they conceived to be a morally superior discipline. In this perspective, stereotypes of sober Jew and drunken Gentile define intoxication among Jews as a threat to the basic claims and defenses of Judaism and as a threat to the particular personalities whose self-esteem and integration derive from the religion. It seems likely that, in association with collective stereotypes, the inner meaning of intoxication for the Jew himself is the degradation of Jewishness. For the Jew to become intoxicated symbolizes the futility of the Jewish moral struggle in a society which holds Jewishness in disesteem. Perhaps, then, these additional factors help to explain the apparent sobriety of ghetto Jews who used alcoholic beverages in convivial situations, such as wedding celebrations, in which drinking might have taken a hedonistic turn. Very likely some Jews were not so pious in these circumstances as always to bless the beverages prior to drinking, but to become intoxicated under these conditions would have been "un-Jewish." * Evidently, the inner and outer social pressures "not to let down" on this *point d'honneur* were and still are very strong for Jews who are solidary with the Jewish community.

The complex reinforcing factors conducive to Jewish sobriety may persist, of course, even where the ceremonial use of alcohol is in decline. Obviously, ritual drinking directly depends upon the vitality of the larger

---

* On this point, see Zborowski and Herzog (39).

religious and ceremonial pattern. Beyond this, ceremonial and ritual evidently are also a powerful mechanism for giving Jewishness and ethnocentric ideas strong inner emotional meaning, while Orthodox beliefs provide a definition of the situation which motivates sobriety in the context of tense ingroup-outgroup relations. Consequently, we suspect that these additional factors lose their power to motivate sobriety among less Orthodox Jews whose identification with traditional Judaism is weak or who situationally identify with Gentiles on a primary-group basis, as in military service or in college. It may be suggested, however, that these additional factors helped to preclude the extensive development of patterns of convivial or hedonistic drinking in alternation with the ceremonial and religious use of beverage alcohol in the closely knit Jewish community.

It is important to note that, theoretically, the effectiveness of norms, ideas, and sentiments in regulating intoxication depends upon their internalization in the personality. They must be anticipated in the drinking situation itself. Social sanctions from members of the group after the individual has reached a state of intoxication or developed a pattern of inebriety are not of primary significance. To be effective, the regulatory norms, ideas, and sentiments must be elicited immediately in the drinking situation and be supported by the consensus or social expectancies of the surrounding milieu. In fact, Bales stresses the specific act of ritual drinking precisely because he believes that the internalization of a controlled attitude toward drinking is facilitated by the overt and repeated practice of drinking in a religious context, and in our opinion this is correct. However, the internalization of the reinforcing ideas and sentiments to which we have alluded need not necessarily depend upon the experience of intoxication or even the experience of drinking. The broader process of socialization is sufficient to structure these elements in the personality. Through the internalization of ideas and sentiments associated with Jewishness and the Jewish situation, and ideas of sobriety as a Jewish virtue, drunkenness as a Gentile vice, Jews bring to the drinking situation powerful moral sentiments and anxieties counter to intoxication. That these factors do not derive from the specific experience of drinking does not preclude their being a part of the normative orientation toward the act of drinking itself. We might say, then, that through the ceremonial use of beverage alcohol religious Jews learn how to drink in a controlled manner; but through constant reference to the hedonism of outsiders, in association with a broader pattern of religious and ethnocentric ideas and sentiments, Jews also learn how not to drink.

References

1. Bales, Robert F., *The Fixation Factor in Alcohol Addiction: An Hypothesis Derived from a Comparative Study of Irish and Jewish Social Norms,* unpublished doctoral dissertation, Harvard University, 1944.
2. ———, "Cultural Differences in Rates of Alcoholism," *Quart. J. Stud. Alc.,* **6**:480–499, 1946.
3. Barron, Milton L., "The Incidence of Jewish Intermarriage in Europe and America," *Amer. Sociol. Rev.,* **11**:6–13, 1946.

4. Bernheimer, Charles S. (Ed.), *The Russian Jew in the United States: Studies of Social Conditions in New York, Philadelphia, and Chicago, with a Description of Rural Settlements,* Philadelphia: J. C. Winston Company, 1905.

5. Clark, Wayne, "Portrait of the Mythical Gentile: One Stereotype Breeds Another," *Commentary,* 7:546–549, 1949.

6. Dollard, John, *Caste and Class in a Southern Town,* New Haven, Conn.: Yale University Press, 1937.

7. Dubnow, Simon M., *History of the Jews in Russia and Poland from the Earliest Times to the Present Day,* I. Friedlander (Trans.), 3 Vols., Philadelphia: Jewish Publication Society of America, 1916–1920.

8. Durkheim, Emile, *The Elementary Forms of the Religious Life: A Study in Religious Sociology,* J. W. Swain (Trans.), London: G. Allen and Unwin, 1915.

9. Fishberg, Maurice, *The Jews: A Study of Race and Environment,* New York: Walter Scott Publishing Company, 1911.

10. Gerth, Hans H., and C. Wright Mills, *From Max Weber: Essays in Sociology,* New York: Oxford University Press, 1946.

11. Glad, Donald D., "Attitudes and Experiences of American-Jewish and American-Irish Male Youth as Related to Differences in Adult Rates of Inebriety," *Quart. J. Stud. Alc.,* 8:406–472, 1947.

12. Glazer, Nathan, "Why Jews Stay Sober: Social Scientists Examine Jewish Abstemiousness," *Commentary,* 13:181–186, 1952.

13. Haggard, Howard W., and E. M. Jellinek, *Alcohol Explored,* Garden City, N.Y.: Doubleday and Company, 1942.

14. Hughes, Everett C., "Social Change and Status Protest, An Essay on the Marginal Man," *Phylon,* 10:58–65, 1949.

15. Infield, Henrik G., "The Concept of Jewish Culture and the State of Israel," *Amer. Sociol. Rev.,* 16:506–513, 1951.

16. Jellinek, E. M., "Classics of the Alcohol Literature. A Document of the Reformation Period on Inebriety: Sebastian Franck's 'On the Horrible Vice of Drunkenness,' etc.," *Quart. J. Stud. Alc.,* 2:391–395, 1941.

17. ———, "Immanuel Kant on Drinking," *Quart. J. Stud. Alc.,* 1:777–778, 1941.

18. ———, *Recent Trends in Alcoholism and in Alcohol Consumption,* New Haven, Conn.: Hillhouse Press, 1947. Also in *Quart. J. Stud. Alc.,* 8:1–42, 1947.

19. Kennedy, Ruby Jo Reeves, "Single or Triple Melting Pot? Intermarriage Trends in New Haven, 1870–1940," *Amer. J. Sociol.,* 49:331–339, 1944.

20. McKinlay, Arthur Patch, "Ancient Experience with Intoxicating Drinks: Non-classical Peoples," *Quart. J. Stud. Alc.,* 9:388–414, 1948.

21. ———, "Ancient Experience with Intoxicating Drinks: Non-Attic Greek States," *Quart. J. Stud. Alc.,* 10:289–315, 1949.

22. ———, "Attic Temperance," *Quart. J. Stud. Alc.,* 12:61–102, 1951.

23. Moore, George Foot, *Judaism in the First Three Centuries of the Christian Era: The Age of the Tannaim,* 3 Vols., Cambridge, Mass.: Harvard University Press, 1927–1930.

24. Myerson, Abraham, "Alcohol: A Study of Social Ambivalence," *Quart. J. Stud. Alc.,* 1:13–20, 1940.

25. Parsons, Talcott, *Essays in Sociological Theory, Pure and Applied,* Glencoe, Ill.: Free Press, 1949.

26. ———, *The Social System,* Glencoe, Ill.: Free Press, 1951.

27. Philips, A. Th., *Transl. Daily Prayers*, New York: Hebrew Publishing Company, no date.
28. Riesman, David, "A Philosophy for 'Minority' Living," *Commentary*, 6:413–422, 1948.
29. Sartre, Jean-Paul, "Portrait of the Inauthentic Jew," *Commentary*, 5:389–397, 1948.
30. Shils, Edward A., "The Study of the Primary Group," *in* D. Lerner and H. D. Lasswell (Eds.), *The Policy Sciences: Recent Developments in Scope and Method*, Stanford: Stanford University Press, 1951.
31. Snyder, Charles R., *Alcohol and the Jews*, Glencoe, Ill.: Free Press, 1958.
32. ———, and Ruth H. Landman, "Studies of Drinking in Jewish Culture, II: Prospectus for Sociological Research on Jewish Drinking Patterns," *Quart. J. Stud. Alc.*, 12:451–474, 1951.
33. Stone, Gregory P., and William H. Form, "Instabilities in Status: The Problem of Hierarchy in the Community Study of Status Arrangements," *Amer. Sociol. Rev.*, 18:149–162, 1953.
34. Straus, Robert, and Selden D. Bacon, *Drinking in College*, New Haven, Conn.: Yale University Press, 1953.
35. Sumner, William Graham, *Folkways: A Study of the Sociological Importance of Usages, Manners, Customs, Mores and Morals* (2nd ed.), Boston, Mass.: Ginn and Company, 1940.
36. Thomas, W. I., and Dorothy S. Thomas, *The Child in America: Behavior Problems and Programs*, New York: A. A. Knopf and Company, 1928.
37. Thorner, Isidor, "Ascetic Protestantism and Alcoholism," *Psychiatry*, 16:167–176, 1953.
38. Warner, W. Lloyd, and Leo Srole, *The Social Systems of American Ethnic Groups*, (Yankee City Series, Vol. III.), New Haven, Conn.: Yale University Press, 1945.
39. Zborowski, Mark, and Elizabeth Herzog, *Life Is with People: The Jewish Little-Town of Eastern Europe*, New York: International Press, 1952.

C.

AGE AND SEX

Introductory Note. Drinking patterns in our contemporary society have been only partially studied in relation to the basic structural variables of age and sex. Alcoholism is known to vary strikingly in incidence between the sexes and to find fullest expression in the middle and later years of life.* It seems probable, moreover, that there is substantial variation in the sex-ratios of alcoholism from one socio-cultural milieu to another. However, despite pronounced differences in the pathological extremes of drinking—which suggest the relevance of broadly conceived sociological inquiry—sociologists have contributed little to the understanding of drinking patterns in terms of age and sex beyond repetition of the statistical significance of these variables as determinants of drinking behavior and attitude, and allusions to differences in the "traditional roles" of men and women, old and young.

Important exception must be taken to this characterization of the existing state of knowledge, however, in regard to one major sector of the total age range of the population, namely, adolescence and young adulthood. It is with this sector of society that the studies in this section are primarily concerned.

In Chapter 12, George Maddox reviews and interprets sociologically the principal findings of several studies of the drinking patterns of teenagers in the United States, studies which collectively sampled more than eight thousand high-school students in different parts of the country. It is clear from his

* The progressive development of alcoholism with age is treated by E. M. Jellinek in Chapter 20, and in other chapters of Section IV. A review of the state of knowledge regarding the woman alcoholic, a subject treated only incidentally in this volume (cf., Chapters 23 and 27), may be found in Lisansky (2).

report that drinking patterns among these adolescents gravitate toward parental practices and are to a high degree predictable from a knowledge of background variables of a socio-cultural nature. Also, the evidence is convincing that the stresses of adolescence, such as they may be, are not manifested on a wide scale in excessive drinking. One could wish that the survey data upon which Maddox's chapter is based had contained richer material on cultural attitudes and adult expectations regarding drinking among youth, and that these studies had been cast in a framework of stratification by age explicitly concerned with the whole structure of relations between adults and youth. Had this been so, it might have been possible for Maddox to explore more fully the social and cultural sources of constraints and the extent of ambivalence in regard to drinking among American youth along lines similar to those suggested by Ozzie Simmons in his study of the learning of drinking in a Peruvian Mestizo community (Chapter 3).

Although the available data lead him to play down the probability that adolescents will be coerced by their peer groups into extremes of drinking, it needs to be emphasized that Maddox is not saying that adolescent peer groups are without consequence in shaping drinking behavior. The point is that either the normative content of these groups or the net balance of reference-group pressures (or both) is *typically* such as not to eventuate in those excesses of youthful drinking which so often fire the imagination of adults. Yet the content and relative weight of peer-group and other reference-group influences upon adolescent drinking, which Maddox treats summarily, are subjects worthy of detailed study, especially, we may suppose, in instances of marked deviation from culturally expectable drinking patterns. Some beginnings toward the systematic investigation of these influences may be found in the reports of research by Rogers (3) and Haer (1). In the present context, it bears mention that Haer's evidence indicates that drinking behavior in the population at large—including older as well as younger drinkers—tends to conform more closely to the patterns of contemporaries (e.g., one's friends or spouse) than to the patterns of older generations. This, incidentally, is a situation which Haer considers quite expectable in a highly mobile and rapidly changing society. The tendency appears to be a function of increasing age, however, and Haer therefore observes, as does Maddox, a relatively close correspondence between parental drinking patterns and those of the younger generation of drinkers.

In Chapter 13, Robert Straus and Selden Bacon report on the results of the application of the broad survey technique to the study of drinking patterns among the slightly older group found in college. Although their college student sample is biased in favor of the higher socio-economic strata, the findings of this vast study seem clearly to show once more that the stresses of youth are not typically and regularly expressed in extremes of drinking behavior. As was the case with high-school students, variations in college-student drinking patterns depend to a significant degree upon socio-cultural background factors, factors which seem altogether extrinsic to the college setting itself. We would be loath to conclude, however, that the informal organization of college student life has no impact upon student drinking behavior. A more appropriate conclusion would seem to be that the differentiation into groups and the corresponding drinking styles among college students in large measure comprise a microcosm expressing and reinforcing the patterns of the various social groups and strata which make up the larger society.

A very important feature of Straus and Bacon's study is the basis it provides for gauging the extent and nature of "problem drinking," including incipient alcoholism, among college youth. Their findings in this connection not only are intrinsically interesting but also have constituted an essential part of the foundation for subsequent, more detailed research, as exemplified by Peter Park's study in Chapter 25.

Finally, in Chapter 14, Albert Ullman directs attention to the first drinking experiences of youth. This is done not so much in the interests of surveying patterns as with an eye to detecting differences in the structuring of initial learning situations of the sort which his theory of the mechanism of addiction would lead him to expect as typical for alcoholics, on the one hand, as opposed to social drinkers, on the other. If the development of alcohol addiction depends, as Ullman believes, upon a definite constellation of conditions of learning, then it is reasonable to suppose that these conditions will be more nearly approximated and occur more frequently among social categories with a high risk of alcoholism (such as males), and be absent, modified, or less frequent in the case of low-risk categories. And it is against the background of such reasoning that Ullman finds it relevant to pursue the question of sex differences among youth in initial drinking experiences.

Ullman's chapter in this book has been necessarily limited to a brief consideration of the first drinking experiences among alcohol addicts and social drinkers and to the exploration of sex differences which logically follows. Yet it deserves mention that his work has definite implications for such problems as differences in rates of alcoholism among ethnic and religious groups, to the extent that these subcultures tend to structure differentially the situations in which drinking is learned. Indeed, this is a problem which Ullman has taken up elsewhere (4). Finally, while we cannot share his view regarding the irrelevance of personality differences to alcoholism (for reasons which will be discussed in Section IV), we would agree that in investigating the nature of the situations in which drinking is first learned in the formative years of life, Ullman may well be calling attention to a crucial link in the chain of factors disposing to alcohol addiction.

References

1. Haer, John L., "Drinking Patterns and the Influence of Friends and Family," *Quart. J. Stud. Alc.*, **18**:179–185, 1957.
2. Lisansky, Edith S., "The Woman Alcoholic," *Ann. Amer. Acad. Pol. Soc. Sci.*, **315**: 73–81, 1958.

3. Rogers, Everett M., "Reference Group Influences on Student Drinking Behavior," *Quart. J. Stud. Alc.*, 19:244–254, 1958.

4. Ullman, Albert D., "Ethnic Differences in the First Drinking Experience," *Social Problems*, 8:45–56, 1960.

chapter 12

Teenage drinking in the United States[*]

George L. Maddox

It has been established beyond question that a majority of American adults drink alcoholic beverages at least upon occasion. Children in our society are generally thought to be abstinent and, excepting youngsters in certain subgroups like the Jews, for the most part probably are. However, what the teenager, the person between childhood and adulthood, does with and thinks about beverage alcohol has been the subject of the most varied speculation. Yet guesswork about adolescent use of or abstinence from beverage alcohol in the United States has become increasingly unnecessary and unwarranted as research has accumulated. Since this work has yet to be summarized in a single source, attention in this chapter will first be directed to this task. The evidence on teenage drinking will then be interpreted within the context of our American social structure.

Relevant Research

Systematic research on drinking among teenagers was begun in 1941 when McCarthy and Douglass made an exploratory study of attitudes toward and uses of beverage alcohol among students in suburban Washington, D.C. Replications of this study were also made in 1945 and 1947 (6). Then, between 1953 and 1956, reports of three coordinated studies of drinking in high school appeared under the auspices of the Mrs. John S. Sheppard Foundation. The first of these studies was made in Long Island's Nassau County (1). Studies in Racine County, Wisconsin (9) and in Metropolitan Wichita and some non-metropolitan counties of Kansas fol-

[*] This chapter was written especially for this book.

lowed (7). Concurrently research under different auspices was being completed in selected areas of Utah (12) and in Michigan (8, 13).

Cumulatively, over eight thousand high-school students have been included in research reported to date. The findings of the various studies have been generally consistent and complementary. There are several limitations, however, in using such data to generalize about drinking among teenagers. First, high-school student and teenager are not necessarily synonymous. Second, it has not been demonstrated that the samples of high-school students which have been studied are, even taken cumulatively, representative of the population of high-school students much less of all teenagers. This remains the case even though students from a variety of regional, religious, and socio-economic subcultures have been studied. Third, every study has relied altogether on the subjective reports of students about their attitudes toward and uses of beverage alcohol. There have been no attempts to verify verbalizations by students about their behavior and no participant observation studies.

These limitations cannot be ignored. It is relevant to emphasize, however, that the data which are available, limited as they may be, seem preferable to impressions and guesses unchecked by any research. Moreover, high-school students as a category probably come nearer than any other social category to being the equivalent to teenagers in this society. This is especially the case if "teenager" refers to a position in the age graded social structure rather than to a numerical age designation alone. If puberty, ordinarily reached between the ages of 12 and 15, is taken as the beginning of the teenage period and the achievement of adult roles, such as marriage, a full-time job, or entrance into the armed forces is taken as the end of the period, then the high-school years provide an approximate but useful definition of the teenage period. The utility of studying drinking among teenagers by studying drinking among high-school students is enhanced by the fact that a majority of young people of high-school age are in school.* Moreover, the studies of high-school students have generally also explored pre-high-school drinking experiences. For these reasons, generalizations about drinking among teenagers in this society based on high-school data are actually less arbitrary than they may appear at first sight. The need for caution, however, is apparent and admitted.

Methodologically, the studies of drinking among high-school students to be summarized here are best classified as descriptive surveys of reported attitudes toward and uses of alcohol with the exception of the Sower, McCall, and Maddox Michigan Study (13), which concentrates on a sociological interpretation of the findings. Generally, specific hypotheses are not advanced to be tested and interpretation is secondary to description.

---

* Some supplementary material on the drinking behavior of teenagers not in high school is available. Incidental reference is made to the drinking of the "out of school" in Wattenberg and Moir (15) and Hollingshead (5). The older teenager in college is considered by Straus and Bacon (14).

These limitations are countered by the fact that adequate sampling procedures were used, that systematic reporting makes possible some comparisons and interpretation of data, and that the research reports are generally well written. The exclusive dependence of the studies on subjective reports of the teenagers about their attitudes and behavior is alleviated somewhat by the consistency of verbalizations among respondents in the various studies and also in those instances in which tests of reliability of response are reported.

In the brief summary of research which follows, most attention will be given to reporting convergences in the data. It will only rarely be possible to do more than hint at variations which occasionally appear to be significant. In the interests of brevity and readability, detailed references to specific research studies will not be made. Instead, in most cases references will be made to a report by naming the state in which it was done. Identification of a study by convenient reference to the state in which it was done does not, of course, imply that generalization from the report to the teenager population of that state is warranted.

The Teenager's Image of Adult Drinking Behavior

When the teenager views adults, his chances are better than one in two of seeing a user of beverage alcohol. The term *user* here excludes those persons who employ alcohol in religious rituals only and those whose use has been confined to an isolated experience only. The term emphasizes recurrence of drinking, however irregularly, and the integration of alcohol to some degree into an individual's style of life. Surveys have consistently reported a majority of adults to be users in this sense. Consistent with such an observation, a majority of students in the Michigan study, for example, believed that most adults drink at least sometimes. The New York, Wisconsin, and Kansas studies are also consistent: a majority of parents were reported to keep alcohol in the home and to make some use of it.

Drinking is perceived not only as common adult behavior but also primarily as a social act. The imagery of adult drinking reported by teenagers in high school has repeatedly focused on the use of alcohol primarily in informal social contexts such as a party or in the celebration of special events. Adults were perceived to drink both in public places and in the home but always emphasis was on drinking in social groups. Moreover, what alcohol was believed to do *to* the user was typically counterbalanced by what it was believed to do *for* him. Hence, adult drinking, as perceived by teenagers, suggests that alcohol is primarily a social beverage rather than a drug with necessarily antisocial consequences attached to its use.

While the teenagers thought of the typical adult as a user, they did not conclude that all adults are equally likely to drink. The Protestant teenager was less likely to report his parents as users than were his Catholic and Jewish peers. The rural teenager was less likely to report his parents as users than was his urban counterpart. All respondents were more likely to perceive the male than the female as a user. In effect, then, perceived differences in adult drinking which are reported by teenagers correspond closely to differences in drinking behavior reported by surveys to be characteristic of persons in various subcultures in the society.

Learning to Drink

The reported association between adulthood and drinking, the predominant image of alcohol as a social beverage rather than a drug, and the reported availability of alcohol in the home anticipate a basic finding of every study of drinking among high-school teenagers: the most frequently reported situation for the first exposure to alcohol is in the home with parents or other adults present. Although the average age at exposure cannot be calculated from the data, it appears to be about the time of entrance into high school, in the fourteenth or fifteenth year, for the majority. For those not exposed by this time, the probability of their exposure increases with age. First drinking experiences are more likely to involve low- than high-alcohol-content beverages.

Regional variation is evident in reports about first exposures. For example, in the New York and Wisconsin studies, almost two-thirds of the users described their first drinking experiences with low-alcohol-content beverages such as beer and wine to be in the home with relatives present. In the Kansas study, however, only half of the users reported this. In the Utah study only one teenager in three described his first exposure as being in the home.

The teenager's perception of adult drinking behavior coupled with descriptions of first drinking experiences in the home both emphasize drinking as legitimate behavior for adults and at least some teenagers under some circumstances. In the New York and Wisconsin studies, in which the perceived legitimacy of drinking among teenagers was investigated, majorities claimed parental permission to drink in the home. Only one in four persons in the Kansas study, however, made this claim. In all three studies claims to parental permission increased with age.

Claims of parental permission to drink outside the home were consistently lower than such claims for permission to drink at home. Yet, 40 per cent of the students in one study and only slightly smaller percentages in the other studies reported drinking more away from home than parents knew about. The significance of this report of drinking more than parents know about is suggested by interview materials from the Michigan study.

In the Michigan study, students differentiated with interesting consistency between "tasting with parents" and "drinking with my friends." Such a qualification would be understandable in a social situation in which decisions about whether, when, what, where, and with whom one drinks are considered an adult but not a teenage prerogative. The teenager appears to perceive this distinction; drinking in the home context is primarily a "playing at" or experimentation with one facet of adult life. He is permitted to anticipate a pattern of behavior which, while premature, is recognized as ultimately legitimate adult behavior. Thus the question of drinking by teenagers appears, for parents of many teenagers, to focus on timing and control rather than on abstinence. Peer groups are presumably more permissive than parents in supporting experimentation. Such an interpretation of parental norms with regard to drinking would help explain why there is so little relationship between community law and drinking among teenagers. Legal rules designed to discourage teenage drinking frequently fail to get either parental or peer-group support.

The teenager, then, does not invent the idea of drinking; he learns it. He learns from both parents and peers and, in the typical case, in that order. It does not follow from this, however, that drinking is pivotal, high-priority behavior for a majority or even a significant minority of teenagers. Although the data permit only tentative conclusions on the point, peer groups do not exert the inevitable and irresistible pressure to make every member a user that is sometimes assumed. It has already been noted that a teenager may be a user in the home context prior to any peer-group drinking experience. Moreover, on the basis of the present evidence, the assumption that the typical teenage peer group is a drinking group may be inaccurate. The possibility of regional and community variations in drinking behavior has already been anticipated. It is certain that drinking is atypical of some teenagers although this is less likely to be true with each advancing year of age. The evidence suggests, moreover, the probability that it is as likely that a teenager will seek out a peer group supporting his preference about drinking as it is for him to be coerced into behavior which is disapproved.

In both the New York and Kansas studies, for instance, only small minorities of users and non-users chose to label each other as "not regular guys" solely on the basis of whether they did or did not use alcohol at parties. Significantly, in the same studies majorities specifically devalued drinking as necessary for social acceptance or a prerequisite of convivial interaction with one's peers. Similarly, while a majority of teenagers in the Michigan study were non-users and perceived a majority of their peers to be non-users, only one in five of them thought drinking among teenagers was unconditionally wrong. The remaining four in five students could imagine some situations in which drinking would be acceptable for their peers if not themselves.

In the same study it was found that, while those students who reported the greatest interest and participation in organized religion were more likely than others to express moral disapproval of drinking, religious identification was not a reliable basis for predicting moral disapproval. A majority of those who attached importance to religious identification did not perceive any necessary connection between this identification and abstinence; they expressed at least conditional moral approval of drinking. The evidence discourages the inference that this permissiveness toward drinking is to be explained by peer-group coercion. It is better explained by the teenagers' awareness of the ultimate legitimacy of drinking for a significant segment of the adult population. Moreover, the relationship between parental drinking or the probability of drinking by the offspring must be considered as basic as the relationship between peer-group drinking and the probability of conformity by any given member of the group.

Drinking among Teenagers

Teenagers learn to drink in a society in which a majority of adults not only drink at least sometimes but also are perceived by the teenagers to do so. They learn to drink in a society in which adult-like roles are typically assumed following graduation from high school. In such a social situation one would expect the incidence of experimentation with or use of alcohol to increase as graduation is approached. The teenager graduated from high school without such personal exposure would be an exception. This is in fact the case. In the Michigan study, for example, the chances were only five in one hundred that a student in the last 2 years of high school had not been exposed at least once personally to the use of alcohol.

Exposure to use is not equivalent to establishing a regular pattern of use, however. For this reason the equation of an experimental taste of alcohol with drinking leads to a serious overestimation of the extent of teenage drinking. If teenagers who use alcohol in the context of religious ritual only and those whose use has been isolated to a single experience are excluded, the proportion of users reported in the various studies ranges from about three in ten in the Michigan and Utah studies to about eight in ten in the New York study. Even these proportions tend to invite overestimation of the extent of drinking among teenagers.

In both the Wisconsin and New York studies, which reported users to be in the majority, only about half of the users had consumed an alcoholic beverage during the week prior to the study. In the Kansas study, which reported a minority of users, only one in four of the users indicated an alcoholic beverage had been used during the previous week. In the Michigan study only one in ten of the respondents identified himself as a "drinker" although about one in three were classified as users; this suggests that only a minority of users considered their drinking as sufficiently frequent or intense to warrant such a self-designation. Moreover, the teenage drinker is typically a consumer of low-alcoholic-content beverages. In all the studies, beer was the most frequently used beverage followed in order by wine and "hard liquor."

Although the various studies do not report measures of intensive drinking in a way that allows for specific comparison, estimation of the proportion of students consuming as much as one drink a day range from about 2 to 6 per cent. Subjective evaluation of drinking experiences led about one half of all users to claim having been "high" or "gay" at some time and about one in four to claim this experience at least once during the month prior to the research in the New York, Wisconsin, and Kansas studies. An estimated one in ten of the teenagers in these studies reported having been "drunk" during this same period, although the terminology is not identical in the various studies.

With the exception of the Washington, D.C., study, there is no available evidence for concluding that the extensiveness and intensiveness of drinking among teenagers has tended to increase or decrease throughout the United States in the last 20 years. In the Washington study a trend toward a larger proportion of users was observed; however, even here the increased extent of use was not matched by a comparable increase in intensiveness of use.

1. *The social characteristics of teenage users*

Only when individuals can place themselves and others in various social situations with some degree of consistency and accuracy is social interaction on a sustained basis possible. Factors of age, sex, socio-economic status, and religion, for example, are associated with identifiable and persisting expectations about the behavior of persons. These shared expectations are typically confirmed by observation of the behavior of persons placed within the society in terms of these characteristics. It follows, then, that such factors would be related to differing expectations about the use of alcohol as well as differences in reported behavior. This is in fact found to be the case.

Age. The probability that a teenager will be a user of beverage alcohol increases with age. Increasing age is also related to the increased probability that the drinker will drink intensively and will experience some physiological effects from drinking such as inebriety. At age 18, the usual age for graduation from high school, the extensiveness and intensiveness of drinking is at its peak for the teenager. Teenage claims to parental permission to drink in the home and away from home also tend to increase with age.

It has already been observed that the typical adult in our society is perceived by teenagers to be a user of beverage alcohol. Drinking is one identifying mark of the adult. If one thinks of the achievement of adulthood as synonymous with reaching age 21, the high proportion of reported users among students in the last year of high school indicates that claims to adult prerogatives frequently antedate legal adulthood. The assumption that drinking is premature before age 21 appears to underlie the legislation of many states designed to discourage or prohibit drinking before this age. However, an interesting commentary on the differing assessments of when one becomes an adult in our society was provided by interview material in the Michigan study.

In these interviews, drinking was frequently associated with "coming of age." Asked to elaborate what "coming of age" meant to them, these students illustrated with references to being graduated from high school, taking a full-time job, being married, or entering the armed forces. The achievement of adulthood was, thus, associated with the playing of adult-like roles rather than the achievement of a particular age. Since only a minority of teenagers postpone playing adult-like roles beyond graduation from high school, the possibility that the teenager being graduated from high school would not think of drinking as premature behavior is quite high.

Sex. Surveys of adult drinking behavior consistently report that males in our society are more likely than females to drink, to drink frequently and intensively, and to drink compulsively. Studies of drinking among teenagers also report that the male is more likely than the female to be a user, although the reliability of the differences in reported drinking behavior tends to decrease with age.

Among teenagers, females were more likely than males to report being exposed to drinking first in the home. They were also less likely than males to claim parental permission to drink outside the home, and less likely than males to drink "hard liquor" and to experience such dramatic effects from drinking as inebriety. Moreover, in the Michigan study both male and female teenagers verbalized a double standard of propriety with regard to teenage drinking. Both sexes perceived drinking to be more permissible for males than for females. This distinction they also imputed to adults.

Religion. Religious preferences and participation in organized religion among teenagers are not uniformly reported in the various studies. The number of Jewish students was large enough to be analyzed comparatively only in the New York study, and even in this case analysis was limited to the reported behavior of parents rather than the teenagers themselves. The proportion of users among Catholic and Jewish parents was found to differ only slightly; moreover, although the proportion of users was higher among both Catholic and Jewish parents than among Protestant parents, the difference was not statistically reliable.

The Wisconsin and Kansas studies compare the drinking patterns of Catholic and Protestant students. However, the findings of the two studies are not comparable since, in Wisconsin, parochial school students were involved while in Kansas only Catholics attending public schools were included. In the former case the Catholic parents were more likely to be users than were their Protestant counterparts, although the difference was not statistically significant. In the latter instance, Catholic parents were more likely than Protestant parents to be users, with a significant difference. Catholic teenagers were also more likely than Protestant teenagers to be users, to drink in the home, and to claim parental permission to drink even though the differences were not reliable.

In the Michigan study, attention was directed to the importance imputed to religious identification and reported participation in organized religious activities. In this study it was found that the minority of teenagers who attached the most importance to religious identification and who reported the most participation were more likely than others to express moral disapproval of teenage drinking and to be themselves non-users. The differences, however, were not significant. Moreover, a majority of those who imputed great importance to religious identification also indicated at least conditional approval of drinking in some situations. Similarly, in the Kansas study, a majority of the users in the metropolitan sample reported attending at least four services in the previous month. Almost half of the users in the non-metropolitan sample described their religious participation in the same way.

The indices of religious interest and participation used in the various studies are admittedly crude. They do indicate, nevertheless, that religious identification and participation in organized religion are not interpreted by teenagers as precluding the use of alcohol.

Socio-Economic Status. Socio-economic stratification may be observed to be a part of the social life of any community. Although the details often vary, power, prestige, and access to the important facilities in communities are unequally distributed. Inequalities may be reflected in the distribution of such rewards as income, occupational prestige, and educational opportunity, or some combination of these or other factors.

Stratification is also reflected in communities in the selective participation or preference for participation of individuals with others who are similarly placed socio-economically. Popularly, categories of individuals who have or are thought to have a common identification as a result of similar socio-economic status have been called "classes." Although sociological research has demonstrated that the common sense characterizations of the classes as "upper," "middle," and "lower" are gross oversimplifications of very complex social processes and arrangements, such designations have attracted attention to the possibility that different styles of life are associated with the various socio-economic positions and that drinking behavior may vary with style of life.

In the absence of consensus among investigators about the criteria for assignment of individuals to one or another social class, research on the relationship between social class and drinking behavior has been both limited and inconclusive. John Dollard (2), one of the first to explore this relationship, noted the existence of widely shared stereotypes of drinking associated with the various classes. Using an impressionistic definition of class, he concluded that "middle-class" individuals tend to be underrepresented in the alcoholic population and hence presumably in the drinking population.

Inadequacies in the studies of adult drinking behavior in relation to socio-economic placement are equally apparent in the studies of teenagers. The New York, Wisconsin, and Kansas studies, avoiding reference to "social classes," use only such socio-economic indices as the number of rooms in the home. In the first two of these studies even this index is related only to whether or not alcohol is kept in the home and not to more general information about drinking behavior. In the New York study a positive relationship was found between the number of rooms in a home and the probability that alcohol would be available there, but no report was made of the reliability of this relationship. In the Wisconsin study a reliable positive relationship was found only where "hard liquor" was involved.

The Kansas report analyzes the relationship between the education of parents and the use of alcohol by the teenager in addition to the "number of rooms" index. A positive and reliable relationship was found for the metropolitan sample only.

If the findings of the District of Columbia study are added to those reported above, one is led to conclude that the probability of teenage drinking increases with socio-economic status. The indices of status used in these studies, however, are inadequate, and the conclusions drawn from their application must be considered quite tentative and suggestive only.

In the Michigan study, more nearly adequate indices of socio-economic status were employed, and the resulting data suggest a modification of the findings of the other teenage studies. In the Michigan study the United States Census classification of occupations and a Warner Index of Status Characteristics were both used in the analysis. Although the differences were not found to be reliable statistically, the data did suggest that teenage users of beverage alcohol were most likely to be found in the upper and lower third of the range of status while non-users were most likely to be found in the middle range. Moreover, among females in the study, users were more likely than non-users to be found in the lower range of status.

The relationship between socio-economic status and teenage use of alcohol, therefore, remains tentative. Adequate indices of status have not been consistently employed, and, even when adequacy has been approached, reliable relationships have not been found. The data do suggest, however, that there are differences in style of life of families with regard to drinking as reflected in whether or not beverage alcohol and what kinds of beverages are kept in the home. Moreover, the Michigan interview material indicates that the teenagers themselves distinguish the drinking of the "country club set" from the drinking behavior of others.*

Rural-Urban Residence. Historically, urban in contrast to rural social life has connoted heterogeneity, complexity, change, and substantial differences in style of life. Recent surveys have pointed out that there are also differences in drinking behavior in urban and rural areas. Urban adults have been found more likely than rural adults to drink and to drink compulsively. Although only one study of teenage drinking specifically investigated rural-urban differences in drinking behavior, reliable differences were found in this instance.

In the Kansas study, reliable differences appeared in the proportion of teenage users in the Wichita metropolitan area and in the non-metropolitan counties of eastern Kansas. Similar differences were found between urban and rural teenagers in the frequency of use, in the experience of unusual

---

* The notion that "upper-class" individuals drink like "ladies and gentlemen" in contrast to the more rowdy and less glamorous drinking behavior of "lower-class" individuals is noted by John Dollard (2). See also Hollingshead (6) on this point.

effects following drinking, and in the proportion of parents who were users. In general, drinking was found to be more common in urban than in rural areas among teenagers as well as adults.

2. A shared "vocabulary of motives"

Why an individual drinks or abstains from drinking is not always apparent to himself much less to anyone else. Most individuals do learn, however, to anticipate in given situations the question, "Why did you do that?" Through interaction with others individual responses to such questions tend to become standardized and to be shared with others. Social interaction through time produces traditional, shared "vocabularies of motives" which are ready answers to questions about motivation (10). Shared verbalizations about motivation for drinking or abstinence are not in themselves always to be taken at face value as explanations for such behavior. These shared vocabularies do, however, provide insight into currently acceptable responses to the question, "Why do you drink?" or "Why did you drink the first time?"

In the Michigan study, teenagers were asked why adults drink. There was agreement among them that adults drink to express social conviviality, to experience personal pleasure, and to reduce anxiety. In assessing why they or their peers drank, the teenagers reiterated the reasons attributed to adults except that "anxiety reduction" was replaced by "experimentation" or "curiosity."

Similarly, in both the Wisconsin and Kansas studies the two most common reasons advanced for first drinking experiences were the celebration of holidays or special events and the satisfaction of curiosity. In the Utah study the two principal reasons for drinking given were to be one of the crowd and to increase gaiety. In effect, then, the shared "vocabulary of motives" for drinking among teenagers focuses on two themes: Drinking is a way of identifying oneself in relation to others in specific social situations and it is a way to experience personal pleasure.

The Michigan data provided additional insight into the significance of drinking as a mechanism for self and social identification among teenagers. In this research, drinking was associated with "coming of age," that is, the assumption of adult roles. Therefore, the teenagers tended to give the same reasons for drinking among both teenagers and adults except that for their age peers "experimentation" or "curiosity" replaced "anxiety reduction" as one of the three principal reasons for drinking. This substitution is consistent both with the teenager's preference for emphasizing the positive aspects of drinking and also with his awareness that, from the adult's standpoint, most teenage drinking is at best premature experimentation with a facet of adult role playing.

A Sociological Interpretation

Drinking is a social act. The evidence reviewed above supports this conclusion. That drinking is patterned, not random, behavior is established by observed regularities in the relationship between the use of alcohol and such socially relevant factors as age, sex, ethnicity, religious affiliation, socio-economic status, and rural-urban residence. It is well established that whether, what, how, when, and with whom one drinks cannot be explained merely by the availability of beverage alcohol or by the peculiarities of individuals. Rather, the existence and persistence of regularities in response to alcohol focus attention on the cultural definitions and social expectations which underlie the response.

Acohol is a culturally defined object. Its use is part of the shared patterns by which a majority of the adult population of the United States, for example, relate themselves to one another and to the world about them. This does not mean that drinking is the pivotal activity around which life revolves for those adults who drink. Obsession with drinking, which characterizes the alcoholic, is always possible for a user but is not typical drinking behavior in this society. Observed regularities in drinking behavior do reflect shared definitions of what alcohol presumably does *for* as well as *to* the drinker. The persistence of these regularities suggests that each new generation does not invent the idea of drinking but rather learns it and that shared definitions of alcohol and its use are a part of the cultural heritage which is passed from generation to generation.*

It is important to understand that responses to alcohol are culturally defined and are a part of the historically created and shared designs for living which serve as potential guides to behavior. It is equally important to recognize that an individual is never exposed to culture in general but to culture as lived by, and hence interpreted by, the significant persons with whom he interacts and from whom he learns. Specific social groups and individuals within these groups who interpret and enact a culture share expectations about situationally appropriate behavior. These shared expectations arise out of continuing interaction and, in turn, structure subsequent interaction. Shared expectations provide the basis for regularity and regulation in group life so as to facilitate the achievement of tasks and goals which group members consider important. The fact that teenagers in our society are typically exposed to groups in which drinking is permissible behavior provides the background for asserting that the teenager does not invent the idea of drinking but rather learns it and for understanding why drinking behavior reflects differences in the social background of users.

Individuals typically participate in and are members of concrete social groups whose standardized symbols allow them to position themselves and others in a meaningful way. This positioning allows them to anticipate the

---

* The observation that an individual may be taught and may learn to drink implies also that he may be taught and may learn not to drink. Abstinence, like drinking, is a social act and is amenable to analysis in similar terms. Focus in this presentation on drinking behavior is primarily a matter of convenience; however, this focus also reflects the fact that teenage drinking research has given little attention directly to abstinent behavior. The principal exception to this generalization is the work of Straus and Bacon (14).

probable sequences of behavior in common interaction situations. The joining of a social position with a definition of appropriate and expected behavior in a given situation is conveniently designated by the concept role.

How one comes to recognize and identify himself and others with various roles is a matter of learning. Or, specifically in terms of understanding drinking behavior, how one comes to associate drinking or abstinence with the various roles with which he identifies himself and others is a matter of learning. In simplest terms, one is taught and ordinarily learns the traditional roles which are defined by others as appropriate for him.

Universally observed age and sex differences illustrate that for a given individual some roles are permitted, encouraged, or required while others are discouraged or prohibited. The teenager in this society, for example, is discouraged or forbidden the premature playing of roles that are reserved for adults although he may at times be allowed to "play at" these roles in anticipation of his later achievement of adult status. Drinking is a case in point.

One cannot understand the drinking or abstinence of teenagers in the United States without recognizing the teenager's position in the social structure and how this position is conceived both by the teenagers themselves and by the adults to whom somehow they must relate themselves. In this society, as in all societies, there are a minimum number of age categories; e.g., infant, child, adult, old person. In addition to prescribing certain occupational and other behavioral expectations, placement in a particular age category provides an individual with patterns of behavior which are proper for his relationship both with his age peers and with those in other age categories.

In the United States, age grading does not involve formal age categorization to any great extent except in the educational system. Nevertheless, age grading constitutes an important point of reference for understanding such diverse phenomena as sexual behavior, kinship relationships, occupational preparation, community participation, and drinking behavior. The absence of rigidity in separating age grades does not lessen their importance. In fact, it is precisely the combination of indistinctness in the lines separating the age grades and the social significance attached to the grades that is of special interest in the study of teenage behavior in this society.

Many societies provide *rites de passage* so that movement from one age grade to another is clearly demarcated. In this society, on the other hand, *rites de passage* which provide an unambiguous transition from adolescence to adulthood are at a minimum. Such disparate events as the debut of the upper socio-economic status female, graduation from high school, entrance into the armed forces, voting for the first time, taking a full time job, and marriage may become improvised *rites de passage*. Yet, these events do not define consistently and unambiguously the "coming of age" when the individual may claim effectively adult prerogatives such as the right to drink. The anomalous social position of the teenager which is occasioned by being no longer a child but not yet an adult has encouraged some observers to characterize the teenage age grade as one of "storm and stress."

Some stresses and strains for the teenager in such a society as this are certainly possible not only with regard to drinking but in other general areas. The experience of discontinuities in enculturation, of conflict between generations in a changing social environment, and of problems associated with occupational and marital choice conceivably contribute not only to tensions but also to the emergence of teenage peer groups which are indifferent or hostile toward the demands of the adult generation. Whether or not the teenager in this society necessarily experiences stress and strain which are productive of a youth culture enacted by peer groups opposed to adult expectations is a question demanding an empirical answer, however. And to the present the evidence has not been consistent.* The teenage drinking studies, while they do not in themselves disprove the "storm and stress" interpretation of the teenage age grade, do not support such an interpretation.

The reviewed studies of drinking in high school suggest the hypothesis that drinking among teenagers in this society is not primarily a response to tensions resulting from an anomalous position in the social structure or an expression of hostility toward adult authority. The association between parental drinking and the probability of drinking by their children, reports of first drinking experience as commonly in the home in the presence of adults, and claims by teenagers of parental permission for some drinking all imply a basic continuity in expectations about drinking behavior from one generation to the next. Moreover, this continuity is also suggested by the fact that comparable associations are found among both adults and teenagers between drinking behavior and such social characteristics as sex, ethnicity, religious affiliation, socio-economic status, and rural-urban residence. It follows, then, that knowledge about the drinking or abstinent behavior of a given adult population is a reasonably accurate basis for predicting the drinking behavior of the associated teenage population. The nearer the teenagers under consideration are to the assumption of adult status the more accurate this generalization becomes.

If this inference is correct, teenage drinking in itself cannot be construed as an act in violation of adult expectations. Among teenagers, the probability that drinking will be observed increases with age, that is, as the assumption of adult status is approached. Many teenagers, particularly those from families in which parents are abstinent, are themselves abstinent. There are no indications from existing evidence that peer-group pressures to drink are

---

* For the argument that a youth culture does in fact exist, see Parsons (11). For a summary and criticism of the "storm and stress" characterization of adolescence in this society, see Elkin and Westley (4, 16). Eisenstadt (3) presents an interpretation of teenage peer groups as a bridge between childhood and adulthood in some societies.

either inevitable or irresistible. Furthermore, there are no indications that drinking produces problems for teenagers any more commonly than it does for the adult population.

Teenage drinking, therefore, appears to be most adequately understood as a social act, as a mechanism of identification, by which many teenagers attempt to relate themselves, however prematurely, to the adult world. Drinking is one of the available mechanisms by which the drinker may say to himself and others, "I am a man" or "I am one of the crowd." This is possible because a segment of the cultural tradition to which he is likely to be exposed has defined drinking in this way. Such a cultural definition permits teenage drinking to become an improvised *rite de passage*, a dissolver of teenage status and an introduction into the life of an adult.

Admittedly there are alternative mechanisms which can and do symbolize the transition to adulthood for some teenagers. For some, drinking is a violation of the cultural tradition to which they have been exposed, but this is not the experience of most teenagers. For the majority the problem is not so much whether or not they will drink but the timing and control of drinking behavior. Younger teenagers, even when they have been exposed to a drinking tradition, may refer disapprovingly to the use of alcohol by their peers as "acting smart." In this way they indicate an awareness of social definitions of premature and precocious behavior. Such references, however, tend to disappear with increasing age so that the older teenager is more likely to accept drinking among his peers even if he himself does not drink.

This interpretation of drinking as a social act, as a mechanism for self and social identification, does not preclude the recognition that alcohol is potentially a drug as well as a social beverage. Drinking which results in unfortunate or undesirable personal or social consequences is always a possibility for the teenager. In a highly mechanized and interdependent society the personal and social consequences of intoxication and "problem" uses of alcohol must be taken into consideration. Furthermore, in a socially mobile society a problem is posed when individuals reared in an abstinent tradition are confronted by others who have been exposed to a different tradition with regard to drinking. Such a situation may pose a serious dilemma for the abstinent individual, one that he does not have the resources to solve satisfactorily. These are, however, possibilities not probabilities. Personal and social problems which can be traced directly to the use of alcohol appear to be the exception rather than the rule in this society generally and among teenagers specifically.

References

1. Chappel, N. M., et al., *The Use of Alcohol Beverages Among High School Students,* New York: The Mrs. John S. Sheppard Foundation, 1953.
2. Dollard, John, "Drinking Mores and the Social Classes," in *Alcohol, Science and Society,* New Haven, Conn.: Journal of Studies on Alcohol, 1945.

3. Eisenstadt, S. N., *From Generation to Generation: Age Groups and Social Structure,* Glencoe, Ill.: Free Press, 1956.

4. Elkin, Frederick, and W. A. Westley, "The Myth of Adolescent Culture," *Amer. Sociol. Rev.,* 20:680–684, 1955.

5. Hollingshead, August, *Elmtown's Youth,* New York: John Wiley and Sons, 1949.

6. McCarthy, Raymond G., and Edgar M. Douglass, "Instruction on Alcohol Problems in Public Schools," *Quart. J. Stud. Alc.,* 8:609–635, 1948.

7. McCluggage, Marston M., et al., *Attitudes Toward the Use of Alcoholic Beverages,* Lawrence, Kans.: The Mrs. John S. Sheppard Foundation, 1956.

8. Maddox, George, *Drinking in High School: A Sociological Analysis of a Symbolic Act,* unpublished doctoral dissertation, Michigan State University, 1956.

9. Miller, John L., and J. R. Wahl, *Attitudes of High School Students Toward Beverage Alcohol,* Madison, Wis.: The Mrs. John S. Sheppard Foundation, 1956.

10. Mills, C. Wright, "Situation Action and Vocabularies of Motives," *Amer. Sociol. Rev.,* 5:904–913, 1940.

11. Parsons, Talcott, "Age and Sex in the Social Structure of the United States," *Amer. Sociol. Rev.,* 7:604–616, 1942.

12. Slater, A. D., "A Study of the Use of Alcoholic Beverages Among High School Students in Utah," *Quart. J. Stud. Alc.,* 13:78–86, 1952.

13. Sower, Christopher, Bevode McCall, and George L. Maddox, *A Study of High School Drinking: The Pattern and Social Context of a Common Illegal Act,* Lansing, Mich.: Social Research Service, Department of Sociology and Anthropology, Michigan State University, 1956.

14. Straus, Robert, and Selden D. Bacon, *Drinking in College,* New Haven, Conn.: Yale University Press, 1953.

15. Wattenberg, William, and John B. Moir, *Teen Age Drinkers,* Detroit, Mich.: Social Science Research Center, 1955.

16. Westley, W. A., and Frederick Elkin, "The Protective Environment and Adolescent Socialization," *Social Forces,* 35:243–249, 1959.

chapter 13

The problems
of drinking in college *

Robert Straus and Selden D. Bacon

Introduction

A survey of drinking customs and attitudes of a group of college students in the United States was initiated in 1947 as part of a larger study of the problems connected with alcohol in American society and their relationship to the customs of drinking. The report of this survey, *Drinking in College*, published in 1953, included data provided by approximately sixteen thousand college students from twenty-seven colleges. These colleges included a broad range of types from different regions of the country: public and private; sectarian and non-sectarian; men's, women's, and coeducational; white and Negro; rural and urban; and those with large and small enrollments. A proportionately large number of Jewish and Mormon students were intentionally included to permit special study of the unique sanctions on drinking characteristic of these cultural groups.

The drinking customs of college students are of special significance to the study of customs and problems relating to alcohol and to the study of youth culture. College students are close to the age when many people start drinking. Because first experiences are fresh in their minds, it is easier for them than for older persons to identify purposes, pressures, sanctions, and reactions associated with the onset of drinking behavior.

College students and their non-college age peers are experiencing a tran-

* This chapter is a revised and somewhat shortened version of sections of the book, *Drinking in College*, by Robert Straus and Selden D. Bacon, published in New Haven by Yale University Press in 1953. The editors express their appreciation to Robert Straus for writing the introduction to this chapter and for the selection of this material.

sition from the dependency of childhood to the independence associated with adulthood. Frequently our culture fails to provide continuities which might smooth this transitional process. For those young people who may be preoccupied with taking on adult roles, the use of alcoholic beverages has particular symbolic meaning. The laws of nearly every state define drinking as adult behavior usually legally permissible only after the age of 21. Some churches impose sanctions on drinking which carry one standard for adults and a different one for preadults. Drinking practices of parents and other adult figures often serve to enhance the attractiveness of alcohol as a symbol of arrival at adulthood. To the extent that restrictions on drinking by young people exist, these, too, may have significant symbolic meaning, for they provide the sometimes confused adolescent with a convenient way of rejecting authority or asserting independence. The many conflicts imposed on the adolescent in our culture can also enhance the apparent value of drinking since the action of alcohol in the human body serves to provide temporary relief from anxiety and to help ease inhibitions. Alcohol may even serve to ease pangs of conscience associated with the conflict over drinking and non-drinking.

An additional factor of conflict imposed on our college students has been the widely prevailing stereotype of college drinking which suggests that most students, because they are students, drink; that they drink frequently and heavily; and that their drinking often results in intoxication. This stereotype is perpetuated by the press, by humorists, by columnists, and even by parents and college administrators; it is not supported by the survey findings. Although 74 per cent of the students in the survey reported that they have experienced some use of alcohol beverages, there were wide ranges of difference according to such criteria as type of college, family income, religious affiliation, ethnic group, and drinking practices of parents. The survey also revealed that the vast majority of college youth do not drink either very frequently or in large amounts and that very few have experienced frequent intoxication.

The major problem of college drinking appears to lie in the confusion, conflict, and anxiety which parents, college administrators, faculty, public officials, and students themselves experience over the question of drinking by young people.

Following are some slightly revised selections from *Drinking in College* which relate to these questions.

College Policy and Student Drinking *

College students are not alone in facing difficult decisions about their drinking behavior. The problem has long bothered college administrators and continues to haunt them. The many letters of inquiry that have come

---

* This excerpt is reprinted with minor changes from Straus and Bacon, *op. cit.*, pp. 66–69.

from college officials in the course of preparing this study bear impressive witness to the deep concern and uncertainty of those responsible for molding college policy.

While giving questionnaires to students, members of the survey staff also discussed college policy toward student drinking with officials of most of the twenty-seven colleges which participated in the study. They found no instance of a clear-cut policy with which deans and other administrative personnel were generally satisfied. Where there were stringent regulations forbidding drinking by students, administrators were aware of deep resentment and rather violent reaction on the part of some students. Where liberal policies were followed, administrators were sensitive to criticism from town residents and parents whenever incidents involving drinking by students occurred. As a result some college administrations have avoided formalizing any policy and have fitted regulations and official statements to the particular circumstances.

A measure of the uncertainty and vacillation in this area can be found in the students' own perception of the policy of their particular college. The question was asked: "In your opinion, what is the attitude of your college officials toward drinking on the part of students?" Space was provided for the students to formulate their own reply. Answers were classified, first independently and then jointly, by two members of the survey staff. Responses were grouped under "unqualified disapproval," "liberality or indifference," and several categories of conditional approval. Just over half of all the students (both men and women) felt that their college's attitude toward student drinking was one of unqualified disapproval, while 21 per cent of the men and 15 per cent of the women felt that college officials were liberal or indifferent to drinking.

These responses represent the students' perception of an attitude or policy. Like all reports on attitude perception they are subjective interpretations of manifest actions. Although not specifically identified as sanctions, these perceptions define the college sanctions of drinking in the most meaningful way possible, not necessarily as they are perceived by those from whom they derive but as they are perceived by those toward whom they are directed. Let us now relate this perception to student drinking behavior.

First it is of interest to consider to what extent individual colleges have clear-cut attitudes, as perceived by their own students, toward drinking. That is, to what extent is there student agreement on the policy of their own school? Of the twenty-seven colleges surveyed, there were five at which at least 75 per cent of the students (men and women) perceived the college attitude as one of unconditional disapproval. At three the vast majority of students perceived either a liberal-indifferent attitude or a conditional attitude (two of these were colleges for men only, the other for women only). At the other nineteen schools substantial numbers of students assigned the college attitude to each of the extremes, indicating no general agreement as to the official attitude.

The students' perception of college policy is not likely to be objective. A college having what an objective observer would term a middle-of-the-road attitude might seem liberal to some abstainers because it tolerates drinking at all, yet disapproving to some heavy drinkers because it opposes heavy drinking. In a majority of the schools where the attitude was not clearly defined, it was found that abstainers were more likely to perceive a liberal attitude while students who were frequent users were more likely to perceive an attitude of disapproval.

It was also found that perception of an extreme attitude on the part of the college (either unqualified disapproval or liberality) was correlated with extreme personal views about drinking. Of the male students who in other questions expressed themselves either as positively disapproving or positively approving of drinking by others, 89 per cent indicated a perception of extreme views on the part of college officials. On the other hand only 67 per cent of those whose personal attitudes were conditional saw the college position as extreme.

To examine the relationship between perception of the college attitude toward drinking and actual student drinking behavior, colleges were ranked according to a liberality score determined by taking the percentage of student responses in each school which indicated a conditional attitude on the part of the college plus twice the percentage of responses which indicated liberality or indifference. When liberality scores are correlated with the per cent of users at each school, it becomes clear that the more liberal the college attitude as perceived by the students, the more users in the college population.*

In a similar manner, the liberality score was correlated with the percentage of the users in each school who had ever reached the level of intoxication defined as "tight." † Findings here indicated no significant correlation, positive or negative.‡ Thus although college sanctions against drinking seem to be definitely associated with a lower incidence of drinkers at a particular school, they have no effect on the extent of drinking among users as measured by the criteria of having been tight. There is some suggestion, illustrated by a few selected schools, that, among male students, drinkers at "dry" schools are more apt to have been tight than those at schools with liberal sanctions.

A definite relationship appeared between the incidence of drinking or abstaining at particular schools and the extent to which male students who drink have experienced intoxication. The five schools having the lowest percentage of users ranked in the highest ten by percentage of users who

---

* Rank correlation coefficient (Spearman); for men $N = 22$, $P = +.70$; for women $N = 17$, $P = +.64$; both significant at the .01 level.

† The term "tight" is used in this study to describe a level of intoxication between "high" and "drunk."

‡ Rank correlation coefficient (Spearman); for men $N = 22$, $P = -.19$; for women $N = 17$, $P = +.12$.

have been tight. Exactly the same relationship was found at the next level of intoxication, defined as drunk. There is certainly a suggestion here that male students who drink in violation of generally accepted practice are apt to go further in their drinking than students for whom the use of alcoholic beverages is more or less accepted behavior. This reaction is illustrated by the comment of a student in a southern "dry" college: "When you go to the trouble of driving 50 miles to drink, you don't have just two drinks."

In summary, it can be noted that the uncertainty and indecisiveness expressed by many college officials in personal conversations with members of the survey staff are reflected in the students' perception of college drinking attitudes and sanctions.

Drinking by Parents *

A review of parents' drinking practices, particularly as they are related to students' own drinking behavior, has revealed several significant facts. The example of parents in drinking or abstaining is seen to be closely correlated with the decision of students to drink or abstain. Parental sanctions against drinking are much more effective than formal sanctions stemming from church or school; and parents' attitudes toward drinking by a son or daughter are usually in line with their own practices. The incidence of problem drinking among parents of college students appears consistent with generally accepted estimates on rates of alcoholism in the entire adult population. Finally, the example of a problem-drinking parent has not acted as a deterrent to drinking by students.

How Much and How Often? †

Findings on amounts consumed and frequency of drinking indicate clearly that stereotypes of college drinking which include notions of widespread, frequent, and heavy drinking are unrealistic. The proportion of students who drink frequently and heavily is very small.

Two facts stand out in relation to frequency of drinking. Less than half the students drink more than once a month; fewer than a fifth of the men and a tenth of the women drink more than once a week.

In terms of quantity, it can be noted that of those who use beer only 9 per cent of the men and 1 per cent of the women usually consume what has arbitrarily been termed "larger" amounts. Of those who drink wine, only 4 per cent of the men and virtually none of the women consume "larger" amounts. Of students who use spirits, 27 per cent of the men and only 7 per cent of the women consume "larger" amounts. Furthermore, a substantial segment of those who use "larger" amounts drink infrequently.

A further comment can be made on the relationship of student drinking to the experience of college. For the more frequent drinkers and for those

---

* This excerpt is reprinted without change from Straus and Bacon, *op. cit.*, p. 85.

† This excerpt is reprinted with minor revision from Straus and Bacon, *op. cit.*, pp. 116–117.

who drink so-called larger amounts, it is clear that attendance at college is not of major significance in their drinking. These are the students who are most apt to have started drinking before entering college and whose parents are most apt to have approved of their drinking. Male students whose pattern of drinking varies between periods of vacation and actual attendance at college are apt to drink more while on vacation. So it can be concluded that maturation and social background have more influence on the quantity and frequency of drinking than does entrance into college.

The Potential Problem Drinker *

It is rare for the subject of drinking to be discussed without some reference to alcoholism. Among the many and varied problems connected with alcohol the hardships and heartaches often associated with chronic uncontrolled drinking are likely to command the greatest share of public attention.

Fortunately, alcoholism is not a significant problem in the college population. There are comparatively few problem drinkers among the age group 17 to 23. Alcoholism is a progressive disorder which, particularly in males, usually takes from 10 to 20 years to develop. To be sure, there are incidents of problem drinking among college students, and there are individuals whose drinking patterns display certain warning signs which may suggest that they are potential problem drinkers. But it is important to differentiate between incidental problem drinking and that which may be repetitive and patterned. It is the latter with which this section is concerned.

While specific causes of alcoholism have not been discovered, studies of alcoholics made in retrospect have identified certain types of behavior which seem characteristic of incipient problem drinking. Next, we shall consider some experiences which are often characteristic of the potential problem drinker, and examine the extent to which they were reported by the students.

1. Social complications

One group of questions which sheds some light on potential problem drinking concerns drinking behavior that inflicts injury or marked inconvenience on oneself or others. Students were asked whether drinking had ever interfered with their preparation for classes or examinations, caused them to lose close friends or damaged friendships, made them miss appointments or lose a job, resulted in accident, injury, or arrest, or brought them before college authorities.

In analyzing the responses to these questions it was possible to employ scaling.† The scalable characteristic was that of social complications associated with drinking. At the lowest point on the social-complications scale

* This excerpt is reprinted with revisions from Straus and Bacon, *op. cit.*, pp. 156–170.

† In scale analysis, the items making up the scale are so related that a positive response to one item implies positive responses on certain other items. The items in a scale represent a variety of magnitudes of some characteristic common to them all.

(most likely to occur without implying occurrence of other items) were the questions about failure to meet academic or social obligations (drinking had at some time interfered with preparation for classes or examinations or resulted in missing an appointment). At the second scale position were the questions on loss of friends or damage to friendship attributed to drinking. Next came the questions about formal punishment or discipline because of drinking (loss of a job, arrest, or coming before college authorities). The scale types of our social-complications scale are here illustrated as Table 1.*

TABLE 1

Scale Types of Social Complications

Scale Type	Item A (Failure to Meet Obligations)	Item B (Damage to Friendships)	Item C (Accident or Injury)	Item D (Formal Punishment or Discipline)
0 (no complications)	—	—	—	—
1	+	—	—	—
2	+	+	—	—
3	+	+	+	—
4	+	+	+	+

The social-complications scale allows us to draw conclusions such as the following: students who have at any time suffered loss of a job or arrest or discipline by college authorities because of drinking have probably also sustained an accident or injury while drinking, damaged their friendships, and failed to meet some social or academic obligations; students for whom drinking has never entailed damage to friendships have probably never suffered injury or formal punishment for drinking but may have failed to meet obligations; students for whom drinking has entailed damage of friendship may or may not ever have suffered injury or formal punishment but have very probably at some time failed to meet obligations.

The distribution of students who drink, according to the social-complications scale, is shown in Table 2. Two-thirds of the men and 85 per cent of the women reported no complications at all and are therefore classified as scale type 0. Seventeen per cent of the men and 8 per cent of the women are scale type 1, indicating that they have at one time or another missed

---

* Irregular scale responses are assigned to the scale pattern which they fit with a minimum of error. For example, the response + — + + would be assigned to scale type 4. A criterion for measuring the reliability of the scale is the frequency of assignment of non-scale patterns to a scale type. An acceptable scale is one in which errors of placement necessitated by assigning non-scale patterns to a scale type constitute no more than 10 per cent of the total placements. Such a scale is said to have a .90 coefficient of reproducibility. The social-complications scale in this study has a .97 coefficient of reproducibility.

social obligations because of drinking but have suffered no other types of complication. Eleven per cent of the men and 6 per cent of the women are scale type 2 and have also at some time or other suffered damage to a friendship which they attribute to drinking. Scale types 3 and 4 contain virtually no women, but 6 per cent of the male drinkers report an accident or injury associated with drinking, in addition to the above complications, and 2 per cent also report formal punishment or discipline.

TABLE 2

Students Who Drink, by Social-Complications Scale

Scale Type	Students Who Drink (in Per Cent)	
	Men	Women
0 (no complications)	66	85
1	17	8
2	11	6
3	4	1 a
4	2	—
Total	100	100

a Actually less than 0.7 per cent.

The usefulness of a measure like our social-complications scale is not limited to determining a meaningful relationship between various items of information. It also serves as an index for comparing with other aspects of behavior the whole complex of behavioral items which it covers. A rather striking correlation was found between the social-complications scale and the quantity and frequency of drinking. It was also found that men with high complications-scale ratings tended to be frequently intoxicated. The scale was also considered in relation to the basic identifying factors of age and religion. Since the probability of experiencing one of the complications increases cumulatively with advancing age, it was expected that the scale would show a direct correlation to age. However, significant differences did not appear for either men or women beyond the age of 18. For both sexes, those 18 or less showed lower complications-scale ratings than all older students.

Students of different religions also displayed rather sharp differences in incidence of social complications. Among men who are users, complications have been experienced by only 20 per cent of the Jewish students, by about a third of the Protestants and Catholics, and by 42 per cent of the Mormons. Sharper distinctions in the same direction are seen among women users, ranging from only 2 per cent of the Jews up to 41 per cent of the Mormons. The low incidence of complications reported by Jewish students and the equally high incidence among Mormons can be explained in part in terms

of the drinking sanctions of these two groups and the nature of certain complications-scale components. It will be recalled that loss of friends and
damage to friendships were items included in the scale. In view of the strong
Mormon sanctions against the use of alcoholic beverages, it is readily conceivable that students who drink even in moderation would risk losing the
respect of their Mormon friends. Nearly half the Mormon men and three-
fourths of the women are abstainers. Also, most of the Mormon students
were attending colleges with predominantly Mormon enrollment, and at
these schools even slight drinking might subject a student to the discipline
of college authorities.

The high complications ratings for Mormons do not seem to be a result of
frequent or extensive drinking, but Mormon male students who drink did
report fairly frequent intoxication. Intoxication and complications together
suggest a reaction pattern. Those students who break away from restrictions
of their religious sanctions seem inclined to react in a more emphatic, perhaps
rebellious, manner than students whose drinking involves less rejection of
their group. Jewish students come from a background which sanctions
moderate drinking. Like the Mormons they did not show high quantity-
frequency ratings, and unlike the Mormons they reported comparatively infrequent experience of the various levels of intoxication. Nearly all the Jewish
friends of Jewish students also drink; and many of the Jewish students were
attending colleges which condoned moderate drinking by students. Furthermore, the sanctions of the Jewish group, while encouraging appropriate
drinking, look with disfavor upon any behavior which reflects unfavorably
upon the individual or the group. It is not moderate drinking but that leading to complications which involves rejection of members of their group by
Jewish students; this behavior is avoided by the majority. Findings on social complications according to religious affiliation are obviously consistent
with those on intoxication.

2. Special stress on drinking

Those factors were considered which suggest a tendency to place greater
than normal stress on the importance of drinking. Students who drink before going to a party and students who like to be one or two drinks ahead
of others tend to drink more frequently and in larger amounts than others
and have more often experienced various levels of intoxication. Altogether
26 per cent of the male users and 9 per cent of the women reported sometimes drinking in anticipation of not getting enough; 10 per cent of the
men and 2 per cent of the women indicated that they sometimes drink surreptitiously. Both these kinds of behavior have been reported by Jellinek as
common to the early phases of problem drinking, although both (particularly anticipatory drinking) are occasionally shown by persons who would
be designated as normal drinkers.

Another attempt to measure the importance students attached to drinking was made by seeking reactions to the hypothetical party or gathering

where it might have been expected that alcoholic beverages would be served but they were not. Thirty-six per cent of the male drinkers and 23 per cent of the women indicated that under such circumstances they would "sometimes feel that a party is a flop." Twenty-seven per cent of the men and 14 per cent of the women would "sometimes make comments" about the absence of drinks. However, only 8 per cent of the men and 2 per cent of the women said they would "probably refuse a future invitation." Just half the men and 69 per cent of the women answered all three questions in the negative, which suggests that they attached no particular importance to whether alcohol is served at such functions or not.

As still another indication of special emphasis on the importance of drinking, the question of whether the cost of liquor had ever caused them to forego other things was put to the students. Eleven per cent of the male users and only 2 per cent of the women reported that this had happened. Four per cent of the men and no women reported that on more than five occasions they had been short of money because of drinking. Women, of course, doing most of their drinking in mixed company, are likely to be treated by their male companions. It was found that students who reported being short of cash tended to have higher family incomes than any of the other students. This was also true, we remember, of students who reported that they abstain because they cannot afford to drink; the economic factor failed to explain why some students reported using beer (which is cheaper) although they preferred spirits (which are more expensive). Again we have evidence that feeling poor is relative to many factors other than actual income. The question about foregoing other things because of the cost of liquor was related to the extent of drinking and to social complications; 66 per cent of the males who reported foregoing other things had high quantity-frequency indices (4 or 5) compared with only 41 per cent of the other users; 72 per cent of them had experienced social complications, as against 29 per cent of the other users.

3. Additional warning signs

Next we shall consider four questions which, while not suggesting special stress on the importance of drinking, have definitely been identified by Jellinek as common warning signs of potential problem drinking. These include a form of temporary amnesia known as the "blackout," becoming drunk when alone, drinking before or instead of breakfast, and participating when drinking in aggressive or wantonly destructive behavior.

The blackout is a term which alcoholics have adopted from aviation, where it is commonly used to refer to anoxemia. Students were asked whether they had ever awakened after a party or a drinking spree with no idea where they had been or what they had done after a certain point, although they had not passed out. This amnesia is not associated with a loss of consciousness. In fact, the drinker may never even have displayed any of the usual signs of intoxication. He may have carried on conversations and complicated activities without having any recollection of it the next day. Blackouts may happen, though rarely, to average drinkers who consume rather large amounts in a state of physical or emotional exhaustion. They have been reported quite frequently by alcoholics as an occurrence which antedated other positive signs of problem drinking. Although comparatively little is known about this phenomenon (it may be associated with malutilization of oxygen), its occurrence, particularly after taking only medium amounts of alcohol, is believed to be characteristic of the prospective alcohol addict. Eighteen per cent of the male student users and 5 per cent of the women reported having experienced it. Only 1 per cent of the women had blacked out more than once; 9 per cent of the men had had only one blackout, and 1 per cent reported more than five.

Becoming intoxicated when alone is also identified as a warning sign of possible deviant drinking behavior. Drinking is primarily a social custom, and most people usually drink in company. While lone drinking is not uncommon among men (52 per cent of the men and 4 per cent of the women in our study reported that they had at some time or other had one or more drinks alone), drinking to the point of extreme intoxication when alone is considered pathological. Thirteen per cent of the male users and 3 per cent of the women reported that they had become drunk when alone. This had occurred more than twice for 6 per cent of the men and 1 per cent of the women.

Another form of behavior quite common in the pathological drinker is early morning drinking, especially before or instead of breakfast. Positive responses to the question, "Have you had one or more drinks before breakfast or instead of breakfast?" were recorded by 16 per cent of the men and 7 per cent of the women; 10 per cent of the men and 3 per cent of the women reported doing it more than twice.

Drinking which had led to aggressive, wantonly destructive, or malicious behavior (such as picking fights without provocation, vicious slander, damaging parked cars or other property, playing dangerous jokes on others) was reported by 11 per cent of the men and less than 1 per cent of the women. For 7 per cent of the men it had occurred more than twice.

Students who had experienced any one of these four warning signs were found to be more extensive drinkers than those who had not, and were much more apt to have experienced social complications. All four forms of behavior together suggest either an abnormal reaction to or desire for alcohol or an asocial drinking pattern.

It should be stressed that the majority of the students who reported any of these four warning signs had experienced only one or two incidents. Two-thirds of the male drinkers had never experienced any of the warning signs, 22 per cent reported only one of the four phenomena, 8 per cent reported two, and 5 per cent reported three or four; 94 per cent of the female drinkers had never experienced any of these warning signs, 5 per cent reported one, and only 1 per cent reported two or more.

4. Anxiety about drinking

The final questions to be considered here were concerned not specifically with behavior which might suggest potential problem drinking but rather with indications of anxiety over the effects of drinking and its possible consequences.

Anxiety over drinking was expressed by 17 per cent of the men and 10 per cent of the women student drinkers; these reported that they either feared the long-range consequences of their drinking, or had felt that they might become dependent on or addicted to drink, or both. These students, whom we shall designate for convenience as "anxious drinkers," have been compared with all other users, whom we shall call "secure drinkers," according to a number of criteria.

Anxiety does not necessarily stem from excessive drinking or from unfortunate personal experience. More than 90 per cent of the students had received some advice about alcohol, and nearly half reported that this advice was designed to make them abstainers.

It was found that advice to abstain had been received by 54 per cent of the anxious male drinkers and only 43 per cent of the secure drinkers; by 50 per cent of the anxious and only 40 per cent of the secure female users. This suggests that for some students anxiety may in part result from advice they have received against drinking. This could explain the anxiety of those students whose own drinking patterns have given them little real reason for concern. For example, it was found that among the anxious drinkers a fourth of the males and three-fourths of the females had never been drunk; half of these men and two-thirds of these women had never had drinking complications. Although these particular anxious drinkers do not appear to have a basis in personal drinking experience for fearing the consequences of their drinking, anxiety is seen to increase in direct proportion to the extent of the experience of drinking complications. While anxious drinkers represent only 12 per cent of the men who have never been drunk, they constitute 27 per cent of those drunk more than five times. Of the men with no social complications only 13 per cent are anxious drinkers, compared with 22 per cent of those with few complications (score of 1 or 2) and 40 per cent of those with more frequent complications (score of 3 or 4). Anxious drinkers included 44 per cent of the students who had experienced at least three of the four warning signs, compared with 20 per cent of those who had experienced one or two of them and only 4 per cent of the students who reported none.

Some anxiety over drinking appears to reflect instruction about alcohol which was couched in terms of threat and fear. However, in the majority of cases where anxiety is expressed by men, it is associated with a relatively high incidence of intoxication, of difficulties resulting from drinking, or of warning signs of potential problem drinking. This is a highly significant finding, for it suggests that the potential problem drinker begins to recognize something different about his own drinking behavior and is often fear-

\ ful of the consequences at a relatively early stage of development. The data of our college study suggest that a large segment of those students whose drinking patterns display some of the warning signs are already, when still quite young, worried about the consequences of their drinking.

5. Summary

This section has examined in student drinking a number of factors which alcoholics have reported retrospectively as characteristic of their incipient problem drinking: the extent to which student drinkers have become involved in various difficulties as a result of drinking, the incidence of special stress on the importance of drinking, and a group of characteristic warning signs of potential problem drinking.

For most of the students who reported any of the complications or warning signs, the experiences were infrequent and often but a single incident; they may have been serious problems at the moment but certainly were not indicative of a pattern. However, a high degree of correlation was found between various warning signs and such factors as the frequency and quantity of drinking, the psychological importance of drinking, and the incidence of complications resulting from drinking.

More immediate and positive significance can be attached to the findings on anxiety over drinking. The fact that large proportions of those students with extreme drinking patterns, more frequent complications, and warning signs are concerned with the long-range consequences of their drinking suggests a susceptibility to constructive counseling aimed at preventing progression into serious pathological drinking. Although our results are not conclusive, the combination of the two tentative findings of this section —that incipient cases can be detected and are susceptible to treatment— gives perhaps some reasonable grounds for optimism about the problem of alcoholism.

chapter 14

First drinking experience
as related to age
and sex *

Albert D. Ullman

An area of investigation with reference to any culturally patterned activity is the manner in which the persons involved are introduced to it. Information on alcohol usage is incomplete without knowledge of the manner in which the drinker first comes into contact with the substance. Essential to our knowledge here are the age of introduction to drinking, whether after introduction it is periodic or regular activity, who is present, who sanctions the activity, and the purposes of drinking as revealed by the reasons for taking the first drink. Thus by studying the person's introduction to alcohol, much is learned about the cultural setting in which this activity occurs and about the values associated with it.

More specific than this is the possible relationship of the first drinking experience to the process of alcohol addiction. To understand the addiction mechanism, one must start with the beginning of drinking by an individual. A decision about what constitutes the beginning is necessary since some facets associated with this cultural element, in most cases, are internalized before the first drink is taken. Group members, particularly those in which the use of alcohol by young children is unusual, tend to be familiar with alcoholic beverages and with the fact of intoxication even before they have had a drink. That is, one comes into the situation in which one takes the first drink with attitudes toward alcohol and drinking already formed. One feels that drunkenness is good or bad and that alcohol has positive or negative effects even before tasting it or experiencing its effects.

The relevance of this to the process of addiction was presented in the

* This chapter was written especially for this book.

writer's paper, "The Psychological Mechanism of Alcohol Addiction" (11). There, the point is made that no matter what else is involved in addiction, a psychological process is part of the complete story. Thus, drinking, in part because of the physiological action of alcohol, namely, its anaesthetic effect, and in part because of the ritual-like activity sometimes involved, is tension reducing. For the alcoholic, however, drinking is a generalized tension-reducing response. That is, drinking is a response which comes to be utilized to cope with tensions derived from a wider and wider range of problems, so that the drinker eventually drinks to meet virtually all problems of ordinary living. This point of view is in contrast with the theory that alcohol addiction rests upon a foundation of rather serious personality disorder, of which the drinking is merely symptomatic.

Based upon experimental evidence, a description of the process of addiction was presented as follows:

It is suggested that the formation of an addiction is dependent upon a psychological state made possible in part by the sociological variable of attitudes toward drinking and the physiological fact of the tension-reducing effect of alcohol. It is posited that (a) when a person is highly motivated to drink or there is some emotional arousal with regard to drinking, and (b) such drinking is accompanied by a stress situation, and (c) these circumstances occur on several occasions when a sufficient amount of alcohol is imbibed to produce a tension-reducing effect, then alcohol addiction will result (11, p. 607).

This summary is quoted in order to indicate the setting in which research on the first drinking experience was done. Sociological considerations in part determine each of the factors quoted above. Although unique experiences of an individual may result in his being emotionally aroused with reference to drinking, knowledge that certain demographic variables are associated with differential rates of alcoholism causes one to investigate this latter variable. Thus, one may suspect that emotional arousal in drinking may be more prevalent among some groups than others. If this is a culturally determined fact, one would expect that such arousal exists from the beginning of experience with alcohol. Vices generally are known as such to the members of a society even before those members indulge in them.

It was reasoned, the stress situation also "required" for addiction may simply be a product of the emotional arousal. Thus, certain kinds of drinking experiences would leave a greater residue of anxiety, affecting the drinker's emotional state at the time of the next drink, than others. In short, it seemed logical to examine the introduction of the individual to this "patterned activity"—drinking.

Background Findings

Some years ago, the writer was involved in an investigation of social characteristics of the inmate population of a county house of correction (10). Close to 70 per cent of these men were problem drinkers, and from that group some 143 were selected because they clearly were compulsive or addictive drinkers.

The 143 men were asked the simple question, "Do you remember the first drink of an alcoholic beverage you ever had?" The question was asked during the course of an interview which covered the essentials of a life history. Of the 143 inmates, 128, or 90 per cent remembered the first drink and proceeded to answer other questions about it.

Since that time, other studies of alcoholic populations have shown a similar pattern of recall. At an institution for women, in which problem drinkers made up the largest category, the percentage remembering the first drink was somewhat lower—80 per cent—but this included all inmates (3). Another penal institution, whose inmates tend to be much older than those at the house of correction, reports that 77 per cent remembered their first drink (1). When we examine the age-specific rates of recall, or when we look at those over and under the median age of 48.5 years, we see that 85 per cent of those 49 and over remember, and 69 per cent of those 48 and under. Another small sample from an alcoholism clinic population showed all 20 members remembering the first drink (5). All but one of 252 male alcoholics in another clinic remembered their first drinks (8).

Descriptions of the first experience with alcohol are in themselves interesting. Several are available in the autobiographic accounts by alcoholics, such as the life stories of Lillian Roth and Norman Brokenshire. One man in the sample drawn from the house of correction population had his first drink at age 17 when he was working with a lumbering crew. He came to town on a Saturday night with the men of the crew, and joined them in a tavern. There he had his first drink—whisky. He did not like its taste, but drank it and more. Eventually he became deeply intoxicated, then sick, and had to be taken back to camp by some of the men. The humiliation of his drinking performance was deep, and he met it by trying to outdrink all others on succeeding Saturday nights. This experience is not at all unusual. Often, alcoholics will report with some pride that they have not been sick from drinking since that first occasion. Others, further along the path of alcoholism, will tell of years of drinking without illness until recent events when the hangovers include illness. A fuller description of alcoholics' first drinking experiences is included in the recent book, *To Know the Difference* (12).

The house of correction population described above was compared with 250 male college students on the same items. Obviously, such a comparison has weaknesses. There was more than 20 years' difference in average ages, the socio-economic classes were not the same, and no attempt was made to match the groups for ethnicity. Yet, small-scale tests of the findings with groups comparable to the prisoners, at least for age, have supported the original findings.

The same questions were posed to college students that had been asked of the inmates, but this time by means of a questionnaire. No particular problems showed up except that the investigator, who was present when the questionnaires were administered, had to point out that any alcoholic beverage, not just a distilled drink, was included, and that the questions referred to the entire drinking episode. That is, if more than one drink were taken at the time of the first experience, the total was to be regarded as one experience. The necessity for these instructions was revealed in pretests when it was discovered that some respondents regarded a drink as being only a distilled beverage such as whisky, and others, who actually had had several drinks at the time and who became intoxicated, reported no effect from the first drink of the series, even though they later were drunk at the same occasion.

The important findings from this study deal with differences in recall of the first drinking experience and in various factors relating to some of the categories of this patterned activity—drinking. The findings were summarized as follows:

a. More addictive than nonaddictive drinkers remembered the first drink.

b. The addictive drinkers had their first drink at a later age than the nonaddictive drinkers.

c. More of the addictive than of the nonaddictive drinkers became intoxicated in some degree on the occasion of the first drinking experience.

d. Most of the addictive drinkers had their first drink in a place other than a private home or one where liquor is usually sold.

e. More addictive than nonaddictive drinkers had their first drink in the company of persons outside the family.

f. There was a longer lapse of time between the first and second drinking experiences of the addictive than of the nonaddictive drinkers (10, p. 190 f.).

The differences between the two groups on all the above items were statistically significant at the .01 level of probability. It was emphasized then that better sample matching was necessary before one could have very much confidence in the results. Lack of resources has prevented accomplishment of this needed investigation.

What has been done to follow up these findings has been more reasonable from the standpoint of availability of resources, but less satisfactory scientifically. It has been based on known differences among groups in their contribution to the population of alcoholics. Even though the statistics may be somewhat unreliable, there are more male than female alcoholics in the United States. We also are reasonably certain that ethnic groups differ from one another in prevalence of alcoholism. Given these differences, then, we can expect that those factors associated with alcoholism ought to appear more frequently among groups with high rates of alcoholism than among groups with low rates. If the six items listed above differentiate alcoholics from normal drinkers then we should find them more frequently among high alcoholism groups. Thus, by drawing a random sample from two groups, one known to have a higher rate of alcoholism than the other, we should expect that we are drawing two samples that can be differentiated on the basis of these six items.

Sex Differences

Calling upon the ever-ready college student, we analyzed data on the first drinking experience of male and female students (9). With a known ratio of male to female alcoholics in the United States of 11 to 2, we hypothesized some differences. Furthermore, social class and ethnic differences were somewhat minimized by using a college population, although minor differences do exist in the sampled university. The predictions were based upon the six items found to differentiate between alcoholics and normal drinkers. Because alcoholism is more frequent among men, the findings of the previous study became hypotheses, but with "men" substituted for "addictive drinkers," and "women" for "non-addictive drinkers." This time the sample consisted of 798 students who had used alcoholic beverages. They were about evenly divided by sex: 401 men, and 397 women.

Analysis of the data yielded some surprises. For example, the first prediction, that more men than women would recall their first drink was not upheld. Indeed, the opposite was found, and the difference was significant. The second prediction, that men had their first drink later than women, was found not to be true; there was virtually no difference between them in this respect. The median age at which the house of correction inmates had had their first drink was in the category of 15 to 19 years, with the mean at 18.2. For the students, the largest number of both male and female had their first drink in the same 15-to-19-year range, but nearer the lower end of the range. It was clear that more men than women became in some degree intoxicated at the time of the first drinking experience. This was in line with the prediction. The women were more likely than the men to have had their first drink at home with their parents, thus confirming predictions (d) and (e). Finally, it was found that more women than men drank a second time in a matter of days or weeks, rather than months or years, confirming prediction (f).

Examples of the first drinking experiences of men and women will illustrate the differences in the experience itself and in the feelings about it. One can see that the male is more deeply committed to the drinking experience than is the female. Drinking is more a part of the male than of the female role. Although the girls succumb to some pressure to drink, they tend to shrug off such pressures as time goes on and become independent in their choice of whether or not to drink. In an interview, a male student describes his first drinking experience in the following replies to questions:

Q. Do you remember the very first drink you ever had?

A. Yes.

Q. Can you tell me about it?

A. I was thirteen. I was on a trip out to California with some boys—about fourteen boys—and there was very little supervision. And we were staying in a hotel in San Francisco and some of the boys, including myself, asked a taxi driver to buy us a bottle of bourbon. It was just sort of a for kicks type thing. I think that was the first time you might say I really had a drink.

The words "you might say I really had a drink" caused some suspicion on the part of the interviewer, so further probing was undertaken. Actually this young man had had sips of wine in his home for as long as he could remember and really did not recall his first drink at all. The incident in San Francisco was important to him, however, and marked the beginning of what can be termed his drinking career.

A contrast is provided by a young woman who clearly recalls her first drink. She was asked to describe the experience, and her story was recorded (12).

I went to a fraternity open house party and got a drink by mistake, because I don't drink. The kids said, "Hurry up! Drink it, because we're leaving." So I did. They were teasing me because they knew I didn't drink. It was some kind of cocktail. It didn't have any effect on me. I had another drink about a year later. I don't remember what it was. I was with some people I didn't know well, and it was easier for me to take it than refuse it. I didn't drink until this time because my mother and father don't and they feel very strongly that I shouldn't drink.

You sort of build up a self-image, and I don't like to think of myself as drinking. I know I feel this way because of my parents, but I don't feel as if I am doing them a wrong. I don't feel that I shouldn't drink because it would disappoint them if I did, although it really would. Rather it's because that's the way I think of myself. My religion (Congregational) is in it somehow. It's not a case of violating my religion, but what I think I should be. That's partly religion. It also has something to do with what other people think of me, like a previous boy friend. The boy I'm pinned to now doesn't drink, so with him I'd be more likely to take a drink if he did. With the other boy friend, he drank, but it meant a lot to him that I didn't.

This young woman's description is particularly interesting because it reveals the various areas of social interaction and personality which are touched by drinking. For her, as for most young persons, drinking is a complicated piece of behavior when viewed in its motivational, social, and cultural setting. In having her first drink somewhere other than at home, and with persons other than her parents, this girl was unusual. Like the majority of the men, but with even greater frequency, girls are given their first drink by their parents. The work of Sower and his collaborators supports this finding (7). In the case of college girls, interviews showed that very often the parents treated the girl's introduction to alcohol ceremonially. She was told that they knew it was likely that she would be drinking at college, and that they wanted her to have her first drink with them so that "she would know what to expect."

But the great difference between the men and women in the nature of their introduction to alcohol is that the women were ego-involved only to the extent of having a drink. Drinking any appreciable quantity of alcohol and feeling some effect of the alcohol, does not really concern them. The girl can meet her obligations by taking an occasional drink, and, as she matures in the college situation, she may decide that she need not make that small concession to community expectations. Many girls report that they felt they had to drink when they were freshmen but that by the time they became upperclasswomen the feeling had gone. A group that would be particularly interesting to study is composed of those who have assumed essentially masculine attitudes toward drinking. Elsewhere, some preliminary evidence of cross-sex identification among women alcoholics has been described (12).

Motivations for drinking are important in describing the differences in male and female drinking behavior. An analysis of public opinion poll data divided the reasons for drinking into three major categories. These were (a) individual reasons, (b) social, or (c) a mixture of both. Social reasons for drinking were given by 33 per cent of the men and 55 per cent of the women while individual reasons were recorded for 49 per cent of the males and 31 per cent of the females. This study indicated that social pressure is greater in motivating young women to drink than young men (6). In this, there is the assumption that the reason for drinking may be either social, as part of ritual, or individual, in order to obtain some effect or to gain whatever pleasure or ease can be derived from the act of drinking, exclusive of the intoxicating effect of the beverage. Glad (4) has emphasized this difference, although in slightly different terms.

We tend, however, to associate individual drinking motivations with the drinking done by alcoholics, who drink because of the intoxicating effect of alcohol. Male drinking, then, tends more to addictive motivation than the female pattern. One can conjecture that the motivational pattern of women's drinking is changing more rapidly than that of men and whether this forces the prediction that we shall have proportionately more women alcoholics in the United States than we have now. Bloch (2) would seem to suggest that at least the first part of this proposition is true: women's drinking habits and motivation are in greater flux than men's. He points out that drinking by women is a late development in America.

In the United States there are differences among men and women in rates of alcoholism, in reasons for drinking, in attitudes in the drinking situation, and in certain aspects of the first drinking experience. All these differences, as they now exist, point to less ego-involvement on the part of women who drink. Women have "nothing to prove" in the drinking situation. Because of these sex differences, it would seem profitable to direct more attention to the woman alcoholic.

References

1. Blacker, Edward, personal communication, 1959.
2. Bloch, Herbert, "Alcohol and American Recreational Life," *The American Scholar,* 18:54–66, 1948–1949.
3. Cramer, M. J., "A Survey of the Backgrounds and Attitudes of One Hundred Inmates of the Massachusetts Correctional Institution for Women at Framingham,

Massachusetts," Report to the Division of Legal Medicine, Office of the Commissioner on Alcoholism, and the Department of Corrections (mimeographed), 1959.

4. Glad, D. D., "Attitudes and Experiences of American-Jewish and American-Irish Male Youth as Related to Differences in Adult Rates of Inebriety," *Quart. J. Stud. Alc.,* 8:406–472, 1947.

5. Kessler, Alice, *A Study of the Relationship Between the Initial Alcoholic Experience and Early Family Life of Twenty Male Alcoholics Under Treatment at the State University Alcohol Clinic at Kings County Hospital, Brooklyn, New York,* unpublished master's thesis, Adelphi College, 1955.

6. Riley, J. W., Jr., C. F. Marden, and M. Lifshitz, "The Motivational Pattern of Drinking," *Quart. J. Stud. Alc.,* 9:353–362, 1948.

7. Sower, Christopher, Bevode McCall, and George Maddox, *Teenage Drinking,* New Haven: Yale Center of Alcohol Studies (in press).

8. Trice, H. M., and J. R. Wahl, "A Rank Order Analysis of the Symptoms of Alcoholism," *Quart. J. Stud. Alc.,* 19:636–648, 1958.

9. Ullman, Albert D., "Sex Differences in the First Drinking Experience," *Quart. J. Stud. Alc.,* 18:229–239, 1957.

10. ———, "The First Drinking Experience of Addictive and of 'Normal' Drinkers," *Quart. J. Stud. Alc.,* 14: 181–191, 1953.

11. ———, "The Psychological Mechanism of Alcohol Addiction," *Quart J. Stud. Alc.,* 13:602–608, 1952.

12. ———, *To Know the Difference,* New York: St. Martin's Press, 1960.

DRINKING CENTERED
INSTITUTIONS AND GROUPS

Introductory Note. The actual contexts within which drinking occurs have received limited systematic examination by social scientists. That there are institutions in Western society, such as the public drinking house, which are organized around the act of drinking and that vast numbers of individuals spend considerable time in these settings are undeniable facts. Identifying the reasons for the conspicuous absence of research on such a pervasive institution as the public drinking house could provide the focus for a study in the sociology of knowledge. Perhaps this omission is a consequence of ambivalent attitudes toward alcohol beverages—stemming from an abstinence tradition—which social scientists themselves still possess. In any event, Marshall Clinard, in Chapter 15, provides the first systematic collation of research studies that have been conducted on public drinking houses or taverns. It is of note that Clinard's students have provided most of the existing systematic data on the public drinking house. These studies, although few in number and limited in scope, do suggest the functions of the tavern in social life and offer a basis for classification of taverns.

Functionally, Clinard indicates, the neighborhood type of tavern located in relatively lower-class areas is extremely important in a complex urban society. The tavern in this context is the neighborhood social center, meeting social interactional and recreational needs and serving as a "counseling center" in which the bartender provides therapy.* Similarly, studies of the Skid-Row subculture reported by Rubington in Chapter 9 indicate that the

---

* For a documentation of this point see Earl L. Koos (3). Koos found that many of the families in his sample, as a matter of course, took their problems to the bartender for solution.

tavern in this locale serves comparable social functions, at least with regard to a provision for a mimimum sociability and insulation against social isolation for these socially disesteemed men. Furthermore, Stone in Chapter 7 has indicated the role of the middle- and upper-class private drinking clubs in the status evaluation and placement of their members in the community. However, research in this area has hardly begun. Clinard, in his conclusion, makes what we believe to be an effective case for using the tavern as a subject for increased sociological, social-historical, and comparative research.

Although sociologists have reiterated to the point of monotony that drinking occurs most frequently in the context of the group, there is a paucity of descriptive studies dealing with natural drinking groups and situations as well as of experimental studies of drinking groups. True, drinking groups such as those on Skid Row have been observed and analyzed by sociologists (Chapter 9), but the most perceptive descriptions of those customary American gatherings, the cocktail party and the cocktail hour, have come from the pens of novelists instead of social scientists.* However, the current studies (7, 8) of David Riesman and his associates on the sociology of sociability do provide some leads for the understanding of the cocktail party in complex urban society, although this is not their primary focus. Having "observed only a few parties in several of the various martini belts of America" (7, p. 332), Riesman and his associates indicate, as does Bacon in Chapter 5, that the party's participants' lack of shared traditions deriving from diverse social class and ethnic origins creates special problems of sociability when coupled with the decline in formality and the emergent "equalitarian ethos" in America. Riesman and his associates' major contention is the view that in analyzing adult play groups concepts derived from laboratory-task or work groups are not particularly germane. Party groups, to their way of thinking, have no task leaders, unless it be their "vanishing hosts" (8), and emotional contagion (6) among the participants establishes the activity and mood of the groups. We would conjecture that Riesman's group is documenting that parties, although perceived by the hosts as expressive mechanisms for integrating their diverse friends, mirror the fragmented and impersonal social relationships of a complex, heterogeneous, and dynamic society.

The second paper in this section is a detailed re-analysis by Kettil Bruun of an experimental study conducted in Finland as part of a program of small group research,† one of the few such programs to have been reported in

---

* Exception might be taken in the case of anthropologist Weston La Barre's (4) satirical account of the cocktail party as viewed through the eyes of a fictional African anthropologist. Allen Drury in *Advise and Consent* (2) and Norman Mailer in *Deer Park* (5), to mention only two of many, provide the novelist's perception of the cocktail party.

† A review of these studies is included as background material for Bruun's larger experimental study reported in *Drinking Behavior in Small Groups* (1).

the literature. Under relatively controlled laboratory conditions, differentials in interaction, expressed attitudes, and role differentiation are examined in terms of differences in levels of blood alcohol. Bruun suggests that increased precision in the use of the method and design of small group research will provide the basis for developing this important approach to the study of drinking behavior.

References

1. Bruun, Kettil, *Drinking Behavior in Small Groups*, Helsinki: Finnish Foundation for Alcohol Studies, 1959.
2. Drury, Allen, *Advise and Consent*, Garden City N.Y.: Doubleday and Company, 1959.
3. Koos, Earl L., *Families in Trouble*, New York: Kings Crown Press, 1946.
4. La Barre, Weston, "The Kocktail Party," *New York Times Magazine*, Vol. VI, p. 17, December 9, 1956.
5. Mailer, Norman, *Deer Park*, New York: Putnam, 1955.
6. Polansky, Norman, Ronald Lippitt, and Fritz Redl, "An Investigation of Behavioral Contagion in Groups," *Hum. Rel.*, 3:319–348, 1950.
7. Riesman, David, Robert J. Potter, and Jeanne Watson, "Sociability, Permissiveness and Equality: A Preliminary Formulation," *Psychiatry*, 23:323–340, 1960.
8. ———, "The Vanishing Host," *Hum. Org.*, 19:17–27, 1960.

chapter 15

The public drinking house and society[*]

Marshall B. Clinard

Since time immemorial, man has enjoyed the use of alcoholic beverages, and for centuries society has argued, fought, and sought to control its use and misuse. The conflict over the use of alcohol has been directed at not only those who consume it but also those who dispense it. As the institutionalized public drinking house became the focal point of the drink, the drinker, and the dispenser, values and conflicts over this institution developed.

Despite the obvious importance of the public drinking house and the perennial controversy over it, most publications about it have been historical accounts, popular articles, or propaganda.[†] Sociological studies of the public drinking house as a contemporary social institution are extremely

[*] This chapter was written especially for this book. The author acknowledges a grant from the University of Wisconsin Research Committee for this research. From part of this grant two research assistants of the author were given aid in the preparation of their doctoral dissertations: Boyd E. Macrory, *A Sociological Analysis of the Role and Functions of the Tavern in the Community,* unpublished doctoral dissertation, University of Wisconsin, 1950; and Simon Dinitz, *The Relation of the Tavern to the Drinking Phases of Alcoholics,* unpublished doctoral dissertation, University of Wisconsin, 1951.

[†] Several popular pamphlets dealing with the tavern have, for example, been issued by the Chicago Juvenile Protective Association but are not what could be termed scientific studies. The pamphlets are entitled: "The Return of the Saloon" (1935), "The Tavern: Chicago's Popular Recreation" (1936), "The Tavern in Community Life" (1939), and Walter O. Cromwell, "The Tavern in Relation to Children and Youth" (1948).

limited. A survey of sociological literature reveals very few published references to its role in contemporary society.*

Although public drinking houses are known by a variety of names, such as taverns, bars, pubs, bistros, wine houses, and beer halls, we shall largely use the term "tavern." For purposes of definition, one might simply say that public drinking houses are establishments whose business consists mainly of selling and serving beer, wine, or other intoxicating liquors for consumption on the premises. Actually this definition is inadequate, for it does not emphasize several important institutional features of a public drinking house.

A more complete definition would include these characteristics: (a) The serving of alcoholic beverages is an indispensable feature and an important source of revenue even if food is served. Because they do not serve alcoholic beverages, such places as soda fountains or milk bars, coffee houses of Greece and the Middle East, or tea houses of the Orient are not public drinking houses as the term is used here. (b) As a drinking establishment it is commercial and public in the sense that theoretically the opportunity to purchase a drink is open to all, whereas the bar of a private club or fraternal organization is restricted to members and their guests. (c) The drinking of alcoholic beverages is *group drinking* in the sense that it is done in the company of others in a public place. (d) It must have a functionary—a tavernkeeper, bartender, or, as in Europe, a barmaid. This person, in addition to serving alcoholic beverages, also acts as a sort of receptionist.†
(e) Finally, it has a physical structure and a set of norms. Patrons are served at a bar, tables, or booths, in specially decorated surroundings, with entertainment or recreational facilities like cards, darts, and shuffleboard available, thus distinguishing it in some way from the customary activities of other similar establishments. Certain norms are also well established, including certain hours of drinking and appropriate drinking behavior.

Tavern Participation and Regulation

The number of taverns in the United States is not known, but a conservative estimate would be at best 200,000. Wisconsin has about 14,000 public drinking establishments, New York City has over 11,000, and Chicago has about 9,000. A Chicago survey (5), some 20 years ago, reported that the annual patronage of the city's taverns was more than 30,000,000, while the motion-picture theaters of the city had an attendance of 20,000,000, and baseball and football alone at least 5,000,000. On this basis the report con-

---

* A few exceptions are Moore's sociological study of Chicago saloons some 60 years ago (13). See also Macrory (11) and Gottlieb (8). An important sociological study has been made of British public drinking houses, or pubs, in an English industrial city of some 180,000 population (12). Because of World War II, this study was published in a very limited edition and is generally unavailable in most American libraries today.
† Hypothetically, if one could serve himself alcoholic beverages through automatic dispensers and drink them with others in a room, without a tavernkeeper, bartender, or barmaid being present, it could not be considered a public drinking establishment.

cluded that taverns at least have more patronage than all other forms of commercial recreation combined. A survey of an English industrial community found that more people spent more time in public drinking houses than in any other buildings except private homes and places of employment. In this city of 180,000 people about 20,000 pub-goers made approximately 140,000 visits to pubs a week. Furthermore, "the pub has more buildings, holds more people, takes more of their time and money, than church, cinema, dance-hall, and political organizations put together" (12, p. 17). From the survey of this community, and other data, it was concluded that about one-twelfth or more of the population of England is consuming alcohol in pubs on Saturday evening and more still at home (12, p. 111).

A random sample of 1,441 persons in Dane County, Wisconsin, was surveyed as to the extent they used the tavern (10, p. 408). Three categories were used, non-patrons, irregular patrons (less than once a month), and regular (more than once a month). Of the 872 men in the survey, one-fourth were non-patrons, one-fourth irregular, and a half regular patrons. One out of ten went to a tavern nine or more times a month. Tavern patronage of the men did not materially differ by farm, village, or urban residence. Among the 569 women, three-fifths were non-patrons, a little over one-fourth were irregular patrons, and only 15 per cent were regular. Urban women appeared to be more frequent patrons than either village or rural women.

As the public drinking house, regardless of its name, has become a firmly entrenched institution in Western society, open conflicts have developed between wets and drys over it and its growing patronage. Extensive propaganda has been disseminated both for and against it, especially in the United States, and the controversy has been intensified and heightened by religious exhortations and heated legislative hearings. The situation in England has differed little from that in this country. In this continuing controversy the wets have generally referred to the tavern as a poor man's club which affords him the same enjoyment and communality as the exclusive country club provides the socially elite. The drys, on the other hand, contend that the tavern constitutes a serious threat to the home and family, leads to crime and delinquency, and weakens the moral standards of society. Largely as a result of these accusations, taverns, especially in the United States, have been more and more strictly regulated. These regulations indicate some of the values * believed to be associated with public drinking houses. Those states which permit the sale of alcoholic beverages for consumption on the premises have two types of regulations, one relating to persons who own and operate taverns, and the other setting standards under which ownership and operation are valid. In other words

* For a discussion of the relation of values to social problems, see John F. Cuber, Robert A. Harper, and William F. Kenkel, *Problems of American Society: Values in Conflict* (New York: Henry Holt and Company, third edition, 1956).

tavern regulations are concerned with the who, where, and when of drinking.*

1. Regulations controlling licensing and qualifications of tavernkeepers and bartenders

The most important instruments of tavern control are state licensing and taxation statutes, and they set forth the various reasons for the necessity to control alcoholic beverages.† The statutes of fifteen states mention the general welfare, sixteen cite health, twelve maintenance of peace, twelve the upholding of morals, and four the prohibition of the open saloon. Eight statutes indicate that the purpose of control is to promote temperance. It would appear that only one-sixth of the states are interested in regulating retailers in the promotion of moderate drinking. However, when one turns to the specific regulations, the picture changes quickly.

Among the requirements which a prospective tavern owner must meet, the one most commonly agreed upon, by forty-one states, is United States citizenship.‡ Thirty-six states insist that no one previously convicted of violating any federal or state liquor laws, or who has had a liquor license revoked, shall be eligible for licensing. Thirty-four states refuse to grant a license to any person who has a criminal record although five of them

---

* Some states permit communities by local option to outlaw, by majority vote, the sale of alcoholic beverages by the drink only. In these states, therefore, it is not drinking but the tavern which is directly on trial. The importance of such ordinances permitting local option elections is second to none in the regulation of taverns. Tavern owners fear the results of being driven out of an area, and in those areas where there is a dry sentiment of some consequence, the local option provisions serve to make the tavernkeepers follow more closely other regulations such as those pertaining to minors and closing hours. There were 2,219 out of a total of 3,070 communities which allowed the sale of liquor in some manner whereas 851 prohibited its sale in any form. As of January 1, 1958, less than one-third (814) of the 3,070 communities in the nation specifically allowed alcoholic beverages to be sold by both package and drink. Five hundred and fifty-five permitted sale by the package only. Some 216 communities allowed distilled spirits to be sold by the package but prohibited the sale of the drink in certain areas. Still another 634 permitted the sale of liquor, whether by bottle or drink, only in certain areas. Close analysis of these ordinances reveals discrimination primarily against the tavern and its drinking function, even more so than against the sale of the alcoholic beverages per se. See *Annual Report 1957*, Washington, D.C.: Distilled Spirits Institute, 1957, p. 52.

† Taverns are heavily taxed both for license fees and on the alcoholic beverages served. These heavy taxes reduce both patronage and profits. On the other hand, it is quite evident that legislative tax enactments reveal basic value conflicts, for in taxing they have sought to curb abuses in the liquor industry as a whole, especially through the retailer, and also to preserve the trade so that the revenues will continue to flow into the treasury coffers rather than into the hands of bootleggers. See *Alcoholic Beverage Control: An Official Study by the Joint Committee of the States to Study Alcoholic Beverage Laws*, 1950, Table 1, p. 69.

‡ Information about regulations controlling the licensing and qualifications of tavernkeepers and bartenders, except where indicated, is from Bertram M. Bernard (2).

provide for licensing if the record is not a recent one. In thirty-two states the applicant must be of "good moral character," and the same number require bona fide state residence, the time limit stretching to as long as 10 years in Kansas.

Twenty-seven states insist on legal maturity, from 21 years of age in most states to 30 in Delaware. Four of these states require the applicant to be a qualified voter. Twenty-one states prohibit interlocking vertical ties between the tavernkeeper and other persons and companies in the liquor trade, an aftermath of saloon days. Seventeen states insist that the applicant be a legitimate party in the place to be licensed. Thirteen states will not license any licensing or enforcement official. In twelve states tavern owners must demonstrate ability to read and write. In six states the applicant must be financially responsible, whereas only four refuse to approve applicants who use alcoholic beverages to excess. In most states many of these provisions can, of course, be evaded by having the license issued to a relative or some other person.

Standards for bartenders are far less rigid than those for tavern owners. The most general rule is that the employee be over 18 or 21 years of age, depending upon the jurisdiction in which he seeks employment. Seventeen states have "anti-barmaid" laws (1). In most cases these rules do not apply to women who work on the premises as waitresses, but only to those who operate behind the bar itself. Exceptions to the latter rule are made in some states where the woman is the wife of the tavern owner.

In many states tavernkeepers are subject to a special type of liability. A tavernkeeper must post a bond which supposedly guarantees payment of damages to any person for injuries suffered as the result of drinking in a tavern. In Illinois this is called the "Dram Act" and because the law has been sometimes used to collect damages unfairly, a subsequent bill was passed setting the limit of $20,000 in damages for injuries or death resulting from intoxication and setting a time limit of 1 instead of 2 years for the filing of a suit against a tavernkeeper.

2. Regulations concerning drinkers

Tavern licenses can be revoked or suspended if liquor is sold, either by the drink or package, to the following major classes of persons (2):

(a) Forty-six states forbid the sale of alcoholic beverages to visibly intoxicated persons.

(b) Thirty-two states do not permit the serving of drinks to known alcoholics, habitual drunkards, or persons of intemperate habits.

(c) Forty-six states prohibit the sale of intoxicating beverages to minors. In nearly all states the minimum age is 21, although in a few it is 18. Frequently the legal age for entering taverns selling distilled spirits is 21, while it is 18 for those serving only beer. Almost without exception the retailer is solely responsible for serving minors, but in a few instances the minor is subject to penalty if he knowingly misrepresents his age in order to procure liquor. It is the seller's responsibility to secure positive proof of a patron's age before any transactions take place.

(*d*) Twenty states forbid the sale of alcoholic beverages to "interdicted" persons. By interdicted is meant any individual whose family, the courts, welfare agencies, mental institutions, public and private officials have specifically notified the licensee that such persons may not be sold intoxicating beverages. These persons are usually persons on public relief, parolees and probationers, and persons judged insane.

(*e*) Four states specifically prohibit prostitutes and keepers of houses of ill repute from patronizing taverns.

3. Time of drinking

Regulations regarding time of drinking vary considerably from state to state. The hours for sale of liquor are fixed by state law, local ordinances, or by rules of the state liquor commissions. Most states call for an 8-hour halt to business, generally from midnight to 8 A.M. The two extremes are South Carolina, which fixes the closing hour at sundown, and Maine, which permits taverns to operate except for one hour daily, from 8 A.M. to 9 A.M. Every state except Wyoming prohibits taverns from operating on election days either entirely or at least while the polls are open, and five states require taverns to close on Christmas Day. In most other states there is considerable informal pressure on taverns, however, to have them close early on Christmas Eve. Three states require the closing of all taverns on Thanksgiving Day, and two of these make this rule apply to Armistice Day as well. Twenty-five states prohibited taverns from operating at any time on Sundays. Six others set specified times on Sundays during which taverns must remain closed. Many of the remaining states leave this decision to local authorities.

4. Tavern associations and regulations

Tavernkeeper associations are well organized, and they are constantly on the alert to protect their own interests in state and national legislatures. The National Licensed Beverage Association has a total membership of some forty thousand taverns in twenty-seven states and the District of Columbia. This group's primary objectives are to keep its members informed on problems relating to taverns, advise them on all things pertaining to their business stemming from federal legislation and regulation, and also to protect their interests through legal counsel. One of the strongest organizations of tavern owners at the state level is The Tavern League of Wisconsin. It was first organized in 1936, and now has 4,300 members.

Types of Taverns

The tavern is often stereotyped by persons not personally acquainted with it. These stereotyped attitudes appear to be based on a combination of "hearsay," half-truths, misinformation, ignorance, prejudice, propaganda, and biased and inadequate data. The stereotyped conception of the tavern is also based on stories of saloon days, newspaper reports, observations of the worst taverns, and the belief that the drinking of alcoholic beverages is its only function. Some people believe tavern patronage is one of the chief causes of alcoholism, broken homes, neglected children, highway accidents, juvenile delinquency, and even crime.

A significant factor in this stereotyped conception of a tavern is the general lack of familiarity with this institution. Actual investigations have shown that the majority of the taverns do not fit the stereotype but are of different types (6, pp. 74–81; 8, pp. 559–562; 10, pp. 366–370; 11, pp. 625–630). Four criteria may be used in describing types of patronage and the functions it performs. A tentative classification is the Skid-Row tavern, the downtown bar and cocktail lounge, the drink and dine tavern, the night club, and the neighborhood tavern.

1. Skid-Row taverns

These taverns are usually located in the deteriorated Skid-Row areas close to the central business district. Many establishments are simply "holes in the wall" with only a bar and stools, while others may have tables and poorly lighted booths. The patronage is largely single and homeless men, migrant laborers, and alcoholics. Although their primary function is to provide a place for cheap drinking, they are often the site of gambling and soliciting for prostitution. There are frequent violations of state and municipal laws relating to taverns, as well as drunk and disorderly conduct and gambling. In this type of tavern, violations of regulations which are strictly enforced in other places are often permitted; for example, closing hours are widely disobeyed, and many establishments virtually operate on a 24-hour basis. While taverns somewhat similar to this description may be found in nearly all cities, the most typical ones are found on New York's Bowery or Chicago's West Madison Street. The reputation of this type of tavern has contributed much toward the development of the stereotype of all taverns.

2. The downtown bar and cocktail lounge

These drinking places are located in business and shopping areas of cities. They usually have long bars, booths, and attractive decorations, and are predominantly patronized by men of the white-collar and business class. Besides drinking, visiting, and talking about business problems the patrons can often watch television or a professional performer, or listen to juke box music. Occasionally a sport like shuffleboard or bowling is available. The downtown cocktail lounge serves primarily mixed drinks and attracts some unaccompanied women. It is open for business chiefly in the early afternoon and caters to afternoon and late evening patrons. Most customers of the bars and cocktail lounges are transients (8). Because of the location and type of patrons there is much less emphasis on the social and recreational activities than in the neighborhood taverns.

3. Drink-and-dine taverns

These taverns are located either in business districts or near the city limits along main highways. The bar is not the center of attraction but is frequently part of a spacious, well-appointed dining room. Patrons are most frequently businessmen, but many women patronize this type of drinking establishment. While serving alcoholic beverages is an important source of income, the primary drawing card is the service of fine foods, and often there is music. Many business deals are transacted over cocktails and steaks. There is little interaction between patrons as they tend to come in small individual groups. Although the frequency of attendance is much less than at a downtown bar, the length of stay is generally longer.

4. Night clubs and roadhouses

Located generally in city amusement centers or along main highways outside of but near the city limits, the night club or roadhouse is usually large and impressive, with neon lights and illuminated billboards attracting the traveler's attention. The bar is usually located adjacent to the dining room whose seating arrangement centers around a stage and dance floor. Although the night club or roadhouse is situated out from the city center, its patronage is predominantly urban couples who come chiefly on weekends. While drinking is encouraged and there is some visiting, the primary functions are dancing, the enjoyment of fine foods, listening to the orchestra, and watching the floor show. Most persons who attend are spectators and there is little social interaction among the patrons.

5. Neighborhood taverns

Of all taverns the most numerous and apparently the most important type functionally is the neighborhood tavern. In a Wisconsin study over three-fifths of all tavern keepers indicated that their taverns were of the neighborhood variety (11, p. 627). Over two-thirds of Wisconsin male tavern patrons, and about half of the women patrons, indicated that they patronized neighborhood taverns (11, p. 627). This type can be divided primarily by location and secondarily by patronage into four subtypes: rural, village, suburban, and city. Neighborhood taverns are more than places for people to drink, visit, exchange ideas, discuss politics and problems, joke, play cards or other games, watch television, and listen to their favorite records on the juke box. Generally speaking, these establishments tend to cater to a local clientele; the bulk of the patrons are "regulars" who are often on intimate speaking terms with one another and with the owner and bartenders. In addition, these taverns do most of their business in the evenings and on weekends and holidays.

Rural neighborhood taverns are located either in the open country along a highway, usually at a crossroad, or in some small unincorporated village. Besides the bar stools they usually have tables and booths, and on weekends many serve fish and chicken dinners. Practically all have juke boxes, many have radio or television, and some have pianos; playing cards are also available. A Wisconsin survey revealed that 85 per cent of the patrons were male and 70 per cent of the patrons were farmers (10, p. 383). Three-fourths of the patrons were under 50 years of age, of which half were under 30. An important function is providing a meeting place for friends and neighbors where they may share like interests and problems, or relax and enjoy visiting together.

Village neighborhood taverns are located in an incorporated village usually at or near the center of the small business district. Structurally and functionally it is about the same as the rural neighborhood tavern. As is the case with all neighborhood taverns, one of the most important functions is to provide a meeting place and social center for patrons and friends.

The city neighborhood tavern is located in a more densely populated area often at or near street intersections, and the suburban neighborhood tavern is located near the city limits, often on highways leading to the city. Structurally they are similar, with a bar, tables, and chairs, although the suburban tavern is usually more modern in appearance with larger and more attractive signs to attract the attention of highway patronage. In a Wisconsin survey about three-fourths of the suburban neighborhood taverns' patrons were men (10, p. 391). The majority of the patronage for both types were in the age group of 30 to 50. Both types drew heavily from their respective areas, and laborers make up at least two-thirds the patronage of both types. In another study this distinction was made between the neighborhood tavern and the cocktail lounge:

The tavern, which develops as a neighborhood center, differs from the lounge which is a sort of private service organization and is, so to speak, non-institutionalized. The tavern is both a phenomenon of the lower social classes and of the immediate neighborhood. Eighty-three per cent of the respondents resided within two blocks of the neighborhood tavern in which they were interviewed (8, p. 560).

Almost all neighborhood taverns have television, juke boxes, card games, and other games. As with the rural and village taverns, both suburban and city neighborhood taverns provide a meeting place for people to talk and relax from the monotony of work.

A British neighborhood pub often represents a combination of several types of taverns (12). Most English pubs have three rooms: the vault, the taproom, and the lounge. The essential difference between them is in the relationship among the people themselves and with the people who run the tavern. The vault has a bar or counter where an exclusively male patronage drink standing. Most men come singly, and some are total strangers. In the taproom, drinking is a male group affair, and they are seated around plain wooden tables and benches. It is like a clubroom and strangers are not welcome. While games are played in both the vault and the taproom, most are in the latter. The lounge, or "best room," is well decorated and comfortably furnished with tables, chairs, and a piano; it attracts women and couples.

There are no games, the demeanor is more homelike, and it attracts mostly middle-class patrons.

The Social Functions of Public Drinking Houses

Most taverns in the United States or the pubs of England are of the neighborhood type. While the consumption of alcohol plays a predominant but not exclusive part in taverns of the Skid-Row type, as well as in downtown bars and cocktail lounges, alcoholic drinking in neighborhood taverns or pubs plays a secondary role. People go to the tavern to drink, but they also go there for other reasons.* In fact to "have a drink in a tavern" actually often means "let's talk" or "play a game or two," in much the same way that "let's play bridge" often means "let us get together and visit." The British pub has been characterized not only as a center of social activities but as the principal locale of the pub-goers' social life.

Worktown working people rarely meet in each other's homes for social activities in the way middle classes do. For some there is the social activity of politics, football or cricket clubs. But participators in these activities are a small minority. The place where most Worktowners meet their friends and acquaintances is the pub. Men can meet and talk of the way of their womenfolk.

A drink is the only price of admission into this society. And so, for the pub-goers, drink becomes inseparably connected with social activity, relaxation, and pleasure. And the picnic, the outing, the angling competition, the bowls match, the savings club, games of cards and darts, betting—all these forms of non-pub social activity become connected with the pub, and thus are "incomplete" without drink.

The forms taken by pub social activity bear on the conclusions that we have drawn from the behavior of drunks. Here, too, the social and the alcoholic motive cannot be disentangled. The alcoholic motive itself is primarily social, if it is given a long term definition; it is a motive that seeks the breaking down of barriers between men, the release from the strain of everyday life in the feeling of identification with a group. And the rituals of the Buffs and the clubs, the merging of groups in singing, all in different ways are part of this process (12, pp. 311–312).

Other than drinking there appear to be three chief functions of the tavern: (a) as a meeting place where social relationships with other persons can be established, (b) as a place for recreation such as games, and, (c) as a place to talk over personal problems with the tavernkeeper or others.

---

* Over 60 years ago, a sociologist attempted to make a scientific analysis of the saloon or taverns of that day believing that any institution so widely patronized must have a function: "What does the saloon offer that renders it so generally useful, in the economic sense, to the great mass of those who patronize it? For it is use, not abuse, that it stands for. It does not personify 'the vilest elements of modern civilization.' It does not 'trade in and batten upon intemperance.' It supplies legitimate needs and is alone in supplying them. It transforms the individual into a *socius,* where there is no other transforming power. It unites the many ones into a common whole which we call society, and it stands for this union amid conditions which would otherwise render it impossible, and intemperance is but its accident" (13, p. 4).

1. *The public drinking house as a meeting place*

The primary purpose of most taverns appears to be that of serving as a place where people can meet, become acquainted, and enjoy social relationships. In one survey a considerable proportion of more than five hundred Wisconsin regular tavern-goers said they felt the tavern played an important social role in their lives and those of others (11, pp. 630–632). About three-fourths felt that the tavern was a social club, two-thirds thought that the tavern provided a place for friends to meet, and one-half felt that meeting friends is an even more important function of the tavern than drinking. In fact, 43 per cent felt that the tavern was as important as the church to many patrons. Persons attending a church, the theater, or various athletic events are usually spectators. Instead of being the audience, tavern patrons are participating actively; instead of having their thoughts and actions patterned for them, they are free to act and think and talk as they wish. To the extent that these needs are met, the tavern acts as an integrating force in the lives of its patrons.

The anonymous opinions of tavernkeepers, while possibly revealing some vested interests, may also be considered valid insomuch as tavernkeepers, both as observers and as tavern functionaries, participate daily in tavern life. Some 150 Wisconsin tavernkeepers indicated that an hour with friends is the most important reason for tavern patronage, followed in order by drinking, talking over problems, and recreation in the form of cards or other games.* Over nine-tenths of all responding tavernkeepers said that their taverns were social centers. Over half of the tavernkeepers commented on their patrons' meeting and visiting together regularly; three-tenths made remarks about patrons discussing work, business, family, social, and political problems; about one-fifth mentioned playing either cards or other games; and about 15 per cent gave as a reason enjoying drinks together. The common thread running through all of these responses is the word or the implication of the word "together."

Chandler (3) has pointed out the importance of the tavern in the social organization of persons living in rooming-house areas. Taverns serve as meeting places for people who have no way of meeting other persons living in rooming-house areas. In the tavern the individual finds a sense of belonging and a place in the community. In the tavern group the individual seeks friendship and prestige, during his leisure hours. At night it becomes the working man's club. The social life of the rooming-house tavern-goer is confined either to a single tavern or to a type of tavern, and the average tavern has a remarkably stable and regular group of patrons. "The tavern-goer could be counted on to appear at a certain place at a certain time.

---

* Nine-tenths of the tavernkeepers were American born and married, and about four-fifths were fathers. Their average age was 45, and the average length of residence in Wisconsin was 39 years. The average length of time spent working as a tavernkeeper was 9 years, and about half of them resided with their families on the tavern premises (11, pp. 632–636).

When others wanted to seek him out they knew exactly where to find him. The tavern-goer met his friends at the bar in the same way that the corner boy met them on his corner. This regular patterned participation involved close interpersonal relations" (3, p. 54).

The extensive participation in British pubs also cannot be explained as merely the desire to consume ale, beer, and other alcoholic beverages. People seldom go to pubs exclusively to drink or get drunk; rather, they go primarily for sociability and recreation. One study has definitely stated:

No pub can simply be regarded as a drinking shop. It may be lacking in facilities for games and music, present no organized forms of social activity, and its actual accommodation be of the crudest; but none the less the activities of the drinkers are not confined to drinking. . . . The pub is a centre of social activities —for the ordinary pubgoer the main scene of social life (12, p. 311).

2. Recreational activities

Recreation in the form of games, music, and other activities is a leading function of the tavern. Most communities provide, except for bowling or billiards, few opportunities for the average person to play games or enjoy other recreational outlets in small groups outside of the home. Some of the games regularly played inside British pubs, for example, are darts, dominoes, cards, and raffles. There is also much singing. It is possible that these activities reduce the amount of actual drinking in a tavern or pub.*

When asked why they went to taverns, a large number of Wisconsin patrons also replied that they went for various recreational activities. Consequently, as one might expect, a survey (11) of 150 Wisconsin taverns indicated that among the recreational outlets offered, 44 per cent provided card games, 41 per cent shuffleboard, and others pinball machines and various mechanical games. Other forms of recreation included the 90 per cent who had juke boxes for their patrons' enjoyment, while others had television, radio, dancing, singing, and bowling. Many provided not one but various forms of recreation. Some of the comments of the tavernkeepers were:

All know each other and gather to play cards for relaxation. Quite a few of them are retired and card games seem to be the only pleasure they have left at a low cost. [City neighborhood tavern, 250–300 patrons a day.] (11, p. 628.)

I believe my tavern is a social center because most of my patrons are the type that enjoy an evening of friendly companionship. They enjoy visiting and singing, and where you have singing you never have arguing. I believe in keeping my customers happy and willing to come back again and enjoy themselves. [Village neighborhood tavern, 100–150 patrons per day.] (11, p. 635.)

3. Talking over problems

Neighborhood taverns often serve as places where one can talk over personal problems. This "talking over" may serve simply as a release for ten-

* These authors claim that the high rate of arrests for drunkenness in a particular community (not the one they studied) occurred because the licensing authorities there tended to discourage games in pubs.

sions while in other instances the person may actively be able to get "help" from the tavernkeeper or others. In one survey (11), responses from regular patrons indicated that the tavern played an important role in offering a place for discussing personal problems.

When Wisconsin tavernkeepers were asked about why people went to one tavern rather than another and what they considered to be the important qualifications of a "good bartender," they obviously mentioned serving good drinks and keeping an orderly place, but they also mentioned, as more significant, being friendly, being attentive, understanding the patron's problems, keeping confidences, sharing the good fortunes and sympathizing with the misfortunes of the patrons, and giving advice to a patron in a "jam." * Some of the patrons' difficulties may involve family problems and problems in personal adjustment and on the job. One bartender stated:

We try to be cheerful. Customers never want to hear your troubles, only to tell us theirs without fear of them being repeated. We are honest and try to show our appreciation of patronage. We try to show interest in their work, crops and family. We greet all by their names and interest ourselves in local things—ball games, legion affairs, etc. [Village neighborhood tavern.] (11, p. 633.)

Tavern Drinking Norms

Certain norms and values often develop in those taverns which have a large proportion of regular patrons. These norms and values control the behavior of the customer to a large extent. Customers are largely known to each other by first names and the bartender is familiar not only with the person's name but with his drinking and other habits as well. In fact one of the ways in which a "regular" tavern patron can be identified is by the degree of familiarity with the staff. In a British pub, for example, a whole system of social norms involve not only the various pub-goers but also the staff. Pub regulars "tend to sit or stand in the same places every night; and this is particularly noticeable with regular groups who stand at the bar; they always retain the same relative positions to one another, and if the room is crowded or they find their usual space in front of the bar partly occupied, though the shape of the group will have to change, their positions relative to one another tend to remain the same" (12, p. 134).

Group drinking whether in a tavern or pub involves other social factors.

---

* Chandler (3) has pointed out the loyalty to the bartender of tavern patrons living in rooming house areas, so that when he moved to another establishment many of the patrons would follow him there. About the saloonkeeper, Moore wrote: "The saloonkeeper is the only man who keeps open house in the ward. It is his business to entertain. It does not matter that he does not select his guests; that convention is useless among them. In fact his democracy is one element of his strength. His place is the common meeting ground of his neighbors—and he supplies the stimulus which renders social life possible; there is an accretion of intelligence that comes to him in his business. He hears the best stories. He is the first to get accurate information as to the latest political deals and social mysteries. The common talk of the day passes through his ears and he is known to retain that which is most interesting" (13, pp. 7–8).

The tavern-goer never sits without a drink, he adapts his drinking pace to the group, and the person who pays for the round of drinks sets the pace for the others. Each person must pay in his turn, and if he misses there is danger of social stigma. If a man knocks another man's glass over, it often means that he must buy him another drink. Often games are played for rounds of drinks.

Regular tavern patrons not only regulate the behavior of other regular patrons but can identify and often will reject the newcomer. Even the extent of drinking and drunkenness which is permitted is subject to social control in taverns where there is a good deal of close social interaction. In some taverns old timers may be allowed more freedom than others. On the other hand the customers of certain taverns may not permit any drunkenness or boisterousness and may ostracize offenders. One neighborhood bartender commented:

Every once in a while one of the fellows will overdo it . . . too much drinking. . . . The others don't go for it, and they tell him . . . . We've got one guy that still comes in here . . . used to be a pretty steady drinker. Then he started drinking heavy. . . . The fellows liked him, and we all tried to get him to cut down. . . . It was no use. . . . After awhile the fellows started to complain so we asked the guy not to come. . . . Well, he still comes in, but they've got nothing to do with him. . . . I guess he's found a new place by now (8, p. 561).

The Tavern and Alcoholism

In 1953 it was estimated that sixty-eight million adults in the United States used alcoholic beverages either regularly or sporadically and that of these some five million persons were estimated to be alcoholics (9). Since millions of drinkers go to taverns and do not become alcoholics, this would indicate that the tavern does not have a direct relationship to alcoholism.* On the other hand patronage of taverns in many cases probably speeds up progression in alcoholism. This was the conclusion of a study (6) of 197 members of Alcoholics Anonymous in Wisconsin where an attempt was made to determine the relation of the tavern to each of the three drinking phases of alcoholism, namely the social, the excessive, and the alcoholic. As a control group estimates of the patronage of regular tavern patrons were secured from 106 tavernkeepers. The alcoholics most frequently cited social rather than drinking reasons for their visits in the social drinking phase, and on most of the variables examined the alcoholics could not be differentiated from regular tavern patrons as social drinkers. As they progressed

* Even taverns are not directly associated with drunkenness, as a study of British pubs has indicated. "If we take a very low estimate of 150,000 pub visits per week in Worktown—nearly eight million a year—we find that the probability of the ordinary drinker getting 'had up' [arrested] after an evening in the pub is one in 60,000. If he goes to the pub five nights a week it might, at that rate, take him two centuries before he was 'had up' for being drunk. He would have died before then; most pub-goers do die before they get 'had up' for drunkenness" (12, pp. 222–223).

from social drinkers to excessive drinkers, and finally to alcoholics, however, there was a statistically significant increase in their tavern participation as measured by chi-square tests and coefficients of contingency. In all phases, taverns were more important than package stores as sources of supply of alcoholic beverages.

1. The social-drinking phase

In the social-drinking phase, the tavern was the principal source of alcoholic beverages, two-thirds procuring and consuming most of their intoxicating drinks in the tavern. For the alcoholic subjects and for the regular customers, however, the tavern did not necessarily serve as the place in which to get drunk. A minority of only about one-third did most of their "serious" drinking, that is, indulgence for the direct purpose of intoxication, in the tavern, and this was approximately the same figure given by tavern proprietors for their regular patrons.*

The mean attendance of taverns by alcoholics at this stage was slightly over once a week. About one in eleven frequented the tavern at least five times a week, although about one in twenty did not patronize taverns at all. According to the estimates of tavernkeepers, regular patrons visit taverns on an average of four times weekly.

It is difficult to see how the tavern during this drinking phase would have significantly affected the drinking patterns of most of these subjects since only a limited amount of time was spent in taverns. About three-fourths of the alcoholics estimated that at this time they spent less than 10 per cent of their leisure time in taverns, and about the same per cent stated that an average visit was an hour or less in duration.

As social drinkers, alcoholics tended to frequent taverns at the same time of day or week as other patrons. The chief times of patronage for the alcoholics, like regular patrons, were weekends, evenings, holidays, and after work. In both groups, however, about 10 per cent of the individuals patronized taverns in the mornings, during lunch hours, and during the working day. The chief places of patronage for the subjects were downtown bars, followed in order of preference by neighborhood taverns near their homes and places of work.

Nine out of ten alcoholics and an estimated three out of four regular patrons drank in the company of others. Some two-thirds of the alcoholics thought that the social contacts in the taverns were more important than the drinking at this stage. Slightly over one-half of the tavern proprietors felt that this was also true for their regular customers. Among the social reasons most often given by both the alcoholic and the regular group were

* If these alcoholics were at all typical in their early drinking, initiation into drinking has little to do with tavern attendance. About nine out of ten alcoholics took their first drink before the age of 20, and this event occurred more often at home, at the home of friends, or at dances, than in taverns. Only 13 per cent of the alcoholics took their first drinks in a tavern. Three-quarters became intoxicated before 20, but only one-fifth first became intoxicated in a tavern.

the meeting of friends, the spending of free time, the lack of anything else to do, the playing of cards, and celebrating.

2. Excessive and alcoholic phases

Between the social- and excessive-drinking phases and between the excessive and alcoholic phases there was a statistically significant increase in the frequency of tavern patronage, the estimated percentage of leisure time spent in taverns, and the amount of time spent per average visit.*
Significantly more of them did their "serious" drinking in the tavern in the excessive phase.

The amount of morning and daytime patronage of taverns, as well as visitation at other times, significantly increased between the social and excessive and the excessive and alcoholic phases. On the other hand, there was a statistically significant shift of patronage from certain downtown bars and neighborhood taverns to the places nearest the subjects when they wanted a drink.†

During the excessive and alcoholic phases, the reasons for patronizing the tavern changed significantly. For most of the subjects social factors became subsidiary, as they most often went to the tavern to drink, get drunk, and forget their problems. There was a decreasing interest in games and friends and a marked increased interest in drinking. This shift was also indicated by the fact that more of the subjects came alone to the tavern and fewer preferred the company of others while drinking, although even as alcoholics about half the subjects still were accompanied by other persons.

3. Tavern practices and alcoholism

Charges are often made that tavern patronage contributes to excessive drinking and alcoholism through encouraging excessive drinking, extension of credit, cashing pay checks, and gambling, and by serving persons already intoxicated. Slightly over half of the alcoholic subjects believed that they were encouraged, at least once, to continue drinking until they were drunk. On at least one occasion, one-third of the alcoholics drank more than they cared to because of friendship with the bartender. Though the extension of credit is generally illegal, 85 per cent were able to buy drinks on credit on at least one occasion, but of those who received credit in taverns fewer than one in three found this to be a reason for drinking more. Only about one-third were also able to procure liquor from package stores on credit. Approximately four out of five at some time in their drinking

---

* Slightly over half of the subjects "slipped" or temporarily reverted to drinking after joining Alcoholics Anonymous. Of these persons, 43 per cent attributed their deviations either directly or indirectly to tavern patronage. In addition, in those cases in which the tavern was thought to be a factor in the first "slip," or return to drinking, it was also thought to be a factor in succeeding "slips."

† As with the other indices, however, there were marked individual variations within all three phases. Some subjects, to the very end of their drinking, remained regular customers at one or a few downtown bars or neighborhood taverns.

histories cashed their pay checks in taverns. Of those who did so, fewer than one out of three, however, felt that this led to greater indulgence.

In general, gambling in taverns appears to have a negligible influence on excessive drinking. Almost two out of five alcoholics never gambled in taverns for drinks as social drinkers. An additional one-fourth gambled for the pleasure of doing so and were not concerned with winning drinks. Of those persons who had gambled for drinks, one-half did so less frequently after becoming excessive drinkers while the other half did so more often than before. Almost all the alcoholics were served drinks on at least one occasion in spite of the fact that they were intoxicated,* as compared with about two-thirds who were able to procure liquor in package stores while intoxicated.

In summary, as the alcoholics progressed through the various phases in their drinking histories, their tavern patronage tended not only to increase quantitatively but to become subjectively more meaningful.† The general social functions of the tavern became of subsidiary importance to the alcoholic, but the tavern did provide a comfortable environment for drinking and this seemed, in part, to account for the added tavern patronage.

Tavern Participation and Juvenile Delinquency

It has been stated that often delinquent acts are committed under the influence of alcoholic beverages, largely obtained from taverns. Likewise, taverns and tavernkeepers are often regarded as a leading source of immoral influence for delinquency and crime among youth. There is little evidence to support such beliefs. In the first place, delinquent or criminal acts seldom appear to be committed under the influence of alcohol (4, pp. 191–192). When drunkenness does occur among juveniles it is an unwarranted assumption to maintain that the tavern was necessarily the source. Undoubtedly one major source of delinquency, however, is the arrest of those under 18 years of age for drinking.

In one of the few specific studies it was found that the tavern was not an important factor in producing delinquency.‡ Taverns which sell to

---

* About fourth-fifths, however, felt that tavernkeepers and bartenders were glad to see an alcoholic "go on the wagon" in spite of the fact that alcoholics are often better customers than most other tavern patrons.

† "While greater and more meaningful tavern participation of the subjects as the drinking phases succeeded one another was a central tendency, particular note should be taken of the fact that differences among the alcoholics within each phase examined tended to be almost as great as the differences between the various phases. Thus, the importance of the tavern varied as much for the different subjects at any one time, as it did for the same persons at different times. Therefore, no unitary role in alcoholism may be assigned to the tavern" (6, pp. 373–374).

‡ See Fagan (7). The study used an anonymous questionnaire which was given to two hundred boys from a single Milwaukee residential area, half delinquents in the Wisconsin School for Boys and the other half attending a high school in the area. Of those who filled out the questionnaire, ninety boys from the high school were matched with seventy-three boys from the training school. Besides the area, the groups were matched on race, parents' marital status, and age range.

minors, however, are a source of trouble among teenagers. Two types of taverns are frequented by teenagers. One type makes an effort to prevent teenage drinking by checking ages, refusing to serve to known minors, and in general upholding the laws concerning minor drinking and tavern participation. This type, classified as the "good" tavern, is in the majority. The second type caters to teenage trade, seldom checks ages, often provides lewd entertainment, and is even sometimes a source of drugs. This "bad" type was generally frequented by delinquents, whereas the control group frequented the "good" type.

The delinquents frequented taverns more often than non-delinquents, and those who did generally had a previous official record of antisocial acts, in high school and among neighbors. They used the tavern more frequently for admittedly antisocial acts, drunkenness, and for the prestige gained through illegal drinking. Their behavior in the tavern was more often loud and boisterous, and invited trouble such as fights and brawls. The delinquents tended to frequent taverns which catered to minors, and because such taverns are checked more frequently by the police, the delinquents' preference for this type of tavern increased their chances of being apprehended and committed to an institution.

In general, taverns did not play as important a part as often assumed among teenagers. There were many teenagers in both groups who did not go to taverns. The chief source of alcoholic beverages for teenagers was the home, and drunkenness tended to occur in the home of friends. Many illegal methods were used by teenagers in both groups to obtain alcoholic beverages, a common method involved adults buying them.

In spite of laws prohibiting a minor from entering taverns, many tavernkeepers are of the opinion that the illegal patronage of minors is their gravest problem. In a Wisconsin survey tavernkeepers generally approved of the Age Certificate Law which provides penalties for minors who misrepresent their age and permits the tavernkeeper to ask for proof of age, but there was noticeable lack of agreement as to its workability and effectiveness (11, p. 624). About one-sixth of them were in favor of permitting minors 18 years of age or over to drink intoxicating liquor in taverns, while approximately half were in favor of raising the age limit to 21 for beer drinking. Some were of the opinion that both the law and a considerable proportion of the public consider teenage business detrimental to the best interests of society and that there exists a lack of cooperation on the part of some public leaders in working with tavernkeepers in attempting to solve the problem of minors drinking in taverns. About one-seventh indicated that minors should be punished more severely for entering taverns unlawfully, for falsifying their ages, and for drunken driving.

Summary and Conclusions

The existence of the thousands of taverns in Western society and the extensive patronage of these public drinking houses bears testimony to their role in contemporary society. Patronage alone, however, cannot convey the role of the tavern in its function of helping to fulfill many social and recreational needs. In spite of this contemporary importance little research has been done by sociologists, and the tavern has continued to be relegated by many persons to a position of low esteem. The ambivalence between an attitude of acceptance and use by large numbers of persons and an attitude of rejection and disregard by others raises several issues. The most important issue is whether or not the tavern is a detrimental institution, as its opponents claim, or a harmless one, as its proponents maintain. It has been accused of being a major factor in prostitution, gambling, alcoholism, crime, and delinquency and of being a threat to basic social institutions. Although the extent to which the tavern actually is associated with these activities can be determined conclusively only by further research on this neglected institution, a number of tentative conclusions can be drawn.

The tavern undoubtedly represents a stereotyped concept to both sides; opponents see nearly all taverns as being the Skid-Row type, while tavern defenders visualize them as the more harmless neighborhood variety. Actually both concepts are valid, as there are several types of taverns and there is wide variation within the various types. The neighborhood type quantitatively is far more numerous than the Skid-Row type.

Attitudes toward the tavern are influenced by one's position in the social structure as well as by one's tavern patronage. While a large proportion of the general population in all social strata drink alcoholic beverages, all do not go to taverns. Many consumers of alcohol, particularly those of the middle and upper classes, drink at home or at private clubs. While they may go to bars or night clubs, they seldom visit neighborhood taverns. Taverns are often not even located in the immediate vicinity of their homes.* Their children are likewise subject to comparatively little pressure to visit taverns since they have other social outlets. Moreover, the issue of acceptance or rejection of the tavern is a complicated problem, with dividing lines not as clearly drawn on the basis of wet and dry sentiments, or patronage or non-patronage, as one might presume. Generally patrons are more favorably disposed than non-patrons, although some non-patrons are favorably disposed to them while some patrons are antagonistic.† This means that in

---

* Public drinking houses, as well as package liquor stores, are disproportionately concentrated in lower class areas and constitute a highly visible symbol of the lower class way of life. There tends to be little distance between the place of residence and public facilities for alcohol consumption. This suggests that "people in the upper reaches of the social hierarchy might do most of their drinking at home or in downtown lounges and hotels, public places for imbibing being separated by some distance from place of residence." (15, p. 455.)

† See Macrory (11, pp. 609–615). Replies were received to a questionnaire from a random sample of 1,441 respondents in Dane County, Wisconsin. Among non-patrons, for example, there appears to be a lack of consensus in relation to the tavern. In this survey many charged the tavern with contributing to drunkenness, unhappy home life, loss of jobs, mental troubles, neglect of children by parents, crime, and personal demoralization. On the other hand, some recognized that the tavern offers social opportunities, that it is better than "bootlegging," that an occasional social drink is all right,

efforts to modify attitudes toward the tavern by both sides, the appeal cannot be made strictly to those who drink or do not drink or who patronize or do not patronize a tavern. These findings also suggest that covert attitudes and overt behavior do not always correspond.

The operation of a tavern and the character of the tavernkeeper and his bartender usually reflect the moral standards of the local community. Taverns located in areas with more conventional norms are likely to be well run and in compliance with legal regulations. Taverns located in the same neighborhoods as pawn shops, flop houses, and burlesque shows are more likely to be lax in enforcing regulations. The amusements or gambling allowed in a tavern of the Skid-Row and "honky-tonk" variety are but reflections of local public attitudes. A British study, for example, indicated that prostitutes largely worked only in those pubs located in the center of the city (12, p. 266). The problem, then, may not be the tavern but local social conditions.

In addition to the local area, the tavern also has reflected broader deviant forces operating in the larger community and in the general society. Even before Prohibition the manufacture and distribution of alcoholic beverages was in many instances associated with shady elements and with political corruption. "Following the repeal of national prohibition, the gangster and criminal element continued to be well-represented in the business of manufacturing, distributing and retailing of liquor. In some instances a number of notorious criminal gangs became a part of the industry, in an open manner. In other instances their interest was an undercover one" (14, p. 133).

In some large cities tavern operations have sometimes been taken over by racketeers who collaborate with wholesale liquor interests and corrupt politicians. The tavern's association with such illegal behavior is partly by chance and is not necessarily intrinsic to taverns generally, as British experience has indicated. Racketeering in America has operated in many forms of business, such as cleaning and dyeing, in addition to the tavern and liquor industry. In fact, it is likely that most of the deviant behavior attributed to the tavern would exist even if there were no taverns and would find expression through other institutions. The tavern cannot, therefore, be thought of as a cause of deviant behavior, although in some areas such deviant behavior may become intensified through tavern influences.

The more sordid aspects of the tavern problem appear to be, in part, outgrowths of negative and inconsistent attitudes toward tavern regulation. In a sense this represents a circular process, for the low status accorded the tavernkeeper, the stringent regulations under which he operates, and the general atmosphere of suspicion may have something to do with the results. Although tavernkeepers at times in the past have been highly respected

---

that the tavern is filling a place which some homes should fill, that the tavern offers relaxation and escape from the rush of the American way of life, and that bartenders by being good listeners are of help to worried patrons.

citizens and still play that role in some areas today, they generally refer to their present position in this country as one of "second-class citizens," socially as well as legally. They complain of "shakedowns" and other injustices which must be accepted as part of the business. In spite of the fact that tavernkeepers have frequent contact with juveniles and are responsible for keeping them out of taverns, they are often not considered respectable enough to serve on community-recreational, delinquency-prevention, or other civic committees. Such attitudes may, in some circumstances, result in attracting the precise type of person which regulations are trying to avoid, or put him in the position of being subject to inducements to violate the law.

The inconsistency of tavern regulations can be illustrated by the rigid exclusion from taverns of anyone under 18 or 21, a regulation which draws a sharp distinction between adults and juveniles. This demarcation makes many adolescents feel that taverns are associated with adult status, a sort of *rite de passage,* thus encouraging their efforts to enter taverns surreptitiously and to drink illegally the alcohol which they associate with adult taverns.* It is debatable whether the encouragement of family participation in the tavern, as in some European countries, might alter this situation.

There are many other regulatory inconsistencies. The moral backgrounds of tavernkeepers are usually checked before a license is granted, but not that of a soda fountain clerk or garage mechanic, who may have closer associations with juveniles. Paroled prisoners are almost always forbidden to enter taverns, yet they are often virtually the only places where they can be reintegrated into the normal society of the people of their local neighborhoods.

Evidence indicates that although people patronize taverns to drink, other factors are equally important. Any reasonable approach to the tavern problem must take these non-drinking functions into account. The reality of such an approach will allow us to proceed in two possible, although by no means mutually exclusive, directions: (*a*) the establishment of substitutes for the tavern, and (*b*) acceptance and improvement of the tavern.

The recognition of this large social and non-alcoholic function of the tavern might result in the broad expansion of soft-drink institutions, such as soda fountains and milk bars, or community centers to serve the same purpose. Such proposals fail to take into account the role that alcohol plays in Western culture or the long historic development of the public drinking

---

* Excluding the minor or late teenager from the tavern without providing alternative places for social participation may mean that such persons may try to gain entrance to the tavern anyway, or they may purchase liquor and consume it under unsupervised conditions with possibly a higher incidence of drunkenness and other immorality. Such a rule, moreover, where applied to the 18-to-21-year-old groups, is far from consistent with other aspects of society. Persons of this age can legally work, operate cars, enter military service, and often marry without consent (if they are girls); except for those going to college, they may often be more or less completely on their own but still not be allowed to enter a tavern. In the case of dating, the 21-year-old rule presents the anomaly of a man being forced to date a girl his own age or older if he wishes to avoid a legal violation in entering a tavern.

house in most Western societies. The use of alcohol is associated with social amenities, many ceremonies, and the conduct of certain business activities. While the phrase "let's have a drink" may mean "let's go to the tavern and talk," the substitution among adults of ice-cream, coffee, or soft-drink places for these social amenities is not likely to be extensive. While substitute arrangements may increase, they are particularly handicapped by the type of beverage, which does not encourage prolonged consumption, and by early closing hours.

Another solution might be the acceptance of the tavern as a part of our drinking culture and its necessary and useful social function. Because of motion pictures, radio, television, and spectator-sports events, people are increasingly playing an inactive role in commercial recreation. One might say that the active and personal social participation which takes place in many taverns is beneficial. In urban areas, they appear to be meeting certain basic social-psychological needs of their patrons. As urbanization has increased impersonality, mobility, formal controls, and individualism in everyday living, men have been hindered in their attempts to adjust satisfactorily to urban life. Furthermore, the monotony of many types of work and the competitive drive of the entire industrial system, with its emphasis on materialism, often result in frustrations. These characteristics of modern urban life may explain, in part at least, the important role of the tavern in contemporary society.

Moreover, a decline of tavern participation and the trend toward package sales in stores and beer depots may mean more solitary consumption of alcohol, either in the home or under unsupervised conditions. Instead of institutionalized social drinking in taverns, alcohol may increasingly be consumed for the sake of intoxication alone.

The tavern should be made a subject for intensive study by sociologists, social psychologists, and recreational workers. As an institution its importance in the lives of Western society can no longer be denied or neglected. Other aspects of the tavern should be studied. These would include the following: the history and function of the modern tavern; the differences in the role of public drinking houses in various societies; the relation between public drinking houses of the West, the coffee houses of the Middle East, and the tea houses of the Orient; and the relation of the tavern to forms of deviant behavior such as juvenile delinquency, crime, alcoholism, marital maladjustment, parental neglect, and sexual promiscuity. The tavern is also an excellent object for small-group research. There is need for studies of social interaction in neighborhood taverns, resort taverns, ethnic taverns, hotel bars, cocktail lounges, and the various other subvarieties found in modern urban life.

References

1. *Anti-Barmaid Laws: A Survey of Laws, Ordinances and Regulations in States and Municipalities Governing the Employment of Women and Bartenders,* Anti-Prohi-

bition Division, Department of Research and Education, Hotel and Restaurant Employers and Bartenders International Union (A.F.L.), Cincinnati, Ohio, December 1948.

2. Bernard, Bertram M., *Liquor Laws of the Forty-Eight States and the District of Columbia,* New York: Oceana Publications, 1949.

3. Chandler, Margaret K., *The Social Organization of Workers in a Rooming House Area,* unpublished doctoral dissertation, University of Chicago, 1948.

4. Clinard, Marshall B., *Sociology of Deviant Behavior,* New York: Holt, Rinehart and Winston, 1957.

5. Cromwell, Walter, *The Tavern in Community Life,* Juvenile Protective Association of Chicago, 1939.

6. Dinitz, Simon, *The Relation of the Tavern to the Drinking Phases of Alcoholics,* unpublished doctoral dissertation, University of Wisconsin, 1951.

7. Fagan, Edward R., *The Tavern and the Juvenile Delinquent,* unpublished master's thesis, University of Wisconsin, 1953.

8. Gottlieb, David, "The Neighborhood Tavern and the Cocktail Lounge: A Study of Class Differences," *Amer. J. Sociol.,* **62**:550–562, 1957.

9. Keller, Mark, and Vera Efron, "The Prevalence of Alcoholism," *Quart. J. Stud. Alc.,* **16**:622, 1955.

10. Macrory, Boyd E., *A Sociological Analysis of the Role and Functions of the Tavern in the Community,* unpublished doctoral dissertation, University of Wisconsin, 1950.

11. ———, "The Tavern and the Community," *Quart. J. Stud. Alc.,* **13**:609–637, 1952.

12. Mass Observation, *The Pub and the People,* London: Victor Gollancz, 1943.

13. Moore, E. C., "The Social Value of the Saloon," *Amer. J. Sociol.,* 3:1–12, 1897.

14. Peterson, Virgil W., "Vitalizing Liquor Control," *J. Criminal Law, Criminol., Police Sci.,* **40**:133, 1948.

15. Pfautz, Harold W., and Robert W. Hyde, "The Ecology of Alcohol in the Local Community," *Quart. J. Stud. Alc.,* **21**:447–456, 1960.

chapter 16

The significance of roles and norms in the small group for individual behavioral changes while drinking *

Kettil Bruun

Research on alcohol problems requires an interdisciplinary orientation. For the individual researcher this means keeping an open mind with respect to problems outside his own particular field; but this demand must not prevent him from following up new theories in his own sphere. It is regrettable to note that sociologists concerned with research on alcohol have paid little attention to newer trends in sociology.

The most revolutionary line of development in sociology during the last 20 years has been the so-called small-group research. Although recognition of the significance of the small group in the formation of norms and behavior is old, only the methodological developments of recent decades have made it possible to use the small group in empirical research in a fruitful way. The small-group researchers themselves, however, have not been the only ones to emphasize the significance of the small group. Research workers at Columbia University have observed in their numerous studies of political behavior that the effect of propaganda and mass media depends to a large extent on how stimuli are interpreted in small groups. Their results have led Katz and Lazarsfeld (2) to speak about "the rediscovery of small groups." Empirical data from research at the Finnish Foundation for Alcohol Studies also show the significance of small groups in drinking behavior. Thus Kuusi (3) has shown that more than two-thirds of the drinking occasions among men in Finnish rural districts involve groups of two to six persons, and

---

* This chapter first appeared as an article in the *Quarterly Journal of Studies on Alcohol*, **20**:53–64, 1959. The original article has been reprinted here with only slight modification.

Allardt (1) has demonstrated that while conformity between drinking habits and drinking norms is the rule, identification with a group is a variable on the basis of which it is possible to explain conflict between an individual's norms and his behavior.

Drinking thus generally takes place in small groups, and within these groups drinking norms are formed. It is assumed that these norms (rules of behavior) may be used in explaining why the group behaves homogeneously in certain respects. In addition, however, role differentiation (a division of labor) develops in the group, causing variations within it. In the sociological study of drinking behaviors, basic similarities and variations in behavior should be explicable against the background of these norms and role differentiation. In the present communication an attempt will be made, employing the results of an empirical study and using the theory of the small group as a starting point, to explain certain hitherto undefined variations in behavior under the effect of alcohol.

In an experimental study Takala, Pihkanen, and Markkanen (7) have shown how the "interaction profile," as measured according to Bales' categories (4), changes remarkably after drinking. Under the effects of alcohol the proportion of reactions related to attempts at problem solving (category B) decreased, while the proportion of negative reactions indicating aggression, antagonism, disagreement, and the like (category D) increased.* However, there was also a difference in the rate of change, related to the type of beverage; at the same blood alcohol level the increase in the proportion of negative reactions was significantly greater when the beverage consumed was brandy than when it was beer.† Takala proposed that physiological responses related to such factors as different volumes of liquid and substances in the beverages (other than alcohol) were responsible for this difference.

This explanation of the different effects of beer and brandy may be quite sound. However, it cannot explain the fact that certain individuals, according to Bales' negative reaction categories, behave rather alike under the effect of brandy and beer while others have a considerably higher proportion of negative reactions under the effect of brandy, though the blood alcohol level is kept constant. It is postulated here that an explanation of these individual differences would also provide an answer to a very crucial problem of alcohol research: Why does the same blood alcohol level affect one person one way and another similar person another way? It is suggested that small-group theory will help to throw considerable light on this prob-

---

* Bales' own definitions of these categories are as follows. B: "Gives suggestion, direction, implying autonomy for other. Gives opinion, evaluation, analysis, expresses feeling, wish. Gives orientation, information, repeats, clarifies, confirms." D: "Disagrees, shows passive rejection, formality, withholds help. Shows tension increase, asks for help, withdraws Out of Field. Shows antagonism, deflates others' status, defends or asserts self."

† The Finnish beer in question is 3.6 per cent alcohol (by weight), the blended brandy 32.6 per cent alcohol.

lem, i.e., that structural characteristics of groups and role differentiation within groups can serve as explanations, at least in part, of such individual differences.

In accordance with this latter point of view, the data of Takala, Pihkanen, and Markkanen have been re-analyzed and supplemented in order to test the following hypotheses drawn from small-group research (5).

I. The proportion of negative reactions after drinking brandy, compared to drinking beer, tends to increase:

a. less among individuals who are "central" persons in the groups than among individuals who are relatively isolated;

b. more among individuals with relatively high identification with the group;

c. more among individuals whose attitude toward aggression is relatively permissive.

Method

In order to test these hypotheses the individuals used in the experiment by Takala, Pihkanen, and Markkanen were interviewed with a schedule of sociometric and attitude questions. Unfortunately these data were not obtained until about three years after the experimental work was completed. However, the fact that a vast majority of the interviewees were still employees of the Finnish State Alcohol Monopoly at the time of the interviews, as they had been during the experiment, indicates at least some stability in the relationships among these informants, which is a necessary condition of this study.

Before testing the hypotheses certain features of the original experiment must be reviewed. A total of forty men were studied. These were divided into eight groups of four to six members, each constituted so as to be socially and culturally as homogeneous as possible. The interaction patterns of the resulting eight groups were studied during two sessions: one a beer-drinking and the other a brandy-drinking session. The program of a session is illustrated by the diagram in Figure 1. A session thus included two discussion periods and a problem task, each limited by time. To determine the blood alcohol level chemically, blood samples were taken twice during each session. The mean first blood alcohol level, drawn between 90 and 120 minutes from the time drinking started, was 0.091 per cent after beer and 0.095 per cent after brandy; the mean second blood alcohol level, drawn 90 min. later was 0.144 per cent after beer and 0.146 per cent after brandy. Even during the first discussion, when the blood alcohol level was comparatively low, there were significant changes in behavior.

In order to test the present hypotheses the subjects were divided into two reaction categories: those with a much increased proportion of negative reactions and those with a relatively constant proportion of negative reactions as between beer and brandy sessions. This dichotomy was made so that the categories would be as equal as possible in size. In each of the eight

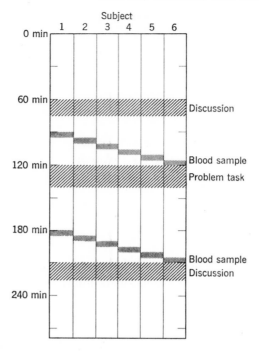

Figure 1. The program of the interaction situations.

experimental groups there is at least one individual in each reaction category. Next the two categories were compared with the sociometric data obtained from the interviews. These data are used as measures of role differentiation, which is determined by the subjects' responses to the three questions: Which person from your drinking group would you prefer to: (a) go out and drink with? (b) work with? (c) have as your foreman? Labeled as "central persons" are all individuals chosen more than once, and as "isolates," those not chosen at all in response to the three questions. Thus sociometric measurements of centrality and isolation were obtained, i.e., individuals central or isolated in respect to drinking, work, and foremanship.

Results

The purpose of Table 1 is not to test hypothesis Ia, that the proportion of negative reactions after drinking brandy, compared with drinking beer, tends to increase less among central persons than among isolates, but rather to test which sociometric criteria can be combined. The table shows very clearly that the group "drinking only" differs from all other groups.

The difference is meaningful, however, only if it can be explained in terms of sociological theory. Recent results in research concerned as well with the family as with small groups indicate the importance of role differentiation in groups, corresponding to the concepts instrumental and expressive leaders (4). In the family the father may generally be seen as the instrumental leader and the mother as the expressive. The same differentia-

TABLE 1

Role Differentiation in Groups and Increase in Proportion of Negative Reactions in Brandy over Beer Sessions [a]

Increase in Proportion of Negative Reactions	Drinking Only	Work or Foreman Only	Work and Foreman	Drinking and Work and/or Foreman
Central Persons				
High increase	3	2	1	1
Low or no increase	1	3	2	3
Isolates				
High increase	0	3	4	6
Low or no increase	4	1	2	5

[a] Figure 2 explains the sociometric groups in the table.

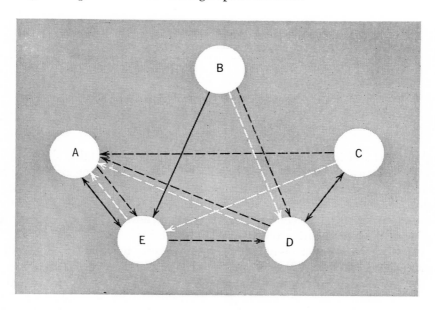

Figure 2. Sociometric choices in respect to drinking, work, and foremanship in a group of five individuals. Solid lines: choices in respect to drinking; black-dash lines: choices in respect to work; white-dash lines: choices in respect to foremanship. E: central in respect to drinking only; A and D: central in respect to work and foremanship; B: isolate in respect to drinking, work, and foremanship; C: isolate in respect to work and foremanship.

tion, however, seems to hold also for small groups in general, and the family may therefore, as Bales suggests, be seen as a special case of the small group. Because drinking, as shown by Takala, Pihkanen, and Markkanen (7) increases the emotionality of the interaction, it seems reasonable to regard the central persons in respect to "drinking only" as expressive leaders, and other central persons as instrumental leaders. Thus the difference in Table 1 is meaningful and it is important to use that distinction in the analysis below.

This distinction having been made, hypothesis I*a* may be tested, and in Table 2 the increase in the proportion of negative reactions among cen-

TABLE 2

Increase in Proportion of Negative Reactions in Brandy over Beer Sessions among Central Persons and Isolates

Increase in Proportion of Negative Reactions	Central Persons, Drinking Only	Isolates, Drinking Only
High increase	3	0
Low or no increase	1	4
	Central Persons,[a] Other Criteria	Isolates, Other Criteria
High increase	3	12
Low or no increase	7	7

[a] Individuals who were central in respect to one criterion but isolate in respect to another were eliminated.

tral persons and isolates is compared. The first part of the table shows how central persons, defined by an expressive criterion ("drinking only"), tend to exhibit an increase of negative reactions in brandy as against beer sessions, while all isolates have a low or no increase. In the latter part of the table the pattern is that central persons tend to show less of an increase in the proportion of negative reactions than isolates.

Although the number of individuals studied was too small to allow statistically acceptable conclusions, the trend is in the direction of hypothesis I*a* stating that central persons increase their proportion of negative reactions less than isolates in brandy as compared to beer sessions. The support is given, however, only in regard to central persons and isolates defined by instrumental criteria, and a contrary pattern seems to hold for centrals and isolates defined by an expressive criterion. The results may be interpreted in the following way.

According to Takala, Pihkanen, and Markkanen, reduction in the control of behavior is inevitable in a drinking situation and the reduction seems to be greater with brandy than with beer. This reduction of control is represented by an increase in the degree of emotionality. Central persons defined by instrumental criteria hold their position in the group because they live up to the expectations of the group in relatively controlled situations. Therefore they tend to behave in a controlled way also in a more emotional situation. The isolates defined by instrumental criteria, however, tend to increase their emotionality. Inasmuch as the groups were formed by individuals who to a certain degree were used to working together, the isolation may indicate a relatively stable position in relation to the group. The isolation may cause frustration; and the increasing emotionality, manifested by negative reactions, may be seen as an answer to this frustration.

Before turning to central persons and isolates defined by an emotional criterion (drinking), it must be stressed that the sociometric choices were made after the drinking situations. This means that the choices probably were influenced by experience with the behavior of the various individuals while under the influence of alcohol. It may therefore be assumed that expressive central persons (central persons—drinking only) are those who were able to meet the expectations of the group in this particular situation. Isolates, however, defined by this criterion, are individuals who were not able to increase their emotionality in a drinking situation. This interpretation is indeed hypothetical but if correct it would have an important bearing on the functions of drinking and warrant studies of the central person in drinking situations.

Unfortunately hypothesis I*b* could not be tested because too many subjects (29 per cent) refused to answer questions designed to measure group cohesiveness. Hypothesis I*c*, concerning attitudes, will therefore be considered next. From the schedule, three scales are obtained, prepared by the H-technique, a special application of the Guttman technique (7). The items used in preparing these scales, the number of items omitted in their preparation, and the coefficients of reproducibility of each scale are listed below.

Scale 1: Permissiveness in Respect to Physical Aggression Items

A real fight now and then is good for a man.
An intelligent man settles things by reasoning and not by force.
To attack another person is under no circumstances permissible.
It is better to hit than to make futile threats.
There are occasions where mischief-makers should be taken by the scruff of the neck and thrown out.
It is good for young boys to get into a real fight now and then.
It is better to give vent to one's rage in violent action than to remain brooding over it.

Getting involved in a hand-to-hand fight is a sign of immaturity.

A proper thrashing would do certain disagreeable fellows a lot of good.

Three items omitted. Reproducibility $(R) = .98$.

Scale 2: Permissiveness in Respect to Verbal Aggression Items

It is good to state things in plain terms without heeding the consequences.

Swearing shows a lack of good manners.

A friend whom you cannot abuse to his face isn't worth a dime.

It is often better to hide one's rage than to show it openly.

There are certain people one simply has to swear at.

Too often people cause unhappiness by being too outspoken.

There are no situations in which it is allowable to call another person a liar.

Persons who are apt to get involved in arguments should keep apart from other people.

One item omitted. $R = .95$.

Scale 3: Permissiveness in Respect to Aggression while Intoxicated Items

Things that people do when they are drunk are forgivable.

An honest man must not defend his foolish behavior by saying that it happened when he was drunk.

Having disagreements when drunk should not influence true friendship.

It is more brutal of a man to beat his wife while he is drunk than to do it when he is sober.

One must not do things when drunk that are unfitting when one is sober.

If you do a person a wrong it is twice as bad to do it under the influence of alcohol.

Intoxication is to be looked upon as an extenuating circumstance in manslaughter.

One item omitted. $R = .92$.

The Pearsonian correlation for scales 1 and 2 is .47, for scales 1 and 3 it is .37, and for scales 2 and 3 it is .17.

The number of individuals is too small to permit any definite conclusions about the unidimensionality of the scales. The fact that items were omitted in preparing all the scales may be considered as a weakness. However, the correlations and the high R values may permit the assumption that three scalable and rather independent dimensions of attitudes measuring the permissiveness of aggressive behavior have been found. The scalability means that individuals can be ranged along continua, measuring degrees of permissiveness of aggression (physical, verbal, and while intoxicated). In these scales, a low value indicates relative permissiveness in respect to aggression while a high value indicates a non-permissive attiude.

In Table 3 the scales and the degree of increase in the proportion of negative reactions in brandy over beer sessions have been cross-tabulated.

TABLE 3

Increase in Proportion of Negative Reactions in Brandy over Beer Sessions Related to Three Scales Measuring Permissiveness of Aggression

Increase in Proportion of Negative Reactions	Individuals Permissive (scale values 0, 1)	Individuals Non-permissive (scale values 2, 3)
Permissiveness in respect to physical aggression		
High increase	5	10
Low or no increase	7	13
$\chi^2 = .07; P < .80$		
Permissiveness in respect to verbal aggression		
High increase	13	4
Low or no increase	9	9
$\chi^2 = 1.61; P < .25$		
Permissiveness in respect to aggression while intoxicated		
High increase	9	8
Low or no increase	3	15
$\chi^2 = 3.62; P < .10$		

The only nearly significant relation is between scale 3 and the increase in the proportion of negative reactions. Thus a non-permissive attitude toward aggression during intoxication appears to inhibit the increase in the proportion of negative reactions. The same tendency, although very weak, appears in the case of verbal aggression. But permissiveness in respect to physical aggression seems to bear no relationship to the increase in the proportion of negative reactions.

The fact that individuals permissive in respect to aggression while intoxicated tend to increase the proportion of their negative reactions in brandy as compared to beer sessions indicates a conformity with their norms in this particular situation. However, there are also individuals who behave in conflict with their norms and these are extremely interesting for the student of the sociology of drinking.

Discussion

The present results indicate that sociological factors are capable of explaining some changes in the behavior of individuals under the influence of alcohol. The results, however, are mainly suggestive for further research on this problem. For instance, the following questions are fundamental: What influence will the nature of the group have on behavior while drinking? How will the group structure change during intoxication? How does the pressure to drink or abstain work in groups? How do different individuals perceive their own and others' behavior in the course of drinking?

These questions have hardly been touched by alcohol research up to the present. The most fruitful way to tackle such problems is probably through small-group research. The following reasons may be given. In the first place, small-group research offers the possibility of both experimental studies and studies of real life situations. In the second place, research on alcohol has heavily stressed the important fact that drinking mostly takes place precisely in small groups (1, 3). Third and finally, small groups are important units in changing behavior and in building up systems of norms (2), and in respect to drinking there are in a great many societies important norm conflicts which will be reflected in small groups.

Summary

The value of putting into practice in research on alcohol problems the theories of the small group developed during the last decades has been emphasized. In order to demonstrate the possibility of explaining individual differences in reactions under the influence of alcohol on the basis of these theories, a re-analysis was performed of material presented originally by Takala, Pihkanen, and Markkanen. The latter, in experiments with 40 persons in 8 groups, showed by systematic observations with the aid of Bales' method that negative reactions increased strongly under the effect of alcohol in such a way that the increase was considerably more noticeable after the consumption of brandy than of beer, though the blood alcohol level was kept constant. By interviewing the subjects afterward and by asking them sociometric and attitude questions, the present inquiry sought to explain why certain individuals had approximately the same proportion of negative reactions during the beer and brandy sessions, while others showed a considerable increase during the brandy sessions. The findings are thought also to illustrate why the same amount of alcohol influences different persons in different ways.

The following hypotheses were formulated: The proportion of negative reactions after drinking brandy, compared to drinking beer, tends to increase less among individuals who are "central" in the groups than among individuals who are relatively isolated and more among individuals whose attitude toward aggression is relatively permissive.

The size of the sample was too limited to permit definite conclusions. The following general results appeared to be explicable, however, in terms of sociological theory.

1. The position of the individual in the group seems to have an important effect on the increased proportion of negative reactions in brandy over beer sessions. According to instrumental criteria central persons tend to increase the proportion of negative reactions less than isolates. According to an ex-

pressive criterion (drinking) the contrary is true; central persons increase the proportion of negative reaction, isolates do not.

2. Individuals with a relatively permissive attitude toward aggression while under the effect of alcohol tend to increase the proportion of negative reactions more than others. Thus the norms of the individual seem to have an important bearing on his behavior while under the influence of alcohol.

These findings were independent of individual differences in the blood alcohol level.

References

1. Allardt, Erik, "Drinking Norms and Drinking Habits," in *Drinking and Drinkers,* Helsinki: Finnish Foundation for Alcohol Studies, 1957, pp. 49–56.

2. Katz, Elihu, and Paul Lazarsfeld, *Personal Influence,* Glencoe, Ill.: Free Press, 1955.

3. Kuusi, Pekka, *Alcohol Sales Experiment in Rural Finland,* Helsinki: Finnish Foundation for Alcohol Studies, 1957.

4. Parsons, Talcott, and Freed Bales, *Family, Socialization, and Interaction Process,* Glencoe, Ill.: Free Press, 1955.

5. Riecken, H. and G. C. Homans, "Psychological Aspects of Social Structure," *in* G. Lindsey (Ed.), *Handbook of Social Psychology,* Cambridge, Mass.: Addison-Wesley, 1954.

6. Stouffer, Samuel, et al., "A Technique for Improving Cumulative Scales," *Public Opinion Quart.,* **16**:273–291, 1952.

7. Takala, Martti, *The Effects of Distilled and Brewed Beverages: A Physiological, Neurological and Psychological Study,* Helsinki: Finnish Foundation for Alcohol Studies, 1957.

THE GENESIS
AND PATTERNING
OF ALCOHOLISM

DEFINITION, EXTENT, AND ECOLOGY

Introductory Note. Demographic and ecological studies of the pathological aspects of drinking behavior have been handicapped by the lack of an adequate and well-accepted definition of alcoholism. This lack of consensus regarding definition is dramatically illustrated in a current study (5) which is investigating social agency and health experts' conceptions of the alcoholic, his disease and its etiology. Three major themes are used by these experts in their definitions. They view the alcoholic in terms of: the *consequences of drinking* for himself or for others—that is, the social, economic, and physical effects of indulgence in alcoholic beverages; the nature of his *drinking behavior*—that is, characterizations of frequency, time of day, presence of companions, and amount ingested; and his *response to alcohol* —that is, the physiological and psychological reactions to the ingestion of alcoholic beverages. These experts, chiefly from psychiatry, social work, nursing, internal medicine, and vocational rehabilitation, seldom stressed all three themes; in fact, the majority were concerned with characterizing the alcoholic in terms of basic economic and social functioning.

Mark Keller, in Chapter 17, grapples with this problem of definition. Finding existing definitions of alcoholism to be inadequate for epidemiological purposes, Keller aims to construct a definition of practical value. Although it may be said that indices to measure the "injury to the drinker's health or to his social or economic functioning" are missing, there is the definite potentiality for operationalizing this qualitative statement.

Having considered the problem of definition, Keller then turns to the problem of estimating prevalence of alcoholism, which is complex and at present shrouded with uncertainty. Historically, prevalence rates have been obtained from the Jellinek Estimation Formula which posits a rather consistent relationship between inebriety and deaths from liver cirrhosis. This formula has been severely criticized recently by John Seeley (4) and Berthold Brenner (1), but Keller maintains that the underlying theory of the formula is sound. From evidence based on statistics of alcohol consumption and numbers of drinkers, Keller reasons that current alcoholic rate estimates have approximate validity but still lack the desired precision.

In Chapter 18, John Seeley presents an interesting ecological analysis of alcoholism which is based on alleged alcoholism rates developed by Keller. Aware that these rates may have deficiencies, Seeley assumes that they are some regular transformation of those rates that would appear if valid techniques for measurement existed. If this is the case, the correlation of .8 which he obtains between population potential and alleged alcoholism rates for the states under analysis is highly significant. From this he establishes that population potential studies can predict expected rates of alcoholism. Population potential, as Seeley indicates, reflects factors of social complexity and urbanism, previously discussed by Bacon in Chapter 5.

Furthermore, Seeley contends that abstinence sentiments toward alcohol as measured by votes of the states on repeal of the Prohibition Amendment do not predict alcoholism. We, however, would desire a better measure of the influence of sentiments in the etiology of alcoholism than voting in America on repeal of the Eighteenth Amendment in the early 1930's.*

The previous paragraphs point up deficiencies in the alcoholism rates as presently constructed. Instead of stating rates per thousand drinkers (the risk population), current researchers state alcoholism rates in crude form —per thousand adults, aged 20 and over, for non-standardized populations. The wide discrepancy between "low" alcoholism rates in South Carolina and Iowa, states with large abstinence groups, and "high" alcoholism rates in Nevada and California, states with small abstinence groups, might partially disappear if rates were constructed on a standardized population only for those who use alcoholic beverages. But this remains an impossibility until more systematic information is collected on drinking behavior by age, sex, race, and geographic location.†

* Voting in these elections, since it involved differential participation by class, racial, and ethnic groups, is not the most valid measure of abstinence. Moreover, where cultural cleavage regarding abstinence is great, alcoholism rates for those who drink might be high. (In Chapter 13, Straus and Bacon's data on Mormon students who drink lend provisional support to this position, as does Ullman's research, by implication, in Chapter 14.)

† The earlier work of John Riley and Charles Marden (3) in obtaining statistical survey materials on drinking behavior by socio-cultural categories in the 1940's has recently been advanced by the work of Harold Mulford and Donald Miller (2) for the state of Iowa. Currently the California Department of Health is engaged in a three-year epidemiological study of the drinking patterns of a "normal" population and will relate these findings to the socio-cultural and economic characteristics of the sample. But as valuable as these last two studies are, they are necessarily limited in time and space. These studies point up the need for a new and more comprehensive national survey of drinking practices.

Finally, Chapter 19 by Arthur Pearl, Robert Buechley, and Wendell Lipscomb takes a critical look at cirrhosis mortality rates from which alcoholism rates are derived. The study areas are three metropolitan centers, and the unit of analysis is the census tract. These researchers find a strong inverse relationship between occupational level and cirrhosis mortality as well as an inverse relationship between family size and cirrhosis mortality, the degree of which is reduced when adjusted for the effect of occupational level. Thus, either liver cirrhosis mortality for higher economic groupings is underreported or class differences strongly influence rates of alcoholism. Their study indicates that more systematic investigation is needed of liver cirrhosis cases on which alcoholism rates are constructed before any credence can be given to the popular assumption that alcoholism is equally distributed among the social classes in American society.

The findings of Pearl, Buechley, and Lipscomb cast considerable doubt on the significance of alleged differential city rates of alcoholism. When their studied cities are arbitrarily assigned approximately equal size, or the total metropolitan areas are compared, much of the difference in alcoholism rates disappears. Thus, differential city rates, in their view, are partially functions of the nature of political boundaries. However, more systematic study of the ecology of cirrhosis mortality as well as the demographic characteristics of its victims should provide a definitive answer to this question.

References

1. Brenner, Berthold, "Estimating the Prevalence of Alcoholism: Toward a Modification of the Jellinek Formula," *Quart. J. Stud. Alc.*, 20:255–260, 1959.
2. Mulford, Harold, and Donald Miller, "Drinking in Iowa: II, The Extent of Drinking and Selected Sociocultural Categories," *Quart. J. Stud. Alc.*, 21:26–39, 1960.
3. Riley, John, and Charles F. Marden, "The Social Pattern of Alcoholic Drinking," *Quart. J. Stud. Alc.*, 8:265–273, 1947.
4. Seeley, John, "Estimating the Prevalence of Alcoholism: A Critical Analysis of the Jellinek Formula," *Quart. J. Stud. Alc.*, 20:245–254, 1959.
5. Sterne, Muriel, and David J. Pittman, "Concepts of Alcoholism Among Community Agency Personnel," unpublished paper delivered at the Midwest Sociological Society, St. Louis, Missouri, April 21–23, 1960.

chapter 17

The definition
of alcoholism
and the estimation
of its prevalence[*]

Mark Keller

The Problem of Definition

If "alcoholics" are to be counted, or the prevalence of "alcoholism" is to
be measured or estimated, obviously an agreement about the meaning of
these terms is needed. What is alcoholism, or who is an alcoholic?

The definition of alcoholism (and alcoholics) has long been marked by
uncertainty, conflict, and ambiguity. This was made evident in the Bowman and Jellinek collection of explicit and implicit definitions two decades
ago (3). The same condition is exposed by Marconi's more recent review
(28) of the historical conception of alcoholism and in other critical discussions (20, 25). The lack of firm definition is not a minor inconvenience in
the alcohol problems field but has sometimes constituted a major impedi-
ment to understanding and progress. In view of heightened interest in alcoholism exhibited by the public health agencies, it seems opportune to try
to formulate a definition suited particularly to the needs of epidemiology.
The accumulation of knowledge over the past two decades provides a foundation of understanding which now promises better success than could have
been expected in previous attempts.

It is necessary to begin by distinguishing between two major problem
areas connected with the use of alcoholic beverages. The first is that of
drinking-related misbehaviors. This includes drunkenness (in many law

[*] This chapter was written especially for this book. The section, "The Problem of
Definition," with minor revision, has also been published as "The Definition of Alcoholism," in the *Quarterly Journal of Studies on Alcohol*, **21**:125–134, 1960.

codes, "public intoxication"). Some but not all of the obtrusive offenders by drunkenness are alcoholics. It includes also automobile driving while "under the influence of alcohol" (below the level of definite intoxication) and many other socially condemned and personally injurious activities. The second problem area is that of alcoholism, a disease. Social scientists as well as biological scientists are interested in both classes of problems. The present discussion, however, is concerned only with the second—with alcoholism.

The assertion that alcoholism is a disease suggests that its primary definition might be sought in medical dictionaries. One of the foremost works of this class has it that "alcoholism" is "alcohol poisoning; the morbid effects of excess in alcoholic drinks."*

This definition indicates that alcoholism is caused by excessive drinking, but provides no criterion of excess, no guide to the morbid effects, and no hint of possible causation underlying the excess. It also takes no account of a different sort of etiological concept, held by many physicians and perhaps by most psychologists and psychiatrists—a concept involving the constitution, personality, and sometimes even the environment of the individual upon whom alcohol may act. At any rate, such a definition can hardly help anyone who would wish to identify alcoholics for the purpose of counting. It is not entirely useless, however. It hints that popular slogans may reflect a medical truth: there is such a disease as alcoholism.

The relevant criteria for a medical definition may be sought in another type of authority, the American Medical Association's *Standard Nomenclature of Diseases and Operations* (31). The classificatory scheme of this master work of medical systematics locates every recognized disease in the organism topographically, to the extent known, and names its etiology to the extent known. Alcoholism (31, p. 91) is "located" as a disease of the "psychobiologic unit." It is assigned etiologically to the "disorders of psychogenic origin or without clearly defined tangible cause or structural change"; more specifically still, to a category of "sociopathic personality disturbances" (which includes such disorders as antisocial and dissocial reactions, and sexual deviations), one of which is "addiction." The addiction subcategory is further divided into "000-x641 Alcoholism" and (other) "drug addiction."

Quite a lot may be learned from this exact classification. Alcoholism is a disease with a history older than the resolutions of medical societies granting it diplomatic recognition as such. It is a disease in the category of addictions. It is a "personality disorder," more specifically of the "sociopathic" variety—apparently a group of behaviors characterized by their obnoxiousness to society. It is a disease of no definitely known etiology. It is not marked by any recognized structural change. Its origin is presumed to be in the "psyche"; at any rate there is no established causative agent. Obvi-

---

* Dorland's *Illustrated Medical Dictionary*, 23d ed. (Philadelphia: Saunders, 1957). Two rival contemporary medical dictionaries (Gould's and Stedman's) do not offer more useful or more meaningful definitions of alcoholism.

ously, alcohol is not accepted as the causative agent. This psychologically oriented conception is in direct conflict with the definitions of the leading medical dictionaries.*

The systematists of the *Standard Nomenclature* have taken the position that the disease alcoholism comes from the man rather than from the bottle, but the superiority and validity of this conception cannot be assumed merely because it appears more sophisticated. A World Health Organization committee of specialists (41) has held that alcohol is a compound whose pharmacological action is somewhere between that of addiction-producing drugs (as morphine) and habit-forming ones (as nicotine). At least it is not ruled out that alcohol may be addictive in its physiological or pharmacological action, and there is some suggestive experimental evidence of this (9). Thus an alternative (more "physiological") form of diagnosis must be considered, and indeed the responsible committees and editors have this under consideration for the next edition of the *Standard Nomenclature*.†

These conceptions allow the conclusion that alcoholism is a chronic disease ‡ and that it is etiologically associated either with personality deviation or with the pharmacological properties of alcohol, and perhaps with both either simultaneously or successively. Based on these premises and on a review of medical and allied writings descriptive of observed symptomatology and behaviors of persons diagnosed as alcoholics—and with concern also for the lexicographic problems—the following is suggested as a medical definition:

> Alcoholism is a psychogenic dependence on or a physiological addiction to ethanol,§ manifested by the inability of the alcoholic consistently to control either the start of drinking or its termination once started, owing to (or caused by) . . .

* It parallels the official classification of the American Psychiatric Association (1).

† Since this was written, the 5th edition of the *Standard Nomenclature* has appeared (1961) and in this volume "000-x641 Alcoholism" has vanished as a diagnostic term. Its place has been taken (p. 112) by "000-x641 Alcohol addiction chronic." The teasing implication of "chronic," that there might be an "Alcohol addiction acute," is left to the user of the new edition to work out. Apparently no other addiction is "chronic," however; thus, for recording opium addiction, there is only "000-x642 Drug addiction."

‡ Alcohol intoxication (drunkenness) or acute sequels of alcoholic debauches (such as delirium tremens), as well as chronic diseases associated with or caused by alcoholism (such as cirrhosis of the liver or chronic brain syndromes), are dealt with in other appropriate divisions and sections of the *Standard Nomenclature*.

§ Specifying ethanol in this formulation may seem to exclude the cases of reported preference for methanol or still other compounds. More faulty still is the absence of recognition that many "alcoholics" may be dependent on intoxication rather than addicted to a particular substance. The suggested model, however, fulfills the practical purpose of its design. If it is desired to provide for other possibilities, the language can be suitably modified—e.g., "Alcoholism is a psychogenic dependence on intoxication or a physiological addiction to ethanol or similar intoxicants, manifested by . . ." The concept of dependence on intoxication would, of course, open to question the appropriateness of the label "alcoholism."

The definer may add "personality deviation," or "immature or deviant personality development," or "injury to the brain by alcohol," or "nutritional defect," or whatever he believes to be the causative agency or agent; or he may prefer tentatively to say, "owing to undetermined causes."

This definition makes explicit the criterion by which the existence of the disease is determined. It makes "loss of control" over drinking the pathognomonic symptom, in agreement with Jellinek (10, 13). The significance of loss of control is that it denotes helpless dependence or addiction, the essence of the disease. The distinction between the two possible forms of loss of control, inability to refrain from drinking and inability to stop, has been elaborated with exquisite logic by Marconi (28), and is of great theoretical importance for the possible physiopathological etiology of the disease. For the present epidemiological interest, however, it is enough to bear in mind that "loss of control" means that *whenever an alcoholic starts to drink it is not certain that he will be able to stop at will.**

The preceding formulation appears to be a satisfactory primary (medical) definition of the disease alcoholism. The lack of physical or biochemical instruments or tests by which the diagnosis can be verified does not prevent a diagnostician from establishing it by adequate anamnesis. However, no single definition is necessarily suitable for all purposes, and the satisfactory medical definition is not adequate for epidemiological needs. The task of determining how many alcoholics there are at any place in any given time by anamnestic verification of loss of control would be extremely difficult to execute even by sampling procedures.

What the public health worker or epidemiologist needs is a set of behaviors or signs which can be recognized by relatively superficial methods of inquiry and yet will allow identification of the alcoholic as defined above. The preceding formulation, and the descriptions of diagnosed alcoholic populations, suggest two main elements of a behavioral-operational definition: (1) drinking—to be described in terms of chronicity or repetitiveness, plus "undesirable" characteristics (of quantity, frequency, pattern, circumstances, and possibly others), and (2) ill effects of the drinking on the drinker. The following is a schematic representation of these elements.

Alcoholism
   I. Drinking (alcoholic beverages)
      a. Implicative (suspicion-arousing) or marked; and
      b. Repetitive (or chronic)
              +
  II. Ill effects (from the drinking, on the drinker)
      a. Health; or
      b. Social (interpersonal); or
      c. Economic

* Distinguished from loss of control over motor activity or temperament as an immediate result of alcohol intoxication.

This schema details the necessary criteria for a definition which in the absence of individual diagnosis, rests on a reasonable inference of the existence of loss of control over drinking and, hence, of a disease.

Before the behavioral-operational definition from this schema is formulated, it will be useful to clarify the function of each element.

I. Drinking is obviously a sine qua non of alcoholism. The question whether alcoholics who stop drinking are still to be designated alcoholics— as the members of Alcoholics Anonymous do—or as ex-alcoholics, or "arrested" alcoholics, is not an unimportant one, and comes up immediately in any attempt to count "alcoholics." If there are several million alcoholics, are the possibly many hundred thousand who were alcoholics but are no longer drinking still to be included in the count or estimate? Theoretical and practical arguments can be made either way. From an epidemiological viewpoint, however, it seems desirable to distinguish between active and non-drinking alcoholics. Thus the present schema and the definition to be derived from it refer to alcoholics who are drinking. Those who once fitted the schema but no longer do, may be distinguished, when identified, by any desired term (former, arrested, ex-, recovered, or whatever).

Ia. The only item in the schema that presents true difficulties is the adjective which describes the "alcoholismic" drinking. This is the place where definers have usually been content to say excessive—or pathological or abnormal or compulsive or undisciplined—or they might have tried pathogenic, dyscrasic, dysfunctional, maladaptive or dysadaptive, and innumerable others. Each of these terms possibly describes the drinking of some alcoholics. None of them describes objectively the drinking behavior or consistent drinking pattern of all alcoholics.* Although "excessive" may come nearest to what is wanted, it fails on two grounds: First, no quantitative measure of "excessive" is possible. Without quantification, "excessive" invites extreme subjective judgment particularly in application to drinking and is thus especially inexpedient for the intended use of the definition. Second, excessive does not actually cover all cases. There can be no question that quantitatively over time many alcoholics drink less than many non-alcoholics,† and this is particularly though not exclusively true of alcoholics who drink only periodically.

For present purposes, therefore, and with the admission that it is for lack of the ideal adjective, the term "implicative (suspicion-arousing) or marked" has been adopted, and implicative will be used here preferentially. Obviously the epidemiologist-public health worker who has to apply the concept of implicative or marked is left to his own resources. It is he rather

---

* The attempt of a World Health Organization committee of experts (42, 43) to describe the alcoholismic drinking or qualify the excess in terms of deviance from social and dietary standards of "the community" is no more adequate, as Seeley (36) has pointed out.

† See, for example, the detailed diaries of a year's drinking, by persons who were quite certainly not alcoholics, reported by Williams and Straus (40).

than the definer who will have to say whether the drinking of the possible alcoholic is such as to allow him to be counted. Quite likely the investigator or his informant will fall back on the defective notion of excess. It may be hoped, however, that not only quantity but also the combination of frequency, pattern, and circumstances will be taken into implicative account, to the extent that they can be determined.

The only justification for this recourse to inexactness is that no matter what term is adopted—pathological, excessive, disorderly, or whatever—the same process is inevitable. While no term or combination of terms as yet proposed is without defect, "implicative (suspicion-arousing) or marked" has at least this advantage: it does not pretend to be exact. It confesses that this element is indefinite, that the applier's subjective judgment is involved. By this frankness it invites caution in the field, and further consideration of the problem for its more satisfactory resolution.

The one question still to be considered here is whether it might not be possible to omit this element (I*a*) altogether and say just drinking—any drinking which results in the ill effects to be specified. To this an unequivocal negative must be asserted, for it is conceivable that very occasional drinking, moderate by any reasonable standards, could result in harm to the drinker in the economic or social spheres, yet not allow the inferences which are essential for alcoholism. Both "marked" and "implicative" are intended to mean that the drinking or drinking pattern suggests to the observer that "there is something wrong with it," sufficiently so to raise the suspicion of alcoholism in the mind of the investigator.

I*b*. The element of repetitiveness or chronicity of the implicative drinking is essential. Any drinking behavior which occurred only once or even on several but rare occasions would not reasonably suggest a disease, alcoholism. It is not impossible that a person with alcoholism (for instance, one whose loss of control is only of the "inability to stop" variety) should, after a single misadventure, deliberately or by force of circumstances never drink again and thus nevermore exhibit the telltale symptoms. With present diagnostic techniques it is impossible to establish the facts indicative of alcoholism in such cases, and they are left out of further consideration here.

II. The ill effects (to be specified) which help to establish the existence of alcoholism must unquestionably derive from the drinking, not be coincidental with it. A moderate drinker whose teetotaler uncle disinherits him may have suffered an economic loss but the damage derives from the uncle's feelings, not from the drinking directly. The ill effects must also affect the drinker himself. If a man's drinking results in a loss to society but not to himself (except as part of the society) it does not meet the criteria of the schema and cannot be counted as evidence for a disease.

The three areas of ill effects specified * are derived from the general evi-

* They are identical with the areas specified by a committee of experts of the World Health Organization (43) but are here made independently sufficient while that committee appeared to regard them as necessary in a combination of all three.

dence concerning the kinds of harms experienced by alcoholics, and were selected because these harms are usually detectable and their relation (or non-relation) to the drinking is commonly determinable. These three areas are, however, not necessarily exclusive. Harm in other areas, provided it is causally connected with the repeated implicative drinking and is suffered by the drinker himself, should count equally. The key criterion, for all ill effects, is this: Would the individual be expected to reduce his drinking (or give it up) in order to avoid the injury or its continuance? If the answer is yes, and he does not do so, it is assumed—admitting it is only an assumption —that he cannot, hence that he has "lost control over drinking," that he is addicted to or dependent on alcohol. This inference is the heart of the matter. Without evident or at least reasonably inferred loss of control, there is no foundation for the claim that "alcoholism is a disease," except in the medical dictionary sense of diseases (of the nervous or digestive system, for example) caused by alcohol poisoning—a sense which leaves out of account a vast part, quite likely the most part, of the alcoholic population.

IIa. Any evidence of continued or repeated ill health resulting from drinking is sufficient to meet this criterion, provided the relationship is definite.

IIb. The kind of "social" or "interpersonal" ill effects encompassed by this criterion is family break-up, actual or threatened, or social isolation or ostracism which would not occur if drinking were stopped or controlled.

IIc. The kind of economic ill effects encompassed by this criterion is illustrated by inability to keep jobs, to perform work efficiently, or to care for one's property as well as would be possible without the implicative drinking.

From the preceding schema and the comments, it becomes clear that an operational definition may take the following form (using only one term wherever a choice is possible):

A. Repeated implicative drinking of alcoholic beverages, so as to cause injury to the drinker's health or to his social or economic functioning, constitutes alcoholism, a chronic disease.

This is restated more conveniently in definition form as follows:

B. Alcoholism is a chronic disease manifested by repeated implicative drinking so as to cause injury to the drinker's health or to his social or economic functioning.

In this restatement "alcoholic beverages" need not be mentioned because of the primary position of "alcoholism." In both formulations the inclusion of "a chronic disease" is justified as a category of information appropriate to the definition and derived from the elements in the schema which describe a repetitive, disabling, uncontrollable behavior—a "dysbehaviorism."

Many other formulations are possible in which an alternative phrase would be substituted for "a chronic disease" in formulation B.* For epidemiological

* Examples are: Alcoholism is a disorder of personality; Alcoholism is a chronic disease or disorder of personality; Alcoholism is a chronic psychological or physiological or psychosomatic disorder; Alcoholism is an addiction. The formulation of choice may give

and other public health uses, as well as for general common use, formulation B appears to have the most advantages and the least disadvantages.

The Problem of Statistics *

None of the attempts to estimate the numbers or rates of alcoholics or to establish these values by means of field surveys used exactly the definition proposed above. Nevertheless, in most cases the underlying conceptions were sufficiently similar to it and to each other so that comparison of the end results is not vitiated. The results may be compared especially with the understanding that they constitute rough approximations, and that—particularly in large populations—they can be useful even if inaccurate by a factor of 20 or 25 per cent. In other words, all past estimates of the prevalence of alcoholism should be thought of not as the equivalents of census values but as rough indices of the magnitude of the problem.

The importance of having some idea of the numbers of alcoholics was recognized about 20 years ago by E. M. Jellinek. In view of the unlikelihood then of obtaining a census even in a few sample areas in the United States, he sought for some indirect measure and believed he had discovered a suitable index in cirrhosis of the liver of the Laënnec type. This disease affects not only alcoholics (or excessive drinkers); its total incidence includes actually more moderate drinkers and abstainers than alcohol abusers. Nevertheless, the disorder is about nine times more frequent among recognized excessive drinkers (6).

Jolliffe and Jellinek (19) carried out a trend analysis of the mortality from liver cirrhosis in many populations, with particular reference to changes during periods of prohibition and scarcity of alcohol. They took into account (a) the incidence of alcoholics among persons diagnosed at autopsy as having liver cirrhosis, as well as (b) the occurrence of cirrhosis among alcoholics who came to autopsy. From this work, Jellinek hypothesized that there was a sufficiently constant relationship between inebriety and the general mortality from liver cirrhosis to allow the estimation of the rate of "alcoholics with complications." † He proposed a formula in which the number of reported deaths from cirrhosis of the liver in a given year, D, is multiplied by the assumed constant percentage, P, of such deaths attributable to alcoholism (different for men and women), and divided by K, another

---

effect to opinion as to the predominantly physiological or psychological order of the involvement, dependence, or addiction; it may be made to conform more or less with the etiological conceptions implied in the *Standard Nomenclature* of the American Medical and American Psychiatric Associations. The choice must be governed by the specific purpose of the definition.

* The collaboration of Vera Efron, Assistant Research Specialist in Documentation, Rutgers University, in all the computations and estimates presented in this section, is gratefully acknowledged.

† Alcoholics with complications (a successor term to "chronic alcoholics") are those who exhibit a diagnosable physical or psychological change caused by inebriety.

constant representing the percentage of all alcoholics-with-complications who die of liver cirrhosis. The result can then be multiplied by R, a presumed ratio of all alcoholics to alcoholics with complications in the given place and time, in order to obtain the total of alcoholics with and without complications. The formula, with $A =$ all alcoholics, thus reads: $A = (PD/K)R$.

The first extensive results of estimates by the Jellinek formula, for the period 1910–1945, were published in 1947 (11). The values assigned then to P were 51.5 for males and 17.7 for females, and to K, 0.693. In line with revision of the International Lists of Causes of Death, the values of P, beginning with the year 1949, became 62.8 for males and 21.6 for females (12). The value of R in the United States generally came to be taken as 4, on the assumption that in this country there were three alcoholics without complications for each alcoholic with complications (43, Annex 2).

A number of surveys and estimates by independent methods in various places, during the next years, yielded enough fairly satisfactory agreements to buttress confidence in the reliability of the formula.*

Estimates of rates of alcoholism in the United States for the period from 1940 to 1948, which indicated a prevalence of nearly 4 million alcoholics in the latter year, were presented by Jellinek and Keller (16) with considerable confidence. They surmised, however, that the rise in the rate between 1940 and 1948 might be an artifact of improved reporting of deaths from cirrhosis. Nevertheless, they did not doubt that the more recent values represented a nearer approximation to the true state of affairs.

Keller and Efron (21, 23), in presenting later estimates which continued to show a climbing rate, emphasized the same view. They analyzed the unequal magnitudes of change in the alcoholism rates in states (21) and big cities (22) with originally low and high ranks and found fairly consistently a much steeper slope of increase in the areas with originally low rates. This seemed to indicate that the increases were indeed artifacts of improved reporting, and they concluded that there was no evidence of any substantial rise in the actual rate of alcoholism. In 1956, the last year for which they published estimates, they calculated (with $R = 4$) that there were approximately 5 million alcoholics in the United States, of whom 4.2 million were males (23); the rate per hundred thousand adults aged 20 and over was estimated as 4,760 (men, 8,270; women, 1,430). These estimates are mentioned here only to facilitate the ensuing discussion, not as representing reality.

The theoretical basis of the Jellinek formula has recently been the subject of critical discussion. Popham (32) in 1956 pointed out that P (the proportion of liver cirrhosis deaths attributable to alcoholism) might not

---

* Popham (32) tabulated ten such independent surveys. Since then two additional estimates have been derived from community surveys, one in a small Michigan town (27) and one in the State of Iowa (30). The first does not lend itself to comparison because the Jellinek formula is inapplicable to small populations. The second is in excellent agreement with the Jellinek formula estimate.

be invariably constant; and that K (the proportion of alcoholics who die of liver cirrhosis) might change with the nutritional status of a population, as Sjövall (37) had noted earlier. Nevertheless, in view of the high frequency of agreement with independently derived estimates, Popham thought that "Jellinek formula estimates of the prevalence of alcoholism in Canada and in the United States in recent years, would probably provide reasonably reliable indications of the magnitude of the problem."

Subsequently Seeley (35) and Brenner (4) presented detailed critiques of these constants. Seeley, on the basis of his analysis, concluded that estimates based on the formula are apparently in error to such an extent that "assertions as to the magnitude of the problem are misleading, and scientific studies based on these data, quite probably, invalid." He viewed the error as decidedly one of underestimation and elsewhere has stated (34) that, with respect to estimates based on the Jellinek formula, "All we can say with reasonable safety . . . is 'You have *at least* this many alcoholics.' "

Brenner, with particular reference to the problem of P, has proposed a modification of the formula in the form of a substitute for PD. Applied to the United States, this modification yields numbers and rates of alcoholics some 56 per cent higher than the original formula.

Jellinek (15) has agreed that the critiques of the "constants" in his formula are justified. He had assumed that P would not fluctuate sufficiently within a decade to distort estimates seriously, but he had been aware and had on occasions indicated that K, and R as well, must require periodic revision. On the basis of approximate changes in the relative occurrence of various complicating disorders of alcoholism prior to 1942 and currently, he has suggested a modification of the values of K and R, while accepting also Brenner's proposed substitute for PD. With these changes, the numbers and rates of alcoholics in recent years are increased by about 18 per cent compared to the original Jellinek formula. This would give, in 1956, nearly 6 million alcoholics (instead of 5 million) in the United States, and in 1957 more than 6.5 million.

The various proposed modifications, it will be noted, all lead to higher estimates than the original Jellinek formula would indicate for recent years. The enormity of the problem of alcoholism in the United States if there should be 5 million alcoholics, giving a total adult rate approaching 5 per cent and a male adult rate above 8 per cent, is sufficiently obvious. The 1957 estimate by the revised Jellinek-Brenner method would raise the total adult rate to above 6 per cent and the male rate to 10 per cent.* In particu-

* The sex ratio is that indicated by the original Jellinek formula, since the Brenner modification estimates apply only to the total population. The Jellinek formula sex ratio has been constant in the United States between 5 and 6 to 1 for half a century. Regardless of the confidence attached to the numerical estimates derived by the formula, the sex ratio can be considered as valid so long as the basic idea of the reflection of alcoholism in liver cirrhosis mortality is accepted, and provided allowance is made (as the Jellinek formula did) for the different rate of non-alcohol-related cirrhosis in the sexes.

lar segments of the population, eliminating unaffected or little affected groups, the rate of alcoholism would rise to values approaching the fantastic. The rate calculated now is based on the population aged 20 and over, because alcoholism is rare in the younger. It might well rather be based on age 25 to 65, as Jolliffe (17) suggested in 1936. There are more urban than rural alcoholics; a rural-urban ratio calculated for 1940 was just about 2 to 1 (11). There are more white than Negro alcoholics; the ratio calculated for the year 1948 was 1.6 to 1 (16). Jews and Italians contribute very few alcoholics; and, of course, the many millions of total abstainers contribute none. If the total of alcoholics is assumed to be more than 6.5 million, a rate based on white urban non-Jewish, non-Italian, non-abstaining males aged 25 years and over would probably involve one out of five or six as alcoholics.

The procedure leads to results that begin to defy credulity. Moreover, the steady rise in the rate cannot indefinitely be explained by more accurate reporting of liver-cirrhosis deaths, that is, by more reliable values of D, since it may be factored by changes in any or all of the several proportions involved: of liver-cirrhosis deaths attributable to alcoholism (P), of alcoholics who die of liver cirrhosis (K), or of alcoholics who have complications (R). It is tempting to declare a moratorium, as Seeley (35) proposes, on all magnitude-of-the-problem claims, or to grant Jellinek his wish (15) that the formula be no longer used for current estimations, but it may be premature to abandon all chances of extracting a reasonable estimate based on this formula.* The possibility of still doing this involves a return to its origin.

The fact remains that the underlying theory of the Jellinek formula—that alcoholism is reflected in mortality from liver cirrhosis—is beyond dispute. The association between the two was solidly established by the analysis of Jolliffe and Jellinek (19) and is in agreement with clinical experience wherever inebriety is observed. Thus, if the values of P and K are established for a particular time, the formula should yield a reasonable approximation of the prevalence of alcoholism with complications at that time, even though the same values cannot be applied with the D of another time.

Jellinek's second attempt to fix the values of P and K took into account the relevant data for the period immediately preceding 1945. It was with these values that he published his first extensive estimates (11), going to the

---

* Jellinek (15) has also suggested an alternative way of estimating the prevalence of alcoholism. This would require accurate statistics of deaths in which alcoholism was a contributory as well as a major cause, with an adjustment for the differential mortality in alcoholics and the general population. Such statistics, and the value of the required adjustment, do not yet exist in the United States, but Jellinek believes special effort on the part of the Public Health Service to establish them might be successful. An earlier alternative was suggested by Ipsen (8)—to use "medical examiner" records with particular reference to deaths from suicide and accidents. This method seemed to yield a fairly reasonable estimate of the prevalence of alcoholism in Massachusetts; but there are few states with comparable records where this method could be tested. Brenner (5) has also offered a further suggestion for estimating the prevalence of alcoholism from vital rates, a method still to be tested.

year 1945, and it is to this work that his recent statement (15) that he had not expected too much fluctuation in the value of P within a decade (i.e., between 1940 and 1950) must refer. Thus the well-known values of P (previously cited) obviously apply to the early 1940's. As for K, Jellinek has stated (15) that its value was derived from data of the period from 1930 to 1941. The vicissitudes of the complications of alcoholism in the next years do not preclude acceptance of the given values of K and P as a reasonable approximation for the early 1940's. It is, indeed, interesting to note the quite stable estimates that result from use of the formula with these values in the entire period of 1940 to 1945 (Figure 1, line B′). Thus it seems reasonable to assume as reliable for this period the average rate of 800 for alcoholics with complications, giving 693,000 alcoholics with complications, 588,000 men and 105,000 women.

The question of total alcoholics, involving the value to be assigned to R in the United States, is a separate one. In the work from which the above averages are derived (11) Jellinek suggested that R in 1945 was probably at least 5. About 5 years earlier (6), evidently based on data for the period from 1930 to 1941, he had thought it might be 3.3 or 4, and some 5 years later (43, Annex 2) he returned to 4, apparently relying chiefly upon reports from a number of outpatient clinics. The latter value has become almost solidly established, perhaps because its use led to agreements with the results of surveys in later years. Most of the agreeing surveys were conducted after 1946. Since the P and K values which lead to the estimate of alcoholics with complications were by then no longer valid, the fact that an R value of 4 produced agreements with a number of findings can be taken as no more than a temporarily gratifying coincidence which tended to mask the mutability of the values. Most recently Jellinek (15) has shown that R requires an adjustment to 5.3 and that this growth, equivalent to a shrinkage in the proportion of alcoholics with complications, was reached at latest by 1950. Actually the enlargement of R must have begun very early in the 1940's when the food enrichment program was initiated. Indeed, by mid-1943, Jolliffe could report * that "since the bread-enrichment program started the incidence of polyneuropathy and pellagra in our wards has been reduced to one-fourth of what it was before . . . ." It thus seems more reasonable to assign a value of 5 to R for the period of 1940 to 1945, when the greatest decline in the complications of alcoholism was taking place.

With this correction, the rate of all alcoholics for that period would be about 4,000 and the total number of alcoholics (with and without complications) 3,465,000 (2,940,000 men and 525,000 women).

To judge the applicability of these considerations to the problem of the prevalence of alcoholism in the late 1950's, it is necessary again to raise the question of evidence for an increase in the rate of alcoholism since 1946. If this rate has indeed risen, if the accretion of new alcoholics has tended to

* In a lecture at the Yale Summer School of Alcohol Studies, July 1943, and published subsequently (18).

exceed the mortality and "arrest" values, then the re-estimation of the rates and numbers of alcoholics from 1940 to 1945 was useful only as an academic exercise. However, if it can be assumed that the rate has not changed substantially, then the 1940-to-1945 data give the means of projecting a reasonable current estimate.

The fact is that nothing acceptable as evidence of a rise in the rate of alcoholism has been brought forward except the Jellinek formula itself— and this evidence is, of course, inadmissible once P and K are no longer regarded as constant. There is the superficial evidence of public appearance and recognition of "more alcoholics." In part this can be accounted for by an actual growth in the number of alcoholics paralleling the gain in size of the adult population in the interval since 1945. An increase of over half a million in the total number of alcoholics could have occurred by 1957 without any rise whatsoever in the rate of alcoholism. In part, however, the greater obtrusiveness of alcoholics can represent better "case finding," easier diagnosis, and franker labeling, a natural consequence—as has been argued elsewhere (16, 21)—of the developments of interest, concern, activity, and facilities precisely in the period under consideration. All that can be said is that there may have been a rise in the rate of alcoholism coincidental with the augmented activity around it, but the appearance of more alcoholics (dramatically illustrated in the growing ease of the public declaration, "I am an alcoholic") cannot be taken as evidence of an actual increase in the rate.

There is, of course, a historical event which could suggest that such an increase ought to have taken place in the 1950's. This is the enormous expansion of the number of drinkers which apparently occurred in the early 1940's. Presumably the new population of drinkers included some who were vulnerable to alcoholism but who would have escaped it had they remained abstainers. On the assumption that it usually takes 8 or 10 years (39) for the development of alcoholism, a higher rate should have come into effect beginning in the 1950's. However, reducing the size of the increase that might be expected is the circumstance that the new drinkers were predominantly women,* who contribute only between one-fifth and one-sixth as many alcoholics as men in the United States. More important are the historical events, whose significance for this outcome is commonly overlooked, which would suggest that some decline in the rate of alcoholism could have been expected. These events are the very activities and developments that have brought more alcoholics more into evidence. It would be strange indeed if all that has happened around alcoholism in the last two decades should have had no salutary effect on the rate of its develop-

---

* Comparison of the Haggard and Jellinek estimate (6) for 1940 with the results of the Riley and Marden survey (33) in 1946 shows that male drinkers apparently increased about 35 per cent and female drinkers over 100 per cent. This involves about 5 million more women than men.

ment. Jellinek and Keller (16) already in 1952 thought they had detected signs of a reductive effect on the incidence of alcoholism in an index of Alcoholics Anonymous activity. There are scattered reports of "cases" of prevention, of the alcoholism pattern aborted before reaching the crucial phase of loss of control, directly related to activities of health and education agencies.* Bacon's exposition suggests that at least secondary prevention related to therapeutic activities may be having an effect in reducing the numbers of alcoholics (2).

It is not possible to gauge the true balance between the forces working for a higher and a lower rate of alcoholism. There is, however, no reason to assume that the rate could only increase.

There remains one line of evidence to be considered; it is an important one, and it goes decidedly against any assumption of an increase in the rate of alcoholism since 1945. This evidence is derived from the statistics of alcohol consumption.

It is always dangerous to make inferences about alcoholism (or even about inebriety) from statistics on drinking.† Certainly it would be possible for alcoholism to wax or wane moderately without great reflection in the consumption of alcohol. However, a very large increment of alcoholics could hardly fail to be reflected in the consumption of alcohol unless there were a simultaneous reduction in the number of drinkers or a marked change in the drinking habits of the rest of the population.

In the United States, in the period between 1940 and the mid-1950's, the number of drinkers, far from declining, rose substantially. Jellinek (11) estimated that in 1940 there were near to 43 million drinkers in the population aged 15 years and over (the "drinking-age" population); in the mid-1950's, Keller and Efron estimated the number of drinkers in this population at not less than 75 million.‡ A considerable proportion of the new drinkers is undoubtedly composed of women and younger people whose drinking perhaps absorbs a relatively small part of the beverage alcohol total. In any case, the huge increment of drinkers raises an expectancy of more alcohol consumption—unless there were grounds for assuming a simultaneous moderation of drinking levels in the population generally.

As for alcoholics, in spite of the observation that some of them may drink less than some non-alcoholics do, the average alcoholic uses up an enormously larger quantity of alcohol in a year than the average non-alcoholic.

* See, for instance, Holmes (7).

† However, the complete divorcement of the two is impossible, as the unavoidable inclusion of drinking in the preceding definition of alcoholism suggests. In France, Ledermann (26) has estimated the prevalence of alcoholism from a combination of alcohol consumption rates with data on mortality from liver cirrhosis and "acute and chronic alcoholism."

‡ Unpublished. Presented in a lecture, M. Keller, "Measures of Drinking in the United States and in Certain Other Countries; Problems of the Interpretation of Statistics," at the Yale Summer School of Alcohol Studies, July 2, 1959.

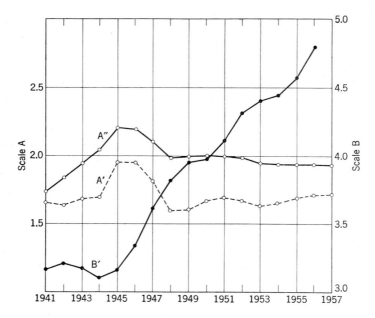

Figure 1. Trends in the rate of alcoholism and consumption of alcoholic beverages, U.S.A., 1941 through 1957. Three-year moving averages. Scale A: U.S. gallons per capita of drinking-age population (aged 15 years or more). Line A′: distilled spirits; line A″: absolute alcohol from all beverages, read against Scale A. Scale B: per cent of adult population (aged 20 years or more). Line B′: rate of all alcoholics, read against Scale B. Two separate graphs have been superimposed to allow better visualization of the lack of association between the apparent trends of alcoholism and drinking in the given time span.

Jellinek (14) has computed the average amount consumed by a male alcoholic in the United States to be nearly 23 gallons of absolute alcohol per year.*

Figure 1 shows the annual consumption of alcohol (per capita of the drinking-age population) from all beverages in the United States during the period from 1941 to 1957 as well as the rate of alcoholism as calculated by the original Jellinek formula. Except for a temporary rise during World War II there has been little change in the average consumption of absolute alcohol (line A″). The consumption of distilled spirits (line A′) rose especially during the latter war years but then dropped and in the postwar

---

* Absolute alcohol is what remains of beer, wine, and distilled spirits when all the water has been "removed" by calculating only the alcohol contained in beverages. This makes it possible to compare the consumption of alcohol rather than of mixtures containing highly variable proportions of alcohol and water. Currently in the United States, beers average 4.5 per cent alcohol; wines of two classes, 13 per cent and 20 per cent; and distilled spirits, 45 per cent.

period has shown a slight upward tendency. At the same time, since 1946, the estimated rate of alcoholism has seemed to rise steadily and steeply. The question suggested by these curves is whether such a vast increase in the number of alcoholics would not require at least some proportional rise in the consumption of alcohol, perhaps especially of distilled spirits. This may be illustrated with a concrete example: between 1947 and 1957 the number of alcoholics apparently rose from 3.4 million to 5.5 million, that is, by over 2 million. So many additional alcoholics would require perhaps 45 million additional gallons of absolute alcohol. The actual consumption of absolute alcohol in 1947 was over 215 million gallons, and in 1957, nearly 238 million gallons. The additional 23 million gallons are enough to take care of only half the estimated higher number of alcoholics and leave nothing for the possibly 10 million other drinkers added through the growth of population.*

If the proportion of drinkers in the drinking-age population had not grown since 1940, the entire alcohol consumption curve would lend itself to an assumption of no change or some reduction in drinking by non-alcoholics and perhaps some decline in drinking by alcoholics. Since the proportion of drinkers has undoubtedly risen, the indication for less drinking by alcoholics is reinforced and it is tempting to infer a reduction in the rate of alcoholism. The situation is complicated, however, by the problem of illicit supplies of liquor. If recent increased operations of large-sized illegal distilleries (38) should mean that the manufacture of "moonshine" has grown substantially in the postwar years above what it was before the war, might this not take care of a vast army of additional alcoholics?

The peak of legal (tax-paid) beverage consumption in the final war years (Figure 1) can be interpreted as representing a total consumption, since at that time the sources of illicit liquor supplies may have been exhausted, owing to wartime limitations on the capacities of moonshine makers to obtain grain and sugar, transport and labor. If so, the subsequent decline could be a measure of the contribution of illicit distillation to the total consumption in the United States. Some part of the peak, however, could have been caused by excess purchases by retailers replenishing stocks depleted during the immediately preceding wartime shortage; † and some part of the postwar decline could be caused by actual reductions in the

* The year 1947 has been taken as a base here, although the 1940-to-1945 average would have been more appropriate, because of the distortions of the alcohol consumption statistics in the war years. Had an earlier base time been used the results of the illustration would appear even more striking, because of the relatively larger increases in alcoholics and other drinkers. The alcohol consumption data are derived from Keller and Efron (24).

† The consumption data are based on deliveries of tax-paid beverages to retailers. This is one reason why a moving average, as in Figure 1, is more representative than the statistics of individual years.

number of drinkers * and average amounts consumed. In any case, the moonshine industry would have to be supplying the equivalent of about 100 million gallons of whisky a year to take care of the 2 million additional alcoholics cast up through current estimates by the original Jellinek formula. A great variety of hypothetical calculations, taking into account many possible combinations of conditions, might be attempted, but none of them can be verified by presently available facts. The one conclusion which seems reasonable, however, is that the alcohol consumption statistics do not indicate any rise in the rate of alcoholism.

All the preceding considerations taken together seem to impel the conclusion that there has not been any rise in the basic rate of alcoholism since 1946. If, then, the apparently reliable Jellinek formula rates for the 1940-to-1945 period are applied to recent times, the following estimate of alcoholics with complications is obtained (for the year 1960): men, 710,000; women, 130,000; both sexes, 840,000.†

To arrive at total alcoholics (with and without complications) we must multiply these results by R, which is set at 5.3 in accordance with Jellinek's recent demonstration (15). This gives 3,760,000 men, 710,000 women, and a total of 4,470,000 alcoholics.

It should be remembered that this estimate assumes that the recent rate of alcoholism with complications is the same as that between 1940 and 1945 —that the 17 million adults who have been added to the population in the postwar years have produced alcoholics at the same rate as the earlier adult population did. The foregoing discussion, however, hardly favors this assumption but rather a lower rate. Thus, it may not be extremely conservative to speak of some 4 million alcoholics rather than of 5 million or 6 million or even larger numbers suggested by other methods of estimating. The seriousness of the problem of alcoholism is not diminished if there should be "only" 4 million alcoholics. Even in a population of 180 million, this is a titanic number of people, mostly in the prime of life, to be suffering from a single disabling disease.

In spite of having arrived at an estimate of the numbers of alcoholics, the preceding considerations have opened up more questions than they have answered. A whole catalog of problems is begging for research. Plowing this

---

* Polls by the American Institute of Public Opinion indicate a postwar decline in the percentage of drinkers (chiefly of women) in the population aged 21 and over, from 67 per cent in 1945 to 58 per cent in 1957. This does not mean a reduction in number of drinkers, since 58 per cent of the 1957 population is almost identical with 67 per cent of the 1945. Keller and Efron, however, in their previously cited estimate of not less than 75 million drinkers in the mid-1950's, have not accepted the reliability of these poll results for recent years. The findings of Mulford and Miller (29) in Iowa in 1958 strongly suggest that the American Institute poll tends to underestimate the percentages of drinkers.

† These projections are based on census population data. The number of adult males (aged 20 years and over) has been taken as 53,339,000 and females as 56,979,000; the estimates are rounded to the nearest 10,000.

field, scientists have a splendid opportunity to serve the public welfare while at the same time developing the theoretical riches of their several disciplines.

References

1. American Psychiatric Association, Committee on Nomenclature and Statistics, *Diagnostic and Statistical Manual, Mental Disorders,* Washington: American Psychiatric Association, 1952.

2. Bacon, Selden D., "Prevention Can be More Than a Word," in *Realizing the Potential in State Alcoholism Programs: Proceedings of the Northeast States Conference on Alcoholism, New Haven, May 18–20, 1959,* Hartford: Connecticut Commission on Alcoholism, 1959, pp. 5–18.

3. Bowman, Karl M., and E. M. Jellinek, "Alcohol Addiction and Its Treatment," *Quart. J. Stud. Alc.,* **2**:98–176, 1941.

4. Brenner, Berthold, "Estimating the Prevalence of Alcoholism: Toward a Modification of the Jellinek Formula," *Quart. J. Stud. Alc.,* **20**:255–260, 1959.

5. ———, "Estimating the Prevalence of Alcoholism from Vital Rates," *Quart. J. Stud. Alc.,* **21**:140–141, 1960.

6. Haggard, H. W., and E. M. Jellinek, *Alcohol Explored,* Garden City, N.Y.: Doubleday and Company, 1942.

7. Holmes, F. S., *The Ultimate Goal: Prevention of Alcoholism,* Worcester, Mass.: County Council on Alcoholism, 1959.

8. Ipsen, Johannes, Merrill Moore, and Leo Alexander, "Prevalence of Alcoholism in the Population and Among Suicides and Accidents from Poisoning, Massachusetts 1938–1948," *Quart. J. Stud. Alc.,* **13**:204–214, 1952.

9. Isbell, Harris, et al., "An Experimental Study of the Etiology of 'Rum Fits' and Delirium Tremens," *Quart. J. Stud. Alc.,* **16**:1–33, 1955.

10. Jellinek, E. M., "Phases in the Drinking History of Alcoholics. Analysis of a Survey Conducted by the Official Organ of Alcoholics Anonymous," *Quart. J. Stud. Alc.,* **7**:1–88, 1946.

11. ———, "Recent Trends in Alcoholism and in Alcohol Consumption," *Quart. J. Stud. Alc.,* **8**:1–42, 1947.

12. ———, "The Estimate of the Number of Alcoholics in the U.S.A. for 1949 in the Light of the Sixth Revision of the International Lists of Causes of Deaths," *Quart. J. Stud. Alc.,* **13**:214–218, 1952.

13. ———, "Phases of Alcohol Addiction," *Quart. J. Stud. Alc.,* **13**:673–684, 1952.

14. ———, "Distribution of Alcohol Consumption and of Calories Derived from Alcohol in Various Selected Populations," *Proc. Nutr. Soc.,* **14**:93–97, 1955.

15. ———, "Estimating the Prevalence of Alcoholism: Modified Values in the Jellinek Formula and an Alternative Approach," *Quart. J. Stud. Alc.,* **20**:261–269, 1959.

16. ———, and Mark Keller, "Rates of Alcoholism in the United States of America, 1940–1948," *Quart. J. Stud. Alc.,* **13**:49–59, 1952.

17. Jolliffe, Norman, "Alcoholic Admissions to Bellevue Hospital," *Science,* **83**:306–309, 1936.

18. ———, "Alcohol and Nutrition: The Diseases of Chronic Alcoholism," in *Alcohol, Science, and Society,* New Haven, Conn.: Journal of Studies on Alcohol, 1945.

19. ———, and E. M. Jellinek, "Vitamin Deficiencies and Liver Cirrhosis in Alcoholics, Part VII: Cirrhosis of the Liver," *Quart. J. Stud. Alc.,* **2**:544–583, 1941.

20. Keller, Mark, "Alcoholism: Nature and Extent of the Problem," *Annals*, **315**:1–11, 1958.

21. ———, and Vera Efron, "The Prevalence of Alcoholism," *Quart. J. Stud. Alc.,* **16**: 619–644, 1955.

22. ———, "Alcoholism in the Big Cities of the United States," *Quart. J. Stud. Alc.,* **17**:63–72, 1956.

23. ———, "The Rate of Alcoholism in the U.S.A., 1954–1956," *Quart. J. Stud. Alc.,* **19**:316–319, 1958.

24. ———, "Selected Statistics on Alcoholic Beverages and on Alcoholism, with a Bibliography of Sources," New Haven, Conn.: Journal of Studies on Alcohol, 1959. (Not for general distribution.)

25. Keller, Mark, and John R. Seeley, *The Alcohol Language*, Toronto: University of Toronto Press, 1958.

26. Ledermann, Sully, *Alcool, Alcoolisme, Alcoolisation. Donnés Scientifique de Caractère Physiologique, Economique et Social,* Paris: Presses Universitaires de France, 1956.

27. Manis, Jerome, and Chester Hunt, "The Community Survey as a Measure of the Prevalence of Alcoholism," *Quart. J. Stud. Alc.,* **18**:212–216, 1957.

28. Marconi, Juan T., "The Concept of Alcoholism," *Quart. J. Stud. Alc.,* **20**:216–235, 1959.

29. Mulford, Harold A., and Donald E. Miller, "Drinking in Iowa: I. Socio-cultural Distribution of Drinkers, with a Methodological Model for Sampling Evaluation and Interpretation of Findings," *Quart. J. Stud. Alc.,* **20**:704–726, 1959.

30. ———, "Drinking in Iowa: V. 'Alcoholic' Drinking," *Quart. J. Stud. Alc.,* **21**:483–499, 1960.

31. Plunkett, R. J., and A. C. Hayden (Eds.), *Standard Nomenclature of Diseases and Operations* (published for the American Medical Association), 4th ed., Philadelphia: The Blakiston Company, 1952; 5th ed., New York: McGraw-Hill Book Company, Inc., 1961.

32. Popham, Robert E., "The Jellinek Alcoholism Estimation Formula and Its Application to Canadian Data," *Quart. J. Stud. Alc.,* **17**:559–593, 1956.

33. Riley, John W., and Charles F. Marden, "The Social Pattern of Alcoholic Drinking," *Quart. J. Stud. Alc.,* **8**:265–273, 1947.

34. Seeley, John R., "How Many Alcoholics?—Under Review," *Alcoholism*, Toronto: **6**:7–8, 1959.

35. ———, "Estimating the Prevalence of Alcoholism: A Critical Analysis of the Jellinek Formula," *Quart. J. Stud. Alc.,* **20**:245–254, 1959.

36. ———, "The W. H. O. Definition of Alcoholism," *Quart. J. Stud. Alc.,* **20**:352–356, 1959.

37. Sjövall, E., "*Alkohol und Lebercirrhose,*" *Dtsch. Z. Ges. Gerichtl. Med.,* **41**:10–14, 1952.

38. U. S. Alcohol and Tobacco Tax Division, Publication No. 425, Washington: Internal Revenue Service, U. S. Treasury Department, 1959.

39. Wellman, W. M., *Time-Ordered Symptomatology of 554 Male Alcoholics,* Pullman, Wash.: Private Publication, 1959.

40. Williams, Phyllis H., and Robert Straus, "Drinking Patterns of Italians in New Haven. Utilization of the Personal Diary as a Research Tool," *Quart. J. Stud. Alc.,* **11**:51–91, 250–308, 452–483, 586–629, 1950.

41. World Health Organization, Expert Committee on Alcohol, First Report, *World Health Org. Techn. Rep. Ser.,* No. 84, March 1954.

42. World Health Organization, Expert Committee on Mental Health, Report First Session of the Alcoholism Subcommittee, *World Health Org. Techn. Ser.*, No. 42, Sept. 1951.

43. World Health Organization, Expert Committee on Mental Health, Alcoholism Subcommittee, Second Report, *World Health Org. Techn. Rep. Ser.*, No. 48, Aug. 1952.

y of alcoholism:

a begin g*

John R. Seeley

The classic ecological procedure, as understood here, is something after the following. We map the phenomena in which we are interested either over space at a given time, or over time within a given space, or both.† We then examine for "pattern"—in the obvious meaning with reference to space, in the sense of trend or in analogy with the spatial pattern, with regard to time. In either case the pattern may be "obvious." This only means that we see immediately in the data so distributed the identity or analogy with the distribution of something else whose distribution in time or space is in the forefront of our minds. If there is no obvious click, we may have to search deeper—either in our minds for knowledge we have or in other data we have or can get—for a parallel pattern to that of our data. When we find it, if we do, we have a correlation or association.

Once established, such a general association serves two purposes, at least. We may be able, by the very nature of the association found, either to establish or to hypothesize fruitfully about an etiological theory. If tooth decay and water-borne fluorides, for instance, correlate highly and negatively, we may have a lead to a remedy or preventive (barring human folly!) and an etiological lead as well. We may, on the other hand, have established a set of "normal expectations," the deviations from which need to be mapped to see what explains *them*. If, for instance, level of industrialization cor-

---

* This chapter was written especially for this book.

† Some scientists refer to the first procedure as falling within ecology and the second within epidemiology. It does not matter. I have let both procedures fall under one term, as seems to be common biological, as against sociological, practice. See, for example, May (9).

relates well with the localization of coal, and if in certain instances we find deviation from expectancy, and if in those instances we find adequate, accessible iron ore present where the deviations are positive, we might be led—if we did not know it by other means—to conclude that industrialization (at a given time) required the compresence of coal and iron ore.

It is to such uses that I would like to see data on alcoholism systematically put. Indeed, it is the purpose of this chapter to make a start in this direction by exploring classic ecological questions with reference to alcoholism.

Problems of Estimation

If the legitimacy and hopefulness of the ecological method be granted,[*] the first question is whether or not we have data about alcoholism sufficiently meaningful and reliable to permit analysis. Yet it is patent that no clear and consistent definition has been applied in studies of alcoholism.[†] This is a serious difficulty. However, although we may expect vagueness of definition (and therefore heterogeneity of data) to weaken correlations, we need not conclude that none will be found.

Accepting this difficulty, then, do we have counts accurate enough under the loose definition to be worth plotting in time and space? Of course, except in rare instances,[‡] we do not have counts at all; we have "estimates." These estimates, almost without exception,[§] rest upon the Jellinek Estimation Formula, which in turn rests upon reported mortality ascribed to liver cirrhosis. We now know that the argument leading to the estimates has defects, and that, hence, we do not know, even within the limits of sampling error, what the proper estimates should be.[¶] We cannot even be sure that the proper figure would be some regular transformation of those actually in use.

In spite of these difficulties, it will be assumed, for trial purposes here, that the true rates are sufficiently close to some regular transformation of the current estimate to permit at least gross analysis. Note the modest re-

---

[*] This is obviously not the place for a full-scale defense of the ecological method even though an influential school of sociological thought seeks to rule it out as a promising way of securing a useful understanding of human affairs. Suffice it to say here that, like any other method, it must ultimately be justified or repudiated by what it produces, rather than by a priori argument.

[†] Keller's discussion in Chapter 17 highlights the problems—summarily treated here— of defining alcoholism in a workable way. For fuller presentation of the writer's views concerning the definition of alcoholism, see Seeley (12) and Keller and Seeley (8). In actuality, the definition implicit in our ways of estimating prevalence comes very close to "persons, in relevant respects, like those who have come to alcoholism clinics."

[‡] The exceptions are the handful of "surveys." See, for example, Gibbins (2).

[§] For an exception—which, however, raises as many questions as it answers—see Ipsen, Moore, and Alexander (3).

[¶] For references to the relevant literature and discussion of Jellinek's formula for estimation, the reader is once again referred to the previous chapter by Keller. The writer's own diagnosis of the weaknesses of the formula is fully set forth in (11).

quirement for the kind of ecological analysis pursued here: not that the
estimates need be accurate (as they *must* be for planning and *should* be for
propaganda) but that they be some regular transformation of the true or
actual numbers or rates. To the degree that this assumption is false, we
may expect difficulty in finding a pattern; any defect in the method of
estimation must militate against confirming the hypothesis that a pattern
exists. At the very worst, if the assumption is unfounded, the things we report about alcoholism will be true not for alcoholism but for ascribed liver
cirrhosis mortality. Such knowledge, however, may be of interest in itself.

Alleged Alcoholism Rates in Space

1. *The states of the United States: 1940*

Since we already have alleged alcoholism prevalence rates for the several
states of the United States in 1940 (4), it might be appropriate to begin by
asking whether any pattern can be discovered in these rates. The answer
seems to be that no pattern is discernible to the naked eye. This may be because the whole of the United States does not form a homogeneous interaction system in consequence of cultural variation by region,* or because
the principle of ordering requires more detailed inspection, or for both
reasons.

To deal with the first problem, that of relevant homogeneity, we shall
limit our analysis to the twenty-eight states which Stewart (14) designates
as "the main sequence." These form, not an arbitrary grouping, but a
"system," by the customary definition of an aggregate whose elements are
in closer interaction with one another than any of them is with any element
outside of the system.

To deal with the second problem, the problem of ordering, we shall use
—because it is available, because it may well be one of those universally
significant variables, and because it is related to a variable significant in
many animal ecology studies—the same author's "population potential" (14).
Population potential is a distance-density function.†

* For the view, in reference to another form of social behavior—philanthropic "giving"—that regionality is a paramount consideration and must be taken into account
before more refined analysis sheds light, see Seeley et al. (13). See also Stewart (14)
for an independent and prior identical conclusion, together with the establishment of
the subsystems of states, one of which is used herein.

† Formally: where V is the potential in question, r is a measure of distance, D is
population density at each "point," and dS an infinitesimal element of the area—
integration being extended over all points of the area where $D \neq 0$:

$$V = \int \frac{1}{r} D(dS)$$

Because of the recurrent emphasis in the literature on the suggestion that alcoholism
rates may well be related to urbanism, some characteristic that may be an index of it is
to be desired. Whatever else urbanism may connote, it must surely be dependent on
the distribution of population over an entire area; that is, it must, in effect, at any one
point be a function of the distribution. This view rules out as unsuitable such common

We shall also designate the alleged alcoholism rates by "A." The data now appear as in Table 1, hereunder, and the fact of correlation is obvious.

TABLE 1

Population Potentials and Alcoholism Rates for Twenty-Eight States of the United States in 1940

State	Population Potential (V)	Alcoholism Rates [a] (A)
North Dakota	14.4	1368
South Dakota	17.3	1920
Texas	20.8	2092
Oklahoma	21.5	2124
Maine	22.8	1548
Kansas	24.4	2448
Nebraska	24.9	2500
Iowa	26.7	1876
Minnesota	26.8	2576
Vermont	30.4	1944
Wisconsin	30.9	3080
New Hampshire	33.3	2676
Missouri	33.6	3332
Kentucky	36.4	2248
Virginia	36.8	2012
West Virginia	36.9	1888
Indiana	41.3	2600
Michigan	46.6	3176
Ohio	48.0	3580
Delaware	48.0	3092
Massachusetts	50.5	3148
Rhode Island	50.5	3480
Maryland	52.0	2744
Connecticut	56.1	3712
Illinois	57.1	3812
Pennsylvania	57.2	3284
New Jersey	86.4	3248
New York	98.7	3888

[a] Per 100,000 adults.

---

measures as the proportion of people living in cities of fifty thousand or over in each state, or the proportion non-rural—even though these may be (indeed are) correlated positively with the measure sought—if a better measure, referable to the "field" (rather than to points in it or sub-areas of it), is available.

The "population potential," which Stewart asserts is the "influence of people at a distance," is, in effect, the approximate, average measure over the sub-area (the state) of those attractions or influences that are constituted by the distribution of the whole population over the whole field (the United States or the twenty-eight states, as the case may be).

For reasons not to be entered upon here,* it was decided to compute correlations, assuming the relation between A and V to be of the form:

$$A = mV^n$$

where m and n are constants fitted by least-squares methods to the logarithmically implied equation.

To a very close approximation, the regression equation † works out to

$$A = 440 \, V^{1/2}$$

and the correlation to

$$r = .80$$

which is significantly different from zero (well beyond the .001 level of confidence). The single variable selected therefore, and moreover a simple function of it,‡ accounts statistically for nearly two-thirds (64 per cent) of all the variance.

2. The cities of the United States: 1940

We may reasonably inquire whether the variation in alleged alcoholism rates between cities can be similarly statistically explained. We might expect, on the whole, less success, since, in general, rates for large areas tend to be less subject to random fluctuation than rates for small areas. Moreover, the population potential measure we are using has been computed only for the state and not for the small sub-area a city occupies.

Since V measures the average potential of the area (the state), and since, to be theoretically consistent, we should take into account the heightened possibilities or necessities of interaction implied by a local concentration of population (a city) within the state, we might explore how closely the city alcoholism rates (A_c) correlate with the state population potential (V_s) and the adult city population, age 20 and over (P_c), assuming the two factors to be operating jointly.§

The data (or rather the logarithms of the raw data) for V_s, P_c, and A_c are found in Table 2, together with another measure S_s to which we shall presently refer.

---

* For convergent evidence suggesting such a function, see Stewart (14, pp. 40–44). See also Zipf (15) and Seeley et al. (13, pp. 177–188).

† The constant (440) is of little except practical interest. The exponent (½) is of theoretical interest as well.

‡ Both aspects need emphasis. The addition of one more variable, an economic one, as an analogue of molecular weight in the analogous physical equations for potential, might well account for a substantial further portion of the total variance. This needs exploration. A less simple—or, at least, a different—function of V might well correlate better with A, without even sacrificing any more degrees of freedom. This also needs exploration.

§ We should still expect, of course, considerable "unaccounted for" variation, based on local ordinances, practices, color, self-image—unless these are themselves substantially affected by V_s and P_c.

The values of V are those employed above. The alcoholism rates and the population data are from Keller and Efron (7). They refer to cities with populations of 100,000 and over, in states of the main sequence, and to "alcoholism with complications." Since the rates for alcoholism-with-and-without-complications are computed simply by multiplying these alcoholism-with-complications rates by a constant, the reasoning is unaffected by the choice of one, as against the other set of rates.

Again correlation was sought around a simplest (logarithmic) regression function that postulates

$$A_c = xV_s^y P_c^z$$

where x, y, z are least-squares constants, as before.

The resulting correlations * (product-moment) are as follows, for the seventy-four cities in the twenty-two states:

Zero-order correlations:	First-order correlations:	Multiple correlation:
$r_{AV} = .4172$	$r_{AP.V} = .3302$	$R_{A.VP} = .5140$
$r_{AP} = .3308$	$r_{AV.P} = .4168$	
$r_{PV} = .0755$		

These correlations tell a most interesting story. City population and state population potential turn out to be virtually independent, as expected ($r_{PV} = .0755$). State population potential accounts for about a sixth of all the variation in city rates ($r_{AV} = .42$) and local population accounts for a ninth ($r_{AP} = .33$). Moreover, the portions of variance so accounted for are quite separate, so that together the two variables account for over a fourth of the variance. This may or may not seem like a great deal, depending on what was expected, but it is quite significantly different from zero and therefore, as I interpret it, points to a pattern in which alcoholism depends (statistically) as a *per capita* risk on the distribution of population in space.

3. The states of the United States: ecology and social psychology

Even with this evidence for the seeming effect of a variable not directly in the actors' nexus of meanings (population, or population potential), it may be profitable to ask whether a "meaningful" measure, a direct expression of attitude towards drinking, correlates any better or worse with alcohol-

---

* Correlations between logarithms of the data, rather than the raw data, of course. If we omit cities of population less than 250,000 (because of excessive variability in year-to-year liver cirrhosis deaths), we get the following correlations: $r_{AV} = .65$, $r_{AP} = .38$; $r_{AP.V} = .08$, $r_{AV.P} = .58$; $R_{A.VP} = .6534$, $R_{A.VS} = .6511$. These not only indicate a higher correlation between A and V, but suggest less importance for either P or S as supplementary explanatory variables. One might, it seems, say, as far as the larger cities are concerned, that neither state-wide sentiment nor local population size adds much to what one can "explain" of local alcoholism rates on the basis of state population potential alone.

TABLE 2

Cities of the United States of Population Over 100,000 and Their
Alcoholism Rates; Population Potential, and "Dry Sentiment"
of Corresponding States

State	Measure [a]		City	Measure [a]	
	V'_s	S'_s		P'_c	A'_c
New Jersey	.937	.146	Camden	0.944	1.167
			Elizabeth	0.903	1.312
			Jersey City	1.324	1.292
			Newark	1.491	1.246
			Paterson	0.996	1.090
			Trenton	0.959	1.233
Connecticut	.749	— [b]	Bridgeport	1.045	1.107
			Hartford	1.097	1.316
			New Haven	1.061	1.182
			Waterbury	0.863	1.045
Massachusetts	.703	.230	Boston	1.747	1.305
			Cambridge	0.924	1.049
			Fall River	0.892	0.886
			New Bedford	0.881	0.833
			Somerville	0.851	0.973
			Springfield	1.053	1.100
			Worcester	1.152	1.114
Pennsylvania	.757	.380	Allentown	0.863	0.826
			Erie	0.949	0.964
			Philadelphia	2.150	1.238
			Pittsburgh	1.664	1.238
			Reading	0.869	1.117
			Scranton	0.929	1.057
Delaware	.681	.362	Wilmington	0.875	1.326
Rhode Island	.703	— [b]	Providence	1.238	1.152
Maryland	.716	— [b]	Baltimore	1.801	1.107
New York	.994	.041	Albany	0.982	1.079
			Buffalo	1.617	1.228
			New York City	2.750	1.190
			Rochester	1.375	1.083
			Syracuse	1.196	1.025
			Utica	0.857	1.176
			Yonkers	1.037	1.223
Ohio	.681	.462	Akron	1.270	0.934
			Canton	0.898	1.140
			Cincinnati	1.534	1.274
			Cleveland	1.792	1.274
			Columbus	1.407	1.045
			Dayton	1.217	1.176

TABLE 2 (*Continued*)

State	Measure [a]		City	Measure [a]	
	V'_s	S'_s		P'_c	A'_c
			Toledo	1.314	1.253
			Youngstown	1.057	1.130
Indiana	.616	.556	Evansville	0.929	1.173
			Fort Wayne	0.949	0.839
			Gary	0.949	1.137
			Indianapolis	1.453	1.124
			South Bend	0.886	1.258
Virginia	.566	.568	Arlington City	0.929	0.756
			Norfolk	1.127	0.732
			Richmond	1.161	1.053
Illinois	.757	.342	Chicago	2.403	1.241
			Peoria	0.892	1.312
Kentucky	.561	.580	Louisville	1.350	1.377
Michigan	.668	.398	Detroit	2.086	1.161
			Flint	1.033	1.134
			Grand Rapids	1.064	0.799
Missouri	.526	.380	Kansas City	1.493	1.149
			St. Louis	1.766	1.210
Wisconsin	.490	.255	Milwaukee	1.624	1.097
Iowa	.427	.602	Des Moines	1.068	0.826
Minnesota	.428	.544	Duluth	0.833	0.763
			Minneapolis	1.533	1.009
			St. Paul	1.310	0.881
Oklahoma	.332	.778	Oklahoma City	1.188	0.690
			Tulsa	1.064	0.851
Kansas	.387	.778	Kansas City	0.934	1.100
			Wichita	1.049	1.033
Nebraska	.396	— [b]	Omaha	1.223	1.104
Texas	.318	.591	Austin	0.924	0.643
			Corpus Christi	0.833	0.826
			Dallas	1.438	1.079
			El Paso	0.914	1.238
			Fort Worth	1.246	1.086
			Houston	1.575	1.079
			San Antonio	1.412	1.086

[a] $V'_s = \log V - 1$; $S'_s = \log S - 1$, where S is the percentage "dry" vote; $P'_c = \log P - 1$ where P is the adult population (twenty years of age and over) in thousands; and A'_c is $\log A - 2$, where A is the rate of alcoholism-with-complications, per hundred thousand adult population (as already defined).

[b] Not known.

ism rates. If it correlates no better, we would ask whether population fact and alcohol attitude account for the same or whether they account for different portions of the variance. If they account for the same portion, we shall almost be driven to conclude that the population facts influence or determine the alcohol attitudes, since it is not reasonable to assume that alcohol attitudes determine the distribution of population over the United States. I say "almost" because we may also choose to assume that some common factor—such as a preference for city life or freedom from traditional restraints—underlies or influences or determines both.

For eighteen states in Stewart's main sequence, we have an indication of attitude or sentiment, as expressed in voting behavior with reference to drinking. For this "Index of Dry Sentiment" (S) we are indebted to Jellinek (4).* The data appear in Table 3.

TABLE 3

Log Population Potential, Log "Dry Sentiment," Log Alcoholism Rate for Eighteen States of the United States

State	V' $Log V - 1$	S' $Log S - 1$	A^a	A' $Log A - 2$
New Jersey	.937	.146	1190	1.076
Massachusetts	.703	.230	1280	1.107
Pennsylvania	.757	.380	1350	1.130
Delaware	.681	.362	1140	1.057
New York	.994	.041	1300	1.114
Ohio	.681	.462	1080	1.033
Indiana	.616	.556	890	0.949
Virginia	.566	.568	630	0.799
Illinois	.757	.342	1200	1.079
Kentucky	.561	.580	760	0.881
Michigan	.668	.398	980	0.991
Missouri	.526	.380	920	0.964
Wisconsin	.490	.255	780	0.892
Iowa	.427	.602	650	0.813
Minnesota	.428	.544	590	0.771
Oklahoma	.332	.778	660	0.820
Kansas	.387	.778	610	0.785
Texas	.318	.591	690	0.839

a State rate: alcoholism with complications.

* The "index of dry sentiment" is simply, for each state, that percentage of the vote in a state referendum which was "Anti-Repeal" (i.e., against repealing the Eighteenth—"Prohibition"—Amendment). In two cases relevant to our series (Kansas and Oklahoma) the referendum vote of the states was not registered, and Jellinek arbitrarily assumed it to be 60 per cent. In this we have followed him. His table also, however, shows no "index of dry sentiment" (S) for four states in our series: Connecticut, Rhode Island, Maryland, and Nebraska.

From these data (on the assumption $A' = xV^yS^z$) we have the following correlations:

Zero-order correlations: First-order correlations: Multiple correlation:

$$r_{AV} = \quad .8671 \qquad\qquad r_{AS.V} = -.251 \qquad\qquad R_{A.VS} = .8761$$
$$r_{AS} = -.7910 \qquad\qquad r_{AV.S} = \quad .616$$
$$r_{VS} = -.8324$$

These results are quite striking. The correlation between A and V in the eighteen states is just about the same as for the whole sequence (about three-fourths of the variance accounted for). The measure of relation between alcoholism rates and "dry sentiment" is about as large, but opposite in sign. Sentiment, holding population potential constant, accounts for only about one-sixteenth of all the variance, so that "prediction" of alcoholism rates is very little improved by the addition of knowledge about "sentiments" over what can be done from knowledge about population potential alone. Indeed, about 70 per cent of the variation in sentiment may itself be (statistically) explained by variation in population potential.

4. The cities of the United States: ecology and social psychology

The corresponding story for the cities is briefly told. The data have already appeared in Table 2.

The results for the sixty-seven cities in the eighteen states are the following:

Zero-order correlations:

$$r_{AV} = \quad .4207$$
$$r_{AP} = \quad .3500 \qquad r_{VP} = \quad .0865$$
$$r_{AS} = -.3625 \qquad r_{VS} = -.8827 \qquad r_{PS} = -.1272$$

Selected first-order correlations:

$$r_{AV.S} = .2300$$
$$r_{AP.S} = .3288 \qquad r_{VP.S} = -.0533$$

Selected multiple correlations:

$$R_{A.VP} = .5254$$
$$R_{A.PS} = .4747$$
$$R_{A.VPS} = .5282$$

The picture is much the same as before. Population potential by itself explains about 17 per cent of the variance; local population explains a further 10 per cent or so; knowledge of "sentiment" adds very little to what has already been explained by these two.[*]

[*] This might have been anticipated from the previous section, since V and S are almost reciprocally related ($VS = 700$ is a close approximation to the regression line). If $\log V$ measures urbanism, therefore, $\log S$ may be a good measure of ruralism.

Alleged Alcoholism Rates in Time

If we have given sufficient evidence to justify further exploration of the proposition that alcoholism rates reveal intelligible spatial patterns, we may turn to the question of whether there is a similar patterning within a given area through time.

1. *Ontario: 1945 to 1953*

The matter is rather simply decided for one large area—Ontario—over a brief 9-year interval.* The data appear in Table 4.

TABLE 4

Alcoholics per 100,000 Population (of 20 Years of Age and Over), Ontario, and Population, for the Period of 1945 to 1953 [a]

Year	Alcoholism Rate	Ontario Population (in millions)
1945	1,042	2.694
1946	1,153	2.759
1947	1,295	2.808
1948	1,403	2.861
1949	1,545	2.921
1950	1,635	2.978
1951	1,605	3.043
1952	1,639	3.138
1953	1,782	3.196

[a] The figures are taken from Popham and Schmidt (10).

Again on the basis of a simple regression equation ($A = mP^n$) we get a correlation between A and P, or, more exactly, their logarithms, of .9368. Even for a nine-point series, this is perhaps a remarkable fit.

2. *The United States: 1940 to 1955*

If we wish to get a much larger area and a slightly larger sweep of time, we may take the data in Table 5 as also conveniently available.

On the basis of these data, and the now standard regression equation, we obtain

$$r_{AP} = .9384$$

which is virtually identical with the Ontario estimate.

Even when, paying attention to the radical difference between male and female rates (roughly, six to one), we separately analyze the sex-specific rates in reference to the sex-specific adult population, we get substantially

* Area and time-span, here and in the next section, were arbitrarily chosen because of ready availability, and not because of any fit, propitious or otherwise, to the hypothesis.

TABLE 5

Population and Alcoholism Rates in the United States, for the Period of 1940 to 1955 [a]

Year	A[b]	P[b]
1940	.4843	0.9365
1941	.4969	0.9445
1942	.5198	0.9518
1943	.5024	0.9590
1944	.4871	0.9638
1945	.4900	0.9685
1946	.5224	0.9754
1947	.5563	0.9809
1948	.5944	0.9859
1949	.5944	0.9917
1950	.5900	0.9983
1951	.6191	1.0030
1952	.6415	1.0086
1953	.6425	1.0191
1954	.6561	1.0253
1955	.6395	1.0334

[a] Sources: for alcoholism rates: Keller (6, p. 6); for adult population: census and intercensal estimates, 1940–1954, provided by Keller; 1955 estimate from *World Almanac*.

[b] A represents the log of the alcoholism rate per hundred adults, P the log of the adult population in tens of millions.

identical correlations (though with rather different regression equations), viz.,

$$\text{For males:} \quad r_{AP} = .9294$$
$$\text{For females:} \quad r_{AP} = .9498$$

It must be recalled at this point that when, as here, we hold space constant, variations in population correspond to variations in population density —and density, as we have already made out, is in turn a factor in communication or interaction potential.

Discussion

It has to this point, perhaps, been sufficiently demonstrated that probably alcoholism rates (and certainly deaths attributed to liver cirrhosis) vary both in space and time with population density or some function thereof. This may be enough to establish the method as "promising." However, some further work has been done and several questions emerge which warrant consideration.

We would like to know, for instance, whether the alcoholism "sex-ratio" is itself a function of P and V, that is, whether, as population density (or some appropriate function thereof) increases, so does the tendency of women to behave more like men in this respect. The answer at this stage appears to be a qualified "Yes," but in a peculiar fashion: in areas of low population potential, the sex differential seems unaffected by local density; in the high population potential areas, local density seems to drive female rates closer to male rates.

We would like to know something of the interplay between such rational interventions as legislation (for example, form of beverage sales control) and such "given" variables as P and V.

We must also "standardize" our data for age and sex, so that we can parcel out the interplay between "urbanism" (if that is what we are getting at by V), differential population composition, and deaths by liver cirrhosis, attributable to alcoholism or something else. Moreover, for the United States, we must standardize for race—or analyze white and Negro data separately—because many state and city rates are what they are in virtue of the pooling of two populations quite differentially at risk, quite differently affected by urbanism, and subject to the influence of separate population densities.

We need to know how the general mortality rate, the disease-specific mortality rates, and perhaps selected morbidity rates behave under the variation of the same variables by which we analyze alcoholism. These and numerous other studies are all under way, at least on a small scale. It might be exaggeration to call them "hopeful," but clearly it would be premature to foreclose so soon this line of inquiry. What is needed now is a determined assault from the beachheads established (and perhaps from others) until there is either a breakthrough or the data offer an impenetrable wall of intractable resistance.

It might well be asked, in view of the opening paragraphs of this chapter, "Interesting mapping apart, where are we now?" The question refers to both held-out hopes: the establishment of "normal expectations" in order to pick out "cases" (for example, cities or states) for further study of marked deviation therefrom, and potential direct light on etiology.

As to the first, the identification of the "non-typical"—states or cities or villages or times—for more detailed study, we must recognize two subsequent stages of which we are only in the first. Stage one consists in trying to account for the unaccounted-for variance by methods essentially similar to those already employed, but using new (and independent) variables. Examples of such variables might be disposable income or an index of an attitude, such as percentage of disposable income spent on such services as education or medical care. This is still a "headquarters," statistical and analytic operation. When, and only when, this process has been pushed to the point of diminishing returns, in my opinion, is it time to send out the field parties, anthropologically and sociologically oriented, into the field to see what other and perhaps more subtle factors account for still more of the variation that is not thitherto accounted for.

As to the second, etiology, it is a little early (we hardly have a thousand man-hours invested!) to speculate, but a convergent line of inquiry in animal ecology opens up some fascinating possibilities. As reported by Deevey (1), newly heightened interest in such phenomena as the cycle of the death-rates (per unit of time) of the Minnesota snowshoe hare, or the Norwegian lemming, reveal not only the previously recognized dependency on (species-specific) population density, but also a curious and suggestive mechanism by which the deaths that readjust the population size actually occur. The triggering mechanism seems to be not, as previously supposed, the Malthusian food shortage based on geometric increase in population accompanied by arithmetic increase in food supply. The mechanism seems to be the very compresence in the given space of the increasing number of organisms of the same species, acting upon one another to heighten excitement or mutual stimulation beyond some critical point.*

In any case, autopsies in the field reveal, not death by starvation, but signs of death by a variety of causes identical with Selye's "shock disease," most notably pathological change in the adrenal cortex, hypoglycemia, and liver cirrhosis or other hepatic damage. The behavior preceding death—in its "manic" character, in its blind rushing through what would normally be "sources of satisfaction" (e.g., a full field of ripe rye), in its evident "excitement" and "compulsive flight"—is all too suggestive of behavior we encounter, suitably translated into human terms, in the alcoholic (as well as other victims of processes of social or collective pathology).

The variable in human affairs corresponding to mere density in animal ecology is not yet known. Presumably it is some function of what communications engineers call "input-overload." Clearly, to the degree that society is differentiated and structured, the actual stimulation impinging on any one member of a group or class or aggregate is a function of the social structure as well as of the distance-density relations implied in such a measure as "population potential." There will be numerous other factors or interplaying causes as well—whether genetic, constitutional, psychodynamic, cultural, social, or historic. However, such other considerations, may well come in later to explain the "fine-grain" variation, once the main lines of the picture of distribution of alcoholism risks has been worked out.

At the very least—even failing any new understanding of etiology—such mapping should lead us to a livelier notion of what we can expect, what we

---

* There seems to be experimental evidence in the same direction, where increasing densities, even with lavish supply of food and other physiological necessities, have peculiar and deleterious biological or biopsychological effects. (These notions stem from a presentation by John B. Calhoun, "Behavioral Sinks," delivered at the American Psychiatric Association Meeting, December, 1959; see also *Proceedings of the Committee on the Environmental Determinants of Mental Health*, National Institute of Mental Health, Volumes for 1958 and 1959.)

must plan for, and what, in the short run, we can do nothing about. Knowledge regarding the last might hopefully release a lot of energy into attempting what we can.

References

1. Deevey, Edward S., Jr., "The Equilibrium Population," *in* Roy C. Francis (Ed.) *The Population Ahead,* Minneapolis: University of Minnesota Press, 1958, pp. 64–86.

2. Gibbins, Robert J., "Alcoholism in Ontario: A Survey of an Ontario County," *Quart. J. Stud. Alc.,* **15**:47–62, 1954.

3. Ipsen, Johannes, Merrill Moore, and Leo Alexander, "Prevalence of Alcoholism in the Population and Among Suicides and Accidents from Poisoning, Massachusetts 1938–1948," *Quart. J. Stud. Alc.,* **13**:204–214, 1952.

4. Jellinek, E. M., *Recent Trends in Alcoholism and in Alcohol Consumption,* New Haven, Conn.: Hillhouse Press, 1957.

5. ————, and Mark Keller, "Rates of Alcoholism in the United States of America 1940–1948," *Quart. J. Stud. Alc.,* **13**:49–59, 1952.

6. Keller, Mark, "Alcoholism: Nature and Extent of the Problem," *Ann. Amer. Acad. Pol. Soc. Sci.,* **315**:1–11, 1958.

7. ————, and Vera Efron, "Alcoholism in the Big Cities of the United States," *Quart. J. Stud. Alc.,* **17**:63–72, 1956.

8. Keller, Mark, and John R. Seeley, *The Alcohol Language,* Toronto: University of Toronto Press, 1958.

9. May, Jacques M., *The Ecology of Human Disease,* New York: M. D. Publications, 1959.

10. Popham, Robert, and Wolfgang Schmidt, *Statistics of Alcohol Use and Alcoholism in Canada 1871–1956,* Toronto: University of Toronto Press, 1958.

11. Seeley, John R., "The Estimation of Alcoholism Prevalence: A Critical Analysis of the Jellinek Formula," *Quart. J. Stud. Alc.,* **20**:245–254, 1959.

12. ————, "The W. H. O. Definition of Alcoholism," *Quart. J. Stud. Alc.,* **20**:352–356, 1959.

13. ————, Buford H. Junker, and R. Wallace Jones, Jr., *Community Chest,* Toronto: University of Toronto Press, 1957.

14. Stewart, John Q., "Demographic Gravitation: Evidence and Application," *Sociometry,* **11**:31–57, 1948.

15. Zipf, George Kingsly, *Human Behavior and the Principle of Least Effort,* Cambridge, Mass.: Addison-Wesley, 1952.

chapter 19

Cirrhosis mortality in three large cities: implications for alcoholism and intercity comparisons*

Arthur Pearl, Robert Buechley, and Wendell R. Lipscomb

The importance of studying mortality from cirrhosis of the liver, apart from its intrinsic significance as a cause of death, lies in its relation to alcoholism. This is because the most widely used method of estimating the prevalence of alcoholism, the Jellinek Estimation Formula, is based upon cirrhosis-mortality data. In this connection, when the three largest California cities—Los Angeles, San Francisco, and Oakland—are compared in terms of cirrhosis deaths as in Table 1, the crude rate for San Francisco proves to be much higher than the rates for the other two cities. Such a finding is not altogether unexpected in view of the fact that San Francisco has been previously estimated to be the most alcoholic large city in the United States (5).

TABLE 1

Number and Rate of Cirrhosis Deaths in California and California's Three Largest Cities (1950) [a]

	Number of Deaths			Total Deaths per
	Total	Male	Female	100,000 Population
State of California	1,791	1,129	662	16.9
San Francisco	327	219	108	42.2
Los Angeles	386	241	145	19.6
Oakland	79	45	34	20.5

[a] *Source:* Death Records—California State Department of Public Health.

* This chapter was written especially for this book.

345

Yet, through analysis of cirrhosis mortality *within* cities, this chapter aims to bring to light certain factors affecting cirrhosis mortality which may qualify conclusions based upon gross intercity comparisons. More specifically, it is our intent to show: (*a*) that cirrhosis mortality distributes disproportionately within, as well as between, cities; (*b*) that cirrhosis mortality is inversely related to measures of economic success, when census tracts of cities are used as the areas for analysis; (*c*) that intercity comparisons of cirrhosis mortality and of its derivative, alcoholism prevalence, have questionable meaning in certain instances, apart from adjustment for the distribution of correlated social factors.

Materials and Methods

Descriptive data permitting the desired kind of comparison were made available in card form by the following city health departments: Los Angeles, for the year 1950; San Francisco, for the years 1950 and 1952; and Oakland, for the years 1951, 1952, 1953, and 1954. These cards had been coded for age, sex, cause of death, and census tract of residence of the deceased.

Census tracts, the basic areal units used in this analysis, are relatively small homogeneous areas into which the Bureau of the Census divides American cities for the purpose of reporting statistical data. These reported data —including distributions by age and sex, occupation, family size, and race —allow computation, for tracts, of mortality ratios and measures of social characteristics. The availability both of population and of mortality data by census tracts made this study possible.

The measures of social characteristic used hereinafter are in substantial agreement with the social measures for tracts developed by Shevky and Bell (8, 9) and by Tryon (11).* The measures actually reported upon in this chapter are as follows:

a. Occupational level. This refers to the weighted mean of the occupational distribution given in Table 2 of the 1950 census tract statistics for tracted cities (12, 13). Low occupational level census tracts are characterized as slums or Skid Rows.

b. Family size. This refers to the mean number of non-institutionalized persons per dwelling unit, as determined from Table 1 of the 1950 census tract statistics (12, 13). The lowest extreme of family size is found in hotel areas, the highest extreme in suburbia and the slums.

Findings

1. *Occupational level and cirrhosis mortality*

As indicated in Table 2 and Figure 1, there is a marked inverse relation

* For an illustration of the similarity between the method employed here and that of Shevky, the reader is referred to (1, p. 35). Cultural group—another measure—referring to the ethnic or racial composition of the tract, was also obtained from 1950 census tract statistics. However, it was not employed in the analysis to follow because it is of doubtful value as an index of possibly important cultural differences. In point of fact, the measure shows little relation to variations in cirrhosis mortality.

between occupational level and cirrhosis death rate. By and large, the higher the occupational level the lower the cirrhosis death rate. The association is seen most strikingly by comparing the tracts of highest occupational level with those of lowest occupational level, which typically exhibit cir-

TABLE 2

Standardized Mortality Ratios [a] of Observed Cirrhosis Deaths to Expected Cirrhosis Deaths, by Occupational Level and Sex, for Los Angeles (1950), San Francisco (1950 and 1952), and Oakland (1951–1954)

Occupational Level	Males				Females			
	Total	Los Angeles	San Francisco	Oak-land	Total	Los Angeles	San Francisco	Oak-land
All Census Tracts	100	100	100	100	100	100	100	100
90–100 High	39	56	36	32	54	61	78	32
80–89	64	82	66	41	53	74	25	51
70–79	50	49	44	122	60	55	64	39
60–69	64	68	73	51	66	86	61	53
50–59	81	80	73	92	102	94	105	107
40–49	86	112	75	82	97	106	85	107
30–39	94	115	79	130	159	161	137	220
20–29	130	150	111	165	162	121	195	291
10–19	208	212	— [b]	206	202	260	— [b]	185
0–9 Low	437	468	461	302	490	526	736	194

[a] The standardized mortality ratio is the ratio of the observed number of deaths for a census tract, or group of tracts, to the age-sex standardized expected number of deaths for the same area, as determined by the age-sex specific rate in all census tracts (multiplied by 100 to avoid decimals). The method compares the experience in subgroup to that of a total group, i.e., the entire city.

[b] There were no census tracts in San Francisco with a score of 10–19 occupational level.

rhosis death rates about ten times those of the former. Striking differences at the extremes, however, hold true both for males and females, in all three cities examined.

2. Family size and cirrhosis mortality

The data in Table 3 show a strong inverse relation between family size and cirrhosis mortality, for both sexes. The association is lessened when the influence of occupational level on family size is removed, and appears strongest in the census tracts of lower occupational level. It is important to note that Skid Row—made up largely of hotels and flophouses and characterized by low occupational level and small family size—has the highest

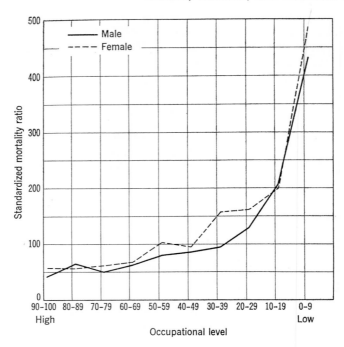

Figure 1. Standardized mortality ratios of observed to expected deaths from cirrhosis of the liver, by occupational level (Los Angeles, San Francisco, and Oakland combined). Source: California Department of Public Health (unpublished data).

cirrhosis mortality,* while the slum of low occupational level but large family size exhibits only moderately high cirrhosis mortality.

3. City boundaries and cirrhosis mortality

The effect on cirrhosis mortality of arbitrary assignment of city boundaries limiting the capacity for new developments can be evaluated if Los Angeles and San Francisco are made geographically comparable by appropriate constriction of Los Angeles or expansion of San Francisco. The former is approximated by delineating an area equal in size to San Francisco from the center of Los Angeles (all census tracts within a 3.7-mile radius of the Los Angeles City Hall). In this area—which, even so, has far less population density than does San Francisco—there is a much higher cirrhosis

---

* The relation of cirrhosis mortality to urbanism has been suggested by a number of other studies employing larger geographical units than were used here. Seeley's previous chapter may be taken as an example along with reports by Berkowitz (2), Mulford (6), and Parkhurst (7). Being restricted to census tract units within urban areas, the findings of the present study are not comparable to these other studies. They are entirely consistent, however, with the earlier findings of Faris and Dunham (3) regarding the concentration of "alcoholic psychosis" in the hobo, rooming-house, and foreign-born-inhabited slum areas of the city.

TABLE 3

Standardized Mortality Ratios of Observed to Expected Cirrhosis Deaths, by Family Size for Each Occupational Level (Los Angeles, San Francisco, and Oakland Combined)

| Occupational Level | Sex | Family Size (Persons per Dwelling Unit) | | | | |
		All Family Sizes	1.5 or Less	2	2.5	3 or More
All Occupational	Male	100	148	131	86	61
Levels	Female	100	202	121	86	80
High 90–100	Male	39	—	34	94	29
	Female	55	—	67	33	55
80–89	Male	64	—	58	75	53
	Female	53	—	22	72	53
70–79	Male	50	17	105	14	50
	Female	60	65	22	89	64
60–69	Male	63	140	68	72	42
	Female	66	108	109	57	62
50–59	Male	81	88	64	88	85
	Female	102	177	68	121	76
40–49	Male	86	152	105	113	70
	Female	97	117	166	101	74
30–39	Male	94	143	126	80	42
	Female	159	287	187	131	140
20–29	Male	130	276	108	149	193
	Female	162	566	191	48	172
10–19	Male	208	220	232	169	87
	Female	202	172	280	132	290
Low 0–9	Male	417	417	584	194	—
	Female	491	811	552	131	—

death rate than for the city as a whole. The total cirrhosis death rate for this small central Los Angeles area is 29.8 deaths per 100,000 population, as compared to rates of 19.6 deaths per 100,000 population of the entire city of Los Angeles and 42.2 for San Francisco. Expansion of San Francisco to Los Angeles dimensions, on the other hand, can be approximated by substituting the San Francisco metropolitan area * (San Francisco, Alameda, Contra Costa, San Mateo, Marin, and Solano Counties) for San Francisco

* Los Angeles cirrhosis mortality would also be reduced, but to a lesser extent, were the Los Angeles metropolitan area to be used as the geographical unit for comparison. However, there would remain important differences, as compared to the San Francisco metropolitan area along the ecological dimensions discussed here. It is important to bear in mind that the intent of this section of this chapter is to question intercity comparison of cirrhosis mortality where wide differences in city ecology exist. More exhaustive analysis of the multifactor conditions which affect cirrhosis mortality awaits more intensive study.

proper. This results in a reduction of the cirrhosis mortality rate from 42.2 per 100,000 population to 23.4 per 100,000. It is entirely consistent with this kind of analysis to find one of the least alcoholic cities, Berkeley (5), and the most alcoholic city, San Francisco, juxtaposed.

Summarized in Table 4 is the extent to which gross adjustments of cities'

TABLE 4

Crude Cirrhosis-Mortality Rates for Los Angeles and San Francisco (1950), Adjusted for City Area

	Crude Rate per 100,000	Constricted Los Angeles	Expanded San Francisco
Los Angeles	19.6	29.8	—
San Francisco	42.2	—	23.4
San Francisco's excess in cirrhosis mortality	23.4	13.6	4.2
San Francisco's cirrhosis mortality "increased risk"	2.2:1	1.4:1	1.2:1

boundaries affect cirrhosis mortality rates. These are not intended to be precise explanations, since other variables which could influence the rates—such as age or sex distribution of the population, or percentage of deaths which are autopsied—are not taken into consideration. The figures indicate, however, the influence of arbitrary boundary factors on estimates of cirrhosis mortality, and the questionable value of intercity comparisons when there is no adjustment for these factors.*

Summary and Discussion

It has been shown in this chapter that cirrhosis mortality is not distributed uniformly in the three largest cities of California. Using groups of census tracts as the unit of analysis, a very strong inverse relation between economic success—as measured by average occupational level of census tract—and cirrhosis mortality was demonstrated. Small family size, measured by census-tract averages, also correlated with cirrhosis mortality, but this association was greatly reduced by adjustment for the influence of occupational level. It was noted, however, that the Skid-Row areas, typified by low occupational level and small family size, exhibited the highest cirrhosis mortality rates. The possibility exists, of course, that the apparent economic influence upon cirrhosis mortality could be partly a function of protective

* After the above was written, we found that a classification of cities has been made (4) which designates San Francisco city as "underbounded," Los Angeles city and Oakland city as both "under- and overbounded." This classification, when combined with our analysis above, would predict that, in comparison with "truebounded" cities, underbounded cities generally would be high in cirrhosis mortality and overbounded cities low.

forces manipulating death certification in higher economic areas. A follow-back analysis of a sample of death certificates might well be inaugurated to investigate this question in future research.

The apparently strong association of social factors with cirrhosis mortality seems to call for the analysis of city ecology to give meaning to inter-city comparisons of cirrhosis mortality rates—or their derivative, alcoholism prevalence rates. Broadly speaking, we may say that the differences in these rates may be a function of the differential capacity of cities to grow within their political boundaries. The influence of political assignment of boundaries is most pertinent here. San Francisco, for instance, is a city of 42 square miles with limited potential for internal growth. Many people with better paying occupations and with families have come to reside in adjoining suburbs, outside the city limits. The city proper is old, with relatively large slum and Skid-Row areas. By contrast, Los Angeles, with an area of 450 square miles, is a relatively new and decentralized city. In 1900 the population of Los Angeles was one-third that of San Francisco, but by 1950 Los Angeles' population was two and a half times that of San Francisco. Los Angeles, with its capacity for internal growth, is in extreme contrast to San Francisco.* As we have seen, even gross adjustment of the boundaries of San Francisco and Los Angeles—so as to make them more comparable sociologically—greatly reduces the difference in the observed cirrhosis mortality rates of the two cities.

The findings of this chapter clearly indicate the need for further study of the phenomenon of cirrhosis mortality within urban areas, as opposed to an exclusive focus upon intercity comparisons. Epidemiologically, further comparative study within cities of those groups or strata which exhibit different cirrhosis death rates should enhance our understanding both of cirrhosis as a cause of death and of its relations to its traditional associate, alcoholism.

References

1. *Alcoholism and California, Related Statistics, 1900–1956,* Berkeley: State of California, Department of Public Health, 1958.

2. Berkowitz, Morris I., "A Comparison of Some Ecological Variables with Rates of Alcoholism," *Quart. J. Stud. Alc.,* 18:126–129, 1957.

3. Faris, Robert E. L., and H. Warren Dunham, *Mental Disorders in Urban Areas,* Chicago: University of Chicago Press, 1939.

4. International Urban Research, *The World's Metropolitan Areas,* Berkeley and Los Angeles: University of California Press, 1959.

5. Keller, Mark, and Vera Efron, "Alcoholism in the Big Cities of the United States," *Quart. J. Stud. Alc.,* 17:63–72, 1956.

6. Mulford, Harold A., and Carl E. Waisanen, "A Summary Report to the Committee for Research on Alcoholism," *A Survey of the Alcoholism Problem in Iowa,* 1957.

* For a more complete exposition of the differences in the rate and pattern of growth of San Francisco and Los Angeles, the reader is referred to Thompson (10).

7. Parkhurst, Elizabeth, "Differential Mortality in New York State, Exclusive of New York City, by Age, Sex, and Cause of Death, According to Degree of Urbanization," *Amer. J. Pub. Health,* **46**: 959–966, 1956.

8. Shevky, Eshref, and Wendell Bell, *Social Area Analysis,* Stanford Sociological Series #1, Stanford: Stanford University Press, 1955.

9. ————, and Marilyn Williams, *Social Areas of Los Angeles,* Berkeley: University of California Press, 1949.

10. Thompson, Warren S., *Growth and Changes in California's Population,* Los Angeles: The Haynes Foundation, 1955.

11. Tryon, Robert C., *Identification of Social Areas by Cluster Analysis,* University of California Publications in Psychology (Vol. 8, No. 1), Berkeley: University of California Press, 1955.

12. United States Bureau of Census, *Los Angeles Census Tracts, 1950,* Washington: Department of Commerce, 1951.

13. ————, *San Francisco–Oakland Census Tracts, 1950,* Washington: Department of Commerce, 1951.

THE PATTERNING OF ALCOHOLISM

Introductory Note. A major line of investigation in clinical medicine has always been concerned with the "natural history" of disease. This approach assumes that typically each disease has a sequence of symptoms which extends from the prodromal to the terminal phases of the illness. In short, the disease, whether alcoholism or diabetes, has patterned symptomatology which can best be discerned if the patient is followed over a number of years. For certain diseases, it is possible for therapeutic intervention to alter the "natural history" of the disease, and the impact of this intervention must be carefully evaluated in each case.

E. M. Jellinek, in one of the most significant contributions to the alcoholism field, applies the natural-history-of-disease assumptions to a questionnaire study of the drinking habits of male alcohol addicts. This study, "Phases of Alcohol Addiction" (which appears here as Chapter 20), is based on the assumption that there are two categories of alcoholics—alcohol addicts and habitual symptomatic excessive drinkers (non-addicts). The crucial differentiating factor is the addicts' "loss of control after drinking begins."

Members of Jellinek's questionnaire group were presented with a set of symptoms associated with alcoholism and were instructed to indicate the sequence in which these features appeared in their own drinking histories. Jellinek's findings are that the symptoms occur in the *typical case in sequence,* but "not all symptoms . . . occur necessarily in all alcohol addicts, nor do they occur in every addict in the same sequence." These symptoms are patterned into four sequential phases; namely, the prealcoholic symptomatic, the prodromal, the crucial, and the chronic phases. Thus Jellinek has documented concrete stages through which alcoholism progresses. This ingenious research study by Jellinek has perhaps had more impact on the alcoholism field than any other and permeates the studies presented by Park (Chapter 25) and Jackson (Chapter 27), among others, in this book.

H. M. Trice and J. Richard Wahl have, in Chapter 21, provided us with, basically, a replication and refinement of the Jellinek study. They were concerned that Jellinek's concentration on the sequential order of symptoms in drinking histories would "mask a significant clustering of individual symptoms" (symptoms occurring simultaneously) and would "create averages that have little individual value." Both the study design and the methodological techniques employed by Trice and Wahl in their analysis of selected symptoms submitted to male alcoholics, both Alcoholics-Anonymous affiliates and non-affiliates, are more complex than those employed by Jellinek. The study group were asked to state the age of onset of fourteen symptoms which were selected to represent early, middle, and late stages of alcoholism; they also could indicate non-recall or the absence of the symptom. The resultant data were analyzed by means of rank order comparisons in which the onset age of each symptom was compared with that of each of the thirteen remaining symptoms.

The results of the Trice and Wahl study indicate that Jellinek's concern with the sequential appearance of symptoms obscures the fact that, particularly during the intermediate stages of the disease, there is a clustering or simultaneous appearance of these signs. They conclude that "only initial and terminal symptoms of the process (alcoholism) were good indicators of stage, and the intermediary stages were obscured."

What do we make of these partially conflicting reports on the patterning of alcoholism? First, both studies suffer from the limitations of their data; they are retrospective and the individuals, although having drinking problems, are not in most cases medically diagnosed alcoholics. Despite this, the studies agree that the initial and terminal phases of alcoholism are quite well defined; their disagreements center on the middle phases. Perhaps the ideal natural-history-of-disease study—that is a long-term study of a cohort of medically diagnosed alcoholics—would be desirable. However, in these study groups there is no disagreement over the patterning of alcoholism, only on whether certain symptoms in the middle phases are clustered or sequential.

In Chapter 22, Jellinek turns his attention to the frequently observed but rarely investigated area of "Cultural Differences in the Meaning of Alcoholism." Most of the alcohol literature is permeated with the Northwestern European and American conceptions of alcoholism which involve the steady symptomatic excessive drinker with or without addictive features. However, as Jellinek points out in his brief essay, there is another pattern of alcoholism found in the wine-growing countries of Southern Europe and South America. France, in many respects, is the ideal case in which may be found alcoholism without the extremes of intoxication—represented by the "inveterate drinker." Jellinek maintains that these two patterns of alcoholism in Western culture carry with them different assumptions concerning etiology and techniques of therapeutic intervention. Jellinek's descriptive essay only scratches the surface of cultural differences in the definition of alcoholism, its patterning and treatment within Western culture, and only implies the existence of different forms of alcoholism in non-Western cultures. (See Section 1.) As this volumes goes to press, Jellinek (1) is attempting to refine the classification of alcoholics, emphasizing physiological factors more than do behavioral scientists.

References

1. Jellinek, E. M., *The Disease Concept of Alcoholism*, New Haven, Conn.: Hillhouse Press, 1960.

chapter 20

Phases
of alcohol addiction [*]

E. M. Jellinek

Only certain forms of excessive drinking—those which in the present report are designated as alcoholism—are accessible to medical-psychiatric treatment. The other forms of excessive drinking, too, present more or less serious problems, but they can be managed only on the level of applied sociology, including law enforcement. Nevertheless, the medical profession may have an advisory role in the handling of these latter problems and must take an interest in them from the viewpoint of preventive medicine.

The conditions which have been briefly defined by the Alcoholism Subcommittee of the World Health Organization as alcoholism are described in the following pages in greater detail, in order to delimit more definitely those excessive drinkers whose rehabilitation primarily requires medical-psychiatric treatment. Furthermore, such detailed description may serve to forestall a certain potential danger which attaches to the disease conception of alcoholism, or, more precisely, of addictive drinking.

With the exception of specialists in alcoholism, the broader medical profession, representatives of the biological and social sciences, and the lay

[*] This chapter presents a summary and refined view of the conception of phases in the drinking history of alcoholics originally set forth in (1). It incorporates those modifications suggested by extensive application and testing of the questionnaire upon which the earlier study was based. The present version was first published under the auspices of the Alcoholism Subcommittee of the World Health Organization (Second Report, Annex 2, World Health Organization Technical Report Series, No. 48, Aug. 1952) and was subsequently reproduced in the *Quart. J. Stud. Alc.*, 13:673–684, 1952. It is reprinted here with only slight modification.

public use the term "alcoholism" as a designation for any form of excessive drinking instead of as a label for a limited and well-defined area of excessive drinking behaviors. Automatically, the disease conception of alcoholism becomes extended to all excessive drinking irrespective of whether or not there is any physical or psychological pathology involved in the drinking behavior. Such an unwarranted extension of the disease conception can only be harmful, because sooner or later the misapplication will reflect on the legitimate use too and, more importantly, will tend to weaken the ethical basis of social sanctions against drunkenness.

The Disease Conception of Alcohol Addiction

The Subcommittee has distinguished two categories of alcoholics, namely, "alcohol addicts" and "habitual symptomatic excessive drinkers." For brevity's sake the latter will be referred to as non-addictive alcoholics. Strictly speaking, the disease conception attaches to the alcohol addicts only, but not to the habitual symptomatic excessive drinkers.

In both groups the excessive drinking is symptomatic of underlying psychological or social pathology, but in one group after several years of excessive drinking "loss of control" over the alcohol intake occurs, while in the other group this phenomenon never develops. The group with the loss of control is designated as "alcohol addicts." (There are other differences between these two groups and these will be seen in the course of the description of the "phases.")

The disease conception of alcohol addiction does not apply to the excessive drinking, but solely to the loss of control which occurs in only one group of alcoholics and then only after many years of excessive drinking. There is no intention to deny that the non-addictive alcoholic is a sick person; but his ailment is not the excessive drinking, but rather the psychological or social difficulties from which alcohol intoxication gives temporary surcease.

The loss of control is a disease condition per se which results from a process that superimposes itself upon those abnormal psychological conditions of which excessive drinking is a symptom. The fact that many excessive drinkers drink as much as or more than the addict for 30 or 40 years without developing loss of control indicates that in the group of alcohol addicts a superimposed process must occur.

Whether this superimposed process is of a psychopathological nature or whether some physical pathology is involved cannot be stated as yet with any degree of assurance, the claims of various investigators notwithstanding. Nor is it possible to go beyond conjecture concerning the question whether the loss of control originates in a predisposing factor (psychological or physical), or whether it is a factor acquired in the course of prolonged excessive drinking.

The fact that this loss of control does not occur in a large group of excessive drinkers would point towards a predisposing X factor in the addic-

tive alcoholics. On the other hand this explanation is not indispensable, as
the difference between addictive and non-addictive alcoholics could be a
matter of acquired modes of living—for instance, a difference in acquired
nutritional habits.

The Meaning of Symptomatic Drinking

The use of alcoholic beverages by society has primarily a symbolic meaning, and secondarily it achieves "function." Cultures which accept this custom differ in the nature and degree of the "functions," which they regard as
legitimate. The differences in these functions are determined by the general
pattern of the culture—for example, the need for the release and for the
special control of aggression, the need and the ways and means of achieving
identification, and the nature and intensity of anxieties and the modus for
their relief. The more the original symbolic character of the custom is preserved, the less room will be granted by the culture to the functions of
drinking.

Any drinking within the accepted ways is symptomatic of the culture
of which the drinker is a member. Within that frame of cultural symptomatology there may be in addition individual symptoms expressed in the
act of drinking. The fact that a given individual drinks a glass of beer with
his meal may be the symptom of the culture which accepts such a use as
a refreshment, or as a "nutritional supplement." That this individual drinks
at this given moment may be a symptom of his fatigue, his elation, or some
other mood, and thus an individual symptom, but, if his culture accepts the
use for these purposes, it is at the same time a cultural symptom. In this
sense even the small or moderate use of alcoholic beverages is symptomatic,
and it may be said that all drinkers are culturally symptomatic drinkers
or, at least, started as such.

The vast majority of the users of alcoholic beverages stay within the limits
of the culturally accepted drinking behaviors and drink predominantly as
an expression of their culture. While an individual expression may be present
in these behaviors its role remains insignificant.

For the purpose of the present discussion the expression "symptomatic
drinking" will be limited to the predominant use of alcoholic beverages for
the relief of major individual stresses.

A certain unknown proportion of these users of alcoholic beverages, perhaps 20 per cent, are occasionally inclined to take advantage of the functions of alcohol which they have experienced in the course of its "cultural
use." At least at times, the individual motivation becomes predominant and
on those occasions alcohol loses its character as an ingredient of a beverage
and is used as a drug.

The "occasional symptomatic excessive drinker" tends to take care of
the stresses and strains of living in socially accepted—that is, "normal"—
ways, and his drinking is most of the time within the cultural pattern. After
a long accumulation of stresses, however, or because of some particularly

heavy stress, his tolerance for tension is lowered and he takes recourse to heroic relief of his symptoms through alcoholic intoxication.* Under these circumstances the "relief" may take on an explosive character, and thus the occasional symptomatic excessive drinker may create serious problems. No psychological abnormality can be claimed for this type of drinker, although he does not represent a well-integrated personality.

Nevertheless, within the group of apparent occasional symptomatic excessive drinkers, there is a certain proportion of definitely deviating personalities who after a shorter or longer period of occasional symptomatic relief take recourse to a constant alcoholic relief, and drinking becomes with them a "mode of living." These are the "alcoholics" of whom again a certain proportion suffer loss of control—that is, become addictive alcoholics.

The proportion of alcoholics (addictive and non-addictive) varies from country to country, but does not seem to exceed in any country 5 per cent or 6 per cent of all users of alcoholic beverages. The ratio of addictive to non-addictive alcoholics is unknown.

The Chart of Alcohol Addiction

The course of alcohol addiction is represented graphically in Figure 1. The diagram is based on an analysis of more than two thousand drinking histories of male alcohol addicts. Not all symptoms shown in the diagram occur necessarily in all alcohol addicts, nor do they occur in every addict in the same sequence. The "phases" and the sequences of symptoms within the phases are characteristic, however, of the great majority of alcohol addicts and represent what may be called the average trend.

For alcoholic women the phases are not as clear cut as in men, and the development is frequently more rapid.

The phases vary in their duration according to individual characteristics and environmental factors. The "lengths" of the different phases on the diagram do not indicate differences in duration but are determined by the number of symptoms which have to be shown in any given phase.

The chart of the phases of alcohol addiction serves as the basis of description, and the differences between addictive and non-addictive alcoholics are indicated in the text.

1. The prealcoholic symptomatic phase

The very beginning of the use of alcoholic beverages is always socially motivated in the prospective addictive and non-addictive alcoholic. In contrast to the average social drinker, however, the prospective alcoholic (together with the occasional symptomatic excessive drinker) soon experiences a rewarding relief in the drinking situation. The relief is strongly marked in his case because either his tensions are much greater than in other members of his social circle, or he has not learned to handle those tensions as others do.

* This group does not include the regular "periodic alcoholics."

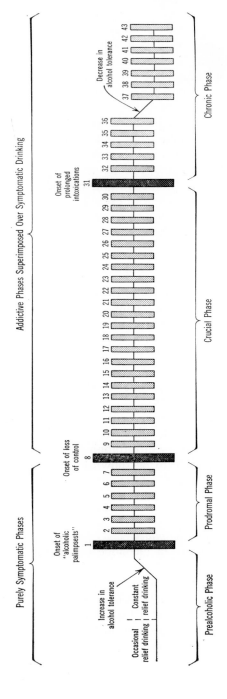

Figure 1. The phases of alcohol addiction. The large bars denote the onset of major symptoms that initiate phases. The short bars denote the onset of symptoms within phases. Reference to the numbering of the symptoms is made in the text, where the numbers appear in boldface type, in parentheses.

Initially this drinker ascribes his relief to the situation rather than to the drinking and he seeks therefore those situations in which incidental drinking will occur. Sooner or later, of course, he becomes aware of the contingency between relief and drinking.

In the beginning he seeks this relief occasionally only, but in the course of 6 months to 2 years his tolerance for tension decreases to such a degree that he takes recourse to alcoholic relief practically daily. Nevertheless his drinking does not result in overt intoxication, but he reaches toward the evening a stage of surcease from emotional stress. Even in the absence of intoxication this involves fairly heavy drinking, particularly in comparison to the use of alcoholic beverages by other members of his circle. The drinking is, nevertheless, not conspicuous either to his associates or to himself. After a certain time an increase in alcohol tolerance may be noticed; that is, the drinker requires a somewhat larger amount of alcohol than formerly in order to reach the desired stage of sedation.

This type of drinking behavior may last from several months to 2 years, according to circumstances, and may be designated as the prealcoholic phase, which is divided into stages of occasional relief drinking and constant relief drinking.

2. The prodromal phase

The sudden onset of a behavior resembling the "blackouts" in anoxemia marks the beginning of the prodromal phase of alcohol addiction. The drinker who may have had not more than 50 or 60 grams of absolute alcohol and who is not showing any signs of intoxication may carry on a reasonable conversation or may go through quite elaborate activities without a trace of memory the next day, although sometimes one or two minor details may be hazily remembered. This amnesia, which is not connected with loss of consciousness, has been called by Bonhoeffer the "alcoholic palimpsests," with reference to old Roman manuscripts superimposed over an incompletely erased manuscript.

Alcoholic palimpsests (1) * may occur on rare occasions in an average drinker when he drinks intoxicating amounts in a state of physical or emotional exhaustion. Non-addictive alcoholics, of course, also may experience palimpsests, but infrequently and only following rather marked intoxication. Thus, the frequency of palimpsests and their occurrence after medium alcohol intake are characteristic of the prospective alcohol addict.

This would suggest heightened susceptibility to alcohol in the prospective addict. Such a susceptibility may be psychologically or physiologically determined. The analogy with the blackouts of anoxemia is tempting. Of course, an insufficient oxygen supply cannot be assumed, but a malutilization of oxygen may be involved. The present status of the knowledge of alcoholism

---

* The numerals in boldface type in parentheses following the designations of the individual symptoms represent their order as given in Figure 1.

does not permit of more than vague conjectures which, nevertheless, may constitute bases for experimental hypotheses.

The onset of alcoholic palimpsests is followed (in some instances preceded) by the onset of drinking behaviors which indicate that, for this drinker, beer, wine, and spirits have practically ceased to be beverages and have become sources of a drug which he "needs." Some of these behaviors imply that this drinker has some vague realization that he drinks differently from others.

Surreptitious drinking (2) is one of these behaviors. At social gatherings the drinker seeks occasions for having a few drinks unknown to others, as he fears that if it were known that he drinks more than the others he would be misjudged. Those to whom drinking is only a custom or a small pleasure would not understand that because he is different from them alcohol is for him a necessity, although he is not a drunkard.

Preoccupation with alcohol (3) is furthur evidence of this need. When he prepares to go to a social gathering his first thought is whether there will be sufficient alcohol for his requirements, and he has several drinks in anticipation of a possible shortage. Because of this increasing dependence upon alcohol, the onset of *avid drinking* (4) (gulping of the first or first two drinks) occurs at this time.

As the drinker realizes, at least vaguely, that his drinking is outside of the ordinary, he develops *guilt feelings about his drinking behavior* (5), and because of this he begins to *avoid reference to alcohol* (6) in conversation.

These behaviors, together with an *increasing frequency of alcoholic palimpsests* (7), foreshadow the development of alcohol addiction; they are premonitory signs. This period may be called the prodromal phase of alcohol addiction.

The consumption of alcoholic beverages in the prodromal phase is "heavy," but not conspicuous, as it does not lead to marked, overt intoxications. The effect is that the prospective addict reaches towards evening a state which may be designated as emotional anesthesia. Nevertheless, this condition requires drinking well beyond the ordinary usage. The drinking is on a level which may begin to interfere with metabolic and nervous processes as evidenced by the frequent alcoholic palimpsests.

The "covering-up" which is shown by the drinker in this stage is the first sign that his drinking might separate him from society, although initially the drinking may have served as a technique to overcome some lack of social integration.

As in the prodromal phase rationalizations of the drinking behavior are not strong and there is some insight as well as fear of possible consequences, it is feasible to intercept incipient alcohol addiction at this stage. In the United States of America, the publicity given to the prodromal symptoms begins to bring prospective alcoholics to clinics as well as to groups of Alcoholics Anonymous. It goes without saying that even at this stage the only possible modus for this type of drinker is total abstinence.

The prodromal period may last anywhere from 6 months to 4 or 5 years according to the physical and psychological makeup of the drinker, his family ties, vocational relations, general interests, and so forth. The prodromal phase ends and the crucial or acute phase begins with the onset of loss of control, which is the critical symptom of alcohol addiction.

3. *The crucial phase*

Loss of control (8) means that any drinking of alcohol starts a chain reaction which is felt by the drinker as a physical demand for alcohol. This state, possibly a conversion phenomenon, may take hours or weeks for its full development; it lasts until the drinker is too intoxicated or too sick to ingest more alcohol. The physical discomfort following this drinking behavior is contrary to the object of the drinker, which is merely to feel "different." As a matter of fact, the bout may not even be started by any individual need of the moment, but by a "social drink."

After recovery from the intoxication, it is not the loss of control—that is, the physical demand, apparent or real—which leads to a new bout after several days or several weeks. The renewal of drinking is set off by the original psychological conflicts or by a simple social situation which involves drinking.

The loss of control is effective after the individual has started drinking, but it does not give rise to the beginning of a new drinking bout. The drinker has lost the ability to control the quantity once he has started, but he still can control whether he will drink on any given occasion or not. This is evidenced in the fact that after the onset of loss of control the drinker can go through a period of voluntary abstinence ("going on the water wagon").

The question of why the drinker returns to drinking after repeated disastrous experiences is often raised. Although he will not admit it, the alcohol addict believes that he has lost his will power and that he can and must regain it. He is not aware that he has undergone a process which makes it impossible for him to control his alcohol intake. To "master his will" becomes a matter of the greatest importance to him. When tensions rise, "a drink" is the natural remedy for him and he is convinced that this time it will be one or two drinks only.

Practically simultaneously with the onset of loss of control the alcohol addict begins to *rationalize his drinking behavior* (9): he produces the well-known alcoholic "*alibis.*" He finds explanations which convince him that he did not lose control, but that he had a good reason to get intoxicated and that in the absence of such reasons he is able to handle alcohol as well as anybody else. These rationalizations are needed primarily for himself and only secondarily for his family and associates. The rationalizations make it possible for him to continue with his drinking, and this is of the greatest importance to him as he knows no alternative for handling his problems.

This is the beginning of an entire "system of rationalizations" which progressively spreads to every aspect of his life. While this system largely originates in inner needs, it also serves to counter *social pressures* (**10**) which arise at the time of the loss of control. At this time, of course, the drinking behavior becomes conspicuous, and the parents, wife, friends, and employer may begin to reprove and warn the drinker.

In spite of all the rationalizations there is a marked loss of self-esteem, and this of course demands compensations which in a certain sense are also rationalizations. One way of compensation is the *grandiose behavior* (**11**) which the addict begins to display at this time. Extravagant expenditures and grandiloquence convince him that he is not as bad as he had thought at times.

The rationalization system gives rise to another system, namely the "system of isolation." The rationalizations quite naturally lead to the idea that the fault lies not within himself but in others, and this results in a progressive withdrawal from the social environment. The first sign of this attitude is a *marked aggressive behavior* (**12**).

Inevitably, this latter behavior generates guilt. While even in the prodromal period remorse about the drinking arose from time to time, now *persistent remorse* (**13**) arises, and this added tension is a further source of drinking.

In compliance with social pressures the addict now goes on *periods of total abstinence* (**14**). There is, however, another modus of control of drinking which arises out of the rationalizations of the addict. He believes that his trouble arises from his not drinking the right kind of beverages or not in the right way. He now attempts to control his troubles by *changing the pattern of his drinking* (**15**), by setting up rules about not drinking before a certain hour of the day, in certain places only, and so forth.

The strain of the struggle increases his hostility towards his environment and he begins to *drop friends* (**16**) and *quit jobs* (**17**). It goes without saying that some associates drop him and that he loses some jobs, but more frequently he takes the initiative as an anticipatory defense.

The isolation becomes more pronounced as his entire *behavior becomes alcohol centered* (**18**); that is, he begins to be concerned about how activities might interfere with his drinking instead of how his drinking may affect his activities. This, of course, involves a more marked egocentric outlook which leads to more rationalizations and more isolation. There ensues a *loss of outside interests* (**19**) and a *reinterpretation of interpersonal relations* (**20**) coupled with *marked self-pity* (**21**). The isolation and rationalizations have increased by this time in intensity and find their expression either in contemplated or actual *geographic escape* (**22**).

Under the impact of these events, a *change in family habits* (**23**) occurs. The wife and children, who may have had good social activities, may withdraw for fear of embarrassment or, quite contrarily, they may suddenly begin intensive outside activities in order to escape from the home environment. This and other events lead to the onset of *unreasonable resentments* (24) in the alcohol addict.

The predominance of concern with alcohol induces the addict to *protect his supply* (25)—that is, to lay in a large stock of alcoholic beverages, hidden in the most unthought-of places. A fear of being deprived of the most necessary substance for his living is expressed in this behavior.

Neglect of proper nutrition (26) aggravates the beginnings of the effects of heavy drinking on the organism, and frequently the *first hospitalization* (27) for some alcoholic complaint occurs at this time.

One of the frequent organic effects is a *decrease of the sexual drive* (28) which increases hostility towards the wife and is rationalized into her extramarital sex activities, which gives rise to the well-known *alcoholic jealousy* (29).

By this time remorse, resentment, struggle between alcoholic needs and duties, loss of self-esteem, and doubts and false reassurance have so disorganized the addict that he cannot start the day without steadying himself with alcohol immediately after arising or even before getting out of bed. This is the beginning of *regular matutinal drinking* (30), which previously had occurred on rare occasions only.

This behavior terminates the crucial phase and foreshadows the beginnings of the chronic phase.

During the crucial phase intoxication is the rule, but it is limited to the evening hours. For the most part of this phase drinking begins sometime in the afternoon and by the evening intoxication is reached. It should be noted that the "physical demand" involved in the loss of control results in continual rather than continuous drinking. Particularly the "matutinal drink" which occurs toward the end of the crucial phase shows the continual pattern. The first drink at rising, let us say at 7 A.M., is followed by another drink at 10 or 11 A.M., and another drink around 1 P.M., while the more intensive drinking hardly starts before 5 P.M.

Throughout, the crucial phase presents a great struggle of the addict against the complete loss of social footing. Occasionally the aftereffects of the evening's intoxication cause some loss of time, but generally the addict succeeds in looking after his job, although he neglects his family. He makes a particularly strong effort to avoid intoxication during the day. Progressively, however, his social motivations weaken more and more, and the "morning drink" jeopardizes his effort to comply with his vocational duties as this effort involves a conscious resistance against the apparent or real physical demand for alcohol.

The onset of the loss of control is the beginning of the "disease process" of alcohol addiction which is superimposed over the excessive symptomatic drinking. Progressively, this disease process undermines the morale and the physical resistance of the addict.

4. *The chronic phase*

The increasingly dominating role of alcohol, and the struggle against the demand set up by matutinal drinking, at last break down the resistance of the addict and he finds himself for the first time intoxicated in the daytime and on a weekday and continues in that state for several days until he is entirely incapacitated. This is the onset of *prolonged intoxications* (31), referred to in the vernacular as "benders."

This latter drinking behavior meets with such unanimous social rejection that it involves a grave social risk. Only an originally psychopathic personality or a person who has later in life undergone a psychopathological process would expose himself to that risk.

These long-drawn-out bouts commonly bring about *marked ethical deterioration* (32) and *impairment of thinking* (33), which, however, are not irreversible. True *alcoholic psychoses* (34) may occur at this time, but in not more than 10 per cent of all alcoholics.

The loss of morale is so heightened that the addict *drinks with persons far below his social level* (35) in preference to his usual associates—perhaps as an opportunity to appear superior—and, if nothing else is available, he will *take recourse to "technical products"* (36) such as bay rum or rubbing alcohol.

A *loss of alcohol tolerance* (37) is commonly noted at this time. Half of the previously required amount of alcohol may be sufficient to bring about a stuporous state.

Indefinable fears (38) and *tremors* (39) become persistent. Sporadically these symptoms occur also during the crucial phase, but in the chronic phase they are present as soon as alcohol disappears from the organism. In consequence, the addict "controls" the symptoms through alcohol. The same is true of *psychomotor inhibition* (40), the inability to initiate a simple mechanical act—such as winding a watch—in the absence of alcohol.

The need to control these symptoms of drinking exceeds the need of relieving the original underlying symptoms of the personality conflict, and the *drinking takes on an obsessive character* (41).

In many addicts, approximately 60 per cent, some *vague religious desires develop* (42) as the rationalizations become weaker. Finally, in the course of the frequently prolonged intoxications, the rationalizations become so frequently and so mercilessly tested against reality that the entire *rationalization system fails* (43) and the addict admits defeat. He now becomes spontaneously accessible to treatment. Nevertheless, his obsessive drinking continues as he does not see a way out.

Formerly it was thought that the addict must reach this stage of utter defeat in order to be treated successfully. Clinical experience has shown, however, that this "defeat" can be induced long before it would occur of itself and that even incipient alcoholism can be intercepted. Since the incipient alcoholic can be easily recognized, it is possible to tackle the problem from the preventive angle.

5. The "alcoholic personality"

The aggressions, feelings of guilt, remorse, resentments, withdrawal, etc., which develop in the phases of alcohol addiction, are largely consequences of the excessive drinking. At the same time, however, they constitute sources of more excessive drinking.

In addition to relieving, through alcohol, symptoms of an underlying personality conflict, the addict now tends to relieve, through further drinking, the stresses created by his drinking behavior.

By and large, these reactions to excessive drinking—which have quite a neurotic appearance—give the impression of an "alcoholic personality," although they are secondary behaviors superimposed over a large variety of personality types which have a few traits in common, in particular a low capacity for coping with tensions. There does not emerge, however, any specific personality trait or physical characteristic which inevitably would lead to excessive symptomatic drinking. Apart from psychological and possibly physical liabilities, there must be a constellation of social and economic factors which facilitate the development of addictive and non-addictive alcoholism in a susceptible terrain.

The Non-addictive Alcoholic

Some differences between the non-addictive alcoholic and the alcohol addict have previously been stated in this chapter. These differences may be recapitulated and elaborated, and additional differential features may be considered.

The main difference may be readily visualized by erasing the large bars of the diagram in Figure 1. This results in a diagram which suggests a progressive exacerbation of the use of alcohol for symptom relief and of the social and health consequences incumbent upon such use, but without any clear-cut phases.

The prealcoholic phase is the same for the non-addictive alcoholic as for the alcohol addict. That is to say, he progresses from occasional to constant relief of individual symptoms through alcohol.

The behaviors which denote that alcohol has become a drug rather than an ingredient of a beverage—symptoms (2) to (6)—occur also in the non-addictive drinker, but, as mentioned before, the alcoholic palimpsests occur rarely and only after overt intoxication.

Loss of control is not experienced by the non-addictive alcoholic, and this is the main differentiating criterion between the two categories of alcoholics. Initially, of course, it could not be said whether the drinker had yet reached the crucial phase. However, after 10 or 12 years of heavy drinking without loss of control, while symptoms (2) to (6) were persistent and palimpsests were rare and did not occur after a medium intake of alcohol, the differential diagnosis is rather safe.

The absence of loss of control has many involvements. First of all, as there is no inability to stop drinking within a given situation there is no need to rationalize the inability. Nevertheless, rationalizations are developed for justifying the excessive use of alcohol and some neglect of the family attendant upon such use. Likewise, there is no need to change the pattern of drinking, which in the addict is an attempt to overcome the loss of control. Periods of total abstinence, however, occur as responses to social pressure.

On the other hand, there is the same tendency toward isolation as in the addict, but the social repercussions are much less marked, as the non-addictive alcoholic can avoid drunken behavior whenever the social situation requires it.

The effects of prolonged heavy drinking on the organism may occur in the non-addictive alcoholic too; even delirium tremens may develop. The libido may be diminished and "alcoholic jealousy" may result.

Generally, there is a tendency toward a progressive dominance of alcohol resulting in greater psychological and bodily effects. In the absence of any grave underlying psychopathies a deteriorative process is speeded up by habitual alcoholic excess, and such a non-addictive drinker may slide to the bottom of society.

References

1. Jellinek, E. M., "Phases in the Drinking History of Alcoholics. Analysis of a Survey Conducted by the Official Organ of Alcoholics Anonymous," *Quart. J. Stud. Alc.*, 7:1–88, 1946. (Memoirs of the Section of Studies on Alcohol, Yale University, No. 5.)

chapter 21

A rank order analysis
of the symptoms of alcoholism *

Harrison M. Trice and J. Richard Wahl

Much of the thinking about alcoholism as a disease process centers around a "typical" sequence of symptoms.† Although Jellinek gave some consideration to the "clustering" of these symptoms, popular usage of the data has tended to describe alcoholism as a series of drinking and related experiences arranged in a sequence, one following the other.

To a degree, the research data have encouraged this interpretation. True that Jellinek warned in his *Grapevine* study that the "trends described here are gross average trends," and gave specific examples of large differences in the order of occurrence of various symptoms in sizable proportions of his alcoholic sample. Nevertheless, the fact that the "over-all picture of the drinking history" was presented serially left an impression of a smooth, steady transition from symptom to symptom. In a similar manner the second "phases" study, republished in the preceding chapter, represents the symptoms as occurring in a regular order, although again the caution was urged that "not all symptoms shown in the diagram occur necessarily in all addicts, nor do they occur in every addict in the same sequence. . . . the sequences of symptoms within the phases are characteristic, however, of the great majority of alcohol addicts and represent what may be called the average trend."

---

* This chapter first appeared as an article in the *Quarterly Journal of Studies on Alcohol*, **19**:636–648, 1958. The original article has been reprinted here with only slight modification.

† Based on Jellinek's original analysis of responses to an Alcoholics-Anonymous *Grapevine* questionnaire (1). This will be referred to in this chapter as the *Grapevine* study.

The problem presented by this serialization of the symptoms is that it may mask a significant clustering of individual symptoms, on the one hand, and create "averages" that have little individual value, on the other. Concerning the latter point, repeated contacts with alcoholics, both in and out of Alcoholics Anonymous, leaves the impression that the "typical" sequence is not quite typical. For example, Table 1 compares mean onset ages of nine selected symptoms of the *Grapevine* study group with those of the Wisconsin study group to be reported on here.

TABLE 1

Mean Onset Ages (Years) of Thirteen Selected Symptoms in the Wisconsin Study Group and in the *Grapevine* Study Group, by Affiliation with Alcoholics Anonymous (A.A.)

| Symptoms | Wisconsin, 1955 | | | Grapevine, 1946 |
	Total (N = 252)	Non-A.A. (N = 133)	A.A. (N = 119)	A.A. (N = 98)
First drink for self	17.6	17.6	17.6	Not Available
First intoxication	18.3	17.9	18.8	18.8
First blackout	29.5	30.2	29.0	25.2
First frequent blackouts	33.6	34.2	33.2	Not Available
First morning drinking	35.6	36.6	34.0	27.6
First "benders"	36.0	36.7	34.5	29.9
First daytime bouts	35.7	37.0	34.6	31.0
First loss of control	36.0	37.1	35.0	31.2
First drinking alone	36.1	37.2	35.5	31.8
First convulsions	37.6	38.4	36.5	Not Available
First protecting supply	37.8	38.8	36.1	32.5
First tremors	38.6	39.5	37.8	32.7
First drunk on less liquor	38.4	39.4	37.2	Not Available

Three non-affiliates drawn at random from the Wisconsin Study group reported the onset ages of their symptoms as in Table 2. Comparison of these random cases with the averages in Table 1 shows very good agreement for "first drink," "first blackout," and "first frequent blackouts." The remainder of the symptoms, however, were either denied by these men or ascribed onset ages 7 to 14 years different from the arithmetical averages of the entire non-affiliate study group. This coincides with the fact that standard deviations around the mean ages in the *Grapevine* study ranged from 7 to 9 years for individual symptoms. This wide variation could obscure tendencies of symptoms to cluster together. Furthermore, it could lead to the placement of one symptom before or after another on the basis of age means produced from an insufficient sample.

In the light of these points, we sought to determine whether symptom data can be analyzed in such a way that clustering and individual variations would be more adequately revealed.

TABLE 2

Onset Ages of Thirteen Selected Symptoms in Three Randomly Selected
Men (Wisconsin Study, Non-A.A.'s)

Symptoms	Case A	Case B	Case C
First drink	19	18	17
First intoxication	25 or 26	24	19
First blackout	30	32	25
First frequent blackouts	33	33	35
First morning drinking	25 to 27	42	37
First "benders"	50	45	37
First daytime bouts	47	32 or 33	36
First loss of control	47	40	36
First drinking alone	Never	38	Never
First convulsions	30	Never	49
First protecting supply	Never	Never	Never
First tremors	Never	Never	49
First drunk on less liquor	Never	43	Never

Method

Further observations of the data in Table 1 indicate that, excluding such symptoms as "first frequent blackouts" and "first convulsions," for which age means were not obtained in the *Grapevine* study, the order of appearance in the two studies is not significantly different. An analogous observation is that the mean age of onset for almost every symptom except "first intoxication" * is about 5 years older in the Wisconsin than in the *Grapevine* study. Notwithstanding this, the chronological orders in the studies are almost identical. Therefore, separation of age of onset from order of onset could reveal the clustering of onset of symptoms for individuals.

The statistical method of rank comparisons can measure the amount of agreement in *order* without regard to assigned numerical values. It is adaptable in part to the analysis of ages at which symptoms appear as recalled by advanced alcoholics. Thus it could aid in meeting the problem at hand.

This type of rank comparison analysis was applied to the onset ages for specific symptoms as reported by 252 male alcoholics, roughly half of whom were members of Alcoholics Anonymous and half non-affiliated. A list of fourteen selected symptoms was submitted to each of these men. These symptoms were selected to represent what are commonly referred to as "early," "middle," and "late" symptoms (see Chart of Symptoms). The instructions asked for ages of onset, to be recalled as accurately as possible, and recorded to the nearest year. Opposite each symptom were spaces for recording the recalled age, or else for checking "do not recall" or "never had it." The symptoms were read aloud to each non-affiliate respondent, but cooperating A.A.

* In questionnaires addressed to alcoholics, this item is usually listed as "first drunk," in concession to popular slang.

members read the list and responded alone. In the analysis, the latter two responses were described as "denials"—denials of onset and of recall.

CHART OF SYMPTOMS

1. Age at first drink.
2. Age at first intoxication ("drunk").
3. Age at first time of "pulling a blank." (*Example:* wake up in the morning after a party with no idea where you had been or what you had done after a certain point.)
4. Age when "pulling blanks" began to occur frequently (at least two or three times out of ten "drunks").
5. Age when you began to notice you got drunk on less liquor.
6. Age when you began to lose control of drinking (intend to have only a couple and wind up "cockeyed").
7. Age when you started going on daytime "drunks" (other than Saturday and Sunday).
8. Age when you began to go on "benders" (staying drunk for at least 2 days without regard for your work or family).
9. Age when you began taking morning drinks (feel the need of and take a drink the first thing in the morning).
10. Age when you started drinking alone.
11. Age when you first had a convulsion after a drinking bout.
12. Age when you began to have uncontrollable tremors (jitters, shakes) after drinking.
13. Age when you began "protecting your supply" (it is always handy and someone won't take it away).
14. Age when you reached what you regard as your lowest point.

Each onset age was compared with every one of the thirteen responses remaining on the symptom list, with a total of 91 comparisons per individual case, or about 23,000 for the entire group. Each symptom in order was taken as a criterion for comparison with those following on the list. If the criterion symptom was "first blackout," then the rank comparisons with the other symptoms indicated whether it began in an earlier year, in the same year as, or in a later year than, for example, "first loss of control" or "first prolonged bouts." [*] If "first blackout" had been checked by a person as "do not recall" or "never had it," all rank comparisons of "first blackout" for the individual concerned had to be eliminated. Therefore, the possible usable classifications were as follows:

1. appeared earlier than the criterion symptom
2. appeared the same year as the criterion symptom
3. appeared later than the criterion symptom

For these data, a more elaborate analysis to measure "earlier" and "later" in years was of interest but was not within the resources of the analysis.

[*] "Benders" in the slang of the questionnaire.

The Subjects

A total of 252 male alcoholics, in part from the Mendota State Hospital and in part from several Alcoholics Anonymous groups in Wisconsin, cooperated in the study. Of these, 119 were affiliates of A. A. and 133 non-affiliates. The mean age of the affiliates was 46.9 years; of the non-affiliates, 46.2 years. The ages ranged between 25 and 70, 43 per cent falling between age 40 and 50. Blue-collar workers and laborers constituted 60 per cent; 30 per cent were white-collar workers and 10 per cent farmers, farm laborers, and the like. The A.A. affiliates had about twice as many of the white-collar workers as did the non-affiliates, and proportionately fewer blue-collar workers.

When asked to estimate their incomes before first contact with A. A., 57 per cent reported incomes of less than $3,000 a year and 95 per cent less than $6,000. The mean income of A.A. affiliates prior to first A.A. contact was $3,240; of non-affiliates, $2,420. This is in line with expectation from the somewhat lower occupational status of the non-affiliates. Similarly, the non-affiliates were somewhat inferior in educational background, only 13 per cent having had some college education in contrast to 25 per cent of the affiliates. While 70 per cent of the A.A. affiliates were married, and the remainder about equally divided among the single, the widowed, and the divorced, of the non-affiliates, only 30 per cent were married and 40 per cent were divorced and widowed. Considering the entire study group, 50 per cent were married, 30 per cent divorced and widowed, and 20 per cent single. More than 95 per cent of both groups had been born in the United States and 87 per cent in Wisconsin. Most of the foreign born were of northwestern European origin. Forty per cent of the affiliates and 60 per cent of the non-affiliates were rural born.

In summary, the study group consisted of native white American males, predominantly in the 40-to-50 age class. The A.A. affiliates were better off in income, occupation, and education than the non-affiliates, and more than twice as many were married. In the subsequent analysis, these differences seemed to have no consequences for the rank orders; hence the following presentation of results is, for the most part, based on the two groups combined.

Results

Table 1 has shown that, for many symptoms, there were identical mean ages of occurrence; therefore, first consideration will be given here to the amount of "clustering" brought out by the rank comparisons with the effect of age of onset removed. Table 3 shows the clustering, which was measured as "the proportion of symptom A occurring with symptom B." This relation is not logically transitive; therefore, if A is highly clustered with B, and B with C, then A might or might not be highly clustered with C. The following observations have two examples of high clustering in three possible

TABLE 3

The Proportions of Onsets Occurring the Same Year as the Criterion Symptom (in Per Cent)

	Criterion Symptoms													
	1	2	3	4	5	6	7	8	9	10	11	12	13	14
1														
2	36													
3	3	6												
4	—	1	13											
5	—	1	7	22										
6	2	3	9	22	33									
7	a	a	9	19	20	36								
8	a	1	5	12	17	22	45							
9	—	a	7	10	17	25	32	42						
10	2	3	8	18	18	22	26	27	30					
11	—	1	8	8	12	23	19	17	24	16				
12	—	a	8	11	17	18	19	25	28	25	35			
13	1	—	8	18	18	19	17	20	25	23	31	34		
14	a	—	2	7	10	9	11	10	8	9	23	13	12	

1 = First drink
2 = First intoxication
3 = First blackout
4 = First frequent blackouts
5 = First got drunk on less liquor
6 = First loss of control
7 = First daytime bouts

8 = First prolonged bouts
9 = First morning drinking
10 = First drinking alone
11 = First convulsions after drinking
12 = First tremors
13 = First protecting supply
14 = First reached lowest point

ᵃ Less than 0.5 per cent.

combinations, and one example of high clustering in two of three possible combinations:

A. "First daytime bouts" with "first prolonged bouts" and with "first morning drinking"; and "first prolonged bouts" with "first morning drinking." One-third to one-half of the cases tended to give the same ages at onset.

B. "First convulsions after drinking" with "first tremors" and with "first protecting supply"; and "first tremors" with "first protecting supply." One-third of the cases tended to give the same ages at onset.

C. "First getting drunk on less liquor" with "first loss of control"; and "first loss of control" with "first daytime bouts"; but not "first getting drunk on less liquor" with "first daytime bouts." Where high clustering existed, one-third of the cases tended to give the same ages at onset.

Besides these three combinations, one strongly clustered pair of symptoms was "first drink" and "first intoxication," in which one-third of the cases ascribed identical ages at onset. This is especially interesting when combined with the results of Ullman's study (3) of first drinking experiences of addictive and "normal" drinkers. His data indicated that the prealcoholic more often became intoxicated in his first drinking experience than did the normal drinker.

Besides clustering, a second consideration was the sequence in symptom appearance. Because ages were recorded to the nearest year, answered "as accurately as possible," clustering obscured the true before-after statuses in the foregoing list of symptoms, if such divisions can occur within a 1-year period.* For a summary table of rank order, however, it was desirable to include not only the proportions of symptoms subsequent to any one as criterion but the proportions that "went along with" the criterion. Hence, Table 4 shows the proportions of the symptoms attributed to the same or a later period than that of the criterion. Ideally, all percentages would be 100, but substantially smaller values were observed.

TABLE 4

Summary Table of Fourteen Symptoms, Showing the Proportions of Onsets Occurring the Same Year as or Later than the Criterion Symptom (in Per Cent)

	Criterion Symptoms													
	1	2	3	4	5	6	7	8	9	10	11	12	13	14
1														
2	98													
3	98	100												
4	99	99	98											
5	98	99	92	80										
6	99	100	79	64	67									
7	99	100	81	69	63	76								
8	99	100	84	66	59	76	83							
9	100	100	79	59	59	68	71	67						
10	99	99	78	67	63	69	66	61	70					
11	100	100	86	76	61	81	84	80	86	84				
12	100	100	91	78	72	82	83	80	84	83	64			
13	99	99	85	72	64	74	75	69	79	74	59	64		
14	99	100	96	98	93	98	99	98	98	97	96	94	98	

1 = First drink
2 = First intoxication
3 = First blackout
4 = First frequent blackouts
5 = First got drunk on less liquor
6 = First loss of control
7 = First daytime bouts

8 = First prolonged bouts
9 = First morning drinking
10 = First drinking alone
11 = First convulsions after drinking
12 = First tremors
13 = First protecting supply
14 = First reached lowest point

* If the respondents had been requested to make paired comparisons of symptoms ascribed to the same year, so as to capture "earlier," "same time," or "later" statuses, the amount of clustering would in all probability have been reduced.

In the first place, Table 4 shows that "first drink," "first intoxication," and "first blackout" have the largest number of high percentages:

A. With "first drink" as the criterion, the assignment of some symptoms to an earlier period seems paradoxical; indeed, only "first morning drinking," "first convulsions," and "first tremors" show values for it of 100 per cent. The differences of 1 or 2 per cent, however, may be explained by errors of reading, listening, or recall on the part of the respondents. It should be noted that "first blackout" as given in the questionnaire (see Chart of Symptoms) makes no mention of drinking; and that both "first intoxication" and "first got drunk on less liquor" have a possible ambiguity in relation to early childhood drink sipping. These were the only symptoms that had an "error" as high as 2 per cent.

B. Considering "first intoxication" as the criterion, fewer errors existed than in the case of "first drink," and these could also be rationalized as due, for the most part, to confusion with childhood drink sipping, whether at parties or by "sneaking" drinks.

C. Considering "first blackout" as criterion, and arbitrarily designating 80 per cent or more as "high agreement" proportions, then only "first loss of control," "first morning drinking," and "first drinking alone" are excluded from high agreement, but only by one or two percentage points.

D. Considering symptoms other than the foregoing as criteria, there are two isolated instances of high agreement: "first frequent blackouts" as preceding "first getting drunk on less liquor"; and "first daytime bouts" as preceding "first prolonged bouts." The remaining instances are not isolated, as is described in the following paragraph.

It is of interest to note that three symptoms are highly agreed upon as following whatever symptom is used as criterion; that is, "first convulsions," "first tremors," and "first reached lowest point" include a large number of percentages in the high-agreement range for all criteria going before, except two which fail of high agreement only narrowly. "Lowest point" especially seems to be the end-point of the process for most of the alcoholics, although 6 or 7 per cent placed "first getting drunk on less liquor" and "first tremors" as subsequent to it.

Table 5 shows in detail the relation between the onset dates of four selected but often-used symptoms associated with the phases. The following observations were notable:

A. Given "first blackout" as criterion, two out of three reported "first loss of control" as later; four out of five, "first prolonged bouts" and "first tremors" as later. In no instance did clustering occur for more than one in ten persons. As shown by Table 1, the rarity of clustering of "first blackout" with other symptoms is consistent with its appearance, on the average, 7 to 9 years before the onset of the others. These, in contrast, hardly differ among

TABLE 5

Relations between the Onset Dates of Four Selected Symptoms, by Affiliation with Alcoholics Anonymous (in Per Cent)

	Given the Date at Onset of								
	First Blackout			First Loss of Control			First Prolonged Bouts		
Remembered Onset Date of	Total	Non-A.A.	A.A.	Total	Non-A.A.	A.A.	Total	Non-A.A.	A.A.
A. First loss of control									
was reported as later	70	67	72						
was reported as in same year	9	10	8						
was reported as earlier	21	23	20						
Totals	100	100	100						
Total Number	195	90	105						
B. First prolonged bout									
was reported as later	79	73	84	54	54	53			
was reported as in same year	5	4	6	22	17	27			
was reported as earlier	16	23	10	24	29	20			
Totals	100	100	100	100	100	100			
Total Number	173	79	94	208	108	100			
C. First tremors									
was reported as later	84	84	85	64	64	64	55	56	55
was reported as in same year	7	6	8	18	18	17	25	27	22
was reported as earlier	9	10	7	18	18	19	20	17	23
Totals	100	100	100	100	100	100	100	100	100
Total Number	174	78	96	209	105	104	187	95	92

themselves in Table 1, and this suggests that among them greater clustering could be expected.

B. With the onset date of "first loss of control" as the criterion symptom, clustering with "first prolonged bouts" and "first tremors" increased from one in ten to one in five. About one in two reported "first prolonged bouts" as later; and about two in three, "first tremors" as later than "first loss of control." As with "first blackout" as the criterion symptom, agreement improved slightly for the symptoms that were later in the Jellinek order. With "first prolonged bouts" as the criterion, about one in two persons reported "first tremors" as later, and about one in four as having them during the same year.

The foregoing observations were made from the totals, without consideration of A.A. affiliation, which had no significant effect on the rank orders.

TABLE 6

Difference in Denial Counts for Thirteen Selected Symptoms, by Alcoholics Anonymous Affiliation

	Total Denial		Denial of Onset		Denial of Recall	
	Non-A.A.	A.A.	Non-A.A.	A.A.	Non-A.A.	A.A.
First drink	0	1	0	0	0	1
First intoxication	0	2	0	0	0	2
First blackout	39	9	37	8	2	1
First frequent blackouts	63	19	62	18	1	1
First drunk on less liquor	46	41	46	34	0	7
First loss of control	12	6	12	2	0	4
First daytime bouts	16	5	15	5	1	0
First prolonged bouts	22	17	22	15	0	2
First morning drinking	16	7	16	5	0	2
First drinking alone	22	23	22	21	0	2
First convulsions	92	89	91	89	1	0
First tremors	26	11	26	10	0	1
First protecting supply	34	25	33	23	1	2
Number of Subjects	133	119	133	119	133	119

Table 6 shows the differences in denial counts between the 119 members of A. A. and the 133 non-affiliates. The non-affiliates tended to deny the onset of symptoms, whereas the affiliates manifested a very slight tendency to deny recall of the dates; therefore the combined denials tended to decrease the differences between the two groups. The large number of denials of onset among non-affiliates, if faithful to the facts, describes chronic excessive drinking with a lower prevalence of complications than among affiliates.

It may be, however, that non-affiliates cannot recall these symptoms because of heavy rationalizations combined with poor memory (2). On the other hand, some of the differences are too great to be entirely attributed to this second factor. For instance, over three times as many non-affiliates denied having experienced "frequent blackouts" as did affiliates. Roughly the same is true for such widely recognized symptoms as "morning drinking," "loss of control," and "tremors." It seems likely that affiliation with A. A. is, to some degree, encouraged by having experienced these pronounced symptoms. Certainly the absence of them would lead an excessive drinker to believe that he was not like other A.A. members. Without such experiences he would be far less inclined to admit that he was "licked" or that he had a drinking problem.

In short, A.A. affiliation appears to depend, in part, upon having advanced well into the syndrome of alcoholism. Until this has taken place it is relatively easy to refuse to "surrender" and "admit" that life has "become unmanageable." These are basic norms in A. A. Since they represent a sharp departure from the use of individual "will power" as encouraged by American society, they are accepted only after repeated efforts to continue drinking in a controlled way. "Hitting bottom" is regarded by many A.A. members as an essential prerequisite to their therapy. The definite differences in denial rates between affiliates and non-affiliates reported here tend to substantiate this concept.

Discussion

Contact with Alcoholics Anonymous, although selective here for persons with better incomes, educations, occupations, and marital status, seemed to have no relation to the order of onset of certain symptoms of alcoholism. However, A.A. affiliates did produce relatively fewer denials of such onsets. This could be explained by at least two factors: (a) the affiliates having more alcoholic complications; or (b) their predilection to admit more complications than the non-affiliates. In short, where better memories do not explain the difference, having been "through the mill" might.

The foregoing results show that the use of mean ages in the analysis of symptom onset has obscured important clustering of symptoms. In considering this clustering, it is important to note the retrospective nature of the material, and how beliefs, guesses, and mental confusion could have affected responses. For example, as many as half of the alcoholics agreed that "first daytime bouts," "prolonged bouts," and "morning drinking" had appeared together. The most plausible explanation is that these are not mutually exclusive events. On the other hand, about one-third of the alcoholics agreed that "first convulsions," "tremors," and "protecting supply" belonged together; here, the appealing explanation is a causal one, e.g., pathological anxiety, which reflects itself in the three symptoms.

The main purpose of the analysis was to evaluate the order of appearance of the symptoms by applying them as if indicating the stages of a disease process. Only the initial and terminal symptoms of the process were good indicators of stage, and the intermediary stages were obscured. Deeply implicated in the process may be more valid and reliable symptoms (chemical, physiological, behavioral) as yet not observed. Among the fourteen symptoms considered here, the alcoholics agreed most frequently on the symptoms belonging to the earliest and the latest stages. The fact that none elicited complete agreement from the alcoholics was not as important as gaining sharper notions about their relevance to and position in the process, as well as about their real complexity. The differences and proportions found in this study might well be artifacts, unique to the study group and the method of data collection; however, this could not be demonstrated by a more elaborate analysis of the data used here.

Because of the retrospective nature of the study design, the data were drawn entirely from persons already diagnosed as being alcoholics; however, younger persons in earlier stages of alcoholism are beginning to appear at clinics, and the person who can be diagnosed with certainty in some current stage of the process would be a better informant. Therefore, a prospective study design, with the subjects drawn from a large variety of treatment facilities and in all stages of the alcoholism process, could reduce errors due to memory and to case selection. Ideally, drinking pattern (quantity, frequency, and regularity in relation to body weight) should be controlled in relation to the rapidity of the process. The possibility of several types of processes could be explored and the essential symptoms of each more sharply identified and defined. Resistance to the process itself, physiological or psychological, regardless of the quantity of alcohol consumed, could be investigated, along with the resistances to treatment after the process has started. In this way, the description of the process of alcoholism as a medical disease distinguishable from popular and folk definitions might be expedited.

Summary

To test the agreement in the order of symptom onset in the phases of alcoholism, rank comparisons of onset ages were made between two groups of native white male alcoholics—119 affiliates of Alcoholics Anonymous, and 133 non-affiliates. Fourteen frequently mentioned symptoms were utilized in the study. The onset age of each symptom in an individual was a criterion for the other symptoms, which were ranked as emerging earlier than, at the same time as, or later than the criterion symptom.

1. Affiliation with A. A. had but slight effect on the rank distributions; hence, only the results of the combined groups were discussed in detail. Non-affiliates tended to deny actual occurrence of some symptoms, whereas affiliates tended to deny recall of the date of onset. This seems to imply that the more symptoms experienced, the more likely is affiliation with A. A.

2. Four groups of symptoms tended to cluster at the same onset age:

(A) "first daytime intoxication," "first prolonged bouts," and "first morning drinking"; (B) "first convulsions after drinking," "first tremors," and "first protecting supply"; (C) "first getting drunk on less liquor" and "first loss of control"; and (D) "first loss of control" and "first daytime bouts."

3. Among the remaining eleven symptoms, "first drink," "first intoxication," and "first blackout" were uniformly first in order of appearance; and "first convulsions," "first tremors," and "first reached lowest point," uniformly last.

4. Isolated additional instances of stable rank orders were (A) "first frequent blackouts" preceding "first getting drunk on less liquor"; and (B) "first daytime bouts" preceding "first prolonged bouts."

5. There is apparently more clustering of symptoms than has been previously assumed. Rather than a steady progression from individual symptom to individual symptom, the present findings strongly suggest that alcoholism is a process of transition from one cluster of symptoms that occur in close conjunction with each other to a new cluster.

6. The findings show that, if the concept of a disease process in alcoholism is valid, only the earliest or the most advanced stages of the process are reliably indicated by the symptoms studied herein.

References

1. Jellinek, E. M., "Phases in the Drinking History of Alcoholics. Analysis of a Survey Conducted by the Official Organ of Alcoholics Anonymous," *Quart J. Stud. Alc.*, 7:1–88, 1946.

2. Trice, Harrison M., "A Study of the Process of Affiliation with Alcoholics Anonymous," *Quart. J. Stud. Alc.*, 18:39–54, 1957.

3. Ullman, Albert D., "The First Drinking Experience of Addictive and of 'Normal' Drinkers," *Quart. J. Stud. Alc.*, 14:181–191, 1953.

chapter 22

Cultural differences in the meaning of alcoholism[*]

E. M. Jellinek

The greater part of the literature on alcoholism is of Anglo-Saxon origin. In these nations the steady symptomatic excessive drinkers (with or without addictive features) are so much in the foreground and engage the interest of the student of alcoholism to such a degree that the terms "alcoholic" and "alcoholism" are applied only to these drinkers, and the problem is seen entirely in the terms of their drinking—to the complete neglect of other important aspects of the problem.

International experience leads to the conclusion that in many countries problems of national magnitude arise more from other types of drinkers than from the steady excessive symptomatic drinkers. The latter do, of course, exist in every country where alcoholic drinks are consumed, but they may form such a small group—or even if they reach a fairly large number—that the problems arising from them may be overshadowed by the problems presented by other types of drinking.

In Finland, for example, alcoholic drinks are sold mainly in urban areas, and the violence displayed by Finnish workers when they come to town from some isolated camps and have a few drinks—nothing that could be called a "drinking spree"—causes such damage and is so dramatic that to the Finnish nation this type of drinking and this form of damage constitutes alcoholism.

The steady excessive symptomatic drinkers are by no means absent in

[*] This chapter is a somewhat shortened version of an article, "The World and Its Bottle," which originally appeared in *World Health,* 10:4–6, July–August, 1957. The chapter contains excerpts from a paper presented to a Joint Meeting (1954) of the World Health Organization Expert Committees on Mental Health and on Alcohol.

Finland (there are probably tens of thousands), and they resemble in their development and behavior their American, British, or Swedish brethren, but their slowly drinking themselves to death seems to present less of a problem than the violence and other damage caused by the occasional explosive relief drinkers. By the same token, one may suspect that the preponderance of the steady excessive symptomatic drinker in the United States of America may lead students of alcoholism there to underestimate and to ignore the damage arising from *occasional* excess.

Serious damage to society by occasional excessive drinkers occurs in many countries and it may be of small, medium, or great frequency. In relation to damage caused by the steady excessive symptomatic drinkers, the occasional excessive drinkers may present an insignificant problem, or, on the other hand, their problem may greatly exceed the problem of the former, either through their greater number or the nature of the damage, or both. In Spain, for instance, the group of alcoholics is small, and the group of occasional excessive drinkers with damaging behavior is considerably larger.

The damage caused by occasional excessive drinkers may be violence (which may occur among steady excessive symptomatic drinkers too, but is by no means characteristic of them), industrial and traffic accidents to which they contribute more than the steady symptomatic drinkers, lowering of disease resistance, and absenteeism and overspending, which may represent extensive damage if their number equals or exceeds that of the steady excessive symptomatic drinkers.

There is a great deal of insistence that the problem of alcoholism varies from country to country. If the term "alcoholism" is extended to occasional excessive drinkers, as is the case in many countries, one may say with justification that the nature of alcoholism shows marked differences throughout the world. According to the accepted ideas about alcoholism in the Anglo-Saxon countries and even in some Latin countries, occasional excessive drinkers—such as weekend or Sunday drinkers, who follow a cultural pattern, or "celebrators," and even the explosive occasional relief drinker— would never be regarded as alcoholics.

The extension of the term "alcoholism" to all forms of drinking which may occasion damage is not impossible, as after all any label or definition is only a matter of convenience and convention, and the essential factor is the consistency in connotation. While such a broad connotation would perhaps eliminate much conflict in international communication on this subject, it would hardly be a useful means.*

A distinction between what in most Anglo-Saxon countries is called alcoholism, on the one hand, and the serious problems arising out of oc-

---

* In his recent book, *The Disease Concept of Alcoholism* (New Haven: Hillhouse Press, 1960), Jellinek did use, however, the word "alcoholism" as a generic term for "any drinking that causes any damage" and has described a variety of "species" of alcoholism.

casional excessive drinking, on the other hand, is a requirement for clear discussion. Treatment and preventive measures of these various problems cannot be considered relevantly without clear-cut distinctions. Such public care and treatment as is advocated in the United States of America, England, and the Netherlands does not make sense in the case of the week-end drinker who follows a cultural pattern and causes vexatious problems, or in the instance of the occasional explosive relief drinker.

The general use of the term "alcoholism" to cover all these forms of drinking could lead, and has led in some countries, to public-care systems with very variable results, because they apply measures which have been designed with the occasional excessive drinker in mind to the exclusion of the steady excessive symptomatic drinker. Instead of the extension of the term "alcoholism" to all forms of excessive drinking and the creation of a new terminology to serve the necessary distinctions, it seems preferable to talk about the problems of alcohol and to regard alcoholism as one of these problems.

In France the picture is not one of alcoholism in the sense of symptomatic alcoholism, with or without addictive features, nor in the sense of problems created by occasional excess. The French conception of alcoholism agrees, however, with ideas concerning alcoholism in some other prominent wine-producing countries or at least concerning one type of alcoholism frequently recognized in those countries. There are differences, however, in the conceptions as to its cause, as well as in the description of the behavior of alcoholics. There is in the French literature on alcoholism frequent mention of l'alcoolisme sans ivresse (alcoholism without drunkenness); that is, it is asserted that a drinker can become an alcoholic without ever showing signs of intoxication. This opinion is held by students of alcoholism, as well as by the population at large. According to an opinion poll, 75 per cent of the men and 82 per cent of the women questioned expressed the opinion that a drinker may become an alcoholic without ever getting drunk. This statement may meet with incredulity in countries where the drinking of distilled spirits is common. Yet, when one observes the French drinking pattern, this contention seems quite plausible.

In the past few years the average daily consumption of pure alcohol from wine and other alcoholic beverages for adult French males was 130 cc (4.3 ounces). The average itself is high and it can result only if a fair proportion of the consumers drink considerably more than the average. According to a fairly reliable computation it appears that, in 1936, 7 per cent of French adult males drank daily amounts of 3 litres of wine or more (the equivalent of 300 cc of absolute alcohol and upwards).

While it cannot be said that a given daily amount of alcohol will produce "alcohol addiction," there can be little doubt that the consumption of amounts from 3 litres of wine upwards per day, over 15 or 20 years, cannot be handled by the organism without much impairment of metabolic and nervous functions, which can be classed as aspects of "chronic alcoholism," even though the ingestion of this amount over 15 hours and the element of adaptation should result in no overt intoxication.

A French laborer—particularly in the wine-producing areas—may distribute a total of 3 litres of wine, beginning with a small glass or two at breakfast. He may drink small amounts almost hourly up to noon, when he may take about half a litre with his lunch. This might be followed again by almost hourly drinks up to the evening meal, when he might take about a litre, with a few small drinks afterwards.

Under these conditions a drinker of average weight will hardly exceed a concentration of alcohol in the blood of 0.02 per cent between morning and noon, and his highest after the evening meal will be somewhere around 0.12 per cent. The latter concentration, although fairly high, would not cause visible symptoms in a well-accustomed drinker. On the other hand, the organism of this drinker will hardly ever be entirely free from alcohol, although the blood alcohol concentration will be at levels of "sobriety" during a large part of the day. The nearly constant presence of alcohol in the organism can hardly be conceived of as not interfering with its normal functioning, and there is a likelihood of acquiring a tolerance which may lead to even larger consumption.

This is not to imply that Frenchmen never get drunk. Intoxication is no rarity in France, but a large proportion of French drinkers may incur some damage characteristic of chronic alcoholism without their having ever shown intoxication or any behavior characteristic of "addictive drinking."

Psychiatrists in the predominantly wine-drinking countries, such as France, the Romande of Switzerland, Italy, etc., have frequently seen delirium tremens and other diseases of chronic alcoholism in men who by their past history could not be described as addictive drinkers, or even steady symptomatic excessive drinkers without addictive features, and whose chronic alcoholic complications came to everybody as a surprise. This type of drinker will be tentatively labeled here as the "inveterate drinker." With the exception of the younger psychiatrists, French students of alcoholism attribute this type of drinking entirely to social habits and attitudes which are greatly influenced by economic factors.

There is a strong tendency in France and some other wine-growing countries to regard alcoholism as an economic problem. In those countries, alcoholism is viewed, except by a few psychiatrists, as a psychiatric problem only after the excessive drinker develops an alcoholic mental disorder. In the origin of the "habit," however, they see no psychological, not to speak of psychiatric, involvements.

Nothing can provoke greater dissent on the part of French physicians and others interested in alcoholism than the contention that prealcoholic maladjustments lead to the heavy use of alcoholic beverages. Particularly, suggestions as to the prealcoholic neurotic character or other marked psychological deviations (let alone the term "psychopathy" with its different meanings) meet with strong rejection.

This antagonism to the "Anglo-Saxon" ideas as to cause, which is not limited to the French alone, is to some extent quite justified in relation to certain types of steady excessive drinkers in wine-growing countries. On the other hand the counterargument cannot be accepted at face value.

The exclusion of psychological factors in the Frenchman's drinking is not borne out by some ideas about the properties of wine in France. In many small restaurants there is on the back of the menu a page with cartoon and slogans, three of which read as follows: "The wines of France create gaiety" —"The wines of France create optimism"—"The wines of France give self-assurance." This leaflet evidently reflects popular ideas about wine. Certainly if optimism and self-assurance are to be derived from wine, there can hardly be any denial of psychological factors in the Frenchman's drinking.

Again, the accent on creating optimism and self-assurance would indicate that these traits are often deficient in excessive drinkers. This deficiency and its remedy through wine, however, suggest a certain psychological vulnerability, although it hardly could be called an abnormality.

Furthermore, despite the wide acceptance of high alcohol intake in France, only 7 per cent of male users consume 3 litres of wine or more per day, and even users of 2 litres of wine per day are greatly in the minority. One may suspect, therefore, a differentiating factor between these heavy drinkers and the majority of wine consumers, who drink much less. The habit and the social acceptance of heavy drinking are facilitating factors, but cannot account for the entire phenomenon.

In international communication on alcoholism and other forms of excessive drinking, understanding could be reached more easily if "psychological vulnerability" rather than any term suggesting psychological abnormality or subnormality were used. Psychological vulnerability has a wide range—from frank neurosis to ill-defined personality weaknesses. In countries such as the United States and Sweden, where there is no social acceptance of heavy alcohol consumption—and on the part of a round third of the population there is disapproval of any kind of drinking—by and large the most vulnerable of the population are liable to drink excessively; while in countries where large alcohol intake is generally accepted by society, much less vulnerable persons are exposed to the risk of developing one or the other forms of alcoholism.

That in France a large consumption of wine is generally accepted by the population is evident from the opinion poll referred to above. One of the questions in the survey referred to related to the amount of wine a man engaged in heavy bodily work can consume daily without any harm. The various amounts stated by male interviewees averaged at 1.8 litres of wine —that is, 180 cc or 6 ounces of absolute alcohol—per day, and amounts of 3 litres and more of wine were acceptable to a fair proportion of interviewees. Female interviewees set the limit for hardworking men 20 per cent lower on the average. Furthermore, 32 per cent of male interviewees regarded wine as indispensable and 58 per cent as useful in the case of men with great physical activity (only 1 per cent said that it was harmful).

Another illustration of the French attitude towards wine is that 88 per cent of the men and 72 per cent of the women expressed the opinion that wine is conducive to health.

In many Anglo-Saxon countries, one-third of the adult population reject the use of alcoholic beverages entirely and the other two-thirds do not favor large individual consumption. Under such conditions it may be expected that largely—but by no means exclusively—persons with high degrees of psychological vulnerability will be exposed to the risk of alcoholism. On the other hand, in countries which have a high degree of acceptance of large alcohol intake—such as France—a small degree of vulnerability may trigger off alcoholism.

There are other factors which influence the ideas about the nature and origin of alcoholism. In Italy, although the "inveterate drinkers" may be smaller in number than symptomatic alcoholics with or without addictive features, a drinker is classed as an alcoholic largely when he develops one of the alcoholic mental disorders. In the absence of such a disorder the excessive drinker is just a "drunk," and this is largely due to the fact the Italian has a great contempt for the drinker who discredits the use of wine, which he regards as one of the traditional fine products of the country.

Swiss students of alcoholism recognize a certain proportion of prealcoholic neuroticism and "psychopathology," but maintain that the majority of alcoholics in Switzerland are "primitive hedonists" who get intoxicated or near intoxicated for the sake of mere pleasure and, in continuing this practice, eventually become "chronic alcoholics." On acquaintance with such a "primitive hedonist," one finds a person with an extremely narrow field of interests and a veritable inability to take interest in anything else but himself and a narrow circle around him. There is also, generally, an inability to respond adequately to the finer stimuli of life. This narrowness of interests constitutes a psychological vulnerability which is the source of the "mere habit" of heavy drinking.

All the ideas about alcoholism in a given country have a good deal of truth in them, but they become modified in the light of experience from other countries. The inveterate drinker, who predominates in France, may be found in every country where alcoholism exists, but in countries where the symptomatic and addictive alcoholics predominate, the ideas derived from them as to origin and behavior are extended to all other heavy drinkers.

The "economic origin" of alcoholism is an idea that is frequently expounded in European countries and some of the South American wine-growing countries. This economic outlook is in gross contrast to the psychiatric theories current in the Anglo-Saxon countries, but it cannot be overlooked without detriment to a clear understanding of the problems of alcohol. By economic origin is meant first of all the vested interest in the production and sale of alcoholic beverages which in some viticultural countries is of extraordinary intensity.

However, the economic insecurity of the individual and poor housing conditions (rather common in France), which induce the dwellers to look for a more pleasant environment in the taverns, may also be designated as economic factors of habitual heavy drinking. In the latter instances, too, some psychological vulnerability of the individual must be assumed, as only a minority of the persons suffering from these conditions succumb to excessive drinking. Such vulnerability may consist of less resistance to these adversities and few resources to cope with them.

When the French speak of the economic origin of alcoholism, they mean that the viticultural interests, and the industrial and trade interest related thereto, are the decisive factors in the genesis of alcoholism. In France, viticulture constitutes a highly important part of the country's agricultural wealth, and millions of its inhabitants earn their living through the production of the raw materials and the processing and sale of alcoholic drinks. The interests of these groups do contribute toward a general acceptance of large consumption. There exists an identification of the general population with these interests, which are recognized as national ones.

These interests dominate public opinion through a variety of propaganda and reinforce customs which make drinking an obligation. Furthermore, the enormous wine production demands a large number of outlets. In France there is about one wine outlet for every ninety-seven inhabitants. The ubiquitousness of alcoholic beverages leads to greater consumption, and the number of alcoholics increases as the number of consumers and the amount consumed increases.

In Italy, the area under viticulture represents 10 per cent of the arable land and is somewhat larger than in France, and 10 per cent of the "active population" earn their living entirely or in part through the production and sale of wine. Nevertheless, France exceeds the Italian alcoholism rate at least five times. In spite of all economic interests the number of inhabitants per outlet in Italy is about two and a half times as great as in France (and is progressively being restricted towards a limit of four hundred inhabitants per outlet), and the consumption of total absolute alcohol per head is half that of the French.

Also, the pattern of drinking in Italy differs greatly from the French pattern (drinking is restricted almost entirely to meals). Furthermore, distilled spirits play an insignificant role in Italy, while in France, where distilled spirits contribute 14 per cent towards the total alcohol consumption, this latter type of beverage nevertheless has a larger consumption rate per head than in countries where it is the predominant source of alcohol (such as Finland, Sweden, and Norway).

These facts indicate that the economic interests alone cannot account for the extremely high alcoholism rate in France; there must be some differentiating factors between France and other large wine-growing countries with marked vested interests. These differentiating factors must be in the nature of cultural patterns as well as collective and individual psychological elements.

DEVELOPMENTAL CONTEXT, PERSONALITY, AND ROLE DEVIATION

Introductory Note. Why, in grossly similar socio-cultural settings, do certain persons become alcoholics while others do not? There is no definitive answer to this question, and perhaps there never will be, but the question itself has given rise to extensive speculation, as well as to a variety of studies concerned with the personalities of alcoholics and aiming to show that alcoholics are somehow different from other people either in kind or degree. The guiding notion is that the key to alcoholism is to be found at the level of personality structure and dynamics and in an appreciation of the developmental context in which the personality is formed.

It must be underscored, however, that the scientific literature contains the gamut of assumptions regarding the relevance of personality factors to the etiology of alcoholism, and their variable or unitary nature, quite aside from speculation as to the specific factors involved. Among sociologists, for instance, Albert Ullman (8) exemplifies one extreme position, cogently arguing that everyone has problems of tension reduction and that the differentia of alcoholism, viewed as a mechanism of relief from tension, are to be found not at the level of personality but rather in variations in the conditions under which drinking is learned and in limitations on the availability of alternative patterns for relieving tensions. For his part, Robert Bales (1) might be said to hold an intermediate position. Recognizing the importance of orienting and alternative factors in alcoholism, he nonetheless acknowledges the role of dynamic factors, as we have noted previously, and repeatedly refers to these as acute or severe needs for adjustment—presumably far more intense and protracted than the needs which most of us experience most of the time. Still, Bales has not attempted systematic

389

examination of these needs and, for the purpose of elucidating other factors in alcoholism, simply rests his case on the conservative assumption that their nature and origin may be highly variable, although he grants the possibility that certain personality types may be empirically predominant. At the other extreme are those writers like William and Joan McCord, a part of whose work appears in this section, who prefer to think of a definite type of personality as peculiarly prone to alcoholism.

Assuredly in the clinical psychological, psychiatric, and psychometric literature there is evidence of a more widespread conviction regarding the relevance of personality factors to alcoholism than is found in sociological writings, but even so there is extraordinary variation of opinion as to their nature. Bold constructions of the personality dynamics of alcoholics have long since been offered by psychoanalysts such as Robert Knight (2) and Karl Menninger (3), while the supposedly more rigorous psychological studies comprise a veritable Pandora's box of findings and related speculations on the subject.

Yet, if the existence of diverse basic assumptions among experts counsels caution in generalizing about personality and alcoholism, a consideration of the critiques by sociologists of the more systematic studies aiming to establish the personality factors involved should only serve to reinforce such an attitude. In 1950, for example, sociologist Edwin Sutherland and his associates (6) examined thirty-seven such studies from the standpoint of their methodological adequacy, concluding that there was no satisfactory evidence that persons of one type are more likely to become alcoholics than persons of another type, and going on to suggest that there is no alcoholic personality prior to alcoholism. Seven years later, sociologist Leonard Syme (7) found recent psychometric studies, both projective and non-projective, either too contradictory in their findings or too suspect from the standpoint of method and design to warrant substantial generalization. In the present book, the reader will find, in Chapter 27 by Joan Jackson, a succinct critique bearing upon many such studies and highlighting both their methodological and theoretical limitations. Hence in this subsection, which is concerned with personality and alcoholism, we have tried to include studies which manage at least to some extent to circumvent some of the major methodological difficulties that inhere in previous work or which hold special possibilities of articulation with a wider body of sociological theory.

A cardinal difficulty with most research on the subject is that we have been forced to consider personality in the terminal stages of alcoholism rather than during or prior to its inception. In consequence, the findings seem to be almost hopelessly contaminated from the standpoint of unravelling etiology, unless we are to be content with clinical reconstruction resting upon a principle of coherence.* Of course, this situation is by no means

---

* For further discussion of this situation, see Snyder (5), where consideration is also given to the promise which systematic cross-cultural study of alcohol-consumption patterns and socialization may hold for bringing a new and independent line of evidence

unique to the study of alcoholism. Nor is its recognition to be construed as implying that it is unimportant to learn what we can about the personality and social relationships of alcoholics in the later stages of the illness. Indeed, such studies not only may have important therapeutic implications but also may reveal durable features of the personality which contributed to alcoholism's onset. However, the possibility remains that this type of investigation will tell us more about the effects of 15 or 20 years of excessive drinking than it does about the causes of alcoholism and the personality factors involved. From an etiological standpoint, then, there is a need for studies which circumvent the dilemma that inheres in studying alcoholics in the later stages of the illness, say, after they have reached Alcoholics Anonymous, the hospital, the clinic, or the jail. It is to this need that Chapters 23, 24, and 25 are addressed.

The first of these studies (Chapter 23), which is longitudinal in nature, makes no attempt to offer a definitive view of the personality type or types found among alcoholics. It might rather be said that the authors—Lee Robins, William Bates, and Patricia O'Neal—have provided some preliminary empirical justification for pursuing these matters, simply as a result of investigating whether or not there is a higher incidence of childhood behavior disorders among persons who in later life become alcoholics than among other, supposedly normal people who do not. Further, their work attempts to specify the kinds of behavioral disorders characteristic of pre-alcoholics in childhood and to delineate gross features of the socialization setting which may be considered as plausible antecedents to the development of alcoholism.

Despite certain similarities in design, the restraint exercised in Chapter 23 with regard to generalizing concerning personality and alcoholism contrasts sharply with Chapter 24 by William and Joan McCord, who have essayed a unitary construction of the personality and developmental matrix of alcoholism. Yet, however much one may object to the McCords' speaking of *the* alcoholic personality, or perhaps to the insufficiency of the supporting evidence, we are of the opinion that they have at the very least made an important contribution heuristically. Indeed, their conception of the alcoholic personality integrates heretofore disparate ideas from several disciplines in a way that should give new directions and criteria of relevance to future research.

In considering these two longitudinal studies, which were undertaken quite independently of one another, the reader will note a certain harmony in the findings; for instance, they point to the inadequacy of parents or the marked aggressiveness of the alcoholics in childhood. In the latter connection, it might be contended that in both studies the operational criteria for inclusion as alcoholics involved a dependence upon institutional records,

---

to bear on the question of etiology. Chapter 4 by Field, in the present book, is, of course, definitely relevant in this connection.

especially records of arrest, which would necessarily bias the samples in favor of the more overtly antisocial elements of the total alcoholic population. From our standpoint, however, this would seem less to counsel despair than to signal the importance of attempting to replicate and extend such studies using indices of alcoholism which would not, a priori, dispose to such a bias.

In any event, it is well to recognize that neither of these investigations represents the perfect longitudinal study nor includes a near-adequate sample of the entire alcoholic population. Assuming such an ideal study may never be made, these studies at least supply practical examples of the kind of research that, if it could be extended to other small samples of the larger alcoholic population, might cumulatively provide an invaluable fund of information about personality and alcoholism.

Chapter 25 by Peter Park is admittedly a compromise between the ideal longitudinal and more typical ex post facto designs. It focuses on a phase of the life cycle much neglected in studies of alcoholism—late adolescence and young adulthood. The factor analysis of incipient alcoholism presented in this study, which owes greatly to Jellinek's phasic formulation reported in the previous section, holds promise for the early identification and interception of alcoholism for therapeutic purposes, as well as for being a useful instrument in research. More than this, Park's study makes a unique attempt to employ the pattern variable scheme of Talcott Parsons (4) so as to generalize the relations between personality dispositions and role structure and to interpret the functions of drinking for the incipient alcoholic. His partially successful effort to operationalize the pattern variables and his development of the dimensions of ambivalence and consistency have, we believe, a methodological significance which goes far beyond the study of alcoholism. However, insofar as alcoholism is concerned, Park not only adds important evidence that personality disturbances precede the full development of alcoholism but restates the problem in sociologically relevant terms so that the tensions between personality dispositions and role demands can be localized in other than the vague descriptive terms that have characterized previous discussion of the matter.

From among the many studies of the personalities of alcoholics in later life we have chosen to present, as Chapter 26, part of the recent work of Ralph Connor on the self-concepts of alcoholics. This choice was made in no small measure because the frame of reference and the tools used in Connor's study articulate well with a wider body of sociological and social-psychological findings and theory regarding personality and role. Broadly speaking, one might say that both Connor and Park have been exploring in detail the general theme, touched upon by Bacon in an earlier chapter, of the relatively total deterioration of the alcoholism-prone personality in complex society. If Park has found among incipient alcoholics indications of deviation from the culturally expected role in the directions of particularism, affectivity, and diffuseness, as well as social deviation in the form of ambivalence in role orientation (all of which foreshadow the isolation of the person from society), these indications seem clearly in evidence in Connor's data on the depletion of adjectives appropriate to secondary-group roles in the self-descriptions of alcoholics in later life, their apparent preoccupation with primary group attributes, and the devaluation and disorganization which their self-characterizations suggest.

The low self-acceptance characteristic of the alcoholics studied by Connor is, of course, consistent with the McCords' finding of low self-confidence which, in turn, contrasts with the apparent (though perhaps compensatory) self-confidence of prealcoholics in childhood. It would be interesting in future research to move the index of self-acceptance back in the life cycle of alcoholics to the point of inception of the illness and beyond to detect where self-acceptance begins manifestly to break down, as it would be equally interesting to complement Park's type of pattern-variable analysis with data phrased in the self-concept terms employed by Connor.

A further important aspect of Connor's data is the demonstration of the enrichment, reorganization, and re-evaluation of the self concomitant with lengthening sobriety. It may be suggested that this constitutes empirical evidence of the personality changes that accompany the resocialization of the person in a supportive, therapeutic group like Alcoholics Anonymous, which is noted by Milton Maxwell in his discussion of A. A. in Chapter 33.

All in all, we are of the opinion that the studies in this subsection add considerable weight to the view that at least part of the key to understanding alcoholism lies in the personality dynamics and the contexts of personality development prior to the onset of the illness itself. This is not to say that such factors offer a necessary and sufficient explanation of the phenomenon, for, in sociological perspective, it is difficult to see their significance apart from the role demands, the cultural meanings of drinking, and the range of alternative modes of adjustment which impinge upon such vulnerable persons in a society like ours. However, it is to say that, in our judgment, the evidence of these studies does not warrant the assumption of some that personality factors are irrelevant to alcoholism or that they are too endlessly variable to merit study. On the contrary, there would seem to be ample justification for assuming their relevance and proceeding in future research along the lines of inquiry suggested by these several studies. In particular, if more data can be gathered on the various points in the life cycle which these studies exemplify, we may hope eventually to see the patterning in the interplay of socio-cultural and personality factors in alcoholism more clearly.

References

1. Bales, Robert F., The "Fixation Factor" in Alcohol Addiction: An Hypothesis Derived from a Comparative Study of Irish and Jewish Social Norms, unpublished doctoral dissertation, Harvard University, 1944.
2. Knight, Robert P., "The Psychodynamics of Chronic Alcoholism," J. Nerv. Ment. Dis., 86:538–548, 1937.

3. Menninger, Karl, *Man Against Himself,* New York: Harcourt, Brace and World, 1938.

4. Parsons, Talcott, *The Social System,* Glencoe, Ill.: Free Press, 1951.

5. Snyder, Charles R., "A Sociological View of the Etiology of Alcoholism," *in* D. J. Pittman (Ed.), *Alcoholism: An Interdisciplinary Approach,* Springfield, Ill.: Charles C. Thomas, 1959.

6. Sutherland, Edwin H., H. G. Shroeder, and C. L. Tordella, "Personality Traits and the Alcoholic: A Critique of Existing Studies," *Quart. J. Stud. Alc.,* 11:547–561, 1950.

7. Syme, Leonard, "Personality Characteristics of the Alcoholic: A Critique of Recent Studies," *Quart. J. Stud. Alc.,* 18:288–302, 1957.

8. Ullman, Albert D., "The Psychological Mechanism of Alcohol Addiction," *Quart. J. Stud. Alc.,* 13:602–607, 1952.

chapter 23

Adult drinking patterns of former problem children [*]

Lee N. Robins, William M. Bates, and Patricia O'Neal

There are at least three established ways of studying the etiology of a disease. The first of these is to attempt to induce the disease experimentally in disease-free individuals. In the case of diseases like alcoholism for which no reliable cure is available, this approach raises serious ethical problems and consequently has been avoided. The second approach is to try to reconstruct events which may have led to the occurrence of the disease by studying persons who currently suffer from it. Such an approach has often been used in research on the etiology of alcoholism, but it contains major and unavoidable drawbacks. Over and above the uncertainties which inhere in attempts to reconstruct the past are the difficulties of disentangling causes or antecedent factors from the effects of the disease. The third approach avoids these pitfalls. It involves studying disease-free cohorts of children or younger persons and studying them again in later life to see who got the disease without experimental intervention. It is this third approach which we have taken to the study of alcoholism.

Advantages and Limitations of the Present Approach

There are, however, problems involved in taking this approach to alcoholism research. The most serious of these is briefly as follows: When a disease occurs in only a relatively small proportion of a population, as does alcoholism, it becomes necessary—barring extremely time-consuming and expensive research—to select a cohort of younger persons whose probability

[*] This chapter was written especially for this book. The research upon which it is based was supported by grants from the Foundation Fund for Research in Psychiatry and the United States Public Health Service.

of manifesting the disease in later life is high. This is essential if enough cases are to be obtained to illuminate etiology in a systematic way. Yet a procedure of this sort sacrifices randomness of selection. The alcoholics, for instance, who emerge in the course of this follow-up study cannot be assumed to be typical of alcoholics in general. If there are alternative sets of factors which antedate the onset of alcoholism but which occur only in pre-alcoholic populations selected by other criteria, they will not be uncovered by such a procedure. The findings from a study of this kind apply, therefore, to a subgroup of the alcoholic population. While they may suggest hypotheses which may ultimately prove to have broader application, the findings should not be generalized to alcoholics as a whole.

The cohort actually selected for this study was the patient population of 30 years ago at a child guidance clinic in St. Louis, a group chosen with the expectation of its yielding a fair number of alcoholics. The high rate of adult deviance—signified by arrests, divorce, mobility patterns, and psychiatric illnesses other than alcoholism—previously found (6, 7, 8) in this "patient group" suggested that it might exhibit an unusually high rate of alcoholism, since alcoholism may also be viewed both as socially disapproved behavior and as a psychiatric illness. As will be noted in detail later on, the findings fully justified this expectation.

The information about these patients as children which was utilized in this research comes from records of the child guidance clinic collected quite independently of considerations as to which children might eventually become alcoholics. Of course the content and scope of this information is necessarily restricted to what the clinic saw fit to record, and it suffers from certain other limitations which will be discussed. It has, however, the decided advantage of obviating the need for reconstruction from the memory of adults and permits the disentanglement of prealcoholic phenomena from the consequences of years of excessive drinking. Moreover, the follow-up investigation of a cohort so studied initially made it possible to identify and compare alcoholics, on the one hand, and a "control group" of persons who exhibited behavior disorders in childhood but did not develop drinking problems as adults, on the other. The follow-up also yielded useful information on spontaneous recovery from alcoholism of a sort that cannot be obtained in many other studies of alcoholism.*

While the particular longitudinal study which we have undertaken has its advantages, it also has definite limitations apart from matters of the scope of the data and of the generality of the findings derived from a "disease-prone" population. In the first place, the information on childhood, which

---

* At the time of follow-up, some of those persons who formerly had difficulties with their drinking no longer evidenced such problems, and the rate of recovery could be studied. By contrast, if one studies a group of known alcoholics who either are by definition *not* recovered (e.g., those currently hospitalized or imprisoned for alcoholism) or are by definition in remission (members of Alcoholics Anonymous, for example), it is not possible to estimate the normal rate of recovery.

was collected quite independently of the follow-up study, is not as systematic as that obtained at the time of the follow-up. The clinic which made these records did use a standard outline of topics so that the same general kinds of data were collected in the great majority of cases. However, identical questions were not necessarily used to elicit information and little attempt was made to record negative evidence. The early records, therefore, fail to meet the most rigorous standards of comparability.

Secondly, the profile of drinking constructed from our follow-up interviews is not as detailed as it might have been had our study been exclusively devoted to drinking patterns. The study of drinking patterns reported here represents only one phase of a broader investigation of the social and psychiatric adjustment of the patient group. While it would have been desirable to ask many more questions about drinking than were actually asked in the interviews, time was limited by other considerations. In the third place, it would have been very desirable, given the tendency of alcoholics to rationalize their drinking, to have interviewed a member of the family in every case as a means of checking statements on drinking experience. This again was beyond the scope of the present study but could well be a part of future follow-up studies of alcoholism.

Details of Method

The patient cohort which is the core of this study consists of every child seen at the St. Louis Municipal Psychiatric Clinic in the years 1924 through 1929 who was white, who had an intelligence quotient of at least 80, and who had been referred for behavior problems of some kind. There were 524 such former patients, 503 of whom survived to age 25 and can therefore be thought of as having made some sort of life adjustment as adults. In addition, this study made use of a matched "comparison group" of normal children who provide a baseline against which the extent of alcoholism in the cohort with childhood behavior problems can be compared. The comparison group consists of students selected from public school records to match the patient group with respect to age, sex, race, I.Q., and census tract lived in. Of one hundred control subjects selected, ninety-nine had survived to age 25.

The members of these two groups were personally interviewed with the use of a standardized questionnaire 30 years after their clinic experience or, in the case of the comparison group, school attendance. With regard to drinking, respondents were asked when they began their drinking, how much and how often they drank in their youth, how much and how often they drink currently, and whether there was ever a period in their lives when they drank more than now. Respondents were asked, too, if they thought there was any period when they drank too much and whether any family member ever complained about their drinking. They were also asked whether they had ever been on a bender, lost a job or been arrested because of drinking, had liver disease, delirium tremens, or any other medical complication of alcohol. Where potential respondents had died, a close relative was interviewed in their stead. Information was also collected from police, hospital, social agency, credit bureau, Veterans Administration, and other records and from death certificates where relevant. At the time of writing, 75 per cent of all subjects who survived to age 25 had been interviewed, the analysis of childhood clinic records was complete for 221 cases, and the collection of data from other records was nearly complete for all cases.

In studying the extent of alcoholism in a total population, it is necessary to set up criteria by which alcoholism can be said to be present or absent. This problem does not, of course, arise if one studies the etiology of alcoholism in a group of known alcoholics selected either by their own definition, as in the case of members of Alcoholics Anonymous, or by the definition of medical personnel, as in the case of hospitalized alcoholics. A review of some of the definitions offered in the literature (see Chapter 17 by Keller) indicates there is a general acceptance of the idea that an alcoholic is a person who gets into *trouble* through drinking, either socially or medically, but there are no clear-cut criteria for the degree or kinds of trouble he must have before he qualifies as an alcoholic.

For the purposes of this paper, two sets of standards for classification of alcoholics were developed: first, criteria for "chronic alcoholics" which are probably rigid enough to include only cases most people working in the field would accept as such, and second, criteria for "probable alcoholics." The criteria upon which these distinctions are based are set forth in the following chart, along with the other criteria and distinctions among drinkers used in this study.

CHART OF CRITERIA FOR THE CLASSIFICATION OF TYPES OF DRINKER

Alcoholic

Chronic Alcoholic

1. Death from acute alcoholism or
2. Medical complications of alcohol (cirrhosis, neuropathy, D.T.'s) or
3. Diagnosis of alcoholism in hospital, army or prison or
4. Arrests, loss of jobs, absenteeism, fighting, serious family complaints * due to alcohol along with chronic unemployment or
5. Five or more arrests for drinking within 5 years, the last arrest being within the last 3 years.

Probable Alcoholic

1. Statement from patient that he cannot control his drinking, in the absence of above criteria or
2. Any of the complaints in 4, above, in the absence of chronic unemployment.

Heavy Drinker

None of the complications above, but over an extended period

1. Drank at least three drinks three times per week or
2. Drank at least seven drinks per sitting.

* Excluded are those cases in which the only known social difficulties were complaints from families which disapprove drinking on principle.

No Excessive Drinking
  1. None of the complications of alcohol and
  2. Has never drunk as much as the minimum above over any extended period.

The criteria established for "heavy drinkers" shown in the preceding chart require both the consumption of relatively large amounts of alcohol and chronicity. Consequently, some persons were classified in the "no excessive drinking" category who had occasionally gotten drunk, provided that this had not been a chronic problem. The heavy drinkers, by definition, include no one for whom there are public records of excessive drinking, since such records would constitute evidence for social difficulties associated with drinking. As a result, the evidence for heavy drinking comes entirely from interviews. Standards for heavy drinking refer to levels reported as *usual* intake. It seems possible, considering the social disapproval of heavy drinking, that many respondents minimized their actual drinking in the interview statements. It may seem to some that the standards chosen for classifying persons as heavy drinkers are rather low. However, as will be seen in the results to follow, only one-fifth of the comparison group reported drinking as much as the minimum standards for heavy drinking require. Therefore, whether or not it is unusual to consume this much, it is surely unusual for respondents to *report* what we have called heavy drinking.

Results

1. *Alcoholism and heavy drinking in the patient and comparison groups*
The data in Table 1 indicate a significantly higher rate of alcoholism for the patient group than for the comparison group. In making these estimates, we assumed that all cases of alcoholism were identified through agency records, whether or not interviews took place.*

Of the entire sample, 89 per cent were located and there was sufficient information on the whereabouts of these cases to permit checks of the appropriate public records. Another 5 per cent who could not be located currently had a known address within the last few years which made possible examination of appropriate records in all locales where they were known previously to have lived. For the remaining 6 per cent, there was little or no information covering the interval between appearance at the clinic as a child and the present. The estimates of alcoholism in Table 1 are therefore probably somewhat below the reality but the increment to be expected if all cases had been located would be small. Moreover, the

---

* It is not anticipated that a significant number of those who are not now alcoholics will become alcoholics later on in life. The average age of the sample is now 43 years and other research indicates that the first symptoms of alcoholism seldom appear after this age. For example, Amark (2) found that 94 per cent of Swedish alcoholics showed symptoms of alcoholism by age 43, 100 per cent by age 54.

TABLE 1

Types of Drinker in the Patient and Comparison Groups (in Per Cent)

		Patients (N = 503)		Comparison (N = 99)	
Alcoholic	Chronic	6 ⎤	15	None ⎤	2
	Probable	9 ⎦		2 ⎦	
Heavy drinker (estimated) [a]			22		18
No excessive drinking			63		80
Totals			100		100

$$\chi^2 \text{ (at } 2df) = 33.18; P < .001$$

[a] Since evidence for heavy drinking comes only from the interview, an estimate was made on the basis of the proportion of heavy drinkers found in the 301 patients and 85 control subjects interviewed who were not alcoholics. Of these, 25 per cent of the patients and 19 per cent of the control subjects were heavy drinkers. The figures in the table assume that the same proportion of the uninterviewed are also heavy drinkers. If none of the uninterviewed are assigned to the heavy drinker category, there are 15 per cent of the patients and 16 per cent of the control subjects now definitely known to be heavy drinkers.

location of the remainder of the cases would probably only serve to enhance the difference between patient and comparison groups, since 98 per cent of the latter had been located as compared to 87 per cent of the patients.

Sex Differences. The differences reported in the literature on alcoholism between American men and women tend toward a ratio in the neighborhood of six male alcoholics for every female alcoholic. It is hardly surprising, therefore, that the male patients in our study included a significantly higher proportion of alcoholics than did the females. However, the difference between men and women was less striking than the differences reported by others. The proportion of male chronic alcoholics exceeded the proportion of female chronic alcoholics by less than two to one, and the proportion of all male alcoholics exceeded the proportion of all female alcoholics by less than three to one.

The relatively high rate of alcoholism among the female patients probably reflects the fact that the clinic population was largely male—as is the case in most child guidance clinics (1, p. 91f.)—and that the girls referred to such a clinic, therefore, tend to be even more atypical of the total population of girls than the males are of boys in general.

While more of the boy than girl clinic patients become alcoholics as adults, the differences are largely accounted for by their greater experience of heavy drinking. Of all the males who were ever heavy drinkers, 55 per cent are classified as alcoholics; among the women who were ever heavy drinkers, 44 per cent are classified as alcoholics. This difference in the rate

TABLE 2

Sex Differences among Types of Drinkers in the Patient and Comparison Groups (in Per Cent)

		Patients [a]		Comparison	
		Men ($N = 367$)	Women ($N = 141$)	Men ($N = 70$)	Women ($N = 29$)
Alcoholic	Chronic	7 ⎤ 21	4 ⎤ 8	—	—
	Probable	14 ⎦	4 ⎦	3	—
Heavy drinker		16	10	19	11
No excessive drinking		41	54	66	79
Uncertain (uninterviewed)		22	28	12	10
Totals		100	100	100	100

[a] For the sex difference among patients (excluding the 83 men and 40 women whose drinking behavior was uncertain): χ^2 (at $2df$) = 16.08; $P < .001$.

of alcoholics between men and women who had experienced heavy drinking is not statistically significant.

2. Rates of recovery

For purposes of this study, an alcoholic was considered "recovered" from alcoholism if he claimed to have had no social or medical difficulties resulting from drinking within the three years prior to interview and if there was no objective evidence to the contrary. Because alcoholism is characterized by periods of temporary remission, shorter periods of recovery were not counted. Heavy drinkers were considered recovered if they claimed not to have had a period within the last three years when they drank as much as is specified by the criteria for heavy drinking in the chart on pp. 398–399.

It is evident from Table 3 that the comparison group contains so few alcoholics and heavy drinkers that the differences in recovery between patient and comparison groups cannot be assessed statistically.

The alcoholic category contains all those who have ever had social or medical difficulties with drinking, that is, both the chronic and probable alcoholics. Most of the alcoholic patients have had social or medical difficulties within the last three years preceding interview (or within three years of their death, if they are deceased). More than half of those who have been heavy drinkers only decreased their drinking as they grew older. The higher rate of recovery found among heavy drinkers may be partly a function of the kind of evidence available. Since evidence for heavy drinking comes from interviews, there was no opportunity to validate the statements of patients who claimed to have reduced their consumption.[*]

[*] With the alcoholics, of course, objective evidence from public records sometimes discounted claims of recovery. In the case of heavy drinkers professing recovery, interviews with relatives would have been especially valuable as a check on their claims.

TABLE 3

Extent of Recovery from Excessive Drinking in the Patient and Comparison Groups (in Per Cent)

	Patients		Comparison	
	Alcoholic	Heavy Drink-ing Only	Alcoholic	Heavy Drink-ing Only
Current Drinking	(N = 84)	(N = 74)	(N = 2)	(N = 16)
Alcoholic	59	—	(0) ᵃ	—
Heavy drinking	7	41	—	69 (11)
Drinking mildly	19	53	(2)	31 (5)
Abstaining	7	5	—	—
No information	8	1	—	—
Totals	100	100		100

ᵃ Numbers of persons shown in parentheses.

Few of the recovered alcoholics claim that they are now abstainers. This is an interesting observation in view of the common belief that alcoholics can never become social drinkers because the first drink leads inevitably to uncontrolled drinking. Yet 26 per cent of those with previous medical or social troubles associated with drinking now claim to be drinking heavily or moderately without complications, and objective evidence does not contradict their claim. It is still possible, however, that they are in fact unable to limit their alcohol consumption but have learned to drink in more discreet settings so that there are no public records of their drinking.

Factors were sought in the records of the patient cohort as children which might distinguish those alcoholics and heavy drinkers who recovered from those who did not. Approximately a hundred and fifty relationships were examined. Of these, only seven were found to be statistically significant and none of these was common to both recovered alcoholics and recovered heavy drinkers. Since this incidence of positive findings is no greater than chance, we conclude that available information about the childhood of these patients does not permit us to predict who will recover from excessive drinking and who will not.

Antecedents of Alcoholism in the Patient Cohort

While the patient cohort has a high rate of alcoholism in contrast with the comparison group, we cannot account for these differences by comparing the childhood records of these two groups since, by definition, the comparison group did not attend the clinic and therefore had no comparable childhood records. We can compare the childhood clinic records of patients who became alcoholics with the records of patients who became heavy drinkers, but never alcoholics, and the records of patients who never drank heavily. These comparisons will give some insight into the etiological factors in the histories of prealcoholic patients, and may permit inferences about why children who come to a child guidance clinic have a high rate of alcoholism as adults.

At the time of writing, analysis of childhood records was complete for all the chronic alcoholics, for 85 per cent of the probable alcoholics and heavy drinkers, and for 37 per cent of those interviewed who were never heavy drinkers.*

1. *Ethnic background*

Because of reports in the literature (3, 11) that the Irish are overrepresented among alcoholics and the Jews underrepresented, it was of interest to see whether ethnicity was an important variable in the patient group.

TABLE 4

Type of Drinker, Patient Group, by Ethnicity (in Per Cent) [a]

	Irish [b] (N = 28)	German (N = 64)	Jewish (N = 15)	Old American (N = 78)	Other [c] (N = 33)
Alcoholic	46	31	20	31	33
Heavy drinker	36	25	20	33	36
No excessive drinking	18	44	60	36	31
Totals	100	100	100	100	100

[a] Ethnicity was determined for all known cases of alcoholism (N = 84) and heavy drinking (N = 74), even where other analysis was not complete, and for all analyzed cases with no heavy drinking (N = 84). Excluded are thirteen alcoholics, seven heavy drinkers, and four with no excessive drinking for whom no information about ethnicity was given in the childhood records.

[b] Irish versus all others: χ^2 (at $2df$) = 7.20; $P < .05$.

[c] Italian, Roumanian, Austrian, English, French, Hungarian.

The ethnic background of patients, as shown in Table 4, was determined by the birthplaces of parents and grandparents and by the ethnicity, if recorded, of American-born grandparents. The German group was kept separate not because of any special hypothesis about its drinking behavior but because in this St. Louis population it was by far the largest ethnic group. Since ethnicity beyond the parental generation had not been previously analyzed, it was necessary to go back to the original records for this

* A far smaller proportion of the no excessive drinking group was analyzed because the 84 cases previously analyzed in the course of this study were enough to permit statistical analysis. While we cannot guarantee that this is an unselected sample of all the cases interviewed which belong in this category, analysis had been previously completed without consideration of the drinking behavior of this group and we have no reason to suspect that this is a biased sample.

information. As a result, it was possible to include all known alcoholics and heavy drinkers, whether or not their records had been totally analyzed. As anticipated, the Irish show the highest rate of alcoholism and were the only group with a significantly different rate, while the Jews have the highest proportion who have never been excessive drinkers.

When only those who have ever been heavy drinkers are compared, however, the rate of alcoholism among the Irish is not significantly higher, nor is the rate for the Jews significantly lower than the rates for other groups. Whatever the ethnic group, between 48 and 56 per cent of the heavy drinkers became alcoholics. Ethnic differences in alcoholism, therefore, appear to be functions of differences in experience of heavy drinking rather than of differences in predisposition to become alcoholic if exposed to such a pattern. These findings are entirely consistent with the conclusions of Bales and Snyder in the works cited above that different cultural patterns for normal drinking account for the *difference* between Irish and Jewish rates of alcoholism.

2. Childhood social status

The patient cohort was largely but not exclusively made up of children of lower socio-economic status. Since referrals were often made by social agencies, many of the children came from families which were not self-supporting.*

Allocation of patients to social-status categories was largely on the basis of their family breadwinners' occupations, since this information was uniformly present in the clinic records. Housing, parents' levels of education, grandparents' occupations, and the neighborhood lived in were used, in addition, to allocate patients when this information was available. The distribution of types of drinkers in the resulting status categories is shown in Table 5.

The lowest socio-economic group, composed of children from families dependent on social agencies or supported by the criminal activities of the parents, yielded a very high rate of alcoholism. Professional and executive families produced few alcoholics. Unlike the findings of differences between men and women and between ethnic groups, these differences are not simply associated with differences in experience of heavy drinking since a strikingly high proportion of the heavy drinkers from the lowest status group became alcoholics and very few of the heavy drinkers from white collar families became alcoholics. Not only do more of the lowest status group drink heavily but when they drink heavily, they are apparently much more likely to have social or medical problems resulting from their drinking [χ^2 (with Yates' correction) $= 11.64$; $P < .05$].

---

* For this reason, even though the comparison group was matched with the patient group on the basis of census tracts, the clinic patients were of lower social status than the comparison group.

TABLE 5

Type of Drinker, Patient Group, by Childhood Family Status
(in Per Cent) [a]

	Professional or Executive (N = 15)	Other White Collar (N = 36)	Self-Sustaining Labor (N = 92)	Marginal (N = 49)	Illegal or Chronically Dependent (N = 23)
Alcoholic	7	19	32	37	65
Heavy drinker	40	31	30	33	9
No excessive drinking	53	50	38	30	26
Totals	100	100	100	100	100

χ^2 (with Yates' correction) = 16.40; $P < .05$

[a] Omitted are six cases for whom there was no information concerning family status; four of these were heavy drinkers, two were never heavy drinkers.

3. Parental adequacy

Evaluation of the "adequacy" of parents with whom the child lived was based on parents' performance of the basic obligations of physical care, financial support, supervision, and provision of a socially acceptable model. No consideration was given to the subtler aspects of interpersonal relations between parent and child. Yet, using these gross criteria of parental adequacy, inadequate parents were found to produce a higher rate of alcoholic offspring than adequate parents, as is evident in Table 6.

Again, while children of adequate parents were less often heavy drinkers, their lower rate of alcoholism could not be explained simply by their lesser

TABLE 6

Type of Drinker, Patient Group, by Parental Adequacy (in Per Cent) [a]

	Both or Only Parent Adequate (N = 51)	Mixed or Somewhat Inadequate (N = 111)	Both or Only Parent Inadequate (N = 49)
Alcoholic	14	34	49
Heavy drinker	31	33	20
No excessive drinking	55	33	31
Totals	100	100	100

χ^2 (2 at 4df) = 18.80; $P < .001$

[a] Ten cases omitted for whom parental adequacy was unknown: one alcoholic, five heavy drinkers, four no excessive drinking.

experience of heavy drinking. A higher percentage of the heavy drinkers who had inadequate parents became alcoholics than of the heavy drinkers who had adequate parents [x^2 (at $2df$) $= 9.43$; $P < .01$].

Parents were judged inadequate if they did not perform the traditional parental roles, regardless of whether their failure arose from irresponsibility or from some incapacitating physical or mental disease. Some parents were therefore judged inadequate because they were confined to hospitals or to their beds at home for long periods during the childhood of the patient. Others we so judged because they wantonly neglected the child, deserted, drank excessively, or committed flagrantly illegal acts with the child's knowledge. Some inadequate parents, therefore, showed antisocial behavior; others were inadequate in other ways. In some instances the child lived with the inadequate parent; in other instances the child was known to have had an inadequate parent but was brought up exclusively by the other parent who was adequate, or by adequate permanent foster parents.

When the father showed antisocial behavior, 40 per cent of the children became alcoholic. When only the mother had exhibited antisocial behavior, or when the parents were inadequate in other ways, they were no more likely to produce an alcoholic child than if they had no known problems (Table 7).

TABLE 7

Type of Drinker, Patient Group, by Parental [a] Antisocial Behavior
(in Per Cent)

	Both Parents Antisocial ($N = 41$)	Only Father Antisocial ($N = 78$)	Antisocial Father [b] (Total) ($N = 119$)	Only Mother Antisocial ($N = 14$)	Other Parental Problems Only ($N = 42$)	No Known Parental Problems ($N = 46$)
Alcoholic	37	41	40	21	24	22
Heavy drinker	31	29	29	29	29	32
No excessive drinking	32	30	31	50	47	46
Totals	100	100	100	100	100	100

[a] Natural parents only, whether or not the child lived with the natural parent.
[b] For antisocial fathers versus others: x^2 (at $2df$) $= 9.94$; $P < .01$.

There were only eight cases in which the father was known to have shown antisocial behavior but in which the child was brought up exclusively by an adequate mother or by adequate permanent foster parents. In none of these cases did the child develop alcoholism. While there are too few cases to draw reliable inference, this finding suggests that the predisposition to alcoholism is not solely genetic but may require the experience of living with an antisocial father.[*]

[*] Our findings support those of Roe and Burks (9), who found that children of alcoholic parents reared in foster homes do not develop alcoholism.

It is interesting that the effect of the father's antisocial behavior does not appear to depend on excessive drinking by the father, assuming our data on this point are in fair correspondence with the reality (Table 8). Fathers

TABLE 8

Type of Drinker, Patient Group, by Nature of Father's Antisocial Behavior (in Per Cent)

	Drinking (N = 76)	Non-support (N = 61)	Arrests (N = 20)	Sex (N = 37)	Cruelty (N = 50)	Desertion (N = 46)	None (N = 81)
Alcoholic	38	46	70	46	42	48	23
Heavy drinker	34	26	15	32	30	26	26
No excessive drinking	28	28	15	22	28	26	51
Totals	100	100	100	100	100	100	100

reported to drink excessively were no more likely to produce alcoholic children than fathers who were arrested, were erratic workers, had deserted, were guilty of sexual misbehavior, or beat their wives or children. Apparently the presence of an antisocial father in the home predisposes a child to excessive drinking whether or not the father sets an example of such drinking.

There are many aspects of the child's experience in the home which are dependent on the adequacy of his parents—for instance, whether discipline is lax, how frequently the family moves, whether the home is broken, whether the child suffers deprivations of food, shelter, clothes, and supervision. All these variables show statistically significant positive correlations with adult alcoholism, illustrating in many ways the relations between parental adequacy and adult drinking behavior.

4. Childhood behavior problems

In previous papers (6, 7, 8) based upon our larger study, it was reported that antisocial behavior in childhood, particularly the severe antisocial behavior that results in juvenile court appearance, is related to different measures of deviance in adult adjustment such as arrests, incarceration, and divorce. Antisocial behavior in childhood is also related to deviant adult drinking behavior (Table 9). Patients who appeared in juvenile court have

TABLE 9

Type of Drinker, Patient Group, by Juvenile Antisocial Behavior

	Juvenile Court Record (N = 105)	Antisocial Behavior (No Juvenile Court) (N = 57)	No Antisocial Behavior (N = 59)
Alcoholic	45	25	15
Heavy drinker	27	38	27
No excessive drinking	28	37	58
Totals	100	100	100

$$\chi^2 \text{ (at } 4df) = 22.36; P < .001$$

a higher rate of alcoholism than do patients without antisocial behavior. Those with antisocial behavior but no juvenile court appearances fall in between, indicating that it is the severity of the antisocial behavior rather than the experience in court which is important in the juvenile-court cases' high rate. Also, the high rate of alcoholism in patients who appeared in juvenile court is not simply a reflection of their greater experience of heavy drinking, since significantly more of the heavy drinkers from the juvenile court group became alcoholic [χ^2 (at $2df$) $= 8.01$; $P < .02$].

Childhood records were analyzed for all types of behavior problems reported, and such problems were categorized in terms of 71 symptoms. Alcoholics had more kinds of childhood symptoms per child than did those who were not heavy drinkers. The median number of symptoms of alcoholics was 12 out of the 71 possible symptoms, for those who were never excessive drinkers, 8 out of 71; but the excess among alcoholics is accounted for only by symptoms of antisocial behavior (such as running away, theft, and assault). Alcoholics did not have more symptoms of a neurotic type (mood disturbances, restlessness, and seclusiveness, for example) as children. Out of 35 symptoms of antisocial behavior, the proportion of prealcoholics showing the symptom was higher than the proportion of those who would never drink excessively in 30 cases. The data on this point are summarized in Table 10.

Moreover, for half of the 30 childhood symptoms of antisocial behavior in which the proportion of alcoholics exceeded the proportion of those without heavy drinking, the differences were statistically significant. For none of the 5 antisocial symptoms where the rate of alcoholics was lower, was the difference significant. Out of 36 neurotic symptoms encountered, half were reported for a higher proportion of the prealcoholics and half for a higher proportion of those who would never drink heavily, exactly what one would expect by chance. For none of the specific neurotic symptoms was the proportion of alcoholics significantly greater than the proportion of those who never drank excessively. The childhood symptomatology of the alcoholics, then, is characterized by many symptoms of antisocial behavior. However, there is no evidence that alcoholics had more neurotic problems in childhood than those patients who never drank excessively as adults.

There are apparently no specific antisocial symptoms which enable us to predict alcoholism. In respect to 15 symptoms of childhood antisocial behavior, significant differences were found in the proportions of alcoholics compared to those with no experience of excessive drinking. However, the higher rate of juvenile court appearances among subsequent alcoholics suggested that these symptoms might be typical of severely antisocial children rather than of prealcoholics in particular. When alcoholics who had appeared before juvenile courts were compared with other patients who had appeared before juvenile courts, none of these symptoms, not even adolescent drinking, was significantly more frequent in the alcoholic group. Children with severe symptoms of antisocial behavior show a high rate of al-

TABLE 10

Relative Proportions in the Patient Group of Alcoholics and Persons
with No Experience of Excessive Drinking, by Type of
Childhood Symptoms (in Per Cent)

	Antisocial-Behavior Symptoms [a] (N = 35)	Neurotic Symptoms [b] (N = 36)
Higher proportion of alcoholics [c]	86	50
Higher proportion of no excessive drinking	11	47
Equal proportions	3	3
Totals	100	100

[a] Incorrigibility, arrests, physical aggression, correctional institutionalization, delinquent associates, impulsive behavior, truancy, poor school achievement, school expulsion, diagnosed "psychopathy," vagrancy, pathological lying, irresponsibility, thievery, poor work history, out late at night, excessive drinking, vandalism, using of aliases, lack of guilt, verbal aggression, sexual perversion, excess masturbation, incest initiating, rape, premarital sex experience, illegitimate pregnancy, exhibitionism, excess sex talk and/or play, hostility toward family, fighting with contemporaries, teasing, discipline problems, attending multiple schools, slovenliness. The first fifteen are those in which alcoholics are significantly higher.

[b] Passivity, learning disabilities, poor coordination, faints, fits, eating problems, bizarre food preferences, eneuresis, sleepwalking, fears, seclusiveness, withdrawn, paranoid ideas, irritability, nausea, apparent stupidity, brooding, being unaffectionate, overdependence, being teased, odd school behavior, somatic symptoms, insomnia, nightmares, nailbiting, thumbsucking, tics, depression, "nervousness," diagnosed psychosis, over-sensitivity, restlessness, daydreaming, suicidal tendencies, low energy, tantrums.

[c] For "higher proportion of alcoholics" versus others: χ^2 (at $1df$) = 12.5; $P < .001$.

coholism as adults, but the knowledge of the choice of antisocial symptoms apparently does not assist us in predicting which of the antisocial children will become alcoholics.

5. *Interrelationships between childhood factors*

We have found three aspects of the childhood of these patients to be related to later alcoholism: the social status of the family, the adequacy of the parents, and the number of (antisocial) symptoms.* These variables, how-

* Since differences in the number of symptoms between alcoholics and other patients depend entirely on the excess of symptoms of antisocial behavior in the alcoholics, differences in the total number of symptoms are equivalent to differences in the number of antisocial symptoms.

ever, are also highly intercorrelated. Inadequate parents tend to be found frequently at the lower end of the socio-economic scale and tend to produce children who exhibit much antisocial behavior. The question therefore arises as to whether or not these variables are independent determinants of adult drinking. Measures of partial association indicate that childhood social status and the number of symptoms in childhood are independent of each other and of parental adequacy. Social status is related to alcoholism controlling number of symptoms ($\chi^2 = 11.31$; $P < .05$) and controlling parental adequacy ($\chi^2 = 8.31$; $P < .05$). Number of symptoms is related to alcoholism controlling social status ($\chi^2 = 15.0$; $P < .01$) and controlling parental adequacy ($\chi^2 = 9.48$; $P < .05$). Parental adequacy is related in the expected direction, but differences do not reach the 5 per cent level of confidence when controlling social status ($\chi^2 = 5.61$; $P < .20$) and number of symptoms ($\chi^2 = 6.72$; $P < .10$). Limiting our definition of parental inadequacy to the presence of an antisocial father in the home would probably delimit this variable sufficiently to obtain significant relationships on partial association.

Summary and Comment

The principal findings of this study may be summarized briefly as follows:

a. Alcoholism was found by follow-up study to be significantly more prevalent among a cohort of former patients of a child guidance clinic than among an otherwise matched comparison group with no childhood clinic experience.

b. Some former alcoholics were found to be drinking heavily or mildly but without evidence of social or medical complications, suggesting that in certain instances alcoholics may be able eventually to drink socially without loss of control.

c. While the extent of alcoholism was seen to differ by sex and ethnic categories, these differences lost significance when the experience of heavy drinking was controlled.

d. Antecedent factors evident in the childhood histories of the clinic patients found to be significantly related to alcoholism in later life were: low family social status; parental inadequacy, in particular antisocial behavior on the part of fathers; and serious antisocial behavior, as evidenced by records of juvenile court appearances and a clinic record of a variety of symptoms of antisocial behavior.

It is important to note that the antecedent factors of low family status, parental inadequacy, antisocial fathers, and antisocial behavior in childhood significantly differentiated the alcoholics from non-alcoholics in later life even when only those who had ever experienced heavy drinking were considered. This is in contrast to the differentiating effect of sex and ethnic factors, which disappeared when only those persons with experience of heavy drinking were considered. This finding suggests that sex and ethnic groups are different kinds of variables from the others. Perhaps the difference is that sex and ethnic status are totally ascribed statuses, assigned at birth, whereas the other variables depend either on the behavior of the patient himself (antisocial behavior in childhood) or on the behavior of his parents (achieved class position, inadequacy, and antisocial behavior of the parents). If we make the assumption that heavy drinking can be normal or accepted social behavior in certain socio-cultural groups but that alcoholism, at least in America, always violates the social norms, we can postulate that alcoholism requires both exposure to the mores of heavy drinking and a pathological individual.

The high rate of alcoholism observed in this and other studies in the Irish as contrasted with other ethnic groups and in men as contrasted with women does not indicate a higher rate of individuals pathologically susceptible to alcoholism in these groups. Rather the fact that these groups accept heavy drinking as normal behavior exposes a larger proportion of their members to heavy drinking and thereby makes alcohol available to a larger proportion of the fixed number of alcohol-susceptible members of the group. The high rate of alcoholism among those who have low status, inadequate parents, and antisocial childhood behavior, on the other hand, reflects not only a greater experience of heavy drinking among these groups but also a higher proportion of alcoholism-susceptible members, as indicated by the higher proportion of alcoholics even when amount of experience of heavy drinking is controlled.

A study of this kind which takes as its population a group of patients referred to a child guidance clinic does not permit generalizations about the etiology of alcoholism. Most alcoholics did not attend such clinics as children, and their alcoholism may have developed from different roots and been reached by different paths. This study indicates, however, that there is among alcoholics a group of still-undetermined size * whose alcoholism

---

* Several other studies suggest that this group may form a significant proportion of existing alcoholics. Amark (2) found a high rate of criminal behavior and alcoholism in the brothers of alcoholics and some evidence that the fathers also had a high rate of criminal activities, suggesting the antisocial family as the origin of alcoholism. The McCords (Chapter 24) support this conclusion, although like this study, it is one that does not have a representative sample of alcoholics. Bleuler's (4) study of the family background of fifty well-to-do hospitalized alcoholics found that even in this upper class group, nineteen had "grossly unfavorable home environment" as children, suggesting parental inadequacy, and twenty-nine had long-standing and intimate contact before the age of 20 with persons who had alcoholic problems, suggesting antisocial behavior in the parents.

Sherfey (10), in studying admissions to the Payne Whitney Clinic, found 11 per cent of those she was able to diagnose to be "asocial psychopathic . . . with a life-long behavioral abnormality." Like Bleuler, she was working with an upper-class group where asocial psychopathy should be minimal. Of the many reports of the psychological test scores of alcoholics, one of the few reliable findings (5) is that alcoholics have a high Pd (psychopathic deviate) score on the Minnesota Multiphasic Personality Inventory, which suggests the intimate relationship between alcoholism and other forms

develops in the context of a long history of antisocial behavior dating from childhood and of childhood experience of grossly inadequate parental care and extremely low social status. A striking finding of this study is that not only is the occurrence of alcoholism highly related to evidences in childhood of pathology in the subjects, and their parents, but the kind of pathology related to alcoholism can best be described as antisocial rather than neurotic behavior.

References

1. Ackerson, L., *Children's Behavior Problems,* Chicago: University of Chicago Press, 1931.

2. Amark, C. A., *Study in Alcoholism,* Copenhagen: Ejnar Munksgaard, 1951.

3. Bales, Robert F., "Cultural Differences in Rates of Alcoholism," *Quart. J. Stud. Alc.,* 6:480–499, 1946.

4. Bleuler, M., "Familial and Personal Background of Chronic Alcoholics," *in* O. Diethelm (Ed.), *Etiology of Chronic Alcoholism,* Springfield, Ill.: Charles C. Thomas, 1955.

5. Chotlos, John W., and John B. Deiter, "Psychological Considerations in the Etiology of Alcoholism," *in* David J. Pittman (Ed.), *Alcoholism: An Interdisciplinary Approach,* Springfield, Ill.: Charles C. Thomas, 1959.

6. O'Neal, Patricia, and Lee N. Robins, "The Relation of Childhood Behavior Problems to Adult Psychiatric Status," *Amer. J. Psychiat.,* 114:961–969, 1958.

7. Robins, Lee N., and Patricia O'Neal, "Mortality, Mobility and Crime," *Amer. Sociol. Rev.,* 23:162–171, 1958.

8. ———, "The Marital History of Former Problem Children," *Social Problems,* 5:347–358, 1958.

9. Roe, Anne, and Barbara Burks, *Adult Adjustment of Foster Children of Alcoholic and Psychotic Parentage and the Influence of the Foster Home,* New Haven, Conn.: Journal of Studies on Alcohol, 1945.

10. Sherfey, M. J., "Psychopathology and Character Structure in Chronic Alcoholism," *in* O. Diethelm (Ed.), *Etiology of Chronic Alcoholism,* Springfield, Ill.: Charles C. Thomas, 1955.

11. Snyder, Charles R., *Alcohol and the Jews,* Glencoe, Ill.: Free Press, 1958.

---

of antisocial behavior. While personality-test scores are influenced to an unknown extent by the long history of excessive alcohol intake, these studies suggest that antisocial personality characteristics are common in alcoholics and that many alcoholics were brought up in homes where male members of the family also exhibited severe antisocial behavior.

chapter 24

A longitudinal study
of the personality
# of alcoholics*

William McCord and Joan McCord

Fruitful search for a basic alcoholic personality pattern has been seriously hindered by the fact that it has been virtually impossible to separate the characteristics of alcoholics that may be the result of alcoholism from those that may be a cause of, or at least precede, its emergence. The clinical import of this situation has been recently summarized by Armstrong (1, p. 45). "One of the most vexing aspects of the situation," writes Armstrong, "is the clinical experience of watching changes in personality take place as a disease situation advances, leaving one in almost complete bewilderment as to what picture existed before the superimposition of a pattern of attitude and behavior which we recognize as alcoholic." Armstrong —and this was in 1958—goes on to say: "There is no report of studies in which it was possible successfully to examine the premorbid or even the early alcoholic history in such a way that a reliable personality profile could be obtained and compared with that observed in the fully developed disease state." In the present study, however, we have been able to investigate the prealcoholic personality of a sample of male alcoholics—and to make comparisons and contrasts with the personality of adult alcoholics—in a way that begins to meet the objections raised against earlier research.

Background of the Study

The subjects for our study were participants in the Cambridge-Somerville Youth Study, begun in 1935 under the guidance of Richard Clark Talbot.

* This chapter is a revised and somewhat shortened version of Chapter 8 in *Origins of Alcoholism* by William McCord and Joan McCord with Jon Gudeman (4). This work was supported by the Ella Lyman Cabot fund and by a grant from the National Institute of Mental Health.

The original project was designed with the dual purpose of preventing delinquency and of collecting valid data on child-training practices of a sizeable section of the lower classes residing in Cambridge and Somerville, Massachusetts. Although the attempt to prevent delinquency seems to have failed (2, 5), the project succeeded in gathering a unique fund of information regarding childhood behavior, family interaction, and the transmission of values in a lower-class urban population.

For an average of 5 years, trained social workers recorded their observations of the 255 boys * and their families whose "treatment" they had undertaken. These records described in detail whatever activities the counselor-observers noticed in the home, at school, during chance meetings on the streets, and in the Cambridge-Somerville Youth Study Center. They reported conversations with parents, friends, neighbors, teachers, and, of course, the subjects themselves. Because of the number of observers covering each case, systematic biases of observation tended to be minimized. In addition, the records included information from a series of medical examinations, school data, psychiatric interviews, summer camps, Y.M.C.A. directors, and other agencies who had contact with the subjects.

The primary virtue of the Cambridge-Somerville records for a study of alcoholism rests upon the fact that the information reported was gathered long before any evidence of alcoholism could have appeared. The boys averaged 9 years in age when the first observations were made; they averaged 11 at the time when regular visits (treatment) began; and they were last seen, on the average, when they were in their middle teens.

To ascertain alcoholism in later life among these 255 subjects, we relied upon official community records: Any of the subjects who had been members of Alcoholics Anonymous, who had been referred to a hospital in Massachusetts for alcoholism, who were known as alcoholics by the Boston Committee on Alcoholism or by other social agencies, or who had been convicted by the courts for public drunkenness at least twice were considered alcoholic. The behavior and attitudes of the 29 boys who, according to these criteria, later became alcoholics were compared to those of the 158 boys who, in adulthood, had become neither criminals nor alcoholics.† The results of this comparison provide evidence on the prealcoholic personality.

The comprehensive records allowed a further comparison: Because a substantial number of the subjects' fathers were addicted to alcohol and were studied in their day-to-day behavior, it was also possible to examine in comparable ways the characteristics of persons after the onset of alcoholism. Consequently, one can begin to specify what syndromes of personality

---

* Of the original 325 boys in the treatment group, we dropped the 65 who were retired from the study in 1941, the 2 who had died, and the 3 who were known to have left the state.

† Subjects who had been arrested only once for drunkenness were omitted from the analyses unless additional evidence identified them as alcoholics. For justification of the criteria of alcoholism used in this study, see (4).

precede the disorder and what characteristics appear to be precipitated by alcoholism.

Characteristics of Male Alcoholics in Adulthood

Eighty-three fathers in the study were defined as alcoholics; that is, their repeated drinking at some time prior to 1945 had interfered with their interpersonal relations or their social or economic functioning. Twenty-three of the men had not been arrested for drunkenness and ten had been arrested only once. These men were classified as alcoholics because they had lost their jobs as a result of excessive drinking or had received medical treatment specifically for alcoholism, or because marital unhappiness was attributable primarily to their excessive drinking. Five of the alcoholics were so classified solely because they had been arrested at least twice for drunkenness. The majority of the alcoholic fathers, numbering forty-five, were considered alcoholics by both criteria.

Since all of these men classified as alcoholics were observed in their routine activities, our analysis of them is unaffected by the methodological defects which inhere in studies of persons confined to special institutions such as jails, sanatoriums, and mental hospitals. When these men were compared with a sample of "non-deviant" fathers (neither alcoholic nor criminal), a number of significant differences became apparent—differences which may be subsumed conveniently under the headings of personality and relations to family and society.

1. The relations of alcoholics to society

It is hardly surprising to note that the alcoholics were social outcasts. Economically, they failed to provide for their families; they found it extremely difficult to hold a regular job. Although the depression hit most of the families in our study, significantly fewer alcoholics than non-deviants were able to find work on a regular basis (Table 1).

TABLE 1

Employment of Alcoholics and Non-deviants (in Per Cent)

	Alcoholics (N = 82)	Non-deviants (N = 105)
Regularly employed	23	58
Irregularly employed	67	33
Regularly unemployed	10	9
Totals	100	100

$$\chi^2 = 24.05; \ P < .001$$

One would also expect that alcoholics, in addition to being economically unstable, would be less actively involved in community organizations. To test this belief, we examined the social activities of the men under study. These activities involved two basic types of social participation: (*a*) "informal" participation, referring to social gatherings that did not involve official "membership rites" (such as parties and poker games); (*b*) "formal" participation, referring to activity in groups with "membership rites" (such as the P.T.A., saloon clubs, neighborhood organizations, and Cambridge Civic Association). The alcoholics, as anticipated, tended to avoid involvement in formal community organizations (Table 2).

TABLE 2

Participation in Community Groups of Alcoholics and Non-deviants (in Per Cent)

	Alcoholics (N = 57)	Non-deviants (N = 89)
Little or no participation	56	43
Participation only in informal groups	40	36
Participation in formal groups	4	21
Totals	100	100

$$\chi^2 = 9.19; P < .02$$

Thus, the alcoholics were, both economically and socially, less stable than their non-deviant counterparts.

2. The relations of alcoholics to their families

How do alcoholics interact with their families? For example, do alcoholics tend to reject their sons or do they, on the contrary, turn to their children as a source of affection? Do alcoholics tend to dominate their families or do they, because of the incapacities caused by their disorder, tend to take a passive role? To explore these and related questions we analyzed the alcoholics' relations to their families.

The alcoholics, as the data in Table 3 indicate, were much less prone than non-deviants to demonstrate their affection in an active manner. It bears mention in this connection that, considering just the affectionate fathers, the alcoholics were significantly more likely to be passive in expressing affection.

Previously (4), we have shown that the combination of paternal alcoholism and paternal rejection is productive of addiction in the son. The data in Table 3, therefore, indicate that alcoholics tend to multiply their own kind in future generations. The reasons for an alcoholic's rejection of his son are difficult to fathom. We would guess (on the basis of causal observation) that the typical alcoholic is unsure of receiving love from other people and is also very unsure of how to give love. The result may often be deep reluctance and hesitation in expressing affection toward his family.

The alcoholics also differed from the non-deviant adults in the type of

TABLE 3

Attitudes of Alcoholics and Non-deviants Toward Their Sons
(in Per Cent)

	Alcoholics (N = 72)	Non-deviants (N = 97)
Actively affectionate	17	43
Passively affectionate	30	33
Alternating	10	6
Passively rejecting	22	11
Actively rejecting	21	7
Totals	100	100

$$\chi^2 = 19.54; P < .001$$

roles which they assumed in the family. The fathers in the study could be categorized into four groups. "Dictators" were those who completely dominated their families and made almost every decision. "Leaders" were men who gave general guidance to family affairs but were flexible in bowing to reasonable arguments from other members of the family. "Passive" fathers, on the other hand, had abdicated direction of the family to the wife or one of the elder sons. As Table 4 shows, the alcoholics clearly tended not to be

TABLE 4

Familial Roles of Alcoholics and Non-deviants (in Per Cent)

	Alcoholics (N = 64)	Non-deviants (N = 95)
Dictator	19	10
Leader	23	63
Passive	58	27
Totals	100	100

$$\chi^2 = 24.3; P < .001$$

leaders and tended, rather, to play a passive role in their families. Considering only the more dominant males, the relatively few alcoholics among them were more likely to be dictators than leaders.

Not surprisingly, a high degree of intense conflict between husband and wife was typical for alcoholics. The majority of the alcoholics' families were rent with dissension, while only a tiny minority of the non-deviants' homes evidenced such conflict (Table 5).

From previous research (3) we have reason to believe that a background of intense parental conflict in childhood leads to alcoholism in later life;

TABLE 5

Husband-Wife Conflict in the Homes of Alcoholics and Non-deviants (in Per Cent)

	Alcoholics (N = 74)	Non-deviants (N = 91)
No conflict	8	58
Some conflict	32	35
Intense conflict	60	7
Totals	100	100

$$\chi^2 = 66.61; \; P<.001$$

thus, the kind of conflict indicated in Table 5 may be an important factor leading to the high rate of alcoholism found in the descendants of inebriates.

The alcoholics varied from the non-deviants in the ways they disciplined their children. The fathers in the study were divided according to their ways of controlling their sons. Some fathers disciplined in a "consistently punitive" fashion; the son knew that if he committed a certain act, his father would respond with physical punishment. Other fathers were equally consistent, but did not use physical methods. These men depended on reasoning and withdrawal of privileges or love as their weapons for controlling the child. We described these men as "consistently non-punitive." Other fathers, however, varied in their demands. At times, they would punish a certain act (for example, staying out in the street beyond a "curfew"); at other times, they would ignore the same action or even condone it. These inconsistent fathers were divided into two groups: "erratically punitive" and "erratically non-punitive," depending on the form of discipline. A fifth group of men simply did not care about their child's activities and imposed no discipline of any sort. These we put under the category of "lax" disciplinarians.

A comparison of the alcoholic and the non-deviant fathers revealed that alcoholics were much more likely to be erratically punitive or lax in controlling their sons (Table 6). This fact bodes ill for the future of alcoholics' sons, for previous research (4) shows that the two forms of discipline more often found in the alcoholics' families—erratic punitiveness and laxity—are significantly involved in the causation of certain types of crime.

Therefore, these alcoholics are unstable members of their families as well as their communities. They perform their roles as fathers in a passive or dictatorial manner; they are prone to express their various frustrations through conflict with their wives, rejection of their sons, and the imposition of erratically punitive discipline on their children. Thus, it seems, people who must live with alcoholics are doomed to an unhappy existence.

3. Values and personality traits

What is the alcoholic's view of his society? How does he view himself?

TABLE 6

Disciplinary Methods of Alcoholics and Non-deviants (in Per Cent)

	Alcoholics (N = 68)	Non-deviants (N = 87)
Consistently punitive	16	26
Consistently non-punitive	10	30
Erratically punitive	50	30
Erratically non-punitive	8	6
Lax	16	8
Totals	100	100

$$\chi^2 = 15.06; P < .005$$

What values does he uphold? What intrapersonal traits differentiate him from the non-alcoholic? To begin to answer these questions, we may note that the alcoholics differed strikingly from the non-deviants in their view of the world. Many of the subjects in the study faced the world with, at least, a façade of self-confidence. Other men felt themselves to be unjustly victimized by society; these tended to be self-pitying individuals who felt that they had been "double crossed" or given a "raw deal." Although a majority of the non-deviants acted in a self-confident way, a majority of the alcoholics thought that they were victims of an unfair society (Table 7). This feeling

TABLE 7

The Views Held toward Society by Alcoholics and Non-deviants (in Per Cent)

	Alcoholics (N = 64)	Non-deviants (N = 93)
Self-confident	19	52
Neutral	22	26
Victimized	59	22
Totals	100	100

of victimization may reflect a need for self-justification on the part of alcoholics, and another tendency of alcoholics may be related to this same need. One might expect that the alcoholics would try to compensate for their inadequacies through "blowing up" their self-image. This phenomenon did occur to some extent: 36 per cent of the alcoholics, as compared to 16 per cent of the non-deviants, exhibited feelings of grandiosity—inflated estimates of their abilities and virtues ($\chi^2 = 8.30$; $P < .005$).

In addition to isolating these more specific attitudes, we classified the general "value orientations" of the men under study. The detailed records

referred to a variety of situations about which the subjects had to make
choices; the primary basis for these choices was classified as being one of
the following five types: (*a*) "security"—a desire to avoid risk, to maintain
or obtain physical security; (*b*) "popularity"—a desire to be liked by others;
(*c*) "achievement"—a desire to do something well; (*d*) "status"—a desire
to be respected (although not necessarily liked) by others, to be thought
better than most people; (*e*) "enjoyment"—a desire for immediate sensual
stimulation. As Table 8 shows, the non-deviants were much more likely to

TABLE 8

The Primary Values of Alcoholics and Non-deviants (in Per Cent)

	Alcoholics (N = 65)	Non-deviants (N = 88)
Security	30	62
Popularity	0	1 [a]
Achievement	0	9 [a]
Status	5	18
Enjoyment	65	10
Totals	100	100

χ^2 (at 2 *df*) = 46.2; $P<.001$

[a] "Popularity" and "achievement" were omitted from the statistical analysis because of the small number of cases.

place security or status highest in their scale of values, while the alcoholics
tended to give priority to immediate enjoyment.* "Enjoyment" as a value
emphasis, in contrast with security, popularity, achievement, and status, involves no deferment of reward. Thus, the alcoholics appeared to be less
strongly inhibited.

A lack of inhibition is evidenced in another trait which statistically differentiates the alcoholics from the non-deviant, namely, unrestrained aggressiveness. Men in the study were classified as "strongly inhibited" because, to the observers' knowledge, they were never openly hostile or angry.
Many of the men showed "moderate aggression"; they expressed feelings of
irritation through "normal" channels—that is, through the forms of behavior
sanctioned by our culture. Another group of men, however, were aggressively "unrestrained"; their expressions of anger often exceeded the bounds

* Closely related to an individual's values is his "conscience orientation." In a recent
article (3) we outlined four basic types of conscience: the other-directed (anxiety
about relations to others), the authoritarian (anxiety about status), the integral (anxiety
about maintaining a consistent self-image), and the hedonist (anxiety concerning repressed dependency). In passing, it should be noted that the majority (52 per cent)
of the non-deviants were authoritarian, while close to a majority of the alcoholics (44
per cent) were hedonistic, the difference in types being statistically significant.

imposed by society. Although only a very small portion of the non-deviants were unrestrained, more than a third of the alcoholics were classified as extremely aggressive (Table 9).

TABLE 9

Manifestations of Aggression in Alcoholics and Non-deviants (in Per Cent)

	Alcoholics (N = 73)	Non-deviants (N = 92)
Aggression strongly inhibited	9	11
Moderate aggression	55	86
Unrestrained aggression	36	3
Totals	100	100

$$\chi^2 = 29.92; \ P < .001$$

In addition to being relatively more aggressive, the alcoholics tended to exhibit markedly dependent behavior in an open fashion. Dependent behavior in a man—overt seeking for comfort, care, and direct guidance—is widely disapproved in American culture. Yet, a small proportion of males in the study did exhibit this type of behavior. At the opposite extreme, some subjects could be described as "highly masculine"—they sought to appear especially strong, resolute, courageous, and responsible. Alcoholics, as Table

TABLE 10

Dependent Behavior in Alcoholics and Non-deviants (in Per Cent)

	Alcoholics (N = 74)	Non-deviants (N = 98)
Highly masculine	11	20
Normally masculine	69	74
Dependent [a]	20	6
Totals	100	100

[a] For "dependent" versus others: χ^2 (at $1df$) = 6.8; $P < .005$.

10 indicates, were significantly more likely to exhibit openly dependent behavior than were the non-deviants.

4. Summary of characteristics in adulthood

The above analysis, based on direct and extended observations, has revealed that the adult alcoholics studied differed significantly from the non-deviants in a number of ways. In relation to their society, alcoholics were more likely to have been irregularly employed and to have participated little in formal community organizations. In relation to their families, alcoholics were more likely to have rejected their sons and to have played a passive role in the family (or else to have been "dictators"). They were more often in intense familial conflict and tended to discipline their sons in an erratically punitive or lax manner. In values and personal traits, alcoholics tended to feel victimized by society, to show compensatory feelings of grandiosity, and to place enjoyment above other values. Also, as compared to non-deviants, more alcoholics exhibited unrestrained aggression and were openly dependent.

It bears emphasis here that this study is not unique in pointing to many of the traits we have mentioned; it does, however, differ from other studies in several respects. First, as we have mentioned, the analyses were based on direct observations of the adult alcoholics within their homes over an extensive period of time. Second, the original observers did not know that *any* study of personality would be based on their reports. Third, reports were made by a variety of observers whose possible biases would tend to cancel one another. Fourth, neither the original observers nor the raters focused on the problem of alcoholic personality, and thus, conscious theoretical biases were minimized. Finally, this sample of alcoholics contains men who had never come to the attention of "official" agencies dealing with alcoholism. For these reasons, we have some confidence that adult alcoholic men are truly distinguishable from adult non-deviant men in their relations to society and their families, and in their personalities.

Nevertheless, this study of adult alcoholics shares with other studies the disadvantage that the subjects were already alcoholics at the time of the observations. Many theories about the alcoholic personality presuppose that the characteristics of adult alcoholics are apparent prior to the onset of alcoholism. To test the validity of this supposition, we turn now to an analysis of the prealcoholics—those twenty-nine boys who in adulthood manifested symptoms of alcoholism.

The Characteristics of Prealcoholics in Childhood

None of the subjects discussed in this section was known to be alcoholic at the time the observations were made (during childhood); nor were any known to be alcoholics by the raters who categorized their traits. As with the adult alcoholics, we discuss here the relation of the prealcoholics to their society and to their families and then turn to their personalities.

1. *The relation of prealcoholics to society*

Adult alcoholics, we have noted, differed from adult non-deviants in tending not to participate in group activities, particularly formal activities. The boys in the study were observed during work and play, and, from these observations, we classified their "group behavior": boys who generally played by themselves; boys who generally played with their peers, yet rarely led them; and boys who were frequently chosen (formally or informally) as leaders of their peers. We found that the prealcoholics did not differ significantly from the non-deviants in any of these categories. Although perhaps not strictly comparable to the data on adults, these data on the childhood group activities of prealcoholics do not seem to presage the relative absence of group participation found among the alcoholics studied in later life.

2. The relation of prealcoholics to their families

We have noted the hostile attitude of adult alcoholics toward their families. Such men tended to reject their sons and fight with their wives. Family rejection was evident also among the prealcoholics.

Most of the children in the study indicated generally favorable attitudes toward their mothers. A smaller group of boys, however, expressed outright disapproval, disdain, or fear of their parents. The prealcoholic children were significantly more likely to reject their mothers than were the non-deviants (Table 11). This relatively disapproving attitude of the alcoholics

TABLE 11

Childhood Attitudes of Alcoholics and Non-deviants toward Their Mothers
(in Per Cent)

	Alcoholics ($N = 25$)	Non-deviants ($N = 143$)
Favorable attitude	64	85
Unfavorable attitude	36	15
Totals	100	100

χ^2 (corrected for small N) $= 5.22; P < .025$

toward their mothers appears, incidentally, to have been somewhat independent of their mothers' attitudes toward them. Also, a higher proportion of the prealcoholic children (48 per cent) than of the non-deviants (31 per cent) disapproved of their fathers; this difference was not, however, statistically significant.

In relation to their brothers and sisters, too, the potentially alcoholic children indicated a lack of affection for their families. Their attitudes toward their siblings were characterized by coolness and apparent indifference. While the non-deviant children tended more often to be companions of their siblings, the prealcoholic boys were more likely to appear totally indifferent (Table 12).

Thus, the attitudes of the prealcoholics toward their parents and siblings seemed to anticipate the attitudes of the adult alcoholics toward their wives and children.

3. The personality of prealcoholics

Although the adult alcoholics lacked self-confidence, tending to feel "victimized" by society, we found no evidence of this trait among the preal-

TABLE 12

Childhood Relationships of Alcoholics and Non-deviants to Siblings (in Per Cent)

	Alcoholics (N = 23)	Non-deviants (N = 124)
Indifferent [a]	43	21
Competitive	9	10
Antagonistic	13	17
Companionable	35	52
Totals	100	100

[a] For "indifferent" versus others: $\chi^2 = 5.4$; $P < .02$.

coholic boys. "Self-confidence" for prealcoholics and non-deviants in childhood was categorized along a three-point continuum. Those boys who demonstrated unusual fearlessness or faced difficult tasks without hesitation were considered "very self-confident." At the opposite extreme, we rated boys as exhibiting strong feelings of inferiority if they talked frequently of their lack of ability and their failures or if they were exceptionally hesitant about attempting even moderately difficult tasks because they feared failure. We discovered that the prealcoholic children *less* frequently appeared to have strong inferiority feelings than did the non-deviants (Table 13). We found,

TABLE 13

Self-Confidence of Alcoholics and Non-deviants in Childhood (in Per Cent)

	Alcoholics (N = 29)	Non-deviants (N = 156)
Very self-confident	10	10
Moderately self-confident	80	58
Strong inferiority feelings [a]	10	32
Totals	100	100

[a] For "strong inferiority feelings" versus others: χ^2 (at $1df$) $= 4.8$; $P < .05$.

too, that the feelings of grandiosity evident among adult alcoholics were not markedly present among prealcoholics. Only a slightly higher proportion of the prealcoholics (36 per cent) than of the non-deviants (27 per cent) gave indications that they held inflated ideas of their own importance.

A further indication that the feeling of victimization was not evident in prealcoholics appeared when we analyzed the relation between boys who had "abnormal fears" during childhood and alcoholism. Some of the subjects felt great concern about unrealistic dangers; they often talked about fears of the dark, of "monsters," of being attacked. The potential alcoholics, as Table 14 shows, exhibited significantly *fewer* of these abnormal fears than did the non-deviants.

TABLE 14

Abnormal Fears of Alcoholics and Non-deviants in Childhood (in Per Cent)

	Alcoholics ($N = 25$)	Non-deviants ($N = 146$)
Abnormal fears	28	50
No abnormal fears	72	50
Totals	100	100

$$\chi^2 = 4.15; P < .05$$

In aggression, however, we found that the prealcoholics resembled the adult alcoholics. We used a three-point scale to rate the aggressive behavior of the boys in the study. Boys who reacted to even slight frustrations with overt and exaggerated aggression, who fought constantly, were rated as "unrestrained" in expressing aggression. At the other extreme, boys who almost never gave overt expression to hostility, regardless of provocation, were considered "strongly inhibited." As Table 15 indicates, the prealcoholic

TABLE 15

Aggressive Behavior of Alcoholics and Non-deviants in Childhood (in Per Cent)

	Alcoholics ($N = 28$)	Non-deviants ($N = 154$)
Unrestrained aggression	36	12
Moderate aggression	50	56
Strongly inhibited aggression	14	32
Totals	100	100

$$\chi^2 = 8.52; P < .02$$

children much more frequently exhibited unrestrained aggression and less frequently appeared strongly inhibited.

In some cases, aggressive behavior manifested itself as sadism—an urge to inflict pain on others. A small proportion of boys exhibited this overtly destructive syndrome. Another group of boys were masochistic—they enjoyed playing games in which they were "victims," in which they placed themselves in a position to receive pain. Although masochism was not related to alcoholism, the prealcoholic boys were more often sadistic (Table 16).

TABLE 16

Sadism and Masochism in Alcoholics and Non-deviants in Childhood
(in Per Cent)

	Alcoholics ($N = 29$)	Non-deviants ($N = 157$)
Sadistic [a]	28	10
Masochistic	3	4
Neither sadistic nor masochistic	69	86
Totals	100	100

[a] For "sadistic" versus others: χ^2 (at $1df$ and corrected for small N) = 4.77; $P < .05$.

We have found that adult alcoholics were markedly dependent in their behavior. The attitudes of the prealcoholics toward their families suggest a tendency for them to deny dependency. Yet one further characteristic of the prealcoholic suggests the presence of dependency conflict; namely, sex anxiety. Although the difference does not quite reach statistical significance, we found that a considerably higher proportion of the prealcoholics (54 per cent) than of the non-deviants (35 per cent) had been preoccupied with fears about sex.[*]

Finally, we found that passive behavior in childhood was negatively related to alcoholism in later life. For this measure, we considered the amount of physical activity or "energy level" of the subjects. Some boys had always to be moving or doing something; these were considered "hyperactive." Other boys participated in activities yet were able to sit quietly for "reasonable" periods of time. Still others of the subjects remained inactive for exceptionally long periods of time; these children were classified as "passive." The findings on this point in Table 17, indicating the greater activity of the prealcoholic, lend themselves to two contrary explanations—both of which may be partly true. On the one hand, hyperactivity may have been a bid for attention; on the other hand, the absence of passivity may have reflected an attempt to deny dependency needs.

Thus, in the prealcoholics, we did not find those feelings of victimization, an absence of self-confidence, which were noted among adult alcoholics. Nor did we find significant evidence of grandiose feelings among the prealcoholics. Yet the prealcoholics like the adult alcoholics, tended to exhibit unrestrained aggressiveness. With respect to dependent behavior, we found conflicting evidence among the prealcoholics: they tended to evidence disapproval of their mothers and indifference toward their siblings, yet they

[*] It should also be noted, in passing, that the prealcoholics did *not* differ from the non-deviants in the degree to which they exhibited homosexual desires or oral tendencies.

TABLE 17

Energy Level of Alcoholics and Non-deviants in Childhood (in Per Cent)

	Alcoholics ($N = 29$)	Non-deviants ($N = 155$)
Hyperactive	31	21
Normal active	62	56
Passive [a]	7	23
Total	100	100

[a] For "passive" versus others: χ^2 (at $1df$) = 4.0; $P < .05$.

showed signs of sex anxiety and a tendency toward hyperactivity—traits which seem to belie their "self-confident" behavior.

4. Summary of characteristics in childhood

An examination of the character of prealcoholics in childhood has revealed a syndrome of personality traits that significantly differentiate them from non-alcoholics. In this analysis, there was no possibility of retrospective bias, for the observations were made when the subjects were children (and had not yet become alcoholics) and the categorizations were done by raters who did not know which subjects might eventually become alcoholics. The findings in this section indicate that alcoholics in childhood were apparently "self-contained." Compared with non-deviants, the prealcoholics were more likely to have been outwardly self-confident, undisturbed by abnormal fears, indifferent toward their siblings, and disapproving of their mothers. Also, they more often evidenced unrestrained aggression, sadism, sexual anxiety, and activity rather than passivity. It is important to recognize that the sample of prealcoholics (observed in childhood) differed in several important ways from the sample of adult alcoholics. The adult alcoholics tended to feel "victimized" by their society; the prealcoholics appeared to be self-confident. The adult alcoholics were often highly dependent; the prealcoholics emphasized their independence. Whereas the adult alcoholics tended to avoid group activities and to express feelings of grandiosity, we found that neither of these traits distinguished the prealcoholics from the non-alcoholics in childhood.

Interpretation of the Basic Characteristics of Alcoholics

Perhaps the most reasonable way of interpreting the contrasts between childhood and adulthood is to assume that traits like dependency, grandiosity, and feelings of victimization were "latent" in the prealcoholics' personality, but were suppressed. Once the disorder had set in, it may be supposed that the person's defenses collapsed and that these latent traits were openly manifested in behavior. In certain other ways, however, the adult alcoholics resembled the prealcoholics—both groups were aggressive, for example, and both tended to reject members of their immediate families. From these types of evidence, it is possible to hypothesize the existence of an "alcoholism-prone" character—a pattern of personality characteristics which is peculiarly sensitive to the attractions of alcohol. In childhood, the alcoholics exhibited several traits—apparent fearlessness, self-sufficiency, and aggressiveness—which, in our society, are generally regarded as being masculine. In terms of common cultural expectations, the potential alcoholics were very "manly" children; they accepted (and sometimes with a vengeance) the American stereotype of the male virtues. Yet, we can assume that this overemphasis on masculinity was a façade, covering up "feminine," dependent tendencies which were repugnant to the boys (and are regarded as undesirable in American society).

This assumption that extreme masculinity was merely a mask for certain disapproved urges can be supported by several pieces of evidence. First, we are aware that in adulthood the alcoholics often exhibited forms of dependent and passive behavior which are in direct contrast to the childhood façade. Unless we believe that alcoholism "spontaneously" created these traits, it seems reasonable to assume that such characteristics were latently present in the alcoholics but were hidden by an elaborate system of defenses. Second, we have noted certain signs of excessive anxiety that seem to be connected with dependency. Third, we know from previous research (4) that alcoholics in childhood were subjected to experiences that, one would expect, should lead to intensified dependency needs and, at the same time, to confusion in self-images. Alcoholics were often raised in conflict-ridden, antagonistic homes by emotionally erratic and unstable mothers. This background seemed to lead to dependency conflict—an unsureness concerning the satisfaction of heightened dependency desires. One way of handling these heightened, yet culturally disapproved, desires would be by attempting to repress the dependent urges. This, in fact, appeared to be the solution preferred by the alcoholics in childhood—through asserting of self-confidence, the alcoholics may have been saying in effect, "I don't care whether I am loved. I am strong, independent, every inch a man. We men don't need maternal care."

The prealcoholic typically was deprived of a responsible example in his early environment (4). Deprived of a stable model to emulate, such children would grasp at any example that would assure them of a secure sense of identity. In stressing his aggressive masculinity, the prealcoholic child seems to have accepted the most readily available self-image of aggressive manhood, an example of which is constantly and attractively offered through the media of the culture. By asserting his "manhood," this type of person could overcome, at least temporarily, his basic confusion.

Thus, it is possible to speculate that the potentially alcoholic personality develops as diagrammed in Figure 1.

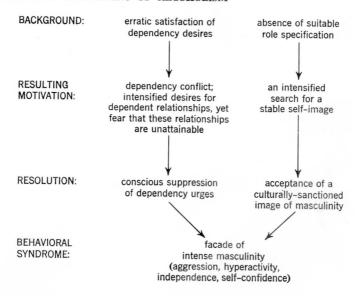

Figure 1. Development of the alcoholic personality.

The resolution of the potential alcoholic's inner conflicts through his "masculine façade" is inherently precarious. His dependency needs continue to plague him, yet his role as an aggressive, independent male leaves little room for their satisfaction. As he reaches adulthood, even further repression of dependent urges is demanded by society; he must become a "breadwinner," the leader of his family, a "pillar of his community." In other words, his cultural role requires that he satisfy the dependent needs of others; he must, according to the cultural restrictions, largely deny dependent satisfactions to himself. Thus, if he tries to live up to this role (and, even more difficult, to maintain his intensified image of masculinity), he dooms himself to continual repression. If he chooses, on the other hand, to strive for open satisfaction of his heightened dependency desires, the price is high: he must relinquish not only his cultural role, but also his masculine self-image—his sense of identity and significance—which has been built up only through intense repression.

At some point in adulthood, this type of person learns that alcohol may provide a compromise solution to his conscious or unconscious dilemma. Through heavy drinking, widely regarded as masculine behavior, he may come simultaneously to satisfy his dependent needs and maintain his precarious grip on a masculine self-image.

References

1. Armstrong, John D., "The Search for the Alcoholic Personality," *Annals,* 315:40–47, 1958.

2. McCord, William, and Joan McCord (with Irving Kenneth Zoal), *The Origins of Crime,* New York: Columbia University Press, 1959.

3. McCord, William, and Joan McCord, "A Tentative Theory of Conscience," *in* Dorothy Willimer (Ed.), *Decisions, Values, and Groups,* New York: Pergamon Press, 1960.

4. ———— (with Jon Gudeman), *Origins of Alcoholism,* Stanford: Stanford University Press, 1960.

5. Powers, Edwin, and Helen Witmer, *An Experiment in the Prevention of Delinquency,* New York: Columbia University Press, 1959.

chapter 25

Problem drinking
and role deviation:
a study in incipient alcoholism *

Peter Park

The growing literature on personal and social orientations of the alcoholic suggests that the reported behavioral disorders of the alcoholic may be analyzed in terms of his deviations in role structuring. This approach appears to be helpful in understanding alcoholism as a sociological problem as well as in trying to unravel the mechanism by which alcoholism develops.

Broadly speaking, the alcoholic can be regarded as a behavioral deviant in two senses: first, he tends to be culturally deviant in that he cannot structure his role in accordance with cultural expectations; and second, he is predisposed to be socially deviant in that he is incapable of playing any role consistently, thus upsetting the stability of a social system. Furthermore, these tendencies which put the alcoholic in conflict with socio-cultural requirements are imbedded in his personality structure and therefore either precede or go hand in hand with the development of alcoholism. These two propositions will be broken down, elaborated, and more explicitly stated in this report, but for now let them serve as our framework.

Role Structure

From an analytic point of view it is convenient to regard social role as the structural element of a social system, on one hand, and to characterize it in terms of its component behavioral traits, on the other. Thus, depending on the generality of analysis, both social system and social role can be analyzed using the same behavioral elements.

* This chapter was written especially for this book. The data upon which it is based are drawn from the author's unpublished doctoral dissertation, *Problem Drinking and Social Orientation,* Yale University, 1958.

The pattern-variable concepts developed primarily by Talcott Parsons denote such behavioral components and provide a general frame of reference suitable for analysis of behavior on the levels of personality, social system, and cultural pattern.* These behavioral components are properly understood as dimensions of behavior that serve to characterize, or locate, unit act, personality, social role, social system, and cultural pattern.

More specifically, the four pattern variables correspond to four dimensions of behavior. The first of these dimensions reflects whether or not the individual relates to and evaluates the object of behavior by injecting subjective significance into the situation. This is designated as the dimension of particularism-universalism. The second dimension is called that of affectivity-affectivity neutrality, and it shows whether a behavior signifies an immediate release of tension or a deferring of tension release. The third dimension, identified as the diffuseness-specificity dimension, indicates the scope of the relationship which the behavior entails. The fourth concerns the mode of relating to the object of behavior in terms of either its ascribed quality or its functional performance, actual or potential. This is known as the quality-performance dimension.†

The four pattern variables are analytical components of a single act. However, since an individual's recurrent patterns of behavior may be assumed to reflect his personality, the pattern variables are also relevant to a description of personality. Furthermore, social role is an aggregate of acts, both expected and actual, incumbent upon the corresponding social status; in this sense, the structure of social role can be analyzed by means of pattern variables. Lastly, culture, which contains the norms concerning allocation of roles to different members of a social system, may be thought of as permitting, prescribing, or prohibiting certain patterns of behavior, and pattern variables are therefore once again useful as descriptive concepts.

This report concerns relationships between cultural and social requirements of role structure and the alcoholic's behavioral tendencies. It is therefore of central importance to present a brief analysis of role structure.

Different structural characteristics of social role arise from the fact of role differentiation in a social system, and the principle of role differentiation is based on the functional and structural requirements of a stable social system. On one level of generality, a social system has four broad areas, or phases, of functional needs, which are identified as follows: adapta-

---

* The germinal ideas of the pattern-variable concepts are to be seen in Parsons (27). These terms are explicitly stated and used in Parsons (28) and are more fully defined in Parsons and Shils (32). In addition, the analysis of role structure in this chapter generally owes to several works of Parsons and his collaborators (29, 30, 31, 33).

† Actually in the frame of reference for the general theory of action, there is another pattern variable referring to the self-versus-collectivity dimension. It is not considered here because the concept is relevant to the inter- rather than intrasystemic organization of behavior.

tion to environment; consummation or gratification of task goals; preservation and integration of the personnel of the social system as a solidary group; and maintenance of the charter or the cultural patterns of the system.*

The adaptive need of a social system refers to that of orienting the personnel to the environment for accomplishing realistic tasks set up for the system. Whatever the nature of the task, carrying it out entails certain modes of behavior on the part of the individuals concerned. Given the goal, it must be objectively evaluated and rational means of achieving it chosen, and certain operations must be performed with specific reference to the end defined. In the meantime, the goal must not be prematurely consummated; that is, gratification must be deferred. In the language of pattern variables, the role of the individual engaged in the adaptive phase of a social system must be universalistic, specific, performance oriented, and affectively neutral.

Once the task of the system has been successfully carried out, the goal may be consummated and the social system fulfils the second of its functional requirements. Here, the object of gratification is no longer a class of rationally related things but a matter of subjective importance which satisfies certain specific needs of the individual or the system. Gratification is immediate and is effected through performance. In contrast to the adaptive phase, the second, or goal-gratification, phase requires a social role that is structured with particularism and affectivity. As in the first phase, however, this phase is characterized by specific and performance-oriented modes of behavior.

The third, or what may be conveniently called the integrative, need of a social system is that of keeping the personnel as a cohesive and boundary maintaining unit. To this end, the promotion of a feeling of solidarity among individuals concerned is essential. Consequently, in the integrative phase of a social system, the attribute of being a member in the group is in ascendency as the basis of social interaction, and each member has a subjective and particular significance to the other, which is not shared by those outside the group. In this context, interactions are regarded as ends in themselves, and activity in general lacks any specific reference. Thus, the role appropriate for the integrative phase is one structured with quality orientation, particularism, affectivity, and diffuseness.

The need underlying the last, or the pattern-maintenance, phase of a stable social system is that of upholding the charter of the system and evaluating the immediate goals set for the system in terms of the charter, on the one hand, and appraising the accomplishments of the system with respect to the goals, on the other. Appreciation of the charter is a prominent

---

* The terms, "personnel" and "charter" are to be understood in the sense that Malinowski (20) used them. On role differentiation and phase phenomenon, see Bales, "The Equilibrium Problem in Small Groups," in (31), Bales (5), and Slater (40).

feature of this phase, and action is not yet in the operational stage but merely potential. Interpersonal relations are not specifically determined by pursuance of a goal, but are diffusely structured through common membership and common adherence to the same charter. Evaluation of goals and accomplishments necessarily involves rational and objective methods. Furthermore, the major concern in the pattern-maintenance phase is an over-all view of the system as a whole, which entails long-range plans. Hence, tensions cannot be released immediately, either in positive or in negative form. To express these ideas in terms of pattern variables, the pattern-maintenance phase of a social system requires that social role be structured with quality orientation, diffuseness, universalism, and affectivity neutrality.

These four areas of functional and structural requirements are the foci of role differentiation when they are fulfilled simultaneously. In addition, they correspond to phases through which a social system moves in time to maintain its equilibrium. The role structure corresponding to each focus of role differentiation, or phase of social system, is summarized in the chart below.

CHART OF TYPES OF ROLE STRUCTURE CORRESPONDING TO PHASES OF A STABLE SOCIAL SYSTEM

Adaptive Phase
Universalism
Affectivity Neutrality
Specificity
Performance

Goal-Gratification Phase
Particularism
Affectivity
Specificity
Performance

Pattern-Maintenance Phase
Universalism
Affectivity Neutrality
Diffuseness
Quality

Integrative Phase
Particularism
Affectivity
Diffuseness
Quality

The chart shows that at least two of the four pattern variables involved differ from one phase to another. It is because of this phenomenon that role differentiation and phase movement take place in a social system. For example, a person cannot play the adaptive and the goal-gratification roles at the same time, because he cannot be universalistic and particularistic, or affective and affectively neutral, at the same time.

What is implied by the statement that both role differentiation and phase phenomena occur in a social system is that an individual has a role in association with his usual status which falls into one of the four above described phases, although he may play other roles at one time or another. Who should play which role is the problem of role allocation, the solution of which is culturally defined. In certain cases, as in the family, this is decided primarily on the basis of ascribed characteristics. Thus, in the American middle class, the man of the family is ordinarily expected to play the occupational role, which is by and large adaptive, while the wife is expected to play a role that is principally integrative.

1. *The role structure of the alcoholic*

Within the frame of reference presented above, the behavioral tendencies of the alcoholic may be analyzed with respect to the structure of the role expected of the male adult (46). The adult male in this industrial society is, normatively, expected to play an occupational role which coincides with the adaptive role in the present frame of reference. To be more specific, the socially mature man is expected to be work oriented, disciplined, and "successful." Expressed in pattern variables, this would mean that he is expected to be universalistic, affectively neutral, specific, and performance oriented insofar as his major social role is concerned. Against this normative expectation, findings on the behavioral characteristics of alcoholics amply suggest that the male alcoholic tends to deviate from this role in the opposite direction.

The observations that the alcoholic has attenuated and even feminine identification, and that he feels deeply inadequate and tends to be homosexually inclined, imply that he tends to deviate from the male role as a whole. When broken down into its components, this in turn signifies that he is inclined to be particularistic, affective, diffuse, and quality oriented instead of being universalistic, affectively neutral, specific, and performance oriented. Indeed, numerous studies (3, 6, 35, 37, 38, 39) may be cited in favor of this hypothesis with respect to the specific elements of role structure.

Bacon (1, 2), writing in a general vein, characterized the alcoholic as being uninterested in objective matters. More concretely, empirical investigations (34, 22) showing a lack of critical ability and of objective judgment in the alcoholic further corroborate this view. These traits of the alcoholic may be relevant to other dimensions of personality, but above all they seem to indicate the alcoholic's leaning toward particularism.

With respect to the affectivity orientation of the alcoholic there is an abundance of supportive findings and observations (1, 6, 22, 45). Psychological traits often singled out by many observers and investigators are those pertaining to emotional immaturity, low frustration threshold, excessive emotionality, uncontrollable emotional reactions, compulsive behavior, immediate gratification, and the like. In one study, for instance, the distinguishing mark between the alcoholic and the psychoneurotic is held by Glueck (9, p. 81) to be that the former "focuses his attention upon a source of immediate relief and satisfaction appreciating at the same time that he will pay in pain and suffering later."

The alcoholic's tendency to establish diffuse relationships frequently enters into the discussion of alcoholic personality in the guise of need for dependency and indulgence. By extension, the often mentioned regressive and infantile tendencies of the alcoholic can be understood in the same light.* Recognizing the etiological significance of this need of the alcoholic,

---

* For examples of discussion in terms of dependence and indulgence, see Bacon (2) and Button (6); regressive infantile tendencies are cited, for instance, by Lolli (19) and by Mowrer (25).

Bales (3) interpreted the diffuse interpersonal relations among the members of Alcoholics Anonymous as culturally approved management of the deviant tendency and attributed the relative success of the A.A. program as a therapeutic measure to this fact.

There appears to be no empirical study directly indicative of the alcoholic's disposition in the quality-performance dimension, although suggestive remarks concerning perfectionism and idealism which cripple action have been made (2). Theoretically, however, it might be anticipated that the alcoholic would deviate from the expected role structure not just in three dimensions but in all four, if role structure and personality makeup are considered as constellations each with interlocking components. That is to say, it may be reasonably hypothesized that the alcoholic is quality oriented rather than performance oriented.

2. Role ambivalence of the alcoholic

The findings discussed above suggest that the alcoholic deviates from the culturally prescribed role by tending to be particularistic, affective, diffuse, and, perhaps, quality oriented in his pattern of behavior, although the role that he is culturally expected to play calls for universalism, affectivity neutrality, specificity, and performance orientation. In this sense, then, the alcoholic may be said to deviate culturally from his role. As further analysis will show, however, there is evidence to suggest that the alcoholic is also socially deviant with respect to role playing.

Social deviation in this context means that the alcoholic tends to upset the social system equilibrium by not playing any one role in accordance with its functional and structural requirements. An example will serve to clarify the distinction we wish to draw between cultural and social deviations: If a man plays what is culturally defined as a woman's role, he is a cultural deviant; but he is not a social deviant in the present sense as long as he plays the woman's role consistently and satisfies the requirements for that role. This is not to imply that such a culturally deviant role identification entails no conflict for the individual; on the contrary, conflict would be expected. However, if a person cannot play either the male or female role decisively and consistently, he constitutes an unstable element with respect to the social system, because he does not fulfill any of the requirements for social stability. It is in this sense that the alcoholic is regarded as a social deviant as well as a cultural deviant.

Socialization, whatever else it may be, is a process by which a person learns to choose and play culturally and socially appropriate roles, and the family is the first and most important agent of socialization. In this light, it is instructive to note that sociological studies bearing upon alcoholism (42, 44) reveal a high incidence of broken homes often indicating undersocialization. What is, however, perhaps more crucial in the present context is that the failure to learn to play consistently an appropriate role results from not only a broken home but also a physically unbroken and yet unbalanced one. Thus, it has been observed (7, 18) that alcoholics come from a family background where one or both parents inconsistently alternate between overindulgence and unrealistic demands for independence with overtones of rejection.

Going a step further, one study (16) concludes that the sibling position of the alcoholic is such as to foster uncertainties about the source of love and role ambiguity in childhood. One result of such a family background is said to be the ambivalence of the alcoholic, particularly toward his parents, manifested by a desire to be independent mingled with strong lingering desires to be loved and indulged. Furthermore, there are indications (6, 38) that this attitude of the alcoholic is generalized beyond his parents to his marital partner and even further to the social system as a whole. For example, while noting the frequent failures of the alcoholic especially in the occupational role, many observers (8, 11, 36) point out that the alcoholic does not lack ambition but that it goes beyond a realistic appraisal of his ability and is mixed with desires to be indulged and even to indulge. To put it differently, it appears that the alcoholic is split between the adaptive and goal-gratification or integrative roles. Considering the pattern-variable elements of these roles, this is basically a dilemma involving the dimensions of particularism-universalism and affectivity-affectivity neutrality.

Thus far, it has been suggested that alcoholism can be understood as an embodiment of deviant behavioral tendencies with respect to the role structure culturally and socially demanded. It is in this sense that alcoholism constitutes a sociological as well as social problem. To be sure, alcoholism is a problem on the individual level, but it is a psychological problem only insofar as it creates conflicts with socio-cultural requirements.

Toward an Empirical Investigation

The rest of this report aims to show that the deviant tendencies of the alcoholic derive from his personality disposition and that they precede or progress together with the development of alcoholism. The method of investigation used for this purpose represents a compromise between the logic of a strict experimental method—so difficult of execution in this field—and the more typical ex post facto studies of alcoholism. Let it be clear that it is not our purpose to show that certain characteristics are present or absent to a significant degree among full-fledged alcoholics. It is rather to demonstrate that certain behavioral tendencies are significantly related to a predisposition toward alcoholism which might be termed incipient alcoholism or "problem drinking." If the individual with high propensity toward alcoholism is defined as a "problem drinker" (and such a propensity as "problem drinking"), then the remainder of this report will hope to show that the behavioral tendencies suggested to this point as characteristic of alcoholics correlate significantly with problem drinking. Such an approach obviates the necessity to sustain a study over the period of time required for the full fruition of alcoholism, and because of this, makes it possible to replicate the study or introduce new test variables with relative ease. Nevertheless, the usefulness of such a study ultimately depends upon the validity of the problem-drinking measure as a prognosticator of alcoholism.

1. Problem drinking

The problem-drinking measure used in this study may now be presented and briefly discussed. This measure was developed by factor analysis on the basis of the data collected by Straus and Bacon (43) on drinking and drinking-associated behaviors among American college students. College students in America normally cluster around the ages between 18 and 22 and therefore as a population cannot be considered to contain any alcoholics almost by definition. Consequently, the signs of alcoholism that may be observed in this population must be regarded as tendencies toward alcoholism rather than denotations of alcoholism itself.

From the questionnaire used by Straus and Bacon in their College Drinking Survey, twenty-eight pertinent items relating to drinking were chosen for analysis.* A majority of these were selected with specific reference to developing an operational definition and measurement of problem drinking. Other items were included because they were concerned with motivations for, feelings about, or manners of drinking whose implications for problem drinking needed to be clarified. The rest were included in order to discover patterns or aspects of drinking other than problem drinking. More generally, it was deemed desirable to include in the factor analysis items that were not obviously related to the hypothesized problem-drinking factor.

Tetrachoric correlations were calculated among the twenty-eight items, and five factors were extracted by the centroid method from the resulting matrix of correlations. These reference vectors were obliquely rotated according to Thurstone's criteria of simple structure. From this, four interpretable primary factors resulted, of which one was identified as the problem-drinking factor. The items that saturated this factor are given in Table 1 with their loadings.

In validating this factor as a measure of problem drinking, the factor items were compared with Jellinek's (14, 16) phasic characterization of the alcoholism process (see Chapter 20), which comprised forty-three drinking and drinking-associated behavioral items from the prealcoholic stage to the final chronic phase. Out of the thirteen items in this factor, five corresponded directly to the symptoms of alcoholism enumerated by Jellinek. These five items were: "blackout," "morning drinking," "aggressive behaviors resulting from drinking," "liking to be one or two drinks ahead without others knowing it" (Jellinek's "sneaking drinks"), and "on the water wagon." Two

* For a list of these items, see Park (26). This source also contains a full exposition of the factor analysis summarily discussed below. Of the total study sample of Straus and Bacon, a 10 per cent subsample was taken. From this subsample, abstainers, women students, and those who reported never having been drunk were excluded; this left a total of 438 students. The rationale for these exclusions is detailed in (26).

TABLE 1

The Problem-Drinking Dimension (Factor) [a]

Factor Loading	Item
.72	has had one or more drinks before breakfast or instead of breakfast (one or more times)
.62	has become drunk when alone (one or more times)
.54	has had one or more drinks alone (one or more times)
.52	has felt that subject might become dependent on or addicted to the use of alcoholic beverages
.50	has incurred social complications due to drinking (Social Complications Scale, Types I, II, III and IV)
.50	had gone on weekend drinking sprees (one or more times)
.44	had been led by drinking to aggressive, wantonly destructive, or malicious behavior (one or more times)
.42	has feared the long-range consequences of own drinking
.39	has experienced black-outs in connection with drinking (one or more times)
.38	drinks large or medium amount of alcoholic beverages at a sitting and more than once a week (Quantity-Frequency Index, Type V)
.27	likes to be one or two drinks ahead without others knowing it
.24	has gone on the water wagon as the result of self-decision or advice of the family or friends
−.36	drinks to comply with custom

[a] Factor loadings below ±.20 are considered negligible and equated to zero.

other items mentioned by Jellinek as referring to consequences of the alcoholic's drinking, namely, breaking ties with friends and leaving jobs, were contained in a single item of the factor, "Social-Complications Scale." * Six other items in Table 1—the "Quantity-Frequency Index," "getting drunk alone," "lone drinking," "fearing that one might become dependent on alcohol," "weekend drinking sprees," and "fearing consequences of drinking" —while not being specifically characteristic of any one phase of alcoholism in Jellinek's scheme, were mentioned or implied by Jellinek and have obvious implications for problem drinking. Finally, "drinking to comply with custom" was negatively loaded in this factor, which was as it should have been if this factor was to be distinguished from another, say, social drinking.

Lest this factor be confused with a measure of alcoholism itself, it must be pointed out that there were important differences in the way Jellinek

* The Social-Complications Scale and the Quantity-Frequency Index mentioned were developed by Straus and Bacon (43). For full explanation of their use in this analysis, see Park (26).

understood the items with which he described the phases of alcoholism and the way their counterparts were treated in the factor analysis. A major difference concerned the frequency with which certain symptoms were manifested, while in regard to certain other items there was also evidence (26) to suggest that college students may have attached rather different meanings to questions than did confirmed alcoholics. These considerations make it clear that what appear to be behavioral traits characteristic of the alcoholic may have much broader and milder implications in the context of the factor analysis. In addition, the participants in the study were virtually at the beginning of their drinking histories, which made it reasonable to interpret this factor as a measure of predisposition toward alcoholism, or problem drinking.*

In the same factor analysis (26), another pattern of drinking was isolated, which was discernibly different from the problem-drinking pattern just discussed. It suffices here to say that analyses in terms of both the behavioral items making up this pattern and the external criteria of incipient alcoholism indicated that this pattern of drinking is devoid of implications for alcoholism and warranted it to be identified as social drinking. It was revealing to note that social drinking, unlike problem drinking, is characterized by what Jellinek would call relief drinking, while implying, like problem drinking, heavy and frequent drinking. This latter point suggested that quantity and frequency of drinking by themselves are not adequate indices of problem drinking.

2. Measuring pattern variables

There are two important assumptions underlying the analysis of role structure in terms of pattern variables that has been presented above. One is inherent in the conceptualization of pattern variables as a frame of reference and is that they pertain to the dimensions of behavior which are logically complete and independent of one another. The other has to do with practicability of measuring pattern variables and is that they can be operationally defined. The measures of pattern variables to be presented in this section at least partially satisfy these assumptions.

The method used to develop the pattern-variable measures was again factor analysis, which made it possible (a) to determine whether or not a battery of behavioral items clustered into more general and more or less mutually independent patterns of behavior which could be regarded as reflections or dimensions of behavior, and (b) to measure persons along these dimensions.

The factor analysis was based on selected portions of the data gathered from 1,047 students in an undergraduate population. These students responded to a mailed questionnaire which, among other things, described

---

* The problem-drinking measure was further validated using independent and external criteria with satisfactory results. For these additional tests of validation, see Park (26).

a series of social situations each posing a dilemma for action in one or another of the four pattern-variable dimensions and asked the students to make a hypothetical choice of action in each situation. These questions were constructed after Samuel Stouffer's model (41), three questions having been taken directly from Stouffer's work with only slight modifications. For each situation, decisions were made a priori as to which pattern variable it would reflect and which answer would correspond to which side of the given dichotomy.

There were thirty-two questions of this kind in the questionnaire, but after a preliminary analysis only twenty-four of them were retained for factor analysis.* The first six questions referred to the particularism-universalism dimension. In each of the situations described by these questions the respondent had the choice of action upholding a general rule at a friend's expense or of making an exception to the rule because of the tie between himself and his friend. The second group of questions, six in number, was designed to elicit the respondent's orientation toward the affective or affectively neutral pattern of action. Here the dilemma in each instance was one between immediate satisfaction and deferred gratification. The next five questions were concerned with the respondent's delimitation of his relationship vis-à-vis social objects. The last group of seven questions dealt with the problem of the extent to which respondents defined persons who are objects of social interaction in terms of attributes such as membership in a social group, or in terms of past, present, or potential achievements. The choice in each instance referred to the quality-performance dimension.

Tetrachoric correlations were calculated between each pair of the questionnaire items and the resulting correlation matrix was factored by centroid method, from which resulted ten reference vectors. Only five of these reference vectors were obliquely rotated for simple structure. Table 2 shows the structure of the primary vectors obtained from the rotation.

In the first column of Table 2, the questions are numbered for identification consecutively from 1 to 24. These are grouped into the dimensions of behavior to which they were supposed to belong. The responses to the questions were scored in such a manner that particularism, affectivity, diffuseness, and quality orientation would be indicated by positive loadings and their opposite members, universalism, affectivity neutrality, specificity, and performance orientation, by negative ones.

Using Table 2 as a guide, one may summarize the findings of the factor analysis. All the items in the particularism-universalism group clustered together with positive loadings in the first factor. However, most of the items from the supposed quality-performance dimension and one from the affectivity-affectivity neutrality group also appeared here. A re-examination of the quality-performance items in the light of this outcome led to two pos-

---

* Eight items were eliminated because their marginal distributions were too extreme. The contents of all questions and a full discussion of the factor analysis of pattern variables may be found in Park (26).

TABLE 2

The Structure of the Pattern-Variable Factors [a]

	Factors				
Pattern Variables	I	II	III	IV	V
Particularism-Universalism					
1	.56		.12		
2	.66		.12		
3	.21			−.25	
4	.19			−.47	
5	.29			−.21	
6	.18			−.48	
Affectivity-Affectivity Neutrality					
7		.67		.20	
8		.86		.41	
9		.78	−.18	.20	.12
10	.13	.59			.17
11		.64			.26
12		.53	.19		.41
Diffuseness-Specificity					
13			.50		
14			.39		
15			.38		−.13
16			.48		
17			.15	−.24	.13
Quality-Performance [b]					
18	.56		−.13		.47
19	.45				.62
20			.28		.25
21	.76				
22	.73				
23	.16			−.17	.17
24	−.11	−.12	.25		.31

[a] Here ±.10 instead of ±.20 is adopted as the critical value of factor loadings, because the number of observations is relatively large (1,047) and the result of the factor analysis correspondingly more stable.

[b] In the discussion of the factors in the text, these items are reinterpreted as indicating particularism-universalism.

sible interpretations. One was that in actual social situations particularism and quality orientation in fact tend to go hand in hand; that is, that empirically particularism-universalism and quality-performance dimensions are positively related to each other. The other was that the situations that were supposed to involve dilemmas of quality-versus-performance dichotomies unwittingly introduced particularism-versus-universalism dichotomies instead. Although these two interpretations were seen not to be mutually contradictory, more weight was given to the second and *it was decided to identify this factor with the particularism-universalism dimension,* and to reinterpret the supposed quality-performance items in other factors as pertaining to particularism-universalism.*

The second factor saturated all the items from the affectivity-affectivity neutrality group, all with positive loadings. No other items appeared here except the already noted erratic one. Consequently, there was little difficulty in equating this factor with the affectivity-affectivity neutrality dimension.

The third factor contained all the items involving the choice between diffuseness and specificity with scattered items from other areas, two of which were negatively loaded. Except for the last-mentioned two, the presence of which could not be explained, all the items were interpreted as having implications consistent with the predominant sense of the factor. Consequently, this factor was identified as the diffuseness-specificity dimension.

There were altogether nine items in the fourth factor. Five of these, all negatively loaded, pertained to the particularism-universalism dimension (as defined by the factor analysis). Three other items, which were positively loaded, came from the affectivity-affectivity neutrality dimension. The remaining item, 17, evidently belonged to the diffuseness-specificity dimension, but its appearance in this factor could not be given a consistent meaning.

Central importance having been attached to the first two clusters, it was interpreted that this fourth factor indicates a mode of behavior characterized by concomitance of two pattern variables—universalism and affectivity or, looking at it upside down, particularism and affectivity neutrality. Since the four types of role structure presented earlier require simultaneous orientations of either universalism and affectivity neutrality or particularism and affectivity, and since no role can be structured with universalism and affectivity or particularism and affectivity neutrality, it seemed sensible to regard this factor as signifying a split, an indicision, between two roles—either between the adaptive and the goal-gratification or between the integrative and the pattern-maintenance roles. For this reason, this factor was called the *ambivalence* dimension, meaning ambivalence in role playing.

The fifth and last factor also showed two main clusters of items, one of affectivity and the other of particularism (as interpreted in the factor analysis) with two items from the diffuseness-specificity area. The latter two

---

* Item 10, which came from the affectivity-affectivity neutrality group, unaccountably appeared in this factor. Since the size of its loading was small, no particular importance was attached to it. Item 24, loaded negatively in this factor, seemed to behave erratically. It was concluded that this was a poorly constructed question to be excluded from further considerations.

were not given weight in the interpretation of this factor since their significance in relation to the main character of this factor was not clear. Like the preceding factor, this one appeared to be mainly relevant to the structuring of social role in terms of two pattern variables. In this instance, however, concomitance of two basically compatible behavioral tendencies was indicated, since one end of the dimension denoted by this factor was characterized by particularism and affectivity and the other end by universalism and affectivity neutrality. Accordingly, this factor was designated as the *consistency* dimension in the sense that it reflects the mode of structuring social role consistently with social requirements.

The labels for the first three factors were shortened for brevity to particularism, affectivity, and diffuseness dimensions, in that order, and this terminology will be used hereinafter. High scores in these dimensions would mean tendencies toward particularism, affectivity, or diffuseness, while low scores would mean tendencies toward universalism, affectivity neutrality, or specificity.* Either a high or low score on the ambivalent dimension would signify a deviant tendency, the former expressing universalism and affectivity and the latter, particularism and affectivity neutrality. However, the middle range of this dimension would indicate non-deviant, or compatible, tendencies. This is because the combined orientations of universalism and affectivity neutrality or particularism and affectivity would both find themselves here. In the consistency dimension, conversely, the consistent role structuring of universalism and affectivity neutrality or particularism and affectivity would be given, respectively, a high or a low score. Inconsistent, or deviant, role structuring would be reflected in the middle region of this latter dimension. These considerations, nevertheless, should not bury the main significance of these two factors, which is that the former mainly portrays a deviant tendency, the latter a stable one.†

* This manner of treating pattern variables as continuous variables, it must be pointed out, does not contradict the basic idea that pattern variables are dichotomous concepts. When analysis concerns a single act it may be proper to regard it as expressing a choice between two horns of dilemma. However, when it describes an aggregate of acts—a personality or a role structure—it is more sensible to view it in terms of tendency or quantity which one can possess more or less of.

† The probable reasons for the failure of a measure of the quality-performance variable to materialize clearly in this factor analysis are fully discussed in Park (26).

Intercorrelations were calculated among the five factors in order to ascertain that they measure different and independent entities and particularly to determine to what degree the particularism, affectivity, and diffuseness dimensions conformed to the assumption of independence. Not negligible correlations were found between particularism and affectivity and between affectivity and diffuseness, with correlation coefficients of, respectively, .35 and .25. Thus the measures of pattern variables tend to overlap somewhat in what they would measure, although the extent and incidence of overlap was not such as would hamper the assumption of logical independence. Not a small correlation was also observed between the ambivalence and the affectivity dimensions, with a coefficient of −.33. This was most likely a reflection of the fact that negative affectivity, namely, affectivity-neutrality, items were loaded on the ambivalence dimension. Aside from these, only negligible associations were seen to obtain among the various factors.

3. Problem drinking and role structure

An attempt has been made to show that the fully developed alcoholic may be characterized by modes of role structuring describable in terms of pattern variables. It has also been suggested that his attitude toward role playing is typically ambivalent. A major aim of this report, however, is to demonstrate that these behavioral traits observed among the fully developed alcoholics actually precede the full development of alcoholism. The measures of problem drinking and pattern variables presented above provide suitable means with which to verify the supposed relationship. The analyses in this section are based on the data collected from the 1,047 undergraduates mentioned earlier.

Pattern Variables. In the way of summarizing the propositions concerning problem drinking and pattern-variable orientations, they may be restated here in the form of hypothesis as follows:

Hypothesis I: problem drinking is positively correlated with the particularism orientation.

Hypothesis II: problem drinking is positively correlated with the affectivity orientation.

Hypothesis III: problem drinking is positively correlated with the diffuseness orientation.

Product-moment correlations were calculated between problem drinking, on the one hand, and the particularism, affectivity, and diffuseness dimensions, on the other. The resulting correlation coefficients are reproduced in Table 3.

TABLE 3

Correlation of Problem Drinking with Pattern Variables

	Particularism	Affectivity	Diffuseness
Problem drinking	.200 [a]	.221 [a]	.025

[a] $P < .05$.

It appears from Table 3 that the particularistic and affective modes of role orientation are significantly related to problem drinking, as was expected from the first two hypotheses. The pattern variable of diffuseness, however, does not show any significant relationship to problem drinking, contrary to the third hypothesis. This failure could well indicate that there is in fact no relationship between problem drinking and diffuseness. It might also result, however, from inadequacies in the operational definition of diffuseness used here. At this point, evidence is lacking to decide which of these alternatives is responsible for the observed lack of association.

Before we consider relationships between problem drinking and social deviation expressed by role ambivalence, it might be instructive to determine just how much of problem drinking is explained by cultural deviation in role structure, that is, by the pattern variables of particularism, affectivity, and diffuseness when they are treated together. This seems to be called for especially in view of the small size of the correlations observed in Table 3. A multiple correlation was therefore calculated between problem drinking and the three pattern variables considered together. The calculation yielded a statistically significant correlation coefficient of .24 ($P < .05$). This coefficient is larger than any of the simple correlations manifest between problem drinking and the pattern variables taken singly, but the gain in correlation size accruing from the combining of the pattern variables does not appear to be appreciable. By themselves, the pattern-variable measures of cultural deviations adopted here, although significant, apparently leave much to be accounted for in explaining problem drinking.

Ambivalence and Consistency. It was stated previously that a juxtaposition either of universalism and affectivity or of particularism and affectivity neutrality is inappropriate for any phase of a social system, while these very juxtaposed orientations are found at the opposite poles of the ambivalence dimension. Therefore, in theory at least, there are social forces imminent upon the individual with an ambivalent orientation to make the component patterns of his role structure consistent with one another and congruent with the various social system phases. Presumably, a stress or strain would be experienced from the combination of universalism and affectivity or of particularism and affectivity neutrality (although this is not to suggest for a moment that the individual necessarily experiences the strain consciously in these terms). It seems reasonable to suppose that for the individual attempting "solutions" to such a dilemma, the drinking of alcoholic beverages might acquire an instrumental importance, given certain reinforcing cultural attitudes toward drinking.*

A person at one extreme of the ambivalence dimension combining, say, universalism and affectivity, could structure his role congruently with the adaptive or pattern-maintenance phase by changing his affective orientation to an affectively neutral one. However, drinking will not help him achieve this, because alcohol tends to increase affectivity as well as to impair universalism.† At first glance, drinking might appear to be more conducive to structuring such an individual's role congruently with the goal-gratification or integrative phase by changing universalism to particularism. Since he is already affectively oriented, however, the alcohol necessary to achieve a sufficient degree of particularism may increase his affectivity beyond the socially acceptable point with social complications as a sequel.

* Animal experiments (23, 24) and experimentation with human subjects (10) suggest that alcohol tends to reduce tensions arising from conflicting demands on behavior. For evidence at the cross-cultural level, see Horton (13).

† This is owing to the sedative properties of alcohol, the psychological implications of which appear to be that drinking relaxes inhibitions and lessens control over emotion (15, 17).

Another person at the other extreme of the ambivalence dimension manifesting the combination of particularism and affectivity neutrality might experience even greater difficulties by relying on alcohol as a means of reducing tensions arising from his conflicting behavior tendencies and of adjusting himself to the requirements of social equilibrium. It would be impossible for such a person to achieve by drinking universalism and affectivity neutrality vis-à-vis the adaptive or pattern-maintenance phase. This is because alcohol is likely to further his particularism while breaking down his affectivity neutrality. If, by drinking, such an individual strives for the goal-gratification or integrative role by achieving affectivity as well as particularism, which he already manifests, he will tend to be unduly particularistic when he reaches the desired state of affectivity. Thus, by drinking, such a person is likely to suffer from a further impairment of universalism in either case. The loss of universalism implies a breakdown in reality orientation in terms of decreased rationality, objectivity, cognition, and evaluation. The sanctions for a person manifesting such extremes of particularism might therefore be much severer than for another at the other end of the dimension manifesting increased affectivity through drinking.

In the above instances, the ambivalent persons may be thought of as attempting to adjust to the requirements of social equilibrium by means of drinking, which not only is unsuccessful, as was shown, but also creates still further problems. When this point is reached, alcohol may no longer be sought as a means of "adjusting" to social situations but as a means of achieving oblivion from social requirements and pressures. Indeed, it is conceivable that some individuals with socially deviant tendencies may drink solely for the purpose of withdrawing from social pressures. In either case drinking will tend to be excessive. Furthermore, since drinking itself is an added source of problems for the ambivalent individual, drinking may tend to progress in a vicious circle.

If role ambivalence actually precedes the development of alcoholism, it follows that the ambivalence of role orientation should be related to problem drinking. To be more specific, it is to be expected that at either extreme of the ambivalence dimension where there are inconsistencies, there will be more problem drinking than in the middle where there is little or no inconsistency in role orientation. It is also to be expected that the particularism-affectivity neutrality end of the dimension will show the greatest association with problem drinking since this inconsistency appears to be the most fraught with difficulties.

These notions and hunches may be restated in the form of hypotheses for the purpose of factual testing as follows:

Hypothesis IV: problem drinking and ambivalence are negatively related to each other.

Hypothesis V: the regression line of problem drinking on ambivalence is in the general form of an inverted J-shape curve.

Hypothesis IV was tested by ascertaining whether there is a significant negative correlation between problem drinking and the measure of ambivalence. The product-moment correlation coefficient between these two variables is —.14, which is statistically significant ($P < .05$). This confirms the hypothesis and signifies that problem drinking decreases with increasing ambivalence of universalism and affectivity, or, to put it differently, increases with growing ambivalence of particularism and affectivity neutrality.*

Hypothesis V signifies that there is less problem drinking in the middle region of the ambivalence dimension where there is compatibility of role orientation. This supposed relationship cannot be adequately expressed by the correlation coefficient but may be tested initially by graphic presentation.

When problem drinking is plotted against ambivalence by taking the mean scores of problem drinking at equal intervals of ambivalence, the graph shown in Figure 1 is obtained. It may be seen from the figure that, while the particularism-affectivity neutrality end is higher than the universalism-affectivity end, both ends of the ambivalence dimension are higher than the approximate middle region, and the line of regression closely resembles the hypothesized inverted J. To ascertain whether there is any significant difference in the mean values of the problem drinking score at the different intervals of the ambivalence dimension shown in the graph, an E^2 was calculated between the two variables. The resulting coefficient of .03 is statistically significant ($P < .05$). Furthermore, a test of linearity based on this E^2 shows that the regression line observed in Figure 1 significantly deviates from a straight line.

Collectively, these findings lend strong support to the view that problem drinking is meaningfully related to role ambivalence, which in turn makes it reasonable to suppose that ambivalence precedes the development of alcoholism.

The relationships between problem drinking and abnormalities in role structuring can be investigated in still another way using the role consistency measure presented earlier. To recapitulate, one end of the consistency dimension is characterized by particularism and affectivity, and the other by universalism and affectivity neutrality. Thus, one extreme of the consistency dimension is congruent with the adaptive and pattern-maintenance phases, and the other with the goal-gratification and integrative phases. Role structuring incompatible with any of the social system phases, however, is re-

---

* It may be thought that since the ambivalence measure is a composite of the two pattern variables, the correlation just observed between it and problem drinking is attributable to the influence of the two pattern variables considered singly. This suspicion can be dispelled by a partial correlation analysis. The partial correlation obtaining between problem drinking and ambivalence with particularism and affectivity held constant is —.30, $P<.05$; the direction of the original correlation remains the same, while its absolute size is increased by .16. This increase undoubtedly results from the elimination of conflicting tendencies between particularism or affectivity, or both, on the one hand, and the measure of ambivalence, on the other. This demonstrates that the ambivalence dimension arises from an interaction between particularism and affectivity dimensions rather than being directly dependent upon one or both variables.

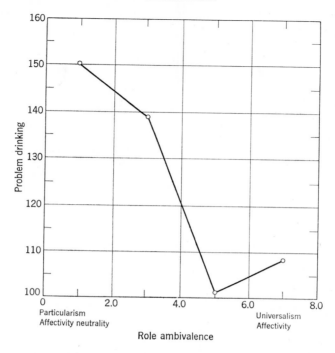

Figure 1. Relationship of problem drinking to role ambivalence.

flected in the middle region of the dimension rather than at the extremes, although this dimension may be thought of primarily as pertaining to the compatibility of the individual's role structuring with requirements of social system phases.

There is no conflict in role orientation at either end of the consistency dimension to precipitate problem drinking and create sequels which might lead to further drinking of a circular nature. Theoretically, then, neither extreme of this dimension should be associated with problem drinking or differ much from the other in this respect. Between the two extremes, however, there are varying degrees of incompatibility in concomitant patterns of role orientation. It is therefore in the middle area of the consistency dimension, if anywhere, that the greatest association with problem drinking might be expected. These considerations lead directly to the formulation of the following hypotheses:

Hypothesis VI: problem drinking is not linearly related to consistency.

Hypothesis VII: problem drinking is curvilinearly related to consistency with a line of regression in the shape of an inverted U.

Hypothesis VI was tested by means of correlation analysis. The product-moment correlation coefficient between the problem drinking and consistency measures is .038, which is statistically not significant ($P > .05$). Hypothesis VI, which implies no problem drinking at the extreme ends of the consistency dimension and no difference between them with respect to problem drinking is thus supported by the data.

The anticipated lack of correlation, which has been confirmed, may, however, reflect the non-linearity of the relationship between these two variables, as Hypothesis VII suggests. The absence of significant correlation does not settle the question of whether or not there is a non-linear relationship between problem drinking and the consistency dimension taken as a whole. This question may be answered by testing Hypothesis VII, which assumes a non-linear relationship in the general form of an inverted U.

Figure 2 shows the mean distribution of the problem-drinking measure at four equal intervals of the consistency dimension. The form of the figure is as expected from the hypothesis, the middle range of the consistency dimension being relatively high on problem drinking, while the two extreme points are low. Nevertheless, according to an E^2 analysis this difference is statistically not significant. Thus, the data do not confirm Hypothesis VII, although the apparent shape of the curve is consistent with theoretical expectations.

It may be added to advantage here that problem drinking was compared to social drinking with respect to the measures of pattern variables and of ambivalence and consistency in order to discern additional features of problem drinking. The findings, reported fully in (26), led to the conclusion that, although certain role orientations are associated with both problem drinking and social drinking, the factors underlying the associations are not the same in each case. Furthermore, it was found that social drinking is related to modes of role structuring not characteristic of problem drinking, namely, to specificity orientation and role consistency. The association of specificity orientation with social drinking could perhaps signify that persons who are able to relate to others in a segmental fashion without making their relationships all-pervasive can also confine their drinking to specific and socially appropriate occasions without letting it encroach upon other areas of life, or vice versa. This is something which an alcoholic, and perhaps also a problem drinker, cannot do.

The fact that social drinking is related to the role consistency dimension while problem drinking is not underlines the already-noted relationship between problem drinking and role ambivalence. Social drinking, unlike problem drinking, is appropriate for certain occasions, especially in the goal-gratification and integrative phases where drinking may be used instrumentally for enjoyment and for facilitating social intercourse, and therefore it is not surprising that the higher end of the consistency dimension should imply more social drinking.*

* It should be recalled that the higher end of the consistency dimension is characterized by particularism and affectivity, which as a combination are compatible with the goal-gratification and integrative phases.

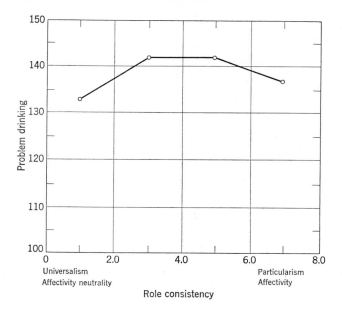

Figure 2. Relationship of problem drinking to role consistency.

Etiological Significance

The significance of these findings for the etiology of alcoholism may be briefly considered. Two aspects of the relationships between problem drinking and role structuring discovered in the preceding section are crucial for an etiological explanation of alcoholism.

The first is that these behavioral characteristics of problem drinking can be reasonably regarded as antecedents of alcoholism by virtue of the likelihood that problem drinking is a precursor of alcoholism. Had the variables of role orientation been related to fully developed alcoholism, rather than to problem drinking, it would have been open to question whether the observed behavioral tendencies are antecedents or consequences of 15 to 20 years of excessive drinking. This question would have been especially pertinent because alcoholism seems to produce the behavioral tendencies that are assumed in this report to underlie alcoholism. However, problem drinking is not alcoholism but an indication of proneness to alcoholism. It is therefore relatively safe to suppose that the observed behavioral correlates of problem drinking precede the development of alcoholism. The soundness of this assumption depends, nonetheless, on the validity of the problem-drinking measure as an index of proneness to alcoholism, validity having been partially and indirectly established for this study.

Another finding which appears to be of special significance for the etiology of alcoholism concerns the problem drinker's role structuring, expressed in terms of the pattern-variable concepts. The problem drinker tends to diverge from the structural requirements of the occupational role of the male adult in the directions of particularism and affectivity. To be sure, the problem drinker in college is not a mature individual and is not expected to play a clear-cut adaptive role. The full impact of his deviant tendencies is likely to be felt when he leaves college. If he continues to manifest tendencies which deviate from the adaptive role when that role is definitely expected of him, his role deviation would be a source of persistent and intensified conflict for him. The problem drinker, by definition, drinks frequently and in relatively large amounts in order, perhaps, to reduce the tensions arising from his role deviation. Drinking further complicates his social adjustment, because alcohol consumed in large quantities appears to have psychological effects which tend to accentuate particularism and affectivity. Hence, inherent in the association of problem drinking and particularism and/or affectivity is the danger that drinking and social maladjustment will progress in a spiral until alcoholism emerges.

A similar interpretation may be given to the problem drinker's manner of drinking and role ambivalence as defined by the ambivalence measure. Specifically, the problem drinker's role ambivalence would signify his inability to play decisively the adaptive role, or any other role, for that matter. One implication of the problem drinker's role ambivalence would be, then, that he is not likely to fit into most social situations with ease. Given this manifest difficulty of the problem drinker, his pattern of drinking heavily and frequently is likely to intensify his problems. Assuming that drinking is a means of releasing tensions arising from his difficulties in role structuring, the familiar pattern of drinking in a vicious circle could very well set in.

An important inference that may be drawn from these findings is that it is not just drinking, nor even drinking to reduce tensions in general, but drinking to relieve particular types of tensions arising from particular types of social situations, that leads to alcoholism. In support of this view, the social-drinking pattern referred to earlier, which is characterized by heavy and frequent drinking, as is problem drinking, does not necessarily imply possibilities of developing into alcoholism. The suggested reason is that this type of drinking relieves strains arising from normative role playing rather than reducing tensions caused by basic deviations from the expected role structure.

References

1. Bacon, Selden D., "Alcoholism: Nature of the Problem," *Fed. Probation*, 11:3–7, 1947.
2. ———, "The Social Impact of Alcoholism," *Conn. St. Med. J.*, 12:1105–1110, 1948.
3. Bales, Robert Freed, "Types of Social Structure as Factors in 'Cures' for Alcohol Addiction," *Appl. Anthrop.*, 1:1–13, 1942.
4. ———, "Cultural Differences in Rates of Alcoholism," *Quart. J. Stud. Alc.*, 6:480–499, 1946.

5. ———, *Interaction Process Analysis: A Method for the Study of Small Groups,* Cambridge, Mass.: Addison-Wesley Press, 1949.

6. Button, Alan D., "The Psychodynamics of Alcoholism: A Survey of 87 Cases," *Quart. J. Stud. Alc.,* 17:443–460, 1956.

7. Chassel, Joseph, "Family Constellation in the Etiology of Essential Alcoholism," *Psychiatry,* 1:473–503, 1938.

8. Clinebell, Howard J., Jr., *Understanding and Counselling the Alcoholic through Religion and Psychology,* New York: Abingdon Press, 1956.

9. Glueck, Bernard, "A Critique of Present Day Methods of Treatment of Alcoholism," *Quart. J. Stud. Alc.,* 3:79–91, 1942.

10. Greenberg, Leon A., and John A. Carpenter, "The Effects of Alcoholic Beverages on Skin Conductance and Emotional Tension: I. Wine, Whiskey and Alcohol," *Quart. J. Stud. Alc.,* 18:190–204, 1957.

11. Halpern, Florence, "Studies of Compulsive Drinkers: Psychological Test Results," *Quart. J. Stud. Alc.,* 6:468–479, 1946.

12. Hewitt, Charles C., "A Personality Study of Alcohol Addiction," *Quart. J. Stud. Alc.,* 4:368–386, 1943–1944.

13. Horton, Donald, "The Functions of Alcohol in Primitive Societies: A Cross-Cultural Study," *Quart. J. Stud. Alc.,* 4:199–320, 1943.

14. Jellinek, E. M., "Phases in the Drinking History of Alcoholics: Analysis of a Survey Conducted by the 'Grapevine,' Official Organ of Alcoholics Anonymous," New Haven, Conn.: Hillhouse Press, 1946. Also in *Quart. J. Stud. Alc.,* 7:1–88, 1946.

15. ———, "Effects of Small Amounts of Alcohol on Psychological Functions," in *Alcohol, Science and Society,* New Haven: Journal of Studies on Alcohol, 1952.

16. ———, "Phases of Alcohol Addiction," *Quart. J. Stud. Alc.,* 13:673–684, 1952.

17. ———, and R. A. McFarland, "Analysis of Psychological Experiments on the Effects of Alcohol," *Quart. J. Stud. Alc.,* 1:272–371, 1940.

18. Knight, Robert P., "The Dynamics and Treatment of Chronic Alcohol Addiction," *Bull. Menninger Clin.,* 1:233–250, 1937.

19. Lolli, Giorgio, "The Addictive Drinker," *Quart. J. Stud. Alc.,* 10:404–414, 1949.

20. Malinowski, Bronislaw, *A Scientific Theory of Culture, and Other Essays,* Chapel Hill, N.C.: The University of North Carolina Press, 1944.

21. Manson, Morse P., "A Psychometric Differentiation of Alcoholics from Nonalcoholics," *Quart. J. Stud. Alc.,* 9:176–206, 1948.

22. ———, "A Psychometric Determination of Alcoholic Addiction," *Amer. J. Psychiat.,* 106:199–206, 1949.

23. Masserman, Jules H., Mary Grier Jacques, and Mary R. Nicholson, "Alcohol as a Preventive of Experimental Neuroses," *Quart. J. Stud. Alc.,* 6:281–299, 1945.

24. ———, and K. S. Yum, "An Influence of Alcohol on Experimental Neuroses in Cats," *Psychosom. Med.,* 8:36–52, 1946.

25. Mowrer, Harriet R., "A Psychocultural Analysis of the Alcoholic," *Amer. Sociol. Rev.,* 5:546–557, 1940.

26. Park, Peter, *Problem Drinking and Social Orientation,* unpublished doctoral dissertation, Yale University, 1958.

27. Parsons, Talcott, *The Structure of Social Action: A Study in Social Theory with Special Reference to a Group of Recent European Writers,* Glencoe, Ill.: The Free Press, 1949.

28. ———, *The Social System,* Glencoe, Ill.: Free Press, 1951.

29. ———, *Essays in Sociological Theory* (rev. ed.), Glencoe, Ill.; Free Press, 1954.

30. Parsons, Talcott, and Robert Freed Bales, *Family, Socialization and Interaction Process*, Glencoe, Ill.: Free Press, 1955.

31. ———, Robert Freed Bales, and Edward A. Shils, *Working Papers in the Theory of Action*, Glencoe, Ill.: Free Press, 1953.

32. ———, and Edward A. Shils (Eds.), *Toward a General Theory of Action*, Cambridge, Mass.: Harvard University Press, 1952.

33. ———, and Neil J. Smelser, *Economy and Society: A Study in the Integration of Economic and Social Theory*, Glencoe, Ill.: Free Press, 1956.

34. Quaranta, J. A., *Alcoholism: A Study of Emotional Maturity and Homosexuality as Related Factors in Compulsive Drinking*, unpublished master's thesis, Fordham University, New York, 1947. Abstracted in *Quart. J. Stud. Alc.*, **10**:354, 1949.

35. Riggall, Robert M., "Homosexuality and Alcoholism," *Psychoanal. Rev.*, **10**:157–169, 1923.

36. Schnadt, Frederick William, *A Study of Alcoholic Personality*, Washington University thesis, St. Louis, 1950. Abstracted in *Quart. J. Stud. Alc.*, **12**:552–553, 1951.

37. Schilder, Paul, *Psychotherapy*, New York: W. W. Norton and Company, 1938.

38. Sillman, Leonard R., "Chronic Alcoholism," *J. Nerv. Ment. Dis.*, **107**:127–149, 1948.

39. Singer, Erwin, "Personality Structure of Chronic Alcoholism," *Amer. Psychol.*, **5**:323, 1950.

40. Slater, Philip E., "Role Differentiation in Small Groups," *Amer. Sociol. Rev.*, **20**:300–310, 1955.

41. Stouffer, Samuel A., "An Empirical Study of Technical Problems in Analysis of Role Obligations," *in* Talcott Parsons, et al. (Eds.), *Toward a General Theory of Action*, Cambridge, Mass.: Harvard University Press, 1952.

42. Straus, Robert, "Alcohol and the Homeless Man," *Quart. J. Stud. Alc.*, **7**:360–404, 1946.

43. ———, and Selden D. Bacon, *Drinking in College*, New Haven: Yale University Press, 1953.

44. Wahl, C. W., "Some Antecedent Factors in the Family Histories of 109 Alcoholics," *Quart. J. Stud. Alc.*, **17**:643–654, 1956.

45. Wexberg, Leopold Erwin, "Alcoholism as a Sickness," *Quart. J. Stud. Alc.*, **12**:217–230, 1951.

46. Williams, Robin M., Jr., *American Society*, New York: Alfred Knopf, 1952.

chapter 26

The self-concepts
of alcoholics [*]

Ralph G. Connor

In broad perspective, contemporary role theory regards personality as action systems arising out of the interplay of self and role. The self is what the person "is," an organization of qualities, the role is what the person "does," an organization of acts. When we come to consider alcoholics, we find that in the main the alcoholic is characterized in terms of acts and very little in terms of qualities; that is, the effective definition of an alcoholic still rests on what he does and not what he is—on role rather than on any real understanding of the self. Furthermore, when we analyze personality in terms of role theory it becomes apparent that anything distinctive of the alcoholic which precedes alcoholism must reside in the self, since role (what there is of it in alcoholism) by definition is learned and could not reasonably be expected to antedate the experience of alcoholism.

Following role theory then, the essential problem facing research into personality factors in alcoholism centers around the question of the self-concepts of alcoholics, and the principal questions are these: What are the self-concepts of alcoholics? Are they peculiar to and characteristic of the alcoholic? Do they precede or follow after the alcoholic experience? What techniques will be used to measure the self-concepts? It is the purpose of this chapter to shed light on such questions, if only in a preliminary way.

Methods of Investigation

One of the most widely used and reported techniques for the measurement of self-concepts is the adjective check list. Gough and Sarbin at Berke-

[*] This chapter was written especially for this book. The data upon which it is based are drawn from the author's unpublished doctoral dissertation, *The Self-Concepts of Alcoholics*, University of Washington, 1960.

ley, using similar lists, have published a number of reports that clearly indicate that adjective check lists do effectively differentiate the self-concepts of persons classifiable according to sociological, social-psychological, and clinical variables. Gough's list (1) has been used somewhat more extensively, and for that reason it is employed in the present study.

The study suffers admittedly from several limitations. In the first place, in common with every other study of alcoholics, it can make no pretense of a random sample. The reasons for this are obvious: there is no generally agreed-upon, effective definition of an alcoholic; the population of alcoholics has never been enumerated so that a random sample could be drawn; and the problem of cooperation is so difficult that one invariably winds up with data only from those who will cooperate and is left with no knowledge of the characteristics of those who will not cooperate. The study has, however, one characteristic not generally shared by previous studies. In the effort to be representative, it includes cases from each of the several alcoholic sub-populations: jail prisoners (or "Skid Row-ers"), Alcoholics Anonymous, sanatorium patients, and penitentiary prisoners. Finally, the study suffers from the lack of a control group. For validity this would have had to be a random sample of the general population, and the expense and unavailability of research funds made this impossible. The study, therefore, settled for a "comparison" group of extension class students.

This report covers data gathered from 347 male alcoholics, including 114 members of Alcoholics Anonymous, 106 jailed alcoholics (mostly Skid Rowers), 102 alcoholic inmates from three prisons, and 25 former patients of an alcoholic sanatorium. The comparison group consists of 230 extension classes' students from the University of Washington. The data were gathered by means of the adjective check list and an extensive questionnaire on social background and drinking history. The findings, in the main, consist of tables comparing the kind of adjectives used and the frequency of their use by the various groupings employed in the analyses.

The tables themselves are the result of three kinds of analysis of the data. The first is the "method of agreement," which indicates the degree to which the members of the various groupings employed in the study agree in the use of a particular adjective as self-descriptive. With an arbitrary cutoff point of .70, if at least 70 per cent of a given group checked a particular adjective, it was selected as descriptive of the self for that group. The second kind of analysis is the "method of proportional differences." This method indicates the percentage by which the groups differ in their selection of a given adjective as self-descriptive. Thus, if 50 per cent of one group selects an adjective as self-descriptive and only 10 per cent of another group selects it as self-descriptive, we would have a 40 per cent difference. The third kind of analysis was developed by Gough (1). He asked thirty judges to rate each of the 300 adjectives as to its "favorability." The highest-rated 25 per cent, or 75 adjectives, were chosen as the basis for his "Index of Self-Acceptance." Its formula is:

$$\text{Index of Self-Acceptance} = \frac{\text{number of favorable adjectives}}{\text{total adjectives checked}}$$

In each of the following sections of this report the three kinds of analysis described above, or variations of them, will be applied to appropriate groupings of the data which will be described at the beginning of each section.

Comparison of the Self-Concepts of Alcoholics and Non-alcoholics

In this section the data for all male alcoholics ($N = 347$) are grouped together and subjected to the three analyses described above. These analyses are then compared with comparable analyses of the data from the non-alcoholic male comparison group aged 30 years and over ($N = 32$). It was early found that age has a direct and progressive effect on the self-concept, and this adjustment in the comparison group was necessary to correct for it and equate the mean ages of the two groups. Hence the substantial attrition in the size of the comparison group.

1. *The method of agreement*

If at least 70 per cent of the group checked a particular adjective it was selected as self-descriptive. Table 1 gives the results of this analysis. The overlapping words are italicized. It is immediately evident from Table 1 that alcoholics describe themselves quite differently from the comparison group of non-alcoholics, and that their self-concepts are not nearly so extended and homogeneous as the self-concepts of non-alcoholics. Furthermore, the character of the adjectives checked is quite different. The non-alcoholic comparison group sees itself almost wholly in terms of qualities important in secondary institutionalized group relations, while alcoholics see themselves only in terms of qualities which would make them liked and accepted in primary group relations.

There are two important aspects of this difference. First, the self, being a socially developed attribute, should reflect in its description those qualities important to the social organization of a given culture, for the major means by which any culture preserves and continues itself is by emphasizing and imprinting on the individual, in the process of socialization, those qualities necessary to the operation of the social structure of that culture. For only if the individual conceives of himself in such terms can he be expected to behave consistently in such a manner. In our present-day, highly complex, institutionalized, technological culture, the qualities important to the operation of the social structure are precisely those we have referred to as important in secondary group relations, and the reasons are obviously related to the increasing importance of secondary relationships in urbanized, industrialized society.*

In this light, then, we might suggest that the alcoholic has become iso-

---

* For relevant discussion of the broad social context, see especially Chapter 5, by Bacon, of the present book.

TABLE 1

Comparison of Words Selected as Self-Descriptive on the Adjective Check List by Alcoholics and the Non-alcoholic Comparison Group [a]; Criterion: at Least 70 Per Cent Agreement

Alcoholics (N = 347)	Non-alcoholics (N = 32)
affectionate	active
appreciative	adaptable
easy-going	ambitious
forgiving	capable
generous	cautious
soft-hearted	conscientious
	conservative
	considerate
	curious
	dependable
	fair-minded
	healthy
	honest
	independent
	intelligent
Overlapping Words	interests wide
cooperative	logical
friendly	loyal
	peaceable
	practical
	reasonable
	reliable
	responsible
	serious
	sincere
	steady
	tolerant

[a] Mean number of words checked: alcoholics, 96.36; non-alcoholics, 107.4.

lated from this aspect of our culture, that he has withdrawn to some extent from participation in secondary relationships, and that the self of the alcoholic appears to be lacking in structure, in organization and integration, as compared to the self of the non-alcoholic.

The second important aspect of the difference between the self-descriptions of alcoholics and non-alcoholics is practically the converse of the first. To begin with, if we simply subtract from the self-descriptions of non-alcoholics the secondary relationship terms they emphasize, we still do not get a self-description that resembles that of the alcoholic. Not only does the alcoholic de-emphasize secondary terms, he places a positive emphasis on primary terms. Thus, if we accept that the self-descriptions of these groups are evidence of the things they are concerned with, we are justified in asking why the alcoholic is so concerned with primary group relationships. The heavy emphasis placed upon secondary relationship qualities by the rewards system of our culture is ample justification for the way in which non-alcoholics emphasize these qualities in their self-descriptions, but the justification for the alcoholic's emphasis on primary relationship qualities, since it does not enjoy such cultural support, may well reside in the alcoholic's felt need for such relationships, in a sense of isolation from their warmth and gratification.

2. The method of proportional differences

This indicates the percentage by which alcoholics and non-alcoholics differ in selecting a given adjective as self-descriptive. Table 2 gives the results of this analysis. In the main, Table 2 extends and reinforces the data and the impression of Table 1. There is, however, one important difference. Nine of the thirteen adjectives listed for alcoholics in Table 2 parallel and overlap a similar list which Sarbin and Rosenberg (2) derived from a study of diagnosed neurotics. Thus, although the non-alcoholic comparison group continues to describe itself in Table 2 in the same kind of terms that appeared in Table 1, alcoholics have added to the cluster of words in Table 1 that centered around permissive friendliness, a separate cluster unrelated to the first and suggesting neurosis. This suggestion is supported and extended by the next analysis.

3. The self-acceptance index

This indicates the degree to which "favorable," self-accepting terms are used in the description of the self. Table 3 compares the self-acceptance index of the alcoholic sample with the self-acceptance index of the non-alcoholics, and with the self-acceptance index of the diagnosed neurotics studied by Sarbin and Rosenberg and referred to in the discussion of Table 2. As Table 3 shows, alcoholics have a much lower self-acceptance index than non-alcoholics, and further, it is practically the same as the self-acceptance index for neurotics. Thus, recalling Table 2, we can say that not only do alcoholics describe themselves in much the same terms that neurotics use, but they have an equally low over-all self-evaluation.

Several important characteristics stand out in the analyses of the data so far performed. First and foremost, the adjective check list self-descriptions of alcoholics are distinctly different from those of non-alcoholics. Secondly, the self-descriptions of alcoholics are far less extended and homogeneous than those of non-alcoholics. This is evident in the fact that where male non-alcoholics agree at the 70 per cent level on the use of twenty-nine adjectives as self-descriptive, male alcoholics only agree on eight. Thirdly, the self-descriptions of alcoholics are almost completely devoid of the secondary-relationship adjectives so characteristic of the self-descriptions of

TABLE 2

Comparison of Adjectives Selected as Self-Descriptive on the Adjective Check List by Alcoholics and the Non-alcoholic Comparison Group, by Proportional Differences in Selection

Difference in Proportion	Alcoholics versus Non-alcoholics	Non-alcoholics versus Alcoholics	
.40 or more	easy-going spendthrift	None	
.30 to .39	worrying	adaptable conservative dependable idealistic independent interests wide inventive logical	mischievous organized reflective reliable responsible serious self-controlled
.20 to .29	confused good-natured high-strung hurried reckless restless self-pitying soft-hearted touchy unselfish	aloof artistic calm conscientious cautious deliberate dignified discreet enterprising foresighted individualistic ingenious initiative mature methodical	moderate modest original painstaking persevering persistent precise resourceful stable steady tactful tolerant thrifty unexcitable versatile

non-alcoholics. Instead, alcoholics employ a cluster of primary relationship adjectives centering around permissive friendliness. Finally, the self-descriptions of alcoholics manifest a distinctly neurotic aspect when subjected to the method of proportional differences, and this impression seems to gain support and confirmation from the application of the self-acceptance index.

To summarize these characteristics, we would like to suggest that two major themes are manifest in the self-descriptions of alcoholics. The first, and the first to appear, and, we suggest, the most important, is the primary-relationship emphasis in the alcoholic's self-description which would seem to indicate a major orientation in the personality structure of the alcoholic. The second, we would suggest, is actually inclusive of the several other char-

TABLE 3

The Index of Self-Acceptance [a] for Alcoholics, Non-alcoholics, and Diagnosed Neurotics

	Alcoholics	Non-alcoholics	Diagnosed Neurotics
Self-acceptance	.376	.433	.380

[a] $\dfrac{\text{Number of favorable adjectives checked}}{\text{total number of adjectives checked}}$

acteristics that have appeared. That is, the heterogeneity and lack of extensiveness, the virtual absence of secondary-relationship terms, and the distinctly neurotic aspects of the alcoholic's self-description are each manifestations of a diffuse lack of structure, and of organization and integration of the self of the alcoholic. Certainly such an interpretation of these characteristics would seem to be indicated by, and related to, the findings so frequently reported in the literature that the alcoholic has difficulty with personal identification and sex identity. Incidentally, such an interpretation makes sense out of one indication in our data which has not yet been explored. There is a strong possibility, which partial preliminary investigation analyses seem to confirm, that the alcoholic employs a distinctly greater number of contradictory or conflicting terms in his self-description than does the non-alcoholic. Investigation and possible confirmation of this indication waits, however, on the effort to develop a suitable "index of conflict" or "index of self-confusion."

These, then, are the self-concepts of alcoholics, and it would seem that they are indeed peculiar to and characteristic of the alcoholic. Thus, we have answered the first two of the questions around which this study of the self-concepts of alcoholics centered. Our third question is more difficult. We asked: "Do these self-concepts precede or follow upon the alcoholic experience?" The present study is an ex post facto design and therefore cannot hope to provide a definitive answer to this question, but the data do permit one form of analysis which, while it does not resolve the question, does cast light upon it, and in so doing provides strong indicators for further research. This is the analysis of the self-concept for changes once the alcoholic achieves sobriety and over time as sobriety is maintained. The second section of this report, which follows, deals with this analysis.

The Relation of Sobriety to the Self-Concepts of Alcoholics

The principal aim of following the self-concepts of alcoholics over the time that sobriety is maintained is to achieve some measure of the stability of the characteristics which have so far been identified. However, it is the nature of this study not to be decisive for etiology but to be exploratory for durable themes for future investigation.

The discussion which follows, bearing on the effects of sobriety on the self-concepts of alcoholics, draws only on the data gathered from male members of Alcoholics Anonymous ($N = 144$). The reasons for this have to do with the characteristics of the several alcoholic subpopulations. It was discovered that the several alcoholic subpopulations differ considerably in the degree to which their self-concepts are depleted of the secondary-relationship adjectives so characteristic of the self-descriptions of non-alcoholics. There is, in fact, a very nearly linear gradient of "self-concept depletion" from non-alcoholics through sanatorium patients, Alcoholics Anonymous, penitentiary prisoners, to Skid Row-ers or jail prisoners. We earlier suggested (see discussion of Table 1) that this "self-concept depletion" reflected social isolation, a withdrawal from participation in the secondary relationships in our culture. This is to be expected from role theory since a sanatorium-patient business or professional man who is still functioning in his occupational role is far less isolated from secondary relationships than a Skid Row-er whose social relations consist almost wholly of primary-relationship drinking groups.

Because of this gradient of "self-concept depletion" the following analysis is limited to a single subpopulation. The choice of Alcoholics Anonymous also rests on the characteristics of the alcoholic subpopulations. Jail prisoners, for example, have only been sober for up to thirty days, and even this is by coercion and not by choice. Penitentiary prisoners have been sober for varying and sometimes protracted periods of time, but it is very doubtful, in their environment, that their integration into, and participation in, the secondary-relationship aspects of our culture could change in any significant fashion during their imprisonment. This leaves only Alcoholics Anonymous and sanatorium patients, and since the self-concepts of sanatorium patients already most nearly approximate the self-concepts of non-alcoholics, the inclusion of sanatorium patients might serve more to obscure than to clarify the effects of sobriety on the self-concepts of members of Alcoholics Anonymous. The one exception is the self-acceptance index which includes all male alcoholics except jail prisoners. The breakdown for length of time sober is given in each table.

1. *The method of agreement*

Table 4 presents the lists of adjectives selected as self-descriptive 70 per cent of the time or more by alcoholics according to the length of time sobriety has been maintained. It is immediately evident that the alcoholic's self-description shifts distinctly with lengthening time that sobriety is maintained, and there are two important aspects to this change. First, the self-description nearly doubles in extensiveness, and second, most of the increase is in the use of secondary-relationship adjectives. It is also worth noting that there is an appreciable decline in the use of adjectives suggesting neurosis.

TABLE 4

Comparison of Adjectives Selected [a] as Self-Descriptive at Least 70 Per Cent of the Time by Alcoholics [b] According to the Length of Time Sobriety Had Been Maintained

0–6 Months Inclusive	Over 6 Months to 2 Years 11 Months Inclusive	3 Years and Over
appreciative	appreciative	appreciative
cooperative	cooperative	cooperative
emotional	emotional	emotional
friendly	friendly	friendly
affectionate	affectionate	
changeable	changeable	
impatient	impatient	
sensitive	sensitive	
sentimental	sentimental	
	conscientious	conscientious
	considerate	considerate
	curious	curious
	honest	honest
	reasonable	reasonable
	reliable	reliable
	responsible	responsible
	sincere	sincere
	sympathetic	sympathetic
forgiving		forgiving

The Following Words Were Used Only by the Group in Whose Column They Appear

capable	active	cheerful
generous	frank	dependable
nervous	healthy	fair-minded
restless	obliging	helpful
	peaceable	interests wide
	serious	kind
	soft-hearted	loyal
	thoughtful	masculine
	trusting	sociable
		understanding

[a] If a word does not appear in the column for a given group it was not selected by that group.

[b] Male members of Alcoholics Anonymous only, $N = 114$.

2. *The method of proportional differences*

In this analysis two lists of adjectives were developed, those for which the frequency of selection increased by 20 per cent or more, and those for which the frequency of selection declined by 20 per cent or more. These lists are presented in Table 5 and here again the increase in the frequency of selection of secondary-relationship adjectives is apparent. Much more

TABLE 5

Adjectives Selected by Alcoholics [a] for Which the Frequency of Selection Either Increased or Decreased by the Percentage Shown in the First Column

Difference in Proportion	*Increase*	*Decrease*
Over 30%	interests wide moderate reliable responsible steady	nervous self-pitying
20% to 30%	considerate contented dependable masculine natural sincere sociable talkative understanding unselfish	awkward bitter changeable conceited despondent dissatisfied excitable high-strung moody preoccupied self-centered shy submissive tense worrying

[a] Male members of Alcoholics Anonymous only, $N = 114$; the range of sobriety is the same as Table 4.

striking, however, is the list of adjectives for which the frequency of selection declined. Without exception, this is a list of the kind of adjectives so characteristic of the self-descriptions of neurotics.

3. *The self-acceptance index*

It was early discovered that changes in the self-acceptance index were fairly uniform among the alcoholic subpopulations, although the actual values among the several subpopulations are somewhat different. Also, since this index rests on the sums of kinds of adjectives used rather than on the frequency of selection of particular adjectives, lumping the subpopulations together for the measurement of this index does not produce the obscuring effect that would occur with the method of agreement or the method of proportional differences. For these reasons, and since it would lend increased confidence in the results, sanatorium patients and penitentiary prisoners are included in this analysis. Jail prisoners are excluded because none of them has been sober long enough to be tested for variation in his self-descriptions with lengthening sobriety.

TABLE 6

The Self-Acceptance Index [a] as Influenced by the Length of Time That Sobriety Has Been Maintained (Included at the Bottom of the Table for Comparison Are the Mean Self-Acceptance Indices for All Male Alcoholics and All Male Non-alcoholics 30 Years of Age and Older)

Time Sober	Self-Acceptance Index
0–under 3 months	.359
3 months–under 1 year	.340
1 year–under 3 years	.380
3 years–under 7 years	.424
7 years and over	.421
Male alcoholics	.376
Male non-alcoholics, 30 years of age and older	.433

[a] Male members of Alcoholics Anonymous only, $N = 114$.

Table 6 presents the self-acceptance indices for alcoholics according to the indicated lengths of time sobriety has been maintained. Included at the bottom of the table, for comparison, is the mean self-acceptance index for all male alcoholics and the mean self-acceptance index for all male non-alcoholics.

Thus, analysis of the data for the effects of sobriety showed that over time the extensiveness of the self-concept nearly doubles, that most of this increase is in the use of secondary relationship adjectives, that almost without exception, words for which the frequency of selection declines are characteristic of the self-descriptions of neurotics, and that the self-acceptance index rises from the value characteristic of neurotics to practically the same value manifested by our non-alcoholics. With a single exception, then, those aspects of the self-description which are characteristic of alcoholics shift with lengthening sobriety until they are no longer distinguishable from the self-descriptions of non-alcoholics. The exception is the primary relationship aspect which not only fails to change with sobriety, but has manifested a high degree of stability throughout a number of other analyses not otherwise reported here.

Conclusions and Implications

Two major themes stand out clearly in the self-descriptions of alcoholics. The first of these, which has been twice pointed out earlier, is the primary-relationship aspect, the pronounced emphasis the alcoholic places on primary-relationship terms when he undertakes to describe himself. This theme is important not only because it is the most emphatic and consistent among the several alcoholic subpopulations, but because it is the only aspect which remains stable through numerous analyses, and particularly for the influence of sobriety on the self-concept.

The second major theme in the self-descriptions of alcoholics is, we suggest, a generalized lack of organization and integration of the self which is manifested by, and includes, the other three aspects of the alcoholic's self-description we have discussed—the lack of homogeneity and extensiveness, the absence of secondary relationship terms, and the use of terms characteristic of neurosis. This second theme, phrased as "personality disorganization" rather than as we have it, is almost a common denominator of the literature on personality characteristics of the alcoholic for the last 20 years. Thus, from this common description, as well as the vast array of psychopathologies and deviant characteristics which have been attributed to alcoholics, it would not seem amiss to suggest that the search for the "alcoholic personality" has partaken of the nature of the examination of the elephant by the five blind men.

We suggest, therefore, as one of our conclusions, that it is just this diffuse and generalized lack of organization and integration of the self, rather than any specific trait, or inventory of traits, which is one of the cardinal characteristics of the alcoholic personality. Such a conclusion has the additional advantage of subsuming the frequent observation in the literature that the alcoholic has difficulty with identification and particularly sex identity. This follows from role theory since individual identity and sex identity are part of the self and the self-concept. Finally, the finding that the alcoholic seems to recover, over time sober, from the characteristics identified here does not permit the suggestion that these characteristics are any less important or influential than the characteristics identified by other studies, because no other study has followed over lengthening sobriety the characteristics it reputedly found, and thus there is no evidence that they are any more stable.

Our first theme, the primary-relationship aspect of the alcoholic's self-description, is not only more stable, it is also more pronounced and clear cut. This clarity and stability endow this aspect with considerably greater importance and confidence than the other three aspects dealt with in the preceding discussion as manifestations of our second theme. Because of the nature of this theme, and the variability of the other aspects under the analyses we have performed, we suggest as our second conclusion that this primary-relationship aspect of the alcoholic's self-description is a basic factor in the self and the personality organization of the alcoholic, and that it actually underlies that generalized lack of organization and integration of the self which is our other theme.

Earlier we suggested that justification for the alcoholic's emphasis on primary-relationship qualities must reside in the alcoholic's felt need for such relationships, in a sense of isolation from their warmth and gratification. We should expect this since the early impact of excessive drinking will be almost completely in the area of primary relationships and will consist of the alienation or deterioration of primary group support and satisfaction from essential sources. In the absence of such support for the self there can be no question but that the individual will experience greater difficulty in the management of the remote, formalized, and demanding secondary relationships which embody so much of the apprehension and stress of our culture. This difficulty produces greater stress, and a correspondingly greater need for primary group supports.

Furthermore, since the self is dependent upon primary relationships not only for support but for actual content, it is not surprising that decreasing primary support, resulting in greater secondary-relationship difficulties, producing a still greater need for primary support, leads to withdrawal from secondary relationships, self-concept depletion, a decline in organization and integration of the self, and heightened emphasis on, and attention to, primary relationships. It is still further suggested that the foregoing process is also the explanation for the gradient of self-concept depletion from non-alcoholics to Skid Row-ers which was mentioned earlier. Certainly, if the alcoholic drinks long enough and hard enough, he ends up on Skid Row, and as we have seen, Skid Row-ers have the most depleted self-concepts, with the only element of homogeneity being the primary-relationship theme.

We suggest, then, that an important aspect of the personality dynamics of alcoholism has to do with the two themes we have discussed above and their interaction as we have sought to describe it. Further, we suggest that the clarity and stability of the primary-relationship theme in the self-descriptions of alcoholics may well be indication that this theme is of even more basic importance to the syndrome of alcoholism than our discussion has so far proposed. In conclusion, therefore, we suggest that fruitful additions to understanding might come from knowledge of the patterns of primary relationships among alcoholics, the ways in which these differ from those of non-alcoholics, and, if they differ, how these patterns came to be established.

References

1. Gough, Harrison G., *Reference Handbook for the Gough Adjective Check-List* (mimeographed), Berkeley: The University of California, April 1955.
2. Sarbin, T. R., and B. G. Rosenberg, "Contributions to Role-Taking Theory: IV. A Method for Obtaining a Qualitative Estimate of the Self," *J. Soc. Psychol.*, **42**: 71–81, 1955.

D.

RELATION TO FAMILY,
TO OCCUPATION,
AND TO SOME TYPES
OF DEVIANCE

Introductory Note. Although implying a good deal about such matters, the studies just presented do not give full consideration to the impact of alcoholism on those social contexts in which most persons in our society experience the bulk of their face-to-face interaction, namely, in the family and at work. Actually this is a two-sided problem. There is, on the one hand, the question of the impact of alcoholism on the familial and occupational systems. On the other hand, there is the question of the effects these systems themselves have on the development and patterning of alcoholism.

Through the vehicle of a critical review of research pertaining to alcoholism and the family, Joan Jackson sets forth, in Chapter 27, a distinctively sociological approach to the behavior of family members in relation to alcoholism. This is done alongside a discussion and appraisal of psychological studies of the personalities of the members of families afflicted with an alcoholic. We noted in the introduction to the preceding subsection that this review has an important bearing upon the evaluation of studies of the alcoholic personality. Furthermore, it has an equally important bearing upon the evaluation of purported characteristics of other non-alcoholic family members and the possible implications of their personality characteristics for the development and course of the illness in the alcoholic. When the view of the family as an ongoing social system threatened by the crises of alcoholism is juxtaposed with more conventional psychological studies, radical questions ensue. To take a single example: The evidences of masculinity or of confusion in sexual identification among the wives of alcoholics which certain personality studies seem to have uncovered can no longer be taken for granted as simply reflecting enduring features of the wife's personality structure—features which may even have contributed to the husband's alcoholism. On the contrary, Jackson suggests that they may with equal plausibility be viewed as manifestations of a reorganization of the family, entailing a reshuffling of roles and efforts by the wife to take over aspects of her husband's roles in the interests of stabilizing the larger family unit.

Indeed as this book goes to press, Edwin Lemert (4) has marshalled evidence in support of Jackson's alternative suggestion. He concludes (pp. 679–680) that the behavior of the wives of alcoholics is "in large part a function of changing interaction patterns, not solely a consequence of personality, or personality type, considered as an independent variable." With regard to Jackson's provocative formulation of seven stages in the family's adjustment to alcoholism, Lemert's very recent results would seem to call for some modification or reformulation of the stages, perhaps involving a tripartite division into early, middle, and latter stages. Whatever reformulation may eventually prove most apt, Jackson's general notion provides, as Lemert's study already testifies, a useful point of departure for research on alcoholism and the family.

In Chapter 28, we turn to the question of the relations of drinking and occupational patterns. Here again, we come upon relatively uncharted ground. Despite an abundance of popular stereotypes about the affinities of certain occupations for beverage alcohol, only a handful of studies have been devoted to investigating the ways in which drinking patterns may be shaped by occupational imperatives.* The study by Harrison Trice which is included here as Chapter 28 takes up one particular facet of this whole question, approaching the matter initially from the point of view of the effects of drinking upon the job, rather than vice versa. Trice's main concern is with alcoholism, especially in the middle stages of its development, and the possible impact of alcoholism on certain key aspects of job performance such as absenteeism, accidents, and job mobility. These, incidentally, are subjects in regard to which there has been considerably more speculation than well-founded generalization, and Trice's study is important for the light which it sheds upon them.

In the course of his analysis, however, Trice effectively shows how differences in the structure of the work situation which are related to occupational type and status influence the form in which alcoholism is expressed. It may even be inferred that some of the variation in the patterning of alcoholism which has been noted in the alcohol literature (in regard to periodicity, for example), and which for want of better explanation has led to vague speculation about fundamentally different types of drinkers, may ultimately prove referable to the different socially structured expectations and pressures which impinge upon problem drinkers in different types of occupational setting. In any event, it is to be hoped that Trice's call for

* For an illustration of suggestive work in this area, see Clark (2), and Straus and Winterbottom (5).

more intensive investigation of the influence of occupation upon drinking patterns will be heeded and that the specific leads which his own work offers will be followed in subsequent research.

As Chapters 29 and 30, we have chosen to present reports which explore the relations of alcoholism to phenomena of deviance that have sustained the interest of social scientists for generations, namely, suicide and crime. In the first of these studies, Ernest Palola, Theodore Dorpat, and William Larson have added substantially to factual knowledge of alcoholism and suicide not only by investigating the involvement of alcoholism in suicidal behavior but also by examining the extent of suicidal behavior among alcoholics. This latter is a subject which has not been studied systematically heretofore, and the findings, while interpreted conservatively, seem quite dramatic. (For example, the overwhelming majority of the members of the Alcoholics Anonymous' subsample reported suicidal tendencies far more serious than the occasional or momentary suicidal thought.) The authors have also made a genuine effort to link their investigation with significant hypotheses about the sources of self-destructive behavior which derive from the diverse traditions of sociology and psychoanalysis. While raising a good many more questions than can be answered by the data, their report suggests points at which the perspectives of these great theoretical traditions converge, as well as a number of problems suitable for investigation at the level of theories of the middle range.

In a recent attempt to consolidate sociological thinking on deviant behavior, Richard Cloward (1) introduced the notion of access to "illegitimate means" to round out and supplement the theory of deviance developed by Robert Merton (3) in his famous essay on social structure and anomie. Merton, of course, had seen pressures to deviance as arising out of the strains engendered by a social structure which limits access to culturally legitimate means for achieving life goals in the context of a cultural configuration which exalts the goal of success for everyone. He further proposed a classification of possible modes of adaptation to this condition of strain, modes which he generalized in terms of such concepts as retreatism, ritualism, and innovation.

Considering the modes of adaptation suggested by Merton in the light of his own conception of differential access to illegitimate means, Cloward was led to speculate that certain retreatist patterns—and he specifically alluded to phenomena such as hoboism and alcoholism in this connection—might be viewed as involving a "double failure." This implies both an inability to utilize legitimate means to success and failure or defeat in the utilization of illicit, innovative modes of adaptation eventuating, for example, in the "successful" criminal career. Cloward was especially concerned to point out that the retreatist mode of adaptation might be arrived at by more than one route. It may come about, as Merton's analysis suggests, in a sort of one step conversion—presumably this would be the case where internalized prohibitions on the use of illegitimate means are strong—but it may, in

Cloward's (1, p. 175) words, "entail intervening stages and intervening adaptations, particularly of the innovating type."

Precisely these same lines of thinking were imminent in the work of David Pittman and Wayne Gordon in their research on the chronic drunkenness offender, a part of which is republished as Chapter 30. This study was conducted prior to and quite independently of Cloward's work, and Cloward was evidently unaware of it at the time of publication of his interesting theoretical paper. In their analysis of the arrest patterns of chronic drunkards, Pittman and Gordon not only anticipate Cloward's notion of "double failure" but present evidence that the alternative route to retreatism which Cloward highlights, and which involves intervening adaptations of the innovative type, may apply to a fair proportion of these offenders. At the same time, it seems equally clear, insofar as arrest patterns are a valid indication, that a substantial number of chronic offenders pass over quickly into the retreatist mode of adaptation.

In the light of Cloward's more general formulation, Pittman and Gordon's material would seem clearly to call for further study of the biographies of chronic drunkenness offenders, beginning with the types which they have delineated empirically on the basis of arrest patterns, and aiming to articulate the selection of these patterns with the dispositional variables suggested by Cloward's theoretical formulation. Finally, it would be well to consider these questions and Pittman and Gordon's study as a whole together with Rubington's discussion of the Skid-Row subculture and social organization presented in Chapter 9.

References

1. Cloward, Richard A., "Illegitimate Means, Anomie, and Deviant Behavior," *Amer. Sociol. Rev.*, 24:164–176, 1959.
2. Clark, Robert, "The Relationship of Alcoholic Psychosis Commitment Rates to Occupational Income and Occupational Prestige," *Amer. Sociol. Rev.*, 14:539–543, 1949.
3. Merton, Robert K., *Social Theory and Social Structure*, Glencoe, Ill.: Free Press, 1957.
4. Lemert, Edwin, "The Occurrence in Sequence of Events in the Adjustment of Families to Alcoholism," *Quart. J. Stud. Alc.*, 21:679–697, 1960.
5. Straus, Robert, and Miriam T. Winterbottom, "Drinking Patterns of an Occupational Group: Domestic Servants," *Quart. J. Stud. Alc.*, 10:441–460, 1949.

chapter 27

Alcoholism and the family *

Joan K. Jackson

Fifty years ago the members of an alcoholic's family were regarded as innocent victims of the willful self-indulgence of an irresponsible, weak, and sinful person. The drunkard was seen as someone for the family to hide, the police to control, and the clergy to reform. The family was to be pitied and shown charity. The "why" of alcoholism was explained by these attitudes, the "what to do" followed logically enough, while failure to change the alcoholic was readily interpretable. Research on alcoholism and the family, if it could be called such, was of the survey kind meant to provide ammunition for social reformers inveighing against the "evils of drink."

Today alcoholism is in the process of being culturally redefined. It is being viewed increasingly as an illness. In this attitudinal context, it follows that alcoholism has a discoverable etiology, course, and treatment, and is a suitable object for systematic research. Members of the alcoholic's family are no longer regarded simply as innocent victims but may be seen, for instance, as etiological agents or as complicating the illness. At times, it seems as though this latter trend has advanced to the point where the alcoholic emerges as the innocent victim of his family. However, there is as yet little evidence that the new cultural attitudes will permit a clearer view of the behavior of alcoholics or provide better tools for understanding the interaction of alcoholism and the family.

The alcoholic and his family are typically caught between these old and

* This chapter was written especially for this book. The investigation upon which it is based was supported in part by Senior Research Fellowship SF262 from the United States Public Health Service and by State of Washington Initiative 171 Funds for Research in Biology and Medicine.

new definitions of the situation in their attempts to conceptualize and resolve their difficulties. The majority of alcoholics and their families still think of alcoholism as willful and as warranting social condemnation. At the same time, the view that alcoholism is an illness is gaining acceptance. Both sets of attitudes may have an important influence upon family interaction and behavior. For those who seek to understand alcoholism, such cultural attitudes may profoundly affect what is observed and how observations are interpreted, theoretically and programmatically.

Some Problems of Research

The investigator of alcoholism in the family setting is confronted with a variety of problems stemming from changing cultural attitudes toward alcoholism which may be illustrated by a few questions. For example, are certain types of family behavior more indicative of conflicting attitudes toward alcoholism, of social disapproval, of the basic personalities of family members, or of alcoholism itself? If the families of alcoholics seek psychiatric treatment either for their alcoholic or non-alcoholic members—and thus, by implication, hold the new attitude that alcoholism is an illness—is their over-all behavior typical of the families of alcoholics in general? Similar questions may, of course, be raised concerning families brought under study because they or their alcoholic members contacted religious organizations, social agencies, or penal institutions. So little is known about family attitudes and behavior in relation to alcoholism that questions such as these have seldom been raised and have yet to be investigated.

Research on alcoholism and the family has also suffered from the premature application of complex research methods on the one hand, and from a lack of concern for scientific method on the other. The latter approach leads to anecdotal articles and case reports, or to theoretical formulations which fail to specify the behavioral evidence on which they are supposedly based. The former yields information which is seductive in its precision but often misleading in its formulation. The fact is that the range of behavior encompassed by the term alcoholism has not been adequately described, nor has that of the alcoholic's family. To apply complex methods before being able to specify the dimensions of the problem to be studied leads to conclusions which are difficult to interpret.

Ample illustration of this may be found in the extensive use of questionnaires and tests of various kinds. These are valuable tools when the area under investigation has been explored to the point where significant questions can be asked. Used prematurely, they close off opportunities to discover relevant variables, arbitrarily impose order on the data, and lead to conclusions which often prove later on to be unjustified. Psychological tests, for instance, often ask the wives of alcoholics how the individual feels at the time and fail to probe how they felt in precrisis days (although, if the writer's interviews with wives of alcoholics attending Alanon meetings are any guide at all, the earlier emotional state may have been considerably different). All too often the conclusions drawn from such tests are that the personality features found during the crisis predated it and were involved in its occurrence. Another illustration may be found in many of the studies of the psychology of the alcoholic's wife which conclude that the ways in which she deviates from test norms are intricately involved in her husband's alcoholism and in its persistence. Yet the majority of the women tested have simply been in situations where they could be tested; that is, they were at agencies providing case work or psychiatric treatment. In no instance has the report of such research specified the range of the husband's alcoholic behavior, its duration, the ethnic or class origins of the family, the extent of the family crisis, or the response of the family's social environment to the alcoholism and to their behavior.

Controls, as a rule, have not been used in research on alcoholism and the family. This omission probably stems in part from the difficulty in selecting suitable controls. The studies of Ballard (4), Mitchell (30), Mowrer (31), and Bullock and Mudd (6) which will be discussed later are unique in having selected other marital couples undergoing crises, drawn from the same source and undergoing the same type of treatment.

Research has been handicapped also by the gaps in knowledge about the range of family behavior which exists in our society. Little is known about family behavior in crises. Still less is known about family responses to the socially disapproved behavior of a member and to situations which are culturally undefined, or to which conflicting norms are applicable. With rare exceptions, knowledge of family behavior in crises is based upon study of a single crisis covering a comparatively short span of time. In consequence, it is not entirely applicable to the alcoholism situation which typically consists of multiple, related crises covering a long period of time.

A Review of Research Findings on Alcoholism and the Family

To date there is no research which could legitimately be called "alcoholism and the family" in the full sense of the phrase. Before such research can occur it must be possible to study the family as a unit. It is still rare to find families in which the alcoholic and all members of the family are willing to be subjects or informants. As a result, the majority of research has focused on one family member or has dealt with one family member's perception of the situation. Most commonly the center of attention is the alcoholic's wife, rather than the alcoholic husband and father.

1. The alcoholic husband and father

The role of the alcoholic in the family unit has not been studied systematically. The published literature contains little in the way of research on his perception of the family situation, of his interactions with family members, and of his ongoing experience in the family.* This is particularly

---

* A start in this direction is evident in the work of the McCords reported in Chapter 24.

peculiar because it is almost impossible in interviewing a married or divorced alcoholic to keep him off the subject. A doctoral dissertation by the present writer (19) contained a chapter on this subject. It was noted that the hospitalized alcoholics appeared to think of their family relationships almost entirely in utilitarian terms of money and service. For instance, if they brought home their pay and did chores around the house, they felt that their wives should be satisfied; at the same time, their demands on their wives for understanding and emotional support appeared to be excessive.

Fox (11), on the basis of observations of a large number of alcoholics in treatment, wrote a discerning description of the alcoholic's part in the marital relationship. It was the chief aim of the compulsive drinker to continue drinking, and the chief aim of the spouse to prevent it. The unpredictability of the alcoholic makes him hard to live with. In rapid succession he may be charming, cruel, aloof, withdrawn, fawning, and hostile. His claims for special treatment and his conviction that he should be free of all responsibilities lead almost inevitably to conflict with his spouse. Family members tend to be the targets for most of his hostility and to be held responsible for most of his difficulties.

Bullock and Mudd (6) clinically observed that the alcoholic spouse has problems in expressing anger constructively in the marriage setting. Additional problems with his wife center around economic dependency on the wife, resentment over attention given to the children, and jealousy over the relations of his wife with parental families and friends. Most alcoholic husbands expressed dissatisfaction with their marriages in relation to the attitudes and behavior of their wives.

Bacon (2) has suggested that excessive drinking is more incompatible with the institution of marriage than with any other. The supposition is that the personality and role problems which led to alcoholism tend to debar marriage or to become intensified if marriage occurs. The institution of marriage, which has primary importance in establishing intimate, affectional relationships, is thought to be uncongenial to the types of personalities who become alcoholics.

Mowrer's (31) study, based on case studies of alcoholics and of their wives, and of controls, indicated that the status of the male alcoholic in marriage tends to become inferior to that of the wife. Sexual relationships tend to be unsatisfactory because of the inadequacies of both partners. By way of conclusion, there is the suggestion that family attitudes towards the alcoholic tend to result from the alcoholism.

2. The alcoholic wife and mother

There are no empirical studies of the alcoholic wife's effect on the family. Clinicians, however, have published some observations.

Fox (11) has the impression that the alcoholic wife is able to hide her drinking from her husband longer than a male alcoholic could hide it from his wife. Because the cultural attitudes towards alcoholism in women are more stringent, the alcoholic woman is more concerned about hiding her drinking. The structure of the housewife's workday permits more frequent drinking, and most of her tasks can be accomplished despite a state of mild intoxication. It is also Fox's observation that the children of an alcoholic mother can hardly be shielded from the impact of drinking. Deep and lasting feelings of rejection tend to occur.

3. The children of alcoholics

In common with much other family research, children, in studies relating to alcoholism, have not been regarded as playing important roles in the ongoing behavior of the alcoholic's family (10). The literature on children has been concerned with the effect of alcoholism on their development. Only Bacon (2) and the present writer (21) have noted that children play a role in the alcoholic's difficulties. Both suggest that fatherhood tends to intensify the alcoholic's problems. In an earlier study (19), the writer found that parenthood is one of the life events which is commonly associated with a sudden and marked increase in the number of the alcoholism behaviors listed by Jellinek (23).

Roe (36) studied the rate of alcoholism and the over-all adjustment in adulthood of the children of alcoholics raised by foster parents as compared with a control group of other foster children. Her findings led to the almost permanent retirement of the hypothesis that alcoholism is biologically inherited.

Newell (32), in a speculative article, raised interesting hypotheses about the psychological effects upon a child of having an alcoholic parent. Unfortunately these hypotheses have been ignored by those engaged in empirical research. She suggested that the children of alcoholics are placed in a situation very similar to that of the experimental animals who are tempted towards rewards and then continually frustrated, whose environment continually changes in a manner over which they have no control. Under such circumstances experimental animals have convulsions or nervous breakdowns.

We know little of what happens to the children of alcoholics. However, Baker (3) notes that children are almost always under emotional strain when they have an alcoholic parent. She comments on the common tendency among such children to feel more affection for the alcoholic than for the non-alcoholic parent, probably because the alcoholic parent is rewarding when sober, while the non-alcoholic parent tends to be irritable and rejecting under the constant situational pressure. Fox (11) points out that the sons of alcoholic males find it difficult to establish stable identifications and are often beset by ambivalent feelings throughout life. The daughter may side with the mother and blame the father or vice versa. Both sons and daughters may identify masculine independence with drunkenness. In the face of society's attitudes towards excessive drinking, they feel deep shame and humiliation. The present writer, on the basis of observations of an Alanon Family Group, noted that children are more affected than any other family member by living with an alcoholic. Personalities are formed in a social milieu which is markedly unstable, torn with dissension, culturally deviant, and socially disapproved. The children must model themselves on adults who play their roles in a distorted fashion. The alcoholic shows little adequate adult behavior. The non-alcoholic parent attempts to play the roles of both father and mother, often failing to do either well.

The child of an alcoholic is bound to have problems in learning who he is, what is expected of him, and what he can expect from others. Almost inevitably his parents behave inconsistently towards him. His self-conception evolves in a situation in which the way others act towards him has more to do with the current events in the family than with the child's nature. His alcoholic parent feels one way about him when he is sober, another when drunk, and yet another during the hangover stage. What the child can expect from his parents depends on the phase of the drinking cycle as well as on where he stands in relation to each parent at any given time. Only too frequently he is used in the battle between them. The wives of alcoholics are concerned that they find themselves disliking, punishing, or depriving the children preferred by the father and those who resemble him. Similarly, the child who is preferred by or resembles the mother is often hurt by the father. If the child tries to stay close to both parents he is caught in an impossible situation. Each parent resents the affection the other receives while demanding that the child show affection to both.

The children do not understand what is happening. The very young ones do not know that their families are different from other families. When they become aware of the difference, the children are torn between their own loyalty and the views of their parents that others hold. When neighbors ostracize them, the children are bewildered about what they did to bring about this result. Even those who are not ostracized become isolated; they hesitate to bring their friends to a home where their parent is likely to be drunk. Moreover, the tendency of the child to examine his own behavior for reasons for parental alcoholism is very often reinforced inadvertently by his mother. When it is feared that the father is leading up to a drinking episode, the children are put on their best behavior. When the drinking episode occurs, it is not surprising that the children feel that they have somehow done something to precipitate it.

Yet some of the children of alcoholics appear relatively undisturbed. The personality damage appears to be least when the non-alcoholic parent is aware of the problems they face, gives them emotional support, refrains from using them against the alcoholic, tries to be consistent, and has insight into her own problems with the alcoholic. It also appears to mitigate some of the child's confusion if alcoholism is explained to him by a parent who accepts alcoholism as an illness.

4. The alcoholic marriage

There has been very little research bearing directly upon the alcoholic and his wife. The works of Gliedman and his associates (14, 15), Mitchell

(30), Ballard (4), Mowrer (31), Bullock and Mudd (6), and Strayer (39) are exceptions. These researchers focused on the interactions of the spouses, whereas, as a general rule, the non-alcoholic spouse is the focus of attention and the alcoholic remains in the background.

Ballard and Mitchell studied couples composed of male alcoholics and their non-alcoholic wives and compared them with control couples whose marriages were also conflicted. The experience of a stressful marital situation was thereby held constant.

Ballard found that on clinical scales the wives of alcoholics showed few differences from the wives in the control group. If anything, they appeared to be better adjusted. The major difference between the alcoholic and non-alcoholic couples was in the relative adjustment of the partners. In the alcoholic marriages the wife appeared less disturbed whereas in non-alcoholic marriages the husband appeared better adjusted. The wives of alcoholics seem to assume masculine roles, to place emphasis on repression, and to avoid responses which suggest a tendency to "act out." Ballard goes on to specify the ways in which the interaction of the personalities of husbands and wives could provide mutual gratifications and defensive reassurances.

Mitchell dealt specifically with the husband-wife pairs of the same groups as those studied by Ballard. He found that alcoholics and their wives were more sensitive to each other than were the partners in marriages where alcoholism was not a problem. Mitchell suggests that this may be a derivative of a marital situation in which both partners are very vigilant of each other's feelings and behavior in order to maintain the relationship and to meet the practical exigencies of family life. In the evaluation of the role relationship of the alcoholic and his wife, power, control, and dominance appeared to be areas of crucial significance. The wives were overwhelmingly viewed as the most dominant figures within the marriage. Both partners had more difficulty than the controls in handling hostility. Mitchell's research led to the conclusion that a major problem in marriages in which alcoholism is present is for the spouses to be able to differentiate their roles. "At the level of interpersonal perception they seem unclear as to what they can expect from each other, who does what, by what authority, at what time and with whom is the core problem in their relationship." (30, p. 557.)

Bullock and Mudd, studying the same couples as had Ballard and Mitchell, reported that both spouses tend to bring personality problems to the marriage and that these problems become intensified during marriage. The failure of each spouse to gratify the overdetermined needs of the other is viewed as the major factor in the marital conflict.

Gliedman and his associates studied nine couples undergoing treatment for the alcoholism of the husband. These investigators agree with Ballard that the wives of alcoholics are better organized than the husbands. The wives in their study tended to be dissatisfied with themselves and their husbands generally, while the husbands, when they were sober, felt satisfied with their wives. Serious sexual difficulties were found in eight of the nine marriages. With treatment the greatest change came in the marital milieu.

5. *The wives of alcoholics*

Research on the wives of alcoholics has taken two major directions—the psychological and the sociological. The psychological approach conceptualizes the family as a unit composed of interacting personalities. The majority of the psychological literature deals with a description and analysis of the personality of the alcoholic's wife. Her behavior towards her husband is regarded as an expression of this personality or as a product of the interactions between her personality and that of her husband. Little is said about the alcoholic's impact on her behavior and personality, but there is considerable speculation about the impact of the wife on the alcoholic.

Students of the alcoholic's wife do not state explicitly that she is the cause of her husband's alcoholism or of its persistence. The reader is often left with this impression, however. Hypotheses concerning complementarity of personalities between the alcoholic and his wife have not been proven, although considerable data have been accumulated on the subject. Some research has tested only the non-alcoholic in each marital pair and has then gone on to speculate on the role of the wife's personality in interaction with that of the unstudied alcoholic. Even when both spouses have been studied, the conclusions about their interactions more often have been based upon group averages than upon data derived from the study of the pairs as social units.

In most of the psychological literature, there is implicit the notion of a constant personality reflected in situations but not altered by them. Despite the existence of a considerable body of psychological theory about the responses of personality to stress and about personality change in therapy, the literature on alcoholism and on the spouses of alcoholics seems to have remained bound to psychological tests and to particular points in time. Notwithstanding the paucity of findings on tests that search for "the alcoholic personality," there is a search for a common personality that can be called "the wife of an alcoholic." There are, indeed, similarities in the behavior of alcoholics and their spouses. However, the contribution which the personality of each spouse makes to the onset, persistence, and alleviation of alcoholism will remain in the realm of speculation until we have firmer knowledge of the etiology of alcoholism, its course, and of its remedy.

The sociological approach to research on the wives of alcoholics reflects, in contrast, basic sociological concerns with the social unit called the family —its structure, functions, and processes. The emphasis is on the behavior of the social unit, the institutionalized norms which govern it, and the behavior of members acting in their institutionalized roles. Sociologists are concerned, in short, with institutional behavior, with social acts. They are more interested in the social behavior which occurs under certain types of social conditions than in the question of behavioral normality or abnormality.

Thus, when commonalities are found in the behavior of the wives of alcoholics, the sociologist turns for explanation to common features of family structure and processes and to common features of the situations which impinge on the family or in which the family is involved. Yet the sociological approach is also open to criticism in the present context. Generally, there is a tendency to ignore personality factors and to concentrate on social roles as if the social structure and situation completely dictated the behavior of the alcoholic's wife. Obviously this yields a very incomplete picture of the wife's behavior.

All studies to date have dealt with the wives of alcoholics who were seeking help, regardless of the duration of the seeking or the motivation behind it. No two studies have had comparable samples. Yet there is no reason to believe that wives who, say, seek help through Alanon Family Groups are similar to wives who go to marriage counseling clinics, or to those who join their spouses in psychiatric treatment at an alcoholism clinic. Nor can it be assumed that they have much in common with those who seek psychiatric aid for themselves or who end up in mental institutions. Wives of alcoholics who do not seek help or who divorce their alcoholic spouses have not been studied. Hence we do not know if the apparent contradictions in certain research findings are attributable to differences in research techniques, sample sources, or the wives themselves.

Most research on the wives of alcoholics is concerned with the psychopathology of the wife—the disagreement in the literature centers on the degree and nature of the wife's disturbance. Gliedman and his associates (14, 15) and Ballard (4) found the wives in the marital pairs they studied to be better organized than their husbands. Ballard found them to be less disturbed than the control pairs caught in conflicted marriages. Price (35, p. 623), while noting deeper insecurities, conceded that some wives of alcoholics "gave the appearance of being completely adequate, capable women . . . ." The majority of investigators, however, have found them to be extremely disturbed people.

In this latter vein, Futterman (12) concluded that the alcoholic's wife unconsciously encourages her husband's alcoholism because of her own needs. He suggested that the needs are so great that, should the husband become sober, the wife often decompensates and begins to show symptoms of neurotic disturbance. MacDonald (29) and Wellman (43) concur in this view. Whalen (44), Lewis (27), and Price (35) have substantially the same view. Whalen delineates four types of personalities commonly found among the wives of alcoholics who come to social agencies for help. Like Futterman, she believes that certain types of women marry alcoholics in order to satisfy deep unconscious needs to be married to weak, inadequate, and dependent males. Price and Lewis differ on the nature of the disturbance, although they agree that it is present. They found the wives of alcoholics to be nervous, hostile, basically dependent people, although on the surface they appear to be adequate. They were unable to cope with the drinking of their husbands and accepted no responsibility for it. The women studied by Lewis and Price appeared to be insecure people at the outset of their marriages who expected their husbands to be strong, dependable, and responsible. They continued to demand that their husbands meet their needs for this type of spouse, thereby making their husbands feel less adequate and, eventually, behave in a less adequate way.

Kalashian (24), Cork (9), and the present writer (21) agree that, during the alcoholism of the husband, the wife tends to be psychologically disturbed. They do not agree with those who contend that, if the husband achieves sobriety, the wife is likely to decompensate; and they have queried the wife's vested interest in maintaining her husband's alcoholism, as well as the basis of her disturbance. Along with Gliedman and his associates, these researchers have noted that the wives they saw were deeply involved in having their husbands achieve sobriety. For instance, only one of the wives seen by the writer over an 8-year period showed an increase in disturbance of more than a temporary nature when the husband's alcoholism became inactive and, apparently, permanently so. On the contrary, the wives' adjustment typically appears to have improved in most respects.

This is not to deny, however, that the onset of sobriety precipitates additional disturbances on the part of all family members. However, the disturbances can be viewed as resulting either from rigidity in personalities or from rigidity in family patterns and processes, or both. When the onset of sobriety is viewed in the context of the total family crisis, rather than as an isolated piece of family history, one may suppose that much of the behavior on the part of the wife which appears to be dysfunctional for the recovery of the alcoholic plays an important part in maintaining the integration and stability of the family as a social unit. An example of this is the wife's reluctance to relinquish her dominance until sobriety is well established and appears to be permanent.

The writer (18) has also raised questions in an earlier report about the ways in which the nature, extent, and duration of the stressful situation contribute to the extent and nature of the wife's disturbance. The behavior of both the alcoholic and his wife is similar in many ways to that of people who are involved in situations characterized by marked and rapid role changes, by social disapproval, by lack of clear-cut definitions for appropriate behavior, by social isolation, by situational ambiguity, and by recurrent auxiliary crises—all of which are ingredients of the family alcoholism crisis.

6. The husbands of alcoholic women

There have been no systematic studies of the husbands of alcoholic women. Lisansky (28), in a study of women alcoholics, found that a sample drawn from a penal state farm typically had husbands who themselves were often in jail, and that abusiveness, irregular employment, and heavy drinking were common. This was not at all characteristic of the husbands of a sample of women alcoholics drawn from an outpatient clinic.

Fox (11) and Bacon (2) comment on their impressions that there is a greater tendency for husbands to leave alcoholic wives than for wives to leave alcoholic husbands. Fox suggests that this results from the tendency of women to mother and sympathize with husbands, from the greater permissiveness towards male drinking in our culture, and from the woman's economic dependence on her husband. Bacon speculates that women in our society have more of an emotional investment in marriage than men. More of their socialization has been directed towards fulfilling the marital and familial roles. In addition, since women have fewer associations than men, the danger of losing such a crucial one is supposedly more threatening. The cultural expectations of the wife's role also permit a woman more readily to remain with an alcoholic husband than a man to remain with an alcoholic wife. Recent research by Bowerman (5) would appear to lend support to Bacon's position. In a study of normal subjects, it was found that the personality adjustment of the wife tended to be seen by her as subordinate to family goals, while for husbands, personal-centered and family-centered goals were of equal importance.

Alcoholism as a Cumulative Crisis for the Family

In recent research, the present writer focused on the alcoholic's family and on the time interval between the onset of the illness and its resolution. The data for the first phase of this research, to be discussed here, consist of verbatim recordings of the regular meetings of one Alanon Family Group during the period 1951 to the present. The basic data thus consist of statements by the wives of alcoholics about their perceptions of the behavior of family members in the past and the present. Such a group stresses the wife's behavior and attitudes and is interested in the alcoholic's behavior largely as background material. An orientation of this kind obviously imposes limits on the sorts of data available for study. In addition, more information was available on regular members than on those who rarely attended meetings. Hence the study deals with women who were either strongly motivated or who derived important satisfactions from group participation. The second phase of the study, now in progress,* consists of a follow-up of the 157 women who attended the group during this period of study. It involves intensive interviews with these women concerning their families' experiences with alcoholism, the administering of psychological tests, and study of a control group composed of friends of these Alanon members who have had no direct family experience with alcoholism.

In this work, the family's behavior in regard to the alcoholism of the husband and father has been approached as a special case of the theory of family crises. The theoretical background may be summarized as follows: When persons live together over a period of time, patterns evolve of relating to one another and of behaving as a unit. In a family, a division of functions occurs and roles interlock. For the family to function smoothly, each person must play his roles in a predictable manner and according to

---

* This research will be reported at a later date.

the expectations of others in the family. When the family as a whole is functioning smoothly, individual members of the family also tend to function well. Each member is aware of where he fits, what he is expected to do, and what he can expect from others in the family. When these expectations are not met, repercussions are felt by each family member and the family as a whole ceases to function smoothly. A crisis is underway.

Family crises tend to follow a similar pattern, regardless of the nature of the precipitant. Usually there is an initial denial that a problem exists. The family tries to continue in its usual behavior patterns until it is obvious that these patterns are no longer effective. A downward slump in organization occurs at this point. Roles are played with less enthusiasm, and there is an increase in tensions and strained relationships. Finally, an improvement occurs as some technique of adjustment proves successful; family organization becomes stabilized at a new level. At each stage of the crisis, there is a reshuffling of roles among family members; there are changes in status and prestige, changes in "self" and "other" images, shifts in family solidarity and self-sufficiency and in the visibility of the crisis to outsiders. In the course of the crisis, considerable mental conflict is engendered in all family members, and personality distortion occurs (42). These are the elements which are uniform regardless of the type of family crisis. The phases of the crisis vary in length and intensity depending upon its nature and the nature of the individuals involved in it.

When one of the adults in a family becomes an alcoholic, the over-all pattern of the crisis takes a form similar to that of other family crises, but there are usually recurrent subsidiary crises which complicate the over-all situation and attempts at its resolution. Shame, unemployment, impoverishment, desertion and return, non-support, infidelity, imprisonment, illness, and progressive dissension also occur. For certain other types of family crises, there may be cultural prescriptions for socially appropriate behavior and for procedures which will terminate the crisis—but this is not the case for alcoholism.

Culturally, alcoholism is subsumed under a general category of undesirable deviant behavior. The culture assumes that if a family is adequate, its members will behave in accordance with social norms. Thus, in efforts to handle problems associated with deviancy, the family labors under a pall of blame. They feel guilty, ashamed, inadequate, and, above all, isolated from social support. Where the husband is an alcoholic this burden falls disproportionately on the wife who, in her own and in society's view, has failed in her major roles. The situation is further complicated in that the culture offers no guideposts to behavior for the family containing a deviant, other than the expectation that the family should bring the deviant back into line. The cultural norms governing how family members should feel and behave with respect to one another are in direct conflict with the prescriptions for how members of the society in general should behave in relation to social deviants. As a result, family members are constantly in conflict about their behavior. If the family accepts the view that the deviant behavior should be labeled illness, the confusion and conflict is likely to be compounded further when this view is not accepted by the sick person, their acquaintances, or those to whom they turn for help (38). The family of an alcoholic thus finds itself in a socially unstructured situation and must find techniques for handling the crisis through trial and error behavior, without social support. In many respects, there are marked similarities between the type of crisis precipitated by alcoholism and those precipitated by mental illness (45).

Alcoholism seldom emerges full-blown overnight. It is usually heralded by widely spaced incidents of excessive drinking, each of which sets off a small family crisis. Both spouses try to account for the episode and then to avoid or alter the family behavior and situations which appear to have caused the drinking. In their search for explanations, they try to define the situation as controllable, understandable, and "perfectly normal." Between drinking episodes, both feel guilty about their behavior and about their impact on each other. Each tries to be an "ideal spouse" to the other. Gradually, not only the drinking problem but also the other problems in the marriage are denied or side-stepped.

It takes some time before the wife realizes that the drinking is neither normal nor controllable behavior. It takes the alcoholic considerably longer to come to the same conclusion. The cultural view that alcoholics are Skid-Row bums who are constantly inebriated also serves to cloud the realities of the situation. Friends compound the confusion; if the wife compares her husband with them, some show parallels to his behavior and others marked contrast. She wavers between defining his behavior as "normal" and as "not normal." If she consults friends, they tend to discount her concern, thus facilitating her tendency to deny that a problem exists and adding to her guilt about thinking disloyal thoughts about her husband.

As Yarrow (45) has pointed out in her work on mental illness and the family, part of the wife's problem in recognizing the illness is that her husband's behavior is unfamiliar, incongruent, and unlikely in terms of social expectations. The cultural expectations and assumptions about behavior screen out certain perceptions and provide her with limited tools for interpreting the evidence. In the case of alcoholism, the sporadic nature of the drunken behavior and the intervals of apparently "normal" behavior tend to prolong the process of defining the behavior as "not normal." During this initial stage the family is very concerned about the social visibility of the drinking behavior. They feel that they surely would be ostracized if the extent of the drinking were known. To protect themselves against discovery, the family begins to cut down on their social activities and to withdraw into the home. Yarrow has noted the parallels between the behavior in this stage and minority group behavior.

The second stage begins when the family defines the alcoholic's drinking behavior as "not normal." At this point, frantic efforts are made to eliminate the problem. Lacking clear-cut cultural prescriptions for what to do in a situation like this, the efforts are of the trial-and-error variety. In rapid succession, the wife threatens to leave the husband, babies him during hangovers, drinks with him, hides or empties his bottles, curtails money, tries to understand his problem, keeps his liquor handy for him, and nags him. Yet, all efforts to change the situation fail. The family gradually becomes so preoccupied with the problem of discovering how to keep father sober that long-term family goals recede into the background. At the same time, the isolation of the family reaches its peak of intensity. Extreme isolation magnifies the importance of all intrafamily interactions and events. Almost all thought becomes drinking centered; drinking comes to symbolize all conflicts between the spouses, and even mother-child conflicts are regarded as indirect derivatives of the drinking behavior. Attempts to keep the social visibility of the behavior at the lowest possible level increase. Moreover, the alienation of husband and wife accelerates. Each feels resentful of the other. Each feels misunderstood and unable to understand. Both search frantically for the reasons for the drinking, believing that if the reasons could be discovered, all family members could gear their behavior so as to make the drinking unnecessary.

There seems to follow, however, a stage of disorganization which could also be entitled "What's the use?" The wife feels increasingly inadequate as a wife, mother, woman, and person. She feels she has failed to make a happy and united home for her husband and children. Her husband's frequent comments to the effect that her behavior causes his drinking and her own concerns that this may be true intensify the process of self-devaluation. Nothing seems effective in stabilizing the alcoholic. Efforts to change the situation become, at best, sporadic. Behavior is geared to relieve tensions rather than to achieve goals. The family gives up trying to understand the alcoholic. They do not care if the neighbors know about the drinking. The children are told that their father is a drunk. They are no longer required to show him affection or respect. The myth that father still has an important status in the family is dropped when he no longer supports them, is imprisoned, caught in infidelity, or disappears for long periods of time. The family ceases to care about its self-sufficiency and begins to resort to public agencies for help, thereby losing self-respect. For her part, the wife becomes very concerned about her sanity. She finds herself engaging in tension-relieving behavior which she knows is without goal. She is aware that she feels tense, anxious, and hostile. She regards her precrisis self as "the real me" and becomes very frightened at how she has changed.

When some major or minor subsidiary crisis occurs, the family is forced to take survival action. At this point, many wives leave their husbands. The major characteristic of this stage is that the wife "takes over." The alcoholic is ignored or is assigned the status of the most recalcitrant child. When the wife's obligations to her husband conflict with those to her children, she decides in favor of the children. Family ranks are closed progressively and the father is excluded.

As a result of the changed family organization, father's behavior constitutes less of a problem. Hostility towards him diminishes as the family no longer expects him to change, while feelings of pity, exasperation, and protectiveness arise. Such reorganization has a stabilizing effect on the children. They find their environment and their mother more consistent. Their relationship to their father is more clearly defined. Guilt and anxiety diminish as they come to accept their mother's view that drinking is not caused by any behavior of family members. Long-term family goals and planning begin again. Help from public agencies is accepted as necessary and no longer impairs family self-respect. With the taking over of family control, the wife gradually regains her sense of worth. Her concerns about her emotional health decrease.

Yet, despite the greater stabilization, subsidiary crises multiply. The alcoholic is violent or withdraws more often; income becomes more uncertain; imprisonments and hospitalizations occur more frequently. Each crisis is temporarily disruptive to the new family organization. The symbolization of these events as being caused by alcoholism, however, prevents the complete disruption of the family. The most disruptive type of crisis occurs if the husband recognizes that he has a drinking problem and makes an effort to get help. Hope is mobilized. The family attempts to open its ranks again in order to give him the maximum chance for recovery. Roles are partially reshuffled and attempts at attitude change are made, only to be disrupted again if treatment is unsuccessful.

The problems involved in marital separation from the alcoholic are similar to the problems involved in separation for any other reason, but certain problems may be intensified. The wife who could count on some support from her husband in the earlier stages of his alcoholism, even though such support was manipulative in character, can no longer be sure of any support. Also, the mental conflict about deserting a sick man must be resolved, as well as the wife's feelings of responsibility for his alcoholism. The family which has experienced violence from the alcoholic is concerned that separation may intensify the violence. When the decision is made to separate because of the drinking, the alcoholic often gives up drinking for a while, thereby removing what is apparently the major reason for the separation.

Other events, however, make separation possible. The wife learns that the family can function tolerably well without her husband. Taking over control bolsters her self-confidence; her orientation shifts from inaction to action. The wife also has become familiar with public agencies which can provide help, and she has overcome her shame about using them. Without the father, the family actually tends to reorganize rather smoothly. Having closed ranks against him, the family members feel free of the disruptions he used to create in the family. This kind of reorganization is impeded, however, if the alcoholic continues to attempt reconciliation or feels he must "get even" with the family for deserting him.

The whole family may become united when the husband achieves sobriety, whether or not separation has preceded, but, for the husband and wife facing a sober marriage after many years of an alcoholic marriage, the expectations for marriage without alcoholism are unrealistic and idealistic. Many problems arise. The wife has managed the family for years and now her husband wishes to be reinstated as head of the house. Usually the first role he re-establishes is that of breadwinner. With the resumption of this role, he feels that the family should reinstate him immediately in all his former roles. Difficulties inevitably follow. The children, for example, are often unable to accept his resumption of the father role. Their mother has been mother and father to them for so long that it takes time to get used to consulting their father. Often the father tries to manage this change over- night and the very pressure he puts on the children towards this end defeats him.

Again, in this situation, the wife who finds it difficult to believe that her husband is sober permanently is often unwilling to relinquish her control of family affairs even though she knows that this is necessary to her husband's sobriety. She remembers when his failures to handle responsibility were catastrophic to the family. Used to avoiding any issues which might upset the husband, the wife often has difficulty discussing problems openly. If she permits him to resume his role of father, she often feels resentful of his in- trusion into territory she has come to regard as her own. If he makes any decisions which are detrimental to the family, her former feelings of su- periority may be mobilized and affect her relationship with him. Yet gradu- ally the difficulties related to alcoholism recede into the past, and family adjustment at some level is achieved. The drinking problem shows up only sporadically, most probably when the time comes for a decision about per- mitting the children to drink or when pressure is put on the husband to drink at a party.

In summation, research has suggested that there may be distinct stages of family behavior associated with alcoholism in the husband and father. Some of the families studied have passed through all the noted stages to a satisfac- tory conclusion, while others have traversed only part of the route. Others have shown no movement to date. Families also vary as to the length of time spent in any one stage. The stages themselves may be summarized briefly as follows: (a) attempts to deny the problem; (b) attempts to elimi- nate the problem; (c) disorganization; (d) attempts to reorganize in spite of the problem; (e) efforts to escape the problem; (f) reorganization of part of the family; and (g) recovery and reorganization of the whole family.

Finally, it bears mention in this context that the writer (22) has also analyzed the changes in family structure with special emphasis on changes in the role and status of the husband and father. The analysis indicates that the alcoholic's status is gradually downgraded when he does not fulfill family and cultural expectations and as other family members assume his traditional roles in order to keep the unit as a whole functioning. Indeed, the alcoholic's major role in some families appears to be that of a spur to the solidarity of the rest of the family who react against him.

Implications

In general, the literature bearing upon alcoholism and the family has been written by persons whose major research interest is the phenomenon of alcoholism itself, or by persons directly or indirectly involved in the amelioration of alcoholism. Even when reports have been primarily research oriented, they tend not to take into account potentially relevant literature other than that directly related to alcoholism, and usually refer only to studies by persons with the same professional identification. Such parochial approaches bode ill both for the acquisition of reliable knowledge by those already interested and for the stimulation of research interest in others.

Gains in knowledge will be made when research on alcoholism and the family is guided by theory and when it is built upon broader awareness of what is already known. There is, for example, a considerable body of information on institutional and family crises. In conceptualizing the experiences of families in which there is an alcoholic, it is illuminating to view what happens to families and their members under other social conditions with ingredients similar to those of the alcoholism crisis. Provocative questions arise about the extent to which the alcoholism situation is unique. These lead to further questions about which variables are dependent or independent and to speculation about the etiology, nature, normality, or abnormality of emotional states found in the members of the alcoholic's family at any given point in time.

In this connection, sociologists such as Koos (26), Angell (1), Kamarovsky (25), Cavan (7), and Cavan and Ranck (8) have studied the impact of the depression and of unemployment on family behavior and structure as well as on family members. These investigators found that the status of the father tended to decline when he was no longer the wage earner and that his roles were taken over by other family members. Families often closed ranks against him and the wife frequently became the dominant figure. In this situation, the father lost more roles than he added, and this left him feeling uncertain of himself and of his position in his family. This loss of roles by the father tended to be accompanied by intense self-criticism, feelings of guilt and shame, and sensitivity to criticism both real and imagined. While roles were in the process of being reshuffled, the family suffered from confusion, and the members experienced great anxiety, hostility, and guilt. The realignment of roles often involved a blurring of the differences between husband and father and wife and mother roles and hence in masculine and feminine behavior. It was no longer possible to predict who had responsibility for doing what. Tasks were performed poorly or not at all. Members of the family who were in the process of assuming new roles or dropping old ones found themselves in conflict when their expectations of their roles did not coincide with what others expected from them. Until new family routines became customary and new role definitions were agreed upon, the family and its members behaved in a disorganized fashion.

In the families studied during the depression, re-employment of the father brought on a crisis for the family similar to the crisis brought on by the sobriety of the alcoholic. As the father attempted to resume his former status, family roles had to be reshuffled again. It was rare, however, that he was able to resume his former status entirely. The family had worked out new patterns of relationships which had become routine and comfortable and which were resistant to change, partly because they were no longer at the level of consciousness. In a similar vein, Nye's (33, 34) findings on the consequences of re-employment of the mother both for family behavior and for the psychological comfort of family members is illuminating because the impact of a crisis involving a phenomenon so different from alcoholism is so similar. Likewise, the studies of Stolz (37) and Hill (17) concerning the effect of the return of the war veteran to the family are provocative in their implications for students of alcoholism and the family.

Some of the questions raised by such studies—questions which have been alluded to at various points in this chapter—are: Is the dominance so frequently attributed to the wives of alcoholics an expression of inherent personality attributes of the wife, or is it in some measure a by-product of taking over the roles of husband and father which have been left unfulfilled and without which the family could not survive intact? Is the blurring of sexual identities in the alcoholic and his marital partner the consequence of inadequate sexual identification as an enduring aspect of their personalities, or is the blurring to some extent the structural outcome of a family in which traditionally sex-linked roles have been reshuffled? How much of the confusion in family behavior can be attributed to the structural changes going on in the family, to inadequate adult personalities, or to alcoholism per se? To what extent is the reticence to restore to the recovered alcoholic aspects of the husband and father roles a product of family processes and past family adaptations to a vacant father status? To what extent is this reticence based upon personality-engendered hostility towards the alcoholic on the part of family members and upon unconscious wishes to impede his recovery because of personality gratifications stemming from persistence of the illness? Finally, is the disturbance shown by wives when their husbands recover attributable to the loss of such gratifications or to the structural necessity of a realignment of roles?

Further examples of differently focused research which has potentially significant implications for understanding the behavior of family members who are trying to adapt to the alcoholic are to be found in the writings of Tyhurst and his associates (41) and of Glass (13). The former studied the behavior of persons under circumstances involving significant changes in their life situations—circumstances such as disaster, retirement, and migration. The subjects of the research were not in treatment situations. From this research the concept of "transition states" was formulated, defined as "the social and psychological circumstances of being in a state of going from one situation to another." Stages of patterned behavior and emotional states were found in people while they made such transitions. Tyhurst and his associates conclude that emotional disturbance in a transition state is normal—normal in the sense that it is usual, and normal in the sense that a lack of emotional disturbance bodes poorly for the successful adjustment of the person in the future. Signs of emotional disturbance, which were very much in evidence, and which could have been given diagnostic labels had the individual been evaluated apart from his total context, were not equivalent to mental illness.

For his part, Glass wrote about soldiers in combat. In discussing how persons reacted to stress situations for which they had not been trained and which they perceived as unstructured and uncertain, Glass suggests hypotheses for students of alcoholism and the responses of family members. He writes (13, pp. 194–195): "The form or type of psychological non-effective behavior displayed in combat is not determined so much by the individual's personality characteristics as it is dictated either by the practical circumstances of the battle situation or by group acceptance of such symptoms or behavior . . . . Pertinent combat circumstances include the intensity and duration of the battle . . . the degree of support given individuals by buddies, group cohesiveness and leadership."

The family of an alcoholic, including the alcoholic himself, apparently goes through a series of social and psychological transition states made without cultural guideposts, without social and emotional support for individuals, and in a milieu of lowered family cohesiveness. What is the range of behavior to be found under such conditions? Tyhurst's position that feeling states and behavior arise which would lead to the diagnosis of emotional pathology if seen apart from their situational and time dimensions is very provocative. Does the behavior of the family and of its individual members vary according to the degree of family isolation, previous family integration, and training in meeting crises? The sociological literature on the family would support such a hypothesis. More generally, it is to be hoped that future research on alcoholism and the family will be not only more rigorous and interdisciplinary in character, but also better articulated with existing theory and knowledge.

References

1. Angell, Robert C., *The Family Encounters the Depression,* New York: Charles Scribner's Sons, 1936.
2. Bacon, Selden D., "Excessive Drinking and the Institution of the Family," in *Alcohol, Science and Society,* New Haven, Conn.: Journal of Studies on Alcohol, 1945.
3. Baker, Sybil M., "Social Case Work with Inebriates," in *Alcohol, Science and Society,* New Haven, Conn.: Journal of Studies on Alcohol, 1945.

4. Ballard, Robert G., "The Interaction Between Marital Conflict and Alcoholism As Seen Through MMPI's of Marriage Partners," *Amer. J. of Orthopsychiat.*, 29:528–546, 1959.

5. Bowerman, Charles E., "Adjustment in Marriage: Over-all and in Specific Areas," *Sociol. Soc. Res.*, 41:257–263, 1957.

6. Bullock, Samuel C., and Emily H. Mudd, "The Interaction of Alcoholic Husbands and their Non-Alcoholic Wives During Counselling," *Amer. J. of Orthopsychiat.*, 29:519–527, 1959.

7. Cavan, Ruth S., "Unemployment—Crisis of the Common Man," *Marr. and Family Living*, 21:139–146, 1959.

8. ————, and Katherine H. Ranck, *The Family and the Depression*, Chicago: University of Chicago Press, 1938.

9. Cork, R. Margaret, "Case Work in a Group Setting with Wives of Alcoholics," *The Social Worker*, Vol. XIV, pp. 1–6, 1956.

10. Ehrmann, Winston Wallace, "A Review of Family Research in 1957," *Marr. and Family Living*, 20:384–396, 1958.

11. Fox, Ruth, "The Alcoholic Spouse," *in* V. W. Eisenstein (Ed.), *Neurotic Interaction in Marriage*, New York: Basic Books, 1956.

12. Futterman, S., "Personality Trends in Wives of Alcoholics," *J. of Psychiat. Social Work*, 23:37–41, 1953.

13. Glass, A. "Observations Upon the Epidemiology of Mental Illness in Troops During Warfare," in *Symposium on Preventive and Social Psychiatry*, Washington, D.C.: Walter Reed Army Medical Center, 1957, pp. 185–198.

14. Gliedman, Lester H., Helen T. Nash, and W. L. Webb, "Group Psychotherapy of Male Alcoholics and Their Wives," *Dis. Nerv. Syst.*, 17:1–4, 1956.

15. Gliedman, Lester H., David Rosenthal, Jerome D. Frank, and Helen T. Nash, "Group Therapy of Alcoholics with Concurrent Group Meetings of Their Wives," *Quart. J. Stud. Alc.*, 17:655–670, 1956.

16. Hey, Richard N., and Emily H. Mudd, "Recurring Problems in Marriage Counselling," *Marr. and Family Living*, 21:127–129, 1959.

17. Hill, Reuben, *Families Under Stress*, New York: Harper and Brothers, 1949.

18. Jackson, Joan K., "The Adjustment of the Family to the Crisis of Alcoholism," *Quart. J. Stud. Alc.*, 15:562–586, 1954.

19. ————, *Social Adjustment Preceding, During and Following the Onset of Alcoholism*, unpublished doctoral dissertation, University of Washington, 1955.

20. ————, "The Adjustment of the Family to Alcoholism," *Marr. and Family Living*, 18:361–369, 1956.

21. ————, "Alcoholism and the Family," *Ann. Amer. Acad. Pol. Soc. Sci.*, 315:90–98, 1958.

22. ————, "Family Structure and Alcoholism," *Mental Hygiene*, 43:403–406, 1959.

23. Jellinek, E. M., "Phases of Alcohol Addiction," *Quart. J. Stud. Alc.*, 13:673–684, 1952.

24. Kalashian, Marion M., "Working with the Wives of Alcoholics in an Out-Patient Clinic Setting," *Marr. and Family Living*, 21:130–133, 1959.

25. Kamarovsky, Mirra, *The Unemployed Man and His Family*, New York: Dryden Press, 1940.

26. Koos, Earl L., *Families in Trouble*, New York: King's Crown Press, 1946.

27. Lewis, Margaret L., "The Initial Contact with Wives of Alcoholics," *Social Casework*, January 1954.

28. Lisansky, Edith S., "Alcoholism in Women: Social and Psychological Concomitants: I. Social History Data," *Quart. J. Stud. Alc.*, 18:588–623, 1957.

29. MacDonald, Donald E., "Mental Disorders in Wives of Alcoholics," *Quart. J. Stud. Alc.*, 17:282–287, 1956.

30. Mitchell, Howard E., "Interpersonal Perception Theory Applied to Conflicted Marriages in which Alcoholism Is and Is Not a Problem," *Amer. J. Orthopsychiat.*, 29:547–559, 1959.

31. Mowrer, Harriet R., "A Psychocultural Analysis of the Alcoholic," *Amer. Sociol. Rev.*, 5:546–557, 1940.

32. Newell, Nancy, "Alcoholism and the Father Image," *Quart. J. Stud. Alc.*, 11:92–96, 1950.

33. Nye, F. Ivan, "Social and Psychological Correlates of the Employment of Mothers: An Introduction" (mimeographed), Pullman, Wash.: State University of Washington, 1959.

34. ———, "Employment Status and Maternal Adjustment to Children," delivered at the Annual Meetings of the Amer. Sociol. Society, Chicago, 1959.

35. Price, Gladys M., "A Study of the Wives of 20 Alcoholics," *Quart. J. Stud. Alc.*, 5:620–627, 1945.

36. Roe, Anne, "The Adult Adjustment of Children of Alcoholic Parents Raised in Foster Homes," *Quart. J. Stud. Alc.*, 5:378–393, 1944.

37. Stolz, Lois M., *Father Relations of War-Born Children*, Stanford, Calif.: Stanford University Press, 1954.

38. Straus, Robert, "Medical Practice and the Alcoholic," *Ann. Amer. Acad. Pol. Soc. Sci.*, 315:117–124, 1958.

39. Strayer, Robert, "Treatment of Client and Spouse by the Same Caseworker," *Quart. J. Stud. Alc.*, 20:86–102, 1959.

40. Stryker, Sheldon, "Symbolic Interaction as an Approach to Family Research," *Marr. and Family Living*, 21:111–119, 1959.

41. Tyhurst, J., "The Role of Transition States—Including Disasters—In Mental Illness," in *Symposium on Preventive and Social Psychiatry*, Washington, D.C.: Walter Reed Army Medical Center, 1957, pp. 149–167.

42. Waller, Willard, *The Family: A Dynamic Interpretation* (revised by Reuben Hill), New York: Dryden Press, 1951, pp. 453–461.

43. Wellman, Wayne M., "Toward an Etiology of Alcoholism: Why Young Men Drink Too Much," *Canad. Med. Ass. J.*, 73:717–725, 1955.

44. Whalen, Thelma, "Wives of Alcoholics: Four Types Observed in a Family Service Agency," *Quart. J. Stud. Alc.*, 14:632–641, 1953.

45. Yarrow, Marian R., Charlotte G. Schwartz, Harriet S. Murphy, and Leila C. Deasy, "The Psychological Meaning of Mental Illness in the Family," *J. Soc. Issues*, 11:12–24, 1955.

chapter 28

The job behavior
of problem drinkers *

Harrison M. Trice

One of the least-studied facets of alcoholism is its job aspects. Other characteristics of the malady have been explored in much greater detail than has its relationship to work. For example, the history of alcohol usage and alcoholism has been widely documented. Cross-cultural comparisons of drinking patterns and pathologies are increasingly available. The physiology of alcohol consumption and of the alcoholic has received close attention from researchers. Many etiological explanations, with accompanying data, have been advanced, ranging from latent homosexuality to impaired metabolism. In addition, the family and community life of the alcoholic has been explored to a considerable extent. His impact on hospitals, jails, courts, and penal systems has been considered. His job life, however, has remained relatively unexplored. Contrary to popular opinion, far less is known about alcoholism as it affects on-the-job work behavior than is commonly believed. Certainly such studies exist. Unfortunately, however, they are usually confined to one company or to a tiny "sample" of subjects. Consequently they are far from conclusive. In addition, they are quite few in number and rarely comparable in any strict sense.

A variety of reasons explain this lack of interest and data regarding the vocational aspects of alcoholism. Probably the most prominent has been the attitude of the industrial community itself. Until recently, there was a "willful blindness" on the part of management—and labor, too—to face up to the simple fact that alcoholics and persons with other types of behavior disorders were on their payrolls in a variety of jobs. As one observer (15)

* This chapter was written especially for this book.

sharply stated the matter: "This attitude is not myopia; nor is it naiveté; it is willful blindness—management has thus created a conspiracy of silence about mental illness in industry; it has become the 'V.D.' of personnel administration and industrial relations."

From such general attitudes has grown the tendency for business managers to deny having any alcoholic employees among their personnel. Unfortunately this attitude has been reinforced by the fact that early- and middle-stage "problem drinkers"—rather than chronic, full-blown alcoholics—make up the bulk of employed alcoholics. These problem drinkers do not show dramatic, bizarre symptoms as do late-stage alcoholics and are thus not easily recognizable. In addition, their developing alcoholism is frequently well concealed on the job either by themselves or their work associates. Consequently, management and union officials do not have specific records or other tangible evidence that identify an employee as an alcoholic. Thus it is not difficult to understand why company and union authorities tend to deny the existence of this kind of employee.

Furthermore, to allow investigators to collect job-related data on persons who elsewhere have been diagnosed alcoholic is a tacit admission that the company does have such employees. New objections to research are thus raised. It is often considered poor public relations for a company to admit to or do anything about alcoholism. It embroils them in the "liquor" question. It invades the private life of the employee and, in the eyes of the union, looks like paternalism.

To this problem of industry's attitude toward the alcoholic employee can be added certain mechanical barriers to research. Even if the cooperation of one large company is obtained, it probably will not yield enough cases for any substantial conclusions. Frequently it is almost impossible to identify specific personnel files as belonging to a problem drinker. Such a labeling may require a second research effort all its own. In addition, personnel files often contain only sketchy data, making a detailed description of work behavior quite difficult.

Recently signs of improvement in this general situation have appeared. Numerous companies have discovered that the popular stereotype of the problem drinker as a chronic "Lost Weekend-er" is not accurate. They have found that they are employing early- and middle-stage alcoholics who are not yet chronic, but whose work has been substantially impaired by their developing alcoholism. As a consequence of this common experience a definition of alcoholism from the job standpoint has emerged: any employee whose repeated overindulgence in alcoholic beverages sharply reduces his or her effectiveness and dependability in carrying out a work assignment is an alcoholic.

Other signs of a decline in apathy include prominent companies who have openly declared alcoholism to be a health problem among their employees and who have developed specific rehabilitation policies regarding the malady. Union counselors have begun to include alcoholism in their educational efforts. A few university researchers are seeking more data about absenteeism, work accidents and efficiency, job turnover, and coverup experiences of problem drinkers by using work histories and in-company studies. Industrial physicians have shown an early recognition of the problem and contributed data on its work features. In addition, many companies have recently begun to manifest an "off-the-record" interest. In contrast to their earlier sharp denial that they had alcoholic employees, this attitude is a cautious inquisitiveness regarding the problem and what can be done about it. It is an attitude of "tell me more about this thing, but keep it quiet—that I ask."

There is also a growing realization among investigators of alcohol pathologies that the earlier phases of alcoholism need more research attention. The major part of the alcoholism process occurs here. Rehabilitation success appears to be greater during the earlier symptoms. Furthermore, since the developing alcoholic typically continues to work regularly during these stages, his work life will come more and more into focus as these earlier phases receive greater attention.

In short, a cautious inquisitiveness on the part of the industrial community, combined with a new research orientation to the earlier stages on the part of some academic researchers, is producing a slow but steady increase in interest regarding the job behavior of alcoholics. To spell out in more detail this rising interest, the present chapter will consider a summary of present data on the job behavior of alcoholics and a report of some new research findings on their job behavior.

Summary of Present Data on Job Behavior

The basic data available on the job behavior of developing alcoholics are less substantial than many people believe. For example, the cost of problem-drinking employees to their employers has often been described as an annual "billion-dollar hangover." Significantly higher rates of on-the-job accidents and job absenteeism are attributed to problem drinkers as compared with the rates of non-alcoholic employees. Evidence to back up these alleged work characteristics is nevertheless quite sparse. There have been some scattered estimates in widely separated companies regarding the cost to the employer of problem drinkers, but these merely suggest that in some job situations such an employee is a costly item while in others he is a relatively minor expense item. Furthermore, his work-related accidents have not been studied in any systematic fashion to discover whether his rate is any higher than that of non-alcoholic employees. Even absenteeism, about which most is assumed to be known, has not been effectively studied with reference to such variables as job types, job status, and stage in the development of alcoholic disease.

Despite this general lack of substantial data about the work behavior of the employee with a drinking problem, some tentative descriptions of the work experiences of alcoholics can be made with a fair amount of confidence. There seems to be little doubt that the alcoholic works regularly while his malady is in its incipient and middle stages (23). Of some seven hundred work histories of members of Alcoholics Anonymous collected by the writer, only four members reported they did not work regularly during the middle phase of their alcoholism. Typically, the developing alcoholic stayed on his job for years as the symptoms of compulsive drinking unfolded at a slow but steady pace. Also, data indicate that problem drinkers are rather evenly distributed through all occupational groups as well as many types of businesses and industries (23, 29). Alcoholic employees appear in substantial numbers in managerial, skilled, unskilled, service, clerical, and professional occupations. They are well represented in construction, transportation, government service, and all other major industrial types.

In addition to this characteristic of dispersion throughout the work world, the middle-stage alcoholic appears to be lodged heavily among male employees in the ages from 35 to 50 years. Certainly female alcoholics exist, probably more than are currently estimated, and many more are in the labor force today than 20 or 30 years ago. There are still grounds for believing, however, that industry will find more alcoholism among men than women. Even more certain is the characteristic that alcoholism is a disorder of the mature years at a time of maximum work expectancy. If it were spread evenly among workers of all age groups, alcoholism's industrial impact would be far less severe. Concentrated as it is in the productive years (age 35 to 50), it can impair a large number of workers at the point of their greatest potential work contribution.

There can be little doubt, also, that work efficiency declines as alcoholism develops. It seems to be quite clear that the hangover, the self-hate, the preoccupation with denying there is anything wrong, the loss of control that leads to continued drinking off the job until something intervenes, and the anxiety about getting alcoholic relief during the workday reduce substantially the developing alcoholic's ability to do his job (10, 24, 27).

This decline in efficiency has numerous facets. The problem drinker begins to procrastinate a great deal, to put off everything except absolutely essential tasks, to fulfill only the immediate requirements of his job. He compromises with quality, accepting second or third "best," because he is unable to concentrate on the details necessary to perform his job well. Fatigue saps his energy, and initiative is forgotten. He has a strong tendency to do his job "any old way" just to get it done. In short, he is content with a mediocre performance. Because he becomes guilt ridden about his poor work, he typically tries to make up for it by spasmodic spurts of output or creativity during which he often does superior work. This frequently serves as a sign that his work is well done. Actually, it is merely a short-lived increase in a general efficiency decline.

Regarding absenteeism, there are data (8, 14, 18) indicating that, in general, the rate for a company's problem drinkers is significantly higher than for non-alcoholics. Beyond this we have only hunches.

Some grounds exist (9, 26) for believing that "no report" and "partial" absenteeism characterize a developing drinking problem in an employee. Failure to report his inability to be on the job appears to be a symptom of the middle-stage alcoholic that distinguishes him from the average absentee. In the early stages, a member of his family may report his absences, but, as his problem worsens, his absences occur without advance notice from anyone. He often comes to the job only to leave before the day is over. He realizes he cannot get through the day without a drink, so he leaves. There is also some exploratory evidence (25) regarding absenteeism among high-status as contrasted with low-status problem drinkers. Alcoholic executives, engineers, lawyers, doctors, and other high-status workers apparently have substantially less actual absenteeism than do low-status alcoholics on semiskilled and unskilled jobs. High-status inebriates, however, seem to have a great deal of "on-the-job absenteeism"; they tend to come to work when they feel badly after an episode of drinking but for all practical purposes are "absent." Low-status workers tend to have much larger amounts of actual "stay-away absenteeism."

Data concerning on-the-job accidents are quite sparse. Jellinek (12) estimated that in 1943 the rate of fatal accidents among inebriate workers was more than twice that of non-alcoholic workers. This figure has often been applied to on-the-job accidents. The figure was based, however, on all types of fatal accidents, one-third of which occurred at work. It is, therefore, invalid to interpret the rates to mean that on-the-job accidents were twice as numerous among problem drinkers as among other employees. Something quite different was found by two industrial physicians (5) who checked a 15-year period in a company of eighteen hundred employees. They found no fatal injury caused directly or indirectly by alcoholism, nor could any non-fatal injury in the last 5 years be attributed to alcoholism.

Furthermore, an exploratory study (26) of the work histories of 98 A.A. members who reported they were exposed to accidents on the job revealed fewer lost-time accidents than expected. Most of the recovered problem drinkers in this study stated they had experienced no increase in their on-the-job accident rate after their drinking reached the problem stage. These findings were subsequently tested by Maxwell (14), who compared the accident rates of 48 alcoholic and 48 matched non-alcoholic employees in a large company. The accident rate of the problem-drinking employees after age 40 was almost identical with that of the controls, but before age 40 the problem drinkers experienced twice as many on-the-job accidents as did the comparison group of non-alcoholic employees.

Probably the area of most speculation and least evidence is that of the extent and cost of alcoholism to American business and industry. There are grounds only for reasonable guesses. Estimates of the number of employed alcoholics have been made in two ways: (a) by taking the estimated number of all alcoholics in the total population and making an educated guess as to the number who are regularly employed, and (b) by using estimates made in specific companies as an indication of the number throughout industry. Both of these methods are questionable at best; however, they provide us with a rough idea of the extent of the problem.

Estimates of the total number of alcoholics have come mainly from the Jellinek Estimation Formula (30). But how many of these incipient and full-blown alcoholics are employed regularly in a definite job? Here the quest becomes very fuzzy. Most observers have played safe and stated that only half of the alcoholics were actively employed. At the same time case histories of clinics and work histories of members of Alcoholics Anonymous suggest a substantially higher number in the employed category. But no one knows how to be more precise in any systematic way about the estimation. The figure usually cited is two million, or approximately 3 per cent of the nation's labor force, but a particular company may have many more or many less than this percentage. Judging from studies in individual companies (19, 22), this figure can range from practically none to 10 per cent. Thus, one careful study of ten small Canadian companies (2) indicated 6 per cent of their employees were problem drinkers.

However, difficulties in estimating really begin when we try to appraise the costs of alcoholism to American business and industry as a whole. This appears to be not only an almost impossible task but also a gigantic one. When the array of factors, both tangible and intangible, affecting the value of an employee to his employer is considered, the difficulty of the task becomes obvious. Furthermore, when an effort is made to attach a dollar value to the way in which alcoholism reduces this value, any nationwide effort is extremely questionable. The best we can do is list the various cost factors that may be relevant to a particular company, leaving to the judgment of those who know the organization any actual estimation of dollar cost (1).

First, cost of reduced work efficiency is the most apparent factor. This can take many forms such as scrap, spoilage, errors in assembly and shipping, slowdown, fewer sales, increased rejects, and customer complaints. Executive and professional error adds another and even more costly dimension. Second, since many alcoholics appear to have a substantially higher absenteeism rate than others, they can be costly from this standpoint. Furthermore, companies make training investments in many employees which are lost if termination for alcoholism occurs, and replacing an employee can be expensive. The public relations impact of an alcoholic employee is also a potential cost item along with the sickness support the company may provide for the many related illnesses that accompany alcoholism.

Briefly, the only meaningful cost items come from specific companies who appraise alcoholic employees in specific jobs and attach a dollar value to their cases. This procedure has been attempted in a few instances, and the results suggest that in many situations problem drinkers are very costly to their employers while in others the cost is relatively modest (16).

Some New Research Findings

Since there are many barriers to in-company research regarding the job behavior of problem drinkers, the best large-scale source of information about their work experiences appears to be the work histories of members of Alcoholics Anonymous. Large numbers of such histories are potentially available, and it seems highly probable that most members are genuine alcoholics, thus simplifying the often difficult problem of identification. On the other hand, work histories so collected suffer from such limitations as errors in recall, unconscious exaggeration, and unusual selectivity (for the simple reason that A.A. affiliation is itself selective). Despite these defects, however, the availability of large numbers of work histories from A.A. members seems to outweigh the disadvantages; consequently the research reported here made use of these histories as the basic source of new information about the job behavior of the alcoholic.

1. *Method of collecting work histories*

Two separate studies were made of how male A.A. members described the effect of their alcoholism on specific work behaviors. Basically, both studies used questionnaires in conjunction with interviews as the method for collecting data on the work behavior of A.A. members. Interviews were geared to questionnaires in order to provide more thorough material with which to interpret questionnaire trends. This basic method did vary, however, between the two studies.

In the first study a series of eighty descriptive statements concerning specific job behaviors constituted the questionnaire. Respondents were asked to indicate how much each one of these described their work experiences during the early and middle phase of their problem. The interviews in the first study were group interviews with three or four members participating in each. No individual interviews were held. From the four hundred members in New York State and Pennsylvania who were asked to do the questionnaire, two hundred usable returns were secured. Group interviews were arranged in Syracuse and New York City by A.A. friends of the writer and were held in private homes, hotel rooms, club houses, and A.A. meeting places. Eighty-six members participated in twenty-three group interviews.

The questionnaire in the second study covered one legal-size page and was designed to secure a volume response. It contained only highlights from the questionnaire of the first study and was not scaled in any fashion. Since the earlier study indicated that respondents usually experienced middle-phase symptoms 5 years before affiliating with A. A., they were asked to concentrate on their job experiences as they recalled them at that time. Interviews in the second study were all individual ones and were more directive than the group interviews in the first study. Eight hundred and seventy-five members from all over the country were asked to respond by mail to the

questionnaire; 602 of these did but some responses were only partly usable.*
Fifty responses from New York City were used for a reliability check in
which the same informant filled out the same form 6 weeks after the first
response. These were not included in the final statistical tables. On two
items, reported absenteeism and accidents, there were correlations of .84
and .79 respectively. In all, 552 questionnaire responses were available for
analysis in the second study. Eighty-three taped interviews, lasting from
30 to 45 minutes each, were conducted. These were done with members
in Syracuse and New York City. Special effort was made to secure interviewees from professional, managerial, and skilled jobs as well as from service, semiskilled, and unskilled occupations.

2. Work behaviors studied

Both studies concentrated on five aspects of job performance during the
middle stage of alcoholism: work efficiency, absenteeism, coverup, turnover,
and on-the-job accidents. Work efficiency was divided into quantity and
quality, and descriptions were sought as to how alcoholism affected these
two aspects. Estimates of number of days per week absent from the job before the drinking problem began were asked for as were estimates of number absent after the problem began. Job changes were defined as either
voluntary or involuntary shifts to a new employer. Coverup was regarded
as self-explanatory, while only information on "lost-time" accidents was
sought.

In addition, data on three job variables were collected in both studies in
order to determine if there was any relationship between variations in the
work behaviors and in these job variables. These job variables were: occupational type (as determined by the *Dictionary of Occupational Titles*),
amount of freedom present in any job (as measured by amount of freedom from scheduling and from close supervision), and off-job drinking
experiences with fellow workers. Statistical tests of significance were applied
to determine if there were meaningful relationships between these variables
and absenteeism, accidents, efficiency, turnover, and coverup experiences.

3. Work efficiency

In both studies practically all respondents reported a substantial decrease
in work effectiveness during the middle stage of their alcoholism. There
were, however, approximately one out of ten who reported that their work
was unaffected. Tiring out very quickly, increased mistakes, and an uneven,
frenzied work pace characterized those who reported a definite decline.
Those who did not report a decline tended to attribute this to their tendency
to work extra hard on some days in order to make up for poor quantity and
quality on others.

* Responses were secured through the efforts of individual A.A. members throughout
the country. Their cooperation was not an official part of A.A. activities in any sense.
There were, however, many members who were willing to respond as individuals. In
short, A. A. did not in any manner sponsor or promote this research.

A jerky work pace was a common description in both studies. Interviewees frequently described a temporary period of increased work effectiveness followed by a sharp decline. Apparently these work spurts served to assure the developing alcoholic that his work was still acceptable.

In short, there was very little variation in reported effect on work efficiency. Consequently none of the three job variables—occupational type, job freedom, or off-job drinking experiences with fellow workers—had any association with work performance. The interviews, as well as the scaled statements in the first study, indicated, however, that the way in which work efficiency declined seemed to vary markedly with occupational type. Thus, professional, managerial, and other white-collar personnel tended to go to work even when feeling unable to do an effective job. Those of lower status, on the other hand, tended to resort both to absenteeism and to further drinking off the job when in this condition. Thus, those in service, semiskilled, and unskilled jobs more often described themselves as "periodics" whose work was impaired by absenteeism and by sharp declines in work efficiency before and after absences, while higher-status workers tended persistently to come to work, but to do practically nothing once there. These latter were the classical "half-men." In contrast, lower-status problem drinkers were inclined to do a substantial day of work whenever they were on the job, if not coming off or going on a spree.

In addition, interviews revealed that the developing alcoholic on a high-status job often got a better, more lucrative position during the middle stage of his alcoholism. Combined with the temporary periods of frenzied work effectiveness, this experience often served to postpone his acceptance of the fact that he had lost control of his drinking.

One specific limitation must be kept in mind regarding these findings. A sizable number (approximately 30 per cent in both studies) reported there were no work standards against which they could determine whether work effectiveness had declined or not. Thus numerous work histories were lost to use and doubt is cast on the reports of respondents who said they could judge what happened to their work performance. On the other hand, there is such widespread agreement among the work histories where efficiency was estimated that it is difficult to discredit the conclusions.

4. Absenteeism

Approximately 70 per cent of the respondents in both studies indicated that absences from work increased as their drinking problem developed. The questionnaire of the second study was analyzed for an estimate of how much absenteeism increased. Fifty-seven per cent of those who reported an increase estimated their absenteeism increased one-fourth to 1 day per week over what it had been before their alcoholism developed. Forty-three per cent increased to 1 or more days per week or to the equivalent during concentrated drinking periods.

These estimated rates are substantially higher than the typical absenteeism rate reported by various industrial and business firms (3, 6, 13). In the case of those who reported a day per week or more, the rate is four to five times greater than typical rates. On the other hand, there was a definite variation in absenteeism experiences. Just over 30 per cent in both studies reported no increase in absences at all during the middle period of their alcoholism. Unlike work efficiency there was variation in absenteeism experience; this provided an opportunity to see if occupational type, amount of job freedom, and off-job drinking experiences with fellow workers were related to different absenteeism patterns.

Only one—occupational type—showed a definite association in both studies. Subjects in higher-status occupations apparently had much less absenteeism than those on lower-status jobs. Interview analysis tended to verify this differential and to provide explanations. A sense of responsibility brought managerial and professional problem drinkers to their jobs despite their condition. Going to work was a sign of "managing" their drinking problem. Furthermore, it was a way of reducing the guilt and self-hate that came from their excessive drinking. Finally, these interviewees often described opportunities to continue drinking while on the job. Such attitudes and opportunities were relatively absent among lower-status subjects.

The findings in this connection are consistent with those on work efficiency. The decline in efficiency of lower-status alcoholics appears to center around absenteeism and the period before and after absences. In contrast, alcoholics on more responsible jobs expressed their job inefficiency by a steady, mediocre performance, intermingled with absences, but relatively fewer absences than among those on jobs of lesser responsibility.

Two limitations to this description of absenteeism should be noted. First, seventy-two respondents in the second study failed to answer either of the questions on the second questionnaire regarding absenteeism. Consequently there were only 480 work histories to use in analyzing the estimated amount of increase per week. Furthermore, many of the subjects used a unit of time other than "per week" in their estimates. For example, some would say "4 days missed per month," or "2 weeks every 6 months." These were all equated on a "per week" basis and, in doing so, additional errors may have been added to the errors of recall.

5. Coverup experiences

Three kinds of coverup experiences were encountered in both studies. First, practically no concealment of a drinking problem would take place on the job. Second, the alcoholic himself would carry out most, if not all, of the stratagems that kept his drinking from becoming common knowledge. For the sake of brevity, we shall refer to this as "self-coverup." The third kind of camouflage was that provided by work associates—immediate bosses, fellow workers, and subordinates.

The two studies produced almost identical results regarding which of these three types occurred most often. Thus, just over 40 per cent reported that they themselves did the most to hide their drinking problems, while relying upon only minor aid from others. The next largest group, approximately 20 per cent, described few coverup experiences or none at all; typically they felt that their drinking was common knowledge and coverup was unnecessary. The third type—coverup by work associates—accounted for the remaining 36 per cent. Fellow workers were the most frequent agents in this type of coverup, accounting for approximately 17 per cent of the total. The immediate boss was next with just over 12 per cent, while subordinates were the least, accounting for only 7 per cent.

Since there was a variety of coverup experiences reported in substantial numbers it was possible to explore whether or not there were any relations between these coverup types and occupational type, amount of job freedom, and off-job drinking experiences with fellow workers. Occupational type did not show a relationship except in the interview data where high-status alcoholics tended to report self-coverup as the predominant type. This was often attributed to the freedom from close supervision enjoyed on these jobs (although there was a definite minority for which this job freedom was not present). Because of the absence of close supervision, they did not have to rely upon work associates but could conceal their drinking problem themselves.

This trend was confirmed by the questionnaire results in both studies. A significant difference was found between the types of coverup and the degrees of job freedom. Apparently self-coverup tended to be concentrated in those jobs with a maximum of freedom from imposed work schedules and from close supervision. This strongly implies a concentration of self-coverup among those managerial and professional positions where these job freedoms are significantly found, more than among lower-status jobs where job freedom is relatively scarce.

The analysis of off-the-job drinking experiences with fellow workers supports this interpretation. Both studies showed that practically all the subjects participated in such drinking situations, although there were instances where this was not the case. There was, however, again a difference between higher-status and lower-status occupations in how this activity was conducted. Higher-status alcoholics participated in such activities but were very careful to drink "normally," waiting until they had separated from work associates to drink heavily. They were inclined to drink relatively small amounts and to avoid being the center of attention in these drinking situations. Lower-status alcoholics, however, frequently described their participation as relatively uninhibited. Thus, they often got drunk with persons from the job with few reservations. As a result their drinking proclivity was visible and easily observed by fellow workers. In sum, high-status alcoholics during the middle phase of their alcoholism continued self-coverup stratagems off the job, but those of lower status were inclined to drink openly with work associates in a manner that exposed their loss of control.* As a result, respondents who had been in service, skilled, semiskilled, and unskilled jobs tended to report that they could not rely on themselves for coverup but depended upon work associates to conceal their drinking, or upon no one at all.

6. Job turnover

The reported number of times the subjects changed jobs during the middle period of their alcoholism was divided into five categories of change: none, one through four, five through nine, ten through nineteen, and over twenty changes. A change was regarded as any shift, voluntary or involuntary, to a new employer. Since the results in both studies were quite comparable, only the percentage distribution of the second study will be reported. Thirty-nine per cent of the respondents reported no change at all; 25 per cent reported one to four changes; 12 per cent reported five to nine changes; 7 per cent had ten to nineteen changes; while 17 per cent reported twenty or more job changes. Thus approximately 65 per cent in both studies reported four or fewer than four job shifts; almost 40 per cent reported no changes at all.

Variations in both type of occupation and amount of job freedom were associated with job changes. There was a significant concentration of "no turnover" in the managerial category, with the service category having a concentration of the job changes. Job changes also accumulated significantly among those with minimum job freedom. These tendencies were observable in both studies. Furthermore, in the second study job changes were in significantly larger numbers among those informants who reported that fellow workers drank together off the job than among those who did not. Turnover thus appears to be associated with lower-status occupations and with work situations where work associates drink together off the job.

Taken in conjunction with the fact that the early and middle stages of alcoholism typically cover from 7 to 10 years, these results seem to reflect turnover patterns of the labor force in general rather than job changes unique to alcoholics. Since a sizable majority of the respondents reported they had only up to four employer changes during this period, their turnover rate would not appear to differ much from the general labor force pattern (20). Their rates of change tend to confirm the findings of Bacon and Straus (23) to the effect that many problem drinkers are more stable occupationally than is generally believed. Apparently, many alcoholics develop their alcoholism in the course of only one or two job changes. Moreover, it is well established that job mobility is relatively low in occupations for which extensive training or experience is required and substantially higher among operatives and laborers (20); rates among the respondents showed such a

---

* This finding is similar to the class origins of "solitary" and "sociable" alcoholics reported by Jackson (11) in that "more solitary than sociable alcoholics come from the middle class."

pattern, as has already been indicated. Finally, it may be that the respondents' rates were influenced by the fact that there is a strong relationship between job mobility and age (7). Since their mean age was 44.8 years, and since rates of job change typically decline sharply during this age period, the rates for the respondents probably reflect this more general feature of turnover.

One substantial limitation must be kept in mind when interpreting these results. The data are not, strictly speaking, for comparable periods of time. For instance, one respondent may have regarded his excessive drinking as having started 7 years before he joined A. A.; another may have felt his alcoholism began 13 years before he affiliated. Thus, the latter is reporting on a 13-year period and the former on only a 7-year span. (In an effort to offset this variation, most of the reported data on turnover were divided into just two groups: "no" turnover and "some" turnover.) In addition, no "before" data on turnover were collected. Consequently, there are no base lines against which to compare job change experiences after the development of a drinking problem.

7. On-the-job accidents

Of those in the first study who said they were exposed to accidents, 18 per cent reported having had, during the middle phases of their drinking problem, at least one accident involving lost time. A similar figure resulted from the second study: 21 per cent of those exposed to accidents on their jobs apparently had had at least one "lost-time accident." When these proportions are roughly translated into a frequency rate per million exposed man hours, they fall about half way between the high and low extremes for various types of industries. This is much higher than the rates found, say, in typewriter assembly plants in New York State (17) and much lower than the rates for such operations as logging, sawmills, and foundries. The tentative conclusion seems to be that the lost-time accident rate reported by the respondents in these studies is not extraordinarily high when compared with median rates. On the other hand, when contrasted with accidents in some specific industries the rate is quite high.

Furthermore, those respondents in both studies who were most exposed to work accidents were congregated among the lower status occupations, i.e., the service, skilled, semiskilled, and unskilled groups. Despite this accumulation, however, respondents in these occupational types did not report a significantly greater number of on-the-job accidents than did those less exposed to accidents. This was also true of the other two job variables; variations neither in job freedom nor in off-job drinking experiences showed any relationship to the number of accidents. On the whole, about one respondent out of every ten in both studies reported work-related, lost-time accidents. This did not provide much range in work-accident experiences. Consequently, there was less opportunity for relationships to emerge between the job variables and the presence or absence of lost-time accidents.

The literature on the subject would lead to the expectation of a higher proportion of accidents per alcoholic respondent than that found in this study. Typically the problem-drinking employee is described as having twice as many work accidents as non-alcoholic workers. This may be true for some types of industries, but, as we have seen, it is doubtful that there is any unusual difference in many industries. On the other hand, accident proneness would be expected from the fact that 80 per cent of the respondents in the first study reported often drinking during working hours.

An explanation of the unexpected lack of work accidents among those exposed to them was found in the interviews of both studies. Time and again interviewees independently explained their safety record during the middle phase of alcoholism in terms of five factors. First, they frequently described an extra cautiousness that slowed them down in the quantity of work performed but acted to prevent accidents. Second, this extra cautiousness was especially manifest when a poor physical condition made accident risk higher than usual. Third, there was a proneness to absenteeism whenever fear of accidents was higher than usual. This tended to remove the alcoholic from the job during a period of high risk and is consistent with the finding on lower-status absenteeism; that is, absences were significantly higher among lower-status occupations where accident exposure was also significantly higher. In short, the problem drinker who is exposed to work accidents apparently tends to stay away from the job when he believes he is unable to perform safely. Furthermore, there was considerable evidence in the interviews that supervisors often acted to remove a problem drinker from the job if they felt he was apt to injure himself.

In the fourth place, many of the interviewees attributed their lack of accidents to the repetitious nature of their jobs. They also felt that they had built up a routine for managing the effects of alcohol—that they had learned what to expect from it. Together, these two factors created a habitual work regularity that helped protect them from injury.

Lastly, a substantial number of interviewees insisted they had had fewer accidents than would be expected because they often drank during working hours in order to "steady" themselves. Drinking moderately during the working day, according to this description, temporarily calmed their hangover symptoms and allowed them to concentrate attention on the job.

One other aspect of on-the-job accidents was explored in the second study. Inquiry into this aspect stemmed from the following question: Do those developing alcoholics who must drive a motor vehicle in the performance of their jobs have more work accidents than those who are exposed to accidents but do not drive a car? No such implied relationship was found despite the fact that it was definitely expected. When the interview analysis was consulted, the explanations for avoiding moving automobile accidents proved the same as those for other accidents, namely, extra caution, absenteeism, and so forth.

Some certain limitations on these findings regarding work accidents bear mention. For instance, the number of reported lost-time accidents tells us nothing about the seriousness of the accident nor the duration of the lost time. Thus a minor accident resulting in a loss of one workday is combined with a major one in which the loss may have been 6 months and the injury quite serious. It is quite possible, furthermore, that some respondents were exposed to risk much longer than this and thus had a greater opportunity for accidents—there being no standardization for exposure in the data. Also, all degrees of exposure were classified as of equal intensity when obviously this could not have been the case in reality.

8. Relationships among various job behaviors

In addition to the relationships found between the job variables (such as occupational type) and job behaviors (such as absenteeism or turnover), other suggestive associations among the specific job behaviors themselves were found in the second study. Thus those respondents who did report lost-time accidents were significantly lodged among the segment who reported the highest absenteeism rates for the period after their drinking problem began.* Moreover, those respondents who reported that work associates did the most to cover up their drinking problems for them, and those who had a strong tendency toward changing employers, were found significantly among those with the highest absenteeism. Since there is a substantial relationship between high absenteeism and low occupational status, it seems reasonable to believe that this cluster of work behaviors is more characteristic of alcoholic respondents in service, semiskilled, and unskilled jobs than of those in professional, managerial, and other white-collar categories.

Then, too, reduced work quantity was highly related to reduced work quality; that is, if a respondent reported that one of these declined, there was a high probability he would report the other also declined. Interview analysis strongly supported these statistical findings, as well as the others previously mentioned. Also, among those who reported decreased work quality or quantity there was the definite presence of some kind of coverup experience, whereas those who reported no such decrease did not show this as sharply. Apparently, coverup on the job tended to characterize respondents who reported reduced work efficiency more than those who did not.

9. Summary

Because of the difficulty of securing in-company work histories of employed alcoholics, members of Alcoholics Anonymous were asked to provide an account of their work experiences during the early and middle stages of their alcoholism. Questionnaires together with taped interviews constituted the basic techniques for securing these data. Two studies of male A.A. members were made, the first involving 200 questionnaire respondents and 86 interviewees; in the second study there were 552 questionnaire respond-

---

* A study of the relationship between absenteeism and accidents among non-alcoholic employees in two New York State companies (4) showed a similar tendency. Thus those who were accident free had fewer total absences in both firms, while those with accidents had more absences.

ents and 83 interviewees. Both studies concentrated on five specific job behaviors: work efficiency, absenteeism, coverup, turnover, and work accidents. Data on three job variables were also collected in an effort to see if
they were related to variations in the job behaviors. These were occupational
type, job freedom, and off-job drinking experiences with fellow workers.

There was almost complete agreement among the respondents that their
work efficiency sharply declined. The manner in which this occurred, however, appeared to vary with occupational type. Those in higher status jobs
tended to manifest "on-the-job absenteeism" by coming to work in poor
condition and attempting to do their jobs despite hangover, fatigue, and
poor memory. In contrast, respondents in lower-status jobs inclined toward
doing an acceptable day's work whenever they were on the job.

Reported absenteeism experiences are consistent with this description of
how the decline in work efficiency varied with occupational type. Thus
actual "off-the-job" absenteeism tended to be concentrated in lower-status
jobs while respondents of higher status reported substantially less absenteeism. Respondents of managerial and professional status apparently came
to work out of a sense of duty, out of a desire to prove by working that there
was nothing wrong, and often because they could easily drink on the job.
These attitudes and circumstances did not motivate lower-status respondents.

Of the three kinds of coverup described, self-coverup tended to characterize those respondents who had a maximum of job freedom in the sense
of freedom from imposed work schedules and from close supervision. Since
there was a relatively strong relationship between occupational type and
job freedom, coverup by oneself was apparently more prevalent among
managerial, professional, and sales occupations. By contrast, no coverup at
all or coverup by associates tended to characterize problem drinkers in jobs
with less job freedom.

Off-the-job drinking experiences with fellow workers tended to confirm
this difference. Practically all respondents reported participating in off-the-
job drinking situations made up of fellow employees. But higher-status
problem drinkers were very careful to engage in "controlled" drinking, while
those of lower status were much less inhibited and readily got drunk with
fellow workers. In short, the developing alcoholism of the latter was more
easily seen by fellow workers than that of the former, who continued self-
coverup stratagems off the job.

The incidence of employer change was related both to occupational type
and to job freedom. Persons in managerial categories had relatively few
changes, while service, semiskilled, and unskilled groups had many. It is
impossible to conclude, however, that these reported job changes differ from
those of non-alcoholics. They appear to represent the pattern of job changes
in general rather than a pattern peculiar to alcoholics.

Fewer work accidents were reported by respondents than would be expected on the basis of estimates suggested in the current literature on the

subject. It is doubtful that the reported lost-time accidents represent an unusual rate. The apparent reasons for this are the extracautious attitude of alcoholics when exposed to accident risk, their absenteeism, the routine nature of many of their jobs, and the protection afforded by fellow workers and bosses. None of the data collected helped to explain those accidents which were reported; for example, accidents were not reported in any greater numbers by those who had to drive a car in the performance of their jobs than by those who did not.

Finally, there were some definite clusterings of variations in the specific job behaviors. High absenteeism was significantly related to lost-time accidents, to high employer change, and to coverup by associates. Since high absenteeism tended to characterize lower-status occupations, this cluster of job behaviors may be more characteristic of such occupations than of skilled, professional, and managerial jobs.

Conclusion

One conclusion seems repeatedly to suggest itself in these studies: occupational type strongly influences how alcoholism is expressed. Absenteeism, coverup, and employer change are apparently experienced by the developing alcoholic according to the content and requirements of his job, not according to a uniform pattern. The way in which job efficiency is affected seems to vary with the type of job. Even accident experience varies as a result of the fact that accident exposure varies from job to job. Thus, instead of focusing exclusively on the alcoholism process as it affects the job, it seems necessary in the future to turn the consideration around and try to understand how variations in occupational type channel and mold the developing process of alcoholism. This is merely another way of saying that alcoholism is not a process developing apart from societal organization but is deeply embedded therein. We must, therefore, consider how occupation and other social phenomena influence the etiology and expression of alcoholic symptoms, rather than the reverse.

References

1. "Alcoholic Workers: 'Problem Drinkers' High Cost to Industry Spurs Rehabilitation Programs," *Wall Street J.*, April 28, 1958, pp. 1, 15.
2. Archibald, H. David, "How Many Alcoholics in Your Firm," *Toronto Financial Post*, June 1, 1954.
3. Bureau of National Affairs, *Computing Absenteeism Rates*, Survey No. 27 of B.N.A.'s Personnel Policies, October 1954.
4. Castle, Peter F. C., "Accidents, Absences, and Withdrawal from the Work Situation," *Hum. Relat.*, 9:223–233, 1956.
5. *Chronic Alcoholism in Industry*, Princeton: Opinion Research Corporation, 1952.
6. Covner, Bernard, "Management Factors Affecting Absenteeism," *Harv. Bus. Rev.*, 28:42–48, 1950.
7. Eldridge, Paul, and Irwin Wolkenstein, "Incidence of Employer Change," *Industr. and Labor Relations Rev.*, 10:101–107, 1956.

8. Franco, S. Charles, "Problem Drinking in Industry: Review of a Company Program," *Industr. Med. and Surgery*, 26:221–228, 1957.

9. ———, "Problem Drinking in Industry—Ten Years with a Company Program," *Edison Electric Institute Bull.*, October 1958.

10. Henderson, Ralph M., and Selden D. Bacon, "Problem Drinking: The Yale Plan for Business and Industry," *Quart. J. Stud. Alc.*, 14:247–262, 1951.

11. Jackson, Joan K., "Types of Drinking Patterns of Male Alcoholics," *Quart. J. Stud. Alc.*, 19:269–301, 1958.

12. Jellinek, E. M., "What Shall We Do About Alcoholism?", *Vital Speeches*, 13:252–253, 1947.

13. Mann, Floyd, and D. Baumgartel, "Absences and Employee Attitudes in an Electric Power Company," *Hum. Relat. Program*, Ser. 1, Report 2, University of Michigan, Survey Research Center, December 1952.

14. Maxwell, Milton A., and Observer, "A Study in Absenteeism, Accidents, and Sickness Payments in Problem Drinkers in One Industry," *Quart. J. Stud. Alc.*, 20:302–312, 1959.

15. McMurry, Robert N., "Mental Illness in Industry," *Harv. Bus. Rev.*, 37:79–86, 1959.

16. Mulford, Harold A., and Carl A. Waisanen, *Alcoholism and Iowa Business and Industry*, Res. Ser. No. 16, State University of Iowa, Bureau of Labor and Management, 1957.

17. "1955 Injury Frequency Rates," *Industr. Bull.*, New York State Dept. of Labor, May 1957, pp. 16–19.

18. O'Brien, Cyril C., "Alcoholism Among Disciplinary Cases in Industry," *Quart. J. Stud. Alc.*, 10:268–278, 1949.

19. Page, Robert C., John J. Thorpe, and D. W. Caldwell, "The Problem Drinker in Industry," *Quart. J. Stud. Alc.*, 13:370–396, 1952.

20. Palmer, Gladys, and Carol Brainard, *Labor Mobility in Six Cities*, New York: Social Science Research Council, 1954, pp. 123–125.

21. Popham, Robert E., "The Jellinek Alcoholism Estimation Formula and Its Application to Canadian Data," *Quart. J. Stud. Alc.*, 17:559–593, 1956.

22. Presnall, Lewis E., *Alcoholism: A Workable Program in Industry*, Salt Lake City: Chino Mines Division, Kennecot Copper Corp., 1956.

23. Straus, Robert, and Selden D. Bacon, "A Study of Occupational Integration in 2023 Male Clinic Patients," *Quart. J. Stud. Alc.*, 12:231–260, 1951.

24. Strayer, Robert, "A Study of the Employment Adjustment of 80 Alcoholics," *Quart. J. Stud. Alc.*, 18:278–288, 1957.

25. Trice, Harrison M., "Absenteeism Among High-Status and Low-Status Problem Drinkers," *I.L.R. Res.*, 4:10–14, 1958.

26. ———, "Identifying the Problem Drinker on the Job," *Personnel*, 33:527–533, 1957.

27. ———, *The Problem Drinker on the Job*, Bull. No. 40, Cornell University, School of Industrial and Labor Relations, 1959.

28. ———, "Work Accidents and the Problem Drinker," *I.L.R. Res.*, 3:2–7, 1957.

29. Wellman, Wayne M., Milton A. Maxwell, and Paul O'Hollaren, "Private Hospital Alcoholic Patients and Changing Conception of the 'Typical' Alcoholic," *Quart. J. Stud. Alc.*, 18:388–404, 1957.

30. World Health Organization, Expert Committee on Mental Health, *Report on the First Session of the Alcoholism Subcommittee, World Health Organization*, Tech. Rep. Ser., No. 42, 1951, pp. 21–24.

chapter 29

Alcoholism
and suicidal behavior[*]

Ernest G. Palola, Theodore L. Dorpat,
and William R. Larson

The aim of this chapter is to explore the relationship of alcoholism and suicide. The report of research is divided into two phases, aimed at a coverage of suicidal and alcoholic behavior from two possible poles. Part One consists of an examination of alcoholism preceding attempted suicide and completed suicide. Part Two is a partial report of research done on suicidal behavior in a group of alcoholics.

PART ONE: ALCOHOLISM PRECEDING ATTEMPTED AND COMPLETED SUICIDE

The Problem

It is our intention to determine to what extent alcoholism with its personal and social consequences is a precondition of suicidal behavior. This investigation will bring evidence to bear on both psychiatric and sociological theories on suicide and its relationship to alcoholism.

Karl Menninger (19) has provided an important link between sociological and psychiatric views with his concept of "chronic suicide." His formulations in this area are of particular interest to workers concerned with alcoholism, inasmuch as alcoholism is seen as a "poison," or "slow death," and a manifestation of self-destructive tendencies. The writings of Freud (7)

[*] This chapter was written especially for this book. The research upon which it is based was supported in part by grants from the State of Washington 171 Fund. The authors wish to express their gratitude to the medical students who assisted in the data gathering process: Carl Allen, William Anderson, John Boswell, Richard Fredericks, Raymond Leidig, and Tore Nielsen.

and Zilboorg (31) make use of such concepts as death instincts and self-destructive tendencies in depressive reactions.

Sociological theories on suicide have proceeded mainly from the investigations of Durkheim (4), which represent the first application of empirical methods and the utilization of sociological variables in the study of suicide. More recently, authors such as Gibbs and Martin (8, 9, 10) and Henry and Short (12) have extended Durkheim's theories on the relationship of lack of social integration to suicide.

As Schmid and Van Arsdol (26), as well as Stengel and Cook (29), have shown, characteristics of persons who attempt suicide are remarkably different from those of persons who complete suicide. It is necessary to include samples of both groups to study the full spectrum of suicidal behavior in alcoholics and to make clear possible differentiating elements between alcoholism and attempted suicide as opposed to completed suicide. Several general psychiatric studies present data on the frequency of alcoholism in samples of attempted or completed suicides. Moore (20), in this country, reported that 11 per cent of 1,195 cases admitted to a general hospital for attempted suicide were alcoholic, while Schmidt, O'Neal, and Robins (27) found that alcoholics constituted 13 per cent of 109 cases of attempted suicide admitted to a general hospital. In a broad compilation of published studies, Dahlgren (2) of Sweden found that the frequency of alcoholism reported in most studies of attempted or completed suicide was about 30 per cent.

Nearly all of these studies were biased because they considered only hospitalized patients or, in the case of completed suicide, were retrospective studies of patients formerly hospitalized. Since many attempted suicides are never reported, there is no way of avoiding bias for that group. To avoid the bias of previous studies of completed suicide this study aims to obtain a completely unselected, consecutive series of completed suicide. There has been only one such study made by Robins, Gassner, and Kayes (23) who report an alcoholism prevalence of 31 per cent.

Samples and Methods

The data on attempted suicide for this portion of the over-all study were obtained by including all admissions for attempted suicide to the King County Hospital, in King County, Washington, during the months of July and August, 1957 and 1958. This hospital is an excellent source for such material, since all known attempted suicides are admitted routinely on mandatory referral from physicians and law enforcement officers.* During the 4 months of data collecting, 121 consecutive admissions were interviewed. A complete work-up was carried out on each patient. Psychiatric histories were taken, using members of the patient's family or other friends

* Washington is one of the four states in the Union in which suicidal attempts are considered criminal violations.

whenever possible. In addition, a lengthy questionnaire was completed on each case, which included material on social background, drinking history, medical history, and psychiatric care.

The initial data on cases of completed suicide were secured through contact with the King County Coroner's office. The completed suicides that were reported to that office between July 1, 1957, and July 1, 1958—there were 114 in all—were included in the study. The basic data were gathered by means of interviews with friends, relatives, and associates of the deceased person. In addition, his physician was asked to provide medical information, and the records of State and local hospitals, social agencies, and the city and county jails were covered for pertinent material. Because of the obvious sensitivity of the material covered in the interview, senior medical students with considerable interviewing skill and experience were used in contacts with the respondents. When the interviews were completed, the questionnaire and interview schedules were edited and coded, and the data were then punched on IBM cards for ease of handling and rapid analysis.

Classification of cases as to alcoholism was carried out by means of the criteria proposed by Jackson (14), who developed a Scale of Preoccupation with Alcohol. The diagnosis of alcoholism was made when at least three items on the Scale of Preoccupation with Alcohol were answered affirmatively.*

Findings

1. *Prevalence of alcoholism*

Twenty-three per cent of the attempted suicides and 31.4 per cent of the completed suicides were diagnosed as alcoholics on the basis of having manifested at least three of the criteria for alcoholism. Information to determine alcoholism status was not available in 3 attempted and 9 completed cases so that percentages given here are based on 118 attempted suicides and 105 completed suicides, rather than the totals of 121 and 114 noted above. Considering all cases where information was available, the differences in the amount of alcoholism in the attempted and completed suicide groups proved not statistically significant.

It is possible, however, that this is an underestimate of the extent of alcoholism in the two suicidal groups. Of the 118 attempted suicides and the 105 completed suicides for whom adequate drinking histories were available, 19.4 per cent and 4.8 per cent respectively could be termed "problem drinkers." Less conservative investigators might well have considered that the fact that these "problem drinkers" manifested at least one, and usually

---

* The relevant items are: (*a*) considering a morning drink to be a necessity; (*b*) staying drunk on workdays; (*c*) neglecting food in favor of drinking; (*d*) needing more alcohol to achieve the same effect; (*e*) feeling anxiety about having enough to drink; (*f*) feeling indifferent to brand or type of beverage alcohol; (*g*) sneaking drinks; (*h*) solitary drinking; (*i*) protecting alcohol supply; (*j*) drinking non-beverage alcohol.

two, of the criteria for alcoholism and, in addition, social, interpersonal, and economic maladjustment associated with drinking, would have warranted a diagnosis of alcoholism.

2. Sex and age distributions

In the attempted suicide group, 28.9 per cent of the males and 20 per cent of the females were alcoholic. Thirty-eight per cent of the males and 17.6 per cent of the females in the completed suicide study were alcoholic. There were no significant differences as to sex in either the attempted or completed groups. There was no significant difference in the rates of female alcoholism between the attempted and the completed groups. In the completed group, the male rate of alcoholism was higher, but not significantly higher, than in the attempted group.

With regard to age, the completed suicides in our study tended to be older than the attempted suicides. The mean age of the completed was 51.3 years as compared with a mean age of 35.1 years for the attempted suicides. There were no significant differences between the alcoholics and non-alcoholics in either the completed or attempted groups. The attempted alcoholics had a mean age of 34.1 years and the alcoholics who committed suicide successfully had a mean age of 49.4 years.

3. Suicidal behavior

Method, Setting, Notes, and Communication of Intent. A striking finding of this study is that the suicidal behavior of alcoholics closely resembles that of non-alcoholics. There were no significant differences between alcoholics and non-alcoholics in either the attempted or completed group in the suicidal method, in the setting within which the suicidal behavior occurred, or in the frequency with which they left suicidal notes. This finding is particularly important because the attempted and completed suicides differed significantly on all these variables.

In the attempted group, alcoholics and non-alcoholics alike tended to select some form of poison or a drug as the method of suicide (44 per cent). In the completed group more lethal methods such as hanging and firearms (40 per cent) were used. Leaving a suicidal note is regarded as a classic part of suicidal behavior, yet notes were found for only 15 per cent of the attempted suicide group. Among the completed cases, 38 per cent left notes.

The setting of the suicidal behavior ranged widely, with 77.7 per cent of the attempts being made in the company of others or with others nearby in the same dwelling. By contrast, 68 per cent of the completed acts occurred in isolated settings.

Those who completed suicide more frequently had communicated their intention to commit suicide than had those who attempted suicide unsuccessfully. Fifty-four per cent of the completed suicides had made statements to others of their intention, whereas only 23.4 per cent of the attempted subjects did so.

Drinking at the Time of Suicidal Behavior. As Table 1 indicates, alco-

TABLE 1

Attempted and Completed Suicide by Drinking at Time of Suicidal Behavior
and Alcoholic Status

		Alcoholics		Non-alcoholics	
		Per Cent	Number	Per Cent	Number
A. ATTEMPTED SUICIDE ($N = 119$) [a]	Drinking at the time	88.9	(24)	38.2	(35)
	Not drinking at the time	11.1	(3)	61.8	(57)
	Totals	100.0	(27)	100.0	(92)
		$\chi^2 = 23.56$; $P < .001$ (corrected for continuity)			
B. COMPLETED SUICIDE ($N = 83$) [a]	Drinking at the time	78.3	(18)	8.3	(5)
	Not drinking at the time	21.7	(5)	91.7	(55)
	Totals	100.0	(23)	100.0	(60)
		$\chi^2 = 36.93$; $P < .001$ (corrected for continuity)			

[a] Information to determine drinking at time of suicidal behavior was not available for two subjects who attempted suicide and for thirty-one subjects who completed suicide. Hence the discrepancy between these totals and the sample totals given in the text.

TABLE 2

Relationship of Alcoholism to Previous Attempts in Attempted Suicide and Completed Suicide

		Alcoholics		Non-alcoholics	
		Per Cent	Number	Per Cent	Number
A. ATTEMPTED SUICIDE (N = 114) [a]	Previous attempt	46.2	(12)	25.0	(22)
	No previous attempt	53.8	(14)	75.0	(66)
	Totals	100.0	(26)	100.0	(88)
B. COMPLETED SUICIDE (N = 88) [a]	Previous attempt	42.9	(9)	28.3	(19)
	No previous attempt	57.1	(12)	71.7	(48)
	Totals	100.0	(21)	100.0	(67)

[a] Information was not available for seven subjects who attempted suicide and twenty-six subjects who completed suicide. Hence the discrepancy between these totals and the sample totals given in the text.

holics in both attempted and completed groups showed significantly more drinking at the time of their suicidal behavior than non-alcoholics. For the purpose of this study, drinking at the time of suicidal behavior was defined operationally as having had two or more drinks in the 24-hour period preceding the attempted or completed suicide.

Previous Suicidal Attempts. Table 2 indicates that alcoholics in both the attempted and completed groups had more frequently made suicidal attempts in the past than had non-alcoholics. While the differences did not prove significant at the 5 per cent level of confidence, the trend is a strong one, particularly in the attempted group.

Many of the subjects studied had made more than one previous suicidal attempt, and in both the attempted and completed groups there was a noticeable tendency for repeated attempts to involve progressively more risk of death. The average number of attempts made by subjects in the various groups was as follows: Alcoholic Attempted Suicide—1.23; Alcoholic Completed Suicide—.47; Non-alcoholic Attempted Suicide—.32; Non-alcoholic Completed Suicide—.57.

Suicidal Intent. The attempted-suicide group, as mentioned earlier, tended to make use of less lethal methods and to make their attempts in settings which were conducive to being found by others. In many instances, other persons were notified by telephone just prior to the attempt so that rescue was assured. Consequently, in order to evaluate the extent to which seriousness of intent might be associated with other variables, the questionnaires and case materials of each individual were examined by a panel of five judges, who made independent ratings for each case. There was a high degree of agreement among the judges (3).

On the basis of these ratings, three classifications of suicidal intent were developed: "gesture," "ambivalent," and "serious." Those who made gestures were those who gave little evidence of intent to die and who tended to be manipulative of others in the course of their suicidal attempt. The ambivalent group is composed of those who made stronger attempts than the gesture group, made use of more dangerous methods, and gave evidence of a generally stronger intention to die, coupled with a vacillation of feelings. Those in the serious group provided much evidence of their wish to die, but ignorance of the methods or the fortuitous intervention of medical aid prevented success.

Seriousness of intent for the study groups as a unit varied directly with age. There were no significant differences between alcoholics and non-alcoholics in this respect (Table 3). For the total sample, the mean ages in the various intent groups are: gesture—27.8 years; ambivalent—34.6 years; serious—44 years. The serious group closely resembled the completed suicide group in such variables as sex ratio, mean age, method used, setting of suicide, and psychiatric diagnoses (3).

As can be seen in Table 3, the majority of attempts reported in this study were rated as ambivalent for both groups, alcoholics and non-alcoholics.

Nearly three-fourths of the alcoholics made ambivalent attempts. These attempts were made in a potentially dangerous way, but very often they were carried out in such a manner that rescue or discovery was possible. Often the victim would take a dangerous poison after making sure an antidote was available. It would appear that suicidal attempts of this caliber are a kind of "gamble with death" (30). Sleeping pills and sedatives were the most frequently used method among the ambivalent group.

TABLE 3

Suicidal Intent in Attempted Suicide by Alcoholic Status

	Gesture	Ambivalent	Serious	Total
Alcoholic	4	20	3	27
Non-alcoholic	20	50	21	91
Totals	24	70	24	118 [a]

[a] Because information to determine alcoholism status was not available in three attempted suicide subjects, this figure is 118 rather than 121 for the entire sample.

Precipitating Events. In the events that were judged to have precipitated the suicide, there were differences between alcoholics and non-alcoholics in the completed suicide group. Differences in the attempted group were less striking.

Among both alcoholics and non-alcoholics in the gesture- and ambivalent-intent categories the most frequent precipitating event concerned disrupted personal relationships with another, such as a "lover's quarrel." From the interview schedules, mixtures of anger and depression were seen, with the individual making use of the suicidal attempt to manipulate the loved one into restoring some former relationship. Spite, as well, was an often-noted motive; many records contain elements which clearly express attitudes of "you'll be sorry" and "you'll miss me when I'm gone."

The most common precipitating factor in the completed-suicide group was serious physical illness. Although alcoholics did not have a greater amount of physical illness just prior to their suicidal behavior than non-alcoholics, a sizable minority suffered from illnesses brought on by the alcoholism (cirrhosis of the liver, for example). Fifty-eight per cent of those alcoholics who committed suicide had a major physical illness which was deemed to have contributed to this suicide. The rate of physical illness in the completed group was nearly twice that in the attempted group. For two of the alcoholics and nine of the non-alcoholics depression associated with recent major surgery appeared to contribute to the suicidal motivation.

The recent loss of a family member was a notable precipitating factor in depressive reactions which led to suicide. Approximately one-third of those in both the attempted and completed groups lost a family member by death, divorce, or separation in the year preceding the suicidal behavior.

Although there were no significant differences between alcoholics and non-alcoholics or between attempted suicides and completed suicides in the rate of such losses, there was a qualitative difference between alcoholics and non-alcoholics. Among non-alcoholics the most common loss was death of a loved one, but among alcoholics there were far more separations and divorces apparently brought about by the subject's alcoholism.

One precipitating event found in the alcoholics who completed suicide but not in other groups was discharge from jobs. Eighteen per cent of these thirty-three alcoholics had been fired from their jobs just prior to their suicide, and in all of these excessive drinking was the reason given for the discharge.

4. Psychopathology and psychiatric diagnosis

There were no major differences between alcoholics and non-alcoholics in psychiatric diagnoses for both the attempted-suicide group and the completed-suicide group. Sixteen per cent of the alcoholics in the completed group and 22 per cent of the attempted group were also psychotic, suffering from either schizophrenia or some type of psychotic depression. The majority of the remaining alcoholics were characterized by a wide range of character or personality disorders.

The prevalence of incarceration among alcoholics was approximately four times that among non-alcoholics in both the attempted and completed groups. Two-thirds of the alcoholics who completed suicide had been in prison, jail, or reform school, and of these about 60 per cent of the internments had been for excessive drinking. In the alcoholic attempted group, 80 per cent had jail records, with 50 per cent of the arrests being for drinking.

A careful study of the case histories of both groups was made by a psychiatrist in conjunction with the interviewers to determine the presence or absence of depressive symptoms. No differences appeared between alcoholics and non-alcoholics in this aspect of the study. Indeed, *all* of the completed-suicide cases, and all but six of the attempted-suicide group, showed evidence of depression at the time of their suicide. The six who showed no evidence of depression were in the gesture category. For some, depression included only expressed feelings of worthlessness and guilt, but in a fairly large number, it included more severe symptoms such as marked psychomotor retardation, severe insomnia, loss of appetite, and feelings of intense self-hatred and hopelessness. A large number found it impossible to meet their daily tasks.

5. Social integration and changes in social integration

For the study as a whole, a Scale of Social Integration and a Scale of Changes in Social Integration were constructed.* The Scale of Social Inte-

* A description of the items and the method for scoring is available from the senior author, E. G. Palola, at the University of Washington School of Medicine, Seattle, Washington.

gration contained items covering: (*a*) steady employment, (*b*) permanent residence, (*c*) membership in formal organizations, (*d*) marital status, (*e*) family status, (*f*) children. The Scale of Change in Social Integration covered the year prior to the suicidal behavior and included measures of changes in (*a*) employment, (*b*) residence, (*c*) religious activity, (*d*) formal organizational membership, (*e*) health, (*f*) interpersonal relationships, (*g*) financial status, (*h*) family status, (*i*) use of alcohol, drugs, and gambling.

When alcoholics and non-alcoholics were compared on the Scale of Social Integration, it was found that in both the attempted and completed groups, alcoholics showed a significantly lower level of social integration. In the attempted group, 62.9 per cent of the alcoholics showed low social integration as compared with 30.7 per cent of the non-alcoholics. In the completed group, 51.5 per cent of the alcoholics as compared with 23.6 per cent of the non-alcoholics were in the low-integration group. The differences, as measured by chi-square, were significant at the 1 per cent level (attempted suicide: $\chi^2 = 11.37$, $df = 2$, $P < .01$; completed suicide: $\chi^2 = 12.89$, $df = 2$, $P < .01$).

On the Scale of Changes in Social Integration, the alcoholics in both groups exceeded the non-alcoholics. In the attempted group, 66.7 per cent of the alcoholics and 30.6 per cent of the non-alcoholics showed a high change in social integration in the year preceding the onset of the suicidal behavior. The equivalent figures for the completed-suicide group are 58.6 per cent for the alcoholics as compared with 23.8 per cent for the non-alcoholics. Again the differences as measured by chi-square are significant at the 1 per cent level (attempted suicide: $\chi^2 = 9.86$, $df = 1$, $P < .01$; completed suicide: $\chi^2 = 10.65$, $df = 1$, $P < .01$).

The change in nearly all subjects involved a decrease in social integration. On the Change of Social Integration Scale, it was also possible to describe the direction of change for each item. A plus score designated an increase in social integration and a minus score a decrease. When these plus and minus scores for changes were added for each subject, it was found that the cumulative direction score was in a minus direction for all of the alcoholics in both groups. Only six of the non-alcoholics in the attempted-suicide group and one of the non-alcoholics in the completed-suicide group showed a cumulative direction score in a plus direction.

There is evidence that both groups, non-alcoholics as well as alcoholics, had a lower than normal degree of social integration. For example, only 53 per cent of completed suicides and 44 per cent of the attempted suicides were married. A more comprehensive study of the data on social integration is being prepared for later publication.

Discussion

The data presented in the first part of this study have clearly shown a high rate of alcoholism among those who attempt suicide and those who complete the act. The finding that 31.2 per cent were alcoholic in the completed suicides is especially significant, since this is only the second study to use clinical psychiatric interviews on an unselected consecutive sample of suicide subjects (23). Also, in the present study, the prevalence of alcoholism for both sexes in both attempted and completed groups is extraordinarily high, since the rate of alcoholism in 1958 for adults in Washington was 4.2 per cent.[*] Since the ratio of females to male alcoholics in this state in that year was one to six, the prevalence of female alcoholics in both groups is even higher than that of males.

Stengel (29) has put forward a strong plea for separate study of those who have attempted and those who have completed suicide. In his view, they represent two different though overlapping populations. The findings in this study for alcoholics and non-alcoholics alike support his formulation. The difference in the two groups is explained by differences in intent, with the serious-intent category most closely resembling the completed-suicide group. Other evidence for the overlap between the groups is the finding in this study that over 40 per cent of those alcoholics who completed suicide had made previous attempts. The extent of overlap between these two groups will be unknown until an adequate follow-up study is made of alcoholics who have attempted suicide. No such studies have been made on alcoholics, and only one long-term follow-up study of attempted suicides has been made. Schneider (28), in France, found that 11.8 per cent of 372 attempted-suicide patients had completed suicide after 18 years.

Karl Menninger looks on alcoholism itself as a kind of "chronic suicide" and a manifestation of self-destructive tendencies. Relating alcoholism to suicide, Menninger (19, p. 168) says: ". . . alcoholism addiction can be thought of not as a disease but as a suicidal flight from disease, a disastrous attempt at self-cure of an unseen inner conflict, aggravated but not primarily caused (as many think) by external conflict." We postulate that alcoholism is in some ways an "ambivalent suicide" which for a time may serve as a substitute or defense against total self-destruction. The data in this paper indicate that alcoholics who make suicidal attempts are on the average about 15 years younger than alcoholics who complete the act. It seems that ambivalent attempts appear early in the alcoholic's drinking career, but that completed suicide is seen after many years of excessive drinking when the problems consequent to excessive drinking are added to those originally present.[†] Those in the ambivalent group take a risk of dying, but they seek relief and rescue from their problems. From them, statements such as the following were obtained: "I just wanted to sleep—I didn't care what happened"; "I wanted to get away." In their wish for a prolonged sleep through the use of sleeping pills there is a similarity to the temporary oblivion sought by alcoholics in their drinking.

From the findings of the present study we have concluded that depression

[*] Department of Health of the State of Washington, Alcoholism Division, 1959.

[†] The authors have known of many members of Alcoholics Anonymous who have seen their membership in that group as the only alternative to suicide.

is invariably present in both alcoholics and non-alcoholics who make serious attempts or who complete suicide. Many psychiatric writings have emphasized the danger of suicide in the depressive psychoses, but little has been said on depressive reactions leading to suicide in others, such as alcoholics. The clinical histories of the alcoholics considered in this study revealed that many had been more or less depressed for years, but that the precipitating factors of loss of health, jobs, or loved ones had brought about a final severe depression leading to suicide * (and alcoholism was the predominant factor in bringing about the loss of jobs and the loss of loved ones).

What sort of bridge is there between various sociological theories (4, 8, 12) having to do with "social integration" and suicide and the psychiatric studies of motivation in suicide? In what way do changes in social integration impinge on the individual? Particularly suggestive leads in this connection are, we believe, provided by a comparison of the psychoanalytical studies of French (6) on the theme of hope with a recent sociological study by Meier and Bell (18) on the subject of anomia and its relation to differential access to the achievement of life goals. Meier and Bell use the concept of anomia in its psychological sense of hopelessness and despair. They showed in their study that individuals who had a high "index of means for the achievement of life goals" † had low anomia scores, whereas those with low index scores had high anomia scores. In their conclusions there is a remarkable congruence with the work of French. Writing of the role of hope in goal-directed behavior French (6, p. 53) says, "Hope is based on present opportunity and on memories of recent sucess," and discusses the channelizing or integrating influence that hope has on behavior. When hope disappears through lack of opportunities to reach life's goals, destructive drives previously subordinated to other goals become discharged. These impulses may then be released against the self in the form of total self-destruction. The findings in the present study on social integration, and changes therein, are consistent with such an interpretation. While the relationship of alcoholism to suicidal behavior is complex, it would appear that alcoholism contributes to suicidal behavior through its disintegrating social and personal consequences.

PART TWO: SUICIDAL BEHAVIOR AMONG ALCOHOLICS

The Problem

The work presented earlier in this chapter has dealt with the phenomena of suicide and alcoholism and has concentrated primarily on the characteristics of those people engaging in some sort of suicidal behavior. An im-

---

* Schmale (25) has summarized many recent studies on the hopelessness and depression which may follow loss of a loved one and which serves frequently as a precipitating factor in a variety of medical and psychiatric disorders.

† The index included the variables "socio-economic status, class identification, age, social isolation, occupational mobility, marital status, and religious preference" (18, p. 201).

portant finding was that the incidence of alcoholism was 27 per cent for the attempted- and completed-suicide groups combined. This figure, however, does not indicate the incidence of suicidal behavior among *alcoholics*. This question is examined here in Part Two for three samples of alcoholics.

Associated with the general problem of the extent of suicidal behavior among alcoholics are other questions for which answers are sought in this study: What is the incidence of suicidal behavior among alcoholics? What role does prior Skid-Row experience play in relation to the presence or absence of suicidal behavior? Has the alcoholic lost control of his drinking at the time of suicidal behavior? What is the extent of drinking prior to and at the time of any suicidal activity? Is an alcoholic more likely to be preoccupied with suicidal intentions while drinking or while sober? Is he most prone toward suicidal acts just at the beginning, during, or after a drinking bender? Since the research being discussed is in progress and involves more data than can be presented at this point, only evidence relevant to the above questions is offered here.

Sample and Methods

1. *The Sample*

The sample ($N = 123$) consists of three subgroups of male alcoholics drawn from the Seattle area between January 1 and July 15, 1959. The first of these subgroups ($N = 49$) was drawn from the Seattle Police Rehabilitation (S.P.R.) Project for Alcoholics. The Rehabilitation Project (16) recruits primarily from the Skid-Row area in Seattle and, in consequence, treats alcoholics who are still drinking. For approximately a 3-month period (April through June, 1959), every white patient with at least a 30-day sentence was interviewed to develop this first subgroup. The second subgroup ($N = 24$) was selected from King County Hospital (K.C.H.) in Seattle where every alcoholic patient admitted to the psychiatric ward was interviewed during June and July, 1959.

Unfortunately, the recruiting procedures involved are biased toward the lower socio-economic class, so that the development of a representative sample from all socio-economic strata was not feasible. The third subgroup of alcoholics ($N = 50$) was made up of members of Alcoholics Anonymous. The only criteria used in selecting A.A. members to be interviewed were that they be male, white, and sober for at least 2 years. Since no list or records of A.A. members were available, a random-sampling technique was not possible. In selecting this subgroup, consideration was given only to balancing the group in terms of geographic distribution in the Seattle area. It is important to note, also, that the questions about drinking and suicidal behavior asked of this latter subgroup referred to experiences which occurred prior to joining A. A.

2. *Instruments, interview format, and statistical analysis*

Initially, ten A.A. members were contacted in order to ascertain the extent of their personal experience with suicidal behavior and the possible resistances which might be encountered in gathering this kind of information from alcoholics. From these preliminary interviews and from the experience acquired during the previously described first phase of our research (Part One of this chapter), a new schedule was developed which was particularly suited for the problem at hand. This new schedule contained about a hundred items which covered aspects of family background, suicidal behavior, characteristics of the drinking patterns (with reference to any suicidal attempt or serious suicidal contemplation), and information concerning perceived links between alcoholism and suicide. In addition, a questionnaire was used to assess the drinking history of each alcoholic. This questionnaire contained about a hundred statements drawn primarily from the work of Jellinek (17). For each of the statements about drinking, the informant was asked to indicate the age at which he first experienced the symptom in question. The statements themselves described behavior directly related to the drinking act, psychological experiences such as periods of depression, resentment, guilt, religious need, family sanctions against drinking, and, finally, help sought for the drinking problem.

The interviews were conducted on an individual basis and were centered on a discussion of alcoholism and suicidal behavior. Suicidal behavior was defined as both the contemplation of suicide * and actual suicidal attempts. The interview was guided by the general schedule mentioned earlier, and attention was focused on the seriousness of the attempt if one had occurred, and on comparisons of multiple attempts. An effort was made to evaluate any tendency for thoughts of suicide, or attempts, to become progressively more serious as preoccupation with and domination by alcohol developed in the drinking history. The actual time required to complete the interview, not including the drinking history which was reserved for the subjects' own time, varied from 30 minutes to 2 hours, depending on the ease with which the subjects could offer information and on the extent of their experience with suicidal behavior.

The drinking-history questionnaire was given to respondents with the directions to read the accompanying instructions and to return it to the interviewer at some later date when it had been completed. This procedure was used so that the subjects could fill out the questionnaire at their leisure when recall for the ages requested would be easier than during the formal interview period itself.

The data from interview schedules and questionnaires were coded and card-punched for IBM 650 analysis, based upon an item-analysis program that produces an output in the form of percentages and frequencies for each of the information sources used. Additional analyses in the form of cross-tabulations were performed in the same manner when preselected variables were held constant.

---

* Thoughts of suicide were considered serious contemplations of taking one's life to the extent that plans were set down but not carried out.

Findings and Interpretation

1. *The prevalence of suicidal behavior among alcoholics*

For the combined samples, 17.1 per cent or 21 of the alcoholics had attempted suicide, 29.3 per cent or 36 evidenced serious contemplation of suicide, and 53.6 per cent or 66 reported no suicidal experience. The active alcoholics (K.C.H. and S.P.R.) reported the least amount of suicidal behavior and the A.A. group reported the most suicidal behavior in terms of both thoughts and attempts (Table 4). Seventy-four per cent or 54 of the

TABLE 4

Suicidal Behavior among Alcoholics

	A.A.		K.C.H.-S.P.R.		Totals	
	Per Cent	*Number*	*Per Cent*	*Number*	*Per Cent*	*Number*
None	24.0	(12)	74.0	(54)	53.6	(66)
Thoughts only	52.0	(26)	13.7	(10)	29.3	(36)
Attempts only	24.0	(12)	12.3	(9)	17.1	(21)
Totals	100.0	(50)	100.0	(73)	100.0	(123)

$$\chi^2 = 31.15; P < .001$$

active alcoholics disclaimed suicidal behavior, as compared with only 24 per cent or 12 of those who are now A.A. members.

Since this was the first investigation of the incidence of suicidal behavior among an alcoholic sample in the United States, no comparable data on suicidal behavior are available in the literature.[*] Assuming that the frequencies of suicidal intention, whether serious contemplations or actual attempts at taking one's life, are reliable estimates of this behavior, several interpretations can be presented to account for the behavior observed in the alcoholics who were questioned.

One possible interpretation of the differences between the groups in suicidal attempts involves the thesis set forth by Karl Menninger (19) that alcoholism, as a kind of "chronic suicide" (a form of self-destructiveness that is less certain than death by shooting, hanging, or drowning), may be thought of as a substitute for suicide. If this thesis is tenable, the higher percentage of attempts among the A. A.'s during their drinking history would suggest that they had reached a point where alcoholism no longer fulfilled their needs for escape from the unpleasantness of life. Something more devastating was required to absolve them of guilt and enforce their self-destructive pattern; this new act could be suicide. Extending this reason-

---

[*] Glatt (11) investigated the frequency of suicidal ideas and suicidal attempts obtained by questioning patients admitted to Warlingham Park Hospital in England. Among seventy-five male alcoholics, twenty-four (32 per cent) had contemplated suicide earnestly and nineteen (25.3 per cent) had actually attempted suicide.

ing, the K.C.H.-S.P.R. alcoholics—that is, people who have not as yet arrested their addictive drinking—apparently were still realizing some satisfaction from the escapism provided by their drinking. Indeed, several of the active alcoholics stated that they were not interested in curbing their excessive drinking, that they enjoyed it and had nothing better to do.

A second possible interpretation involves questioning the initial assumption made above concerning the reliability of the expressed suicidal experiences. Considering the groups individually, one could probably say that the incidence of reported suicidal activity among the A.A. group is the most reliable. Joining A. A. and living in accordance with its principles are essentially processes of resocialization or relearning. The actual procedures involved in realizing this transformation necessitate a free and honest appraisal of one's past experiences—not only relating past drinking and the way in which it has dominated one's life, but also discussing relationships with others and especially appraising oneself as an individual. Within this type of environmental context, the admission of suicidal thoughts or attempts may assume a socially desirable tenor. External to the A.A. environment—that is, in society at large—few socially desirable expressions are registered toward people contemplating suicide or relating past experience of a suicidal attempt; society places a stigma upon those individuals who toy with suicidal undertakings. Moreover, evidence in the present study that there was a freer flow of information in the A.A. interviews was found in the overwhelming willingness of the A. A.'s to discuss their drinking histories and suicidal behavior. In contrast, more interviews among K.C.H. and S.P.R. alcoholics, who had had no A.A. experience, involved active or latent hostility toward the interviewers and toward the subject being discussed. Implied here is the notion that practicing alcoholics, in displaying hostility and defensiveness during the interviews, may have been denying their experiences with suicidal behavior.* If this was so, then the actual amount of suicidal behavior involved with alcoholism is probably much greater than reported in this study.

Still a third interpretation of the differences in reported suicidal behavior may be offered after we consider the possible impact of Skid-Row experience on the lives of alcoholics.

2. Skid-Row experience and suicidal behavior

It can be seen from Table 5 that, while there is a relationship between

---

* Some measure of the relative defensiveness or self-protection of the alcoholics in this study might assist in checking the hypothesis that the amount of suicidal behavior by the practicing alcoholics is actually low as compared to the A.A. group. In consequence, data relevant to the testing of this hypothesis are now being processed. That hostility and defensiveness were present in the interviews is exemplified in such remarks of practicing alcoholics as the following: "Nobody but an alcoholic can understand an alcoholic." "What's the use of studying alcoholism . . . it's with us and we've got to live with it." "Why do you guys waste your time studying something that can't be beat?"

Skid-Row experience and suicidal behavior, the direction of the relationship is different for the two groups shown. For those in the still actively drinking group (K.C.H.-S.P.R.), Skid-Row experience was related to thoughts of suicide, and its absence to attempts. For the A.A. members, the opposite relationship was found: attempts were associated with the presence of Skid-Row experience and thoughts with the absence of Skid-Row experience (A. A.: $\chi^2 = 6.64$, $df = 2$, $P < .01$; K.C.H.-S.P.R.: $\chi^2 = 6.01$, $df = 2$, $P < .05$).

TABLE 5

Skid-Row Experience and Suicidal Behavior

Suicidal Behavior		Skid-Row Experience						Total
		Yes		No		No Response		
		Per Cent	Number	Per Cent	Number	Per Cent	Number	Numbers
None	A.A.	9.4	(5)	10.4	(5)	9.1	(2)	(12)
	K.C.H.-S.P.R.	54.7	(29)	41.7	(20)	22.7	(5)	(54)
Thoughts only	A.A.	5.7	(3)	29.2	(14)	40.9	(9)	(26)
	K.C.H.-S.P.R.	15.1	(8)	2.1	(1)	4.5	(1)	(10)
Attempts only	A.A.	11.3	(6)	6.2	(3)	13.6	(3)	(12)
	K.C.H.-S.P.R.	3.8	(2)	10.4	(5)	9.1	(2)	(9)
Totals		100.0	(53)	100.0	(48)	100.0	(22)	(123)

In interpreting these findings and their relevance for the findings in the preceding section, let us suppose, in the tradition of Durkheim (4), that integration into social groups sustains the individual; that the groups to which one belongs provide the goals, rewards, and satisfactions which make life worth living; that without a group structure toward which one can look for guidance and support, life for the individual has no meaning.* From this standpoint, we are inclined to note at once that the chronic Skid-Row drunkard is usually considered (24) to be closely attached to alcohol and relatively detached from people and, further, that his interest in other people decreases as his interest in alcohol increases. He is, then, generally viewed as being influenced minimally by the normative structure of society and as exemplifying anomic traits. Pittman and Gordon (21, p. 145) in their study of the chronic police case inebriate conclude that he is "the product of a limited social environment and a man who never attained more than a minimum of integration in society. He is and has always been at the bottom of the social and economic ladder; he is isolated, up-rooted, unattached, disorganized, demoralized and homeless, and it is in this context that he drinks to excess." Accordingly the chronic drunkard of this type is an individual realizing little gratification from participation in an integrated and organized societal environment. However, as Rubington (24) points out, a

* With regard to the importance of primary groups in this context, Faris' (5, p. 255) observations are noteworthy: "Because of the strength and near universality of the desire for primary relations it is almost impossible to find individuals in daily proximate association who do not spontaneously form into a number of small primary groups. It is apparently necessary that most persons find at least some groups of very small size."

most important factor common to chronic drunkenness offenders is their participation in a deviant subculture of a compensatory nature.* Jackson and Connor (15, p. 479) have also pointed to the subcultural experiences of the Skid-Row alcoholics in stating:

The Skid Row alcoholics, like other types of deviants, have tended to seek out social relationships with others who share their particular pattern of deviant behavior. On Skid Row they find a congenial atmosphere where the condemnation of their behavior by the larger society is missing, and a group which enables them to survive. Once they have become members of such groups they become isolated from the larger society; the new group reinforces their deviant tendencies and all those characteristics which are useful to the group. Socially approved motivations and patterns of behavior which are not useful to the group go unrewarded or are actively discouraged.

Participation in the Skid-Row subculture by chronic alcoholics can thus be viewed as an experience leading toward a partial reduction of social isolation. The Skid-Row alcoholic has a supportive social organization in the social acceptance and security offered in group interactions of the deviant subculture.† This way of life may be quite primitive from other points of view, but may be sufficient nonetheless to sustain the will to live in the Skid-Row alcoholic. It would therefore be considered a depressor of the suicide rate among Skid-Row alcoholics. The greater prevalence of thoughts of suicide rather than actual attempts among the K.C.H.-S.P.R. group having had extended Skid-Row experience in the present study would then be explained.

By contrast, as Charles R. Snyder has suggested in personal communication, the greater incidence of attempted suicide, rather than thoughts of suicide, for the A.A. members who had Skid-Row experience might be explained by hypothesizing that this group of alcoholics had essentially no supportive social group to which they were socially and psychologically assimilated. The A. A.'s, being typically middle-class alcoholics,‡ may have been alienated both from "middle-class society," in consequence of their recalcitrant drinking behavior, and from the Skid-Row subculture, because of their unfamiliarity and dissatisfaction with, and lack of acceptance by, that world. Hence, these alcoholics might experience more guilt, psychic impoverishment, and sense of worthlessness which could rapidly precipitate

---

* Indeed, Pittman and Gordon have also commented on group participation by Skid-Row inebriates in stating, ". . . observation of these men in their free milieu, Skid Row, revealed the existence of drinking cliques or groups. In many respects these groups are not different from those found in the larger society among non-inebriates; at any rate, they are characterized by norms, expectancies and status differences among the members" (21, p. 69).

† The fact that subcultural support is evident in the lives of Skid-Row alcoholics who are typically of lower-class origin with an unskilled occupational status would seem to indicate a necessary qualification to Powell's (22) notions concerning the relationship between dissociation among unskilled occupations and high suicide rates.

‡ Evidence for this in the present study was gleaned from such factors as occupation, religious affiliation, and educational attainments.

dramatic acts of self-destruction in the form of attempted suicide. In contrast, the Skid-Row alcoholics do have a rather well-developed group structure from which sympathy and a "sense of belonging" can be realized. Social support, which the respectable world withdraws, can be found with a minimum of effort from one's associates on Skid Row. It would be of considerable interest, incidentally, to study the frequency of suicidal behavior among alcoholic and non-alcoholic Skid-Row habitués to assess more fully the impact of the Skid-Row subculture in maintaining the lives of alcoholics.

3. *Loss of control over drinking and suicidal behavior*

Initially, the attempt to correlate the presence of suicidal behavior with the phases of alcoholism as outlined by Jellinek (17) was a task set for this study.* However, it was observed early in the study that the symptom order coincident with the various phases described by Jellinek did not pertain sufficiently. Since Jellinek derived his four phases from grouped data, the symptom order and phase sequence described was the one which best described his group of alcoholics. In the present study, an attempt was made to look at the individual's drinking and suicidal patterns so as to pinpoint the relationship between the two. Individual variation being what it is, attempts to reproduce the symptom order described by Jellinek were thwarted; it was found, for example, that frequently "benders" appeared before "blackouts" when analyses were carried out on an individual basis. At this point, additional work is being carried out to fulfill the initial task set forth, but results are not available.

An alternative procedure for approaching this problem was undertaken instead, using but a single item in the drinking history questionnaire. This item inquired as to the age at which the alcoholic thought he had lost control of his drinking. Loss of control of drinking was chosen on the assumption that this is the cardinal sign of alcoholism. Comparing this age to that at which suicidal behavior occurred provided some indication of the relationships involved. It is apparent from Table 6 that suicidal behavior (both

TABLE 6

Suicidal Behavior and Loss of Control Over Drinking

	Had Lost Control	Had Not Lost Control	No Response	Totals
Thoughts only	4	24	8	36
Attempts only	6	15	—	21
Totals	10	39	8	57

thoughts and attempts) was most likely to have appeared before the alcoholic admitted a loss of control over his drinking.

* See, also, Chapter 20.

This particular finding lends support to the hypothetical interpretation reviewed earlier that chronic drinking may serve as a substitute for suicidal behavior since it is known that the persons reporting no loss of control at the time of their suicidal behavior did ultimately become alcoholic. Self-destructiveness in the form of suicidal behavior was typically evidenced in their earlier drinking history, and the subsequent development of a full-blown alcoholic syndrome could therefore be viewed as a substitute for suicide. A key question at this point—and for which evidence was not gathered in the present study—is an assessment of whether or not and in what ways excessive drinking had become inadequate as an escape mechanism at the time suicidal intention emerged.

4. Drinking in the context of suicidal behavior

What is the extent of drinking prior to and at the time of any suicidal activity? Is an alcoholic more likely to be preoccupied with suicidal intentions while drinking or while sober? Is he most prone to suicidal acts just at the beginning, during, or after a drinking bender?

Table 7 indicates the distribution of responses to the question of whether

TABLE 7

Suicidal Behavior and Drinking at the Time

	Drinking	No Drinking	No Response	Total
Thoughts only	24	11	1	36
Attempts only	16	5	—	21
Total	40	16	1	57

drinking was taking place during suicidal thoughts and attempts. In this table, we find that drinking * was predominant at the time of both types of suicidal behavior.

Batchelor (1), in a study of 200 consecutive cases of attempted suicide, found 39 (19.5 per cent) had been drinking at the time of their attempt. In this part of the present study, 16 (76.1 per cent) out of 21 attempts were drinking at the time of the attempt. The higher percentage found here may result from the probabilities involved in drinking when comparing a relatively non-alcoholic sample (Batchelor's cases) with a strictly alcoholic sample. In the present chapter (Part Two), the proportion of alcoholics who reported drinking at the time of suicidal *thoughts* (66.7 per cent) is comparable to the proportion reported for the alcoholic *attempt* group. In Part One, by contrast, in an unselected sample, 88.9 per cent of the alcoholic attempted group and 78.3 per cent of the alcoholic completed group were drinking at the time of the attempt.

* The same definition for "drinking at the time" of suicidal behavior is used here as in Part One of this chapter.

In regard to the question of drinking prior to suicidal thoughts (Table 8), it can be seen that "no drinking" * was most common; for attempted

TABLE 8

Suicidal Behavior and Prior Drinking

	Drinking	No Drinking	No Response	Total
Thoughts only	9	13	14	36
Attempts only	15	6	—	21
Totals	24	19	14	57

suicides, "drinking" was most common. However, the difference, as measured by chi-square, is not significant at the 5 per cent level of confidence.

With reference to prior drinking and suicidal thoughts, "no drinking" was the most prevalent response which contrasts with the picture for drinking at the time. Yet prior drinking in conjunction with actual attempts at suicide suggests a pattern contiguous with drinking at the time of the attempt. The alcoholics frequently commented: "I thought suicide was the best way out . . . but we're all too yellow . . . more drinking helps us get the nerve to do it . . . ."; "Alcoholics are, in general, too scared to really take their own life . . . even though they may want . . . it takes a lot of drinking just to get confidence enough to try it . . . but still we don't succeed . . . ." Consistent with these statements, which imply a considerable degree of ambivalence about suicidal intentions, are the findings in Part One showing "ambivalent" attempts to be most frequent among the alcoholics.

Combining the results from Parts One and Two, we can realize some glimpse of the developmental pattern of suicidal behavior and alcoholism. Before a potential alcoholic has lost control of his drinking, he has experienced considerable dominance of his behavior by drinking. In fact, he has reached a point where his close friends, family members, and employer are commenting frequently about his excessive drinking. Thoughts of suicide as well as ambivalent and, to a lesser extent, gestural attempts † are observed at about this time also. At some later point, the potential alcoholic actually loses control of his drinking and enters into a period of chronic alcoholism. According to many of the A.A. interviews, this period of compulsive drinking, which leads to "hitting the bottom" where everything looks hopeless, would terminate in either of two ways: the alcoholic would join

---

* Defined as continuous drinking preceding the 24-hour period during which the thoughts or attempts occurred.

† From Jackson's (13) compilation of data on approximately 600 alcoholics, the mean age of onset of alcoholism was about 34 years. In Part One of the present study, the mean age of those alcoholics (26 out of 114) who attempted suicide was also about 34 years.

A. A., or he would commit suicide. This scheme implies that "hitting the bottom" after an extended term of alcoholism is a necessary prerequisite to forcing the alcoholic into either of the two alternative behaviors. Those alcoholics having had and still continuing to experience subcultural support in a Skid-Row environment may never attain the proverbial "bottom" in their drinking and hence not reach a situation of hopelessness which apparently requires some measure of action, or solution. A research effort concentrating primarily on tracing the *development* of suicidal behavior among people who eventually become alcoholic would shed some light on the above hypothesis.

SUMMARY OF PARTS ONE AND TWO

Two studies on the relationship of alcoholism to suicidal behavior have been reported in this chapter. Part One, "Alcoholism Preceding Attempted and Completed Suicide," is a sociological and psychiatric study of 114 completed suicides and 121 attempted suicides.

In this first study, there was a high prevalence of alcoholics in both the attempted and completed groups, with an especially high prevalence of female alcoholics. Alcoholics shared the characteristics of their respective groups in regard to the following variables: age distribution, degree of suicidal intent, method of suicide, suicidal notes, setting of suicide, and the communication of suicidal intent. Alcoholics had made more previous suicidal attempts than had non-alcoholics, and more often were drinking at the time of their suicidal behavior. Although there was a generally low level of social integration among the cases studied, alcoholics in both groups showed a significantly lower degree of social integration and greater change in social integration than did non-alcoholics.

Among alcoholics and non-alcoholics, depressive reactions leading to suicide were precipitated by the loss of family members and by serious physical illness, although for alcoholics these events were frequently caused in part by the excessive drinking. Psychiatric theories on the role of depression in suicide and theories relating suicide and alcoholism, as similar kinds of deviant behavior, were discussed. Suicide, it was suggested, appears in settings of hopelessness where the loss of social integration had denied the individual effective avenues to life goals. These are often lost to the alcoholic by the social and personal consequences of his drinking.

Part Two, "Suicidal Behavior Among Alcoholics," was concerned with the study of the extent of suicidal behavior among alcoholics, including the impact of Skid-Row experience, the role of drinking at the time, prior drinking, and the loss of control over drinking.

About half of the alcoholics contacted reported suicidal behavior, either serious contemplations of suicide or actual attempts. A considerable difference was observed in the amount of reported suicidal experience by the alcoholics who were still drinking and those who had arrested their drinking at the time of the interviews. It was suggested that the low incidence of attempted suicide observed among Skid-Row alcoholics, as compared with non-Skid-Row alcoholics, might be attributed to the subcultural support realized by this Skid-Row group, which would have the effect of maintaining the will to live.

In terms of both thoughts and attempts at suicide, it was observed that loss of control of drinking typically had not occurred. Drinking itself was found to be predominant at the time of both types of suicidal behavior. In contrast, the relationship between prior drinking and suicidal behavior was seen to be different for each kind of suicidal act.

References

1. Batchelor, I. R. C., "Alcoholism and Attempted Suicide," *J. Ment. Sci.*, **100**:451–461, 1954.

2. Dahlgren, K. G., *On Suicide and Attempted Suicide—A Psychiatrical and Statistical Investigation*, Sweden: Lund, 1945.

3. Dorpat, Theodore L., and J. L. Boswell, "Evaluation of Suicide Intent." (Paper in preparation.)

4. Durkheim, Emile, *Suicide* (trans. by John A. Spaulding and George Simpson), Glencoe, Ill.: Free Press, 1951.

5. Faris, Robert E. L., *Social Psychology*, New York: Ronald Press, 1952.

6. French, Thomas M., *The Integration of Behavior*, Vol. 1, Chicago: University of Chicago Press, 1952.

7. Freud, Sigmund, "Mourning and Melancholia," in *Collected Papers*, Vol. IV, London: Hogarth Press, 1925.

8. Gibbs, Jack P., and Walter T. Martin, "A Theory of Status Integration and Its Relationship to Suicide," *Amer. Sociol. Rev.*, **23**:140–147, 1958.

9. ———, "On Status Integration and Suicide Rates in Tulsa," *Amer. Sociol. Rev.*, **24**:392–396, 1959.

10. ———, "Status Integration and Suicide in Ceylon," *Amer. J. Sociol.*, **64**:585–591, 1959.

11. Glatt, M. M., "Alcoholism and Attempted Suicide," *Brit. Med. J.*, **2**:991, 1954.

12. Henry, Andrew F., and James F. Short, Jr., *Suicide and Homicide*, Glencoe, Ill.: Free Press, 1954.

13. Jackson, Joan K., Personal Communication.

14. ———, "Definition and Measurement of Alcoholism," *Quart. J. Stud. Alc.*, **18**:240–262, 1957.

15. ———, and Ralph G. Connor, "The Skid Road Alcoholic," *Quart. J. Stud. Alc.*, **14**:468–486, 1953.

16. Jackson, Joan K., Ronald J. Fagan, and Roscoe C. Burr, "The Seattle Police Department Rehabilitation Project for Chronic Alcoholics," *Fed. Prob.*, **22**:36–41, 1948.

17. Jellinek, E. M., "Phases in the Drinking History of Alcoholics: Analysis of a Survey Conducted by the Official Organ of Alcoholics Anonymous," *Quart. J. Stud. Alc.*, **7**:1–88, 1946.

18. Meier, Dorothy L., and Wendell Bell, "Anomia and Differential Access to the Achievement of Life Goals," *Amer. Sociol. Rev.*, **24**:189–202, 1959.

19. Menninger, Karl A., *Man Against Himself*, New York: Harcourt, Brace and Company, 1938.

20. Moore, Mary E., "Cases of Attempted Suicide in a General Hospital: A Problem in Social and Psychologic Medicine," *New Eng. J. Med.*, **214**:291–303, 1937.

21. Pittman, David J., and C. Wayne Gordon, *Revolving Door*, Glencoe, Ill.: Free Press, 1958.

22. Powell, Elwin H., "Occupation, Status and Suicide," *Amer. Sociol. Rev.*, **23**:131–139, 1958.

23. Robins, Eli, Seymour Gassner, and Jack Kayes, "The Communication of Suicidal Intent: A Study of 134 Consecutive Cases of Successful (Completed) Suicides," *Amer. J. Psychiat.*, **115**:724–733, 1959.

24. Rubington, Earl, "The Chronic Drunkenness Offender," *Ann. Amer. Acad. Pol. Soc. Sci.*, **315**:65–73, January 1958.

25. Schmale, Arthur H., "Relationship of Separation and Depression to Disease," *Psychosom. Med.*, **20**:259–277, 1958.

26. Schmid, Calvin F., and Maurice D. Van Arsdol, Jr., "Completed and Attempted Suicides," *Amer. Sociol. Rev.*, **20**:273–283, 1955.

27. Schmidt, E. H., Patricia O'Neal, and Eli Robins, "Evaluation of Suicide Attempts as Guide to Therapy," *J. Amer. Med. Assn.*, **155**:549–557, 1954.

28. Schneider, P. B., *La Tentative de Suicide*, Paris: Neuchatel, 1954.

29. Stengel, E., and N. G. Cook, *Attempted Suicide*, London: Chapman and Hall, 1958.

30. Weiss, J. M. A., "Gamble with Death in Attempted Suicide," *Psychiatry*, **20**:17–25, 1957.

31. Zilboorg, Gregory, "Differential Diagnostic Types of Suicide," *Arch. Neurol. Psychiat.*, **35**:270–291, 1936.

chapter 30

Criminal careers
of the chronic
drunkenness offender*

David J. Pittman and C. Wayne Gordon

The present study is concerned with an analysis of the criminal careers of the particular category of excessive drinker commonly referred to as the chronic drunkenness offender. The data reported here were obtained chiefly from the arrest and incarceration records of the 187 men who comprised the sample of a comprehensive study of the chronic police case inebriate; additional data were obtained by interview. These men were selected at random from those serving 30-day sentences or longer for public intoxication at the Monroe County Penitentiary, Rochester, N.Y., during a period of 1 year from October 1953 through September 1954. Only recidivists, men who had served at least one previous sentence for public intoxication at a short-term correctional institution, were included in the sample. These are men who are involved in a circular process of arrest, incarceration, release, and rearrest for public intoxication. They comprise a group for whom both the penal sanctions of the society and the existent community resources for rehabilitation have failed.

Description of the Sample

The socio-cultural characteristics of the chronic police case inebriates in the sample may be briefly summarized as follows:

Age. The average age of the men was 47.7; nearly half (45 per cent) were over 50 years of age.

* This chapter first appeared as an article in the *Quarterly Journal of Studies on Alcohol,* **19:**255–268, 1958, and later as part of the book, *Revolving Door,* Glencoe, Illinois: Free Press, 1958.

Racial Background. The sample was marked by a high proportion of Negroes (18 per cent) in comparison to their representation in the general population of Monroe County (2 per cent).

Nationality. The most frequent national groupings were English and Irish. Italians composed only 2 per cent of the sample, although between 15 and 20 per cent of the general population of Monroe County fall into this group.

Community Background. Thirty-eight per cent were born in New York State. Only 9 per cent were foreign born, a proportion that declined with decreasing age.

Marital Status. Although 59 per cent of the sample had at one time married, only four of these 187 men were "married and living with spouse" at the time of the study. The observed frequency of divorces and separations is far higher at all age levels than in the general population. For example, the expected frequency of never-married status was 13 per cent, the observed frequency, 41 per cent. The expected percentage of marriages terminating in divorce, widowerhood, and separation was 11, but the observed frequency was 96 per cent.

Educational Attainment. On the whole, the sample was an educationally disadvantaged group. Seventy per cent of the sample had not gone beyond grammar school, compared with 40 per cent in the general adult population of the area.

Occupational Status. Sixty-eight per cent had been unskilled workers, mainly laborers, 22 per cent had been skilled workers, and 3 per cent had been professional and allied workers, compared with 13, 46, and 22 per cent, in the respective categories, in the general population.

Religious Affiliation. Forty-two per cent of the men in the sample were Protestants, 40 per cent were Catholics, and 18 per cent professed no affiliation; there were no Jews.

Residential Mobility. The sample exhibited a moderate degree of stability in a geographic sense: 63 per cent lived in the community of present residence for a period of 2 years; 3 years or more of continuous residence may be taken as average stability. On the other hand, the sample was marked by high residential instability in terms of the number of places of residence within the community and the type of residence reported at arrest. Only 5 per cent were living in their own homes or apartments and only 6 per cent with relatives or friends, while 39 per cent could give no permanent address.

Social Class Background. The chronic police case inebriates were drawn heavily from the lower-class groupings in society, as reflected in the educational and occupational status of their fathers. Only 4 per cent of the fathers had completed grammar school, and 29 per cent had had no schooling whatsoever.

Despite the fact that the sample was drawn from a single penitentiary in a single metropolitan area, there is reason to believe that in their essential personal and social characteristics these men are representative of the general population characterized as chronic drunkenness offenders.

Criminal History

Students of social class, such as Warner (3) and Hollingshead (2), have pointed out in their empirical studies of communities that arrest and incarceration are phenomena alien to middle- and upper-class positions in a society and would be viewed by these classes with shame and abhorrence if either occurred to a member. Lower-class groups, on the contrary, are particularly vulnerable to arrest and incarceration in our society, and exposure to jailing is recorded in the folk music that appeals to lower-class groups in such songs as the recent "I'm in the Jailhouse Now" and the older "Birmingham Jail." Thus the music as well as other facets of the culture inform the observer that the lower class has had experience with the process of jailing and arrest. However, the society as a whole views the person who is arrested and incarcerated for any offense in a negative light, since this is a violation of the values that center around middle-class respectability.

On the cultural front, the individual who is constantly arrested and imprisoned has a stigma attached to him by the rest of society and is outside the pale of respectability. However, just as crucial as the cultural values, which define the responses of the class groups to arrest and incarceration, is the psychological impact of these two events on the individual who experiences them. It may be argued with logic that an isolated arrest without incarceration may have little influence on the personality, and this is perhaps the case. However, the psychological impact of a continual process of arrest and incarceration on the individual and on his self-conception are of a different order. Imprisonment, which occurs in American society in a framework of repression, authoritarianism, and rigidity, is not conducive to the development of initiative and maturity in the individual. The effects are perhaps more severe in the individuals who have committed only nuisance offenses such as public intoxication and vagrancy and whose behavior in many cases is symptomatic of an illness or disturbance in the personality.

Whatever be the value of this belief, the fact remains that society's accepted manner of dealing with the public drunkard is to place him in a county or city jail or penitentiary, along with other misdemeanants, where the framework is one of repression instead of treatment. In the process, the resources of the individual suffer further deterioration and the development of the institutionalized offender occurs—one whose pattern of life becomes a constant movement from incarceration to release and reincarceration, with increasing dependency on the institution.

The extent to which this revolving-door policy for the chronic inebriate is in operation can be discerned from a detailed examination of the criminal histories of the sample. These histories were obtained from the arrest and incarceration records of each offender as maintained by the county penal authorities. Admittedly these records are not accurate in all respects; like all criminal statistics they suffer from lack of reliability in reference to recording and from ambiguity in the behavioral categories. Nevertheless, these records do furnish a general picture of the minimum number and types of arrests which these men have experienced during their life careers.

Lifetime Arrest Experiences

Table 1 summarizes by four age categories the lifetime arrest experience

Table 1

Recorded Arrests for all Offences, by Age Categories

Frequency of Arrests	Under 35		35 Through 44		45 Through 54		55 and Over		All Ages	
	N	Per Cent	N	Per Cent	N	Per Cent	N	Per Cent	N	Per Cent
2 to 5	12	63.2	13	26.5	11	16.2	10	20.0	46	24.6
6 to 9	2	10.5	12	24.5	12	17.7	12	24.0	38	20.4
10 to 19	5	26.3	15	30.6	27	39.6	8	16.0	55	29.5
20 to 39	0	0	8	16.3	9	13.3	11	22.0	28	15.1
40 and over	0	0	1	2.1	9	13.2	9	18.0	19	10.4
Mean		6.8		11.6		18.1		22.9		16.5
Median		4.0		9.0		12.0		13.0		10.2
Total cases	19	100.0	49	100.0	68	100.0	50	100.0	186	100.0
Total arrests	129		571		1,234		1,144		3,078	

of the chronic police case inebriates. For the group as a whole, a total of 3,078 arrests were recorded for all offense categories ranging from criminal homicide to vagrancy. The individual number of arrests ranged from 2 in ten cases to the exteme of 110 arrests in one case. The mean frequency of arrests was 16.5, and the median for the entire group, 10.2. When the data are examined in terms of age categories, a significant though not unexpected finding emerges. The number of arrests increases progressively with increase in age. The mean number of arrests for offenders less than 35 years of age was 6.8, with a median of 4.0; for offenders aged 35 to 44 years, the mean was 11.6 and the median 9.0; for offenders aged 45 to 54, the mean was 18.1 and the median 12.0; while for the oldest group, aged 55 years or more, the mean number of arrests was 22.9 and the median 13.0. The difference in the medians between the two oldest categories, however, is only 1.

The difference in the means between these two groups is due to the presence of a larger number of the extreme cases (in terms of number of arrests) in the oldest category. Despite the increasing number of arrests related to increasing age, it should be noted that in the two older age brackets there are individuals who have had the minimum number of incarcerations to meet the sample criterion, and this evidences the fact that arrests and incarcerations for certain problem drinkers may be phenomena of later life, when all other props have been removed and complete deterioration of resources has occurred. In the younger age groups, those under 45, the pattern of excessive arrest and incarceration has already established itself; this is revealed by the fact that approximately 85 per cent of them have been arrested or incarcerated four or more times.

Arrests for Intoxication

In this investigation the focus is on the public inebriate who has been a problem to the constituted sources of authority; we are therefore especially concerned with the extent of public intoxication as viewed from the arrest records. Public intoxication was responsible for 2,387 arrests of the sample and accounted for 77.5 per cent of all their recorded arrests. This record, however, definitely underrepresents the number of arrests involving the excessive use of alcohol, since in many jurisdictions the individual is booked on a charge other than public intoxication—disorderly conduct or vagrancy, for example. Since there is no accurate means of assessing this factor, however, the official record must suffice for the present analysis.

Table 2 presents a frequency distribution of the arrests of the men in the

Table 2

Recorded Arrests for Public Intoxication, by Age Categories

Frequency of Arrests	Under 35		35 Through 44		45 Through 54		55 and Over		All Ages	
	N	Per Cent	N	Per Cent	N	Per Cent	N	Per Cent	N	Per Cent
2 to 5	15	78.9	24	48.9	21	30.9	18	36.0	78	41.9
6 to 9	3	15.8	12	24.5	17	24.9	7	14.0	39	21.0
10 to 19	1	5.3	9	18.4	14	20.5	8	16.0	32	17.2
20 to 39	0	0	3	6.1	9	13.3	11	22.0	23	12.3
40 and over	0	0	1	2.1	7	10.4	6	12.0	14	7.6
Mean		4.1		8.2		14.4		18.6		12.8
Median		2.3		5.3		8.3		9.0		6.0
Total cases	19	100.0	49	100.0	68	100.0	50	100.0	186	100.0
Total arrests	78		404		977		928		2,387	

sample for public intoxication, by four age categories. For all age groups combined the mean number of arrests is 12.8, with a median of 6.0. It is of interest to note that Bacon (1), in his survey of individuals arrested for intoxication in Connecticut in 1942, found the same median. The age category reveals a trend for the mean and median number of arrests to increase with age. For the offenders less than 35 years of age, the mean number of arrests is 4.1 with a median of 2.3; for those between 35 and 44 years of age, the mean is 8.2 and the median 5.3; for those of ages between 45 and 54, the mean is 14.4 and the median 8.3; and for those 55 years of age or older, the mean is 18.6 with a median of 9.0. Again the difference between the medians of the two upper age categories is small.

Substantial differences exist also in the range of the number of arrests for public intoxication. The range of the entire sample is from 2 to 110 arrests, but the widest ranges are in the two upper age categories. For those 55 and over the range is from 2 arrests to 110, but with the concentration in the frequency categories of less than 10 arrests. The same is true of the men in the 45 to 54 age bracket, which shows a range of 2 to 72 arrests. In the younger age brackets the ranges are much smaller: from 2 to 19 arrests in those under 35, and from 2 to 40 in those aged 35 to 44. From this analysis it appears that the offender who is marked by 30 or 40 or more arrests for public intoxication is atypical, and that the typical chronic police case inebriate has experienced fewer than 10 arrests on this particular charge.

Arrests for Other Offenses

As has been noted previously, 22.5 per cent of the arrests experienced by these men are on charges other than public intoxication. The mean number of arrests on other charges is 3.7, with a median of 2.0. When analyzed by age categories, the pattern of increase with age observed in public-intoxication arrests does not hold true for other charges. For those under age 35, the mean number of arrests on other charges is 2.7, the median 1.0; for those aged 35 to 44, the mean is 3.4 and the median 2.0; for those aged 45 to 54, the mean is 3.8 and the median 2.0; and for those aged 55 years and older, the mean is 4.3 and the median 2.1. On the whole, the number of arrests on charges other than public intoxication does not show a significant increase with aging after 35. This is reflected in the medians of the groups, although the means do increase slightly because of a subgroup of men whose offenses increase continually with age, resulting in a distortion of the total picture.

It is suspected that the increase in means with increasing age would be less if each bout with alcohol were accurately recorded as public intoxication instead of disorderly conduct or vagrancy. The explanation for the failure of other offenses to increase with age lies in the fact that at the end of the first-utilized age period, 35, there is a trend for the inebriates who have been involved in more serious crimes, such as automobile theft and burglary, to cease this type of criminal activity, and for the intoxication pattern of behavior to emerge as an adaptation to the life situation.

It should be noted that 31 per cent of the offenders (58 cases) have never been arrested on any charge other than public intoxication. However, the full meaning of this statistic cannot be discerned until an examination is made of the types of "other" offenses committed by the inebriates and their frequency. These data are presented in Table 3.

As is indicated in Table 3, the men in this sample have been arrested for a variety of offenses in their careers, ranging from the least frequent categories of gambling and criminal homicide to the more frequent one of vagrancy, for which they have a recorded 175 arrests. Following this in terms of frequency are 106 arrests for disorderly conduct and the same num-

ber for larceny, 48 for "aggravated assault," and 41 for burglary. It is interesting that these 187 chronic inebriates have among them experienced only
22 arrests for driving while intoxicated. In addition, they have recorded
100 arrests on a variety of miscellaneous charges such as trespassing and
begging.

TABLE 3

Distribution of Arrests for Offenses Other than Public Intoxication

Offense	Frequency	Number of Offenders	Percentage of All Offenders
Criminal homicide	2	2	1.1
Rape	5	4	2.2
Robbery	14	11	5.9
Burglary	41	24	12.8
Larceny	106	44	23.5
Car theft	10	7	3.8
Forgery, counterfeiting	6	5	2.7
Embezzlement, fraud	6	3	1.6
Carrying and possessing weapons	8	8	4.3
Offenses involving family and children	19	13	7.0
Narcotics law violations	12	6	3.2
Liquor law violations	9	2	1.1
Gambling	2	1	0.6
Aggravated assault	48	24	12.8
Disorderly conduct	106	41	22.0
Vagrancy	175	66	35.5
Driving while intoxicated	22	14	7.5
All other offenses	100	51	27.4
Total	691		

The statistics of arrest for offenses other than public intoxication raise
certain pertinent questions concerning the behavioral differences which can
be attributed to these categories. That these offense categories on the whole
are not qualitatively the same is obvious, but of what relevance are they for
the behavior of the inebriate?

We can divide the other offense categories into two groups: those which
appear to be related to the problems that are engendered by excessive drinking, and those that seem to bear little relationship to drinking behavior in
general. The offenses which appear to be closely associated with problems
of chronic inebriation, and which at times may be the official way of recording drunken behavior, are vagrancy, which becomes a high-risk category in the inebriate's excessive mobility and lack of steady employment,
and disorderly conduct, which may be the charge used instead of public
intoxication by the arresting officials. The same situation may prevail in the

case of aggravated assault, which may happen during the drinking bout. The married inebriate also tends to have problems with his family and children, particularly in reference to financial support. The offense categories of liquor law violations, driving while intoxicated, gambling, and the carrying and possessing of weapons have been assumed by some to be alcohol-related offenses, too. However, whether these offense categories bear a closer relationship to public intoxication than do certain others is very uncertain, and for that reason they have not been grouped with the public intoxication cases. In all, 59 of the men, 32 per cent of the sample, have been arrested not only for public intoxication but also for driving while intoxicated, vagrancy, disorderly conduct, aggravated assault, gambling, violation of liquor laws, offenses involving family and children, carrying and possessing weapons, or for one of the miscellaneous offenses designated "other" in Table 3.

Serious Crime

A substantial number of the incarcerated inebriates, however, have more serious criminal arrest records from the viewpoint of society as reflected by their arrest and conviction on felony charges which appear to have less relationship to the problem of excessive drinking. This group is comprised of sixty-nine men, 37 per cent of the sample, who have been charged with criminal homicide, rape, robbery, burglary, larceny, automobile theft, forgery, counterfeiting, embezzlement, fraud, and narcotics-law violations. Table 3 reveals that almost one-fourth of the sample have been arrested for grand or petit larceny, one out of eight has been arrested for burglary, one out of twenty for robbery, and one out of twenty-five for automobile theft.

Many of these offenses may have been committed under the influence of alcohol, yet the overwhelming majority of drinkers in general and inebriates in particular do not commit these acts under the same influence. The search for causation must delve deeper into the personality than noting that a man was inebriated when the act occurred. However, the finding that over one-third of the incarcerated inebriates have had ordinary criminal careers which were unsuccessful lends some support to the belief, hitherto unsupported by empirical fact, that a significant portion of the population incarcerated for public intoxication has spent time in state and federal correctional institutions, and that the pattern of excessive drinking is an adaptation to the lack of success in the criminal career.

One more conclusion can be drawn concerning this group of primarily felony violators. Examination of their arrest records reveals that the criminal career is generally divided into two distinct phases. The first covers the earlier years of life, generally when the man is under 40 years of age, and is marked by arrests and incarcerations for offenses that are seemingly unrelated to excessive use of alcohol. However, these arrests and incarcerations mean that their attempted criminal careers have been unsuccessful. They then drop out of active crime, not only because of ineptness and age, but also through the emergence of the new pattern of adaptation to societal norms and requirements which is reflected in increased drinking and life on Skid Row. In terms of their perception of the life situation, drinking forms a part of a new pattern of gratifying psychological needs, replacing the unsuccessful attempt to achieve that gratification in a career of crimes against property. However, this phasic pattern is neither rigid nor universal, since arrests and convictions for public intoxication do occur earlier in many histories, though not in great frequency. This pattern can perhaps best be demonstrated by the brief case history of one of the men in the sample.

Howard Raymond is at present 66 years old; he characterizes himself as a "worn-out drunk," but there is more to his history than that. At the age of 14 he was committed to an institution for juvenile delinquents in New York State for a series of thefts in his home town. At this reformatory, he states, he "learned a lot" which aided him in his later career, which is punctuated by numerous incarcerations in penal institutions. A chronological review of his criminal career reveals the following history.

At the age of 14 he was sentenced to a juvenile reformatory for theft. He was paroled, violated parole, was returned to the institution, and was paroled again. At 19 he was incarcerated in the state reformatory for theft and, while on parole from this institution, was sentenced to the state prison for rape. Again he was paroled, violated the conditions, and was returned to prison. At 28, because of his frequent violations of parole and a grand larceny offense, he was sentenced to an indeterminate term in prison. At 30 he was released from prison to join the Army, but he spent most of his time in the detention barracks for absence without leave, insubordination, and breaking arrest. He was given a dishonorable discharge from the Army. At 35 he was committed to the state prison after a conviction for grand larceny. He was released on parole. At 40, convicted of assault, he was once again sentenced to prison, this time for the rest of his natural life, but after 7 years his case was reviewed and he was paroled.

In the 19 years since then, his record has been free of any major infractions of the criminal code, but the significant point to note is that arrests for public intoxication, formerly isolated and infrequent in his arrest history, now show an increase in frequency. From the age of 47 to his present age of 66 his record shows more than 45 arrests for public intoxication. As far as society is concerned, Howard Raymond is no longer a serious problem in terms of the type of the offense he commits. He has drifted into a drinking pattern which may be viewed as an adaptation in substitution for his previous unsuccessful career in crime.

The case of Howard Raymond, though extreme in terms of its criminal history, amply illustrates the phasic quality of the career pattern. The early career in crime was unsuccessful and covered the first decades in the individual's attempted adjustment. The later pattern, which may have been foreshadowed in the earlier drinking history, is a rapid involvement in the pattern of public intoxication as an adaptation to the individual's disorganized life situation.

Three Offense Categories

The chronic police case inebriates are, in reality, a heterogeneous category in respect to their criminal behavior as reflected in their arrest records. This is true on two counts. First, there are wide variations in the number of times they have become involved with constituted authority as reflected in arrest and incarceration records. It is worth re-emphasizing, however, that the stereotyped picture of a man with 30 or 40 or more arrests and incarcerations is not an accurate statistical portrayal of the group, though many individuals in the sample reflect this attribute of frequent incarceration. Second, there are wide variations in criminal experience. There appear to be, indeed, three major subgroupings in reference to criminal records. One subgroup is composed of fifty-eight men (31 per cent of the sample) who have never been arrested on any charge other than public intoxication; a second is composed of fifty-nine men (32 per cent) who have been arrested not only for public intoxication but on charges which are probably associated with excessive use of alcohol, or on charges of a minor nature; and a third is composed of sixty-nine men (37 per cent) who not only are chronic police case inebriates but have been involved in serious violations of the legal norms of the society, such as felony offenses.

At this point, however, a word of caution concerning the reliability of criminal arrest records must be entered. Criminologists have long been aware that many more violations of the legal norms occur than are officially recorded by the arresting authorities. Non-reporting of criminal behavior occurs in many cases because the offense is known only to the one who commits it, or the victim is unwilling to report it. Thus, the number of recorded arrests of the inebriates must be presumed to under-report the violations which actually occurred. Furthermore, the particular charge on which an individual is booked may not represent the true violation, since offense charges are frequently altered according to the discretion of the functionaries of the legal system.

In spite of these limitations in the police recording system, an attempt was made to determine by statistical test whether any significant differences existed among the three subgroups in terms of their major social characteristics. The results were negative with respect to racial status, nationality background, religious affiliation, occupational status, and marital status. In terms of their previous criminal records, the three subgroups evidenced slight differences which may have been due to chance, failing to attain a .05 level of confidence. Thus, the criminal records of the men in this sample do not serve to differentiate them into distinct behavioral subcategories, at least with respect to these variables.

Notwithstanding these negative results, the interviews with the men revealed that the criminal record and type of activity in which the inebriate has engaged are used as means of evaluation and status placement by his colleagues. Since the system of clique differentiation and rating within the larger category of inebriates was not a major focus of the present investigation, only certain insights which relate to the status hierarchy can be offered, and they should not be viewed as conclusive until empirical studies are made. Among the men in the present sample, the individual with a record of convictions for felony offenses is not highly rated by the majority, who have only been in difficulty with the law as a result of their drinking pattern and were arrested only for public intoxication and related offenses.

However, certain types of offenders are viewed with more disfavor than others, and one of the least favored is the petty thief whose proclivities lead him to prey not only on society but on his fellow inmates as well. The petty thief may attempt to conceal his previous convictions on this charge, not only from officials and researchers but also from his fellow inmates, because of the negative values attached to his behavior. Negative evaluation is also made of the man who becomes abusive and engages in assaultive behavior under the influence of alcohol, since the aggression may be directed toward his peers as well as other members of society. This type of offender may have a history of arrests on the charge of aggravated assault. Unlike the situation in many long-term penal institutions, no positive status is granted the individual who has had an active criminal career with service in the "big leagues" of state and federal prisons. Perhaps the most disesteemed of all are those inebriates who are "panhandlers" and ply their trade even while incarcerated by attempting "to put the bite on" a fellow inmate.

The least disesteemed are those whose only encounter with legal authority has been for intoxication or closely related offenses, such as disorderly conduct and vagrancy. This is apparent in two ways: (a) the tendency on the part of some men to conceal their previous active criminal history, and (b) the graphic and emphatic assertion by those who have only alcohol-related offenses on their record that their problem is not with the law but with drinking.

Conclusions

From this detailed presentation of the previous criminal records of the chronic police case inebriates, certain generalizations may be drawn:

a. These men exhibit a high degree of heterogeneity in respect to their previous offenses in terms of types and frequency. The most common violation is public intoxication, with a mean of 12.8 arrests per man and a median of 6.0. But there is also a mean of 3.7 arrests per man, with a median of 3.0, on charges other than public intoxication. Moreover, the recorded number of arrests decidedly underrepresents the actual number of violations of the criminal code, many of which remain unreported, reflecting the vicissitudes of crime detection and reporting.

b. A biphasic pattern of criminal career was discovered in the history of many of these men: an early pattern marked by arrests chiefly for offenses other than intoxication; and a later pattern, representing substantial abandonment of the criminal career usually after age 35, of arrests chiefly or exclusively for intoxication.

c. An examination of the criminal histories of the chronic police case inebriates reveals that many have become what may be termed institutionalized offenders. This is reflected in their constant movement from the protective institutional environment of the penitentiary to the sheltered milieu of Skid Row or other forms of semi-communal living—such as work in hospitals or labor camps, and residence in public shelters, cheap rooming-houses, or hotels—and then back again to the most protective environment of all, the penal institution. Thus their problem is not simply one involving difficulties in the sphere of drinking behavior but a much more deep-seated disorder referable to the psychological and social factors of dependency and security.

The penal institution is thus functional for those inebriates who show long and continuous histories of incarceration, in that it meets, although in a socially disapproved way, the basic psychological needs of their personality structure. Incarceration, on the other hand, is dysfunctional in the sense that it provides the situation in which the developing dependency can be fixed in the personality pattern where it is already evident as an inability to develop autonomy in adulthood.

References

1. Bacon, Selden D., "Inebriety, Social Integration and Marriage," *Quart. J. Stud. Alc.,* **5**:86–125; 303–339, 1944.
2. Hollingshead, August B., *Elmtown's Youth,* New York: John Wiley and Sons, 1949.
3. Warner, W. Lloyd, Marchia Meeker, and Kenneth Eells, *Social Class in America,* Chicago: Science Research Associates, 1949.

RESPONSIVE MOVEMENTS AND SYSTEMS OF CONTROL

Introductory Note. Broadly speaking, the social control of the drinking of alcoholic beverages and related behaviors is a theme which runs throughout this book. Yet in another and narrower sense there are special phenomena and problems relating to the social control of alcohol use in contemporary society which merit particular consideration. In Chapter 5, Selden Bacon outlined the basis in increasing societal complexity for the breakdown of diffuse and effective controls characteristic of a certain type of simpler society—though surely not of all simple societies—and pointed up the formidable tasks confronting societal-wide efforts at control in complex society. His discussion also spelled out the general conditions for the emergence of those relatively differentiated movements, specialized agencies, and activities with which our recent history is replete and which aim variously at the social regulation of alcohol consumption, drunkenness, alcoholism, and related "alcohol problems." While it is not within the province of this book to review these developments in historical perspective, we are concerned to call attention in this final section to some of the currently important alcohol-centered movements and control systems which have been, or hold promise of being, excellent subjects for sociological investigation.

Here, Edwin Lemert presents and discusses in Chapter 31 four "models" of the social control of alcohol use—models derived from the present and past experiences of societies. These models of control, while not applicable to alcoholism, have as their goal minimizing the costs of intoxication and drunkenness. However, as Lemert indicates, none of them has been particularly successful. In his discussion, Lemert cogently presents the dilemma facing the state in regard to the control of alcohol use; namely, the fact that those groups which place a high premium on sobriety and a low value on intoxication have little need for governmental regulation of their drinking behavior. (The classic illustration here is that of the Jews, discussed by Snyder in Chapter 11.) Conversely, those groups or societies which at times value intoxication more than sobriety effectively sabotage or reject governmental controls.

Despite the lack of success of state control plans for alcohol use, Western societies, in particular, have a vast but realistic problem in bringing controls to bear on alcoholism and alcohol-related behavioral problems. In the past quarter of a century, a variety of social movements have arisen throughout the Western world to cope with the economic, social, psychological, and physical costs of alcoholism. These movements and programs run the gamut from massive governmental programs in Sweden and Finland, through the efforts of private voluntary health agencies such as the National Council on Alcoholism in the United States, to the activities of alcoholics themselves in their fellowship of Alcoholics Anonymous. Although exact data are not available, it is perhaps the case that more alcoholics have found sobriety through the vehicle of Alcoholics Anonymous than by means of all other agencies combined. Again, the striking feature of this latter movement is that its program was developed and continues to operate not through professional therapists or governmental supports but solely through the activities of alcoholics themselves.*

In Chapter 32, the first of two selections devoted to Alcoholics Anonymous, we have chosen to republish the major portion of an article by Robert Bales, originally published almost 20 years ago. The selection of this article was made not for want of more recent material on Alcoholics Anonymous but because it presents in compact form a definitely sociological view of the organization which is lacking in the bulk of writings on the subject and because it raises questions still germane today about the impact of Alcoholics Anonymous' social organization on its future direction. A basic observation is that all spontaneous social movements such as Alcoholics Anonymous have a tendency through the years to move through a cycle of institutionalization which "greater clarification, regularization, and, finally formalization and rigidity" of both structure and function occur.

Bales examines the structure of Alcoholics Anonymous and attempts to relate the characteristics of the organization to the major purpose of the group—staying sober. Certain problematic features such as crises in sponsor-protégé relationships, political conflicts among older members, tendencies to schism, and pressures to define future activities in a way which would necessitate the elaboration of counter-therapeutic "overhead" structure are considered alongside an appraisal of the strengths of the organization. Concluding on an optimistic note, Bales states that as long as the emphasis re-

---

* One of the best brief descriptions of the Alcoholics Anonymous program and its history is provided by Trice (6). This should be supplemented by the organization's own account of its history (1).

mains squarely upon helping other alcoholics, a protection is built in against the dangers of conflicts and institutionalization. Yet the characterization of the organization in its earlier years which he provides and the questions which he raises about possible loci of stresses in its development provide excellent starting points for new and comprehensive sociological study of Alcoholics Anonymous.

Chapter 33, the second selection dealing with Alcoholics Anonymous, is by Milton Maxwell. He presents a social psychological interpretation of the organization's therapeutic effectiveness, building his analysis on the hypothesis that there are prerequisite conditions in the alcoholic's life which form the basis of seeking help. When these conditions are coupled with the contents of the Alcoholics Anonymous program and the gemeinschaft-like quality of the subculture, a new sober and productive way of life with its constituent mores and folkways can be learned. Of importance is the fact that this therapeutic context is potentially available to the alcoholic 168 hours a week compared with the professional therapist's maximum availability of 4 or 5 hours.

Because of the dramatic therapeutic results obtained by many alcoholics in their affiliation with Alcoholics Anonymous, there has been an understandable tendency to present the organization as the ultimate answer to the alcoholism problem and to eulogize its therapeutic features (4). However, Alcoholics Anonymous does possess certain dysfunctionalities from a therapeutic point of view. Trice (5), for example, has pointed out in his study of affiliation with Alcoholics Anonymous that certain local groups do not provide adequate sponsorship for new members. Other researchers (2) have begun to chart the effects of differences in social-class position upon the readiness of local groups to incorporate the potential member. Some Alcoholics Anonymous groups, although accepting the view that alcoholism is a chronic disease, apparently have a low tolerance for those members who have "slips" or relapses. In these circumstances, the centering of the member's total life around the Alcoholics Anonymous group makes it virtually impossible for him to admit that he has had a slip, thus setting the stage for dissociation from the group and new cycles of uncontrolled drinking.

Moreover, if a relative autonomy from special external therapeutic supports be taken as a goal of therapy, then Alcoholics Anonymous tends to fall short of this objective. It is evident, too, that the movement fails to reach a great many alcoholics, some of whom, at least, may be presumed to be amenable to other types of therapy.* Also, the movement has clearly had its

---

* While the question of social psychological factors effecting affiliation or non-affiliation with Alcoholics Anonymous has begun to receive systematic attention in the work of Trice, noted above, the question of socio-cultural influences predisposing toward the rejection of Alcoholics Anonymous and the acceptance of therapeutic alternatives has yet to be thoroughly investigated. The remarks of Stone in Chapter 7 concerning the appeal and effectiveness of Alcoholics Anonymous vis-à-vis certain status levels of

greatest impact among cultures of "Anglo-Saxon" derivation and has very probably appealed especially to the type of alcoholic predominant in such cultures (cf. Jellinek, Chapter 22). These limitations need not detract, however, from the great importance which this social invention, Alcoholics Anonymous, has had in helping alcoholics. They may be understood simply as posing problems for future inquiry. As Maxwell observes, the spiritual terms of Alcoholics Anonymous have perhaps disenchanted certain investigators of naturalistic inclinations, but this hardly constitutes sufficient grounds for avoiding the sociological analysis of Alcoholics Anonymous from which, we would contend, social scientists have much to learn.

However, Alcoholics Anonymous is only one of a variety of movements, agencies, and activities which have evolved in complex society manifestly to cope with alcoholism. Many others, whether of a governmental or private nature, stand in especially close, reciprocal relation to the emerging societal definition of alcoholism as an illness or disease, having facilitated this definition and having received ideological support therefrom. Placing alcoholism in a disease frame of reference, instead of a moralistic one, has far-reaching consequences for social policy, and it is to this question that John Seeley addresses himself in Chapter 34.

Although Seeley is primarily concerned to reflect upon and analyze the conditions under which phenomena may be appropriately termed disease, his conclusions highlight the programmatic nature of the proposition that alcoholism is a disease and the logical implications for social policy. There would seem to be no doubt but that this proposition has already done much to legitimate the shift of the alcoholic's custody and care into the hands of the so-called "helping professions" of the medical, social-work, and applied behavioral-science variety. Perhaps most important, given the present structure of the helping professions, alcoholics as sick individuals become legitimate concerns of governmental health programs, and the stage is set for the intervention of government into all areas upon which alcoholism impinges, including the conditions which are predicated as significant in the disease's etiology.

It is in documentation of this tendency that we have concluded the book with Chapter 35, a brief survey by Archer Tongue of existing governmental programs on alcohol and alcoholism as seen from an international point of view. Since World War II most governments have taken direct action to provide programs in alcohol education, in the treatment and rehabilitation of the alcoholic, and in the organization of research. Over-all programs in European countries are better organized and more "research oriented" than those in the United States. Alcohol programs in the United States are still caught in the controversy of whether they should be specialized—that is,

---

"localites," on the one hand, and "cosmopolites," on the other, provide a lead for inquiry here, as does the apparent resistance to the Alcoholics Anonymous program of certain indigenously lower-class alcoholics of the Skid-Row variety who may nonetheless be open to other modes of rehabilitation.

directed only toward treatment and rehabilitation of the alcoholic because of his supposed uniqueness—or whether they should be integrated into well-established state programs dealing with physical and mental health of which alcoholism as a disease is an integral part.

Tongue has, in our opinion, provided excellent documentation of the multiplication of governmental programs in the alcoholism area, as well as testimony to their growing articulation with one another at the higher administrative levels, nationally and internationally. Yet it is not within the scope of his article to ask the fundamental question of whether or not these programs have basically altered the prevalence of alcoholism in any country, or whether in their very nature they are capable of doing so on any significant scale.* Certainly these programs have been instrumental in altering to some extent the treatment procedures for alcoholism, and they have been instrumental in calling public attention to the alcoholism problem. They have also played a growing part in sponsoring research of varying quality, with—if our own experience may be taken as a guide—different degrees of sympathy and understanding as to what scholarly and scientific endeavor is about.

Advocates of these programs would, no doubt, justly plead that the programs are in their infancy and are frankly experimental in nature, and that, as Tongue suggests, it is premature to evaluate them in terms of their professed long-term goals. This is a situation which, of course, heightens their dependence at various points upon scientific research for legitimation and direction. In these circumstances, there are at once dangers and challenges to social scientists interested in gaining support for research on alcohol problems. A first danger, as we see it, is that of being drawn into pseudo-research activities where the explicit or implicit concerns for and defense of these programs and their bureaucratic structure limit the selection of problems and the vision of research to administratively safe questions of a pedestrian nature. This would preclude, among other things, realistic appraisal of the

---

* Whatever the eventual form and impact of these programs, their extraordinary proliferation in advance of theoretical solutions to the riddles of alcoholism—and on a tack quite different, at this stage, from the empirical solutions offered by such movements as Alcoholics Anonymous—suggests serious examination of their latent functions. In this regard, we are forcibly reminded of Michels' (3) contentions concerning the tendencies of state bureaucracy, in times of societal instability, to expand in the form of an endless screw, offering middle-class status and security to those who might otherwise be proletarianized and, thereby, add substance and voice to the dissident elements of the populace. Whether or not such a view (or alternative explanations in terms of latent functions) can account for the remarkable growth of governmental programs in the alcoholism area and in other perennially enigmatic areas (such as delinquency, crime, and mental illness) is an open question. We would deem such questions worthy of investigation, however. Nor should the possibility be overlooked that these programs may be symptomatic of a basic change in values and a reintegration of social structure which, in turn, might have an important impact upon drinking patterns and alcoholism —however virile or impotent the programs themselves prove to be in their direct assaults upon alcoholism.

programs themselves. A second danger is in the temptation to responsible persons in these programs and to social scientists themselves to oversell social science as a panacea for the problems of alcohol. If these dangers can be avoided, the development of these programs may well present social scientists in the next few decades with unparalleled opportunities to study alcoholism, in particular, and drinking patterns in general.

References

1. *Alcoholics Anonymous Comes of Age: A Brief History of A. A.*, New York: Alcoholics Anonymous Publishing, 1957.
2. Lofland, John F., and Robert A. Lejeune, "Initial Interaction of Newcomers in Alcoholics Anonymous: A Field Experiment in Class Symbols and Socialization," *Social Problems,* 8:102–111, 1960.
3. Michels, Robert, "Bureaucracy and Political Parties," *in* Lewis A. Coser and Bernard Rosenberg (Eds.), *Sociological Theory,* New York: The Macmillan Company, 1957.
4. Ripley, Herbert S., and Joan K. Jackson, "Therapeutic Factors in Alcoholics Anonymous," *Amer. J. Psychiatry,* 116:44–50, 1959.
5. Trice, Harrison M., "A Study of the Process of Affiliation with Alcoholics Anonymous," *Quart. J. Stud. Alc.,* 18:39–43, 1957.
6. ———, "Alcoholics Anonymous," *Ann. Amer. Acad. Pol. Soc. Sci.,* 315:108–116, January 1958.

chapter 31

Alcohol, values, and social control*

Edwin M. Lemert

A general analysis of alcohol and social control deals with the universal qualities of alcohol, the values and costs of its use, the distribution of power in social structures, the available means of control, the probabilities of resistance, and patterns of values in cultures and individuals. These concepts are designed for a kind of "action analysis," being oriented to research into problems of alcohol use which have emerged from the impact of rapid technological change in Western societies and from the spread of modern technologies and ideologies to non-literate and "underdeveloped" societies of the world. Central to this analysis is the hypothesis, well grounded in empirical findings of alcohol research, that values are crucial factors in the social control of alcohol use.

The Attributes of Alcohol and Values

The values which have been assigned to alcoholic beverages throughout the world partially rest upon their physical qualities and certain of their recurrent or universal physiological effects. It has been pointed out that alcohol is distinctive for the ease and cheapness of its preparation. Other physical properties permit it to be stored for long periods and transported with facility (14, 15). In many societies alcohol is valued as a food, as a promoter of digestion and sleep, as a protection against cold and fatigue, and as a medicine to relieve pain or to treat specific illnesses. This is not to say that alcohol metabolism determines symbolic associations among human beings. It should be emphasized that the ascription of values to alcoholic

* This chapter was written especially for this book.

beverages diverges from and transcends their demonstrable physiological functions.*

The more important symbolic associations of alcohol derive from its function as a behavior modifier. Mild to severe intoxication promotes the expression of a variety of idiosyncratic values in the individual and a large measure of socially shared and communicable values. Perhaps the most important of the former is the relief or relaxation from fatigue, tension, apathy, and the sense of isolation.

The social values facilitated by the consumption of alcoholic drinks spring from a recognition of their function in diminishing social distance and strengthening group bonds. These values revolve around fellowship, social amity, and group morale. Often these values are expressed through rituals which symbolize the solidarity of kin groups and work groups or the collective willingness of warriors and soldiers to die for a leader or a cause. Alcohol is further valued for its ritual functions in symbolizing status changes at birth, marriage, coming of age, and bereavement. Alcohol also finds an important place in some societies in the specialized culture of ecstasy and in Dionysian communion with gods. A number of societies have institutionalized groups in which drinking and drunkenness are terminal rather than mediating values.

There are other positive values of alcohol use, less concerned with interpersonal interaction, which come to the fore in larger nation-state-type societies. One of these is the recognized ease with which revenue for state purposes can be raised through taxing alcohol production. This, of course, is a more specialized valuation of alcohol held by political or administrative elites. Closely related to this is the recognition of the value of induced dependence upon alcohol as a means of social control. This can be seen in connection with contract labor and peonage, in connection with sex behavior, and in connection with diplomacy and power struggles between ruling elites. Finally, there is a set of sharply defined values attached to alcohol by those whose economic livelihood and occupational status rest upon the production and distribution of alcoholic beverages.

There is a tendency, perhaps universal, for valuations of alcoholic beverages to become polarized. At one extreme, liquors, wine, and beer are glorified in song, poetry, and drama as keys to ecstasy and sublimity; at the other extreme, they are viewed as perverters of human morality and the chief causes of the ills of society as well as of the sorrows of individuals. This imparts a marked ambivalence to attitude and opinion concerning the proper place of alcohol in social life (37). In part this ambivalence stems from an awareness that satisfactions brought by imbibing alcohol not infrequently have a spurious quality. What seemed to be love to the intoxicated maiden turns out in sober retrospect to have been sex exploitation. The comradeship of the college reunion in afterthought is seen realistically

---

* Function in this article means operation or process; value is an object or a state which is desired. Functions may or may not be valued.

as largely inspired by the martinis rather than by common interest long since gone.

A more important ingredient of this ambivalence towards alcohol comes from the perception of its previously mentioned function as a behavior modifier. Modifications in human behavior brought by intoxication are socially and personally destructive as well as socially integrative. The same object which makes human pleasures makes human pain and unhappiness. Although this can be said of many other objects used by human beings, alcohol is distinctive in that it is difficult to predict which will be the consequences of its consumption.

The Costs of Alcohol Use

It is a reasonable assumption that there is some kind of hierarchy in the values held by human beings. This signifies that in a hypothetically free situation with unlimited means at hand there is an order in which values are satisfied. However, this order is imperfectly manifested in actual choice making by individuals because the environmental situation limits choices, often excluding opportunities for satisfying some values and allowing only a partial or compromised satisfaction of others. The cost of a value, stated most simply, is the degree to which other values must be sacrificed in the process of its satisfaction (8). Generally speaking, the cost of a value is estimable in terms of time, energy, and the amount of discomfort expended to satisfy it.

Indulgence in alcohol, while promoting fulfillment of previously mentioned values, frequently does so at the cost of others. This is most apparent in the tendency for intoxication to encourage or "release" aggression and deviant sex behavior (15). Intoxication also impairs physiological functions, making for the neglect or inadequate performance of roles as well as accidents. The values commonly sacrificed by drunkenness are respect for person, life, property, health, longevity, family integrity, parental responsibility, regularity of work, and financial dependability. Apart from these general or universal costs chargeable against intoxication are countless others which are more variable and understandable only in relation to a particular socio-cultural system.

The strictly economic costs of drunkenness and alcoholism in our society have been subject to estimates and can be considerable (22). The theoretical limits to such costs can be only speculative. Adam Smith (43) stated that "there is no risk that nations will destroy their fortunes through excessive consumption of fermented liquors." However, the production of alcohol may take place at the cost of necessary commodities and services, as happened in the Hawaiian Islands at one time (47). The mutineer colony of Pitcairn Island came perilously close to annihilating itself through drunkenness and conflict over women (38).

It is possible that rapid social change in the last 150 years, which has been strongly felt in Western societies and is emergent throughout the world, has enhanced the values of alcoholic intoxication. Such things as culture conflict, stress, and anomie may have grown to such proportions that alcohol in many societies is increasingly valuable as a social reagent and as a sedative for personality conflicts (1). This hypothesis is a large one and, with the present state of sociology, a difficult one to test.

Modern technology changes the costs of satisfying values even though the order of the values may remain unchanged. This is to say that technological and related cultural changes very definitely affect choice-making behavior in relation to social control. As applied to alcohol consumption, this means that intoxication and drunkenness levy critically higher costs in certain contexts of technologically mediated, interdependent, high-speed, high-productivity, health-oriented societies. Thus to older, more universal, costs of drunkenness are added death and injury from traffic accidents, lowered productivity and absenteeism in industry, disease, disturbances of public order, crime, and weakening of military discipline. Furthermore, with the growth of statism and welfare values, costs of policing and treating the chronically inebriate population must be reckoned in the over-all economy of alcohol use.

Values and Power Elites

It should not be concluded that policies or lines of action or inaction followed by societies in relation to the control of drinking result from a simple summative economy of values and costs. For this reason serious questions have to be raised about the sufficiency of research into such things as "basic personality," "themes," "cultural patterns," and "national character" in order to predict the course and results of social control. Social action and control usually emanate from elite power groups who have their own systems of values, which differ from those of the general population, from those of other groups, and even from those of individual members of the elites. The organizational values of such elites and their rules of procedure also have a strong bearing on controlling events. Furthermore, elites are limited by the amount of power they exercise, the kinds of alliances they make, and the means of control available to them to reach their goals.

The position of groups and individuals at the point of their interaction in a social structure is of great significance in predicting the resultant action taken by a society or government to control or decontrol alcohol consumption. Groups and individuals whose values are being sacrificed by intoxication and drunkenness may have no structure to formulate their vaguely felt dissatisfactions. On the other hand, minorities, because their programs are defined and their power is organized and well-timed, more readily have their values cast into the emergent pattern of social action (8).

Resistance

Action by groups or whole societies to change the drinking behavior of a population necessarily alters the costs of satisfying values that have been sought directly through the medium of alcoholic beverages. At the same time other costs may be assessed through modification of laws and reorganization of the political and socio-economic structures required to institute the new controls. Many of these costs are likely to be unanticipated and to carry the risk that resistance will follow. A consideration of the amount, the duration, and the form of the resistance must be part of the study of social action to control drinking.

If resistance arises, decisions must be made as to how it will be met and dealt with by control agencies. Such choices may be constricted by social structures and generalized values which make some means of control available but exclude others. For example, coercion may be an acceptable sanction in some societies but not in others. The organization of power in space and time may prevent the application of coercive controls to resisting populations, even where they are morally and legally permissible.

A special factor complicating the choice of controls over drinking is the irrationality of the intoxicated person and his unresponsiveness to symbols which limit the responses of sober persons. Added to this is the fact that socially deleterious behavior of the drunken person is often followed by acceptable or even praiseworthy behavior. While the inebriated person is nowhere regarded as mentally disordered, some societies have sought to solve this problem by treating him as irresponsible. However, this is not a solution in the sense of control.

The Absence of Social Control—Laissez Faire

A substantial number of societies appear to exercise little or no social control over consumption of alcoholic beverages; they approximate a condition of *laissez faire*. In these societies there is no organized public opinion unfavorable to drinking or drunkenness. With respect to the drunken person the attitude seems to be *caveat socius* rather than *caveat potor*—let society beware of the drinker rather than the reverse. Efforts at control in such societies are directed to avoiding the costly consequences of drunkenness rather than to controlling it. Speeches are made prior to feasts or drinking sprees, or rituals are performed urging drinkers to avoid quarreling and fighting or to "have a good time." Sober persons are told to stay away from quarrelsome drunks and even blamed for not doing so if they are injured. In extreme cases, fighting drunks may be separated and passively restrained. They may be tied to trees or, as in a case familiar to us among Salish Indians of British Columbia, placed in cooking retorts ordinarily used to pack canned salmon. When the drunken person passes out he may have a pillow placed under his head or be covered with a blanket or wrapped in a hammock pending his return to sobriety (15).

The apparent tolerance and lack of direct control of the inebriated persons in such societies are attributable in part to the high value placed upon intoxication by individual members. The attenuation of control is also consistent with the fact that the integrating functions of drinking for society are perceived and collectively valued. When urgent and persistent needs are met thereby, drunkenness may assume institutionalized form, as it did among Northwest Coast Indians (25, 27). Correspondingly, losses from drunkenness in these societies may be relatively low. Consuming beverages of low alcoholic content, such as beers, may mitigate the drunkenness or shorten its duration. The presence or absence of toxic congeners in the beverages and adulteration are additional variables predictive of unwanted consequences of intoxication.

Even when drunkenness is widespread and destructive at the time, its occurrence in the form of sprees or festivals following or preceding planting, harvest, hunting, and fishing seasons minimizes interference with economic activities.* If the production of food is carried out by isolated families the costs of drunkenness will not be felt by the whole community. Finally, in those societies living close to a subsistence level, the withdrawal of labor from the food quest tends to be a self-limiting phenomenon. With all of these facts to consider, it is probably correct to say that many primitive and rural societies adjust to rather than control intoxication and drunkenness. In all cases there are costs, but they seem to be written off or absorbed.

The gemeinschaft qualities of many primitive and isolated rural societies make them ill adapted to take action towards drunkenness even though the costs are substantial and are realistically perceived. Their dependence upon locality and kinship groups as units of control does not seem to work well because they are bound together on an intensely personal basis. This happens because the aggression and aberrant sex behavior released by intoxication come from impulses in the drunken person which were never fully integrated in social interaction with family members, companions, and neighbors (19). The latter people seem to sense this, and furthermore they realize that they must "live with" the drunken person for years to come. This fosters ambivalence and deters forceful action, a condition which exists in families and neighbors of drunken persons even in modern urban societies.

When societies are organized into clans a drunken person may be an especially vexatious problem because attempts to restrain him may backfire and lead to demands for damages or they may trigger warfare. When this is combined with a diffuse kind of authority in leaders and the absence of supra-clan or "superordinate" organization, control over the drunken person may be at a minimum (15). Wives, who often bear the heaviest costs of drunkenness, have low status in most primitive and rural societies and often are products of out-group marriages. Hence, the values they hold are more easily sacrificed.

Ritual and Drunkenness

Evidence from several societies indicates that notwithstanding a high tolerance for drunkenness, serious difficulties are created when drinking

---

* Where hunting is a continuous necessity rather than seasonal, drunkenness may be more disruptive in a hunting society than in an agricultural society. This seems to have been true of Eastern Woodlands Indians (18).

coincides with ritual performance. Efforts to integrate the two may be made, but they are seldom successful. The Snohomish of Puget Sound say that intoxication spoils their spirit dancing. Likewise the Kwakiutl of Kingcome Inlet in British Columbia and the Bella Coola farther north say that drinking is contrary to the sacred value of their potlatch dances (26, 35). Yet attempts at control on these ritual occasions more often than not were completely absent or at best they were token efforts. The Pomo Indians of California on one occasion decided that a 4-day winter ceremonial dance had been spoiled by drinking. No one, however, was reprimanded or punished. Instead the entire ritual was repeated (33).

To the degree that basic values of a society are widely expressed in ritual, drunkenness becomes more costly to the community. It is quite possible that the detailed, complicated, and interlocking ceremonial life of the Zuni Indians, in which all feel a sense of participation, may explain why they went through the experience of first accepting then rejecting alcoholic beverages (3). The high degree of organization of Pueblo societies seems to have prepared them better to establish policing agencies and to use authoritative controls than was true for most other American Indians. Their response to temperance propaganda was more broadly based, and early nineteenth-century temperance societies among them were less a missionary implant and more an indigenous growth (6). Yet some accounts suggest that the problem of drunkenness was not completely solved by the Pueblo peoples (48).

Contact and Interaction with White Society

The relation of social structure to the deficiency of social control over intoxicating drinks comes into clearest focus in American Indian societies which experienced direct and continuing contact with white explorers, traders, missionaries, settlers, and soldiers. The introduction of strong liquor into these societies was accompanied by a great deal of social disruption, destructive behavior, and demoralization (16, 31, 40). None of these societies was able to take effective action in the matter. Chiefs and high-ranking Indians in a number of tribes clearly appreciated the social costliness of immoderate liquor consumption, and they themselves sometimes showed restraint. In several instances, in the territories of the Iroquois and the Shawnee, efforts were made to install prohibition but without success (31, 49).

The problem, while obviously concerned with values, hinged also upon the importance of clans and kin groups as agencies of control in these societies and upon the need for complete unanimity of public opinion before taking action (32). The typical way in which nobles and chiefs sought to influence the behavior of others—through precept and example—also proved to be a poor technique for restraining those—often younger men—who chose to get drunk or enter into dealings with liquor sellers.

Looming over the immediate situation was a larger context in which American Indian societies were caught in conflicts of power between imperialistic nations of Europe, especially France and England. Jealous colonial governments and rival fur trade companies gave added dimensions to these struggles. Later the United States became a party in the conflicts. In some cases warring nations deliberately used rum or brandy as a means of weakening Indian tribes allied with their enemies (31). The few agreements reached by competing fur companies to curtail the sale or trading of liquor to Indians quickly fell into disuse (7). Many colonial governments and, later, states and Canadian provinces passed prohibition laws, but their history has been one of evasions and unenforceability.

Although missionaries tried to aid the American Indians in their struggles with liquor, their policies and methods were not readily accepted. The price they demanded in return for the Christian sobriety they promised was one the Indians could not afford to pay, being more or less a complete repudiation of deeply cherished values as well as their culture-sustaining rituals. Thus, drunkenness often took on a reactionary virtue—becoming a means of resistance and of discrediting the "missionary way" and at the same time reaffirming older values (27).

While control and, indeed, the idea of control over drinking, as we have shown, have been weakly developed or absent in many societies,* other societies, particularly those of the Western world have followed a much more positive course of action. They have recognized drinking and its consequences as a problem to be solved or as a threat to the integrity of society itself which calls for removal. This has been undertaken through decrees, passage of laws, and the indoctrination of special ideologies. A variety of control systems and methods have been devised; specialized agencies and organizations have been instituted and given responsibility for control over alcohol consumption. To discuss all of these in the detail they merit is impossible here; at best we can examine a few of the salient ideas around which they have been built.

Four Models of Social Control

A reasonable working assumption is that the objective of social control over alcohol use generally is to minimize the costs of intoxication and drunkenness. For purposes of determining whether and how such an objective can be reached, it is helpful to formulate a number of hypothetical models of social control. These are drawn from the experiences of whole societies and also from the ideologies and programs of power elites which at different times and places have actively sought to bring alcohol use under control.

---

* It is not intended to claim here that lack of control over drinking is a characteristic of primitive societies in general. Indeed, recent research has revealed the existence of reasonably successful "disciplined" drinking in certain Polynesian societies. See Edwin M. Lemert, "Alcohol Use in Polynesia," *Trop. and Geo. Med.* (in press).

Model I

The costs of intoxication and drunkenness can be reduced by a system of laws and coercive controls making it illegal to manufacture, distribute, or consume alcoholic beverages.

This, of course, is a familiar model—prohibition. It has been tried in several forms, for long and short periods of time, in Aztec society, ancient China, feudal Japan, the Polynesian Islands, Iceland, Finland, Norway, Sweden, Russia, Canada, and the United States. The well-documented failures of the model can be attributed to its high costs, the instability of power elites favorable to prohibition, the limitations of power and available means of control, and the growth of resistance unresponsive to coercion.

The prohibition model in effect sacrifices all of the values of moderate drinking as well as those associated with intoxication, plus the vested values of those who earn a livelihood or receive investment returns from the production and distribution of fermented drinks and liquor. In order for such high costs to be willingly paid a large number of power elites must either see positive value gains in prohibition laws or see them as a means of protection against threatened value losses (24). Consequently the prohibition model most likely can be established only through a social movement during periods of rapid social change, culture conflicts, conquest, or nationalistic movements.

Reform movements, from which prohibition springs, tend to be ephemeral in nature because new issues supplant the old, undermining or destroying the alignments of elites supporting them. Disillusionment of their individual adherents and defection of groups through changing policies are speeded by difficulties of enforcement and consequences of resistance.

Resistance can be predicted for any model of control requiring the abandonment of values deeply held by large segments of a population. In the case of prohibition the problem of enforcement is augmented because it is a form of sumptuary legislation which affects the more personal aspects of human behavior and individual choice making in intimate or private behavior. In the absence of a reinforcing public opinion the application of coercive controls seldom has succeeded. Even the most severe punishments, such as death among the Aztecs and exile to Siberia in Russia, failed to abolish bootlegging in those societies (28).

In large, complex societies a control model which prohibits a highly desired item increases its scarcity value and also the probabilities that collective enterprise will grow up to supply it. The large variety of foods which can be converted into alcohol and the ease and cheapness of its production and its movement make bootlegging and smuggling inevitable. The costs to the state of discovering and stamping out such illegal industry can reach a point where governing elites are unable or unwilling to pay them. The organization of evasion poses threats to other values such as respect for property and life, and even the value of government under law. This contributes further to resistance and reaction against prohibition.

The power of a given state to enforce prohibition may be insufficient if the economic and political values of other states are threatened thereby. In 1841, France intervened under threats of bombardment and compelled the reigning monarch of the Hawaiian Islands to end prohibition there (46). France, Germany, Russia, and Spain at different times variously applied pressures to Finland, Norway, Iceland, and Turkey in order to prevent interference with liquor imports and smuggling (5).

It may be more profitable to speculate on the conditions under which the prohibition model can succeed rather than to inventory the reasons for its failure. Probably it would require conspicuously high costs of drunkenness on one hand and on the other a positive replacement of the drinking values or substitution of new means for achieving the old values. A precondition of this would be relatively complete geographic isolation, similar to that found on islands, where behavior deviations have a high visibility. A social structure in which power is concentrated and little affected by public opinion or is upheld by supernatural sanctions perhaps would make for successful prohibition. Needless to say, conditions such as these are increasingly anomalous in the world of the present.

Model II
The costs of intoxication and drunkenness can be reduced by a system of indoctrination of information about the consequences of using alcohol— thus leading to moderate drinking or abstinence.

The assumption behind this control model is that a causative relationship holds between controlled presentation of information and change in attitudes and values. The general idea is favored by some research on attitudes in specified areas of behavior. The findings, however, are not altogether consistent and where giving information has been found to modify attitudes and values the change is not always in the anticipated direction (4). In general it would be hard to say whether exposure to information leads people to change specific values or whether the reverse is true—that is, whether the adherence to certain values stimulates people to inform themselves of pertinent facts. Currently there is no conclusive research from which judgments can be made about the kinds of information or educational content best calculated to achieve the goals of abstinence or moderation in drinking.

In the absence of data, the content of alcohol education has tended to be influenced by values and policies of temperance groups. This has been especially true of alcohol education in the schools of countries where forms of this model have been tried. Those whose values are more directly involved—parents—are not inclined to resist the inclusion of special curricula on alcohol education in the schools because many believe that some guidance is needed, especially in the United States where education is apotheosized as a solution for social problems. On the other hand some evidence from England and America speaks of indifference to or lack of sympathy with the alcohol curriculum on the part of teachers who do not subscribe to temperance values. This may reflect a failure to reconcile religious and scientific orientations in the recommended curricula (29). Resistance from these sources, of course, need not necessarily be fatal to the working of this model.

A more serious flaw in the educational model of alcohol control lies in the probability that values surrounding drinking and embedded in drinking patterns are primarily shaped by experiences in the family and in peer groups rather than by formal educational agencies (29, 42, 45). No problem is created for the society relying upon the educational model if it is homogeneous with reference to its drinking or abstinence habits. In the absence of such homogeneity, educators are faced with discontinuity between the learning process in the schools and what goes on in primary groups outside. Examples set by parents at home or pressures to conform in friendship groups easily cancel out the abstinence or moderation precepts of the school.

Education for restraint in drinking might be directed to parents instead of youth, through agencies outside or peripheral to the school. Yet prospects for this kind of enlightenment are not promising. Family-life education generally considered has yet to prove its worth (13). Other programs, such as those promoted by state mental hygiene departments or by local alcoholism committees, or by citizens' committees as in Russia, are still largely untested by research or extensive empirical trial. In some places it has been shown that mental hygiene education can have effects opposite to those intended (9, 10).

The means which can be made to work for alcohol education have not been well adapted to the ends sought. Pamphlets, charts, movies, and lectures which dwell upon the results of excessive drinking often seem to run afoul of the ambivalence underlying popular reactions to alcohol. The arousal of fears, implied warnings, or threats as to what will happen if one drinks too much have been noted to provoke avoidance reactions towards further propaganda. There also seems to be an unwillingness of audiences to particularize such propaganda. This is very apt to be true if the educational materials are pointed to alcoholism as an end result of drinking.

Research into the factors which account for the long history of Jewish sobriety makes it fairly certain that the indoctrination of values is significant. It has not yet been settled what the values are, nor whether they are generalized or specific in nature. Furthermore there is a good possibility that such values may be functional only in a special context of ongoing social control represented by the Jewish community (12, 44). Comparable research into drinking by Italian Americans and Italians concludes that valuation of wine as a food is an important part of their relative sobriety (30). Yet this scarcely seems to be a complete explanation, and even if it were, there are no investigations to clarify the process by which such a value is inculcated or maintained in the ethnic population.

A final necessary comment on the educational model of control is that in a mobile, culturally diversified society which changes rapidly it becomes difficult to predict what pattern of values indoctrinated in children will best serve to adjust them as adults. To the extent that drinking is a response to situations, to adventitious groupings, and to stresses generated by role conflicts or social isolation, reliance upon a preconceived pattern of drinking values to control excessive use of alcohol may fail. Attention must be directed to the controls functioning in the drinking situation.

Model III

The costs of intoxication and drunkenness can be reduced by legal regulation of the kinds of liquor consumed, its pecuniary cost, methods of distribution, the time and place of drinking, and its availability to consumers according to age, sex, and other socio-economic characteristics.

This model rests upon the conviction that the state or its agencies can determine what amounts and what forms of drinking have costly consequences. In most comprehensive form the model defines drinking as a privilege which, if abused, can be withdrawn from the individual; corollary to this is withdrawal of privileges, such as that of driving an automobile, which are affected by drinking. Archetypes of this model are found in the history of Scandinavian countries—particularly Sweden, home of the Gothenberg and Bratt systems of liquor control. Examples also come from the temperance orders of medieval Germany, possibly including the apocryphal *jus potandi,* the drinking code of orders given to heavy drinking (41).

Government regulation of alcohol consumption grew up historically largely from non-moral considerations. Among these were popular agitation that governments make fermented beverages equally available to localities and demands that the quality of such drinks be insured against fraud. The willingness of populations to accept taxes on alcohol production as a revenue measure has been an enticing path to regulation for financially hard-pressed governments (5). This last possibility has caused a persistent dilemma for governing officials who have to choose between raising money the "easy way" and at the same time taking steps to diminish heavy drinking which has the effect of decreasing revenue. The dilemma has been conspicuous in the history of Russia, where, under the Tsar's *kabak* system, and subsequently under the "farming out" system of vodka monopoly, the government abetted or encouraged widespread drunkenness (11, 17). The dilemma still lives today in muted controversies over the respective merits of licensing versus monopoly and trust systems of alcohol distribution.

Effective alcoholic beverage control may strike heavily at the economic values of producers and distributors even when it does not threaten drinking values of the population. If these elites are numerous and well organized, their resistance may well nullify efforts at regulation. A well-documented case in point is France, whose parliaments passed a series of regulatory laws after the First and Second World Wars. Yet the great power of the wine industry there has prevented anything beyond token enforcement of the laws. The presence of approximately a third of the electorate who are either workers in the wine industry or their family members does much to explain this phenomenon (34). The so-called *bouillers de cru,* home distillers, who are entrenched in certain areas of France seem to openly defy regulation, protecting their traditional privileges largely through sheer power of numbers at the polls.

In the latter part of the nineteenth century, in some countries pressures from temperance groups exerted a mounting influence on government regulation. The result has been that regulation more and more reflected a power conflict between temperance organizations and those of the liquor industry. Regulations formulated by legislative bodies have been the incorporation less of consistent policy and designed control than of compromises, special concessions, exceptions, and arbitrary requirements. The atmosphere of mutual distrust between the two power alignments, of which these have often been the products, is not conducive to enforcement.

As other power elites, such as health, welfare, and law-enforcement people, researchers, and tax officials, become more professionalized and articulate their values, regulatory laws can become more symmetrical. Administrative rule making also permits a more rational adaptation of means of control to ends. If the regulatory model is to work efficiently, however, conflicting elites must be able to believe that their values can be realized or preserved through regulation. Those persons and groups who have to bear the heaviest sacrifice of values must be able to find alternatives.

The organization and jurisdiction of regulatory agencies present as yet unsolved problems of this control model. In large, heterogeneous societies like our own and perhaps that of Russia, a high level of uniformity in regulations coupled with centralized control over alcohol use carries a strong probability of resistance. On the other hand extreme decentralization of control and dependence upon purely local agencies invite connivance and circumvention of rules where they deviate from local drinking customs or run counter to interests of local power elites.

Although this model is not designed to liquidate values associated with drinking or even drunkenness, it may nevertheless have this effect through regulations which significantly alter the form or pattern of drinking. In areas where public opinion does not support such regulations or the actions of the enforcing agencies, the result often is simply to add extraneous behavior to the form of drinking without appreciably modifying it. Thus a rule specifying that children and youth may not enter a liquor establishment unless food is served there may do nothing more than cause proprietors to install a bare minimum of restaurant equipment. Requirements that wine and liquor can only be served with meals may simply have the effect of adding the cost of a meal to the liquor bill.

Where lawyers or legal-minded elites set the policies of regulatory agencies there may be little understanding of the functions and values of drinking groups and related institutions. Historical studies and research reports both have shown a significant relationship between drinking groups and the persistence of primary groups' values (20, 29, p. 25 f.). Ignorance or disregard of such facts easily vitiates regulation. In this country many states have regulations against extending credit in bars and taverns. Yet frequently the success of such a place depends upon personal ties between customers and barkeepers. Hence many of the latter put drinks "on the tab" or "hold" personal checks as a means of giving credit. Not only does the regulation often fail in its purpose, but it also plays a part in many bad-check offenses.

The chief means for implementing regulatory rules are suspensions and withdrawal of distributors' licenses or, in the case of monopoly systems, manipulating the number of outlets and their hours of sale. Along with these are the withdrawal of ration cards or "buyer surveillance" (23), techniques aimed at errant individual drinkers. Behind all of these is the possibility of police action for persistent and flagrant violators.

Distributors and retailers unquestionably can be hurt economically and made more receptive to rules by suspension or revocation of licenses. Furthermore, experiments in rural Finland have shown that placement of sales outlets does have some limited effects upon the kinds of alcoholic beverages consumed in certain population categories (21). No workable methods yet have been invented to control the individual drinker or drinkers who want to "beat the system." If motivation is strong enough such persons will find ways of circumventing the regulations. Furthermore, controls focused upon the excessive drinker often inconvenience or alienate persons who comply with the form and meaning of the regulations. Even in Scandinavian countries, where a strong tradition of government paternalism prevails, ration cards and "buyer surveillance" have not been popular (23).

This underscores the importance of public opinion in securing cooperation necessary for regulatory control. The cooperation of local law-enforcement officials is equally important. A broad area of responsibility for dealing with consequences of drinking must always remain with the local community because it must deal with disturbances of public order, offenses against the family, and juvenile offenses, which in varying degrees involve drinking and drunkenness. Legal procedures and coercive controls, such as fines and jail sentences, are poor methods for handling such cases because the consequences of punishment often are worse than the offense.

Model IV
The costs of intoxication and drunkenness can be reduced by substitution of functional equivalents of drinking.

This model has received most attention in England where it has been the subject of investigation under the heading of "moderating influences" and "counter attractions" (29). It has interested those who see excessive drinking as a symptom of some kind of "deprivation" of human beings due to defects or omissions in social structures (2, 39). It carries the assumption that values satisfied through drinking or drunkenness can be fulfilled through other activities. It calls for an engineering-type reorganization of community life so that time, money, and interests devoted to drinking will be redirected into sports, games, gardening, radio listening, motion picture, travel, and similar diversions. Improved housing to make family life more attractive and building of community centers also are envisioned as part of this model.

In certain kinds of internally controlled or isolated community situations where boredom and apathy or social isolation have reached critical proportions, diversionary activities may very well decrease the extent of drunkenness. This has been observed in military encampments and isolated outposts (36). Comparable data are also at hand in the history of a missionary system of control among Salish Indians of British Columbia where religious pageantry organized by Catholic Oblates for a time, at least, successfully replaced whiskey feasts and decreased other forms of drunkenness (26).

If is, of course, naive to expect to convert urban communities into analogues of military camps or missionary societies. Short of this the best that can be done is to introduce new programs, such as recreation, into situations where many other variables cannot be controlled, and to look for changes in the amount and forms of drinking. This is a crudely empirical procedure and can be very costly. Where heavy economic costs must be met, as in housing development, business and governing elites will not easily support the programs.

Despite these reservations this model may have usefulness in many situations which occur in contemporary societies. Here we think of logging camps, long-term construction projects in sparsely settled areas, technical research teams, and diplomatic corps in foreign countries, as well as of military installations throughout the world. Wherever there are situations in which centripetal social integration operates, manipulation of social participation may be significant in reducing drunkenness.

This model has an appeal to the researcher because in the kinds of situations which have been specified it may lend itself to rigorous testing. An important task in such research would be to ascertain whether in given cultural contexts drinking is inescapably associated with attaining certain value satisfactions. The obverse of the question is whether drinking or drunkenness is symptomatic for societies in the same way that some psychiatrists hold it to be for individuals. This also merges into a query about the influence of values on the selection of narcotics, stimulants, and sedatives by societies, similar to the problem of "symptom choice" in psychiatry.

Conclusion

As yet, no model of social control has been evolved which has been greatly effective for diminishing the costs of excessive drinking. Research is complicated by the fact that the adoption of control programs and a decline in drunkenness both may be functions of changes in larger value systems. In general, those societies and groups which place a high value on sobriety and a low value on intoxication do not have a need for extensive social control. This is subject, however, to the qualification that drunkenness among a small number of persons whose roles express basic values of the society or drunkenness at vulnerable junctures in an industrial system magnifies the need for control. Presumably the necessary controls are more easily established under such conditions.

Societies which place a high premium upon the pleasures of drink and which have the greatest need for control are inclined to reject programs of control or to sabotage them if they are established. Members of these societies who do not share the drinking values or who perceive their high costs may be unable to make their voices heard in the arena of government or in community councils. If they do, they risk unpopularity and ostracism. France is an almost classic example of this situation.

Large societies with mixtures of ethnic minorities, diverse locality, and occupational groups make it unlikely that any one model will suffice to eliminate socially harmful drinking. The problem of choice of a model is complicated by the fact that drinking may be, in turn, a culture pattern, a symptom of psychic stress, a symbolic protest, or a form of collective behavior. Yet a technologically oriented society inexorably demands that drinking, whatever its form, not be permitted to disrupt crucial social integrations which cut across many groups. Formulation of these requirements in the areas of industry, communications, health, and family life probably can only be done by controlling elites "from above." Achievement of these minimum conformities in drinking behavior can best be implemented at the "grass roots" level in particular groups where resources for control at the level of informal interaction can be tapped and brought into play (23).

An example of the possibilities in such a process was the decision of English labor groups and associations in the nineteenth century to remove their meetings from public houses. According to some writers (41), this was important among other influences bringing about a decline in drunkenness during this period. Returning to our present-day situation, there is little hope that state officials or police can directly control such indigenous cultural growths as office parties at Christmastime, New Year celebrations, "martini luncheons," "beer-bust" picnics, and general weekend and holiday drinking behavior. It does seem possible, however, that employers' groups, professional groups, unions, clubs, and civic associations which are close to drinking phenomena can assume a larger share of responsibility for such control.

The problem of establishing communication between these groups and responsible control agencies is formidable, and it requires more than legal instrumentation. When drinking takes place adventitiously or when it is a form of protest or alienation from society—as with much teenage drinking and with "bottle gangs" in Skid Row—control through the co-optation of groups is difficult if not impossible. It is here that direct regulation, unsatisfactory though it may be, must be applied.

Control of any kind is a marginal influence in social and cultural change —a consideration no less true of action to reduce the costs of intoxication and drunkenness. Control cannot create behavior *de novo,* but it can strengthen existing tendencies by articulating unspoken values and by organizing the unorganized dissidents in a population. Further, it can define programs of action in a way to minimize resistance or gain the support of otherwise opposed or indifferent groups. Whether this can be done best at the local, regional, or national level is a question best left to research and open-minded experimentation.

No effort has been made here to devise and discuss a model of control for the addictive drinker. Models suitable for limiting drunkenness in whole societies most assuredly will not apply to the alcoholic. The nature and ordering of values in these persons is such that they usually are unmoved or even made hostile by symbols of control which have an effect upon other drinkers. The extreme tensions under which they labor and their disturbed social interaction distort their value systems in complex ways which preclude the communication necessary for control. Such pathological drinkers presumably can be made responsive only through specially invented therapeutic models of control.

References

1. Bacon, Selden D., "Alcohol and Complex Society," in *Alcohol, Science and Society,* New Haven, Conn.: Journal of Studies on Alcohol, 1945, pp. 190–193.
2. Bales, Robert F., "Cultural Differences in Rates of Alcoholism," *Quart. J. Stud. Alc.,* 6:482–498, 1946.
3. Benedict, Ruth, *Patterns of Culture,* New York: New American Library (Mentor Books), 1958, pp. 78–82.
4. Bonner, Hubert, *Social Psychology,* New York: American Book Company, 1953, pp. 185–192.
5. Catlin, George, *Liquor Control,* New York: Holt, Rinehart and Winston, 1931.
6. Cherrington, Ernest H., *Standard Encyclopedia of the Alcohol Problem,* Westerville, Ohio: American Issue Publishing Company, 1925, pp. 5–7; 37–39.
7. Chittenden, Hiram M., *The American Fur Trade of the Far West,* Vol. 1, New York: Frances P. Harper, 1902, Chapter IV.
8. Cottrell, W. F., *Research for Peace,* Amsterdam: North Holland Publishing Company, 1954.
9. Cumming, Elaine, and John Cumming, *Closed Ranks: An Experiment in Mental Health Education,* Cambridge, Mass.: Harvard University Press, 1957.
10. Davis, Kingsley, "Mental Hygiene and Class Structure," *Psychiatry,* 1:55–65, 1938.
11. Efron, Vera, "The Tavern and Saloon in Old Russia: An Analysis of I. G. Pryshov's Historical Sketch," *Quart. J. Stud. Alc.,* 16:484–505, 1955.
12. Glad, D. D., "Attitudes and Experiences of American-Jewish and American-Irish Male Youths as Related to Differences in Adult Rates of Inebriety," *Quart. J. Stud. Alc.,* 8:406–472, 1947.
13. Goode, William J., "Social Engineering and the Divorce Problem," *Ann. Amer. Acad. Pol. Soc. Sci.,* 272:86–94, 1950.

14. Haggard, H. W., and E. M. Jellinek, *Alcohol Explored,* Garden City, N.Y.: Double-day, Doran and Company, 1942.

15. Horton, Donald, "The Functions of Alcohol in Primitive Societies: A Cross-Cultural Study," *Quart. J. Stud. Alc.,* 4:199–319, 1943.

16. Howay, F. W., "The Introduction of Intoxicating Liquors Amongst Indians of the Northwest Coast," *British Columbia Hist. Rev.,* 6:157–169, 1942.

17. Johnson, W. E., *The Liquor Problem in Russia,* Westerville, Ohio: American Issue Publishing Company, 1915.

18. Kelbert, M., and L. Hale, *The Introduction of Alcohol into Iroquois Society,* un-published manuscript, Department of Anthropology, University of Toronto, no date.

19. Kluckhohn, Clyde, *Navaho Witchcraft,* Papers of the Peabody Museum, Vol. 22, No. 2, Cambridge, Mass.: Harvard University, pp. 52–54.

20. Kolb, John H., *Emerging Rural Communities,* Madison, Wis.: University of Wisconsin Press, 1959, p. 60 f.

21. Kuusi, Pekka, *Alcohol Sales Experiment in Rural Finland,* Helsinki: Finnish Foundation for Alcohol Studies, 1957.

22. Landis, Benson Y., "Some Economic Costs of Inebriety," in *Alcohol, Science and Society,* New Haven, Conn.: Journal of Studies on Alcohol, 1945, pp. 201–221.

23. Lanu, K. E., *Control of Deviating Drinking Behavior,* Helsinki: Finnish Foundation for Alcohol Studies, 1956.

24. Lee, Alfred, "Techniques of Social Reform: An Analysis of the New Prohibition Drive," *Amer. Sociol. Rev.,* 9:65–77, 1944.

25. Lemert, Edwin, *Alcohol and the Northwest Coast Indians,* Publications in Society and Culture, No. 2, Berkeley, Calif.: University of California Press, 1954, pp. 303–406.

26. ———, "The Life and Death of an Indian State," *Hum. Org.,* 13:23–27, 1954.

27. ———, "The Use of Alcohol in Three Salish Indian Tribes," *Quart. J. Stud. Alc.,* 19:90–107, 1958.

28. ———, "An Interpretation of Society's Efforts to Control the Use of Alcohol," in *Alcoholism—Society's Responsibility,* Berkeley: California State Department of Health, 1958.

29. Levy, Hermann, *Drink: An Economic and Social Study,* London: Routledge and Kegan Paul, 1951, pp. 136–141.

30. Lolli, Giorgio, et al., *Alcohol in Italian Culture,* Glencoe, Ill.: Free Press, 1958.

31. MacLeod, William C., *The American Indian Frontier,* London: Kegan Paul, French, Trubner and Company, 1928, chapter III.

32. Mead, Margaret, "Public Opinion Mechanisms Among Primitive People," *Pub. Op. Quart.,* 1:5–16, 1937.

33. Meighan, Clement, Personal Communication, Department of Anthropology and Sociology, University of California, Los Angeles, 1952.

34. Mignot, André, *L'Alcoolisme: Suicide Collectif de la Nation,* Paris: Cahiers des Amis de la Liberté, 1955, p. 83 f.

35. McIlwraith, T. F., *The Bella Coola Indians,* II, Toronto: University of Toronto Press, 1948.

36. Moore, Merrill, "The Alcohol Problem in Military Service," *Quart. J. Stud. Alc.,* 3:244–256, 1942.

37. Myerson, A., "Alcohol: A Study in Social Ambivalence," *Quart. J. Stud. Alc.,* 1:13–20, 1940.

38. Nordhoff, Charles B., and J. N. Hall, *Pitcairn's Island*, Boston: Little, Brown and Company, 1934.

39. Poirier, Jean, "Les Sources de L'Alcool," *Alcool en Oceanie*, Paris: Mission des Iles, No. 66, 1956.

40. Salone, Emile, "Les Sauvages du Canada et les Malades Importées de France au XVIIIe Siècle: La Picote et l'Alcoolisme," *Journal de la Société des Américanistes*, 4:1–17, 1904.

41. Samuelson, James, *The History of Drink*, London: Trubner and Company, 1878, chapter VIII.

42. Sariola, Sakari, *Drinking Patterns in Finnish Lapland*, Helsinki: Finnish Foundation for Alcohol Studies, 1956.

43. Smith, Adam, *The Wealth of Nations*, London: Methuen and Company, 1950, pp. 456–457.

44. Snyder, Charles R., *Alcohol and the Jews*, Glencoe, Ill.: Free Press, 1958.

45. Straus, Robert, and Selden Bacon, *Drinking in College*, New Haven, Conn.: Yale University Press, 1953, chapters 6 and 9.

46. Thursten, Lauren A., "The Liquor Question in Hawaii . . . ," Manuscript Collection, University of Hawaii Library, no date.

47. *Translation of the Laws of the Hawaiian Islands Established in the Reign of Kamehameha III* (manuscript), Hawaiian Missionary Children's Society Library, Honolulu, 1842.

48. White, Leslie, *The Pueblo of Santa Ana*, Pub. Amer. Anthrop. New Series, 44, 1942, p. 69.

49. Wraxall, Peter, *An Abridgment of the Indian Affairs, Contained in Four Folio Volumes, Transacted in the Colony of New York, From the year 1678 to the year 1751* (edited by Charles H. McIlwain), Cambridge, Mass.: Harvard University Press, 1915.

chapter 32

The therapeutic role
of Alcoholics Anonymous
as seen by a sociologist*

Robert F. Bales

In the long run, of course, the kind of social organization that Alcoholics Anonymous is, by reason of its origin, mode of growth, and day-to-day life, has a great deal to do with the job of staying sober, both for the old and for new members. Perhaps it would be useful to examine some of its principal structural features as a "going concern" and consider how these features affect the principal job of the members—staying sober.

Alcoholics Anonymous is a group which was virtually started by one man —at least there is a strong tendency on the part of the members to look back to the "founder" for guidance and, in spite of his modesty, to regard him with an unusual degree of respect, even reverence. Many religious sects and popular movements start in this way, and it is likely to be a major crisis in their existence when the key figure is removed, as eventually he must be, by death if for no other reason. If he has been able to transfer his "magic," or in other cases his "sacred" character, to a set of ideas, sentiments, and procedures, perhaps expressed in a body of writings, or to some other impersonal source that can live after him, the organization has a chance to survive. His unique place as founder and father can never be filled by another, but his place in the functioning organization can be taken over by a more pedestrian executive; in fact, the more pedestrian the better for the preservation of the original tradition.

This particular crisis is still to come for Alcoholics Anonymous. Steps have already been taken to meet it. The "magic" has been transferred to "The

* This chapter is an excerpt from an article which originally appeared in the *Quarterly Journal of Studies on Alcohol*, **5**:267–278, 1944.

Book," *Alcoholics Anonymous,* apparently with a considerable degree of success. One quite often hears of members who have become sober by the aid of The Book alone. The Book is the charter of the organization, and the "Twelve Steps" are the core of its established procedure. The outlines laid down in The Book and in the Twelve Steps, however, are actually very broad, and require "filling in" according to local needs, resources, and types of members before they become sufficiently concrete to function as stable guides for day-to-day activity.

Thus far, Alcoholics Anonymous has gotten along with remarkably little articulation of what may be called "the minimum degree of structure necessary to the successful functioning of the group as a social organization." To cite only one example of this lack of articulation, the individual is encouraged to recognize the existence of a "Power greater than the self" and to transfer his worries and the direction of his will to that Power, as far as possible. The group does not attempt to go further than this in a theological way. From the point of view of those structural features which are necessary to the continued functioning of the organization as such, this is a distinct gap. Whether it is "according to plan" or not, it can be confidently expected that there will be pressures to fill in such gaps in structure. At the present stage of development the gaps are held open by an active tolerance wisely exercised by the founder and by the leading members of certain of the local groups. In certain other local groups the process of filling in the gaps with a more definite content of ideas and procedures can already be recognized.

This tendency toward crystallization, which might be called a "normal process" for all social organizations, whatever their purpose or type of membership may be, is particularly crucial to Alcoholics Anonymous because one of the great sources of strength in the group is the fact that it is largely residually defined. The very name of the group makes an initial appeal to the harassed compulsive drinker, since in it he will be "anonymous"— technically not known and not censured. He qualifies as a member of the group because for some undetermined reason he cannot drink like his friends who are social drinkers; and he is not required to determine what this reason is—at least, not immediately. He comes into a group which is unregimented, which is not specifically Protestant, Catholic, or Jewish, not Republican or Democratic, not upper, middle, or lower class, nor specifically anything else which can be placed neatly in the ordinary categories of social structure. The members are "a bunch of ex-drunks," as some of them put it, and even this is a residual definition.

So far as the job of staying sober is concerned, there are definite dangers in the inevitable pressures toward greater clarification, regularization, and, finally, formalization and rigidity, to which Alcoholics Anonymous, like every living social organization, is subjected. There is the constant danger that local groups will fall under the control of individuals who have not only imaginative and persuasive powers but also "ideas of their own" sufficiently unique to lead the group out of its loose and tentative structure into a rigidified form of organization and procedure which may destroy, or at least seriously hamper, the therapeutic effectiveness of the group, particularly where its appeal to new members is concerned. On the other hand, there are many organizational models which exercise a potential attractive influence on local groups—the model of some particular religious sect, perhaps, or of some lodge, service club, charitable organization, crusading organization, or the leisure club of some particular social class, according to the composition of the membership. The discerning observer can see the struggle both toward and away from such a crystallization in many of the local groups. Projects, plans, and opportunities are constantly presenting themselves which lead toward some more familiar and comfortable state of affairs.

To a certain degree the development of overhead organization is unavoidable. Meetings have to be arranged and the rent has to be paid. Less obvious, perhaps, but just as important for the job of staying sober, is the fact that the method of reproduction of the group results in an intimate network of friendships and mutual obligations which constitutes a major structural feature in its own right. This structure also has its dangers—it contains within it the seeds of jealousy, just as the human family does. The sponsor obtains a protégé. That man is "his baby." When another "baby" comes, the first is likely to be somewhat neglected, and to resent it. He may even have a "slip" to regain his place as a center of attraction. Another crisis appears when a protégé begins to be attracted to other members of the group, to listen to their views and explanations, and is "weaned away" from his original sponsor. This time the sponsor himself may "slip" from an excess of resentment or a need for attention. Still another crisis may be precipitated when the man who was a protégé "comes of age," as it were, and becomes more productive and successful in obtaining followers than his sponsor. This is the time of "old age" for the original sponsor. What he lacks in reproductive powers he may compensate for in political direction of the group on a less intimate level than that of the sponsor-protégé relationship. As long as he can command the veneration and respect which are likely to fall to an "old member" he may be safe, but when he begins to fall into the discard, as he may in a rapidly growing group, he is in danger of slipping again.

There is a more or less definite limit to the number of old members who can retain top positions of veneration and direction in any one local group, and when this limit is approached the political conflicts may be expected to grow more acute. This is the time when the local group is subjected to the most severe strains toward splitting into rival factions or cliques. One possible solution to such a conflict, if it arises, is to make such a clique formation the basis of a new group in a territorial setting somewhat removed—perhaps in a separate part of the city. If allowed to continue in one setting, these clique strains are a potential source of competition, irritation, jealousy, and resentment—a whole series of emotional disturbances which may lead to slips.

Against these potentially disturbing structural features, Alcoholics Anonymous has a very broad and sound basis of solidarity which can be positively defined. The things the members have in common which hold them together are their past drinking experiences, an intimate knowledge of the places and people the compulsive drinker inevitably gets to know, a bag of tricks, ruses, rationalizations, and defenses which they have been forced to build up in the course of their compulsive drinking, an odyssey of adventures and misadventures too often ending in tragedy, and the sense of a common fate: they are all alcoholics to whom drinking has become so dangerous and unmanageable that they can only go on by living a life of complete abstinence. It is upon these things that their solidarity rests.

Since the solidarity of the group depends upon past experiences which cannot form the basis for future action except in a negative way, that is, as an encouragement toward abstinence, the question as to what the group as such is to do in a positive way is one of the most obvious gaps in its structure. This gap is not actually filled in but simply blocked off by a program which aims only at the present "twenty-four hours," by the caution that "easy does it," and by the warning against "screwy alcoholic thinking," a type of thinking which, in part, consists of grandiose plans for the future. This simple blocking off of the future appears to be a sound feature, both for the individual who tends to be grandiose and for the continued successful functioning of the group.

When plans for concerted action begin to be considered in detail, the pressures toward more specific and rigid organization increase, political jealousies and divisions are likely to appear, and the vital relationship between the sponsor and his protégé, which is both the heart of the therapeutic process for the individual and the means of reproduction for the group, is likely to be endangered. One might say that, as a result of the group's particular basis of solidarity, the articulation of ideas and sentiments relevant to action, which are necessary and natural products of group life, can take place only in the areas of orientation toward the past and the immediate present, rather than toward the future, if the solidarity of the group is not to be endangered.

There is one positive course of action which would seem to offer a generalized protection against this whole series of potential dangers. This procedure is to emphasize above everything else, and to value above everything else, the activity of the individual member in bringing the Alcoholics Anonymous program to other alcoholics, and to direct all common or collective efforts of the group to the creation of ways and means of expediting these individual active efforts.

In the first place, this procedure brings into prominence the central purpose of Alcoholics Anonymous which distinguishes it from all other groups —devotion to the job of keeping sober and helping others to keep sober. The dangers of developing toward the pattern of some other more familiar type of organization, with therapeutically irrelevant purposes and features, are thus minimized.

In the second place, the continued activity of every individual member in bringing the Alcoholics Anonymous program to other alcoholics is the best generalized preventive measure against the overdevelopment and excessive prolongation of the individual attachments of sponsor to protégé which are bound to arise if the therapy is effective. The advantage is similar to that which large families, generally speaking, have over families with only one or two children, in the minimization of excessive attachments, jealousies, and suppressed conflicts.

In the third place, this emphasis brings into prominence and utilizes to the fullest extent the one general basis of solidarity in an organization otherwise residually defined—the past common experiences and present common characteristics of the members as compulsive drinkers. The exploration, articulation, and emphasis of this fund of past experience, as it applies to the present situation of the compulsive drinker, is the main resource of material for the meetings, and the central reason for their being. This resource can be utilized to the fullest extent without incurring any of the dangers of developing an irrelevant and therapeutically dangerous overhead organization which would follow from a more explicit articulation of future plans and features for the organization as a whole.

Finally, in the activity of the individual as he attempts to help other alcoholics, this basis of solidarity comes into the sharpest focus and is, in general, the most effective and unique feature of the therapeutic process as it goes on between the Alcoholics Anonymous sponsor and his protégé. In this fund of common experience, and in the particularly intimate friendship it fosters, every member has a resource for helping other alcoholics that can hardly be duplicated by any other type of therapist.

chapter 33

Alcoholics Anonymous:
an interpretation[*]

Milton A. Maxwell

It is probable that more contemporary alcoholics have found sobriety through the fellowship of Alcoholics Anonymous than through all other agencies combined. Yet the "A.A. recovery program" remains an unknown quantity to many, and at least something of an enigma to most. It is agreed that, for many alcoholics, the A.A. program "works," but what makes it work? What are the therapeutic dynamics? At this point, even social scientists and clinicians close to the alcoholism problem are often baffled. They find it difficult to reconcile what they know or think they know about A. A. with their theoretical assumptions about the nature of alcoholism on the one hand and the imperatives of the therapeutic processes on the other. The interpretation that follows—limited and incomplete as it must be—is based on the assumption that enigmatic qualities of A. A. are more apparent than real, and that the A.A. program "makes sense" in the light of contemporary social science concepts and assumptions.

Conditions for Change

How then, we may ask, can the alcoholic change? If the more he uses alcohol as his means of relief the worse he gets, and if he is unable to control its consumption, how can he escape his dilemma? Paradoxically, the answer seems to be that he cannot escape his predicament until he faces the fact that by himself he cannot escape it. It appears, furthermore, that the alcoholic has to become completely disillusioned, not only with his own ability to solve his alcohol problem, but also with alcohol as his method of solving any problems. This includes the conviction that his drinking which

[*] This chapter was written especially for this book.

577

for years was considered to be an asset has definitely become a liability and, if continued, will lead only to more suffering, degradation, and perhaps insanity, or even death. For the disillusionment with alcohol to be complete, however, it apparently must include the conviction that any compromise goal of safe, controlled drinking is utterly impossible for him. The average alcoholic knows what the ultimate outcome of compulsive drinking is, but he finds it difficult to believe that this fate is in store for him until he is completely convinced that he is an "uncontrolled drinker."

Such disillusionment was reported in a study of 150 A.A. members (6). Asked what had happened just before joining A. A. to make them ready for A. A., some of the respondents simply expressed their over-all feeling of despair. For example, the comments ran as follows: (a) "Complete feeling of being 'licked.' Dejected and remorseful—'down and out' "; (b) "The feeling [that] I was just in a sort of whirl-pool which was slowly taking me beyond hope"; (c) "A beaten, hopeless person, my back to the wall"; and (d) "At the end of the rope."

About 25 per cent replied in terms similar to these, obviously implying their inability to control their drinking, but another 35 per cent specifically listed the conviction of being an uncontrolled drinker as the factor which made them ready for A.A. help. For example, one respondent stated: "I finally faced the obvious fact that my drinking was completely out of control. I'd tried many so-called systems to limit my drinking and failed." Still another 28 per cent mentioned some jolting event which gave a disillusioning, crisis definition to their use of alcohol. Most often listed was the loss or threatened loss of job or spouse. Also listed were such events as arrest for drunken driving, hospitalization or illness because of drinking, fractured skull in a fall while drunk, rejection of a life insurance application, insane behavior during a drinking bout, blackouts, and hallucinations.

Apparently, however, disillusionment is only one of the major prerequisites for readiness to seek help. A certain number, obviously implying their disillusionment with their alcoholic way of life, reported the discovery that there was a way out as the factor which made them ready for A. A. This is the prerequisite of "hope," without which an active movement toward help is not conceivable.

In the case of these particular subjects, the hope was usually introduced by a recovered alcoholic—an A.A. member. And here we can pinpoint one of A.A.'s great strengths. The mere information that A. A. (or any therapeutic program) can work introduces hope into an alcoholic's situation. How much more convincing, then, is the flesh-and-blood example of a person for whom the program has worked! In addition, if this same "recovered" alcoholic, through his accepting and understanding attitude, can also help the prospect face and accept an honest, disillusioning appraisal of his drinking problem, it is much easier to bring about the particular intersection of disillusionment and hope which constitutes "readiness" to move toward help.

Such a meaningful coming together of disillusionment and hope seems to be a very individual matter. It may occur early as in the case of what A.A.'s call "high bottoms." It may not occur until after many years of suffering ("low bottoms"), and it may not occur at all, but there is nothing fateful about it. More early-stage and early-middle-stage alcoholics are affiliating with A. A. and are being seen in the growing number of alcoholic clinics as a result of alcoholism education and the therapeutic success of A. A. and other programs.

Whether disillusionment and hope intersect early or late, it appears that both are prerequisites for readiness to seek or accept help. It follows, accordingly, that these prerequisites should be the first two steps in the A.A. program of recovery:

1. We admitted we were powerless over alcohol—that our lives had become unmanageable.
2. Came to believe that a Power greater than ourselves could restore us to sanity.

The Greater Power Concept

The naturalistically oriented reader who has been following this analysis without difficulty up to this point finds himself up against language which may block his understanding of A. A. at a crucial point. What is he to make of William James' phrase, "a Power greater than ourselves," especially if this is then equated with "God as we understood Him"? It may therefore be appropriate to point out that a naturalistic interpretation of the "Greater Power" concept is possible.

The reader can, for example, recognize the fact that there are powers—resources of many kinds—to help an alcoholic recover. He can also recognize the fact that these resources for recovery are quite beyond the isolated, alibi-ridden, and anxious alcoholic. If one is sophisticated in the use of the concept of "self," one can recognize that these resources believed to be within the individual are nevertheless beyond and outside the "self" as the alcoholic knows himself. These resources are not effectively but only potentially present.

Moreover, it can be accepted that the potential resources are empirically identifiable resources. They consist of real energies locked up or wasted in conflict, burned up in anxiety, and depleted through neglect of health. They consist of blocked and unused mental powers. They consist of the potential capacities to be "productive" in Erich Fromm's sense of being able to love, to give, and to accomplish. All these and other potential resources are "there"—they are "real."

As far as the alcoholic is concerned, however, they are anything but "there." It is even difficult for him to believe that they are potentially present. Yet, to move out of his dilemma, he has to develop some belief, tentative and partial though it may be, that the potential resources are real—are available to him—and are capable of restoring him to normalcy. This is the hope of Step 2.

Next the alcoholic is asked to turn himself over to this potential—to abandon his constricted and hopeless position and to "surrender" or "give in" to the "life forces" potentially available. This would be the naturalistic interpretation of the third step:

3. Made a decision to turn our will and lives over to the care of God *as we understood Him.*

It might be added that, in actual practice, atheists, agnostics, naturalists, and a great variety of supernaturalists have found it possible to take this important step thanks largely to the phrase *"as we understood Him,"* and to the general practice of requiring nothing more than some concept of some power or powers other than what the particular alcoholic is able to command at the time. This may be the group. It may be the program. It may be a liberal or orthodox concept of God. It may be anything which meaningfully symbolizes to the individual the potential resources on which to base his hope of recovery.

Thus the first three steps in the A.A. program are seen to consist of the necessary admission of powerlessness over alcohol and a hopeful willingness to let the more productive forces in the individual and his situation prevail. To the degree that the three prerequisites are met, the formerly impossible begins to happen. The log jam is broken. The emotional constriction is relaxed. The release of potential resources begins. Satisfying interactions with other persons again become possible. In short, the movement toward health begins.

The Twelve-Step Program

Many of the elements of the Twelve-Step Program are seen in sharper relief in the original formulation of the steps by which Bill, A.A.'s cofounder, achieved sobriety. These are: you admit you are licked; you get honest with yourself; you talk it out with somebody else; you make restitution to the people you have harmed; you try to give of yourself without stint, with no demands for reward; and you pray to whatever God you think there is, even as an experiment, to help you to do these things (1).

In this series of steps will be seen the admission of "powerlessness over alcohol" already discussed. Also implicit is the hope of a way out—faith in potential resources and complete reliance upon these resources. The other steps constitute quite an additional order: honest self-analysis and catharsis; the mending of social fences; the practice of out-going, giving, productive behavior for its own sake and not for ego-defense or reassurance; and, finally, the cultivation of the "potential resources" as understood by the individual. Much could be written about the therapeutic value of these steps, for there is wide consensus about the importance of an honest facing of oneself and the unburdening of guilts, fears, and repressed material in the presence of an accepting person, and about the importance of cultivating the desired attitudes and practicing the desired patterns of behavior. However, the Twelve Steps do not exhaust the A.A. program. The interpersonal and group aspects of the A.A. fellowship also play a very important therapeutic role.

The Personality Changes

That personality changes occur in A. A. is accepted. It is true that the degree or range of change varies greatly from person to person. Some merely achieve sobriety without any other observable change. Yet, in perspective, even this achievement is a dramatic one. In the writer's opinion, however, the majority exhibit additional and sometimes very substantial changes in personality.

The changes and direction of change may be seen in the case material upon which the writer has previously reported (5). The following seven replies are representative of the kinds of "attitudes, desires, fears, etc." which A. A. had helped its members to "give up" to some degree:

a. I gave up intolerance, jealousy, self-pity, anger as much as possible, desire for power and a lot of money, being critical.

b. Self-pride, conceit, headstrong attitude, fears of others and their opinion of me, fear of my thoughts, fear of inadequacy and fear of insecurity.

c. The attitudes of egotism, vanity, selfishness, etc., and the desire of wanting to be a big shot—the big I (without of course trying to even deserve such a title).

d. Have tried to give up selfishness, "Big I" attitude, running others my way, desire for money as such, false social position, procrastination, fear of what people might say.

e. Gave up the fear of loving anyone wholeheartedly, even my child; fear of life for myself and others; thinking it smart to be caustic and overbearing.

f. Am relinquishing the attitude of self-importance and the feeling of the need to emphasize my qualifications compared to those of others . . . .

g. Gave up formless fears, fear of failure, sense of inadequacy, fear of people or love . . . and pretense of being other than one of the "little people" who are bound by the limitations of their own undeveloped potentialities.

More systematically summarized, the list of reported changes was led on the one hand by the reduction of interpersonal anxieties, ego-inflation, hostility, and intolerance, and, in a listing of values gained, by an increase in the ability to interact more satisfyingly with other persons. Reportedly gained was the greater enjoyment and appreciation not only of other persons but also of other facets of life; a greater ability to face and accept reality; greater objectivity with regard to self—honesty, humility, and sense of humor and of proportion; an increase in the sense of security, adequacy, confidence, worth, and accomplishment; physical and emotional relaxation; and, finally—and frequently listed—"peace of mind."

If any one trend stands out in these reported changes, it is the modification of self-other attitudes and perceptions in the direction of what we have been calling a more productive orientation.

A complete accounting of personality changes is beyond the scope of present knowledge. We assume that such changes are the products of learning. We assume furthermore that the learning processes in A. A. are of the same kind found in any psychotherapy leading to the same changes. The language of psychotherapy could be used to describe and explain many aspects of the therapeutic dynamics to be found in A. A.* It is, however, possible and appropriate to conceive of the personality-changing dynamics in A. A. in more sociological concepts.

The A.A. Group and Its Subculture

Kurt Lewin and Paul Grabbe (2) have provided us with a bridge in their suggestion that a change in personality may be conceptualized as a change in culture. Specifically, they suggested that to change is to accept a change in "facts" which are accepted as true, a change in values, and a change in the perception of self and others in a social field. To this we could add that the personality changes may also be seen as the acceptance of new norms —folkways and mores, new roles in a new role-status system, a new charter, and new sanctions. These are all aspects of culture—of a group-shared way of life.

We may accordingly conceptualize the alcoholic's recovery in A. A. as the joining of a new group and, in that group, gradually learning that group's culture. The A.A. subculture, moreover, constitutes a way of life which is more realistic, which enables the member to get closer to people, which provides one with more emotional security, and which facilitates more productive living. Thus, the A.A. group becomes an important new reference group—a new point of orientation.

The A.A. group must also be seen as a primary group which provides exceptionally favorable learning conditions for the internalizing of this new way of life. Primary groups were so called by Cooley because they are more influential than other groups in shaping our attitudes. Among primary groups, however, some are more influential than others. The more intimate the group and the more totally involved its members become in each other and the group life, the greater is the influence of the group upon its members.

The writer's experience as a participant observer in an A.A. group for a summer impressed upon him the unusual quality of relationship to be found there—the intimacy, mutual acceptance, and identification. Unless these qualities of relationship are recognized and unless the "relearning potency" of such a group experience is appreciated, the observer will miss something very important about A. A.

To summarize the points just made: the A.A. group is to be understood as an unusually intimate primary group which sponsors, in a potent learning situation, a new way of life—a new subculture. Within this frame of refer-

---

* See for example Tiebout (11, 12, 13), Stewart (9, 10), Ripley and Jackson (7), and Lindt (3).

ence, it is possible to analyze the content of this new learning and how it deals with the linkage of stress to alcohol drinking.

First, the A.A. subculture provides the member with much more objective knowledge about alcohol and particularly about alcoholism. This includes a redefinition of alcoholism as an illness rather than as moral degeneracy.

Second, the A.A. subculture requires and facilitates an honest facing of the connection between drinking and stressful situations; the alcoholic begins to define his disorder as involving an obsession of the mind. The impotency of will power to handle the obsession and the necessity of other help are emphasized. Myths and rationalizations concerning drinking are debunked. The "screwy alcoholic thinking" is dissected and exposed, frequently in a humorous fashion.

Anxieties against drinking are buttressed. Alcohol is associated with all the harm it has done to the alcoholic and with the tragic increase rather than the solution of problems. The member is given perspective on the first drink—that he will always be just one drink from a drunk, and that he can never again drink socially. He is taught that he can "arrest" his problem but that he will always remain an alcoholic. This fact is reinforced each time he presides and introduces himself with "I'm Joe Doakes and I'm an alcoholic." Then, to handle the anxiety aroused by the dread of a lifetime without alcohol, he is provided with the "24-hour plan"—sobriety just one day at a time. Because of his association and identification with sobriety models, the A.A. system is made easier to accept and learn. Then when he steps out to help a new prospect (Twelfth-Step calls), he furthers his learning by becoming a teacher and a representative of the A.A. way of thinking and acting. Thus, the A.A. ideology not only attacks vigorously the use of alcohol for the relief of stress, it provides alternative methods of tension relief.

Important is the A.A. structuring of the freedom and the formal and informal opportunities to gain relief from tensions by the "talking-out" process. Important also are the club activities: the fellowship of the coffee bar, the bull sessions, the games, the parties, or the hours of private conversations over a cup of coffee somewhere. In countless ways, A. A. provides the rewards of satisfying social activities to replace the rewards previously sought in a drinking group, or simply sought in the bottle itself.

Outgoing activity in the form of "Twelfth-Step" work—working with other alcoholics—is another important mode of tension relief expected in A. A. In addition, the A.A. culture encourages the cultivation of hobbies, interests, and other means of tension relief. Included are meditation and prayer.

Not only does A. A. provide and encourage the learning (or relearning) of alternative relief methods, but the A.A. way of life also reduces the amount of stress for which relief is needed. When the compounding of stress through years of alcoholic drinking is considered, the reversal of the isolation, anxiety, and rationalization trends adds up to a substantial reduction of stress. In addition, acceptance of the A.A. way of life reduces the predrinking level of stress. This is done by providing the group member with values and norms and ways of perceiving his social world which are simply less anxiety-producing, which enable him to relate more satisfyingly to other people and, in general, to find more of the satisfactions of a productive orientation.

Other stress-reducing aspects of the A.A. way of life can be mentioned. There are the slogans repeated in the literature and usually posted in meeting places. "Live and let live" reminds the member of the importance of tolerance for others. "Keep an open mind" asks for tolerance of new ideas. "Easy does it" suggests relaxation in various tension-producing contexts. "But for the Grace of God" expresses thankfulness and reminds him of his dependence upon more than his own efforts. The value placed upon "honesty" and "humility" are a constant encouragement to a greater objectivity with regard to himself.

To be rated also are the low-pressure methods encouraged in A.A. This permissiveness has the function of reducing initial resistance. It constantly encourages respect for the rights of the other fellow—even his right to get drunk if he wants to.

Many other aspects of the A.A. way of life could be cited, but the above are sufficient to illustrate the present frame of reference through which the changes in the A.A. member's personality are seen as the learning of a new culture—a new way of life—in the favorable learning milieu of an exceptionally intimate primary group.

Lest too idealized an impression be left, however, it should be acknowledged that A.A. groups often fall short of providing an ideal learning environment. Even in the same group, the constellation of factors is less favorable for some members than for others.

In studying the favorable and unfavorable factors involved in affiliation with A. A., Trice (14, 15) found not only differences in attitude and knowledge on the part of those attempting to affiliate, but also differences in the receiving groups. Despite the injunctions of the program, prospects were not always provided with sponsorship. Nor were efforts always made to draw one into close relationships with the members.

The writer's own observations in many A.A. groups have led him to similar conclusions. Some groups are less energetic in reaching out to new members, less successful in sponsoring them and in overcoming their early fears. Some groups, furthermore, fail to provide as warm and intimate a climate as others. Thus they create group situations which are less favorable not only to affiliation but also to effective relearning.

It also appears that groups vary considerably in the psychological insight collectively possessed by their members—insight into the causes of alcoholism, the dynamics of personality, and even the personality-changing factors of the program and group activities of A. A. itself. Groups also vary in the maturity of the actual patterns of behavior prevailing in the group. This refers not only to the amount of rivalry, conflict, or other "immature" behavior, but also to the level of productive living which is espoused and to the seriousness with which this goal is pursued.

That these and other differences exist in A.A. groups should, of course, surprise no one, nor should the differences obscure the recognition that even the more ineffective groups, if they continue to exist at all, have achieved at last some success in learning and applying the A.A. way of life. Furthermore, the group differences should not obscure the appreciation that A. A. is an amazing phenomenon on the modern scene.

Not least remarkable is the fact that its program was worked out not by professional therapists but by a group of alcoholics themselves. A.A.'s success alone demonstrates that these laymen did indeed weave together a very effective pattern. Their lay language and spiritual concepts, however, have made it difficult for some social scientists and clinicians to appreciate fully the dynamics involved.

References

1. *Alcoholics Anonymous Comes of Age: A Brief History of A. A.*, New York: Alcoholics Anonymous Publishing, 1957.

2. Lewin, Kurt, and Paul Grabbe, "Conduct, Knowledge, and Acceptance of New Values," in Gertrud W. Lewin (Ed.), *Resolving Social Conflicts*, New York: Harper and Brothers, 1948, pp. 56–68.

3. Lindt, Hendrik, "The 'Rescue' Fantasy in Group Treatment of Alcoholics," *Inter. J. of Group Psychotherapy*, 9:43–52, 1959.

4. Maxwell, Milton A., *Social Factors in the Alcoholics Anonymous Program*, unpublished doctoral dissertation, University of Texas, 1949.

5. ———, "Interpersonal Factors in the Genesis and Treatment of Alcohol Addiction," *Social Forces*, 29:443–448, 1951.

6. ———, "Factors Affecting an Alcoholic's Willingness to Seek Help," *Northwest Science*, 28:116–123, 1954.

7. Ripley, Herbert S., and Joan K. Jackson, "Therapeutic Factors in Alcoholics Anonymous," *Amer. J. Psychiat.*, 116:44–50, 1959.

8. Ritchie, Oscar W., "A Sociohistorical Survey of Alcoholics Anonymous," *Quart. J. Stud. Alc.*, 9:119–156, 1948.

9. Stewart, David A., "The Dynamics of Fellowship as Illustrated in Alcoholics Anonymous," *Quart. J. Stud. Alc.*, 16:251–262, 1955.

10. ———, *Preface to Empathy*, New York: Philosophical Library, 1956.

11. Tiebout, Harry M., "The Act of Surrender in the Therapeutic Process with Special Reference to Alcoholism," *Quart. J. Stud. Alc.*, 10:48–58, 1949.

12. ———, "Surrender Versus Compliance in Therapy with Special Reference to Alcoholism," *Quart. J. Stud. Alc.*, 14:58–68, 1953.

13. ———, "The Ego Factor in Surrender in Alcoholism," *Quart. J. Stud. Alc.*, 15:610–621, 1954.

14. Trice, Harrison M., "A Study of the Process of Affiliation with Alcoholics Anonymous," *Quart. J. Stud. Alc.*, 18:39–43, 1957.

15. ———, "The Affiliation Motive and Readiness to Join Alcoholics Anonymous," *Quart. J. Stud. Alc.*, 20: 313–320, 1959.

chapter 34

Alcoholism is a disease: implications for social policy [*]

John R. Seeley

The statement, "Alcoholism is a disease," is now so widely heard in scientific and lay circles that one can hardly safely begin any undertaking in reference to alcoholism without first repeating it as, presumably, a sign of piety and a promise of right performance. If it is to function as something more than a shibboleth, a distinction between the "good guys" and the "bad guys," it would seem profitable to ask what is being contended in the assertion, what is its legitimacy, and what is the implication of what is asserted.

In order to gain perspective, it may be helpful at first to drop the preoccupation with alcoholism and to ask instead what is meant by any proposition of the form "X is a disease," where some noun appears in the place of X.

One's first impression may well be that anything men are willing to call a "disease" belongs in the class of things that they do not desire—or, to put it more actively, that they counter-desire. A moment's thought will indicate, however, that this is not the case. The slightest acquaintance with modern psychology and psychiatry, let alone with earlier common-sense observation, would indicate that not all diseases are undesired by all men, either for themselves or for others. Indeed, many processes that are destructive to the person are desired by him, either intrinsically for their very destructiveness, or because of some inseparable effect which is valued above other considerations. Even if we seek to exclude from the definition the judg-

[*] This chapter is based upon an unpublished paper prepared at the Alcoholism Research Foundation of Ontario as part of a series aimed at conceptual analysis of basic problems of research and policy in the alcoholism field.

ment upon the disease of the patient himself, we cannot, unfortunately, even assume that the disease in the patient is undesired or counter-desired by his immediate primary (or often secondary) group. The reasons are many and complex, but among them one must recognize the commonplace occurrence in everyday life of conscious or unconscious *schadenfreude*, even in reference to loved or valued others. Whatever else we may say, therefore, we cannot say that disease is a subclass of the class of things that are universally unwanted or counter-wanted by individuals.

If we cannot say that disease is something that is undesired, we can probably safely assert, if we are clear as to what we mean, that disease is something that is undesirable. However, we must make clear that, by "undesirable," we do not mean the probably null class of things which men cannot desire, but the class of things none of which is to be desired in the sense that men *ought not* to desire them. The message of the moralist, in season and out, is that, sadly for human happiness, this class includes a large part of what we actually do desire.

The discussion of what is desirable in this sense is as long as human history, and as acrimonious and blood-soaked, perhaps, as the discussion of any other question. Whether or not there is an "objective moral order," whether or not we can know about it with any security, and whether or not from such knowledge we can derive necessary propositions as to what ought to be desired, are all such vexed questions and so hopeless of proximate satisfactory answers that there is no profit now to be had from debating them here.

Failing such answers, then, what meaning may be given to "undesirable" that does not assume that we have the answers we actually haven't? The only remaining resort would seem to be, at least for now, to take a purely relativistic and sociological stand and to say that, from the viewpoint of any one person, the undesirable is that which those persons whom he regards as competent in such matters say is undesirable; and that, from the viewpoint of public communication, those things are undesirable which those officials whose official right it is so to declare, declare to be so. In this view, then, a disease is simply something in the category of those things that warranted judges (such as doctors, clergymen, and philosophers) declare as not to be desired.* The discriminant is thus a moral judgment intended presumably in full generality, even though all the judges may, and some certainly will, themselves desire what they say is not to be desired.†

---

* What is to be done if the warranted judges do not agree, as between categories of themselves or as between individuals, is by no means clear. Presumably, we should have to retreat to the definition of the top of the hierarchy, arranged in order of warranted capability of judgment.

† No amount of scientific haggling can, I think, get us off this ethical hook. Even if we say that disease is something that interferes with normal functioning or destroys or abbreviates life, there is an implicit prior judgment that normal function is to be desired, or the destruction or abbreviation of life to be not-desired.

Within the category of things to be not-desired, a disease is presumably moreover within the subcategory of transactions between the organism and its environment. This leaves logically open the possibility of defining as disease what is not-to-be-desired from the viewpoint of either, but habit and custom incline us, I think usefully, to make the criterion the effect on the organism rather than on the environment. What happens to the air around an advanced cancer patient is thus not the disease (even though it may be inseparably connected with it); the locus of the disease is from this viewpoint "in" the patient. However, the category we have reached— of not-to-be-desired transactions between an organism and its environment —is still too broad, especially when we are talking of the human organism. The category still includes more than diseases: "accidents," "sin," "crime," and deterioration (when taken as "natural" and inevitable). Accident is fortuitous.* Death is fated. Disease is differentiated from both by the view that it belongs in the category of the conceivably escapable—that is, by the view that we are not denied access to its control by an infinity of infinitesimal causes (chance) or an irresistible weight of cause (fate). This leaves us, within the category of the conceivably escapable, with disease, sin, and crime.

Crime and sin may be distinguished from one another in terms of their respective violations of the mandates to render unto Caesar that which is Caesar's and unto God that which is God's. What unites them and at the same time differentiates both from disease is the again-inescapable notion of culpability. Disease falls into a naturalistic matrix; sin, into a moral one; crime, into a legal one.

Even so, the distinction is not as clear cut as one might wish. If in a series of transactions with the environment every stage (except the first) follows in natural sequence from the preceding one, the whole series may be a disease. However, the first stage—or the reaching of it—may or may not be clear of culpability. Indeed, even later stages in the "natural process"— rather, the acts of omission or commission by which they are reached— may not be held to be blame free.

As to the first, it is widely believed that any person who permits himself to become infected with small-pox (under circumstances where effective preventive measures are available) is, in effect, a sinner or a criminal (in that respect). As to the second stage, a similar view is taken, by many specialists in the field, of those persons who, having contracted a venereal disease, leave the sequel to nature in the presence of and with adequate knowledge about mitigating, palliative, therapeutic, or abbreviating measures. The disease itself is a "natural process" and therefore outside the realm where praise and blame are relevant. However, the entertainment by the host of the disease will continue to be a matter of culpability assessment wherever two elements are held to coexist: (a) means that, if em-

* Unless we change the essential meaning of the term as in discussing the "accident-prone." What we then mean to say is that (some) accidents are no accidents!

ployed, would positively affect the probability of minimizing the undesirable; and (b) capacity in the person being judged to put these means into use.

A special category of "diseases" emerges, perhaps, where the natural course of the "disease" acts significantly upon the second condition for culpability—capacity to put potentially "saving" means to use. If we knew of a drug or other agent such that, once ingested, it literally and utterly paralyzed all capacity to entertain any other idea except further consumption, and if this further consumption led on to dissolution and death, the entire element of culpability (after the first act of ingestion) would disappear, and the subsequent sequence would be treated, without ambivalence, as a disease. The opposite ideal type would be the one where nothing connected with the natural process (of the disease) itself affected at any point capacity to make an imputed "free" choice as to next steps.

In the case of some or all mental disorders, or processes in which there occur specifiable, sensible, psychological alterations (in the inevitable natural course of the "disease"), the very capacity to act or to act appropriately in reference to "saving" means is affected, and to that extent culpability is diminished in part or altogether. The problem, therefore, of separating an organism-environment behavior sequence of the kind we have been talking about into disease components and non-disease components— the latter being justiciable and the former not—depends on an assessment, specific for the stage in the process and for the organism's situation, as to what is "free" and what is "determined" behavior. Logically then, what is "in" the disease and what is outside it depends on an act of judgment as to what may properly be brought under judgment.*

The imputation of "sickness" also carries with it a whole series of consequences †—consequences which, foreseen, as ends-in-view, enter into the decision as to whether or not to make the imputation. An obvious consequence is that the imputation itself may (indeed, mostly will, in the case of many sequences substantially affected by psychological components) enter as a difference-making element (therapeutic or counter-therapeutic, public-interest adient or abient) into the behavior sequence of the imputee.

A second and most important consequence is the shift in moral responsibility for care, palliation, cure, and control from one set of professions to another: from the defenders of the society to the defenders of the individual, from the police function to the protective function, from the rule-administrative to the exception-providing, from the enforcing to the "helping"

---

* This view, of course, would rule out of the universe of discourse the views of pure determinists, for whom the legitimacy of acts, including acts of judgment, must be a meaningless category; and the views of pure indeterminists—if such there be—for whom any discussion of policy must be trivial, since the notion of policy rests on foreseeable regularities of relation between acts and their sequels.

† The profound and pioneer analysis of the social meaning of being sick stems from Talcott Parsons and is reported in (1). Something of what is said here is already inferentially obvious in his treatment; see especially pages 436 and 437.

professions. Of course, this is not to say that the roles are not complementary, or that mixed cases do not exist, or that elements from one function do not have to be discharged sometimes by persons performing the other; but the main distinction is clear enough. The act involved is—in reverse— the analogue of the act of excommunication and turning the heretic over to the secular arm of the medieval church. The imputee is withdrawn from secular responsibilities and the secular view, and drawn into a special communion where his transcendent value as an individual is given operative paramount effect.

A third consequence, not wholly separable from the preceding, is a redefinition of the total expectation or demand system upon the imputee. This may well extend beyond the elements of the disease itself, or even further than matters closely related to it. Indeed, in another phrasing, the imputation carries by implication a new license, radically different from the preimputational one, and in many cases a near contrary. The imputee may be permitted (or even enjoined) to be instead of to do; to absorb and consume instead of to produce; to be self-centered or (temporarily) "regressed" instead of other- or system-centered and "mature"; and to constrict his time span from either past or future orientation to present orientation. ("Learn to live a day or even an hour at a time.") It is difficult to resist the generalization that the imputation of the term "sickness" both defines the imputee out of the general, public, and secondary-group life and relations into a special, private, and primary-group one, and, in effect, permits or encourages or commands him to orient himself primarily (temporarily or otherwise, and in more or less radical degree) to those values which are the contraries of the acknowledged ones in the culture.

One might also be tempted to add, in terms of one's relation to self rather than others' relation to one, that the imputation of sickness constitutes an invitation to the sick one to take himself out of the atmosphere of overconcern, overintimacy, overresponsibility for himself, and to move towards a view of himself (in the relevant regards) as a natural object in a natural sequence—that is, as the "stage" for an event rather than as an actor in a situation. Put another way, the dual effect of the imputation on the imputee is (a) in his relation to others, to bring him from a secondary-group relation into a primary-group one, and (b) in his own relation to himself, to move his view from the highly overconcerned, very personal, primary-group view to a more detached, natural-sequence, objective, secondary-group view. In many cases, this is not only a prelude to engagement in therapy, but the very first and most essential step thereof.

One more consequence is that the imputation carries with it the legitimation of claims to "outside" help—help from outside the self, outside the primary group, very often outside the circle of those who could be rewarded, by pay or otherwise, for helping. Indeed, it may go further—toward an implicit moral injunction to seek outside help or all the way to coercion in accepting "help" (as in commitment for mental disease).

The decision as to whether or not to call something a "disease" seems therefore to turn on an evaluation of the foreseen consequences of so designating it—as against designating it otherwise—in terms primarily of the effect of the designation (and what it carries with it) on what would be either the natural sequence without designation or the sequence consequent upon some other designation. The decision to call something a disease is hence a programmatic decision as well as or instead of a diagnostic establishment of the presence or absence of a given state of affairs.

Withal, is nothing more than social or therapeutic policy involved? Are there not some characteristics about behavior sequences that limit, if they do not determine, what may and may not come under the process of decision at all? More particularly, are there not some reality characteristics (independent of considerations in terms of the effect of the adjudication) that make a class of behavior sequences candidates for such judgment, and/or, if present, force the judgment to one verdict or the other, if judging takes place at all?

The feeling that there must be positive answers to these latter questions springs certainly in part from the fact that the word "disease," as commonly employed, belongs to the biological sciences, as against the physical or social sciences. Since within the biological sciences crime and sin are not terms in the universe of discourse, and since the desire of the non-human organism cannot be determined, nor what is desirable for it made a matter of aesthetics or morality, disease, even from the "viewpoint" of the organism, must be defined in quite other terms. For an organism, a disease is a process in which its specific characteristics are diminished or their increase toward a maximum or an optimum militated against. One would have to emphasize the word "process" as against an episode—e.g., an accident; and one would have to invoke the notion of evitability—otherwise, aging beyond a certain point would come as a case under the definition.

The two characteristics of an organism that seem most general, and whose reduction or evitable non-increase (where increase is otherwise potential) are involved, are its order and complexity.* Whatever conceivably evitable process, therefore, leads toward an increase in the organism's entropy or a reduction in its complexity (or both) may be labeled a "disease." It is an article of faith—or an overarching hypothesis—that all such changes will be accompanied by observable changes in the elements of the system under observation, or in the relations of those elements, or both. If the process is the disease, these alterations, or, rather, altered states, may be thought of as the pathology.

* By its order is meant nothing more than the degree of improbability, in comparison with a random distribution, of the state that it is in. Rationality and self-control, for instance, are hence most improbable and highly ordered states. By its complexity is meant simply the number of "bits" of information that would be required to give a description of it. I do not think that these are wholly dependent or wholly independent dimensions.

When we examine human beings in terms of behavior or in terms of psychological states, we have no reason to abandon this fundamental biological orientation, though it may fail in a given state of knowledge and practice to be of much practical guidance. If we speak of "functional psychoses," we should recognize that this is but a loose shorthand for a set of states of increased entropy or decreased complexity (or both) for which we do not *yet* know the correlated alterations in biological structure. To *state* that there are none postulates omniscience; that is, we would have to know everything to know that there were no such correlates. To *postulate* that there are none takes the data into a wholly new domain of phenomena with a special ad hoc metaphysics.

If we take this view—that every behavior sequence presumably involves altered bodily states—then no behavior sequence is ruled out from the possibility of being labeled a disease simply because we do not know what those states or their interconnections are. Hence, if "alcoholism" or "delinquency-as-a-career" recommend themselves for inclusion in the disease category on other grounds, it is difficult to see what could be said from the side of biology—except *ignoramus*—that would make for their exclusion as contrary to good biological usage. Indeed, their labeling as diseases will quite probably make for that kind of research which has the best chance of discovering the observable biological connections which, if now known, would have justified the label "disease" in the more obvious or narrower sense.

We have now come close to saying, I believe, that, in the domain of well-marked, evitable, undesirable behavior sequences, the question of what is to be designated as a disease and what otherwise is a matter of social policy is to be decided in terms of its consequences for (primarily) the continuation or sequel of the behavior process itself. Such a view clearly opens the door to more humane, physician-like "treatment" of many sequences or conditions, but it opens also a veritable lawyer's nightmare of a door to far more than we might wish. What is to prevent, on this view, a gradual process of apostasy from the Church or the Communist Party—or, per contra, the increasing conservatism that accompanies maturation in many—from being defined as a disease, and the exhibitor of the behavior from being consigned to a compulsory "treatment," more dangerous than persecution (more dangerous, of course, because it comes garbed ostensibly in love rather than hate and invites "surrender" rather than resistance)? There is nothing to prevent such dangerous extension of the view except insofar as we can tie the use of the word "undesirable" to some high-friction social process (such as court adjudication); and even then we are not sure. In any case, we already face such risks—in the imputation of "insanity," for instance. Such safeguards as there are lie in the character of persons and in the institutions of the society. We are no safer against them if we use terms arbitrarily instead of consistently.

On the foregoing view, then, there is little difficulty in concluding—without any long arguments about "craving" or about the physical correlates, if any, of "loss of control" —that we *may* choose to speak of "alcoholism" as a "disease." The behavior sequence is relatively well marked. The judgment of undesirability would be a matter of nearly universal consent among the socially warranted judges. It is clearly within the domain of organism-environment transactions, and equally clearly in the realm of the conceivably evitable.

If we may without impropriety define it as a disease, we may next ask *should* we—a question for wisdom—and, if so, how should we report our decision—a question for communication or education expertise.

On the first question, I think we might safely rest a positive answer on the sheer historic unavailingness of measures taken upon the basis of other definitions. Punitive measures based upon a view of alcoholism as crime seem to have a classic nugatory effect matched only by hortatory measures based upon a view of alcoholism as sin. What, then, is left as hopeful except the third definition, as disease? And do we not have some indications in the field itself of some differential favorable outcome under such a redefinition, as well as some reasons for hope in this direction from fields analogical to our own? If this is so, and if we are to be as prudent as may be, might not wisdom indicate an experimental procedure in which we commit ourselves to the disease view on a trial basis and judge finally the soundness of our definition by its consequences?

As far as public communication is concerned, however, I think the bare statement that "alcoholism is a disease" is most misleading, since (*a*) it links up with a much-too-narrow concept of "disease" in the public mind, and (*b*) it conceals what is essential—that is, that a step in public policy is being *recommended,* not a scientific discovery announced. It would seem to me infinitely preferable to say, "It is best to look on alcoholism as a disease because . . . ," and to enumerate reasons. This would both take the public into our confidence (and hence really educate) and permit withdrawal of the recommendation if it seemed wise at a later date. The latter ought to be much easier and more comprehensible than a first announcement of a seeming scientific fact and its later contradiction with no new evidence.

References

1. Parsons, Talcott, *The Social System*, Glencoe, Ill.: Free Press, 1951.

chapter 35

What the state
does about alcohol
and alcoholism:
an international survey[*]

Archer Tongue

In many of the international congresses on alcohol and alcoholism which have been held over the past 75 years, the subject of state activity in this field has often been considered. Discussion has, however, usually tended to be from the point of view of legislative enactment or fiscal measures, and the various systems of regulation, license, and monopoly have been thoroughly examined.

The last 15 years, however, have seen the emergence of a new pattern of development, namely, the overall state program or direct action by the state in the whole field of alcoholism and alcohol problems. In many countries the state is now not just concerned with legislation but is also taking direct action as regards education, treatment, and rehabilitation, as well as the organization of research.

Some reference to the historical development in this regard since the end of the Second World War may be helpful. It was in 1947, in Connecticut, that there appeared the first American state commission on alcoholism which grew out of the Board of Trustees of the State Fund for Inebriates set up two years earlier. This was followed by the New Jersey Commission on Alcoholism, and now some thirty-five to forty of the United States have programs on alcoholism either maintained by an independent commission or integrated in the various state health services. In 1949, the first Canadian program, the Alcoholism Research Foundation of Ontario, was established,

[*] This chapter is a revised and somewhat shortened version of a paper presented at the 26th International Congress on Alcohol and Alcoholism in Stockholm, July 31 through August 5, 1960.

and some five or six Canadian provinces have since developed their own programs.

In Europe also there was considerable activity in this period. In Switzerland, in 1945, the Federal Commission on Alcoholism was appointed. The year 1954 saw the inauguration of several new programs. An important event in France was the creation in that year, through the initiative of Mr. Mendes-France, of the Government High Committee of Study and Information on Alcoholism. In 1954, in the Soviet Union, the Ministry of Health issued directives on alcoholism education and treatment to doctors and medical personnel which led to the development of a nationwide program organized through the Central Research Institute of Health Education.

In 1954, also, a State Council on Alcoholism was set up in Iceland. In the same year a state program on alcoholism was initiated in Yugoslavia by the Yugoslav Red Cross. During this period other state programs were developed in Eastern Europe—in particular, in Poland, where a Central Committee to deal with alcoholism throughout the country was inaugurated, and where in 1957 an Interministerial Commission under the Minister of Labor and Social Service was established to coordinate effort and planning in this field. In Czechoslovakia, a Central Committee to promote a national program was formed in the Ministry of Health.

In 1947, the Indian Government, on attaining independence, established a program of prohibition which, however, went beyond mere legislative measures and was applied differently in the different states of the country.

During the 1950's in Latin America various types of programs were put into operation, such as, for instance, that growing out of the Commission on Delinquency of the Ministry of Justice in Venezuela and the program organized by the Ministry of Health in Peru, stimulated by the National Conference on Alcoholism held there in 1957. In Chile, over some years, there has been a developing program with particular emphasis on research.

It is clear from these facts that in recent years there has been a remarkable development of state activity in the alcoholism field. It is too early, and it would involve a considerable amount of research, to present a really comparative evaluation of the results of these various state programs. It is, however, useful to examine the structure, aims, and activities of some of these programs.

In considering these state programs it is necessary to make clear one rather important distinction between North American and European practice. In Europe, programs on alcoholism usually include, as well as questions regarding alcoholism in the strict sense of the word (that is, the treatment and rehabilitation of the problem drinker), the intoxication-caused problems. In North America, on the other hand, such problems would appear to have been much less emphasized in state programs. Moreover, in North America, state programs of education on alcohol problems have tended to develop within state departments of education, such as those of Mississippi and Florida. In some states, cooperation between the commission on alcoholism and the education department is now developing towards a comprehensive plan for instruction on alcohol problems.

From the foregoing the impression might be gained that state programs on alcoholism have emerged only in the postwar period. This is not the case, however, for in the Nordic countries state programs have been in existence for many years. Usually, however, these older programs differ from the more recently established ones in that they rely to a very large degree, as concerns education on alcoholism and alcohol problems, on private organizations subsidized by the state. It would be appropriate in commencing this survey to refer briefly to one of these earlier programs, and Norway may be taken as an example in this respect.

In Norway, in 1936, a body known as the State Temperance Council was set up consisting of five members appointed by the King. This body is responsible for ensuring liaison between different state departments on legislative and administrative matters concerning alcoholism. Its major activity, however, is that of helping and guiding the municipal "Sobriety Boards," which are established in almost all areas in Norway and have as their duty the care of alcoholics and the promotion of education on alcohol problems. In particular, the State Temperance Council arranges courses for the orientation of these committees in their duties.

Then the State Temperance Council maintains liaison between the Ministry and the various private temperance education bodies who receive grants from the state for education and research. One of the most important of these is the State Board of Temperance Education, which was actually set up as long ago as 1902 and which includes in its management, in addition to representatives of private bodies, board representatives of the Social Affairs Ministry, of the Ecclesiastical and Educational Ministry, of the Central Board of Statistics, and of the University of Oslo.

One of the recent initiatives undertaken by the State Temperance Council of Norway shows a particular field in which the organ of a state program may have a significant role to play. This is in reaching the broad masses of the people who are not always responsive to private organizations, particularly if some kind of membership is involved. In Norway, recently, this action in the field of alerting the larger public took the form of what was known as the *Bred Front* (Broad Front), which introduced and stimulated attention to alcoholism problems in a variety of organizations which had no direct connection with the subject.

This particular function of a state program may also be seen in the activities of the High Committee of Study and Information on Alcoholism in France dating from 1954. The duties of this committee, which is directly responsible to the Cabinet and not to any ministry, are to assemble all information relative to the problem of alcoholism, to propose to the Government any measures which would tend to the diminution of this problem, and to undertake with other interested bodies an extensive campaign of information directed to the general public, public authorities, and large public utilities on the dangers of alcoholism and the possibilities of arresting its development.

The composition of this committee is interesting. The members who are elected in their own right are not more than eighteen in number and consist of three doctors, two members of the teaching service, five parliamentarians or former parliamentarians, several high officials, an industrialist, an agriculturalist, a manual worker, and a journalist. There is a permanent panel of thirteen experts called into consultation on the different subjects under examination as required. There are broadly three fields of activity: the first, that of general information; the second, the modification of the production of alcoholic beverages, as, for instance, dealing with problems posed by the prevalence of home distilling, eliminating wines of poor quality, and encouraging non-alcoholic beverages; thirdly, the harmonization of the policies of different ministerial departments with regard to alcoholism.

The cooperation between this committee and the Ministry of Health, which has its own particular program for the treatment and rehabilitation of alcoholics, is close; also, relations are maintained with private organizations, such as the National Committee of Defense against Alcoholism. A continuing feature of the committee's activity has been the promotion of research in a variety of fields which has included such diverse subjects as the effects of alcohol on the human organism, the occurrence of factory accidents resulting from alcoholism, and regional surveys on the incidence of alcoholism.

The Federal Commission set up in Switzerland in 1945 is of a rather different character, reflecting the constitution and organization of the country in which executive authority in many questions, such as health, resides in the governments of the twenty-five cantons which make up the country. This commission is comprised of representatives of the medical and teaching professions, of the Federal Health Service, of the Federal Alcohol Monopoly, and of the temperance societies. It works through four main subcommittees dealing with questions of finance, legislation, scientific research, social questions, and prevention. Its main tasks are to encourage research and inquiries on the effects of alcohol consumption, to advise on the setting up of treatment institutions and other facilities, to pronounce on proposals regarding alcohol policy which may be submitted to the authorities, and to see that the employment of the "alcohol-tenth" is in accordance with the Federal constitution. This "alcohol-tenth" is a feature of the Swiss system.

The net receipts of the Federal Alcohol Monopoly arising from taxation of spirits are, after deduction of administration expenses and expenses incurred in the utilization of fruit and potatoes without distillation, divided into two parts, one part going to the Federal Old Age Insurance Fund and the other to the cantons. At least one-tenth of the part received by the cantons (the alcohol-tenth) must be employed by them to support organizations and institutions dealing with alcoholism. It is thus one of the duties of the Federal Commission to ensure that this tenth is correctly employed. The commission, although not executive, deals also in its advisory capacity with a variety of intoxication-caused problems, such as legislation on alcohol and traffic and alcohol-caused offenses in the army.

Several countries of Eastern Europe have evolved state programs on alcohol problems and alcoholism in the last few years. In Poland, a National Committee against Alcoholism was set up, subsidized by the Ministry of Health and operating through regional committees, to inform the public on the question and to organize treatment facilities throughout the country. In 1957, the state program was supplemented by an Interministerial Commission on Alcoholism. One of the outstanding problems in a number of countries is the question of harmonizing the policies followed by the governmental departments which are responsible for the production and sale of alcoholic beverages and the policies of the departments which deal with alcohol problems and alcoholism. Moreover, there are numerous government departments whose activities touch alcohol and alcoholism problems at some point. This Interministerial Commission in Poland was composed of the vice-ministers of nine ministeries concerned in some way with alcoholism problems under the leadership of the Minister of Labor and Social Service. The task of the commission was to work out an over-all plan for dealing with alcoholism, and this has gradually led to the important legislation promulgated at the end of 1959. This legislation, which covers the reorganization of the treatment of alcoholics as well as taxation of alcoholic beverages and includes such detailed questions as the conditions of sale and consumption of alcoholic beverages on boats, is comprehensive, and the directives to implement its operation are drawn up by the appropriate ministries: Health, Labor, Communications, Marine, etc., in consultation with the Central National Committee.

In Czechoslovakia a Central Committee to devise an over-all program was set up within the Ministry of Health. Its work is carried on through four commissions, one dealing with the development and encouragement of the production of non-alcoholic beverages, a second with the protection of children and young people from the effects of alcohol abuse, a third with legislative proposals, and a fourth with scientific research.

In 1954, in the Soviet Union, a directive was sent out by the Ministry of Health requiring doctors and health personnel, physicians as well as psychiatrists, to undertake an educative action on the subject of alcoholism. This program has been developed into a nationwide one by the Ministry through the Central Research Institute of Health Education. Some of the principles of this program are stated here. The health education work must first of all emphasize that abuse of alcohol and drunkenness cannot be tolerated, that alcoholism is treatable and the wish of the alcoholic to be cured is of paramount importance for the result. As in most countries, alcoholism is recognized as an illness. However, in the Soviet Union, it is emphasized that alcoholics must not always be regarded as patients, since that would imply condonement of their antisocial behavior and doubt of their responsibility for their actions.

There is a tendency in some countries to separate prevention measures and treatment facilities as two distinctive programs. In the Soviet program, treatment and rehabilitation are also used as means of effective education on alcoholism, and the treatment program in itself performs an important public education service. A similar use of treatment facilities may be noted in the Netherlands where the numerous consultation bureaus for alcoholics are in touch with a wide section of the population—that is, families, neighbors, employers, and the like—who thus become informed on the subject.

In the United States since the creation of the Connecticut Commission on Alcoholism, there have developed state programs in one form or another in about 35 to 40 states. The second program set up, that of New Jersey, later became a Bureau on Alcoholism of the State Department of Health. The programs in Connecticut and New Jersey are examples of the two general types which have emerged in the United States, the independent state program (or agency) and the integrated program.

There has been much discussion as to which of these plans is most effective, and the discussion is of interest not only in North America but wherever these problems are being examined. The principal argument in favor of the program integrated in a state health service would seem to be that responsibility for alcoholism is placed with an established health agency which is administratively equipped for the purpose, has had a long experience with treatment programs and has experience in transmitting research findings into educational programs for professional and public use. In addition, financing of such a program may be less burdensome because it is possible to draw upon existing facilities.

The argument in favor of an independent agency seems to be that an integrated program may easily lose its identity in a larger program of mental health. Also, the complexity of the problem demands the setting up of special clinics with specialized personnel, particularly for the early and middle stages of alcoholism. The most effective therapy has often seemed to be that which combines medicine and drugs, psychiatry, psychology, social casework, and Alcoholics Anonymous in a team under the leadership of a physician or a psychiatrist. When we extend the question beyond the treatment of alcoholism to the wider education of the public, there may be even more advantages in having a specialized agency because alcohol and alcoholism problems do affect a whole series of departmental agencies and some kind of outside coordinating body would seem to be an advantage.

Most of the state programs in the United States in addition to establishing treatment facilities have characteristics of special interest. For example, the Connecticut Commission has certain police powers under which different courts—superior, municipal, and judicial—can commit to the custody and control of the commission habitual drunkards (or any persons three times convicted of intoxication in any such court, or who have lost self-control as a result of the intemperant use of intoxicants) for a period of not less than 4 months and not more than 3 years. In some state programs particular emphasis has been placed on research; such is the case in Virginia where the Division of Alcohol Studies and Rehabilitation in the Virginia State Department of Health has given special prominence to this field. The North Carolina Alcoholic Rehabilitation Program places great emphasis on public relations and includes journalists in its Board. The Massachusetts Commission on Alcoholism has given attention to such specialized subjects as the role of the public-health nurse and the family-centered approach to the control of alcoholism and has convened conferences on these and allied subjects.

In 1949, the first Canadian program, the Alcoholism Research Foundation, was established in the Province of Ontario. This agency was given the authority to make agreements with universities and hospitals for experimentation on methods of treating alcoholics as well as to establish clinics and to disseminate information. The Foundation has concerned itself with a wide variety of topics such as consumption statistics, sales trends, the alcohol language, and treatment of alcoholism. International cooperation has been encouraged by the exchange of research workers between the Finnish Foundation of Alcohol Studies and the Alcoholism Research Foundation.

To review, briefly, state programs dealing with alcoholism, the important role of private or ancillary organizations in this field should not be minimized. They are certainly indispensable whether they are set up specifically to deal with the question of alcohol problems and alcoholism, or whether they are existing agencies such as the Red Cross, trade unions, or youth organizations, which in a number of countries supplement the state programs in the field of education on alcohol and alcoholism.

The increasing tendency to establish over-all state programs on alcoholism and alcohol problems is significant, however, since it indicates the need to achieve certain results which can only be obtained with great difficulty and in some cases not at all by private organizations. In the first place, the state program can promote a unification of the highest levels of national policy on alcohol and alcoholism problems. Secondly, it can establish a pattern of procedure to be followed by the local authorities and agencies throughout the country in dealing with these questions. Thirdly, in respect to the dissemination of information, it can make a considerable impact upon the general public, who often may not be responsive to other approaches. Fourthly, it can effectively mobilize research facilities.

In the future, and in spite of the differences existing in drinking habits and customs in different countries, it will certainly be useful if international discussion and consultation can develop between those who are responsible for the administration of state programs.

Name Index

Subject Index

Date Due